D0706580

REFIGURING ANTHROPOLOGY

First Principles Of Probability & Statistics

David Hurst Thomas

American Museum of Natural History

Waveland Press, Inc.
Prospect Heights, Illinois

For information about this book, write or call:

Waveland Press, Inc.
P.O. Box 400
Prospect Heights, Illinois 60070
(312) 634-0081

Copyright © 1986, 1976 by David Hurst Thomas
The 1976 version of this book was entitled *Figuring Anthropology*.

ISBN 0-88133-223-2

Printed in the United States of America.

This book is thoughtfully dedicated to T. D. and T. B. O. In several places, this book is just for them.

Preface

A preface has always struck me as an odd tradition: read by the reader first, written by the author last. As the completed manuscript lies mounded before me, I remember first sitting down to write this book, over three years ago. I felt much like a five-year-old kid shopping at Christmastime, "Oh, I can't give him a book, he's already got a book." And it was true. We already had a book about statistics. We had dozens of books about statistics. At this very moment, my desk is cluttered with exactly 33 such books. At times over the last few years, I've pondered why I should bother reading another introductory statistics book, much less trouble myself with writing one.

But, as you can see, yet another book was indeed written, and for what I think is sufficient reason. Despite muffled grumblings from my students, I've always felt that quantitative techniques could be readily mastered by most anthropologists and their students. Elementary statistics is simply not so difficult a subject as we have been programmed to believe. I readily admit to a certain impatience with slide rules, logarithm tables, computers, and even numbers, for that matter. Yet despite these handicaps, I remain convinced of the critical importance of quantitative procedures in modern anthropology. I am therefore quite eager to encourage my younger colleagues to master the basics of statistical methodology as part of a sound anthropological background.

Most up-to-date anthropology advisors encourage their students to take at least an introductory statistics course, but such courses are too often "farmed out" to other departments (especially economics, psychology, and mathematics). The obvious shortcoming with this procedure is that the subject matter is not tailored to the unique needs of the anthropologist. The approach often waxes overly mathematical with an overemphasis upon proofs and mathematical elegance. Or else the course is too generalized, failing to establish the relevance of statistical machinations to anthropological reality. I recall, during my own undergraduate days, puzzling over exacting exercises concerning the "mean annual number of faulty television sets" and "variance of gross hog weight." In what possible way could problems such as these be helpful to my anthropological interest? (Of course these problems were relevant in the long run, but try to convince a college sophomore of that!) An alternative, and I believe more fruitful approach, is to teach statistics in an explicitly anthropological context, and the present text has been designed with this specialized approach in mind. The book itself is largely an elaboration of notes developed between 1968 and 1973 for classroom use at the University of California (Davis) and the City University of New York. Several former students have assisted in the preparation of the manuscript, and I gratefully acknowledge their patience and ingenuity.

My more mathematically inclined colleagues will immediately note that this is a statistics book, not a mathematics book. The approach is "user-oriented." Because "user" in this case means anthropologists and their students, the lack of mathematical rigor is deliberate on my part. Formal proofs, elaborate step-by-step deviations, and the like have been shunned. Inconspicuous references have been provided where convenient to guide the curious reader to the relevant literature. Exposition proceeds largely through illustration, with examples drawn from anthropology where possible. Because I am primarily an archaeologist, the examples are often drawn from areas most familiar to me: demography, artifactual correlates of behavior, settlement pattern, typology, and the like. But the scope is by no means strictly archaeological and several exercises deal with ethnology, cross-cultural research, primate and human anatomy, psychological anthropology, genetics, and a host of other anthropologically relevant subjects. I have merely selected some convenient topics of anthropology and attempted to illustrate the common statistical procedures upon these data. The techniques themselves are not so limited.

No prerequisites are assumed herein, save an elementary working knowledge of high school algebra. Where possible, computations are simplified, but not at the expense of using real-world social science data. To those who might still feel uncomfortable with their mathematical backgrounds, I heartily recommend *Mathematics Essential for Elementary Statistics* by Helen M. Walker (revised edition, Holt, Rinehart and Winston, 1951). With this little volume firmly in hand, no anthropologist should fear the statistical procedures considered here.

A word about computers and multivariate statistics

> *. . . the fundamental requirement of anthropology is that it begin with a personal relation and end with a personal experience, but . . . in between there is room for plenty of computers.*—C. Levi-Strauss

When I began writing this book, a couple of my anthropology colleagues not so subtly berated me for not taking a "computer-oriented perspective." Computers are, after all, the wave of the future. With the current availability of digital and desktop computing machines, who needs to learn the outmoded pencil-and-paper methods of mathematical statistics? The computers can do all of that. Computers should work so people can think.

Of course I won't argue against the ubiquity and general utility of computers; my own Ph.D. dissertation bristled with computer simulations and multivariate analyses. But I contend that the very availability of computers and statistical programs to feed them even more directly places the onus upon social scientists to learn statistical fundamentals. I see a real danger in the computer-assisted, push-button brand of statistics which threatens to overtake our graduate schools and research museums. Despite some rather lengthy sessions with computing machines, I've yet to hear the computer warn me: "Stop. Think. Is this calculation really necessary? Are you just playing number games?" Indeed, is not the computer mentality geared for more and more numbers in less and less time?

There is nothing wrong with using computers for statistical purposes; I've done so more times than I'd care to relate. In fact, most of the examples in this book have been verified by computer. The simple point I wish to make is that computers are seductive devices which tend to lure the unwary down the endless trail toward numerical obscurity. I think that a solid understanding of the calculations and underlying theory of statistics minimizes the temptation to reify sheer statistical data. Hence this book proceeds with simple examples, designed to reveal the mechanics of simple statistical operations. Then more complex data are introduced until finally computers become a necessity to handle the sheer bulk. But to dispense with the pencil-and-paper stage of statistics is to set a faulty foundation for more complex applications. What good is an orthogonal multiple-factor multivariate analysis if one doesn't understand the meaning of elementary correlation?

As this book unfolds, you'll realize that I'm not the most gung-ho statistician around. In fact, I'm not a statistician at all. I'm an anthropologist. But statistics are a very, very important tool to the modern anthropologist; if this were not so, I'd have written a very short book. But by the same token, let us not be led astray. Statistics are not the answer to all anthropological issues. It is just as important to learn when *not* to statisticize. Sometimes, the solutions to anthropologically relevant inquiries are obvious, and only the hardened zealot would insist upon computing complex statistics in such cases. My vote is firmly cast against obfuscating the obvious, and this is why basic statistics must be thoroughly understood before one turns to the buzzing, whirring brand of statistics all too commonly dispensed by the local computer center.

A word to the instructor

> *. . . he told the truth, mainly. There was things which he stretched, but mainly he told the truth.*—H. Finn

The scope of this book seems somewhat unusual to me. It is a statistics book prepared by a nonstatistician for use by other nonstatisticians. Furthermore, the instructors teaching from this book are not expected to be statisticians either. This is as it should be. The rationale for writing the book is to introduce elementary statistical procedures and logic in an explicitly anthropological context. Who is better equipped to convey an anthropological context than a practicing anthropologist? I hope that the coming decade will see more anthropologists who feel comfortable teaching elementary quantitative methods. Only then can we seriously hope to pass on a statistical familiarity without undue anxiety on the part of our students.

Appended to each chapter are a few exercises covering the newly presented subject matter. These problems involve, where possible, nontrivial applications to actual anthropological data. The exercises are roughly graded in difficulty, and the answers to the odd-numbered problems are supplied at the end of the text. I cannot express too strongly the importance of assigning at least some of these exercises as problem sets, to be completed out of class. While the specter of "homework" in a college-level anthropology course strikes some as outdated, or even distasteful, experience has shown that the positive results of such exercises should more than counterbalance any reluctance. I also recommend that the previously assigned problem sets be reviewed at the beginning of each classroom session so that difficult problems and concepts can be explained while difficulties are still fresh in the students' minds. Care should be taken to insure that the problem sets are adequately corrected and promptly returned to the students, so that misconceptions can be *immediately* remedied before proceeding to more difficult concepts. You are, of course, urged to present your own exercises in class, problems that reflect a personal involvement with statistical methods in your own anthropology.

In the course of preparing this book, I stumbled upon an interesting and surprisingly effective technique which might prove of some use to others. From time to time, I require students to prepare sample exercises such as those found at the end of each chapter. Students are asked to supply their own anthropological data, either from the literature or from other anthropology courses. In fact, several of the exercises included in this text were originally generated by beginning students as part of their classroom assignments. Feedback from former students indicates that even the more elusive statistical concepts are often readily mastered during the construction of these sample problems. Such exercises also have the advantage of forcing the student to assume an *active* posture in applying statistical methods.

The topic of examinations is always a problematical subject with instructors, particularly so in recent years. There are probably as many testing procedures as there are testers. Yet regardless of frequency and composition of examinations in a course such as this, I wish to enter a plea that such tests should be *open book*. This text has been prepared with a strong de-emphasis upon mathematical rigor, memorization, and computational manipulation. Students should be presented with new ideas in the classroom, and then they should apply these new concepts and procedures on carefully designed problem sets until the mechanics become familiar. But I can see no particular virtue in memorizing even the most elementary formulas. This relatively low-priority information is readily available in scores of statistics books. What matters is that students learn correct application, especially underlying logic and the implications of each of the standard procedures. This sort of sophistication comes only from the discerning instructor (since no book can replace the good teacher) and honest effort on the part of the student. It seems to me that the cram-type examination does little in such situations except to force students into the untenable position of learning formulas as one memorizes nonsense syllables. Even the best students turn off at such treatment (and I don't blame them).

> *Granted that they did not find the riches of which they had been told; they did find the next best thing—a place in which to search for them.*
> —P. Casteneda (Spanish historian who traveled with Coronado during exploration of the New World)

A word to the student

> *This book suffers from the same disadvantage that has proverbially been attributed to the study of Latin, which is that the chief thing it fits you for is the study of more Latin.*—A. Gingrich

Although I don't wish to scare anybody off—the prevalent "statistical mystique" has probably done a credible job of that already—perhaps a friendly word of caution is in order. In my own teaching experience with introductory statistical courses, I have noticed a couple of common pitfalls which seem to plague fledgling anthropologists. For one thing, you should not expect to master statistics with a quick skim through the book. We all know that many college courses do not require daily preparation; in fact, almost no anthropology courses require daily study. One can often simply spend a few days cramming at the end of the term and pass an essay (or even an objective) examination without a great deal of difficulty.

But such is not generally the case with statistical methods. I start from scratch in this book, assuming that you know virtually nothing about statistics. Each chapter progressively builds upon the concepts and operations introduced in previous chapters. There is a continuing thread of development. I strongly suggest, if you're serious about anthropology, that you *keep up*. Don't let this material slide because you can easily find yourself hopelessly mired after only a couple of weeks.

If you've glanced at my advice "To the Instructor" earlier in this preface, you will have noted that I entered a plea for *open book* testing, stressing insightful applications rather than memorization. Lest you think this advice was motivated by some anomalous compassion for the lot of today's student, let me hasten to add that instructors have also been urged to assign a wealth of problem sets, each to be completed out of class. (A former student of mine once described these "problem sets"—a pusillanimous alias for *homework*—as "excessive, tedious, and damned demanding, but a necessary evil, I suppose.") My primary concern is with what you retain *after this book is closed* rather than with what can be painfully memorized and then promptly forgotten. Exact formulas, procedures, and symbolism can always be looked up in this (or another) statistics book. That is why we have library cards. I want you to retain the *flavor* of the statistical perspective, a certain finesse when approaching the data of social science, and a general sophistication toward empirical research. *Nothing in this book should be memorized* (except possibly this statement.)

A word to colleagues and friends

One pleasant obstacle remains before we plunge into the numbers; this is the section where the author thanks those friends and colleagues without whose indispensable suggestions the text would have been completed months earlier. More seriously, however, this manuscript benefited significantly from the critical review of others. I thank George Collier, William Tulio Divale, and George Spindler, each of whom reviewed and commented upon early drafts of the manuscript. I am especially thankful to Marvin Karson of the Department of Statistics, University of Alabama, for ferreting out numerous mathematical *faux pas.* It's a surprisingly difficult task to find a professional statistician willing to sacrifice mathematical rigor for substantive relevance, and Dr. Karson's contribution is gratefully acknowledged.

Several former students lent their hands to the task. Four students in my introductory quantitative methods course at the City University of New York deserve thanks for conducting the literature survey discussed in the first chapter: Eileen Fruchter, Tom Horoszewski, Joseph Privitera, and Rona Rosenberg. Roberta Fischer literally spent weeks proofing text and recomputing examples in the earlier chapters.

Warren Kinzey graciously allowed me to use his unpublished dental measurements on the pygmy chimpanzee. Stanley Freed and Robert Bettinger were especially helpful in directing me toward relevant quantitative examples.

The onerous task of final typing, copyediting, and indexing fell to Carol Slotkin, who performed admirably. It was Carol who trenchantly observed that *somehow* my typing has become even more abysmal than my handwriting. Thanks also are due my long-suffering spouse. Despite an almost allergic reaction to things numerical, Trudy consented to edit and re-edit the more cumbersome chapters.

Finally, I would be remiss if I didn't acknowledge the influence of my former professor and advisor, Martin A. Baumhoff. Although not directly contributing to the writing of this volume, Marty's influence has so pervaded my thinking over the years that I can scarcely touch pen to paper without somehow reflecting this unspoken guidance. Thanks.

New York City   D.H.T.
December 1975

1986 Preface

I love being a writer. What I can't stand is the paperwork.

— Peter De Vries

This book is a slightly revised version of *Figuring Anthropology: First Principles of Probability and Statistics*, originally published in 1976 by Holt, Rinehart and Winston, Inc. As stated in the Preface, my objective at the time was to provide anthropology students with a readable, user-friendly introduction to statistical methods.

The book met with some success, having been adopted in several dozen classrooms throughout the country. I have been told that, as I had hoped, many students responded to the slightly irreverent tone, realizing that quantitative methods need not be deadly dull and stultifying. Several thousand copies of *Figuring Anthropology* were sold before the book went out of print in 1983.

Since that time, a number of anthropology professors wrote to urge an updating and revision of the text. While part of this interest doubtless stemmed from the professorial disinclincation to rewrite one's lecture notes, I also sensed that some instructors and their students honestly liked the book and wanted to continue using it. But I repeatedly declined to prepare the revision because of pressing archaeological fieldwork and previous publication commitments.

Until now. Having agreed to teach an introductory course in anthropological statistics at New York University, I realized that no comparable volume had come along to replace *Figuring*. Although that honor is something like being the first in a race of one, I realized that *Figuring Anthropology* filled a void in the literature.

Despite the fan mail, *Figuring Anthropology* had a serious problem that inhbited its usefulness. Within a year after publication, it became clear that the original text was littered with dozens (and dozens) of typographical errors. Although no author likes typos, these seemingly trivial mistakes are particularly disconcerting in a quantitatively oriented textbook. I have it on good authority that a former student (now my wife) was ready "to wring my neck" after using *Figuring* as a textbook. The mathematical typos drove her — and her instructor — up the wall.

In 1978, we attempted to remedy the problem by releasing an extended errata sheet. But we found this sheet of corrections both incomplete and difficult to use. The only workable solution was to recompute the mathematics line-by-line, attempting to ferret out and correct all typographical errors. In the process of doing this, I learned one sterling lesson: Never again will I attempt to correct galley proofs around the campfire.

But I have resisted the temptation to rewrite the text. No effort has been made to update the reading list, add new material to the exercises, or extend the treatment beyond elementary statistics.

I am particularly grateful to Ms. Margot Dembo and Ms. Lorann S.A. Pendleton, both of the American Museum of Natural History, for their extended efforts in preparing the revision. Had it not been for their assistance, the book would still be out-of-print. I also thank Mr. Neil Rowe (Waveland Press) for his encouragement in the project, and Mr. Bob Woodbury (Holt, Rinehart, and Winston, Inc.) for his cooperation in making *Figuring Anthropology* available once more.

Very special thanks go to those teachers and students who provided me with detailed errata sheets, based on their classroom experience: Dr. Eleanor Bates (California State University, Long Beach), Dr. Paul A. Erickson (Saint Mary's University), Dr. Jay K. Johnson (University of Mississippi), Dr. Robert L. Munroe (Pitzer College), and Dr. Richard Scaglion (University of Pittsburgh).

Although every effort has been made to purge the text of typographical errors, anybody finding additional errors is encouraged to convey the information to me directly, c/o Department of Anthropology, American Museum of Natural History, Central Park West at 79th Street, New York, New York 10024.

D.H.T.
Nyack, New York
February, 1986

Contents

1 Statistics in Anthropology

● *The fact that for a long time Cubism has not been understood and that even today (circa 1930) there are people who cannot see anything in it means nothing. I do not read English; an English book is a blank book to me. This does not mean that the English language does not exist. Why should I blame anyone but myself if I cannot understand what I know nothing about?*—P. Picasso

Introductory statistics texts generally begin by attempting to convince the reader that a thorough knowledge of statistics is almost imperative for survival in modern society. Without an elementary statistical awareness, one is incapable of appreciating, for example, the extraordinary predictability of baseball batting averages, the economic merit of industrial quality control, or even the findings of the now-familiar Harris and Gallup polls, which monitor (and modify) current political and social trends. A more philosophical perspective suggests that better Science — and hence a general betterment of mankind — can result only from the more rigid and insightful application of statistical thinking.

There are likewise a number of forceful justifications to encourage a basic understanding of statistics for the anthropologist. Unfortunately, these justifications assume working knowledge of statistical procedures; and if you knew enough statistics to appreciate the justification, you would not need this book. So, the only point of this initial chapter is to demonstrate the simple, pragmatic fact that anthropology is rapidly becoming a quantitative discipline and that without an appreciation of elementary quantitative methods the student will be left behind.

Let us consider, for example, current practices in teaching anthropology. Despite an obvious educational trend away from rigid requirements, many graduate programs in anthropology have recently been significantly modified to

1

prepare students to cope with the increasingly quantitative methods in anthropology. In 1974 over half (52.6 percent) of the graduate departments of anthropology in the United States and Canada required (or at least strongly recommended) of their Ph.D. candidates a basic acquaintance with the fundamentals of statistics. In fact, a number of graduate programs encouraged the student to substitute a statistical proficiency for the time-honored foreign language requirement. Also in 1974, nearly 30 percent of the master's degree candidates in anthropology were required to demonstrate a familiarity with common statistical concepts and practices. There are even forward-looking undergraduate programs in anthropology which require statistics of their undergraduate majors, and it seems probable that many of the students now using this book have been coerced to do so by curriculum requirements.[1]

In short, a working knowledge of statistical inference and cognate testing procedures has become virtually essential for anybody wishing to deal with anthropological data and to truly comprehend the findings of up-to-date anthropology. To those who disagree with this position, I offer the professional literature itself.

Scholarly journals not only serve to disseminate the research results of practitioners of the profession, but also function as lasting archives in which the very development of a discipline is recorded. As such, professional journals undoubtedly provide the single, best barometer of significant trends and patterns within a discipline. It seems clear that within the past two decades there has been a notable increase in the application of statistical thinking brought to bear on anthropological problems. To illustrate this point, I conducted a simple survey in which a major journal was selected from each subfield of anthropology. These journals were then evaluated with respect to their dependence upon statistical procedures: The *American Journal of Physical Anthropology* (the official journal of the American Association of Physical Anthropology) was selected as representative of physical anthropology; *American Antiquity* (the official journal for the Society for American Archaeology) was chosen to reflect American archaeology; *Language* (vehicle of the Linguistic Society of America) was selected to represent anthropological linguistics; the *American Anthropologist* was included to represent not only ethnology but also anthropological theory in general. Each periodical was selected because of its long-range perspective and its generally unbiased coverage of the respective subdiscipline. The total run of each journal was analyzed. Each of the 7903 articles was examined to determine whether the author had relied upon statistical inference in his research.[2]

Just how important has statistical reasoning been in the development of today's anthropology? Figure 1.1 illustrates the findings of this survey and answers this question. We note immediately that physical anthropology has relied upon statistical inference to a much greater degree than any other

---

[1]These figures were derived from the *Guide to Departments of Anthropology 1973–74*, published by the American Anthropological Association, in which 134 graduate departments described their own programs and degree requirements.

[2]"Statistical inference" means using known principles of probability theory to derive sensible conclusions about an entire population, based upon a small sample from that population. This concept, the very bulwark of statistical reasoning, is explored in greater detail in Chapter 2.

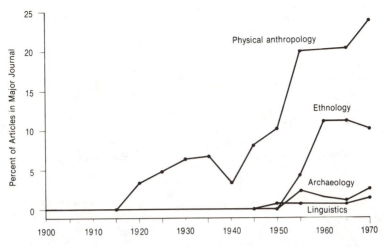

Fig. 1.1   The use of *statistical inference* in anthropology since 1900.

subfield of anthropology. In fact, statistical inference became a common research tool for physical anthropologists a full three decades before its consistent application to ethnology and archaeology.[3] Even more striking is the overall trend in quantification: The use of statistical inference has been markedly increasing over the past two decades in *all* of anthropology (except anthropological linguistics). Beginning in the early 1950s, anthropologists have increasingly used statistical procedures as a vital tool in analyzing their field data, and this trend shows no indication of declining in the 1970s—quite to the contrary.

These findings illustrate both the increasing importance of statistical thinking in anthropology and the relative consumption of quantitative procedures by anthropology's subfields. But there are those anthropologists (and their students) who still question the overall importance of statistics to today's anthropology. To see just what is going on in modern anthropology, a recent volume (1972) of each journal was dissected in greater detail.

What proportion of the papers relies upon *simple quantification*, such as graphs, numerical tables, or codified informant responses?

What proportion relies upon *fundamental statistics* (essentially those topics covered in this book)?

What proportion includes analysis by *advanced statistics* (mainly multivariate techniques beyond the scope of this text)?

The findings of this more detailed survey are displayed on the circle graphs of Fig. 1.2.

[3]The earliest use of statistical methods in anthropology is generally ascribed to the physical anthropologist Morton, who analyzed measurements from a large series of crania in 1839. E. B. Tylor's paper, "On a Method of Investigating the Development of Institutions" (1889), in which Tylor attempted to determine evolutionary sequences by analyzing "adhesions" of social traits, is generally acknowledged to be the earliest application of statistical procedures to ethnological data (see Driver 1953:50).

4

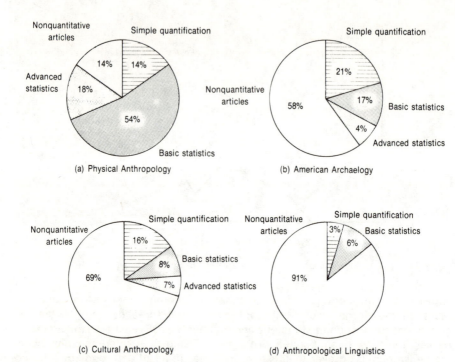

Fig. 1.2   Relative importance of quantitative and statistical analyses in modern anthropology. Source: (a) *American Journal of Physical Anthropology*, 1972; (b) *American
Antiquity*, 1972; (c) *American Anthropologist*, 1972; (d) *Language*, 1972.

It is again obvious that physical anthropology remains the most quantitative,
most statistically sophisticated of anthropology's subdisciplines. While this
result was probably predictable from the previous survey of the literature, the
actual degree of dependence upon statistical reasoning seems startling: Over
85 percent of the 1972 articles in the *American Journal of Physical Anthropology*
employed at least elementary quantitative techniques. More than half of the
1972 papers assumed at least a preliminary grasp of basic statistical operations
and reasoning on the part of the reader, and at least one article in six employed
advanced statistical techniques. In other words, readers with a diffidence toward
things quantitative could critically evaluate *fewer than one article in seven* in
the modern literature of physical anthropology.

Over one-third of the articles for 1972 in modern archaeology and ethnology
employed at least elementary quantitative analysis [Figs. 1.2(b) and 1.2(c)],
and more than one in 25 articles utilized rather sophisticated statistical
procedures. As expected, anthropological linguistics rarely turned to quantitative measures, with fewer than 10 percent of the 1972 articles using even
elementary statistics. Most linguistics still proceed in purely qualitative fashion,
without recourse to either mathematics or statistics.

Yet, despite this almost meteoric shift to quantification, statistical thinking in anthropology remains a relatively recent venture—especially in ethnology and archaeology—when viewed in the perspective of the rest of the social and biological sciences. Anthropology has been rather reluctant to come about. In fact, as late as 1927, anthropologist Franz Boas—known in many circles as the "Father of American Anthropology"—could note cryptically that "attempts have been made to apply statistical methods to ethnographical phenomena. The success of these attempts is more than doubtful" (Boas 1927). Because of this reluctance on the part of many to accept the use of statistical methods on anthropological data, quantification in anthropology lacks the maturity evident in other social sciences, and errors in even elementary statistical operations are still alarmingly common. It has been said that some anthropologists use statistics much as the drunk uses a street lamp—more for support than for illumination. There is even an occasional anthropologist who attempts to disguise shoddy research under the veneer of statistical jargon and symbolism in the belief that few colleagues are so statistically aware as to check his results. Practices such as this cannot be allowed to pass unchallenged: It requires just as complete a grasp of statistical technique to judge when *not* to apply them as to know when statistics are imperative. All things considered, it seems clear that students planning a serious study of anthropology owe it to themselves to learn at least the fundamentals of quantification, if for no other reason than to properly assess the results of other anthropologists.

● *It began oddly. But could it have begun otherwise, however it began?*—P. Roth

SUGGESTIONS FOR FURTHER READING

Detailed titles and sources are given in References at the end of the text.

General

Driver (1953). Considers historical development of statistical methods in anthropology; separate discussions dealing with physical anthropology, archaeology, ethnology, and social anthropology.

Kay (1971). A brief discussion of the *who, what, when, where, how,* and *why* of mathematics in anthropology. Kay suggests that the major themes in mathematical anthropology are (roughly in order of importance): (1) abstract algebra, (2) computing technology, and (3) probability and statistics, with deemphasis on correlational methods and tests of significance.

Spaulding (1960). Interesting paper considering uses of statistics for archaeological description and classification. The discussion of this paper by several archaeologists is particularly enlightening, as it indicates the status of statistical thinking in the archaeology of the mid-1950s.

White (1973). A general introduction to use of mathematics in the analysis of ethnographic data; White's emphasis is largely upon probabilistic statements rather than upon conventional statistical inference.

Modern Mathematical Anthropology

Buchler and Selby (1968). An introduction to traditional and mathematical approaches to kinship and social organization.

Clarke (1972). An edited volume of papers using various models (mathematical and otherwise) in archaeological research.

Cohen and Naroll (1970). Discussion of need for comparative approaches in anthropology and the importance of quantitative methodology to the comparative approach.

Hodson, Kendall, and Tăutu (1971). Fifty-two papers presenting substantive applications of mathematical models to archaeology and the historical sciences in general.

Hoffman (1970). General review of literature and trends in mathematical anthropology.

Kemeny and Snell (1972). The authors present a number of mathematical models dealing with preference ranking, ecology, marketing systems, and problems of scheduling; not for those afraid of mathematical symbolism.

Anthropology and the Computer

Burton (1970). Paper summarizes several major projects in which computers are used to analyze uniquely anthropological data.

Hymes (1965). A compendium of 18 papers discussing statistical applications to anthropology; volume particularly strong on approaches to anthropologic linguistics.

Pelto (1970). Appendix C briefly discusses general computer nomenclature and some of the author's personal encounters with counting machines.

> ● We have modified our environment so radically that we must now modify ourselves to exist in this new environment.
> —N. Weiner

2 What Are Anthropological Data ?

● *The subject of anthropology is limited only by man.*
—A. Kroeber

2.1 INTRODUCTION

This chapter begins in backward fashion. Rather than considering what data *are,* we must first peruse what data *are not*. For one thing, the word "data" is not singular; "datum" is the singular form, although this term is rarely used in statistical contexts. So, statements about a set of measurements are properly worded "the data are..." rather than "the data is...."

More importantly, even though anthropology is generally defined as the study of people, *people do not constitute the data of anthropology*. People are people. What anthropologists study are observations *about* people rather than the people themselves. Along this same line, skulls and bones are not the data of physical anthropology any more than artifacts, temple tombs, or housepits are the data of archaeology. Data are not people, objects, or things; data are counts, measurements, and observations *made on* people, objects, and things. Twenty Neanderthal crania are not in themselves a set of data; the cranial capacities, cranial lengths, or nasal widths of these skulls comprise the data. There are no data until an anthropologist observes them. Data do not passively exist. Data must be generated.

A couple of major points follow from this active definition of data. For one thing, those who would accuse anthropologists of "using people as data" neither understand what data are nor how they are collected. Clearly, anthropologists manipulate observations (the *real* data), not people.

Secondly, data can hardly be destroyed once they are generated. A society might become extinct, an archaeological site may be bulldozed to make way for a parking lot, a skeletal series might be lost or destroyed, but all these disasters

7

occur only to people or objects or things, not to data. One case in point is the strange, unfinished saga of the famous Peking man fossils, which has been related in marvelous detail by Harry L. Shapiro (1971). At this writing, the fossils are lost to science, their whereabouts unknown. The fossils disappeared in 1941 when a Japanese invasion of the Chinese mainland seemed imminent. Professor Franz Weidenreich, who had been studying the fossils at the Peking Union Medical College, was forced to flee to the United States, crating the *Sinanthropus* fossils for secret transport. But they disappeared. It appeared for a while as though the fossils might have been lost overboard during loading onto the *S.S. President Harrison*. But new evidence has recently come to light indicating that the fossils safely reached Camp Holcombe in Chinwangtao, where Japanese soldiers confiscated and apparently ransacked the crates. The fossils may have been discarded as worthless junk. But there is also the possibility that some of the crates—those destined for shipment to a Swiss warehouse, the Pasteur Institute, and the homes of reliable citizens in Tientsin— were stored in Chinese warehouses, or perhaps even taken to Tokyo as war booty (as was the Solo skull, which had been taken from G. H. R. von Koenigswald in a Japanese prison camp). Perhaps the fossils miraculously reached the United States and will someday surface. But, even assuming the worst—that the fossils were totally destroyed—the *data* on *Sinanthropus* have not been lost to science because detailed measurements, photographs, and observations were published by Weidenreich in 1943.

In order to actually "destroy data," one would have to destroy every original and every copy of the published descriptions, a virtual impossibility. Whatever the fate of the fossils, the Peking man *data* remain as viable as the day the finds were first analyzed. Of course, if the original fossils could be found, then *new* data could be generated, using modern techniques developed in the three decades since the fossils disappeared.

Data can also take a number of forms. Data can be recorded as counts or as measurements or as observations. Data can also be generated from other data, as with ratios and powers. Data can be in the form of variables and constants, variates and populations, samples and statistics. This chapter is concerned primarily with how the individual observations—the "raw" data—are transformed into statistically meaningful forms, a discussion which supplies the foundation for much of statistical theory.

2.2 CONSTANTS AND VARIABLES

● *Freedom is the freedom to say that two plus two makes four. If that is granted, all else follows.*—G. Orwell

Philosopher Bertrand Russell once pointed out that the reason some people have so much trouble understanding what X means is that X doesn't mean anything at all. X is nothing but a symbol, and symbols assume meaning only after they are assigned to a particular characteristic. Symbols such as X, Y, and π have no natural or necessary relationship to their assigned referent. Symbols are merely arbitrary notations.

Anthropology is often concerned with the meaning and significance of symbols. In fact, there is even a movement within modern ethnology whose adherents term themselves "symbolic anthropologists." Symbols pervade our everyday life to such an extent that we cannot think without them. Leslie White (1940) has gone so far as to term symbols "basic units of all human behavior and civilization ... the symbol is the universe of humanity."

But if symbols are truly basic to humanity, then why do so many humans (especially social science undergraduates) seem to fear X? X is just a symbol. Why should X be any more terrifying a symbol than, say, a stop sign, the peace sign, or the Star of David? A recent report by the Mathematical Association of America cautioned statistics instructors to allow for "symbol shock" suffered by many introductory college students. The problem, of course, is that X belongs to a very special class of symbols—*mathematical symbols*—and a large segment of the Western population has been covertly programmed to fear the encroachment of mathematical logic and methodology. Nowhere is this aversion to mathematical symbolism seen more clearly than in the application of statistical methods to social science. Perhaps by looking more closely at what statistical symbols actually symbolize, we can make some inroads at dispelling "symbol shock."

The most elementary use of mathematical symbols is to denote a constant. In this case, the symbol and its referent have a one-to-one relationship.

A constant is a quantity (denoted by a symbol) which can assume only one value.

Mathematics is rife with constants, often assigned a conventional symbol.

$$\pi = 3.14159265 \quad \text{(ratio of diameter to circumference)}$$
$$e = 2.71828183 \quad \text{(base of natural logarithms)}$$

Constants are named according to scientific convention rather than because of any natural isomorphism between the symbol and its characteristic. The Greek letter π is no more suitable to designate 3.14159265 than is any other symbol.

Anthropology has its share of constants too, but the symbols for these constants are more tractable than those of mathematics. Since each specimen of *Homo sapiens* has exactly two ears, for example, we could say that 2 is a constant for our species. Ego has precisely two biological parents or four biological grandparents, so these numbers are other biological constants. But anthropological constants need not always be so trivial. *Naroll's constant*, for example, attempts to relate the floor area of a settlement to the size of human population living in that area. In general, the population of a given settlement is about one-tenth of the floor area, expressed in square meters (Naroll 1962a):

$$\text{population} = 0.10 \text{ (floor area in square meters)}$$

Naroll's constant ($c = 0.10$) is particularly useful to archaeologists; once the floor area of a prehistoric settlement or structure is known, the prehistoric population can be estimated. At the Thomas Riggs site in South Dakota, for example, a longhouse was excavated which covered about 260 square meters. Applying Naroll's constant,

$$\text{population} = 0.10 \, (260 \text{ m}^2)$$
$$= 26.0 \text{ individuals}$$

Naroll's constant thus estimates the prehistoric population of the structure at the Thomas Riggs site to be about 26 people. The longhouse contained four hearths, so if each hearth served a single nuclear family, the average family size must have been about 6.5 people. This estimate corresponds closely with the known ethnographic information for this area, and provides some support for the proposition that Naroll's constant is *in fact* relatively constant (that is, invariant).

Another useful constant in anthropology is *Shapiro's constant for cranial deformation* (Shapiro 1929). Artificial deformation of the skull is a cultural trait worldwide in its distribution, with the primary occurrence in pre-Columbian America (especially among the Classic Maya), Peru, and the American Southwest. The specifics vary from region to region, but in all cases the infant's skull was altered to correspond with the local ethnic conception of beauty. Sometimes the skull was simply flattened by pressure from a cradleboard, while other groups deformed the frontal portion of the skull as well. The difficulty for physical anthropologists is that the cultural deformation of crania renders many anthropometric measurements virtually useless for comparison to undeformed skulls. Because of the frequency of artificial deformation, the craniometry of several areas of the world was simply unknown.

Shapiro attacked this problem by reasoning that while the shape of the cranial vault is drastically altered by deformation, the facial and frontal areas are left essentially unchanged, even in highly deformed skulls. Thus, the diameter from basion to nasion ought to reflect undeformed cranial characteristics even in deformed skulls, although the cranial length would be much too short (Fig. 2.1). This relatively constant basion–nasion diameter could then be used to correct the deformed length. Shapiro tested his idea upon a series of 1400 undeformed skulls from throughout the world, and computed a "constant":

$$\text{cranial length} = 1.49 \, (\text{basion-nasion diameter})$$

For every unit change in cranial length, there is a corresponding change of roughly 1.49 units in the basion–nasion diameter. To obtain the corrected head length, the difference between the averages of the basion–nasion diameter in deformed and undeformed crania is multiplied by Shapiro's constant ($c = 1.49$). This product is then subtracted from the undeformed head length to obtain an estimate for length in deformed crania. Earnest Hooton (1930:39) provides the following example to illustrate how Shapiro's constant enabled him to correct for cranial deformation in the skeletons from the Pecos Pueblo in central New Mexico:

Cranial length (undeformed males), mm	175.74
Cranial length (deformed males)	(?)
Basion–nasion diameter (undeformed males), mm	102.70
Basion–nasion diameter (deformed males), mm	101.58

The difference in basion–nasion diameter between the deformed and undeformed crania is

$$101.58 - 102.70 = -1.12 \, \text{mm}$$

which corrects to -1.67 mm when multiplied by Shapiro's constant ($c = 1.49$).

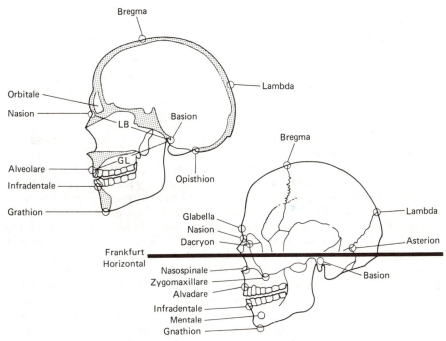

Fig. 2.1 Principal craniometric points and measurements of the human skull (after Brothwell 1963:fig. 33).

When this correction factor is added to the undeformed cranial length, the corrected head length of the deformed series can be estimated to be 174.07 mm. Hooton used Shapiro's constant to correct for deformation in over 300 crania, which otherwise would have been useless for further comparative analysis.

Symbols can thus denote a handy set of constants, but symbols are even more frequently used in statistics to denote *variables*. Most people know that variables are what scientists observe, and variables are most commonly assigned conventional letter symbols such as X, Y, or Z. What makes variables different from constants is that while *constants* must remain *constant*, *variables vary*.

A *variable* is a measurable quantity (represented by a symbol) which is free to assume more than one value.

By this definition, variables must always have *at least two* "states" or potential values.

A *variate* is an individual measurement of a variable.

Variables are thus abstractions, while the real data of anthropology consist of variates—the observations themselves and their measurements.

Cranial capacity is an example of a variable, which we can symbolize by the term X (or any other symbol). When dealing with a series of measurements, the variates are often denoted by the symbol X_i (read as "X sub i"), where i is a subscript specific to each variate. The cranial capacities of four individual Neanderthal skulls can be conveniently recorded in this shorthand (data from Coon 1971a: table 39):

Specimen	Symbol		Variate, cc
La Ferrassie I	X_1	=	1641
Spy 1	X_2	=	1525
Spy 2	X_3	=	1425
Gibraltar	X_4	=	1300

Using this symbolic form of notation, one can summarize even massive sets of variates with relative ease.

All variables vary, but it is important to note that all variables do not share the same underlying mathematical structure. Some variates are exact observations, while other variates are mere approximations of unknown measurements. A variable is called *discrete* if it can assume only certain fixed, predetermined values. "Number of teeth per species" is a discrete variable, for instance. We know that some primitive mammals had 44 teeth and that some varieties of South American monkeys have 36 teeth, while others have 32 teeth. Both humans and apes generally have 32 teeth. This variable is discrete because tooth number can assume only certain values—in this case, positive integers—even though the number of teeth varies between species. We can eliminate on logical grounds the possibility of ever discovering a mammalian skull with exactly 33.38 teeth. Teeth may be broken, of course, but we can be certain that, regardless of the true number before breakage, the total number was a positive integer. Thus, discrete variables are always exact measurements.

Most discrete variables common to anthropology are counts: the number of sacral vertebrae in gorilla, the number of sites located in an archaeological survey, the number of individuals whom ego calls FaBr, the total number of female children born in society Y during the last calendar year. Each case involves exact whole number measurements, but not all discrete variables are counts. Expected Mendelian genetic frequencies can generally assume only a few fixed values, such as $3:1$, $2:1$, or $9:3:3:1$. These ratios are not free to assume all possible intervening values, so Mendelian ratios are also discrete variables.

Variables are termed *continuous* if the variates can logically assume any interval of measurement. The precision of observations generally determines which measurement interval should be applied, and these intervals are mere approximations. Discrete variables are always exact, but a continuous variable can never be exact because its measurement is an approximation. The cranial capacity of the La Ferrassie I Neanderthal skull, for instance, was estimated at 1641 cc (cubic centimeters). Unlike a discrete variable, cranial capacity is perfectly free to assume any possible value measurable in cubic centimeters. There would be no objection to a variate of 1641.2 cc or even 1641.34920593 cc, provided the measurements could be sufficiently accurate.

Continuous variables generally involve variates measured by common physical units: time, length, or mass. Body stature, body weight, the average score on the Graduate Record Examination, population density, daily caloric intake, and birth rate are all continuous variables because the final figure is determined by the accuracy of measurement rather than by logic.

Sometimes a continuous variable might be purposely defined as discrete. "The relative degree to which a society depends upon animal husbandry," for example, is a continuous variable measured as a percentage. But because of the difficulty in estimating accurately, and also to facilitate coding upon computer punch cards, column 10 in the *Ethnographic Atlas* (Murdock 1967) lists the variable "relative dependence upon animal husbandry" in ten categories:

0   0–5 percent
1   6–15 percent
2   16–25 percent
.
.
.
9   86–100 percent

The opposite situation can also occur: A seemingly discrete variable can be refined into a continuous variable, and this is precisely what happened in the case of measuring human skin color. For decades, physical anthropologists characterized skin color by discrete categories such as "very light," "light," "intermediate," "dark," and "very dark." But a reflectometer has recently been used to measure light reflectance from human skin. The darker the skin, the more light is absorbed; therefore skin color can now be characterized by "the percent of light reflectance," a continuous variable which allows for greater precision and objectivity. There are even laboratory methods for determining the precise amount of melanin present in human skin, but these techniques remain impractical for massive population surveys.

The refinement of discrete variables into more precise, continuous variables is sometimes considered an obvious sign of progress in science. But one must remember that while each method of testing may purport to characterize a variable such as "skin color," a change in measuring technique usually involves a new operational definition of the variable. The skin color determined by visual inspection does not exactly correspond to skin color measured by reflectometer readings. Caution must be exercised when comparing findings resulting from different techniques.

> ● *SYMBOL, Nn. Something that is supposed to typify or stand for something. Many symbols are mere "survivals"—things which having no longer any utility continue to exist because we have inherited the tendency to make them; as funereal urns carved on memorial monuments. They were once real urns holding the ashes of the dead. We cannot stop making them, but we can give them a name which conceals our helplessness.*
> —A. Bierce

2.3 OPERATIONALLY DEFINING THE VARIABLES OF ANTHROPOLOGY

Much of the literature of modern science is involved with describing conditions and outcomes of experimentation. As long as the scientist has properly reported his experiments, other investigators should be able to repeat the initial procedures and obtain similar results. Science is grounded in establishing the *repeatability of results*, and these procedures apply to some anthropological research, especially in genetic and dietary studies conducted by physical anthropologists. But as Pelto (1970:48–49) has pointed out, anthropological data are not always collected as the result of experimentation, but are collected frequently through the systematic observation of unusual, aperiodic events such as ceremonies, kinship interactions, subsistence practices, and even disasters such as floods or fires. When dealing with phenomena of this sort, anthropologists cannot provide for true repeatability of observation, no matter how well the field techniques are described. In fact, the very nature of some anthropological research—particularly in archaeology and hominid paleontology—involves the destruction of archaeological and paleontological sites during the process of data extraction. Pelto suggests that rather than attempt to refine experimental repeatability, anthropologists should address themselves to a more realistic proposition: "If another observer had been at the particular event, and if he used the same technique, would he have obtained the same results?" (Pelto 1970:49). The true test of adequate definition and technique in anthropology often involves *objectivity* rather than strict repeatability.

Some anthropologists, of course, still object to quantification and statistical manipulation of anthropological data in any form. Social phenomena are too complex, too subjective—the argument goes—to be approached in a "scientific" (that is, objective) manner. What these skeptics overlook is that the larger the errors involved, the more imperative become statistical methods. Statistics is often called the *science of variability*, so clearly the mere presence of error in no way vitiates use of statistical procedures. In fact, statistical methods were developed to meet the needs of those who must deal with imperfect data.

But all treatments of anthropological data, whether statistical or otherwise, can have no more validity than the basic definition of concepts. The most important criterion for adequate operational definition requires one to specify the procedures or processes through which data have been generated. Operations should be so specified that the same procedures can be repeated "in an unbiased manner by an intelligent person after a period of training" (Krumbein and Graybill 1965:69). But it is impractical (and, in fact, impossible) to define every term operationally, since there must always be certain "primitive" terms which remain undefined. Physicists have difficulty in defining absolutes such as time, length, and mass. But anthropological definitions can neatly sidestep such difficulties by simply taking given primitive terms and using them as undefined physical terms to build operational criteria relevant to anthropology (Harris 1964:3–6). Rather than consider at length the theory behind a good operational definition, let us examine some practical attempts by anthropologists to clarify their definitions operationally.

● *No member of a crew is praised for the rugged individuality of his rowing.*—R. Emerson

2.3.1 Operationally Defining Acculturation

In a study of rural Buganda in Uganda, Robbins and Pollnac (1969) attempted to establish the relationship between drinking patterns and acculturation. Not only is alcoholic consumption in Buganda considered to be an overt symptom of psychic disorder, but also the actual mechanisms involved in drinking behavior are thought to be indications of more far-reaching social changes. The fieldworker can readily define and observe alcoholic consumption, but the problem of operationally defining acculturation is a more elusive task. Robbins and Pollnac decided that "degree of acculturation" should be considered as two major aspects in the overall acculturation process: the self-identification of informants with Western society (as seen through the use of material items) and general exposure to Western behavior and values (through formal education). To achieve a rough approximation of the various acculturative factors operating within Bugandan society, the researchers devised a survey questionnaire involving a variety of economic and social topics. This questionnaire was administered to 109 randomly selected households in six rural villages of Buganda.

From these results, Robbins and Pollnac abstracted criteria to distinguish traditional from acculturated households. The pilot study provided investigators with empirical evidence on Bugandan acculturation. The scale items consisted of 25 discrete variables, each readily observable by the ethnographer (Table 2.1). Each item is an indicator of westernization, and can be answered only by one of two possible responses: acculturational or traditional (this is why they are *discrete* variables). Ownership of common items of material culture—clocks, radios, stoves, and the like—indicates Western influence, while the relative degree to which the *kanzu* (native dress) was worn indicates traditional behavior. The sum of the acculturative responses thus proves an operational measure of westernization within any Bugandan household.

Using this scheme, independent workers should be able to scale any household from "highly acculturational" to "highly traditional" with a high degree of accuracy and repeatability. This ordinal scale (see Section 2.4.2) could in turn be compared to various aspects of drinking behavior (beverage preference, degree of alcoholic consumption, and various material aspects involved with drinking, such as bar furniture). Not only does the Robbins-Pollnac acculturation scale satisfactorily describe the processes used to rank households, but the items are also explicitly defined so the results can be repeated by other independent investigators.

2.3.2 Operationally Defining Projectile Point Attributes

The initial step in most archaeological analyses involves classifying the artifacts into rough categories. This preliminary classification is undertaken for several purposes: to condense the data, to establish time markers for dating the sites, to determine functional artifact types, perhaps even to reflect prehistoric "mental templates" reputed to exist in the mind of the maker. Regardless of the motive for classification, archaeological typology is always based upon the relatively fine-grained analysis and grouping of variables.

TABLE 2.1 Acculturation Scale Items for Bugandan Households (after Robbins and Polinac 1969: table 1).

---

1. The ability to read Luganda.
2. The ability to speak English.
3. The ability to read English.
4. Education of spouse, one or more years.
5. Education of spouse, four or more years.
6. Education of spouse, nine or more years.
7. Owns clock.
8. Owns watch.
9. Owns radio.
10. Owns iron.
11. Owns stove.
12. Respondent thinks it is proper for the husband and wife to eat at the same table.
13. Wearing *Kanzu* (native dress) at home with relatives and friends or when visiting relatives and friends (trad.).
14. Wearing *Kanzu* to work, to the local market, to towns and cities (trad.).
15. Wearing *Kanzu* all of the time (trad.).
16. Prefers drinking from a glass instead of gourd.
17. Has been to the bank to do business.
18. Goes to the cinema.
19. Purchases and reads magazines.
20. Visits Kampala (city).
21. Likes to straighten hair.
22. Presence of photographs on the inside walls.
23. Education of respondent one or more years.
24. Education of respondent four or more years.
25. Education of respondent nine or more years.

Sometimes these variables are quite crude and can be readily defined operationally: artifact length and width (as measured by vernier calipers), weight (as determined by a three-beam laboratory balance), color (as measured by a Munsell color chart), and so forth. But few archaeologists limit their analyses to such straightforward and easily defined attributes. Significant variables are more often rather subjective in nature, and observation becomes a matter of past experience rather than objectivity. Consider the projectile points in Fig. 2.2. Is artifact (a) basally indented? What about artifact (b)? Is projectile point (e) a basally notched point, or is it corner-notched? What about artifact (d)? Such questions cannot be answered objectively until we know how the variables are defined operationally. Such impressionistic variables are often defined by the naming process itself: basal indention means just that; corner-notched points appear just as the name implies; side-notched artifacts are notched from the side. Not only are these definitions circular, but they are also not operational because we are not told just how to determine the amount of basal indention or corner-notching in given artifacts.

Operational definitions must tell other researchers exactly how the variables are defined and measured:

$$\text{basal indention} \equiv \text{basal indention ratio} = \frac{\text{axial length}}{\text{total length}}$$

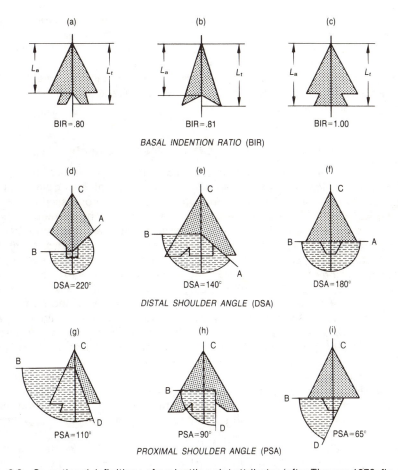

Fig. 2.2   Operational definitions of projectile point attributes (after Thomas 1970: fig. 2).

The variable "basal indention" is defined as the ratio (BIR) of two other continuous variables, "axial length" and "total length." "Total length" (L_t), in turn, is defined as the longest dimension of the projectile point. "Axial length" (L_a) is the distance along the line of symmetry (the midline). "Length" is a primitive term and hence is undefined. We'll let the physicists worry about that! Basal indention is thus operationally defined by two simple and relatively objective measurements. The measurement BIR = 1.00 [Fig. 2.2(c)] indicates that the point is not at all basally indented, but BIR = 0.80 [Fig. 2.2(a)] denotes a high degree of basal indention. The smaller the BIR, the more an artifact is basally indented. After a little practice, any novice can determine a BIR measurement as accurately as the most grizzled dirt archaeologist.

Notching position is a trickier attribute to define operationally. Rather than deal with position of notching directly, we must define a totally new variable, the Distal Shoulder Angle (DSA). In this case, DSA has not been assigned a written definition, but is defined graphically in Fig. 2.2. This case illustrates that good operational definitions need only be objective, and not necessarily stated in words. Discussing projectile point morphology in terms of such operational variables obviates the use of vague categories such as "corner-notching," "side-notching," and so forth, since we now have more precise methods of expression. Furthermore, DSA is on the interval scale of measurement (defined in Section 2.4.3) and is amenable to more sophisticated quantitative analysis than are mere categories.

2.3.3 Operationally Defining Cranial Measurements

Nowhere in anthropology has the operational definition of variables progressed so far as in craniometry—the measurement and analysis of human skulls. In fact, there are even those who suggest that craniometry has progressed *too far* (for example, Boyd 1950) and that excessive zeal in measuring human skulls has unduly overshadowed other lines of study in physical anthropology. Perhaps this is true, for surely no portion of mammalian anatomy has been more extensively probed, poked, X-rayed, and photographed than the human skull.

The recording of cranial measurements seems to date back to Petrus Camper, an eighteenth-century Dutch anthropologist who measured the degree of facial angle in order to determine the amount of prognathism of the human skull (Hulse 1963:427). But Camper's work and most subsequent attempts were rather clumsy approximations and quite lacking in precision. The problem of establishing objective cranial measurements was discussed in 1884 at the Congress of the International Anthropological Association in Frankfurt. A standardized plane of reference for craniometry, the so-called Frankfurt Horizontal (FH), was established as the plane defined by the left and right poria, and the right orbitale (see Fig. 2.1). Since that time, the phrase "measured in the Frankfurt horizontal" has assured that common cranial measurements are indeed comparable.

But the definition of the Frankfurt horizontal is itself dependent upon the objective placement of the two cranial reference points: the porion and the orbitale. Krogman has operationally defined these terms as follows (1962:316–317):

orbitale: The lowest point on the lower margin of the orbit.
porion: Most lateral point on the roof of the external auditory meatus (bony ear hole).

Both definitions contain primitive terms ("lowest point," "lower margin," "most lateral point") which must themselves be undefined. Figure 2.1 presents these and other cranial reference points in common use by modern physical anthropologists.

2.4 LEVELS OF MEASUREMENT

If anthropologists measured only skulls, then almost all relevant variables could be expressed in metric units such as millimeters, cubic centimeters, or degrees of arc. But the study of mankind embraces a range of topics and specialized subject matter, and such purity of measurement does not exist. In fact, most observations in social science are not measurements at all, strictly speaking, but are rather counts or ranked orderings. In order to cope adequately with the diversity of anthropological data, it is necessary to consider the common scales of measurement: their definition, their properties, and their restrictions.

2.4.1 Nominal Scale

The most elementary measuring operation involves the sorting of individual objects into homogeneous categories. This procedure (*classification*) is a necessary first step in nearly all social, biological or physical sciences, and many branches of science—especially the social sciences—have yet to evolve beyond the stage of primitive item classification. Although classification must never be treated as an end in itself, few worthwhile projects in science can proceed until individual phenomena can be treated in operational classes rather than as mere raw variates.

In nominal scales, symbols are assigned to categories which represent the range of possible values any given variate might take. These symbols are often words, such as "male" and "female" or "left" and "right," but other symbols such as numbers, pictures, colors, or even simple signs (+, −, and *) can label nominal categories. Creating a nominal scale involves merely assigning symbols to categories, subject to only one rule: Do not assign the same symbol to different categories, or different symbols to the same category (Stevens 1951). In a more formal sense, a nominal scale requires only that the classification be exhaustive (classify all possible items in the array) and mutually exclusive (classify each item into only one category). Beyond these elementary restrictions, anything goes on the nominal scale.

The nominal scale is anthropology's most primitive form of measurement, but this simplicity must not be allowed to obscure the practical difficulties and pitfalls involved in applying the nominal scale to real data. Numerals, for instance, are sometimes used to symbolize a set of nominal classes. The mere application of a numeral to a class, however, in no way justifies the use of ordinary arithmetic operations on that scale. It is arithmetically possible, for example, to add several license plate numbers, but the outcome is logically absurd. The arithmetic manipulation of any nominal scale, regardless of the symbol, is meaningless because nominal scales reflect only differences in *kind*, not of *degree*.

Some variables can be characterized in a number of different ways—that is, on several different nominal scales. "Blood type," for instance, has been observed on literally dozens of operational scales: ABO system, MN system, P system, Lutheran system, Lewis system, Duffy system, Kidd system, and Diego system, to name but a few. Each scheme defines its own categories and each involves a different nominal scale. These scales may or may not be independent. Which scale is selected usually depends upon a variety of factors such as the exact objectives of research, feasibility, cost, and previous experience. But once a given scale has been selected, the operational definitions of a successful classification divide all possible variates into exhaustive and mutually exclusive categories. Table 2.2 presents several examples of other nominal scales commonly used in modern anthropology.

TABLE 2.2 Some Common Nominal Scales in Anthropology.

Variable	Symbol	Common Operational Definition
"Regional identification" (col. 1, *Ethnographic Atlas*)	A	Africa, exclusive of Madagascar and the northern and northeastern portions of the continent.
	C	Circum-Mediterranean, including Europe, Turkey, and the Caucasus, the Semitic Near East, and northern and northeastern Africa.
	E	East Eurasia, excluding Formosa, the Philippines, Indonesia, and the area assigned to the Circum-Mediterranean but including Madagascar and other islands in the Indian Ocean.
	I	Insular Pacific, embracing all of Oceania as well as areas like Australia, Indonesia, Formosa, and the Philippines that are not always included therewith.
	N	North America, including the indigenous societies of this continent as far south as the Isthmus of Tehuantepec.
	S	South America, including the Antilles, Yucatan, and Central America as well as the continent itself.
"Slavery" (col. 71, *Ethnographic Atlas*)	H	Hereditary slavery present and of at least modest social significance.
	I	Incipient or nonhereditary slavery, that is, where slave status is temporary and not transmitted to the children of slaves.
	O	Absence or near absence of slavery.
	S	Slavery reported but not identified as hereditary or nonhereditary.
"Ground plan of dwelling" (col. 80, *Ethnographic Atlas*)	C	Circular.
	E	Elliptical or elongated with rounded ends.
	P	Polygonal.
	Q	Quadrangular around (or partially around) an interior court.
	R	Rectangular or square.
	S	Semicircular.

"Blood group (ABO system)"	A	Antigen A present
	B	Antigen B present
	AB	Antigens A and B present
	O	Neither antigens A nor B present
"Epicanthic fold"	Present	"... consists of a fold of skin that when the eye is open, comes down over and runs on a line with the edge of the upper eyelid" (Kelso 1970:253–254).
	Absent	—
"European Mousterian" (after Bordes 1968: chapter 8)	Typical Mousterian	Handaxes rare, percentage of scrapers between 25–50%; points well developed and carefully worked; limaces (double-pointed scrapers retouched all around) rare; few backed knives; notched flakes and denticulates; relatively small percentage of Levalloisian technique.
	Quina-Ferrassie Mousterian	50–80% scrapers; few or no handaxes; no backed knives; relatively few denticulates; non-Levalloisian technique.
	Denticulate Mousterian	No typical handaxes; no typical backed knives; few or no points; 5–25% scrapers (of poor quality): 35–55% denticulated tools; notched flakes common; technique may or may not be Levalloisian.
	Mousterian of Acheulean tradition, Type A:	8–40% handaxes; 20–40% scrapers; prevalence of points; some notched flakes; fairly large number of denticulates; some tools of Upper Paleolithic type; backed knives.
	Type B:	2–8% handaxes; great development of denticulates and backed knives; occasional double burins.

22

As mentioned earlier, operational definitions vary in both precision and accuracy. The ABO blood-grouping system is virtually infallible, since classification depends strictly upon the comparison of the antigen-antibody reaction of a drop of blood. "Sex" is another nominal scale which is relatively clear-cut, although there are a few borderline cases. But dichotomizing a lithic tool assemblage into "core" and "flake" tools, or estimating the predominant familial organization within a given society can introduce a high degree of personal judgment and intuition. Obviously, such cases involve nominal scales which are neither totally exhaustive nor completely mutually exclusive. But these difficulties arise as a result of inadequate definition of categories (a strictly anthropological matter) rather than from any inherent insufficiency in the mathematical grounding of nominal scales.

2.4.2 Ordinal Scale

An *ordinal* (or *ranked*) scale involves a relevant ordering of discrete categories into a meaningful sequence, obviously a significant logical advance over mere classification on the nominal level. Ordinal categories rank classes along a continuum, but the distance between each category in the continuum is either unknown or undefined because of imprecise measurement techniques or some quality inherent in the variable. It is impossible to specify *how much* of a variable each ordinal category represents.

Ordinal scales possess all properties of nominal scales, but have the additional property of *asymmetry*. That is, if the ordinal relations indicate that $A > B$ and $B > C$, then it must follow that $A > C$. In the case of ethnographic settlement pattern (Table 2.3), we know that since B (fully migratory) is less sedentary than H (separated hamlets), and since H is less sedentary than N (neighborhoods of dispersed homesteads), then B must also be less sedentary than N. But note that there is no indication in this—or in any other—ordinal scale regarding the *magnitude* of difference between categories. "Separated hamlets" are not necessarily twice as sedentary as "fully migratory," any more than "separated hamlets" are half as sedentary as "neighborhoods of dispersed homesteads." Because equal distances between ordinal categories can never be assumed, it is improper to add two ordinal scores, or to attempt to take an average of an ordinal scale. A large body of "rank-order statistics" has evolved to handle problems on the ordinal scale (as discussed in Chapters 12 and 14).

The line between nominal and ordinal scales occasionally becomes fuzzy and indistinct. Peruvian archaeologists, for example, sometimes classify their sites as "ceramic" or "preceramic." This distinction can be applied as a simple descriptive label, without necessary implications of chronological priority. This is a nominal scale. But when presence of pottery is used to seriate sites into a temporal sequence, then a rank ordering is definitely implied and the scale becomes ordinal. These distinctions are discussed in more detail when nonparametric statistics are considered.

2.4.3 Interval Scale

A scale of measurement is termed *interval* if it possesses all the properties of an ordinal scale but also implies *equal distances between the symbols.* A weather-

TABLE 2.3 Some Common Ordinal Scales in Anthropology

Variable	Symbol	Common Operational Definition
"Settlement pattern" (col. 30, *Ethnographic Atlas*)	B	Fully migratory or nomadic bands.
	H	Separated hamlets where several such form a more or less permanent single community.
	N	Neighborhoods of dispersed family homesteads.
	S	Seminomadic communities whose members wander in bands for at least half the year but occupy a fixed settlement at some season or seasons, for example, recurrently occupied winter quarters.
	T	Semisedentary communities whose members shift from one to another fixed settlement at different seasons or who occupy more or less permanently a single settlement from which a substantial proportion of the population departs seasonally to occupy shifting camps, for example, during transhumance.
	V	Compact and relatively permanent settlements, that is, nucleated villages or towns.
	W	Compact but impermanent settlements, that is, villages whose location is shifted every few years.
	X	Complex settlements consisting of a nucleated village or town with outlying homesteads or satellite hamlets. Urban aggregations of population are not separately indicated, since column 31 deals with community size.
"Male genital mutilations" (col. 37, *Ethnographic Atlas*)	0	Absent or not generally practiced.
	1	Performed shortly after birth, that is, within the first two months.
	2	Performed during infancy, that is, from two months to two years of age.
	3	Performed during early childhood, that is, from two to five years of age.
	4	Performed during late childhood, that is, from six to ten years of age.
	5	Performed during adolescence, that is, from 11 to 15 years of age.
	6	Performed during early adulthood, that is, from 16 to 25 years of age.
	7	Performed during maturity, that is, from 25 to 50 years of age.
	8	Performed in old age, that is, after 50 years of age.

Table 2.3 (*cont'd*)

Variable	Symbol	Common Operational Definition

"Human hair form"
(after Kelso 1970:253)

Straight — a, b
Wavy — c, d
Curly — e, f
Tightly Curled — g, h, i, k, l

"Human nasal flatness"
(after Kelso 1970:245)

1   2

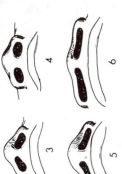

3   4

5   6

Free wandering	Remains should represent initial occupation of region; wide distribution of artifact types that are simple in nature and limited in variety; camps which moved frequently, evidence of occupation undetectable or at best scanty; consisting of ash or charcoal; split or burned animals bones and a few artifacts.
Restricted wandering	More limited distribution of characteristic artifact types; more specialized tools; food-grinding implements and stone-lined hearths; awls and needles (reflect basketry making and skin working).
Central-base wandering	Indications of seasonal occupation; thicker midden accumulations than above; shell middens were used; cave occupations common; occasional graves unusually rich (shaman?).
Semipermanent sedentary	Refuse deposits thin; potsherds common; house structures patterned in relation to one another; isolated graves in village; or burial may be in cemetery; evidence of ceremonial activity discernable; storage or cache pits common.
Simple nuclear centered	Ceremonial structures (earthworks) long-term habitation refuse; pottery differentiation into utilitarian and ceremonial wares; cemeteries have a few graves of very high status; stone sculpture; mosaics; engraved shell common; house structures of adobe or stone have patterned arrangement; ceremonial areas show planning.
Advanced nuclear centered	Contrast between remains at "capital" and relative simplicity of satellite communities; public buildings show planned construction and uniformity of architecture; crafts indicate occupational specialization; head deformation and tooth mutilation common in upper class.
Supranuclear integrated	Presence of roads between centers; extensive irrigation works; evidence of conquest; construction of forts in architectural style of conquerer at strategic places.

man who describes the daily temperature in New York City as "cold, cool, mild, or hot" is operating on an ordinal scale, since the distances between the categories are not specified. But if these identical temperatures were expressed in degrees Fahrenheit, the scale would be interval because each symbol (degree) represents exactly the same temperature interval as every other degree. We could say, for instance, that the difference in temperature between 70 and 75 F is exactly equal to the difference between 95 and 100 F. In the strict sense, interval scales are the first truly quantitative measures we have discussed—ordinal and nominal scales are generally considered qualitative— and most statistical and arithmetic manipulations are applicable to interval variates. Interval scale variates may be added or subtracted, and the addition of a constant does not change the internal relationships of such scales.

Few interval level measures are more intrinsically interesting than the Maya calendrical system. The Maya calendar crops up several times in this text; not only does the system have chronological significance but it also has arithmetic properties that are common to all interval scales. The basic element of the Maya calendar is the day (*kin*), and days can be grouped into several larger temporal divisions:

20 *kins* = 1 *uinal*, or 20 days
18 *uinals* = 1 *tun*, or 360 days
20 *tuns* = 1 *katun*, or 7200 days
20 *katuns* = 1 *baktun*, or 144,000 days

Groupings such as these are impossible on both the nominal and the ordinal scales because exact intervals are required between each basic category (see Coe 1966:chapter 3 for more details of the Maya calendar).

This additive property enabled the Maya to construct the systems of "Long Counts," which placed an event within the span of historic time. Long Count dates were commonly inscribed on monuments to commemorate great political events, to dedicate temples, or to celebrate a particularly important military episode. Long Count dates are obviously invaluable to archaeologists studying Maya cultural history.

When translated, all Maya Long Count dates read "*X* days since the end of the last Great Cycle," somewhat like the Christian calendar which records time as "*X* years since the birth of Christ." A system of numerical notation has been devised by Mayan epigraphers to express the Maya dates in more comprehensible form. The Long Count date of 9.10.19.5.11, for example, can be interpreted as follows (example from Coe 1966:58):

9 *baktuns* = 1,296,000 days
10 *katuns* = 72,000 days
19 *tuns* = 6,840 days
5 *uinals* = 100 days
11 *kins* = 11 days
1,374,951 days (since the end of the last Great Cycle)

In other words, the Maya calendar works because the constant intervals (the *kins*) can be grouped *through addition* into precisely equivalent larger units. This property does not hold for ordinal or nominal scales.

Interval scales can also be meaningfully manipulated by subtraction. Suppose, for example, that two monuments were found at a particular Maya site: Monument A had the above date (9.10.19.5.11 = 1,374,951 days since the end of the last Great Cycle) and stela B had a date of 9.10.12.2.3 (1,372,363 days since the end of the last Great Cycle). Since both counts date from the same zero point, and since we know that interval variates can be subtracted from one another, it becomes an easy matter to determine that the two stelae were erected exactly 1,374,951 − 1,372,363 = 2,588 days apart.

But note that the zero point in this, and in all, interval scales is arbitrary. Maya Long Count dates are expressed in "days since the end of the last Great Cycle." In fact, the zero point of the Long Count is so arbitrary that epigraphers and archaeologists labored for years trying to pin down that elusive date. The search was narrowed to a series of discrete time intervals, however, since any given *katun* can recur only once every 260 Maya years. As a result, it was possible for scholars to correlate any given Long Count date with only a few intervals along the Christian calendar, depending upon which *katun* was selected for the zero point. According to a correlation by George Spinden, the zero year corresponded to 3373 B.C. on the Christian calendar, while a second hypothesis, the Goodman–Thompson–Martinez correlation, set the magic year at 3113 B.C. Any Maya date could be converted to Christian years by either correlation, and the Spinden correlation is always 260 years older than the dating by the Goodman–Thompson–Martinez correlation.[1] Incidentally, radiocarbon evidence now strongly supports the Goodman–Thompson–Martinez correlation, by methods discussed in Chapter 7.

The lack of a true zero point restricts the utility of interval scales in some respects. Since zero is arbitrarily assigned, the *ratios* of two interval variates cannot be meaningfully compared. Consider the statement "80°F is twice as hot as 40°F." In effect, this statement implies the following ratio:

$$80°F:40°F = 2:1$$

Because the zero point on the Fahrenheit scale has been assigned by convention only, the ratio of these two variates is a logical absurdity. So, for that matter, is the assertion that A.D. 975 is twice as old as A.D. 1950, or that today is twice as hot (half as cold?) as yesterday. Only when zero points are dictated by the phenomena themselves—as is the case of ratio scale variates—can comparisons such as "twice as," "half as," or "three times as large as" be meaningful.

2.4.4 Ratio Scale

The ratio scale is the most advanced counting system considered here, and ratio variates are still rare, unfortunately, in most of anthropological research. What sets the ratio variates above those of the interval measurement scale is that the

---

[1]Note that correcting from the Spinden to the Goodman–Thompson–Martinez date is precisely the same logical operation as converting daily temperature from degrees Celsius to degrees Fahrenheit by the formula

$$F = (9/5)C + 32$$

There is nothing intrinsic about the zero point in any interval scale, whether it be the Long Count, an IQ score, height above sea level, or years before present (B.P.) which archaeologists arbitrarily take to be A.D. 1950.

zero point of a ratio scale is fixed rather than arbitrarily assigned. The most common ratio scales in anthropology involve the quantitative expression of physical properties such as length, width, size, weight, and so forth: Body stature, projectile point width, cranial capacity, basion–nasion diameter, mean distance travelled per year, and average weight are all ratio variables.

Anthropology also makes use of ratio scales in the enumeration of cases: the minimum settlement size, the number of cervical vertebrae, the number of same-sexed siblings, the number of storage cists in a habitation cave. While the counts themselves are discrete variates, they form a sophisticated set of measurements; not only are the counts exact—rather than approximations, as with continuous variates—but also a zero point is always implicit in the enumeration process.

Ratio variates can also be derived from other primary variates. Population density, for instance, is generally defined as

$$\text{population density} = \frac{\text{number of people}}{\text{unit area}}$$

An estimate of 500 people per square mile is one such derived ratio variable, in which the numerator and denominator are themselves ratio levels. Many common demographic indices—mortality, fecundity, rate of immigration, intrinsic rate of increase—are derived ratio variates, as are the ratios common to physical anthropology (cephalic index, nasal index, metabolic rate) and also to archaeology (the room-to-kiva ratio, the number of beta emissions per 1000 minutes in radiocarbon dating, the ratio of domesticated to nondomesticated foodstuffs).

Ratio variates admit a wide range of mathematical properties because ratio scales are totally *isomorphic* to arithmetic (meaning that, since the structures are identical, all arithmetic operations can be performed upon ratio variates without destroying the relationships among the variates). As the name implies, ratio scales can also be meaningfully compared as ratios: A population density of 50 people per square mile is exactly twice that of a city with only 25 people per square mile; a 5.0 gram projectile point has only one-third the mass of a 15.0 gram point; a nuclear family of four individuals is exactly half the size of a family of eight. In addition, unlike interval scaling, ratio level variates can be transformed through multiplication by a constant. Inches are readily converted by multiplication to feet, for example, by using the correction factor of $1/12 = 0.083$.

Table 2.4 summarizes the arithmetic operations permissible for each level of measurement.

TABLE 2.4 Permissible Operations for Measurement Scales.

Scale	$=, \neq$	$>, <$	$+, -$	$\times, \div$
Nominal	Yes	No	No	No
Ordinal	Yes	Yes	No	No
Interval	Yes	Yes	Yes	No
Ratio	Yes	Yes	Yes	Yes

2.4.5 Refining Levels of Measurement

The preceding sections have characterized measurement scales into four basic (ordinal) categories. At this point, one might justifiably question: So what? Was this merely another academic exercise in number games and classification, or do the levels of measurement have some practical worth?

Two reasons justify our consideration of the various levels of measurement. First of all, these levels of observations dictate to some degree the statistical operations which can be applied to particular sets of data. Nominal measures are often termed "weak" because few arithmetic operations are applicable to simple unordered categories. Ratio scales, on the other hand, are "strong" because these measures are applicable to all mathematical operations. Every statistical test makes certain explicit assumptions about the underlying structure of the data and generally requires some minimal level of measurement. All statistical procedures to be considered here can be legitimately applied when strong measurement is available, but weak measurements severely restrict the potential avenues of analysis. The relationship between scale of measurement and statistical test is a complex topic and not so straightforward as social scientists once thought. It is sufficient to recognize at this point that the kinds of measurements available will influence the mode of analysis.

Levels of measurement can also be taken as a rough gauge of scientific maturity within a given discipline. Physics, for instance, is generally considered to be a most sophisticated science, and nearly all physical measurements are "strong." Social science measurements, on the other hand, are often only nominal and ordinal, indicative of a more primitive state of investigation. As Kemeny (1959:143) has pointed out, many sciences (and especially the social sciences) have yet to pass beyond the stage of preliminary classification. Students in introductory anthropology courses, for example, often complain about the strange names and categories which they are expected to assimilate: Paleolithic, Mesolithic, cross-cousin marriage, couvade, morpheme, australopithecine, cognatic, animistic, moiety. While, admittedly, learning these elementary categories can be tedious for the novice, the procedure is essential. Science usually begins with classification in one form or another, and the fact that a young science can characterize two objects as sharing a single variable state is a significant milestone. That is, when two objects are judged to be the "same" with respect to a variable, the conclusion is a primitive form of generalization, and a unifying thread throughout science is the consistent search for more encompassing generalizations. To say, for example, that the Nisenan Indians of central California have the "same" cousin kinship terminology (the Hawaiian system) as the Blackfoot of the Plains is an important step toward understanding kinship systems in general.

A second important signpost of scientific maturity is the introduction of orders of magnitude. Not only may two objects be judged "equal" with respect to variable X, but ordinal scales allow the additional judgment that some categories contain *more* of variable X than do other categories. A simple order is sufficient for many purposes, but a higher level of measurement is generally preferred so that the more advanced mathematical techniques are available. The more sophisticated the measurement system, the more precise will be the theories which result.

But the real problem in developing adequate systems of measurement lies outside the scope of mathematics and statistics. Statistics deals only with symbols, and statistical methods work equally well regardless of the referents which these symbols represent (see Hays 1973:89). Progress in measuring systems requires a deeper understanding of anthropological phenomena rather than more sophisticated mathematical statistics. Once the variables have been defined on solid anthropological grounds, then appropriate manipulative techniques are readily available from established mathematics. Some examples should illustrate how measurements progress in anthropology.

Anthropologists have faced few more truculent problems than in their efforts to measure *cultural evolution*. In fact, the effectiveness of measuring cultural development reflects in large part the maturation of anthropological inquiry. Most primitive sciences commence substantive research with a lengthy period of name giving, and these early classifications are generally nominal scales. But the scientific study of cultural evolution has progressed somewhat differently because the name-giving phase began directly with the ordinal level and bypassed the nominal phase altogether. By its very nature, the study of cultural evolution is concerned with the sequences of events. Ordering was implied right from the start. Even when discussion involved simplistic dichotomies—such as civilized versus noncivilized or hunter versus farmer—an ordering was always implied. The categories of cultural evolution were never nominal.[2]

Literally dozens of ordinal scales have been suggested to measure the cultural progress of man. One notable effort was Condorcet's ten-stage scheme in the *Outline of Intellectual Progress of Mankind*, originally published in 1795:

1st   Tribal society.
2d   Pastoral society.
3d   Agricultural society to the invention of the alphabet.
4th   The progress of the human mind in Greece up to the division of the sciences about the time of Alexander the Great.
5th   The progress of the sciences from their division to their decline.
6th   The decadence of knowledge to the restoration about the time of the Crusades.
7th   The early progress of science from its revival in the West to the invention of printing.
8th   From the invention of printing to the time when philosophy and the sciences shook off the yoke of authority.
9th   From Descartes to the foundation of the French Republic.
10th   The French Republic.

Not only are Condorcet's categories impressionistic, but they are also ethnocentric, dealing largely with European history and ignoring cultural evolution throughout the rest of the world. Marvin Harris (1968:35) has succinctly characterized Condorcet's perspective as "the more remote the age, the duller

---

[2]Although the approaches to the study of cultural evolution have varied enormously over the past century, the basic definition of cultural evolution has changed surprisingly little. Robert Carneiro (1973:90) recently defined evolution as a "change from a relatively indefinite, incoherent homogeneity to a relatively definite, coherent heterogeneity, through successive differentiations and integrations." The essence of this statement is little modified from the 1862 definition by Herbert Spencer.

the mind, the less enlightened is man's social life." But regardless of the shortcomings, Condorcet's scheme illustrates the principles of ordinal scaling.

Refined ordinal classification was later framed by Lewis Henry Morgan in *Ancient Society* (1877). Morgan divided the progress of human achievement into three major "Ethnical Periods": savagery, barbarism, and civilization, which were scaled to seven categories according to status as follows:

I. *Lower Status of Savagery:* commenced with the infancy of the human race in restricted habitats, subsistence upon fruits and nuts. No such tribes remained into the historical period.

II. *Middle Status of Savagery:* commenced with acquisition of fish and use of fire. Mankind spread over greater portion of earth's surface. Exemplified by Australians and Polynesians.

III. *Upper Status of Savagery:* commenced with invention of the bow and arrow. Exemplified by Athapascan tribes of Hudson's Bay Territory.

IV. *Lower Status of Barbarism:* commenced with invention or practice of pottery. Exemplified by the Indian tribes of the United States east of Missouri River.

V. *Middle Status of Barbarism:* commenced with domestication of animals in the Eastern hemisphere, and in the Western with cultivation by irrigation and use of adobe brick and stone in architecture. Exemplified by villages of New Mexico and Mexico.

VI. *Upper Status of Barbarism:* commenced with manufacture of iron. Exemplified by Grecian tribes of the Homeric Age and Germanic tribes of the time of Caesar.

VII. *Status of Civilization:* commenced with use of a phonetic alphabet and production of literary records; divided into *Ancient* and *Modern*.

The ordinal stages of Condorcet and Morgan can, of course, be faulted on several scores, but these early classifications were important steps in sharpening the perception of cultural evolution.

After decades of strong disfavor, the definition and study of evolutionary stages has again become the subject of legitimate anthropological research. Service (1962), for example, defined three stages of primitive human social organization—bands, tribes, and chiefdoms—and some archaeologists, such as Sanders and Marino (1970), have directly adopted Service's sociocultural stages in interpreting the archaeological record. Other archaeologists have attempted to apply schemes of stages based upon technological criteria (such as the Beardsley classification presented in Table 2.3). In fact, most archaeological research is from time to time synthesized using similar ordinal frameworks, as in the Willey and Phillips' (1958) scheme of "historical-developmental stages" of New World prehistory: Lithic, Archaic, Formative, Classic, and Postclassic. Yet, regardless of sophistication (or lack of it), all such scales remain subject to the limits of ordinal level measurements.

In 1948, Carleton Coon prepared a six-part classification of cultural development, basing his stages upon four quantitative measures: number of specialists, amount of trade, number of institutions to which an individual may belong, and the complexity of those institutions (Coon 1948:612f). In other words, Coon bridged the gap between ordinal and ratio level variates. Somewhat later, Raoul

Naroll (1956) furthered this line of investigation by devising a single index of cultural evolution. Naroll's *"Preliminary Index of Social Development"* is based upon three equally weighted and operationally defined indicators: craft specialization, organization ramification, and urbanization. The 1960s saw an important series of related studies in which literally hundreds of traits were considered for use as measures of cultural complexity (see Tatje and Naroll, 1970, for a comprehensive discussion of these indices). The more recent studies indicate that several of these indices are highly interrelated and often produce nearly identical results. The single best indicator of cultural evolution seems to be the *maximum settlement size* variable, defined earlier (Section 2.2).

The point is that when substantive research began on cultural evolution, the level of measurement consisted of relatively crude—and usually ethnocentric—ordinal scales such as Morgan's "Ethnical Periods." Stages of evolution were redefined on several occasions, sometimes for rather specialized objectives and at other times to provide more precision, but they remained on the ordinal scale and were therefore subject to the restrictions which apply to all rank-order variables. Finally, a second line of metric investigation led to more sophisticated measurements: Naroll, Carneiro, and others were able to derive interval and ratio scale indices to characterize cultural evolution. It was ultimately discovered—largely as a result of attempts to redefine such measures—that a single ratio scale indicator, the maximum settlement size, is sufficient to adequately characterize cultural complexity throughout the world. This discovery is of particular significance to archaeologists, since settlement size can often be estimated from the maximum floor areas of archaeological sites by using Naroll's constant; thus, much of the prehistoric record can be applied to the study of cultural evolution. The scientific investigation of cultural evolution progressed hand in hand with the progressive definition of more adequate operational indices, which in turn raised the overall levels of measurement.

Similar refinements in measuring technique have occurred in physical anthropology. One prime example is the measurement of the PTC taste-deficiency trait. In 1931, A. L. Fox observed quite by chance that while some individuals were unable to taste the synthetic compound phenylthiocarbamide (PTC), others reported the taste as quite bitter, somewhat like quinine. Subsequent investigation revealed that the ability to taste PTC is inherited as a simple Mendelian dominant. The test was initially administered by instructing informants to directly ingest crystals of PTC or to touch the tongue with a PTC-impregnated paper strip. The results of this procedure were based upon informant response, and subjects were characterized as "taster" or "nontaster," two dichotomous classes on the nominal scale. The test was later refined by administering to informants a series of diluted PTC solutions, and then asking them to describe their sensations. While this test was largely subjective—determined by the informant's ability to articulate his sensations—the refined test indicated a range of sensitivity among tasters which could be expressed in terms of crude rank orders of tasters along a scale of sensitivity.

The test was even further improved when informants were given a series of unlabelled tumblers, half of which contained a PTC solution and half of which contained just water. Subjects were then asked to discriminate the bottles containing PTC. If the groups were successfully sorted, then the next lowest concentration was used. The lowest concentration at which a completely correct answer was given can be operationally defined as the tasting threshold. In order to standardize the results, the following standardized solutions were applied (after Harris and Kalmus 1950:table 1):

Solution No.	PTC, mg/liter
1	1300.00
2	650.00
3	325.00
4	162.50
5	81.25
6	40.63
7	20.31
8	10.16
9	5.08
10	2.54
11	1.27
12	0.63
13	0.32
14	0.16

In this manner, taster threshold is characterized by the solution number, a ratio-level variable. This test is repeated over a large series of subjects in the same biological population, producing a bar graph which characterizes a population's thresholds (see Fig. 2.3) in percentage. The horizontal scale refers to solution number. Such graphs frequently exhibit two peaks (or *modes*) distinguishing tasters from nontasters.

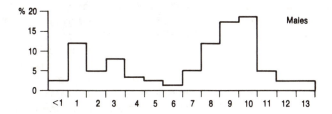

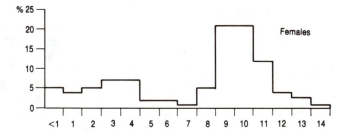

Fig. 2.3   PTC thresholds for 100 females and 114 males between the ages of 20 and 59 (after Harris and Kalmus 1950:fig. 3).

The case of PTC tasting is an excellent illustration of the principle that progress in science is generally paralleled by an increasing refinement in the level of measurement. Similar progress has occurred in the study of skin and hair pigmentation, color blindness, and nutritional ecology, to mention but a few areas of ongoing research in physical anthropology.

2.5 POPULATION AND SAMPLES

> ● *It is like the North Carolina mule which a tourist once stopped to admire. He asked the mule's owner what the animal's name was. The farmer replied, "I don't know, but we call it Bill."*
> —S. Ervin

In Winick's *Dictionary of Anthropology*, the word "population" is defined twice:

"*population, amphimictic.* A population which has freely crossing fertile descendants."
"*population, inbreeding.* A group of persons among whom mating takes place." (Winick 1966:428)

Ecological populations are groups of living organisms of a single species found in a circumscribed area at a given time. This definition of population is frequently used by physical anthropologists with reference to both living and extinct animals. In this sense, one can study the chimpanzee population of the Gombe Stream reserve in Tanzania, the hunting behavior of *Australopithecus* populations in South Africa, or the gene frequency of the sickle-cell trait in Afro-American populations. Cultural anthropologists also use "population" in this sense. Human *society*, for instance, has been defined by Marvin Harris as a "population that has an organized way of life" (1971:654); societies are groups of people (populations) who depend upon each other for survival. Similarly, archaeologists often discuss the "prehistoric Pueblo III populations" or the "nomadic population of Clovis hunters," and a linguist might refer to his informants collectively as "the Shoshoni-speaking population." In general, anthropologists tend to use the term "population" in a phenomenological sense, denoting a concrete set of living (or once-living) individuals. All populations of this sort could be physically delimited under ideal conditions, enumerated, and assembled in one place.

The word "population" takes on a rather different meaning in statistics, but this difference is subtle and could easily be overlooked. A statistical population does not consist of physical objects at all (people, lemurs, or microbes), but rather of variates measured upon those objects. Arikara Indians could comprise a biological or sociocultural population, but they could never be a statistical population. Only a set of related variates—such as the stature of Arikara Indians—could be a statistical population. Body weight, daily caloric intake, marriage to cross-cousins, presence of the Rh blood factor, frequency of reflexive verb usage, and cranial capacity are all variates comprising statistical populations characteristic of the aggregate of Arikara Indians.

A *statistical population* is a set of variates (counts, measurements, or characteristics) about which relevant inquiries are to be made.

Unlike the phenomenological populations of biology and anthropology, statistical populations are *ideational*. Statistical populations include only observations; and observations have in themselves no objective reality. Statistical populations are comprised of variates, not objects.

Populations in this sense are arbitrary and must be carefully (that is, operationally) defined. Some populations may consist of a finite number of variates, such as the stature of all living Arikara Indians. Populations could also be defined to include not only living Arikara, but also all Arikara who lived in the past, and also those who will ever live in the future. So populations could also be infinite. Clearly, there is nothing "natural" about a statistical population because it is defined to satisfy specific research objectives. All these definitions, however, must be based upon *anthropological* rather than *statistical* considerations. Statistical methodology comes into play only after the relevant populations have been defined to suit the research objectives at hand.

It would be onerous indeed for an anthropologist to attempt to interrogate, measure, observe, or photograph the entire physical population of all living Arikara. And, if the statistical population had been defined to include Arikara of all times and all places, complete observation would be patently impossible. One characteristic of most statistical populations is that they are *incompletely observable*. Physical anthropologists can never hope to measure the entire population of *Australopithecus robustus* crania, for example, and in fact, primatologists have trouble dealing with an entire biological population of living nonhuman primates.

Thus it is that populations of variates must usually be estimated from a small subset of the actual statistical population.

A *sample* is defined as any subset of a statistical population. While many samples are (or should be) formed through random selection of variates, *any* subset of a statistical population can be termed a sample. Some methods of sampling are more efficient than others, while other sampling procedures produce more reliable results. Regardless of the sampling procedure, however, samples are bound to reflect the character of the parent population at least to some degree.

Neither statistical populations nor their samples are thus comprised of objects per se, but rather are variates measured upon the objects. These sets of variates can be characterized by certain fundamental measures.

A *parameter* is any quantitative measure which seems to characterize a population.

Chapter 4 considers several indices (the mean, mode, standard deviation, and so forth) which estimate certain characteristics of populations. Since parameters, by definition, must always refer to populations, the phrase "population parameter" is redundant.

A *statistic* is any quantitative measure which seems to characterize a sample.

Note that this usage of the term "statistic" differs from that heard in ordinary parlance.

A parameter is a constant, fixed for the referent population. Parameters are generally unknown because most populations are incompletely observable. If a population is defined as the cranial capacity of all living mountain gorilla, then clearly the mean of that population (the mean is a parameter in this case) will never be known. For this reason, parameters are usually *estimated* from statistics which have been derived from samples. Statistics are never constant for a population, since several possible samples could have been drawn from the same population. Greek letters such as μ, σ, and ρ are conventionally assigned to represent populations, whereas Latin letters such as S, X, and r are traditionally reserved for statistics.

2.6 WHAT ARE STATISTICS?

● *After all, the higher statistics are only common sense reduced to numerical appreciation*—K. Pearson

We are finally in a position to answer a question which I hope has been troubling you throughout this chapter: What exactly are statistics? We know that a *statistic* is a measure characterizing a sample, but is this all there is to statistics?

Statistical procedures assume basically two objectives when applied to anthropological data. The initial objective is to provide precise description of phenomena, and the branch of statistics which enables one to characterize diverse data sets is called descriptive statistics. The other major objective of statistical analysis is to provide a systematic procedure of predicting unknown parameters through the application of inferential statistics.

2.6.1 Descriptive Statistics

An archaeological student has just finished excavating a 19-room pueblo; a graduate student has returned from his initial ethnological fieldwork; a novice physical anthropologist has just administered a questionnaire on heredity. What do they do with their data?

Descriptive statistics consists of a battery of standardized procedures through which masses of data can be reduced to manageable proportions. Sometimes the variates are grouped into categories, which are then ordered into a frequency distribution (discussed in Section 3.2). Or perhaps a bar graph would better illustrate the relationships of interest (Section 3.3.1). If the data are in percentages, then perhaps a circle graph should be used instead (Section 3.3.3). But occasions arise when the data are too complex for simple schemes of graphing; then new measures must be applied in order to ferret out fundamental information within the data. Measures of central tendency, such as the mean, the mode, and the median are handy for finding whether the data tend to group about a single point or whether there are several clusters of variates on each variable. There are also measures of dispersion, which summarize the tendency of variates to disperse about the central tendencies. Chapter 4 examines the usefulness, applicability and computation of common descriptive statistics.

2.6.2 Statistical Inference

This chapter began with A. L. Kroeber's adroit observation that the subject of anthropology is limited only by man himself. While such ambitious objectives make for a colorful kaleidoscope of observational potential, problems raised by the oppressive bulk of "relevant data" can be overwhelming for a fledgling science. Anthropology's holistic cornerstone is at once its greatest virtue and also its most severe handicap. Anthropologists are spread so thin that one can never hope to observe all of anything that is truly important. In fact, it is impossible to make a complete set of observations about *any* variable relating to mankind, relevant or otherwise. Not only must one consider the three billion people currently billeted on the planet, but also the millions who have already died. And, if the goal is truly to generalize about the total human condition, then unborn humanity must be considered as well. So it is that anthropologists have (at least tacitly) resigned themselves to working with *samples* from the human spectrum. These samples have been chosen by any number of criteria: for convenience, for quantity, for representativeness, for uniqueness. Samples are, by definition, incomplete representatives of a specific population.

Thus, a knotty problem facing anthropologists—and in fact, facing all scientists—is to determine just what claims about a population can reasonably be made from a sample. Consider the ethnological example of Tikopia, a small Polynesian island in the extreme east of the British Solomon Islands. In 1929, anthropologist Raymond Firth (1957) took a house-by-house census and determined that 1281 people lived on Tikopia. One Tikopian village, Siku, contained 38 adults. Suppose a psychological anthropologist travelled to Tikopia and administered a TAT test to the adults of Siku. How far could he generalize his results? Does his test refer just to the population of all adults in Siku, or are the results relevant to all living adults on Tikopia? What about those Tikopians who just recently died? Perhaps one could even claim that these tests represent all Polynesians in the Solomon Islands. Or perhaps even humanity?

Physical anthropologists face the same problem. Earlier in this chapter we considered four Neanderthal crania. One can readily determine that their average cranial capacity is 1473 cc, which is a descriptive statistic. But what does this average tell us? Since all four fossils were classified as the "temperate glacial" variety of Neanderthal, is one justified in stating that the average cranial capacity of the glacial Neanderthal *population* is 1473 cc? But do we really expect that the population average is exactly 1473 cc, or is this just a reasonable approximation? What if somebody else claimed that our sample average is good enough to represent the population of *all* Neanderthal varieties; is this claim justified?

Further suppose that we also had a sample of temperate *interglacial* Neanderthals (data from Coon 1971a:table 37).

Specimen	Symbol	Variate, cc
Tabun 1	Y_1	= 1271
Skhūl 4	Y_2	= 1554
Skhūl 9	Y_3	= 1587

The average of these cranial capacities is 1471 cc. Since this statistic is 2 cc less than the average for the temperate glacial variety, can we justifiably conclude that the interglacial population had a cranial capacity which is on the average 2 cc smaller than the glacial variety? Or is this 2 cc difference too small to worry about? Are the two varieties identical with respect to cranial capacity?

Anthropologists almost always work with samples and are continually faced with similar problems. How far can they generalize their findings? Researchers sometimes try to use their common sense for such generalizations, but psychological experiments have shown that few individuals are capable of assimilating large batches of data, mentally weighing each bit of relevant information and arriving at a good, unbiased generalization (Mendenhall 1971: 176). Fortunately, a powerful tool exists which can help in analyzing sample results, and, that tool is called *statistical inference*.

Statistical inference is the process of reasoning from a sample statistic to a population parameter using the principles of probability.

The main objective of statistical inference is to make a sensible conclusion about the whole when only a part is known. Because statistical inference is always based upon incomplete data, the conclusions are only tentative. The main objective of the theory of sampling is to determine the chances of error in making inferences from a sample to a population. The degree to which such a statistical decision is reliable is often expressed in the form of *probabilities*, or the odds of making a correct decision. Chapters 3 and 4 consider various descriptive statistical methods, Chapter 5 presents the basics of probability theory, and Chapter 6 combines potentiality with description to provide the rudiments of statistical inference.

● *Know then thyself, presume not God to scan!*
*The proper study of mankind is man.—*A. Pope

SUGGESTIONS FOR FURTHER READING

General

Clarke (1968:chapter 1). A systems perspective of archaeology and its data base.
Kemeny (1959:chapter 15). General look at the limits of social science data.
Kerlinger (1973:chapters 1, 2 and 3). A detailed and quite sophisticated treatment of the nature of science and its relationship to social phenomena; Kerlinger carefully defines the categories of variables encountered in social research.
Naroll (1962b:chapter 1). Consideration of the nature of errors within ethnological data.
Simpson, Roe, and Lewontin (1960:chapters 1 and 2). Readable introduction to measurements and data of the biological sciences; especially relevant to physical anthropologists.
Sokal and Rohlf (1969:chapter 2). A more advanced look at biological data.

Levels of Measurement

Blalock (1972:chapter 2). Detailed consideration of the specific problems involved with common measurements scales of social science.

Pelto (1970:chapter 7). Excellent introduction to levels of measurement as applied to kinship studies.

Steger (1971:section 1) This reader reprints several articles, especially from psychology, which debate the virtues of "strong" versus "weak" measurement theory in statistics.

Operational Definitions

Benjamin (1955). General introduction to issues of operationalism in science; discusses Bridgman's initial thesis, its modifications by the physical and social sciences, and presents a plea for sensible operationalism.

Harris (1964). A rather abstract proposal for an operational data language in ethnology.

Kemeny (1959:chapter 7). Kemeny, a former research assistant to Albert Einstein, discusses the necessity and shortcomings of rigidly operational definitions.

Krumbein and Graybill (1965:chapter 3). Several excellent examples of how common field concepts can be assigned precise, graphic definitions.

Naroll (1970a). Discusses problems with operationally defining "tribe" or "society"; Naroll proposes the *cultunit* as the basic culture-bearing unit of anthropology.

Pelto (1970: chapter 3). Gives several examples of attempts by ethnologists to operationalize their field concepts.

3 Grouping Data for Analysis

● *The stature of a science is commonly measured by the degree to which it makes use of mathematics.* —S. Stevens

3.1 INTRODUCTION

Anthropology's holistic perspective on man and his works generates a phenomenal quantity of data. In theory at least, anthropology's field of observation is the largest in all of social science because no aspect of the human condition is a priori excluded. Since data never speak for themselves, an initial step in the analysis of anthropological data generally involves summarizing raw field data.

There are basically two techniques for consolidating and presenting the primary data. The first method involves the direct summary of raw numbers into tabular form. Such tables may often prove adequate for some purposes, but data tables and frequency distributions commonly preface more intensive analysis. Another option is to display the summarized data as graphs or diagrams. Diagrams can serve either as explanatory devices—to elicit proper responses from the reader—or as preliminary aids to the investigator in deciding upon the proper direction for further analysis.

3.2 DATA TABLES AND FREQUENCY DISTRIBUTIONS

Anthropologist A. L. Kroeber spent much of the first quarter of this century in fieldwork among the California Indian population, and after two decades of study he summarized his findings in the monumental *Handbook of the Indians of California* (1925). Although much of his text considers the religious, social, and economic characteristics of various California groups, Kroeber was concerned largely with the impact of White contact upon the native Californians.

Population density is a quantitative matter, and Kroeber spent an entire chapter evaluating various estimates of the decline of population density among aboriginal populations. Kroeber's chapter 57 (entitled simply "Population") considers such diverse demographic factors as ecological determinants of aboriginal settlements, the impact of the early mission period, inroads of disease, and influences of reservations. He ultimately synthesized the available information into a quantitative estimate of the population decline over the past 125 years.

Kroeber *could have* presented his concluding findings in textual form as follows: The best estimator for the aboriginal population of California in 1800 is 260,000; for 1835, 210,000; for 1849, 100,000; for 1852, 85,000; for 1856, 50,000; for 1860, 35,000; for 1870, 30,000; for 1880, 20,500; for 1890, 18,000; and for 1900, 15,500. The data are all there, but what is Kroeber's point? Although a decreasing trend is apparent, the true nature of the decrease is somehow lost in a textual presentation. Kroeber, in fact, rejected this textual mode of presentation and summarized his findings in population change in a concise data table (Table 3.1). Tabulations such as Table 3.1 not only underscore the salient trends, but also relieve the text of wordy and redundant summaries. The *variable* in this case is "aboriginal population of California" and each annual estimate of that population is a *variate*. Kroeber's material was succinctly displayed in this rather simple tabular format because only ten variates were involved. Tables can become awkward and cumbersome as the number of variates increases.

Table 3.2 presents the weights of 96 Elko series projectile points (probably dart tips) recovered from the Reese River Valley of central Nevada. Projectile point weight is an engaging variable for archaeologists because the heavier points seem to be older, and weight can be a functional indicator (arrowheads are lighter than spear points). But one can tell almost nothing by inspecting the raw data in Table 3.2. Most anthropological data must be grouped into a less cumbersome, more compact format conventionally termed a *frequency distribution*.

Basically, a frequency distribution comprises a large set of variates into a few summary classes. The first step is to determine the *range* of the observed data. In Table 3.2, the lightest artifact weighs only 2.7 grams and the heaviest is 9.0 grams. The most serviceable frequency distributions generally contain between 8 and 20 classes; excessive information is lost when data are compressed into too few classes, and tables with more than about 20 classes tend to lose their effectiveness as summary statements. These data run from 2.7 to 9.0 grams;

Table 3.1   California Indian Depopulation (after
            Kroeber 1925:891).

Year	Total	Year	Total
1800	260,000	1860	35,000
1835	210,000	1870	30,000
1849	100,000	1880	20,500
1852	85,000	1890	18,000
1856	50,000	1900	15,500

TABLE 3.2   Weights (in grams) of 96 Elko Series Dart Points from the Reese River Valley, Central Nevada (data taken from Thomas 1971a).

3.7	4.0	3.5	6.6	6.7	4.0
6.0	5.0	4.0	3.5	5.0	4.3
3.0	4.5	4.9	6.0	4.5	4.0
8.0	3.3	3.8	5.0	3.1	4.2
3.3	3.3	4.2	4.6	3.4	3.8
3.0	3.5	3.0	4.7	4.5	5.0
5.0	4.0	4.0	4.4	3.5	5.6
3.3	5.0	8.6	3.3	3.0	3.1
4.0	3.1	7.7	3.8	7.3	7.8
3.0	6.0	3.5	3.9	3.1	9.0
4.0	4.0	4.0	3.2	5.0	3.5
3.4	4.0	3.5	3.0	8.0	3.3
3.5	4.0	4.0	3.1	5.0	4.8
4.3	3.1	5.5	4.9	2.7	5.0
7.0	8.2	7.0	4.0	3.2	5.1
4.0	5.0	3.5	5.5	3.9	4.8

thus, the range is the total interval of 6.3 grams. By applying a class interval of 0.5 gram, all variates can be compressed into 14 classes.

Table 3.3 presents a standard frequency distribution for the raw projectile point data of Table 3.2. In effect, the *class midpoint* replaces the variation within each class by a single indicator. The class midpoint, *X*, is simply the average of the upper and lower class boundaries. The number of variates falling into each class is termed the *class frequency, f*.

The frequency distribution is an analytical tool enabling the social scientist better to visualize the trends and distributions within his data. The precise

TABLE 3.3   Frequency Distribution of Projectile Point Weights on Table 3.2.

Class Boundaries, grams	Class Midpoints, X	Tallies	Frequency, f	Cumulative Frequency
2.5–2.9	2.7	|	1	1
3.0–3.4	3.2	ЖЖЖЖ||	22	23
3.5–3.9	3.7	ЖЖЖ	15	38
4.0–4.4	4.2	ЖЖЖЖ	20	58
4.5–4.9	4.7	Ж ||||	9	67
5.0–5.4	5.2	ЖЖ|	11	78
5.5–5.9	5.7	|||	3	81
6.0–6.4	6.2	|||	3	84
6.5–6.9	6.7	||	2	86
7.0–7.4	7.2	|||	3	89
7.5–7.9	7.7	||	2	91
8.0–8.4	8.2	|||	3	94
8.5–8.9	8.7	|	1	95
9.0–9.4	9.2	|	1	96

arrangement of class intervals may vary between investigators. Although an interval of 0.5 gram was selected for illustration here, somebody else might wish to group the data in intervals of, say, 0.6 gram (which would result in 12 classes). The larger the interval, of course, the more information is lost in forming the table. Decisions such as this are left to the worker because he is more familiar with the measurements at hand and he knows what tasks the data will be called upon to perform.

All frequency distributions must obey two simple rules:

1. The classes must be *mutually exclusive*. There can be no ambiguity as to the class in which any variate belongs. If, for instance, the two lower classes of Table 3.3 were defined as "2.5–3.0" and "3.0–3.5," then a variate of 3.0 would fall into both classes. This situation must be avoided.
2. The classes must be *exhaustive*. That is, the entire range of observed variates must be reflected by the classes. Had one of the Elko projectile points weighed 10.2 grams, additional classes would have been necessary: "9.5–9.9" and "10.0–10.4." There is generally no purpose in extending the number of classes beyond the observed range of the sample.

There must always be a gap between the upper boundary of one class, and the lower boundary of the adjacent class. The distance between boundaries depends upon the accuracy of measurement (that is, the number of significant figures). But since all frequency distributions must have exhaustive classes, you should be aware that the *implied class limits* extend infinitely beyond the significant figures. In other words, it is the true limits of the frequency distribution which must be exhaustive, even though rounding of the actual data leaves gaps in the actual stated limits (excepting the case of discrete measurements, in which there is no rounding error). By convention, all digits less than 5 are rounded to the lower class, measures 5 or greater go into the higher class. The stated limits for Table 3.3 are 2.5–2.9, 3.0–3.4 . . . . The true or implied limits are understood to be

$$2.455\cdots - 2.9499\cdots$$
$$2.9500\cdots - 3.4499\cdots$$
$$\vdots$$

The theoretical class boundaries are not influenced by the rounding of particular variates or the accuracy of particular measuring devices. Such inaccuracies influence only the stated limits.

The *cumulative frequency* is generally also included in the frequency distribution table. As we will see subsequently in this chapter, cumulative frequency is useful for constructing ogives and for determining the median class.

It should be mentioned that the practice of grouping data into frequency distributions is becoming something less than universal. In the early days of statistical methods, when nearly all computations were performed by pencil and paper means, grouped data were absolutely necessary for further analysis. But with the recent advent and increasing availability of computers, the need to reduce data to frequency distributions has decreased somewhat. Computers and desk calculators can handle raw variates and grouped distributions with equal facility. As we proceed to examine the various quantitative techniques, we will alternate between grouped and nongrouped data, providing computational formulas for each procedure.

A particularly salient aspect of frequency distributions, quite aside from computational ease, is that such grouping is often a first step in graphically presenting the data. Graphs not only provide a cogent summary of the data for publication, but also often dictate methods of further analysis of data by the actual *shape* of the distribution curve.

3.3 GRAPHS

● *Man is the only nonlinear computer able to be mass produced by unskilled labor.*—Anonymous

The anthropologist generally wishes to establish at least two points in his published results. The data must initially be presented in a relatively complete manner so other workers can check and duplicate the results. The basic data are commonly published as frequency distributions. But anthropological reporting is rarely restricted to mere data cataloguing because most anthropologists have a theory in mind regarding the particular variables under study. In fact, fieldwork is almost always undertaken in order to find support (or lack of it) for a particular theory or a set of theories. Frequency tables serve admirably for the factual presentation of data, but rarely are tables sufficient in themselves to convince the reader to favor one theory over another.

Graphs provide one illustrative method for a researcher to recast his data into a more forceful mode. Graphs clearly illustrate trends inherent in the data, and serve to overcome the psychological hurdle with which anthropologists are still faced—the segment of intelligent readers who simply have an aversion to numbers. One of the best ways to avoid symbol shock is through the graphic presentation of frequency data. Graphs are especially well suited to a concise summary of a mass of relevant data so that efficient comparisons can be made. These comparisons may either document a change in the variates of a single variable or may compare a number of similar or related variables. It is the task of the investigator to fit the data into the graphic mode best illustrating the particular trends of interest.

3.3.1 Bar Graphs

The simple *bar graph* demonstrates the relationship between two variables by means of vertical or horizontal rectangles. Bar graphs (as opposed to the *histograms* discussed in Section 3.3.5) are of especial importance when the data on one variable are measurable only on the *nominal scale*. Figure 3.1 is a bar graph representing the worldwide frequency of the A blood-group allele. Even if ignoring the numbers on the graph, one can readily see that Greenland has over three times the frequency of the A allele as found in the eastern United States. Africa and India have moderate concentrations. Although the frequencies themselves are expressed in percentages (a ratio-level measurement), the

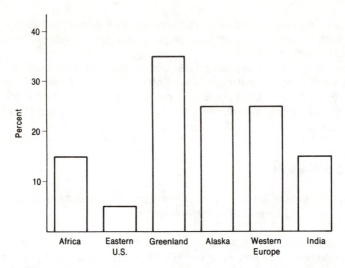

Fig. 3.1 Distribution of the A blood-group allele (data from Hulse 1963:300).

geographical areas are only on the nominal scale. Note that no ordering is implied in the arrangement on the horizontal axis. Single bar graphs such as Fig. 3.1 are generally used for expressing relations between nominal variates.

In his extensive study of the Pueblo Indians, anthropologist Edward Dozier (1970:130) illustrated the changing ratios between the various ethnic groups within the American Southwest with a *component bar graph* (Fig. 3.2). The population figures have been included at the *end* of each bar, so a reference scale on the x-axis is unnecessary. Sometimes the bars are broken when the data are extremely diverse, as with the years 1900 and 1960. Had all bars been drawn to exact scale, the critical interactions during the early historic period— when the total population was relatively small—would have been over-shadowed. Note that the bars denoting the Pueblo Indians have been accented by shading, since Dozier's book was concerned primarily with the Pueblo groups. The component bar technique is especially useful in demonstrating changing interrelationships between component parts, in this case, ethnic groups.

3.3.2 Broken-Line Graphs

Kroeber's data on California Indian population have been plotted on a *broken-line graph* in Fig. 3.3. This graphic format is particularly handy when comparing two variables which tend to covary (in this case, time and population). The vertical axis is generally termed the *ordinate* (or y-axis) and the horizontal axis is known as the *abscissa* (or x-axis). For Kroeber's data, the population size appears on the ordinate and time is on the abscissa.

As with the bar graph technique, broken-line graphs effectively demonstrate bivariate change. Bar graphs also handle data on the nominal scale; each class interval is taken to be equal, without ordering. Both variables must surpass the

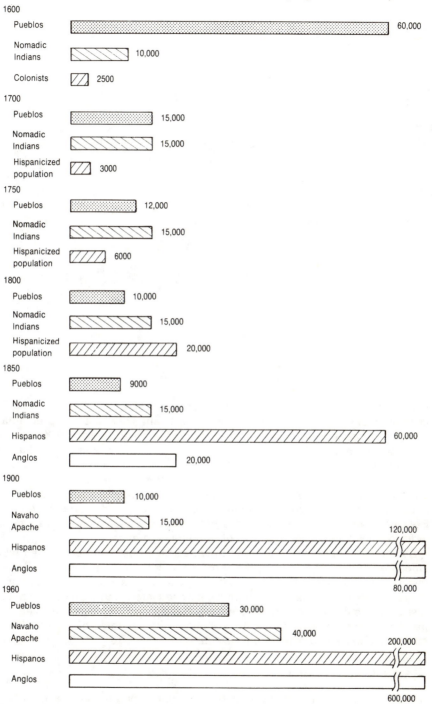

Fig. 3.2 Ethnic composition of American Southwest, 1600–1960 (after Dozier 1970:fig. 9).

48

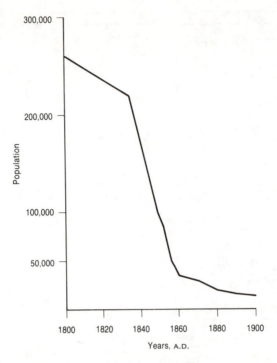

Fig. 3.3 Depopulation of California Indian groups.

nominal scale on the broken-line graph (population size is ratio scale, and time is an interval variable). This distinction is important since neither variable has been measured along a constant increment, and hence a bar diagram cannot be constructed. In order to draw a bar graph of population change, for instance, time must be measured in constant units with equal spacing such as years, decades, or perhaps centuries. Much of anthropology's data come from historic documentation, archaeological estimates, or other irregular, nonexperimental sources, and data are commonly partitioned more by accident than by design. Because constant interval spacing is not required, cases such as this can be more readily handled through use of broken-line graphs.

Sometimes graphs are presented in which data points are connected by a *smoothed curve* rather than by the short, straight lines used in Fig. 3.3. Unless the data are of extremely high quality, or the curve is known to be of some standard theoretical distribution (to be discussed later), anthropologists should resist the temptation to smooth the irregularities from the curve. Broken-line graphs represent unbiased reporting of facts, whereas smoothed curves inject interpretations which may be unwarranted.

3.3.3 Circle Graphs

Circle graphs provide a forceful method for illustrating the interrelationships between components of a unitary whole. Figure 3.4 arrays the data from the

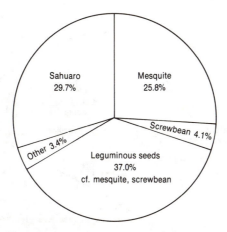

Fig. 3.4 Relative seed frequencies from trash levels of Snaketown, southern Arizona (after Bohrer 1970: fig. 4).

archaeological site of Snaketown, located in southern Arizona. As a result of careful laboratory analysis, Bohrer (1970) was able to estimate the relative proportion of seed foods in the Snaketown trash levels. These percentages are taken to reflect the dietary habits of the prehistoric Hohokam farmers of this area. In general, circle graphs such as Fig. 3.4 should be kept simple because too many categories can obscure the overall relationships. Rare items should be grouped into a component labelled "other."

Circle graphs are also useful in illustrating *cyclical* phenomena. Since circles have neither beginning nor end, continuous cycles can be parsimoniously arrayed. In Fig. 3.5, Savishinsky analyzed the subsistence cycle of the Hare Indians of Canada. Not only can seasonal activities— such as trapping, fishing, and caribou hunting—be represented on a single circle graph, but also the degree of dispersion or agglomeration of the Hare bands can be demonstrated with differential shading. This single graph probably saved pages of redundant text. Similar comparative graphs could well be assembled for other nonagricultural peoples—such as the Australian aborigines, the Bushmen of the Kalahari and the Great Basin Shoshoni—and comparisons made between these hunter-gatherer subsistence patterns. Straightforward, relatively simple graphic displays of this sort contribute significantly to the synthesis of cross-cultural patterning and regularities.

● *Thou hast spoken right; 'tis true.*
The wheel is come full circle; I am here. — King Lear

3.3.4 Ogives (Cumulative Curves)

Ogives, special versions of the broken-line graph, are used to express graphically the cumulative frequency distribution of a set of variates. Instead of concentrating upon the relationship of class intervals to their frequency, as was

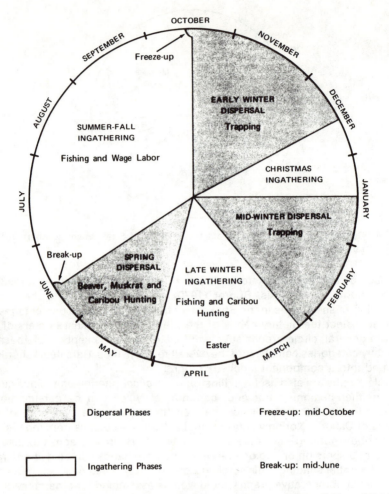

Fig. 3.5 Major population dispersals, ingatherings, and economic activities of the Hare Indians (after Savishinsky 1971: fig. 1).

the case with the ordinary broken-line graph, the ogive illustrates relations between a class interval and the frequency at or below its upper limit. Ogives, in other words, accumulate variate frequencies so that the curve rises as the variable increases. Figure 3.6 compares a broken-line graph with an ogive, using the Elko projectile point data from Table 3.3. The ordinate of the broken-line graph in Fig. 3.6(a) is expressed in terms of raw frequencies (ranging between zero and N), while the ogive [Fig. 3.6(b)] deals with percentages along the y-axis. The initial entry on all ogives is 0 percent (zero frequency) and the final entry on the right-hand side represents 100 percent. Ogives are generally cast in terms of proportional change (percentage), but sometimes such graphs are also computed in terms of absolute frequencies.

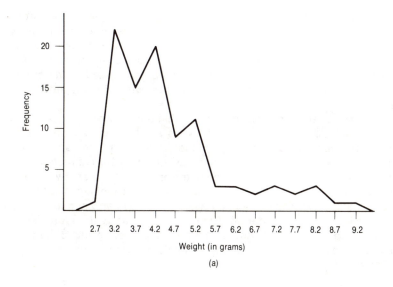

(a)

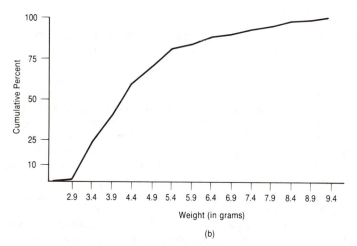

(b)

Fig. 3.6 Comparison of broken-line graph with an ogive, using Elko projectile point weights listed in Table 3.3. (a) Broken-line graph. (b) Proportional ogive.

Note further that the x-axis intervals of the broken-line graph refer to *class midpoints*, while the abscissa of the ogive expresses weight in terms of *stated upper-class boundaries*.

The ogive must rise as long as the frequency increases. When the line forms a horizontal, we know that the frequency has become constant. The steepest part of the curve always indicates the vicinity in which most of the variate scores occur. As we will see in subsequent sections, ogives are particularly useful in determining the shape of various frequency distributions.

A word of caution is in order regarding the use of ogives in anthropology. Since the x-axis refers to a quantitative measure of increasing intensity, and since the intervals between classes are assumed to be constant, the abscissa must always attain the level of at least interval scale measurement. Nominal variates have no ranking, so the classes could be expressed in any order along the x-axis. A different ogival curve emerges with virtually every possible ordering.

Ogives have been employed from time to time by archaeologists to compare prehistoric artifact assemblages. Tool types are commonly plotted along the abscissa, and cumulative percentage of tool frequency plotted on the y-axis (for example, Bordes 1972). Then the ogive is taken to be characteristic of the "shape" of the cumulative distribution of the artifacts; the more two assemblage curves differ, the more different are the overall assemblages. But since archaeological tool types are almost always expressed in only nominal categories, there is no inherent rank ordering. The shape of the ogive therefore depends, in part, upon the arbitrary ordering of the artifact types. Results obtained in this manner should generally be viewed with suspicion (see Kerrich and Clarke 1967, and Thomas 1971b).

3.3.5 Histograms

The *histogram* is unquestionably the most helpful graph for understanding basic statistical and probabilistic concepts. The histogram provides, in effect, a two-dimensional map of the frequency distribution table. Histograms concisely summarize the raw data and also serve as heuristic devices introducing key statistical concepts.

Let us return to the frequency distribution of Table 3.3 in which the 96 Elko projectile points were grouped into 14 analytical classes. Turn the frequency distribution on its side, placing the right side of the chart along the bottom of the graph. Note how the frequency tallies tend to "grow" from the abscissa of Fig. 3.7(a). As the stack of tallies becomes higher, we can clearly see that more measurements are represented in that class. A rapid inspection of Fig. 3.7(a) tells a great deal about the relative distribution and central tendency of the projectile point weights.

A *histogram* is formed when the tally marks are converted into vertical bars similar to those of a bar graph, shown in Fig. 3.7(b). The difference is that histograms employ only the class midpoints instead of class boundaries. In other words, by considering only the midpoints, the histogram tallies the original variates of 3.1, 3.2 and 3.4 to be analytically equal to 3.2, the class midpoint. The loss of information in this reduction, known as *grouping error*, is generally slight as long as larger quantities of variates are involved.

Note also that there is no space between the histogram bars, as was the case with a bar graph. Since histograms function primarily to convert metric tallies of frequency distributions into two-dimensional maps, empty spaces would only distort such a map. Histograms translate numbers into space. This is important for illustrating that the relative frequency of any class is *directly proportional to the area contained under that section of the histogram.*

The basic advantage of spatial (rather than numerical) interpretation of

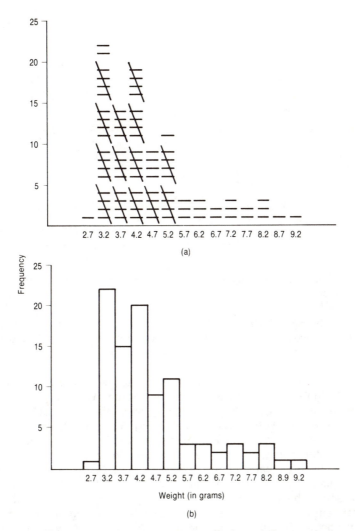

Fig. 3.7   (a) Tallies from Table 3.3; (b) histogram from Table 3.3.

frequency distributions is the ease with which one can determine the *shape of the distribution.* Analysis of shape generally consists of two aspects: symmetry and modality. A histogram is said to be symmetrical if it can be divided into two halves and each side is a "mirror image" of the other. Figure 3.8(a) is a hypothetical histogram displaying perfect symmetry. The center of gravity lies directly in the midline of a symmetrical histogram.

Asymmetrical graphs are further characterized by the direction of *skewness* (distortion). The Elko point weights of Fig. 3.7(b) are obviously not symmetrical, since the two halves do not approximate mirror images. The histogram forms a "tail" trailing off toward the right of the graph, so Fig. 3.7(b) is said to be

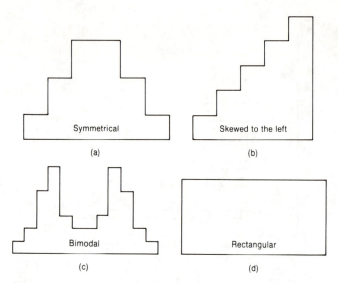

Fig. 3.8 Histogram shape: (a) perfect symmetry; (b) skewed—asymmetry; (c) bimodal; (d) uniform.

"skewed to the right."[1] Conversely, the hypothetical histogram in Fig. 3.8(b) is said to be "skewed to the left." The direction and magnitude of skewness will become important in later discussions of the binomial and normal distributions (Chapters 6 and 7).

A second important aspect of distribution shape is *modality*, referring to the number of high points or "peaks" of the histogram. When a graph has but a single apex as in Figs. 3.8(a) and 3.8(b), then the distribution is termed *unimodal*. The hypothetical distribution in Fig. 3.8(c), containing two distinct peaks, is termed *bimodal*. The uniform distribution in Fig. 3.8(d) has no modes at all. Real anthropological data, of course, contain considerably more variability than do hypothetical textbook examples. The Elko projectile point data produce a histogram with several minor peaks (at 3.2, 4.2, and 5.2 grams). These effects are probably due more to the variability of the small sample than to the actual tendency of the data. Had 960 points been weighed, these minor peaks would probably disappear and the contours of the histogram would be smoother and more regular. That is, Fig. 3.7 is probably a unimodal curve which is significantly skewed to the right.

> ● *If you are hunting rabbits in tiger country, you must still keep your eye peeled for tigers, but when you are hunting tigers you can ignore the rabbits.*—H. Stern

EXERCISES

> ● *We only think when we are confronted with a problem.* —J. Dewey

[1]Sometimes histograms which are skewed to the right are called "positively skewed," while histograms skewed to the left are termed "negatively skewed."

3.1   What are the *class limits* implied by the following midpoints?
    (a) 3.7, 4.2   (d) 3.75, 4.25
    (b) 0.017, 0.022   (e) What difficulty is encountered in (d)?
    (c) 3.0, 4.0

3.2   What are the *true limits* for the following class intervals?
    (a) 3.5–3.9   (d) 0.045–0.049
        4.0–4.4   0.050–0.054
    (b) 1.5–2.4   (e) 15,900–15,949
        2.5–3.4   15,950–15,999
    (c) 1695–1699
        1700–1704

3.3   What are the class midpoints for the intervals in Exercise 3.2?

3.4   The following data represent infant mortality rates under one year of age for 1969 (data from Ehrlich and Ehrlich 1972:table 4–1):

Continent and Country	Rate per 1000 Live Births	Continent and Country	Rate per 1000 Live Births
Africa		Europe	
Kenya	49.9	Austria	25.4
Madagascar	75.0	Belgium	22.9
Mauritius	69.1	Bulgaria	30.5
Réunion	62.4	Czechoslovakia	22.9
United Arab Republic	118.5	Denmark	15.8
North and Central America		Finland	13.9
Barbados	45.7	France	16.4
Canada	20.8	Germany, East	20.4
Costa Rica	62.3	Germany, West	22.8
Dominican Republic	72.6	Greece	31.9
Guatemala	93.8	Hungary	35.6
Mexico	65.7	Ireland	20.6
Puerto Rico	28.3	Italy	30.3
Trinidad and Tobago	36.6	Netherlands	13.1
United States	20.8	Norway	13.7
South America		Poland	34.3
Argentina	58.3	Portugal	61.1
Chile	91.6	Spain	29.8
Colombia	78.3	Sweden	12.9
Ecuador	87.9	Switzerland	16.1
Peru	61.9	United Kingdom—England	
Venezuela	41.4	and Wales	18.3
Asia		Yugoslavia	56.3
Taiwan	19.0	Oceania	
Hong Kong	20.9	Australia	17.8
Indonesia	87.2	Fiji	24.8
Israel	23.0	New Zealand	16.9
Japan	15.3		
Kuwait	35.9		
Philippines	72.0		
Thailand	27.9		

(a) Construct a frequency distribution for infant mortality, using a class interval of 10 live births per 1000.
(b) Construct a histogram for these data.
(c) Based upon this tabulation, what worldwide trends are apparent in the data?

3.5 The following variates are fluted projectile point lengths from Mecklenburg and Dinwiddie counties in Virginia (data from Fitting 1965). Draw the histogram for these data.

Class Interval, cm	Frequency
1.0–1.9	0
2.0–2.9	8
3.0–3.9	30
4.0–4.9	56
5.0–5.9	60
6.0–6.9	35
7.0–7.9	33
8.0–8.9	12
9.0–9.9	13
10.0–10.9	5
11.0 plus	4

3.6 The following variates are vital lung capacities (measured in cubic centimeters) for 40 informants:

4499	4383	4192	4273
4281	4296	4396	4780
4742	4680	4023	4115
4656	4006	4320	4222
4191	4050	4106	4092
4566	4596	4812	4623
4222	4623	3614	4186
3767	3780	4419	3801
5022	3923	4546	3923
4593	4110	4323	4124

(a) Construct a frequency diagram using 100 cc class intervals.
(b) Construct the histogram representing this frequency distribution.
(c) What is the form of this histogram?

3.7 What type of chart or graph would best illustrate the following circumstances? Why?

(a) To compare one informant's blood pressure on each day of July with each day in January.
(b) To indicate how one informant's blood pressure varied from month to month through the year.
(c) To compare the average blood pressure of 16 informants over the same time period.
(d) To compare blood pressure on January 1 with that on July 1 for 16 informants.

3.8 The *Ethnographic Atlas* (Murdock 1967:column 36) codes the following societies on *post-partum sex* taboo:

Somali	2	Egyptians	2
Amhara	4	Riffians	2
Bako	4	Neapolitans	0
Wolof	4	New England	1
Songhai	2	Lapps	2
Woodabe Ful	5	Bulgarians	1
Zazzagawa	4	Druze	2

The following coded categories are used:

No taboo	0
Taboo less than 1 month	1
1 month–6 months	2
6 months–1 year	3
One to two years	4
More than two years	5

(a) What is the level of measurement?
(b) Is the underlying nature of the variable different from its operational measure as defined in the *Ethnographic Atlas*?
(c) Construct a frequency distribution.
(d) Construct a histogram.
(e) How can the form of this graph be described?

3.9 The *Ethnographic Atlas* (column 80) codes the following 20 African societies on *ground plan of dwelling*:

Lango	Circular	Ngala	Rectangular
Songhai	Elliptical	Turu	Quadrangular
Cerusé	Circular	Kung	Semicircular
Yako	Rectangular	Lele	Rectangular
Ekiti	Quadrangular	Chagga	Circular
Dogon	Quadrangular	Kutshu	Rectangular
Mbum	Circular	Diola	Elliptical
Tiv	Circular	Lendu	Circular
Kowa	Circular	Mao	Circular
Minianka	Rectangular	Dinka	Circular

(a) Construct a *bar graph* representing these data.
(b) Construct a *circle graph*. Which graph seems to better depict the trends?
(c) Can you construct a frequency distribution? Why or why not?

3.10 Construct the graph which best illustrates the change in cranial capacities (data from Brace 1967:108).

Australopithecus	500 cc
Paranthropus	600 cc
Sinanthropus	1000 cc
Neanderthal	1500 cc
Skhūl	1500 cc
Přĕdmost	1465 cc
Modern	1400 cc

58

3.11 Compare the trend in Exercise 3.10 with the size of post-canine dentition[2] (data from Brace 1967:108).

Australopithecus	825 cc
Paranthropus	1000 cc
Sinanthropus	590 cc
Neanderthal	600 cc
Skhūl	500 cc
Prĕdmost	525 cc
Modern	540 cc

3.12 The following data represent the population of Europe between the years A.D. 1000 and 1700 (data from Ehrlich and Ehrlich 1972:13):

Year	Population (in millions of people)
1000	56
1100	60
1200	64
1300	76
1400	61
1500	63
1600	90
1700	120

Construct the graph which best illustrates the effect of the bubonic plague epidemics on European population size during this period.

3.13 Construct a graph to illustrate the weights (in kilograms) of various recent primates (data from Buettner–Janusch 1973:317):

Man	61.5
Chimpanzee	56.7
Night monkey	9.2
Sykes monkey	4.9
Vervet	4.0
Capuchin monkey	3.1
Galago	0.2

3.14 Construct the graph which best illustrates the following data (from Ehrlich and Ehrlich 1972:41):

	Population density in 1960, people/square mile
Earth (land area only)	65
United States	55
Japan	700
Tokyo	20,000
New York City	25,000
Manhattan	75,000

[2]Post-canine dentition is measured by the summed cross-sectional area of the teeth on one side of the upper dental arch.

3.15 The following figures represent the amount of cultivated land in the major continents, measured in billions of acres (data from Ehrlich and Ehrlich 1972:114):

Continent	Total	Potentially Arable	Cultivated
Africa	7.46	1.81	0.39
Asia	6.76	1.55	1.28
Australia and New Zealand	2.03	0.38	0.04
Europe	1.18	0.43	0.38
North America	5.21	1.15	0.59
South America	4.33	1.68	0.19
USSR	5.52	0.88	0.56

Construct the most appropriate graph to illustrate each of the following statements:

(a) Europe is the most heavily cultivated continent in the world.

(b) Roughly two-thirds of the potentially arable land in the USSR is under cultivation.

(c) Africa is the largest continent in the world.

4 Measures of Central Tendency and Dispersion

● *If a man will begin with certainties, he shall end in doubts; but if he will be content to begin with doubts, he shall end in certainties.* —F. Bacon

4.1 INTRODUCTION

Chapter 3 considered some initial steps of descriptive anthropological statistics, attempting to create an orderly arrangement from otherwise chaotic data. We now turn to more precise methods for measuring the tendency for data to *aggregate* (central tendency statistics) and to *disperse* (statistics of variability). But before discussing these important descriptive statistics, it is first necessary to learn some new statistical symbolism.

4.2 SUMMATION NOTATION

● *I don't know what he's talking about, but I'm glad he's talking.*—S. Ervin

The quantitative approach to anthropological data requires a somewhat specialized new language. But anthropologists are constantly required to learn new languages as part of their fieldwork and, with sufficient practice, such languages may become second nature for serious students of science.

By the same token, the effective usage of everyday statistics requires a certain amount of specialized notation, and no symbol is more important than a form of the Greek letter capital sigma, usually written as Σ and and representing "summation." To see just what this symbol does, let us consider a set of variates, say, measurements of cranial capacities on a group of modern human crania. The variable "cranial capacity" is denoted by X, and we can refer to each successive measurement of cranial capacity (that is, each variate) by successive terms of X_1 (read as "X sub one"), X_2, X_3, and so forth. If n is the total number of measurements at hand, then the raw data can be expressed as follows:

$$X_1 = 1430 \text{ cc} \qquad X_2 = 1580 \text{ cc} \qquad X_3 = 1693 \text{ cc}$$
$$X_4 = 1520 \text{ cc} \qquad X_5 = 1720 \text{ cc} \qquad X_6 = 1410 \text{ cc}$$

An initial step in nearly all statistical analysis requires that all of the X_i be *added* together, and this is the definition of Σ:

$$\Sigma_{i=1}^{n} X_i = X_1 + X_2 + X_3 + \cdots + X_n \qquad (4.1)$$

The symbol $\Sigma_{i=1}^{n} X_i$ is to be read as "the summation of X sub i, where i refers to all values between 1 and n, inclusive." More succinctly, one generally says "sigma X, as i goes from 1 to n." For the cranial capacity measurements given above,

$$\Sigma_{i=1}^{6} X_i = 1430 + 1580 + 1693 + 1520 + 1720 + 1410$$
$$= 9353 \text{ cc}$$

You will find that in most circumstances the subscript and superscript can be dropped, since statistical procedure generally requires summation of all numbers from 1 to n.

In this more simplified notation, the cranial measurements above can be summed as

$$\Sigma X_i = 9353 \text{ cc}$$

It should be noted, however, that if there is any chance for confusion, the complete subscript and superscript notation should be included.

4.2.1 Rules of Summation

In the following discussion of elementary descriptive statistics, we will have occasion to frequently refer to the summation of several numerical series, and it is useful at this point to establish three general rules which simplify the use of Σ.

Rule 1: $\qquad\qquad \Sigma(X + Y) = \Sigma X + \Sigma Y$

This first rule is intuitively obvious and will prove a boon when we develop alternative computational formulas for common descriptive statistics.

Example 4.1

An anthropological team, studying subsistence maritime economy, observed informants fishing on two consecutive days.

Informants	Day 1, X	Day 2, Y	Total Catch, $X + Y$
A	23	13	36
B	24	18	42
C	32	5	37
D	18	3	21
	$\Sigma X_i = 97$	$\Sigma Y_i = 39$	$\Sigma(X + Y) = 136$

Note that the total catch for the two days can be determined either as $\Sigma(X + Y)$, as above, or by the more simple method

$$\Sigma(X + Y) = \Sigma X + \Sigma Y$$
$$= 97 + 39 = 136 \text{ fish}$$

Rule 2: $\Sigma aX = a\Sigma X$

Rule 2 tells us that the summation of a constant times a variable is equivalent to that constant multiplied by the summation of the variable. In other words, constants can be factored out prior to summation.

Example 4.2

Suppose that the fish caught in the first day of Example 4.1 weighed 40 grams each:

Informants	Day 1, X		Individual Weight, grams		Total Weight, grams
A	23	×	40	=	920
B	24	×	40	=	960
C	32	×	40	=	1280
D	18	×	40	=	720
	$\Sigma X_i = 97$				$\Sigma aX = 3880$

Rather than multiplying each value of X_i by 40, the sum of the X_i can be multiplied, thereby saving four multiplication operations:

$$a\Sigma X = 40 \text{ grams} \times 97 \text{ fish} = 3880 \text{ grams}$$

Rule 3: $\Sigma a = na$

The final rule tells us simply that the summation of a constant is merely n (the total number of cases considered) multiplied by the constant.

Example 4.3

Suppose that on a third day the hypothetical fishermen caught the same number of fish.

Informants	Day 3, Z
A	17
B	17
C	17
D	17
	$\Sigma Z_i = 68$

On this third day, the number of fish is no longer a variable; it is a constant, so

$$Z = b = 17$$

and by Rule 3,

$$\Sigma Z_i = nb = 4 \times 17 = 68$$

These three simple rules of summation can save the alert investigator literally hours of the mindless tedium resulting from useless calculation. Furthermore, the longer the computations, the larger the probability of error.

In addition to the summation rules, the student should verify for himself that some relations *do not hold* for summation notation:

$$\Sigma XY \neq \Sigma X \Sigma Y$$
$$\Sigma X^2 \neq (\Sigma X)^2$$

although $(\Sigma X)^2 = (\Sigma X)(\Sigma X)$

It is strongly suggested that you now turn to the summation exercises (4.1–4.6) at the end of this chapter so that the use of Σ is rather firmly planted in your mind prior to the consideration of measures of central tendency.

4.3 MEASURES OF CENTRAL TENDENCY

Chapter 3 concentrated upon methods for concisely summarizing large masses of empirical data. While graphs and frequency distributions provide important first steps in synthesizing raw data, these devices still leave us with rather cumbersome summary statements. It is necessary, for most statistical purposes, to summarize the data still further, and the single most important characteristic in a set of data is their tendency (or lack of it) to agglomerate about a single central point. The mean, median, and mode are all common measures of central tendency, each with its particular strong points, yet none suitable to fulfill all needs.

● *Troubles never come singly.*—L. Peter

4.3.1 Mean

The *mean* (or *arithmetic mean*) is unquestionably the most versatile of the various estimates of central tendency. The mean carries with it an intuitive understanding of that which is being measured. The mean expresses the *average*, the *center of gravity* in a set of variates. In fact, the mean is commonly compared to the fulcrum of a seesaw, since the forces on either side (mass $\times$ distance) must sum to zero.

For our purposes,[1] the *sample mean* $\bar{X}$ (read as "X bar") is defined as

$$\bar{X} = \frac{X_1 + X_2 + X_3 + \cdots + X_n}{n} = \frac{\Sigma X_i}{n} \qquad (4.2)$$

Example 4.4

Find the sample mean of the cranial capacity measurements discussed in Section 4.2.

$$\frac{\Sigma X_i}{n} = \frac{1430 + 1580 + 1693 + 1520 + 1720 + 1410}{6}$$

$$= \frac{9353}{6} = 1558.8 \text{ cc}$$

While the computation of the sample mean for small samples such as this is relatively simple and easily accomplished by Eq. (4.2), larger sets of data often require grouping variates into a frequency distribution. The sample mean for grouped data is defined as

$$\bar{X} = \frac{\Sigma_{i=1}^k f_i X_i}{n}$$

where k denotes the number of groups.

---

[1]The purpose of this introductory discussion is to introduce the preliminary concepts of central tendency. As explained in Section 2.6, statistical indicators can serve either as statistics or parameters, depending upon whether the data represent a sample or a population. Unless stated to the contrary, the indices in this chapter refer to sample statistics. The *population mean* will be denoted by μ (read as "mu"), and is computed in exactly the same manner as $\bar{X}$ except that N is substituted for sample size n.

Example 4.5

Find the mean weight of the sample of Elko projectile points in Table 3.3 (which have been incorporated into Table 4.1).

To compute $\bar{X}$, the various values of $X_1 = 2.7$, $f_1 = 1$, and so forth, must be substituted into Formula (4.3).

$$\bar{X} = \frac{(2.7)1 + (3.2)22 + \cdots + (9.2)1}{96}$$

$$= \frac{440.7}{96} = 4.59 \text{ grams}$$

It is generally advisable to compute the sample mean of grouped data from a conventional frequency distribution table such as Table 4.1. Only the column labeled "$X_i f_i$" is of importance in finding the mean, but the other columns will be used in the subsequent computation of the sample variance.

When data are converted from raw variates into frequency distribution form, a certain amount of information is always lost. This loss is termed the *error of grouping*. Had $\bar{X}$ for the Elko points been computed directly from the raw variates without grouping into the frequency distribution, the mean would have been

$$\bar{X} = \frac{431.9}{96} = 4.50 \text{ grams}$$

The error of grouping in this case is only $(4.59 - 4.50) = 0.09$ gram, which is a relatively trivial error.

4.3.2 Weighted Mean

Publication of raw field data is expensive, and for this reason the actual variates rarely appear in anthropological monographs. But with only $\bar{X}$, n, and the standard deviation (to be introduced later in this chapter), almost any other necessary summary statistic can be derived.

It is sometimes critical, for example, to generate additional statistics which involve the combinations of various sample means. There is no difficulty in computing the *grand mean* of several sample means, provided the groups are of the same size. The standard formula for sample mean can be employed and one is, in effect, taking the "mean of the means."

Consider a study of racial stature in which samples of 30 informants each have been selected from the major areas of the world:

Geographical Area	$\bar{X}$, cm	n	Geographical Area	$\bar{X}$, cm	n
Africa	164.9	30	Oceania	167.3	30
Asia	163.0	30	New World	163.7	30
Europe	167.2	30			

TABLE 4.1 Frequency of Elko Projectile Point Weights (raw variates on Table 3.2).

Class Boundaries, grams	Midpoint, X_i	Frequency, f_i	Cumulative Frequency	$X_i f_i$	$|X_i - \bar{X}|$	$|X_i - \bar{X}|f_i$	$|X_i - \bar{X}|^2$	$|X_i - \bar{X}|^2$
2.5–2.9	2.7	1	1	2.7	1.89	1.89	3.5721	3.5721
3.0–3.4	3.2	22	23	70.4	1.39	30.58	1.9321	42.5062
3.5–3.9	3.7	15	38	55.5	0.89	13.35	0.7921	11.8815
4.0–4.4	4.2	20	58	84.0	0.39	7.80	0.1521	3.0420
4.5–4.9	4.7	9	67	42.3	0.11	0.99	0.0121	0.1089
5.0–5.4	5.2	11	78	57.2	0.61	6.71	0.3721	4.0931
5.5–5.9	5.7	3	81	17.1	1.11	3.33	1.2321	3.6963
6.0–6.4	6.2	3	84	18.6	1.61	4.83	2.5921	7.7763
6.5–6.9	6.7	2	86	13.4	2.11	4.22	4.4521	8.9042
7.0–7.4	7.2	3	89	21.6	2.61	7.83	6.8121	20.4363
7.5–7.9	7.7	2	91	15.4	3.11	6.22	9.6721	19.3442
8.0–8.4	8.2	3	94	24.6	3.61	10.83	13.0321	39.0963
8.5–8.9	8.7	1	95	8.7	4.11	4.11	16.8921	16.8921
9.0–9.4	9.2	1	96	9.2	4.61	4.61	21.2521	21.2521
		96		440.7		107.30		202.6016

Assuming these samples to be without significant bias, what is the mean stature of the world's population?

Rather than return to the original variates (which in this case are unavailable to us), the grand mean can be computed as

$$\bar{X} = \frac{164.9 + 163.0 + 167.2 + 167.3 + 163.7}{5}$$

$$= \frac{826.1}{5} = 165.2 \text{ cm}$$

Note that Formula (4.2) can be applied to compute a grand mean only when the samples are of equal size. In effect, each sample is treated as a new variate, each with equal weight. But had 60 Asian informants been measured, for example, then the Asian sample must be weighted with its greater contribution to the grand mean.

To handle the more general case, with unequal sample sizes, the following formula should be used:

$$\bar{X} = \frac{\Sigma \bar{X}_i n_i}{\Sigma n_i} \tag{4.4}$$

This grand average is termed the *weighted mean,* since the number of variates involved in each original mean determines the overall contribution of that particular mean. When the sample sizes are equal, as in the case above, the weighted mean will be equal to the unweighted "mean of means."

Example 4.6

In Richard B. Lee's study of the !Kung Bushmen of Botswana, South Africa, the average camp sizes were found to be (after Lee 1969: table 1):

Name of Waterhole	No. of Camps	Average Population per Camp (people)
Dobe	2	15.5
!angwa	1	16.0
Bate	2	15.0
!gose	3	17.3
/ai/ai	5	18.8

What is the average population per Bushman camp?

Since the number of camps at each waterhole varies from 1 to 5, the contribution of each camp must be weighted by Formula (4.4).

$$\bar{X} = \frac{2(15.5) + 1(16.0) + 2(15.0) + 3(17.3) + 5(18.8)}{2 + 1 + 2 + 3 + 5}$$

$$= \frac{31.0 + 16.0 + 30.0 + 51.9 + 94.0}{13}$$

$$= \frac{222.9}{13} = 17.1 \text{ people per camp}$$

The mean (weighted or unweighted) exhibits several properties which explain its popularity in social science and biometric research. First of all, the mean is the *most efficient* measure of central tendency because every variable has an impact upon the final computation. No data are wasted. The mean is also the *most stable* measure of central tendency. When one draws samples from a population, the mean will generally be found to vary only minimally between successive samplings. So, the sample mean is generally a good approximation of the overall population mean (which generally is unknown). Because of the high degree of stability, the sample mean often provides a good benchmark against which to predict future data from the same population.

On the other hand, it is not always desirable to consider each variate when assessing central tendency because sample means are easily skewed by one or two extreme measurements. Although random errors in measurement are known to cancel out in the long run, a few extreme variates can badly skew the sample mean. As we will see, other measures of central tendency are more robust toward the skewing effect of extreme variates.

The mean is also important in elementary statistics because it is *readily manipulated algebraically.* For one thing, if we know $\bar{X}$ and n, we can instantly find the sum of all variates in the group. That is, since

$$\bar{X} = \frac{\sum X_i}{n}$$

then

$$\sum X_i = n\bar{X}$$

This relationship is useful when only summary data are provided in published reports. Suppose, for instance, that an investigator reported that a camp of 35 hunter-gatherers consumed an average of 1967 calories per day; one could easily find that the camp required a total of 68,845 calories per day. Further algebraic examples of the computational facilities of the sample mean will be discussed at the conclusion of this chapter.

A final property of the sample mean is that the sum of the deviations about the mean, $\sum(X_i - \bar{X})$, is always zero. That is, any number other than $\bar{X}$ will provide a greater sum.

4.3.3 Median

One way to minimize the impact of extreme variates is to compute the *median*, defined as that statistic which has an equal number of variates above and below it. The median of a set of n variates is simply the "middle term," and hence is unaffected by the magnitude of extreme values.

More explicitly, when n is an odd number, then the median is *exactly* equal to the middle term. But when n is an even number, then the median is defined as the arithmetic mean of the middle two variates.

Example 4.7

Find the median of 7.8, 9.4, 3.4, 2.6, and 11.6.

There are five variates, so the median is simply the middle term, which is 7.8.

Example 4.8

Find the median of the following cranial capacities:

1430, 1580, 1693, 1520, 1720, 1410

Since $n = 6$, the median is known to be the arithmetic mean of the two middle terms:

$$\text{median} = \frac{X_3 + X_4}{2} = \frac{1520 + 1580}{2} = 1550 \text{ cc}$$

While the median can generally be found using the method described above, occasionally one must find the median of a frequency distribution. To do so, the *median class* must first be determined. Median class is defined as the lowest class for which the cumulative frequency exceeds $n/2$. The median per se is found within the median class by using the following formula, which is merely a version of linear interpolation:

$$\text{median} = L + c \frac{(n/2 - F_c)}{f_m} \tag{4.5}$$

where

L = lower boundary of the median class
c = *class interval* (that is, the difference between successive class midpoints)
n = total number of variates in the frequency distribution
F_c = cumulative frequency of the class below the median class
f_m = frequency of the median class

Example 4.9

Find the median for the Elko projectile point weights given in Table 4.1.

Since $n/2 = 48$, the class 4.0–4.4 is the median class because the cumulative frequency first exceeds 48 in this class.

$$\text{median} = 4.0 + 0.5 \frac{(96/2 - 38)}{20}$$

$$= 4.0 + 0.25 = 4.25 \text{ grams}$$

It is clear that even for grouped data such as those in Table 4.1, the median is *much simpler to compute* than is the mean, and this can often be an advantage. Whenever a quick measure of central tendency is necessary (such as in preliminary fieldwork), the median can be a useful indicator of overall central tendency. The median is often used when a desk calculator is unavailable. The mean is a more complex statistic because it considers *all* of the information in any set of variates. Each score contributes its full numerical value and this explains why the mean can be so readily manipulated algebraically. The mean is therefore rather heavily weighted by large variates.

But in computing the median, one considers only the *order* into which the variables have fallen. Each variate contributes exactly as much to the median as do its higher and lower neighbors. In other words, the contribution of an individual variate to the median depends upon where it falls in the rank-ordered sequence, rather than strictly upon its magnitude. So the median preserves only ordinal relationships between the X_i, regardless of the original level of measurement.

Because the median uses less information than the mean, the median is *less sensitive to the influence of extreme cases.* The median is often used when the investigator feels that a few wild variates would render the mean misleading. In most industrial societies, for example, the effect of a few very rich individuals would badly skew the *mean* per capita income, so the *median* per capita income is a preferable statistic. Medians are also handy when only a *limited sample of data* are available and the investigator feels that the extreme values of X_i are not represented.

But the loss of information involved with the median is not necessarily a desirable condition, since the median is much less stable under repeated sampling than is the mean. Suppose that one wished to determine the average size of local communities in the New World. The *Ethnographic Atlas* (Murdock 1967) lists 307 societies in North, Central, and South America. Assume a 25 percent sample has been randomly selected ($n = 77$). The median has the advantage of easy computation, and the median would also dampen the skewing effect of those few large societies with inordinately high populations (such as the Aztec, with over 50,000 inhabitants). But suppose that the initial sample were somehow lost or destroyed, and a second sample of 77 societies had to be selected anew from the *Atlas*. Experiments of this sort have shown the mean to be generally more stable than the median, so we could expect the means of the two independent samples to be somewhat closer than the two medians. The robust nature of the mean becomes a critical asset as we move further into the area of statistical inference.

There is no clear-cut rule regarding the use of the median in preference to the mean. In most cases, the mean will prove more useful than will the median. But whenever a distribution is known to be badly skewed, or whenever variates reflect only ordinal scale relations, the median will be more appropriate.

4.3.4 Mode

The third indicator of central tendency to be considered here is the simplest of all. The *mode* of a distribution is merely the most common variate. Here are some common examples referring to modes:

Most hunter-gatherers are nonsedentary.
Most "civilized" societies have descriptive kinship terminologies.
Archaeologists usually operate within a normative framework.
Most Homo erectus crania have poorly developed mastoid processes.
The "magic number" of American Indians is generally four.[2]

[2] Note how the mean and median take on almost absurd implications in this context.

Modes are more readily applied to discrete variables, since "most common" implies presence of clear-cut categories. When a mode is cited for continuous data, the divisions are derived either from a lack of precise measurement or from artificial categorization in the frequency distribution. When continuous variates have been grouped, then the most populous category is defined as the modal class. In Table 4.1, for instance, the modal class is 3.0–3.4, which has a frequency of 22.

Like the median, the mode is uninfluenced by extreme variates, but is hampered by ambiguity and a lack of computational potential. The mode is a nonunique measure because there can be several modes within the same population. In fact, if all variates are different, then each variate is itself a mode. This serious defect is not suffered by either arithmetic mean or the median. In defense of the mode, however, I should point out that the well-tempered gambler had better place his money on the *modal* outcome of a roulette wheel rather than on the median or the mean. The point is to find a measure of central tendency which fits the task at hand. All measures suffer some sort of defect or another.

4.3.5 Other Measures of Central Tendency

Two additional means will be mentioned but not discussed in detail (see Alder and Roessler 1972: 35–38 for details on usage and computation).

The *geometric mean* is applied to data for which the ratio of any two consecutive numbers is thought to be constant. Geometric means are useful in problems of population growth or for computing compound interest rates.

The *harmonic mean* is sometimes used to assess "hybrid ratios" in which units of measurements differ between numerator and denominator, such as miles per hour or tons per acre.

4.4 MEASURES OF DISPERSION

● *The history of mankind is an immense sea of errors in which a few obscure truths may be here and there found.*—C. De Beccaria

Obviously, every measure of central tendency has drawbacks, although each serves to measure some aspect of the center of a frequency distribution. But data do not only agglomerate; in another sense, data tend to disperse. Figure 3.8 indicates some of the extreme ways in which data can distribute. The distributions are quite dissimilar with respect to dispersion even though the four histograms have identical means. Let us consider some measures of relative and absolute dispersion.

4.4.1 Range

The observed range is merely the difference between the highest and lowest variates. The observed variates for the raw Elko projectile point weights (Table

3.2) run from 2.7 to 9.0 grams. The range is thus 6.3 grams. Grouped data range from the upper boundary of the upper class to the lower boundary of the lower class. The range for the grouped Elko point data is $9.4 - 2.5 = 6.9$ grams (Table 4.1).

The range is neither a stable nor a particularly useful statistic because it considers only the two extreme observed values. But note that for Fig. 3.8(d) the range is better, in a statistical sense, than the mean. One can never assume that the entire range has been observed when working with samples (rather than populations). Thus, the sample range is always a conservative estimator. The observed range is nevertheless often included in quantitative summaries of anthropological variables, probably because of the intuitive simplicity and because no computations are required. Records of extreme occurrences are no more than rather lengthy tabulations of the range of exotic phenomena (such as the *Guinness Book of Records*). Much of the so-called popular anthropology (the far-away-places-with-strange-sounding-names school) emphasizes the *range* of the human condition, often with a profound neglect of *central tendencies*.

4.4.2 Mean Deviation

It should be clear that adequate measures of dispersal must do more than consider merely the extreme variates. More meaningful measures must likewise heed the distances of each variate from a central reference point, such as the mean or the mode. In a highly dispersed set of variates, the distance from this central point may become quite large. We can operationally define *variability* as the distance of a variate from the mean of the distribution. The larger the distance, the more disperse are the data.

Consider the following sample of variates: 2, 4, 6, 8, 10. The mean is obviously $\bar{X} = 6.0$. The measure of dispersion suggested above is the *sum of the deviations of variates about the sample mean*, expressed as $\Sigma(X_i - \bar{X})$:

$$\Sigma(X_i - \bar{X}) = (2-6) + (4-6) + (6-6) + (8-6) + (10-6)$$
$$= (-4) + (-2) + 0 + 2 + 4$$
$$= 0$$

The sum of the deviations about the mean, in this case, totals zero. In fact, a theorem in mathematical statistics states that the sum of the deviations about the mean *must always* equal zero, regardless of the dispersion. Although $(X_i - \bar{X})$ provides some indication of dispersion, we still must find a way to always keep the deviations about the mean from summing to zero.

Since we are concerned only with the *magnitude* of the deviations, (not the *direction*), this measure of dispersion can still be salvaged by taking the absolute value of each deviation.[3] All deviations are thus expressed in position terms. In other words, we elect to ignore "negative distances"—which do not exist anyway. Returning to the sample variates,

$$\Sigma|X_i - \bar{X}| = |2-6| + |4-6| + |6-6| + |8-6| + |10-6|$$
$$= 4 + 2 + 0 + 2 + 4$$
$$= 12$$

[3] The absolute value of any X_i, symbolized as $|X_i|$ means simply that negative signs are ignored; so, $|-5| = 5$, and $|5| = 5$.

This new measure—the sum of the absolute values of deviations about the mean—provides a serviceable indicator of dispersion. But a problem still remains because this sum is a direct consequence of the *number of variates* considered. Had there been twice as many variates in this sample, then the sum of the absolute deviations would have been greatly inflated. A new deviation is added for each new variate. One can free this measure from sample size by dividing the sum by *n*, the total number of variates. The new measure of dispersion is termed the *mean deviation* (MD) because the sum of the deviations has been averaged.

$$MD = \frac{\Sigma|X_i - \bar{X}|}{n} \tag{4.6}$$

For the data in our example,

$$MD = \frac{12}{5} = 2.4$$

The mean deviation tells us that, on the average, each variate deviates approximately 2.4 units from the sample mean. Since MD is an arithmetic mean, the outcome is independent of sample size. The larger the mean deviation, the more dispersion is present in the sample.

Example 4.10

Find the mean deviation for the cranial capacities in Example 4.4.
Since $\bar{X} = 1558.8$ cc,

$$\begin{aligned}
\Sigma|X_i - \bar{X}| &= |1430 - 1558.8| + |1580 - 1558.8| + |1693 - 1558.8| \\
&\quad + |1520 - 1558.8| + |1720 - 1558.8| + |1410 - 1558.8| \\
&= 128.8 + 21.2 + 134.2 + 38.8 + 161.2 + 148.8 \\
&= 633.0 \text{ cc}
\end{aligned}$$

$$MD = \frac{633.0}{6} = 105.5 \text{ cc}$$

Expression (4.6) can be applied only to raw variates. When the data have been compressed into a frequency distribution, the following formula for mean deviation should be applied:

$$MD = \frac{\Sigma|X_i - \bar{X}|f_i}{n} \tag{4.7}$$

where *n* denotes the total number of variates in the frequency table and X_i refers to each successive class midpoint.

Example 4.11

Find the mean deviation for the Elko projectile point weights in Table 4.1.

The computation of MD involves several simple, yet cumbersome, arithmetic steps. For this reason it is wise to follow the standardized format of Table 4.1 until you are totally familiar with the various steps involved. The sample mean was computed in Example 4.5 to be

$$\bar{X} = 4.59 \text{ grams}$$

To find the mean deviation, first compute the absolute deviation of each class from the sample mean (column 6 in Table 4.1). These values are then multiplied by their respective frequencies (column 3) and then summed at the end of column 7. To find MD, the summation is then divided by n; in this case, $n = 96$:

$$MD = \frac{\Sigma|X_i - \bar{X}|f_i}{n} = \frac{107.30}{96} = 1.118 \text{ grams}$$

Example 4.12

Find the mean deviation for Bushman camp size (Example 4.6).

Since $\bar{X} = 17.1$ individuals per camp.

$$\Sigma|X_i - \bar{X}|f_i = |15.5 - 17.1|2 + |16.0 - 17.1|1 + |15.0 - 17.1|2$$
$$+ |17.3 - 17.1|3 + |18.8 - 17.1|5$$
$$= 3.2 + 1.1 + 4.2 + 0.6 + 8.5$$
$$= 17.6$$
$$MD = \frac{17.6}{13} = 1.35$$

As an overall measure of dispersion, the MD has the advantage of including all the variates in the computation rather than merely the extremes (as with the observed range). In addition, the mean deviation is relatively simple to compute. Thus, MD provides an adequate method for emphasizing those variates with extreme values, since the more extreme the variates, the larger the mean deviation. A critical disadvantage of the mean deviation is the absolute value operation required to keep the deviations from summing to zero. For reasons not discussed here, dropping the signs precludes further algebraic manipulation of MD, so the mean deviation does not lead to more sophisticated mathematical results. In addition, although the mean deviation is much more stable than the range, repeated random sampling experiments from a single population indicate that the successive values of mean deviation fluctuate too wildly for common usage.

In fact, the mean deviation is rarely considered when working with a run of real data and MD's are almost never published in modern anthropological literature. The reason that MD has been discussed at all is that the operation provides insights into the general problems of characterizing dispersion in data sets. MD has been a necessary prelude to the discussion of a more effective measure of dispersion, the variance.

4.4.3 Standard Deviation and Variance

We took the absolute value of the deviations about the sample mean in calculating MD in order to eliminate the minus signs. A second way of accomplishing this same objective is to *square* all deviations prior to summation. The mean of the squared deviations about the population mean (μ) is termed the *population variance,* and symbolized by σ^2. The equivalent statistic from a sample is the *sample variance,* symbolized by S^2:

$$\sigma^2 = \frac{\sum_{i=1}^{N} (X_i - \mu)^2}{N} \tag{4.8}$$

$$S^2 = \frac{\sum_{i=1}^{n} (X_i - \bar{X})^2}{n - 1} \tag{4.9}$$

Aside from the substitution of $\bar{X}$ for μ in the sample statistic (S^2), there is a second important difference between the population and sample variances. Both measures reflect the variance—the average dispersion of the variates about the mean—but the population variance (σ^2) is simply averaged, divided by the population size N. But the sample variance has been computed by *dividing by one less than the sample size,* $(n - 1)$. This is a critical distinction, but the reason for this discrepancy will not become apparent until we study Chapter 8, when we consider the estimation of parameters by sample statistics in more detail.

Table 4.2 summarizes the sample and population notation introduced thus far. Where possible, population parameters have been designated by Greek letters (such as μ and σ), and sample statistics are represented by italic letters ($\bar{X}$ and S). In the following discussion, reference will be to sample statistics unless noted to the contrary.

When data are grouped into frequency distributions, the variances are found by

$$\sigma^2 = \frac{\sum_{i=1}^{k} (X_i - \mu)^2 f_i}{N} \tag{4.10}$$

$$S^2 = \frac{\sum_{i=1}^{k} (X_i - \bar{X})^2 f_i}{n - 1} \tag{4.11}$$

where k is the number of classes in the frequency distribution.

TABLE 4.2

Characteristic	Parameter, Population	Statistic, Sample
Number of variates	N	n
Mean	μ	$\bar{X}$
Variance	σ^2	S^2
Standard deviation	σ	S

Variances are always expressed in units which are the *square* of the original variate units of measurement. The variance of a set of cranial capacities, for instance, would be in cubic centimeters squared, the weights of projectile points in grams squared, and so forth. But it is often desirable to deal with the same units of measurement throughout an analysis, and for this reason a second related measure is more commonly reported than the variance. The *standard deviation* is merely the square root of the variance:

$$\sigma = \sqrt{\frac{\Sigma(X_i - \mu)^2}{N}} \tag{4.12}$$

$$S = \sqrt{\frac{\Sigma(X_i - \bar{X})^2}{n - 1}} \tag{4.13}$$

For grouped data, use the following formulas for standard deviation:

$$\sigma = \sqrt{\frac{\Sigma_{i=1}^{k} (X_i - \mu)^2 f_i}{N}} \tag{4.14}$$

$$S = \sqrt{\frac{\Sigma_{i=1}^{k} (X_i - \bar{X})^2 f_i}{n - 1}} \tag{4.15}$$

Example 4.13

The following head lengths in millimeters are from a sample of temperate glacial variety Neanderthal specimens. Compute the sample mean, variance, and standard deviation (data from Kelso 1970:184).

Neanderthal	201
Spy I	200
Spy II	198
La Chapelle	208
La Ferrasie	209
La Quina	203
Gibraltar	190
Monte Circeo	204
Shanidar	207

In this case, the data are ungrouped, so $X_1 = 201$, $X_2 = 200$, and so forth, where $n = 9$.

The sample mean is computed as

$$\bar{X} = \frac{201 + 200 + 198 + \cdots + 207}{9}$$

$$= \frac{1820}{9} = 202.2 \text{ mm}$$

The variance is computed as

$$S^2 = \frac{(201 - 202.2)^2 + (200 - 202.2)^2 + \cdots + (207 - 202.2)^2}{(9 - 1)}$$

$$= \frac{279.56}{8} = 34.95 \text{ mm}^2$$

The standard deviation is found to be

$$S = \sqrt{34.95} = 5.91 \text{ mm}$$

Example 4.14

Find the sample variance and standard deviation for the Elko projectile point weights listed in Table 4.1.

Using the standard format, one need find only the values for $(X_i - \bar{X})^2$ and $(X_i - \bar{X})^2 f_i$ (cols. 8 and 9), and then substitute into the generalized formulas:

$$S^2 = \frac{202.60}{95} = 2.13 \text{ cm}^2$$

$$S = \sqrt{2.13} = 1.46 \text{ cm}$$

The advantages of using the sample standard deviation and variance far outweigh those of all other measures of dispersion. Like the arithmetic mean, the standard deviation is remarkably stable in repeated sampling experiments from large populations. The squaring operation involved in the definition of S does not detract from the algebraic properties of the standard deviation, so that further manipulation in more sophisticated statements is quite permissible.

The exact meaning of "variance" is unfortunately sometimes obscured by the lengthy formulas, and few beginning students can intuitively feel how variances express variability. Just what does "one standard deviation from the mean" tell us anyway? The emphasis here must not be upon what to divide by—is it n or N or $(n - 1)$?—but rather upon what these statistics and parameters have to tell us. Once the normal distribution has been considered (in Chapter 7), we will see how the variance is used to predict the distribution of variates. It turns out that roughly two-thirds of the variates should land between $(\bar{X} + \sigma)$ and $(\bar{X} - \sigma)$. An approximation such as this is quite useful when assessing errors in radiocarbon dates, for example, or when trying to tell whether two samples could have been drawn from the same population.

But for now, it is sufficient to point out the essential similarity between variance and arithmetic mean. Both measures are averages. The arithmetic mean expresses central tendency by measuring the *average* value of a set of variates. Similarly, variances express variability by figuring the *average* amount of dispersion of variates within a sample (or within a population). Taken together, the mean and variance form a useful pair of summary measures.

4.4.4 Computing Formulas for Standard Deviation

Now that population and sample standard deviations have been introduced by formulas in Section 4.4.3, I must implore you to promptly ignore this method of computation for most actual cases. Although these formulas define the concept of variance, there are more efficient, and often more accurate, means of finding σ^2 and S^2.

It can be shown that, algebraically, Formula (4.13) can be reduced to a much simpler computational formula for S:

$$S = \sqrt{\frac{\sum_{i=1}^{n} X_i^2 - ((\Sigma X_i)^2/n)}{n-1}} \qquad (4.16)$$

The computing formula for the sample standard deviation is

$$S = \sqrt{\frac{\sum_{i=1}^{k} X_i^2 f_i - ((\sum_{i=1}^{k} X_i f_i)^2/n)}{n-1}} \qquad (4.17)$$

where k is the number of classes in the frequency distribution.

Similar computing formulas can be derived for the population standard deviation:

$$\sigma = \sqrt{\frac{\sum_{i=1}^{N} X_i^2 - ((\sum_{i=1}^{N} X_i)^2/N)}{N}} \qquad (4.18)$$

$$= \sqrt{\frac{\sum_{i=1}^{k} X_i^2 f_i - ((\sum_{i=1}^{k} X_i f_i)^2/N)}{N}} \qquad (4.19)$$

While these formulas may seem more complex, in fact they are particularly well suited for rapid computation either by hand or with a desk calculator. The computing formulas do not directly involve the mean, thereby eliminating the tedious subtractions for each variate, as in column 6, Table 4.1. In addition, since a single division is required to find the sum of the squared deviations, the resulting standard deviation is generally more accurate than the result supplied by the earlier formulas. When using these computing forms, care should be taken to round off as little as possible during the actual computations.

Example 4.15

Using the computing formulas, find the sample standard deviation for the nine Neanderthal head lengths in Example 4.13.

Only three quantities are necessary to find S by the computing Formula (4.16): $\Sigma(X_i^2)$, $(\Sigma X_i)^2$, and n.

	X_i, mm	X_i^2, mm^2
Neanderthal	201	40,401
Spy I	200	40,000
Spy II	198	39,204
La Chapelle	208	43,264
La Ferrasie	209	43,681
La Quina	203	41,209
Gibraltar	190	36,100
Monte Circeo	204	41,616
Shanidar	207	42,849
	1820	368,324

$$S = \sqrt{\frac{368{,}324 - ((1820)^2/9)}{9-1}} = \sqrt{\frac{368{,}324 - (3{,}312{,}400/9)}{8}}$$

$$= \sqrt{\frac{279.56}{8}} = 5.91 \text{ mm}$$

Note that this answer is in exact agreement with that obtained earlier (Example 4.13) using the more tedious formulas in Section 4.4.3.

Example 4.16

Use the computing formula to find the standard deviation of the Elko projectile point weights listed in Table 4.1.

(1) Class Midpoint, X_i, grams	(2) Frequency, f_i	(3) $X_i f_i$	(4) X_i^2	(5) $X_i^2 f_i$
2.7	1	2.7	7.29	7.29
3.2	22	70.4	10.24	225.28
3.7	15	55.5	13.69	205.35
4.2	20	84.0	17.64	352.80
4.7	9	42.3	22.09	198.81
5.2	11	57.2	27.04	297.44
5.7	3	17.1	32.49	97.47
6.2	3	18.6	38.44	115.32
6.7	2	13.4	44.89	89.78
7.2	3	21.6	51.84	155.52
7.7	2	15.4	59.29	118.58
8.2	3	24.6	67.24	201.72
8.7	1	8.7	75.69	75.69
9.2	1	9.2	84.64	84.64
	$n = 96$	440.7		2,225.69

$$S = \sqrt{\frac{2225.69 - ((440.7)^2/96)}{96-1}} = \sqrt{\frac{2225.69 - 2023.09}{95}}$$

$$= \sqrt{2.13} = 1.46 \text{ cm}$$

Computing formulas provide a substantial saving in time over the more cumbersome methods shown in Table 4.1, although both methods are correct. Note that by using the computing formula in Example 4.16, only five computing columns were necessary, rather than the seven columns required on Table 4.1. In practice, columns 3 and 5 in Example 4.16 would generally be carried upon separate registers on a desk calculator, so the numbers would not even be recorded longhand. For a more detailed consideration of the efficient use of desk computing machinery in determining standard deviations, see Sokal and Rohlf (1969: 57–62).

4.4.5 A Further Note on Sample Statistics and Population Parameters

Because it is critically important to understand the relationship of σ to S, let us consider an empirical example of the difference. Table 4.3 presents a series of 99 breadth measurements of the lower first molar of pygmy chimpanzee, *Pan paniscus*. These measurements were taken from an unpublished study by physical anthropologist Warren Kinzey, who measured all of the available *P. paniscus* crania in the Musée Royale de l'Afrique in Tervuren, Belgium. If the intent were to generalize from these measurements to the first molars of *all living pygmy chimpanzees*, then the data in Table 4.3 should properly be considered a *sample* representing the population of all living pygmy chimpanzees. The sample variates can be summarized as follows:

$$\bar{X} = 8.83 \text{ mm}$$
$$S = 0.4818 \text{ mm}$$
$$n = 99$$

The sample standard deviation has been determined using the computing Formula (4.16), in which the divisor is $(n-1)$. In order to generalize from the Tervuren museum sample to the worldwide population of all pygmy chimpanzees, the investigator must assume (and hopefully demonstrate) that all pygmy chimpanzees in the world had a roughly equal chance for inclusion in the Tervuren collection, as discussed in Section 2.6.

If, on the other hand, the research objectives were restricted to the Tervuren collection as a whole, then the collection becomes a statistical *population*, characterized by the following *parameters*:

$$\mu = 8.83 \text{ mm}$$
$$\sigma = 0.4793 \text{ mm}$$
$$N = 99$$

TABLE 4.3 Breadth Measurements (in millimeters) of Lower First Molar in *Pan paniscus* (data supplied by Warren Kinzey).

8.2	8.6	8.7	9.8
8.8	9.0	8.2	8.4
8.0	8.0	9.3	9.3
9.2	8.9	8.8	8.8
8.5	8.7	9.2	9.2
9.0	9.2	8.4	8.7
8.9	8.2	8.9	9.4
8.1	9.3	7.9	9.4
9.3	8.8	8.7	8.5
7.9	8.5	9.7	9.1
9.3	8.9	8.2	9.3
8.6	8.5	9.4	8.6
8.2	9.2	8.0	9.6
9.4	8.7	8.6	8.3
8.7	7.9	8.8	9.0
8.0	9.0	8.5	9.5
8.8	8.7	9.3	8.8
8.4	9.6	9.2	8.8
8.9	8.1	8.2	9.5
8.5	9.0	9.1	8.4
9.1	9.3	8.9	9.5
9.2	8.5	9.3	9.5
8.1	9.1	8.3	8.5
9.3	9.4	9.7	9.3
8.7	8.9	8.9	

We will see these 99 variates treated as a population in the sampling experiments discussed in Chapter 8. Note that while the population and sample means remain identical ($\mu = \bar{X} = 8.83$ mm), the sample standard deviation is slightly larger than σ because of the $(n - 1)$ factor in the denominator. In fact, this difference is exactly $\sqrt{n/(n - 1)}$, as one would expect. In this case, n was of sufficient size so that the difference between S and σ is negligible, but such is not always the case.

4.4.6 Coefficient of Variation

● *The particular characteristic of our own age is that no evidence is regarded as acceptable unless it is statistical, that is to say, that it is of a kind which can be expressed in numbers. Nothing counts, we might say, unless it can be counted.* —G. Rees

All measures of dispersion considered to this point are *absolute*, that is, expressed in units of measurement identical with the raw variates (centimeters, counts, grams, and so forth). Now that such measures have been explained, let's ask "What good are they?" The best overall measure of dispersion—that is, the one carrying the most information—is the standard deviation, which indicates the amount of variability about the mean. But sometimes one must compare the relative (rather than absolute) dispersion of two or more groups. Can standard deviations from different samples be directly compared?

Beginning with the simplest case, let us compare the relative homogeneity of two samples having the same mean. Suppose that two societies are known to have the same average IQ scores. Their respective standard deviations would be quite adequate to compare the dispersion of IQ scores between the two societies, or if two varieties of pottery were known to contain approximately the same average volume, then S would be a sufficient measure to compare the relative variability of each variety. The standard deviation is an adequate indicator of relative homogeneity as long as the sample means remain roughly identical.

Would the standard deviation remain a useful measure for comparing samples with different means? Let us consider a concrete example. There is an apparent trend in evolution for adaptive characteristics to exhibit less variability than nonadaptive traits. Specifically, some think that the stronger the intensity of selection acting upon a particular morphological characteristic, the more stable will be that trait (Wolpoff 1969). Consider the following cranial capacities for (1) australopithecines[4] and (2) Homo sapiens[5]:

(1) $\bar{X} = 574.3$ and $S = 84.9\,cc$
(2) $\bar{X} = 1367.9$ and $S = 100.2\,cc$

The standard deviation is large for the sample of Homo sapiens. Can we conclude that this sample of Homo sapiens crania is more variable than the australopithécine crania?

The answer is no. The sample standard deviation cannot be used in this case. The reason for this follows from Formula (4.13), which defined sample standard deviation as the root mean square deviation. The magnitude of S is a direct result of the amplitude of the fluctuation about the sample mean. As long as two means are identical, then the fluctuation about the common mean is comparable, but when the means diverge, the same relative dispersal appears larger in samples with larger means. Standard deviation becomes useless for comparison because S is a direct function of $\bar{X}$. Since the mean cranial capacity of the Homo sapiens sample is twice that of the australopithecines, the standard deviation of the Homo sapiens sample must be inflated.

The solution to this difficulty is simple. We need a new measure which expresses the sample variability in terms independent of mean size. This new measure, called the coefficient of variation (CV) is defined as follows:

$$CV = \frac{100 \times S}{\bar{X}} \tag{4.20}$$

The CV is designed to express group variability (as measured by S) in terms

[4]Hypothetical data.
[5]Taken from Hooton (1930: 50), from all Series A undeformed male crania at the Pecos pueblo in New Mexico.

relative to the central tendency of that group ($\bar{X}$). CV is a "pure measure," since the result is expressed in percentages rather than in the absolute units of the standard deviation. The coefficient of variation is particularly well suited for comparing two groups for which the relative homogeneity must be assessed independent of the respective sample means.

Returning to the example at hand, the coefficients of variation are found to be

(1) *Australopithecus*:
$$CV = \frac{100 \times 84.9\ cc}{574.3\ cc} = 14.78\%$$

(2) *Homo sapiens*:
$$CV = \frac{100 \times 100.2\ cc}{1367.9\ cc} = 7.33\%$$

From this comparison of the coefficients of variation, it is clear that this sample of *Australopithecus* crania is almost twice as variable as the *Homo sapiens* sample with respect to cranial capacity, despite the fact that the standard deviation for *Homo sapiens* was in fact larger.

Interpreting the exact meaning of coefficients of variation is largely a matter of experience with the actual data, and should be handled with caution. In general, comparison of CV should be restricted to categories within similar modes of measurement. The coefficient is not always a reliable indicator, for instance, when comparing a continuous variable with a discrete one. In addition, there is no set boundary between wholly acceptable and unacceptable values of CV, although Simpson, Roe, and Lewontin (1960) feel that most CV (measured upon biological variables, at least) should lie between 4 and 10 percent, with 5 and 6 percent being good average values. Observed values much below this range often indicate that the group selection was inadequate to represent the overall variability of the variable. Groups showing values greater than 10 percent or so are probably impure, possibly because the underlying distribution is bimodal. In this case, unrecognized subcategories would tend to inflate the CV.

Example 4.17

It has been suggested that the "Classic" form of Neanderthal particularly lacked variability, which implies that this variety must have been under the influence of extremely strong selective pressure. Do the following data (abstracted from Brose and Wolpoff 1971: table 2) support this contention with respect to cranial capacity?

	$\bar{X}$, cc	S, cc
Solo Neanderthals	1154	84.5
"Classic" Neanderthals	1399	145.5

Since the sample means are quite different, the CV rather than the sample standard deviations must be compared.

$$CV_{Solo} = \frac{100 \times 84.5}{1154} = 7.3\%$$

$$CV_{Classic} = \frac{100 \times 145.5}{1399} = 10.4\%$$

On the basis of these (and several other) CV indicators, Brose and Wolpoff (1971:1168) concluded that the "Classic" form of Neanderthal was in fact *more variable* than other Neanderthal varieties.

Example 4.18

Since quantification is a relatively new venture in anthropology—as compared, say, to biology or psychology—many of the common anthropological variables are as yet untested in terms of overall reliability and repeatability. An experiment was conducted by Thomas (1970) in which six archaeologists were asked to repeat, independently, three common measurements on the same arrowhead to determine reliability of the measurements. (See Thomas 1970, for definitions of variables.)

Archaeologist	Thickness, mm	Length, mm	Max. Width Position
A	5.6	44.0	8.7
B	5.5	47.0	8.9
C	5.5	44.1	4.0
D	5.6	45.0	8.0
E	5.5	40.0	4.3
F	5.5	47.4	3.5
$\Sigma X_i =$	33.2	267.5	37.4
$\Sigma X_i^2 =$	183.7	11,961.6	265.6
$\bar{X} =$	5.53	44.58	6.23
$S =$	0.05	2.67	2.55

What do these results indicate about the reliability of the three variables?

From simple comparison of standard deviations, the length seems to be the worst variable (and hence the least desirable for analysis). But since the means of the variables are far from equal, S is not directly suitable for such comparison.

The CV are as follows:

$$CV_{thicknesses} = 0.90\%$$

$$CV_{length} = 5.99\%$$

$$CV_{MaxWpos} = 40.93\%$$

These results clearly indicate that while thickness and length are acceptable, the maximum width position (MaxWpos) is a thoroughly erratic variable, since independent investigators cannot reproduce the measurement within acceptable degrees of accuracy. In fact, MaxWpos is almost seven times worse than the other variables considered (Thomas 1970); for this reason, Thomas rejected the measurement of MaxWpos from further consideration in projectile point typology.

4.5 CODING DATA FOR EASIER COMPUTATION

One reason for the popularity of the mean and standard deviation in everyday statistical usage is that both $\bar{X}$ and S are amenable to simple algebraic manipulation. This is how the computational formulas were derived. In many cases, data may also be "coded" to more simple forms so that computations can be performed on integers or other numbers which are easy to manipulate. Specifically, several rules can be determined for coding data.[6]

4.5.1 Coding the Sample Mean

1. Addition of a constant to each variate increases the mean by that constant:

$$\frac{\Sigma(X_i + c)}{n} = \bar{X} + c \qquad (4.21)$$

Since subtraction is the algebraic equivalent to addition of a negative number, subtraction of a positive constant from the X_i decreases the mean by that constant.

$$\frac{\Sigma(X_i - c)}{n} = \bar{X} - c \qquad (4.22)$$

2. Multiplication of a constant times each variate results in a mean multiplied by that constant.

$$\frac{\Sigma(cX_i)}{n} = c\bar{X} \qquad (4.23)$$

Since division is the algebraic equivalent to multiplication by the reciprocal of a constant $(1/c)$, division of each variate by a constant results in division of the mean by that constant:

$$\frac{\Sigma X_i / c}{n} = \frac{\bar{X}}{c} \qquad (4.24)$$

4.5.2 Coding the Standard Deviation

1. The addition or subtraction of a constant from the variates has no effect upon the standard deviation.
2. The multiplication (or division) of all variates by a constant results in a standard deviation multiplied (or divided) by that constant.
3. The multiplication (or division) of all variates by a constant results in a *variance* multiplied (or divided) by the *square* of that constant.

---

[6]Rigorous proofs for these statements can be found in Sokal and Rohlf (1969: appendix A1.2).

Example 4.19

The Neanderthal head-length data from Example 4.3 can be readily coded for more efficient computation by subtracting 200 from each raw variate.

$(X_i - 200)$	$(X_i - 200)^2$
201–200 = 1	1
200–200 = 0	0
198–200 = −2	4
208–200 = 8	64
209–200 = 9	81
203–200 = 3	9
190–200 = −10	100
204–200 = 4	16
207–200 = 7	49
20	324

The coded mean and standard deviation are

$$\bar{X}_{coded} = \frac{20}{9} = 2.22 \text{ mm}$$

$$S_{coded} = \sqrt{\frac{324 - (20^2/9)}{8}} = 5.91 \text{ mm}$$

These interim coded values can then be *decoded* according to the simple rules presented above:

$$\bar{X} = \bar{X}_{coded} + 200 = 2.22 + 200 = 202.22 \text{ mm}$$
$$S = S_{coded} = 5.91 \text{ mm}$$

Example 4.20

Calculations upon frequency tables are often facilitated when the midpoints are simplified to round numbers. In general, midpoints can be reduced to sequential nonnegative integers by applying the following simple conversion;

$$\frac{\text{(class midpoint)} - \text{(initial midpoint)}}{\text{class interval}}$$

For the Elko projectile point data given in Table 4.1, consecutive integers result for class midpoints when the following code is applied:

$$X_{i(coded)} = \frac{X_i - 2.7}{0.5}$$

The final mean and standard deviation can then be found by simply reversing the sequence of coding.

X_i	$X_{i\text{(coded)}}$	f_i	$X_i f_{i\text{(coded)}}$	$X_{i\text{(coded)}}^2$	$X_i^2 f_{i\text{(coded)}}$
2.7	0	1	0	0	0
3.2	1	22	22	1	22
3.7	2	15	30	4	60
4.2	3	20	60	9	180
4.7	4	9	36	16	144
5.2	5	11	55	25	275
5.7	6	3	18	36	108
6.2	7	3	21	49	147
6.7	8	2	16	64	128
7.2	9	3	27	81	243
7.7	10	2	20	100	200
8.2	11	3	33	121	363
8.7	12	1	12	144	144
9.2	13	1	13	169	169
		96	363		2183

The coded mean and standard deviation are

$$\bar{X}_{\text{coded}} = \frac{363}{96} = 3.78$$

$$S_{\text{coded}} = \sqrt{\frac{2183 - (363^2/96)}{95}} = 2.92$$

These figures are then decoded:

$$\bar{X} = (0.5\,(\bar{X}_{\text{coded}})) + 2.7 = 4.59 \text{ grams}$$

$$S = (0.5\,(S_{\text{coded}})) = 1.46 \text{ grams}$$

Note that these results agree with those obtained earlier (Examples 4.5 and 4.16), but the actual computations have been vastly simplified.

It is important when decoding results such as these to remember to *reverse the order of coding*. Note, for instance, that $\bar{X}_{\text{coded}}$ must be multiplied by 0.5 *prior* to adding 2.7 cm.

● *I'm lost, but I'm making record time!*—A pilot, somewhere over the Pacific (L. Peter)

SUGGESTIONS FOR FURTHER READING

Adkins (1964: chapters 5–8).
Blalock (1972: chapters 5 and 6).
Campbell (1974: chapters 6 and 7). An amusing and elementary presentation of the misuse of averages and the problems arising ignoring dispersion.

*Hays (1973: chapter 6). In-depth development of central tendency in terms of discrete probability distributions.

*Kerlinger (1973: chapter 6). Advanced consideration of variances based upon set theory; excellent introduction to the logic of analysis of variance.

Langley (1971: chapter 4). Detailed introduction of various measures of central tendency; especially good on the logarithmic mean.

*Mendenhall (1971: chapter 3). Excellent discussion of coding data; measures of dispersion presented in terms of Tchebysheff's theorem.

Simpson, Roe, and Lewontin (1960: chapter 6). Good discussion of Coefficient of Variation.

Welkowitz, Ewen, and Cohen (1971: chapters 3 and 6). Detailed introduction of transformation (standardization); particularly useful in psychological testing.

EXERCISES

● . . . for I made no haste in my work but rather made the most of it . . .—H. Thoreau

Note: Those exercises with the star (*) are designed to provide practice with machine calculation. Only the masochistic should attempt hand computation on the starred problems.

4.1 Simplify the following expressions, using Σ and its appropriate limits:
   (a) $W_3 + W_4 + W_5$
   (b) $X_1 Y_1 + X_2 Y_2 + X_3 Y_3 + X_4 Y_4$
   (c) $(X_1 - 3) + (X_2 - 3) + (X_3 - 3) + (X_4 - 3)$
   (d) $(Y_6 - 6) + (Y_7 - 7) + (Y_8 - 8)$

4.2 Write out in full the sums represented by these expressions:
   (a) $\Sigma_{i=3}^{4} Y_i$ (b) $\Sigma_{i=1}^{5} (Y_i + 4)$
   (c) $(\Sigma_{i=1}^{3} X_i)^3$ (d) $a \Sigma_{i=1}^{7} (X_i - 2)$

4.3 If $Y_1 = 19$, $Y_2 = 2$, $Y_3 = -6$, and $Y_4 = 3$, find the numerical values for the following expressions:
   (a) $\Sigma_{i=1}^{3} (Y_i - 1)$ (b) $\Sigma_{i=2}^{4} (Y_i - 2)^2$
   (c) $\Sigma (Y_i)^i$

4.4 Use the Rules of Summation (Section 4.2.1) to simplify the following expressions:
   (a) $\Sigma_{i=1}^{4} 8$ (b) $\Sigma_{i=1}^{4} (X^2 + 4i)$
   (c) $\Sigma_{i=1}^{5} (X_i^2 + i^2)$ (d) $\Sigma_{i=1}^{5} i^4$

4.5 Express the following words in symbols:
   (a) Take 10 variates and subtract 20 from each. Then find the sum.
   (b) Add up all Y variates. Then add all X variates and multiply these two terms. Square the result and add 43. Then take the square root and divide this by n.
   (c) To each X add 4 and multiply by X. Then take the sum and find the square root.

*More advanced treatments.

4.6 Express the following statement in symbolic notation: Sum the X variates, square this sum, and divide by n. Subtract this from the sum of the squared X variates. Multiply by the squared sum of the Y variates divided by n subtracted from the sum of the Y variates squared. Take the square root and then divide this into the sum of the XY products minus the sum of X divided by n times the sum of Y divided by n. (This is, incidentally, the formula for the parametric correlation coefficient, introduced in Chapter 14).

4.7 A worldwide survey was conducted to determine the average family size desired by women in several Latin American cities (data from Ehrlich and Ehrlich 1972: table 10.2).

Latin American Cities	Average Number of Children Wanted
Bogota, Colombia	3.6
Buenos Aires, Argentina	2.9
Caracas, Venezuela	3.5
Mexico City, Mexico	4.2
Panama City, Panama	3.5
Rio de Janeiro, Brazil	2.7
San Jose, Costa Rica	3.6

(a) What is the mean desired family size in Latin American cities based upon this limited sample?
(b) What is the variance of the mean?
(c) Find the coefficient of variation.
(d) Find the median number of children desired.

4.8 For the following sample,
4 10 9 18 22 1 21
find the
(a) mean
(b) median
(c) range
(d) variance
(e) standard deviation

4.9 If variates in Exercise 4.8 were a *population* rather than a sample, which of the measures of central tendency and dispersion would change? Find these new values.

4.10 Refer to the Virginia fluted point lengths in Exercise 3.5.
(a) What is the median length?
(b) What is the modal class?
(c) Find the sample mean.
(d) Find the sample variance.
(e) What is the coefficient variation? What does it tell us?

4.11 Brose (1970: table 2) has determined the following diameter measurements for the 290 postmolds excavated in the Middle Woodland component at the Summer Island site in northern Lake Michigan:

Class Limits, ft	Number of Occurrences
0.06–0.15	9
0.16–0.25	47
0.26–0.35	89
0.36–0.45	23
0.46–0.55	24
0.56–0.65	49
0.66–0.75	33
0.76–0.85	10
0.86–0.95	3
0.96–1.05	2
1.06–1.15	1
	290

(a) Compute the sample mean, standard deviation, and CV.

(b) Find the median.

(c) Determine the modal class.

(d) Which, if any, of the measures of central tendency are poor summaries of these data? Support your answer.

4.12 Referring to the frequency distribution constructed for worldwide infant mortality rates in Exercise 3.4,

(a) Find the median.

(b) Find the modal class.

(c) Determine the CV.

(d) Find the mean and standard deviation using the grouped data.

(e) Find the mean and standard deviation for ungrouped variates.

(f) Which measure of central tendency do you feel best illustrates the worldwide trends in infant mortality rate? Support your answer.

*4.13 A census of 11 villages throughout the Andaman Islands indicates the following figures for maximum community size (data from Divale 1972: table 4):

Name of Village	Total Population
Chariar	39
Kora	96
Tabo	48
Yere	218
Kede	59
Juwai	48
Kol	11
Bojigyab	50
Balawa	19
Bea	37
Onges	672

(a) Compute the sample mean and standard deviation.

(b) Find the sample median.

(c) Which is the better measure of central tendency, the mean or the median? Why?

*4.14 The following variates are maximum length of the mandibular canine in *Gorilla gorilla* (data from Pilbeam 1969: appendix 1d):

Specimen No.	Max. Length, mm
Z1224	13.5
Z6592	13.8
Z5685	13.4
Z6595	14.6
Z6593	14.4
Z Fr. Cam.	13.2
Z6600	12.0
Z6676	13.0
Z6840	13.2
Z6594	12.7
B1939–935	13.6
B1939–925	12.6
B1939–933	11.3
B1939–936	—
B1939–927	13.2
A G20	—
A G21	11.8
A G22	12.4
A G23	12.1
A G30	12.4

(a) What is the sample range?
(b) Find the median.
(c) Find the sample mean.
(d) Find the variance.
(e) Determine the coefficient of variation.
(f) Do you think the mean is a suitable indicator of central tendency in this case? Why?

4.15 Marriages in northern India are exogamous by village (that is, wives are obtained from nearby villages, and daughters marry elsewhere). Thus, every marriage, whether wife or daughter, has a distance associated with it. Stanley Freed and Ruth Freed (1973: table 2) obtained the following data from Shanti Nagar, a small rural village in northern India:

Caste	n	$\bar{X}$, miles
High	102	11.02
Low	53	11.39

(a) What is the average distance of marriage for the 155 recorded marriages in Shanti Nagar?
(b) For these 155 marriages, it is known that the mean distance for wives is 11.31 miles, and for daughters is 10.28 miles. How many daughters married outside Shanti Nagar (round off your answer)?

4.16   The mean cephalic index for a sample of African informants was found to be 76.59 percent. If the 52 South Africans (Bushmen and Hottentots) in the sample had a mean cephalic index of 75.10 percent, and the rest of the informants averaged 77.89 percent, how large was the total sample (you must round off the answer)?

4.17   The Scholastic Aptitude Test (SAT) is an examination designed to provide college admissions officers with standardized measures of ability. The test has a range of possible scores from 200 to 800, and the questions are constructed to produce a mean score of 500.
   (a) If a student has an SAT score of 610, should he hope for a large or a small sample standard deviation? Why?
   (b) If the SAT results were found to be positively skewed, which would be larger, the mean or the median?

5 Basic Probability Theory

● *The race is not always to the swift—nor the battle to the strong—but that's the way to bet.—*D. Runyon

5.1 INTRODUCTION

The time has come for a rapid shift of gears. This chapter launches into consideration of fundamental probability theory. The Preface promised a streamlined approach which would minimize lengthy proofs, elaborate notation, and generally played down mathematical elegance. This chapter departs from that tradition slightly to consider probability in a somewhat more formal manner. Three axioms are presented and then several theorems are introduced which follow from the axioms. Exposition proceeds in terms of elementary set theory and Venn diagrams. Because this method differs from earlier chapters and because many anthropologists seem quite susceptible to symbol shock, a further word of explanation is in order.

First of all, probability theory provides the basic framework and structure for the remainder of the book. In fact, the theory of statistics is grounded almost entirely upon probabilistic thinking. Many basic statistical notions cannot even be defined in terms other than probabilistic: independent, mutually exclusive, random. Even this elementary presentation of statistical theory must lean heavily upon the probabilistic foundation.

A second reason for detailed attention to probability theory has to do with the present state of mathematical thinking within anthropology. There are those who argue that procedures of statistical inference and hypothesis testing represent an old-fashioned, out-dated mode of thinking which will eventually disappear from social science. Some feel that the strict testing of hypotheses will soon give way to a more thoroughly mathematical consideration of probability, set theory, logic, and axiomatic method. Mathematical anthropologist Paul Kay has written (1971: xvi) that "there is little doubt that anthropology students would benefit if their probability and statistical training were more probability and less statistics." While questioning Kay's evaluation regarding the relevance of statistical theory per se, I surely endorse his proposal that anthropologists should adopt a more probabilistic orientation to their subject.

This chapter presents a very brief look at probability theory, both as a foundation for statistical theory and also as a *sui generis* mode of inquiry.

5.2 STATISTICAL EXPERIMENTS

Our consideration of probability theory must begin with the common-sense term "experiment." Statistical experiments do not necessarily involve scientists at work in a laboratory, psychologists running rats through a T-maze or physicists monitoring their geiger counters in a radiocarbon laboratory. There are everyday conceptions of scientific experiments, but a scientific experiment is not necessarily a statistical experiment. A *statistical experiment* is any well-defined act which leads to a well-defined outcome. Thus, our usage of the term "experiment" will be much broader than the commonplace notion of experiment.

A common statistical experiment involves flipping a coin in midair. When the coin lands on the ground, one of two well-defined outcomes will result: The side with the head will be facing upward or it will be facing downward. Rolling dice, drawing cards, and picking roulette numbers are gaming phenomena which often are used to illustrate probabilities. Gaming devices are particularly useful because the rules are well defined and the possible outcomes are clear-cut. But if appropriate care is taken, many everyday situations can also be phrased in terms of the statistical experiment. Wait patiently, for example, for 5 minutes by your telephone. Assuming the device to be in working order, the telephone will either ring during those 5 minutes, or it will not ring. Your 5-minute episode of observation is a "statistical experiment" because one of two well defined outcomes will undoubtedly occur: Ringing or not ringing. All the necessary conditions for a statistical experiment are present.

Every statistical experiment must have at least two potential results. The set of all possible distinct outcomes for a specific statistical experiment is called the *sample space S.* Any individual element within that sample space is known as an *event.* If the experiment is properly defined, we can tell whether a specific event has *occurred* or *not occurred* as a result of the experiment. Properly executed statistical experiments allow no middle ground. Either the telephone rings or it does not; either the coin has "heads" facing up or it does not; the little roulette ball either lands on space 13 or it does not. An event which has occurred is often denoted as A, and the nonoccurrence of event A is $\bar{A}$ (read as not-A). A and $\bar{A}$ are thus events within the sample space, and either A or $\bar{A}$ must occur, but they cannot occur simultaneously. $\bar{A}$ is the *complement* of the event A.

A dart-throwing contest is another example of a statistical experiment.[1] The

[1]The approach to probability developed here follows, to some extent, that found in McFadden (1971) and Hays (1973).

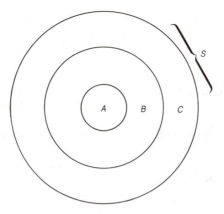

Fig. 5.1

circular dart board can be taken as representing the sample space, S, on Fig. 5.1. The center bull's-eye is labelled A, the intermediate ring designated as B, and the outer ring is called C. The rules of the game are quite simple. A dart is thrown in the direction of the board. If the dart misses the board, it is retrieved and thrown again until finally the target is hit. That is, this experiment required that S occur. S is a certain outcome.

The dart board in Fig. 5.1 is also known as a Venn diagram, named after the British logician J. Venn. Venn diagrams are simple pictures representing a set of points within some geometrical format. Venn diagrams can be circles, squares, ellipses, or even irregular forms. Figure 5.1 contains all necessary components for a statistical experiment. The target represents the sample space S, and exactly three possible outcomes exist for our experiment: A, B, or C, depending on where the dart lands. (Note that Fig. 5.1 could be redefined into two possible outcomes, A and $\bar{A}$, in which case $\bar{A} = B + C$.)

A slightly more complex statistical experiment is represented by the Venn diagram in Fig. 5.2. In this case the experiment is to roll a single die and record

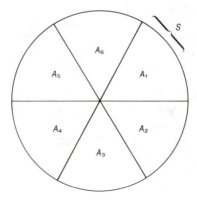

Fig. 5.2

the outcome. The face of the circular dart board once again represents the sample space S, but this time there are six different outcomes possible: 1, 2, 3, 4, 5, and 6. Each individual event is assigned a symbol: "one" corresponds to A_1, "two" corresponds to A_2, and so forth. The Venn diagram representing these events within the sample space consists of a circle neatly partitioned into six areas. We can, symbolically, roll our single die by tossing a dart in the direction of Fig. 5.2. Once again, the dart must land within the circle for the experiment to have taken place.

These two elementary statistical experiments can also be represented in terms of elementary set theory. In both cases, the sample space is the target, containing the set of all possible outcomes. Each distinct event is thus a subset of the total sample space. Events A, B, and C in Fig. 5.1 are all subsets of the set S.

$$A \subset S$$
$$B \subset S$$
$$C \subset S$$

The expression $A \subset S$ is read "A is a subset of the set S." These individual statements can also be summarized into a single listing for the set S.

$$S = \{A, B, C\}$$

This statement reads: "The set S consists of the elements A, B, and C." Similar statements could be framed for the six events of Fig. 5.2, each of which comprises a subset of the set S.

Once these relations are established, it becomes possible to generate a number of useful statements about our experiment. The Venn diagrams and set notation allow us to proceed in an abstract manner without actually referring to the specifics. We know, for example, that because A_1 and A_2 are both subsets of the total sample space in Fig. 5.2, the combination of A_1 with A_2 must likewise be a subset of S. The combination of any two subsets is termed their union, symbolized in set notation by $\cup$, as in

$$A_1 \cup A_2 \subset S$$

This statement is read "the union of subsets A_1 and A_2 is a subset of set S." A_1 and A_2 are both original events of a statistical experiment. $A_1 \cup A_2$ is also an event of the same experiment. The event $A_1 \cup A_2$ occurs if either a "one" or a "two" is obtained in a roll of a die. Or, symbolically, $A_1 \cup A_2$ occurs whenever a dart lands in the shaded portion of the target on Fig. 5.3, the shaded portion representing $A_1 \cup A_2$.

Similarly, the intersection of two subsets of S is also an event. The set term "intersection" refers to the area (or points) held in common by two or more subsets. Intersections are denoted by $\cap$. The intersection of A and B is yet another subset of the sample space S. Hence $A \cap B$ is itself an event in a statistical experiment. In Fig. 5.1 we can see that two nonzero intersections occur within the set S:

$$A \cap B = A \qquad B \cap C = B$$

In this case, $A \cap B = A$ because every point within A is also squarely within B.

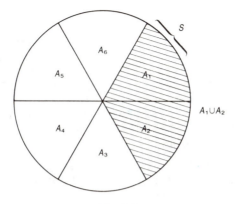

Fig. 5.3

There are no intersections at all on Fig. 5.2. Whenever the intersection of two subsets of S contains no points, this intersection is called the *empty set,* symbolized by ϕ. Every possible intersection between subsets of S in Fig. 5.2 results in the empty set. For example, $A_1 \cap A_3 = \phi$. Whenever the intersection of two subsets of S corresponds to the empty set, these two events are *mutually exclusive* because they cannot occur simultaneously. All six subsets of S in Fig. 5.2 are mutually exclusive. In other words, the six possible outcomes of the single die experiment must be mutually exclusive.[2]

To summarize: A statistical experiment consists of selecting some discrete subset from the set S which contains all possible outcomes of that experiment. This outcome is a *simple* subset of S if the event cannot be decomposed (such as A_1, A_2, and so forth, on Fig. 5.2). Or the outcome can be a *compound* subset of S, itself comprised of two or more subsets. Both the intersection and the union of any two subsets of S are themselves discrete events which may or may not occur, depending upon the specific rules of the experiment.

5.3 THE PROBABILITY OF A SIMPLE EVENT

The next step is to assign numbers to all possible events within an experiment. These numbers will be called *probabilities.* The probability of event A is symbolized as $p(A)$. As before, A refers to a specific event of an experiment, some subset of the sample space; A is not a number. The number is $p(A)$, and we will now consider how to assign appropriate numbers to events within S.

Chapter 2 briefly introduced the process of reasoning from a specific sample to some more general population. This procedure, statistical inference, involved an *inductive* method of reasoning. The conclusions of statistical inference are

[2]You should be slightly bothered by the intersection of contiguous subsets such as $A_1 \cap A_2$ and $A_5 \cap A_6$ in Fig. 5.2. The intersections of these subsets must correspond to the empty set for the die analogy to hold. We must qualify the Venn diagram in Fig. 5.2 so that the line separating each quadrant is infinitely small. That is, we can use the *ideal* properties of mathematical constructions to make our Venn diagrams. These conditions will not hold for any real dart board.

really strategic guesses based upon some initial body of data (the sample). Assigning probabilities, on the other hand, involves a *deductive* mode of reasoning. Deduction sets forth some reasonable assumptions, derives necessary quantities from the assumptions, and then evaluates experimental findings in light of the deduced quantities. That is, the deductive process commences with assumptions and proceeds toward a definite conclusion.

The "reasonable assumptions" in the case of probability are three critical statements called *axioms*. An axiom is a presupposition necessary for one to proceed with a given train of reasoning. These axioms, in fact, constitute our formal definition of probability.

Axioms of probability: For any event A in the sample S, there exists a number, called the probability of that event and denoted by p(A), for which the following three properties must be true:

Axiom 1. The probability is nonnegative:

$$p(A) \geq 0$$

Axiom 2. The probability of a certain event is unity:

$$p(S) = 1$$

Axiom 3. If two events A and B are mutually exclusive, then

$$p(A \cup B) = p(A) + p(B)$$

The axioms of probability are really no more than the Venn diagrams and set notations of Section 5.2 transcribed into systematic form. The first axiom asserts that probabilities must be nonnegative. Returning to the dartboard of Fig. 5.2, we see that events A_1 through A_6 represent all areas in which the dart might possibly land. Figure 5.2 represents six equal subsets of the sample space S.

$$A_1 = A_2 = A_3 = A_4 = A_5 = A_6$$

Each subset contains a finite space within the total sample space. The numbers associated with these areas are the probabilities of each event in a statistical experiment: $p(A_1)$, $p(A_2)$, $p(A_3)$, $p(A_4)$, $p(A_5)$, $p(A_6)$. Negative spaces can never exist, and hence we will not allow a negative number to represent one of these spaces. Axiom 1 forbids a negative probability.

The second axiom arbitrarily sets the probability of a certain event at unity. On Fig. 5.2 the union of the six areas must equal the entire sample space of S:

$$A_1 \cup A_2 \cup A_3 \cup A_4 \cup A_5 \cup A_6 = S$$

Axiom 2 sets this value at $p(S) = 1$. The event S must occur and its probability is equal to 1. Taken together, Axioms 1 and 2 establish the total range for all probabilities:

$$0 \leq p(A) \leq 1$$

By convention, all probabilities must range between zero and 1, inclusive.

Finally, Axiom 3 defines the probability of the union of two mutually exclusive events as the sum of their individual probabilities. The union of A_1 and A_2 is shaded on Fig. 5.3. Each area has some discrete number associated with it,

$p(A_1)$ and $p(A_2)$. The total area contained within $A_1 \cup A_2$ is established by Axiom 3 to be $p(A_1 + A_2)$.

A host of new deductions follow from the three axioms of probability. Each of these subsidiary deductions is called a "theorem." A theorem must be true as long as the original axiomatic conditions have been fulfilled. None of the axioms, for example, actually stated that all probabilities must range between zero and 1. The statement $0 \leq p(A) \leq 1$ is a logical deduction following from Axioms 1 and 2; the statement that probabilities must range between 1 and zero is a theorem. Similarly, the axioms imply that the probability of an impossible event must be zero. Once again, no axiom has directly stated this property; it is simply implied in our formal, axiomatic definition of probability. A number of probability theorems could be derived and proved to be true strictly on mathematical grounds. In fact, some weighty volumes have been filled with theorems of probability, all of which derive from the three basic axioms. There is a certain abstract beauty in this system, and those inclined toward mathematical elegance are urged to consult Hays (1973: chapter 2) and Mood and Graybill (1963) for more detailed consideration of probability functions.

But we need not clutter the present path with a tangle of theorems and derivations. The point is that we can find literally hundreds of rules which probability must obey, even though we have not stated what a probability *really means*. That is, the theory of probability can be considered as a perfect abstract system without any practical interpretation at all.

5.4 PROBABILITY AS RELATIVE FREQUENCY

The probabilities of Section 5.3 are the probabilities of ideal objects. The dart board was a perfect circle, the line separating subsets within the target were of zero width, the six segments of Fig. 5.2 were of exactly equal size. That is, the dart board exists only as a mathematical abstraction.

Ideal probabilities are inherent in the nature of their system. The die we rolled wasn't loaded because we said it wasn't. The probability of obtaining a head is exactly equal to the probability of a tail if we specified a perfectly *fair* coin. The ideal roulette wheel has exactly 38 equally probable niches because we say it has.

Consider a standard coin-tossing experiment. By the rules of Section 5.3, we could specify that this coin is *fair*. That is, as long as we toss an ideal coin—a mathematical abstraction—the probability of obtaining a "head," $p(H)$, can be specified to be exactly equal to the probability of obtaining a "tail," $p(T)$. Thus, $p(H)$ must be equal to $p(T)$ because we say so. We are allowed such excesses with perfect mathematical systems. Figure 5.4 is a Venn diagram representing the perfectly *fair* coin. A dart tossed at this target has an exactly equal chance of landing in area H or T.

Earlier I promised a "user-oriented" introduction to probability and statistics, a method approaching the real world of social science. So let us discard our "fair" coin (which didn't really exist anyway) and toss a real, everyday coin. I have removed a 1972 U.S. quarter from my pocket, a coin which looks "fair" enough to me. It is round, seems well balanced, and appears to be quite

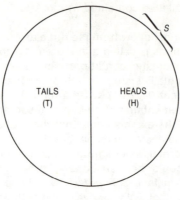

Fig. 5.4

symmetrical. There seems to be no obvious reason for favoring either heads or tails, but I cannot categorically state that it is perfectly "fair" in the sense that p(H) is *exactly* equal to p(T). I suspect this to be roughly the case, but I cannot be absolutely sure, and neither can you. This is the price we pay for using real money instead of pretended money.

To test the fairness of my 1972 quarter, I tossed it 200 times in a row and recorded the frequency of heads and tails. My 200 tosses resulted in exactly 96 heads and 104 tails. These findings are not exactly 100 heads and 100 tails, as a perfectly *fair* coin would perform, but the results are not very far off. The results of this little experiment can be generalized into relative frequencies. The relative frequency of an event is simply the ratio of its occurrence to the total number of trials.

$$\text{relative frequency of } A = \frac{\text{frequency of event } A}{\text{total number of trials}}$$

Defining "heads" as event A, the relative frequency of heads is

$$\text{relative frequency of heads} = \frac{96}{200} = 0.48$$

Similarly, the relative frequency of tails is $104/200 = 0.52$. My 200-trial experiment can now be summarized as follows:

Outcome	Absolute Frequency	Relative Frequency
Heads	96	0.48
Tails	104	0.52
	$\Sigma = 200$	$= 1.00$

This experiment could have been repeated using other gambling devices. For example, we could chart the frequencies of *actual* roulette numbers, or real dice, or a particular Keno game. In fact, casino gamblers are sometimes seen running exactly this kind of experiment. Their objective is to find a particular device which is "unfair" and then bet on this tendency. Professional gamblers tend to keep most casinos "fair" (if not honest).

Flipping my 1972 quarter suggests a rather obvious alternative to axiomatic probability. Why not use the observed relative frequency as an *approximation* of the formal probability? The axioms tell us that $p(H) = p(T)$ for the ideal coin. But I am interested only in my 1972 quarter, which has relative frequencies of 0.48 and 0.52 for heads and tails, respectively, after 200 flips. The axioms do not apply here. The alternative perspective suggests we use the relative frequencies of heads and tails to *estimate* the true probabilities, whatever they might be. From coin flipping, let us call the relative frequency estimates $p(H) = 0.48$ and $p(T) = 0.52$. We now have *two* distinct conceptions of probability, the axiomatic definition and the relative frequency definition. The two approaches complement one another.

Why is there disagreement between the ideal values and the experimentally observed frequencies? Perhaps my quarter is really not fair. Maybe the eagle's tail is somehow lighter than George Washington's head, so the tail lands upward more often. Perhaps one side is more streamlined than the other. My experiment might be trying to tell me that tails really are more "probable" for this particular 1972 quarter. If that is true, then "tails" is the way to bet on this given coin.

But perhaps my coin is really "fair" after all, and the result indicates only that the experiment was too brief for the probability to stabilize. It could be that, *in the long run* (a very important phrase), the two probabilities might have approached a stable ratio of $p(H) = p(T)$. When an approximately fair coin is tossed a few times in succession, the relative frequency of heads should fall near 0.50. The relative frequency can be expected to be *very* close to 0.50 when the same coin is tossed dozens of times in succession. If this same coin were flipped thousands of times, we could be practically certain that the relative frequency would be $p(H) = p(T) = 0.50$. In general, the relative frequency of success will stabilize as the number of trials increases under constant conditions. This constant value is known as the *theoretical limit*. We simply postulate that there exists a limit to the relative frequency probability. On the other hand, it may not exist.

The first time I tossed my 1972 quarter the result was a "head." The initial tally stood at one head and zero tails. On the basis of this single toss, the relative frequency probability was computed to be $p(H) = 1.0$ and $p(T) = 0.0$. These figures are "estimates" of the long-range probability, based upon a single trial. I retrieved my coin and tossed it again. Another head came up, so the tally now stood at two heads and no tails. The relative frequency probability remained unchanged: $p(H) = 1.0$ and $p(T) = 0.0$. The third toss finally produced a tail. In three trials, I had two heads and one tail, and the relative frequency probability for three trials changed to $p(H) = 2/3$ and $p(T) = 1/3$. The fourth toss was another tail, moving the relative frequency to $p(H) = 1/2$ and $p(T) = 1/2$. But the fifth toss produced another head, moving the relative frequency probability of $p(H) = 0.6$ and $p(T) = 0.4$.

I have charted the first 25 trials of this experiment on Fig. 5.5. You can see how the first two trials, both heads, kept $p(H) = 1.0$. Then two tails appeared, moving $p(H)$ to 0.5. As the number of trials increased, the relative frequency kept

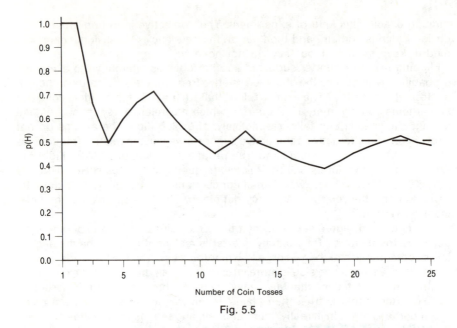

Fig. 5.5

changing somewhat, but its oscillations about 0.5 became smaller. The dotted line for p(H) = 0.50 is the *theoretical limit* of the relative frequency. When the number of trials is very large, we expect p(H) to fall very close to the theoretical limit.

The practical link between relative frequency probability and axiomatic probability is suggested by the concept of theoretical limit. This principle was first established by the eighteenth-century mathematician James Bernoulli, and it bears his name.

Bernoulli's Theorem: If the probability of an event occurring is p(A), and if N independent and identical trials are made, then the probability that the relative frequency of occurrence of A differing from p(A) approaches zero as N becomes large.[3]

Bernoulli's theorem codifies what we observed already from my flipping of the 1972 quarter (Fig. 5.5). At first, the relative frequency probability of heads was vastly different from the formal probability, p(H) = 0.50. On the first trial, $N = 1$, there were only two possibilities for the observed relative frequency. If a head appeared, then p(H) = 1.0; if a tail appeared then p(H) = 0.0. The difference between the formal probability and the relative frequency must be 0.5 in either case. There is no middle ground for a single trial. As I tossed the coin again and again—that is, as N increased—p(H) began to oscillate about 0.5. Bernoulli's theorem tells us that as N becomes larger, the oscillation about 0.5 should almost cease, assuming the coin is actually fair. If the coin is really "unfair," then the relative frequency probability should eventually approach that "unfair"

[3]"Independent" is a key word examined in Section 5.11.

probability, such as $p(H) = 0.6$, or $p(H) = 0.4$, or whatever. This is what Bernoulli's theorem really tells us.

Probabilities are often expressed in terms of the ratio between successful and unsuccessful trials.

$$\text{probability} = p(A) = \frac{s}{s + f}$$

where s denotes the frequency of event A and f denotes the frequency of $\bar{A}$. The sum of the frequencies of $A + \bar{A}$—the same as $s + f$—must equal N, the total number of trials. When the events are theoretical, as in throwing a dart at an ideal dart board or tossing an ideal coin, then the ratio of $s/(s + f)$ is a formal probability. When actual successes and failures are enumerated, the probability is a relative frequency ratio.

It should be clear that probability has no "true" meaning any more than X has a true meaning in algebra. X and $p(A)$ mean whatever we say they mean. But keep in mind just which meaning of probability is used at any given time.

● *In the long run, we are all dead.*—Lord Keynes

Example 5.1

What is the probability of drawing the ace of spades from a well-shuffled deck?

Because we are using an *ideal* deck of 52 cards, this is an exercise in axiomatic probability. If selecting the ace of spades is considered success, then

$$s = 1 \quad \text{and} \quad f = 51$$

The probability of selecting the ace of spades is thus

$$p(A) = 1/52$$

Example 5.2

What is the probability of not drawing the ace of spades?

This time, the ace of spades is a failure, so

$$s = 51 \quad \text{and} \quad f = 1$$

The probability of not drawing the ace of spades is thus

$$p(A) = 51/52$$

Note that the same results could have been obtained by subtraction:

$$p(A) = 1 - p(\bar{A}) = 1 - (1/52) = 51/52$$

Example 5.3

While ethnographer Roy Rappaport was working among the Tsembaga of Highland New Guinea, he discovered that in his sample of 381 Tsembaga gardens, 91 gardeners were working upon land to which they had no "legal" claim (Rappaport 1968:20). What is the probability that any particular gardener is working upon his own land?

If we define a gardener working on his own land as a success, then $f = 91$ and $s = 381 - 91 = 290$.

The probability of finding a gardener with legal claim to his land is

$$p(A) = \frac{s}{s+f} = \frac{290}{381} = 0.76$$

The probability is $p(A) = 0.76$ that any given gardener is working his own land. This is a relative frequency probability based upon an actual (rather than ideal) statistical experiment.

5.5 PROBABILITY AND THE "LAW OF AVERAGES"

● *As for the "law of averages," it doesn't exist, certainly not in the sense that he who has lost over a considerable length of time must, on the strength of all that accumulated defeat, inevitably begin to win. There is no such mechanism in life anymore than at the gaming tables.* —P. Roth

Bernoulli's theorem suggests that the relative frequency will be significantly different from its theoretical limit only when insufficient trials have elapsed. As N increases, the relative frequency should very gradually fall into line with the limit. Bernoulli's theorem works because it *averages out*, or *smooths over*, a few aberrant outcomes. The bulk of more typical trials will eventually smother the short-term variability. Only "in the long run" can we be confident that the relative frequency adequately reflects its theoretical limit.

But intuitive feelings can suggest a different mechanism for Bernoulli's theorem. Most of us have observed hundreds of experiments involving chance events—rolling dice, playing poker, flipping coins, and so forth. After this long period of casual observation, we seem to develop an intuitive "feeling" for the odds in each case.[4] We know that heads should come up about half the time, that there is usually a 5:1 chance of rolling a 5 (or any other number) with a single die, and that there is a 1:4 chance of drawing a heart from a deck of cards. How do we know these things? In effect, our period of informal observation corresponds to flipping my 1972 quarter: The relative frequency of

[4]"Odds" are usually expressed in a manner slightly different from relative frequencies, but the principles are the same. If $p(A) = 1/6$ and $p(\bar{A}) = 5/6$, then the odds are 5:1 against A. A "ten-to-one shot," for instance, reflects one success and ten failures, so $p(A) = s/(s+f) = 1/11$. $p(A) = 1/3$ reflects "two-to-one odds against."

success, $p(A)$, is thought to be an adequate estimator of the theoretical limit of probability. The degree to which our odds prove ultimately true is a good operational measure of how well the theoretical limit has been estimated.

But this intuitive approach to probability can lead the unwary astray. Even the consistent loser will keep gambling, maintaining that he is bound to win shortly "because of the *law of averages.*" What is the "law of averages?"

Let us peek over the shoulder of a particular roulette loser. This game involves tossing a little ball about a fancy wheel which contains 18 red numbers, 18 black numbers, and a green "0" and "00." Gamblers can bet either red, black, or a particular number or group of numbers. This gambler has bet on red for the last eight times, and he has lost every time. With only enough money for one final bet, he contemplates his decision when a stranger nudges him. "Bet the black, stupid. The law of averages is on your side—it's *got to* come up black next time." When the disconsolate gambler fails to respond, the stranger on his other side scornfully argues that the law of averages is a myth. In games of chance, he is told, every trial is totally independent. It makes no difference what has happened in past games because the roulette wheel had no memory or conscience. The past can make no difference. The second stranger urges our gambler to bet on red, figuring that a wheel landing eight times in a row on red must be biased in favor of red. The second stranger has, in effect, rejected the proposition that $p(\text{red}) = p(\text{black})$. He thinks $p(\text{red}) > 0.5$.

But our gambler disregards all of this free advice, simply shrugs, takes his last silver dollar from his pocket and flips it, muttering "Heads I bet red, and tails I bet black." And, even though he has been losing, the gambler is the smartest of all. He knows that the friendly advice can not improve his chance of winning. Each spin of the roulette wheel is independent of all past spins. There is no "law of averages." He also knows that eight observations are totally insufficient to establish the theoretical limit of a probability. So he simply pays the last of his money, and takes his chances.

Roulette, and all other games of chance, remain profitable at Monte Carlo, Nassau, and Las Vegas for two simple reasons. First of all, the house always maintains a slight advantage in the odds. The roulette wheel has two green segments marked "0" and "00." Whenever the ball lands on either of these numbers, the house wins all "color" bets because the color is neither red nor black. So the color bets have odds which are actually only $p(A) = 18/38$, less favorable than $p(A) = 0.50$. An even more critical factor is that gambling houses stay in business because there is no infallible "system" of winning on games of chance. As long as superstitions such as the "law of averages" or the perfect "system" survive, Monte Carlo will thrive. Enough people will "best the odds"—itself a predictable event—to keep the losers systematically losing.

● *"All life is 6–5 against."*—D. Runyon

5.6 THE UNION OF COMPOUND EVENTS

All statistical experiments considered so far involve *simple events*, experimental outcomes which cannot be decomposed into smaller units. Also of interest are those events known as "compound." As the name implies, a *compound event* comprises two or more simple events. Basically, two kinds of compound events are possible: the union of two simple events and the intersection of two simple events.

Consider the Venn diagram in Fig. 5.4. Events A and B must be *mutually exclusive* because they cannot occur simultaneously on a single trial. The axiomatic probability of the two events are $p(A)$ and $p(B)$. Axiom 3 tells us that if A and B are mutually exclusive events, the probability of their union is equal to the sum of their individual probabilities:

$$p(A \cup B) = p(A) + p(B)$$

The union of these formal (and simple) probabilities readily produces a new compound probability.

Consider a relative frequency approach to the same situation. Let S be the dart board in a neighborhood pub. This dart board can be represented by the Venn diagram in Fig. 5.1, but be certain to realize that this is now a real dart board rather than a mathematical abstraction. Because the target is located in a particularly busy pub, we can safely exclude the possibility of skill. Darts are simply thrown in the general direction of the board and they are counted only when they hit the target. The thrower is given another chance when his dart misses.

We have no way of finding the axiomatic probability for this particular dart board. The best estimates for the probabilities are the tallies of tournament results for the past week, kept by the watchful bartender. The *relative frequency probability* for hitting the bull's-eye (event A) on a single trial is

$$p(A) = \frac{s}{s+f} = \frac{\text{number of hits on } A}{\text{total number of hits on } S}$$

Similarly, the tallies could be used to find $p(B)$ or $p(C)$, the other two simple subsets of S.

What, then, is the probability of hitting either the bull's-eye (event A) or the intermediate ring (event B)? What is $p(A \cup B)$? Axiom 3 holds here as long as $(A \cap B) = \phi$. This is true even though we are dealing with relative frequency probabilities. The probability of a dart landing in either A or B, given that the dart hits the target at all, is the sum of the two relative frequencies:

$$p(A \cup B) = p(A) + p(B)$$

The union is found for mutually exclusive events from Axiom 3 for both axiomatic and relative frequency probability, even though two rather different notions of probability underlie these statements.

This example stipulated that a dart could not land in both A and B simultaneously. The intersection of A and B is the empty set, so $p(A \cap B) = 0$. But how does one find the union of two events which are *not* mutually exclusive? Can the individual simple probabilities still be combined by simple addition?

Consider Fig. 5.6. What is the probability of $A \cup B$, given that $(A \cap B) \neq \phi$? The probability of either A or B occurring on a single trial is given by a new theorem:

$$p(A \cup B) = p(A) + p(B) - p(A \cap B) \tag{5.1}$$

The individual probabilities are combined as in Axiom 3, but a correction must

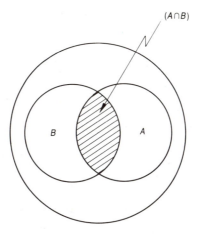

Fig. 5.6

be applied to account for their nonzero intersection. When the probability of event A is added to $p(B)$, the intersection $(A \cap B)$ is included *twice.* Because area $A \cap B$ should be considered only once, its area must be subtracted in order to find $A \cup B$. Note that this expression does not mean the probability of "A or B but not $A \cap B$." If this were so, then $p(A \cap B)$ must be subtracted *twice*, since it is covered once by $p(A)$ and once by $p(B)$.

Expression (5.1) can be illustrated by our ideal deck of playing cards. The probability of drawing a five of hearts on a single trial is

$$p\text{(five of hearts)} = 1/52$$

Replacing our theoretical card and reshuffling the deck, let us complicate matters a bit. What is the probability of drawing any 5? This time, not only does the five of hearts (event A_H) count, but so does the five of diamonds (A_D), or spades (A_S) or clubs (A_C). These four events are mutually exclusive for a single trial, and Axiom 3 provides the overall formal probability as

$$p(A) = p(A) \cup p(A) \cup p(A) \cup p(A)$$
$$= 1/52 + 1/52 + 1/52 + 1/52 = 4/52$$

The probability of drawing any 5 is the union of the probabilities of drawing the individual 5's, and the intersections are all the empty set.

Reshuffling our imaginary deck once again, let us ask yet a third question: What is the probability of drawing *either* a 5 *or* a heart? We must now combine the probability for obtaining a 5, $p(A)$, with the probability for obtaining a heart, $p(B)$. Axiom 3 is inapplicable because the intersection of the 5's (event A) with hearts (B) is now the five of hearts. Formula (5.1) is now relevant. The probability of selecting a 5 is known to be $p(A) = 4/52$, and the probability of selecting a heart is $p(B) = 13/52$ because a deck of cards contains exactly 13 different hearts. The intersection of the subsets, hearts and 5's, has an associated probability of $p(A \cap B) = 1/52$, the probability of the five of hearts.

Hence, by Formula (5.1), the overall probability of selecting a 5 or a heart is

$$p(A) + p(B) - p(A \cap B) = 4/52 + 13/52 - 1/52 = 16/52$$

Had we simply combined $p(A)$ with $p(B)$, the resulting probability would have erroneously counted the five of hearts twice, once for the subset hearts and once for the subset of all 5's. Formula (5.1) removes one of the two values for $p(A \cap B)$.

Example 5.4

What is the probability of obtaining either a 1 or a 2 in the single roll of one die?

Let the probability of rolling a 1 be $p(A) = 1/6$ and the probability of obtaining a 2 be $p(B) = 1/6$. The intersection of events A and B is the empty set. So the union of A and B is simply their sum:

$$p(A \cup B) = 1/6 + 1/6 = 1/3$$

The formal probability of rolling either a 1 or a 2 is 1/3.

Example 5.5

Suppose a survey of Crow males revealed the following population distributions (after Lowie 1935):

Clan	Population
Sore-Lip Lodge	250
Filth-Eating Lodge	200
Kicked-in-Their-Bellies Lodge	250
Whistling Lodge	200
	900

A Crow is always born into the class of his mother, so clan membership is hereditary. Chieftainship, on the other hand, is achieved through one's military prowess. What is the probability that the tribal chief (the *batse'tse*) belongs either to the Sore-Lip Lodge or the Filth-Eating Lodge? Since one cannot belong to more than one lodge, the intersections between clan memberships consist of the empty set. The probability that an individual is a Sore-Lip is $p(A) = 250/900$ and the chances of one being a Filth-Eater are given by $p(B) = 200/900$. The probability of a *batse'tse* belonging to either clan is

$$p(A \cup B) = \frac{250}{900} + \frac{200}{900} = \frac{450}{900} = 0.50$$

Example 5.6

An urn contains 50 cubes labelled 1 through 50. What is the probability of drawing a cube with either an even number or a number under 15?

Let us call the subset of even numbers A. Because there are 25 even numbers less than or equal to 50,

$$p(A) = 25/50$$

The intersection of subsets A and B (even numbers with numbers under 15) contains only 7 cubes: 2, 4, 6, 8, 10, 12, 14:

$$p(A \cap B) = 7/50$$

The union of subsets A and B is given by

$$p(A \cup B) = p(A) + p(B) - p(A \cap B)$$
$$= 25/50 + 14/50 - 7/50 = 32/50$$

The probability of drawing an even number or a number under 15 on a single draw is thus 32/50.

5.7 CONDITIONAL PROBABILITY

The intersection of A and B (Fig. 5.6) must be examined more closely. Suppose that we know that event A has *already* occurred. Given this previous knowledge, what is the probability that B has *also* occurred. That is, our dart has landed somewhere in area A—we are told that—and we must find whether this same dart has also landed in area B, $(A \cap B)$.

This situation involves a *conditional probability.* Conditional probabilities comprise two or more interdependent subsets of the sample space. That is, whether or not B occurs may somehow depend upon the occurrence of A. The situation can be illustrated with a deck of cards. There are exactly four chances of finding an ace in 52 cards. The initial probability of selecting an ace is $p(A) = 4/52$. Suppose that we were successful on the first trial and in fact drew an ace. If we replaced the ace and reshuffled, there would be once again four chances in 52 of fetching an ace. This situation is *unconditional* because the first draw had absolutely no influence on the second draw. The first card in no way "conditions" the probabilities of the second card.

But suppose the first ace was withdrawn and then destroyed. If we were to attempt to draw another ace from this same deck, the probabilities would have changed. The first draw had a probability of $p(A) = 4/52$, as before. But the number of possible successes is reduced for the second draw to 3—because one ace is now gone—and the size of the deck is also reduced by one card. The new probability for the second card stands at $p(B) = 3/51$. A *condition* has been placed upon the second draw by holding out one of the aces. The probability of drawing an ace *on the condition that an ace has already been drawn* is denoted as $p(B|A)$. This statement is read: "the probability of B, given that A has already occurred." In the example, A indicates drawing an ace on the first draw and B indicates drawing an ace on the second draw.

In a somewhat more formal sense,

A and B are two events within the sample space S. The conditional probability $p(B|A)$ of B's occurring, given that A has already occurred, is given by

$$p(B|A) = \frac{p(A \cap B)}{p(A)} \tag{5.2}$$

where $p(A) > 0$.

Before examining these conditional probabilities in more detail, let us return to the intersection of two subsets. The probability of the intersection of two subsets can be found by multiplying Expression (5.2) by $p(A)$:

$$p(A \cap B) = p(B|A)p(A)$$
$$= p(A|B)p(B) \tag{5.3}$$

In terms of the relative frequency approach, Expression (5.3) tells us that A is expected to occur in a large number of N trials with a relative frequency of about $p(A)$, where $p(A) > 0$. Of these successful A trials, B must also sometimes occur. The event $A \cap B$ (*both* A and B) should occur with a relative frequency equal to the product of $p(B|A)$ and $p(A)$, or $p(A|B)$ and $p(B)$, depending upon how the probabilities are phrased.

A more general version of Expression (5.2) can be easily derived by substituting $p(B)p(A|B)$ for its numerator and dividing $p(A)$ into its component expressions:

$$p(B|A) = \frac{p(B)p(A|B)}{p(B)p(A|B) + p(\bar{B})p(A|\bar{B})} \tag{5.4}$$

where B and $\bar{B}$ are mutually exclusive and exhaustive possibilities for event B. This more general expression of Expression (5.2) is called "Bayes' theorem," after the eighteenth-century clergyman and scholar Thomas Bayes. Later in this chapter Expression (5.4) will be expanded to handle several outcomes, that is, several $p(B_i|A)$. An example will illustrate the mechanics of conditional probability.

I once taught a large anthropology course in which 60 percent of the students were male. On the first day of class, I asked how many people in the class smoked; 70 percent of the males and only 50 percent of the females were smokers. Because the classroom was overcrowded and the room rather stuffy, I requested students to refrain from smoking in class, and everyone agreed. But one day during a film showing, several of us noticed somebody smoking in the corner. Because the lights were out, we couldn't tell whether the surreptitious smoker was male or female. What is the probability that this antisocial individual was male?

The overall probability that any given student in the class is male is $p(B) = 0.60$. This is a simple probability based upon enrollment figures with no "conditions" involved. But we have the prior knowledge that our culprit is a smoker, and this bit of information *conditions* the probability that the unidentified student is male. We really want to know $p(B|A)$: What is $p(B)$, given that A has occurred? The Expression (5.4) of conditional probability is

$$p(B|A) = \frac{p(B)p(A|B)}{p(B)p(A|B) + p(\bar{B})p(A|\bar{B})}$$

Consider first the numerator. $p(B)$ is the unconditional probability that any given student is male: $p(B) = 0.60$. The expression $p(A|B)$ is the probability that a student smokes (A), given that student is a male (B). We know that 70 percent of the males of the class smoke, so the numerator of Expression (5.4) is

$$p(B)p(A|B) = (0.60)(0.70) = 0.42$$

The denominator consists of the product $p(B)p(A|B)$—which was just computed for the numerator—plus the product $p(\bar{B})p(A|\bar{B})$. The probability of $\bar{B}$ (the probability of a given student being female) is known to be 0.40 and $p(A|\bar{B}) = 0.50$ because 50 percent of the females in the class smoke. The entire denominator is

$$p(B)p(A|B) + p(\bar{B})p(A|\bar{B}) = 0.42 + (0.40)(0.50) = 0.62$$

Substituting into Expression (5.4),

$$p(A|B) = \frac{0.42}{0.62} = 0.68$$

Note that the conditional probability $p(B|A) = 0.68$ is larger than the simple probability $p(B) = 0.60$. Given no prior information, we must guess that the probability any student is male is $p(B) = 0.60$. But since we know this student is a smoker, the knowledge that more men than women smoke increases our probability to $p(B|A) = 0.68$.

Bayes' theorem, Expression (5.4), has been used to illustrate the logic and mechanics of conditional probability. You should convince yourself that the simpler Expression (5.2) would produce identical results.

Example 5.7

A certain prehistoric culture is known to have manufactured 25 percent jars and 75 percent bowls. About 50 percent of the bowls were decorated, while only about 20 percent of the jars were decorated. If an archaeologist finds a decorated sherd of this culture, what is the probability that the sherd came from a bowl?

Let A indicate that a pot is decorated. B denotes a bowl and $\bar{B}$ denotes a jar. We must find the probability $p(B|A)$ of B, given A. Expression (5.2) tells us this quantity is equal to

$$p(B|A) = \frac{p(A \cap B)}{p(A)}$$

First we must find the intersection of A and B, given by Expression (5.3):

$$p(A \cap B) = p(A|B)p(B)$$

The probability of *(A|B)* is the probability that a bowl has been decorated, *p(A|B)* = 0.50. The probability of its being a bowl is *p(B)* = 0.75. Hence, the numerator of $p(B|A)$ is

$$p(A \cap B) = (0.50)(0.75) = 0.375$$

The denominator, $p(A)$, is the total probability of finding a decorated bowl:

$$p(A) = p(A|B)p(B) + p(A|\bar{B})p(\bar{B})$$
$$= 0.375 + (0.20)(0.25) = 0.425$$

The conditional probability $p(B|A)$ is thus

$$p(B|A) = \frac{0.375}{0.425} = 0.88$$

The probability is 0.88 that a given decorated sherd came from a bowl. The same results occur when Bayes' theorem is used.

Example 5.8

If there are five green and five red marbles in a bag, what is the probability that a blindfolded player will first draw a green marble, and then *without* replacing the first marble, draw a second green marble?

The probability of withdrawing the first green marble is $p(A) = 5/10$. If this green marble is not replaced, the probability of drawing a green marble is changed to $p(B|A) = 4/9$. The probability of first drawing a green marble thus "conditions" $p(B)$ by leaving one less success available.

The overall probability of *both* events occurring, $p(AB)$, is given by Expression (5.2):

$$p(A \cap B) = p(B|A)p(A)$$
$$= (4/9)(5/10) = 2/9$$

5.8 SUMMARY: RULES OF PROBABILITY FOR UNCONDITIONAL COMPOUND EVENTS

● *God casts the die, not the dice.* —A. Einstein

This section introduces three axioms of probability and their major consequences, thereby setting the foundation for the general theory of statistics. But the study of probabilities as such can also be relevant to anthropologists. The following three rules were developed in Section 5.2, and are summarized here to provide operational guidelines for computing actual compound probabilities.

I. *The Addition Rule*: Given the *mutually exclusive* events A and B which have associated probabilities $p(A)$ and $p(B)$. The probability that two mutually exclusive events will occur in a single trial is given by the sum of the individual probabilities:

$$p(A \cup B) = p(A) + p(B)$$

II. *The Multiplication Rule for Independent Events*[5]: Given the *independent* events A and B which have associated probabilities of $p(A)$ and $p(B)$. The probability that two independent events will occur on a single trial is given by the product of their associated probabilities:

$$p(A \cap B) = p(A)p(B)$$

III. *The Multiplication Rule for Dependent Events*: Given the *dependent* events A and B which have the associated probabilities $p(A|B)$ and $p(B)$. The probability that two dependent events will occur in a single trial is given by the product of their associated probability:

$$p(A \cap B) = p(A|B)p(B)$$

Example 5.9

What is the probability of rolling either a 1 or a 6 on a single roll of a die?

The probability of rolling a 1 is $p(A) = 1/6$ and the probability of rolling a 6 is $p(B) = 1/6$. Because these events are mutually exclusive for a single roll, probability Rule I applies and the individual probabilities are combined by addition:

$$p(A \cup B) = p(A) + p(B) = 1/6 + 1/6$$
$$= 1/3$$

Example 5.10

What is the probability of rolling both a 1 and a 6 on two consecutive rolls of a single die (or on two dice rolled simultaneously—take your choice)?

The two probabilities are independent of one another, so probability Rule II indicates they should be multiplied:

$$p(A \cap B) = p(A)p(B) = (1/6)(1/6)$$
$$= 1/36$$

---

[5]The terms ''independent'' and ''dependent'' will be defined in a mathematical fashion in Section 5.11. For now, it is sufficient to recognize two events as *independent* if the probability of the first in no way influences the probability of the second; otherwise, these events are *dependent*.

Example 5.11

A die is rolled once and the outcome recorded. It is rolled again until a different number appears. What is the probability that the first number is a 1 and the second number is a 2?

The probability of a 1 on the first roll is $p(B) = 1/6$. On the second roll, only five outcomes are possible, so the probability of obtaining a 2 is $P(A|B) = 1/5$. The probability of both these dependent events is given by probability Rule III:

$$p(A \cap B) = p(A|B)\ p(B) = (1/5)(1/6)$$
$$= 1/30$$

Example 5.12

A single die is rolled twice. What is the probability of rolling a 1 exactly once?

The probability of rolling a 1 on the first trial is $p(A)$ and the probability of a 1 on the second trial is $p(B)$. Both $p(A)$ and $p(B)$ are themselves intersections of independent events:

$$p(A) = p(\text{rolling a 1})\ p(\text{not rolling a 1})$$
$$p(B) = p(\text{not rolling a 1})\ p(\text{rolling a 1})$$

Probability Rule II for independent events applies here:

$$p(A) = (1/6)(5/6) = 5/36$$
$$p(B) = (5/6)(1/6) = 5/36$$

Events A and B are mutually exclusive, so probability Rule I gives us

$$p(A \cup B) = 5/36 + 5/36 = 10/36$$

5.9 COMBINATIONS AND PERMUTATIONS

As probability statements become more complex, the exact number of successful outcomes becomes more difficult to assess by inspection alone. Everyone can readily tell that when a coin is flipped, the outcome will be either a head or a tail. But when ten coins are flipped simultaneously, it becomes impossible to tell by simple inspection how many possible outcomes there might be. Because of this complexity, it is necessary to resort to the concepts of combinations and permutations for the more sophisticated probability computations.

A *permutation* is an arrangement or ordering of items into a definite sequence.

Suppose that there are two people (A and B) who are attending the theater together. There are only two possible arrangements (permutations) in which they can stand in line:

AB   or   BA

If three people arrived together, A, B, and their friend C, then there are now six possible permutations in the way in which they can line up:

ABC   BAC   CAB

ACB   BCA   CBA

Further enumeration of this sort would reveal that had four people lined up, there would be 24 possible permutations.

This is an important numerical series which should be clearly understood. Let us extend our example to five people, but this time consider the situation in which the five people must be seated about a circular table. When everybody is standing, there are exactly five ways of filling the first chair, since anybody can sit there. After the first person is seated, there remain only four people to fill the remaining four chairs. When another guest is seated, there are only three people for the three chairs, and so forth. The total number of possible arrangements can be found by taking the *product* of all the possible ways in which each chair can be filled, so the situation is solved as follows:

Total number of permutations = $5 \cdot 4 \cdot 3 \cdot 2 \cdot 1 = 120$

The formula for this general series is

Total number of permutations = $n(n-1)(n-2) \cdots (2)(1) = n!$

The number of permutations in such cases is found by the sequential product of all integers from 1 to n. The symbol "$n!$" (to be read as "n factorial") is a shorthand method of denoting this sequence. The total number of permutations can also be denoted as "$P_{n,n}$" (to be read as "the number of permutations of n things taken n at a time"). In the case of the five dinner guests to be seated in five chairs, we wish to consider the permutations of five things taken five at a time, symbolized as $P_{5,5}$.

The general formula to find the number of permutations is

$$P_{n,n} = n! \tag{5.5}$$

Example 5.13

In how many different orders can ten books be arranged upon a library shelf?

This question asks the value of $P_{n,n}$, where $n = 10$. By Equation (5.5):

$$P_{10,10} = 10! = 10 \cdot 9 \cdot 8 \cdot 7 \cdot 6 \cdot 5 \cdot 4 \cdot 3 \cdot 2 \cdot 1$$
$$= 3{,}628{,}800 \text{ arrangements}$$

This problem obviously could not be answered without Equation (5.5), since one would be physically unable to tally such problems by simple enumeration (except with sophisticated computing machinery).

As useful as Equation (5.5) may be, however, one is generally not concerned with all n objects n at a time. Suppose there were ten books, but room for only three on the bookshelf. How many permutations would there be in this case? To handle this more general situation, it is necessary to consider the permutations of n objects taken r at a time, where $r \leq n$. We know that the first position on the shelf can hold any one of the ten books. There are nine possible alternatives for the second position, and only eight choices left for the third niche. So there are only $10 \cdot 9 \cdot 8 = 720$ permutations in this case.

The formula to express this general relationship is given by

$$P_{n,r} = \frac{n!}{(n-r)!} \qquad (5.6)$$

Equation (5.5) has been modified by truncating the unused $(n-r)!$ positions, which become redundant with $r < n$. In the preceding example, $P_{10,10} = 10!$, but $P_{10,3}$ requires only the first three factorial digits $(10, 9, 8)$, which is analogous to the books fitted into the three spaces on the shelf:

$$P_{10,3} = \frac{10!}{(10-3)!} = \frac{10!}{7!}$$
$$= \frac{10 \cdot 9 \cdot 8 \cdot 7 \cdot 6 \cdot 5 \cdot 4 \cdot 3 \cdot 2 \cdot 1}{7 \cdot 6 \cdot 5 \cdot 4 \cdot 3 \cdot 2 \cdot 1}$$

All the digits less than 7 cancel between the numerator and the denominator, so the equation reduces to

$$P_{10,3} = 10 \cdot 9 \cdot 8 = 720$$

which agrees with the answer obtained above without the use of Equation (5.6).

You should also note that Equation (5.6) applies to *all* permutations, including the case of $P_{n,n} \cdot (r = n)$. For example,

$$P_{10,10} = \frac{10!}{(10-10)!} = \frac{10!}{1}$$
$$= 3,628,800$$

which agrees with the answer obtained from Formula (5.5).

By convention, zero factorial (0!) is always taken to equal 1.

● *Nothing is new except arrangement.* —W. Durant

Example 5.14

In a particular graduate school, all students are required to write three term papers. If there are eight possible paper topics from which to choose, how many options does a student have?

$$P_{8,3} = \frac{8!}{(8-3)!} = \frac{8!}{5!}$$
$$= \frac{8 \cdot 7 \cdot 6 \cdot 5 \cdot 4 \cdot 3 \cdot 2 \cdot 1}{5 \cdot 4 \cdot 3 \cdot 2 \cdot 1}$$
$$= 8 \cdot 7 \cdot 6 = 336 \text{ options}$$

Example 5.15

How many four-letter permutations can be constructed from the letters in ANTHROPOLOGY?

$$P_{12.4} = \frac{12!}{(12-4)!} = 12 \cdot 11 \cdot 10 \cdot 9$$
$$= 11{,}880$$

In many cases, one is interested only in the proper subsets of items in a collection, regardless of their order. If a committee of 3 people is to be selected from 12 candidates, for example, the *order* in which the candidates are selected is irrelevant to the composition of the committee. This is a problem in *combinations*, not permutations.

A *combination* is a subset of items in which order is defined as irrelevant.

The number of combinations is symbolized by $C_{n,r}$ (to be read as "the number of combinations of n things taken r at a time"). By discounting order, we are in effect stating

$$P_{n,r} \geq C_{n,r}$$

In other words, combinations are permutations with the redundancy of order removed. To compute the number of combinations, the total number of permutations must be found, and then the redundant orderings must be eliminated.

The number of ways in which 3 individuals can be selected from a total of 12 candidates, for example, is the number of permutations of 12 things taken 3 at a time:

$$P_{n,r} = P_{12.3} = \frac{12!}{(12-3)!} = 12 \cdot 11 \cdot 10$$
$$= 1320$$

But the figure 1320 includes the various orderings in which these same people could have been selected. As we saw earlier, three items (A, B, and C) could be selected in six possible orders:

$$\begin{array}{ccc} ABC & BAC & CAB \\ ACB & BCA & CBA \end{array}$$

or alternatively,

$$P_{3.3} = 3! = 6$$

So the correct number of ways in which the three people fill the committee must be reduced by $3! = 6$:

$$\frac{P_{12.3}}{P_{3.3}} = \frac{12!}{3!9!} = \frac{1320}{6}$$
$$= 220 = C_{12.3}$$

For the general case, the number of combinations is given by

$$C_{n,r} = \frac{n!}{r!(n-r)!}$$ (5.7)

Example 5.16

In a survey of the Mexican Highlands, an archaeologist located 12 Formative temple mounds. How many alternative research strategies are there open to him if his funds permit him to excavate only four of the mounds?

Since the order of excavation is irrelevant, the number of combinations is

$$C_{12,4} = \frac{12!}{4!8!}$$

$$= 495 \text{ possible samples}$$

● *Most competent men throughout history have had their lapses. Conversely, the habitually incompetent can, by random action, be right once in a while.*—L. Peter

5.10 BAYES' THEOREM FOR MULTIPLE OUTCOMES

Expression (5.4) of conditional probability was said to be a simplified version of Bayes' theorem. Formula (5.4), defined for two mutually exclusive and dichotomous outcomes of B (B and $\bar{B}$), can be generalized for k alternatives of B as follows:

$$p(B_i|A) = \frac{p(B_i)p(A|B_i)}{p(B_1)p(A|B_1) + p(B_2)p(A|B_2) + \cdots + p(B_k)p(A|B_k)}$$

$$= \frac{p(B_i)p(A|B_i)}{\sum_{i=1}^{k} p(B_i)p(A|B_i)}$$ (5.8)

where the alternative events B_1, B_2, ... B_k are mutually exclusive and exhaustive. This new version of Bayes' theorem simply generalizes Formula (5.4) for more than two possible outcomes of event B. An elementary example should illustrate this expanded version of the Bayes' theorem.

During the spring of 1973, I was reanalyzing the projectile points from Danger Cave. This important site was originally excavated in 1949–1951 and the artifacts are now stored at the Department of Anthropology at the University of Utah. Because the Danger Cave artifacts have been handled a great deal over the past two decades, a few of the original catalog numbers have disappeared from the artifacts. While measuring Danger Cave artifacts, I found an Elko Eared type point without a catalog number. The number had once been there, but is now illegible. There is no question that the artifact is from Danger Cave, but its exact provenience is unknown.

Here is a complete listing of projectile point frequencies at Danger Cave (from Aikens 1970: table 6):

Stratum	Total Points	Elko Eared Points
DV	146	7
DIV	46	9
DIII	171	54
DII	85	7
	448	77

Over two-thirds of the Elko Eared points came from DIII. What is the probability that the numberless Elko Eared point came from DIII?

Let us first label stratum DV as event B_5, stratum DIV as B_4, and so on; we have four possible outcomes for event B. The probability that just any point came from stratum DIII is simply the relative frequency of points in DIII: $p(B_3) = 171/448 = 0.38$. This situation is *unconditional* because the relative frequency has not been "conditioned" by any other probability.

But we also know that the errant artifact is an Elko Eared type. This typological assignment gives us an added insight into guessing at the provenience, since the Danger Cave artifacts tend to sort stratigraphically; typology in this case *conditions* the stratigraphic probabilities. In terms of conditional probability, we must find the probability that this point came from DIII, given that it is an Elko Eared type. In other words, find $p(B_3|A)$. This quantity can be readily found using Bayes' theorem, Formula (5.8), which involves four sets of probabilities, one for each stratum:

$$p(B_3|A) = \frac{p(B_3)p(A|B_3)}{p(B_5)p(A|B_5) + p(B_4)p(A|B_4) + p(B_3)p(A|B_3) + p(B_2)p(A|B_2)}$$

The quantities necessary to find these terms are available from the stratigraphic and typological information cited above.

Stratum	Total Points	$p(B_i)$	Elko Eared Points	$p(A|B_i)$	$p(B_i)p(A|B_i)$
DV	146	$B_5 = 0.33$	7	$p(A|B_5) = 0.05$	0.017
DIV	46	$B_4 = 0.10$	9	$p(A|B_4) = 0.20$	0.020
DIII	171	$B_3 = 0.38$	54	$p(A|B_3) = 0.32$	0.120
DII	85	$B_2 = 0.19$	7	$p(A|B_2) = 0.08$	0.015
	448				0.172

The relative frequencies of points per stratum, $p(B_i)$, are found as before. The relative frequencies of Elko Eared points *within* each stratum, $p(A|B_i)$, is the frequency of Elko Eared points divided by the total point frequency in that

122

stratum. The final column computes the products for each pair of $p(B_i)p(B_i|A)$. Substituting into Expression (5.5), the probability of a given Danger Cave point coming from stratum DIII, given that point is an Elko Eared, is

$$p(B_3|A) = \frac{0.120}{0.017 + 0.020 + 0.120 + 0.015} = \frac{0.120}{0.172}$$
$$= 0.70$$

The conditional probability in this case involves a prior knowledge of the relative frequencies of types within strata at Danger Cave. This information allowed us to refine our probability from simply $p(B_3) = 0.38$ to a much more satisfying value of $p(B_3|A) = 0.70$.

The probabilities from Bayes' theorem have been used to establish a rather new and controversial form of statistical inference. Bayes' theorem is not controversial as a mathematical statement. All resultant probabilities derive directly from axiomatic probability theory. The controversy comes about when Bayes' theorem is harnessed as an apparatus of decision making. The *Bayesian approach*, as it is called, attempts to go beyond the bald information available from a sample by including additional sources of auxiliary information. Bayesian probabilities may include previous experimentation, theoretical considerations, and even the experimenter's own opinions. It is in the assignment of these *prior probabilities* where the Bayesian approach differs from "classic" statistical inference discussed earlier in Chapter 2.

One interesting aspect of the Bayesian perspective is given by Savage (1954), who sets forth "rational man" as a decision-making creature. Behavior is constrained only by five definitions and seven postulates. Rational man operates on the consistent principles of *utility*—what's in it for me if I decide A instead of B. For his strategy to succeed, rational man must be given prior information regarding the likelihood of his alternatives. Savage extends the notion of prior knowledge to include *personal probabilities* by assigning degrees of belief to specific outcomes. A personal probability is just that: "I am 95 percent confident that this is a Neanderthal cranium," *or* "I think it's likely that this informant suffers from malnutrition," *or* "I'll bet we don't hit the bottom of Gatecliff Shelter during this field season." The acceptability of these statements of personal belief as probabilities is a controversial philosophical issue. Some philosophers, such as Hans Reichenbach, have argued that personal probabilities will ultimately be analyzed in concrete, strictly mathematical terms, phrased as precisely as probabilities derived by the frequency concept. Other distinguished philosophers, including Bertrand Russell and Ernst Nagel, also stress the importance of subjective probability statements, but doubt that these statements will ever attain the precision of reactive frequency probabilities. Still other philosophers reject the notion of subjective probability entirely (see Kemeny 1959: chapter 5).

At the extreme, the Bayesian approach sets forth a total framework for statistical inference and decision making. The full implications and methodology of the Bayesian statistical approach are yet unknown. To date, Bayesian methods have had little impact on the research methods of anthropology, but as general mathematical awareness grows among anthropologists, it seems inevitable that these methods will ultimately prove useful. The present discussion is restricted to more conventional "classic" statistical inference, and the interested reader is provided references on Bayesian methods at the end of this chapter.

Example 5.17

Coccidioidomycosis is a very serious infection transmitted by minute spores present in many dusty soils of the American West. Nearly all residents of highly endemic areas have been mildly infected by coccidioidomycosis before reaching adulthood. Also known as "valley fever," this disease has become a major hazard to archaeological crews working throughout the western United States. In fact, the most serious valley fever outbreak on record occurred in 1970 on an archaeological excavation conducted near Chico, California (Werner 1974). A total of 103 students participated in the project and of these, 90 students came from New York State (hence they had never been previously exposed to valley fever). Sixty-seven of the excavators were stricken by valley fever, and only two of these were not New Yorkers. What is the probability that a given student suffering from valley fever also came from New York?

Let $p(A)$ be the probability that a student contracted valley fever, $p(B_1)$ be the probability that a student came from New York, and $p(B_2)$ be the probability that he came from someplace other than New York.

	$p(B_i)$	$p(A\|B_i)$	$p(B_i)p(A\|B_i)$
From New York	$90/103 = 0.87$	$65/90 = 0.72$	$(0.87)(0.72) = 0.626$
Not from New York	$13/103 = 0.13$	$2/13 = 0.15$	$(0.13)(0.15) = 0.020$

The probability that a valley-fever sufferer came from New York is given by Bayes' theorem to be

$$p(B_1|A) = \frac{p(B_1)p(A|B_1)}{p(B_1)p(A|B_1) + p(B_2)p(A|B_2)}$$

$$= \frac{0.626}{0.646} = 0.969$$

Given only the knowledge of where students live, the probability of randomly selecting a New Yorker on this dig is only $p(B_1) = 0.87$. But by restricting choice to the valley fever cases (that is, given a certain degree of prior knowledge), the probability that the randomly selected student hails from New York jumps to $p(B_1|A) = 0.97$.

5.11 STATISTICAL INDEPENDENCE

We considered the situation of student smokers in Section 5.7. Because males tend to smoke more than females, the knowledge that a particular student was smoking gave a probabilistic edge in predicting that student's sex. Males smoke more, so a smoker was more likely to be a male than an individual who does not smoke. The smoking habit set a *condition* on the other variable, and the mechanics of conditional probability allowed us to assign numbers to these events.

But suppose that a census on the first day of another such large lecture course revealed that roughly 60 percent of *both* males and females smoked. In this class, we lose our probabilistic edge because the same proportion of males and females smoke; smoking no longer sets a condition on the second variable. This situation is sometimes called *symmetrical* because one variable (smoking habit) is symmetrically distributed across the other variable (sex). This contrasts to the conditional (or asymmetrical) example involving 70 percent male smokers and only 50 percent female smokers. This symmetry (or lack of it) is also reflected in the overall sample space.

The contrast between conditional and unconditional probability (or between symmetrical and asymmetrical relations) brings us to the question of *independence*. We already have an intuitive notion of the meaning of independence. Conditional probabilities somehow involve variables which depend upon one another. The value of $p(A)$ somehow conditions the value of $p(B)$, or perhaps the reverse. *Independence* can readily be defined in terms of conditional probability.

Two events A and B with $p(A) > 0$ and $p(B) > 0$ are *independent* if and only if

$$p(B|A) = p(B) \qquad (5.9)$$

Two events are independent whenever the probability of A has no quantitative effect on B. A bit of algebraic manipulation also allows us to reverse Expression (5.9). Using the earlier definition given by Equation (5.2) and multiplying both sides of (5.9) by $p(A)$, we find

$$p(A \cap B) = p(A)p(B)$$

Again using the definition of conditional probability expressed by Equation (5.9), and dividing by $p(B)$,

$$p(A|B) = p(A)$$

In other words, if A is independent of B, then B must also be independent of A.

Take our ideal deck of cards once more and draw two cards. The probability that the first card is a heart is $p(A) = 13/52$. If this first card is indeed a heart and not replaced in the deck, the probability that the second card is also a heart is $p(B|A) = 12/51$. Holding out that first card will *condition* the probability of the second card. But if the first card is replaced, the probability that the second card is a heart becomes $p(B|A) = 13/52$, the same as the probability for the first card. That is, with replacement, $p(B|A)$ is equal to the probability of drawing a heart from the full deck: $p(B|A) = p(B) = 13/52$. Therefore, by Expression (5.9), the second draw is independent of the first draw, as long as the first card is returned to the deck.

Some people seem to confuse independent events with events which are mutually exclusive, two concepts which are rather different. Two events are mutually exclusive when their intersection is the empty set: $A \cap B = \phi$. Hence, the probability of the intersection of A and B must be zero. If these same events A and B were also to be independent, then it must be true that $p(A \cap B) = p(A)p(B)$, from Expression (5.9). But they can be so only if either $p(A)$ or $p(B)$, or both, are zero—a possibility excluded in the definition of independence. Thus, two events can be both mutually exclusive and independent only if at least one event has an associated probability of zero.

5.12 RANDOMNESS AND RANDOM SAMPLING

Because of its importance to general statistical theory, *independence* has been defined in a rather rigorous manner. Every statistical test in this book will assume independent events. This assumption allows us to deal strictly with *unconditional* probabilities in routine statistical computations.

The notion of independence brings us directly to the closely related concept of randomness. To this point, we have taken a commonsense approach to random events. Randomness has been introduced simply by shuffling a deck of cards, or by shaking a die vigorously. Dictionary definitions also imply this commonsense meaning, generally setting *random* as synonymous with haphazard, casual, or desultory. But in the strictly statistical sense, there is nothing haphazard, casual, or desultory about a random event. Sampling of random events in social science is plain hard work, often tedious, time consuming, and expensive. And yet without randomness, there can be no statistical inference.

We will follow Kerlinger (1973:121) and define randomness in a slightly backhanded manner:

Events are said to be *random* if their outcomes cannot be predicted.

So, *randomness* really means that there is no known law to explain the outcomes of certain events; if the results could be predicted beforehand, then the event is not random. The only limit on a truly random event is the size of the sample space itself. Any one of 52 possible cards can be drawn from a well-shuffled deck. Rolling a single die will result in one of six outcomes, but since this is a random event, we have absolutely no way of knowing which of the six faces will appear faceup.

It's interesting to note that random events can be predicted only *in the aggregate.* We cannot tell which of six numbers will turn faceup when a die is rolled, but we do know that 1 will appear about 17 percent of the time, 2 will appear about 17 percent of the time, and so on. Random events cannot be predicted individually—otherwise they would not be random. But *in the long run*, random events are quite predictable, and it is this long-term behavior upon which statistical inference is based.

Now we can move from randomness as an abstract concept to the applied problem of sampling random events. A *random sample* assumes that every member of the statistical population has an equal and independent probability of selection. Variates in the sample space must all be equally likely to be included in the sample: $p(A) = p(B) = p(C)$, and so forth. This follows because we have no way of predicting which random event in the sample space will occur on a single trial. Furthermore, every *combination* of variates must be equally likely to occur as any other combination of variates. The only method of insuring equally likely combinations is to deal with variates which are independent in the sense of Expression (5.9). That is:

> *Simple random sampling* is a method of generating samples such that every sample of size n has exactly the same probability of selection.

A sample was defined earlier as simply any subset of a statistical population. We now equate the statistical population with the sample space of a statistical experiment. The experimental outcome becomes an element of the sample subset of S, and there are n sample elements corresponding to the n trials of the statistical experiment. If the elements are returned to the sample space after selection—*sampling with replacement*—then the same variate is allowed to occur in the sample more than once, although each selection constitutes a different event. More commonly, simple random samples are selected *without replacement*, and elements may occur only once in a given sample. When sampling without replacement, the sample space initially contains N variates; after the initial draw, the sample space contains $N - 1$ variates; after the second draw, $N - 2$ variates, and so forth. Technically speaking, these probabilities are not completely independent because the chances of selection in later experiments is slightly higher than in the first draw (because N is smaller). But, as long as N is rather large, sampling without replacement causes no appreciable error. When statistical populations are infinite, there's no error at all.

The *sample element* is the basic unit in all random sampling. In a population census, for instance, the element might consist of counts of individuals, or of families, or of city blocks, or even of neighborhoods. The element in archaeologic site survey is generally the "site," although artifacts, house depressions, or even artifactual tracts of land can all function as elements in specific samples. The nature of the element is dictated strictly by the purpose of the sample—not the reverse.

In general, the sampling element corresponds to a single event in a sample space, and the set of all sampling elements corresponds to the sample space itself. In other words, the sample space consists of the set of N elements, and the probability that a given element will be selected on any particular draw is equal to $p(A) = 1/N$. This follows from the preceding definition of a random sample.

In theory, therefore, social scientists should always deal with strictly random samples, and a number of methods exist to generate randomness in social samples. Probably the most common techniques of random sampling involve numbering all population elements and then selecting the samples from a *random-number table* (such as Table A.2, Appendix I). A random-number table is literally that—an extensive tabulation of random digits arranged into rows and columns. The investigator simply picks a page, finds a row or column, and proceeds to read the sequence of numbers. Sometimes the page number itself is selected as a random digit, and the investigator often begins by haphazardly placing a pencil on any page and choosing that as the first number. Subsequent digits may be read horizontally, vertically, or even diagonally. Some people select only every other random digit, and others insist on moving from right to left. The premise behind these various methods is that *there are no instructions* for using a random-digit table—nor should there be. Rigid directions would eventually lead to *pattern* samples, and this is exactly what random sampling is designed to avoid. Tables of random digits are readily available.

A small table of 5000 random numbers has been reproduced in Table A.2. These numbers were generated by hand in the 1930s, but this is not the only method of constructing random-number tables. Rohlf and Sokal (1969: table O), for example, employed an IBM 7040 computer to generate 10,000 random digits. The actual numbers arose from the recurrence equation, using integer arithmetic:

$$X_{i+1} = \frac{X_i \times 5^{13}}{2^{35}}$$

The subsequent random number X_{i+2} was then computed from the *remainder* rather than from the quotient. These numbers were then scaled between zero and 1.0, multiplied by ten, and then truncated into integers. An analysis of their preliminary table indicated that some digits (3 and 7) were slightly too abundant and others (2 and 8) were somewhat too rare, so a suitable transformation was developed to adjust the overall frequency. The RAND Corporation (1955) even published a large book containing nothing but random digits—one million of them. Captivating reading.

Most modern anthropologists have confronted the random-number table at one time or another, and the table of random digits is about the only denominator common to all sampling. Beyond this point, samples must be carefully designed to reflect the specifics of the actual data. Cross-cultural samples, for instance, must consider bias and data quality problems quite different from archaeological survey sampling, and physical anthropologists sample geological strata (or museum collections) in a manner quite distinct from that of ethnologists taking genealogies. The underlying principles of random sampling are similar, but the specifics vary with the data. A number of the references suggested at the end of this chapter deal directly with sampling strategies in social science.

Before we finish discussing anthropological sampling, let me describe a couple of applications from my own archaeological fieldwork. These two instances are not really "typical" at all, but they should at least suggest the flavor of the sampling process.

Between 1968 and 1971, I directed several archaeological field schools in the Reese River Valley of central Nevada. The students were involved in a number of field projects: collecting surface sites, excavating rock shelters, mapping house rings, and preliminary typological studies. Literally thousands of stone tools were collected during these three field seasons, and every artifact was gingerly cleaned and assigned a catalogue number in our field laboratory. The system of cataloguing is simple. Every artifact receives the prefix "RR" (to denote the

Reese River), followed by a four-digit catalogue number.[6] The first artifact catalogued at Reese River received the number RR1000; the second artifact, RR1001; and so on. Appropriate entries were made in the field catalogue to record the exact provenience of individual artifacts. By looking up the accession number, one can locate exactly where each artifact was found. At the end of the 1971 field season, the last number in the field catalogue was RR8000.

It became clear to me when I brought these stone tools to the American Museum of Natural History in New York that I would need the help of a geologist to identify the various types of stones. At least two dozen stone types seem to be involved at Reese River, including obsidians, several varieties of chert, rhyolite, opalite, chalcedony, and basalt. While I could make a rough sort, I felt that a trained geologist should also verify my identifications. But identifying 7000 stone tools is an onerous job, and geologists are not generally known for their patience at such mundane tasks. After some searching, prodding, and cajoling, I convinced a geologist from the U.S. Geological Survey in California to examine the Reese River artifacts. But he had only enough time (or inclination) to identify a fraction of the 7000 artifacts. In a fit of generosity, he consented to identify 25 percent of my "Shoshoni rocks," as he called them. We both figured that this would be adequate to substantiate the identifications I had already made.

So, my problem was to select the 25 percent of my 7000 artifacts to ship back to California. A number of legitimate factors could influence that choice. To reduce the shipping cost, I could have selected the 1750 *lightest* artifacts for short shipment from New York to California. Or for greatest speed, I could have pulled out the *first 1750 artifacts accessioned* (since all the artifacts were stored in sequential order); this subset *S* would consist of the catalogue numbers RR1000–RR2750. For the greatest scope, I could have gone to my original identifications and carefully included all the *exotic and unusual specimens*, to be certain that every conceivable stone type was included. Or I might even select the *most perfect* specimens because those are the ones most likely to be illustrated in the final site report.

Any number of realistic operations were open to me at that point. The problem was to select some subset (size $n = 1750$) from the total sample space of $N = 7000$ stone tools. Each of the options mentioned would produce a sample of the appropriate size, and each sampling method has its strong point: low cost, easy access, or special information. But I decided to select a *simple random sample* over all the other potential kinds of samples. Why a random sample?

Consider first the more general question of why sample at all—to reduce the number, you might say, because my geologist friend was willing to look at only 1750 rocks. That's true enough, but a good sample should have some virtue beyond simply $n < N$. Remember that Chapter 2 went to great pains to stress that data are not things. Data are observations made by scientists upon people, or specimens, or things. The *things* in this case were artifacts, prehistoric stone tools. The *data* are the observations to be made by my geologist friend upon the stone tools. He would identify the rocks. His report might tell me: obsidian, 230 artifacts; banded chert, 367 artifacts; silicified rhyolite, 95 artifacts; and so forth.

---

[6]Four digits were always used to facilitate computer coding of the field catalogues.

These frequencies are sample statistics because they summarize some characteristic of a sample.

But the sample was not my real interest. At the outset, I tried to get him to identify all 7000 tools, but he wouldn't do it. Although only one-quarter of the total artifacts would be identified, my real interest remained in the original collection of 7000 tools. There are some frequencies which characterize the rock types for the 7000 artifacts. These figures, the *parameters*, were unknown to me and would remain so because I could only collar a geologist who would identify 25 percent of the total. My real interest was to generalize about the population parameters on the basis of my sample statistics. This procedure, called *statistical inference*, was introduced earlier in Section 2.6.2.

Now that my objective was clear, a rational decision could be made in choosing the 1750 artifacts to ship to California. The overarching factor, given a wish to generalize about a population from a given sample, was not cost nor convenience. My only concern was strictly with generating an unbiased sample to represent the population. "Unbiased" in this case refers to how well the sample statistics reflect the unknown population parameters, and all statistical inferences require (and assume) a random sample. A sample selected at random in this case meant that no artifact in the 7000 would have any greater chance for inclusion in the sample than any other artifact; this is stated in the definition of random sampling.

Random sampling is thus a method of generating statistics which estimate their parameters in an unbiased manner. Unfortunately, we are never that positive that our random sample is totally *representative* of its population. All we can do is to assume that the characteristics "typical" of the population are those which are the most frequent, and hence the ones most likely to appear in a random sample (Kerlinger 1973: 119). But there is never a guarantee. Random sampling simply provides us with a method for obtaining unbiased results within a predictable amount of variability. Some of the practicalities (and impracticalities) of actual random sampling in anthropology will be considered in Chapter 15.

Let us examine the Reese River project in a bit more detail, since a somewhat more complex random-sampling design was used in the actual archaeological fieldwork. The Reese River Valley was inhabited in historic times by the hunting-gathering Shoshoni peoples. The Western Shoshoni established two or three base camps each year, and specialized work parties lived in perhaps a dozen additional task-specific localities. The main purpose of the research was to see whether this ethnographic Western Shoshoni pattern could serve as a model for prehistoric economic practices. It became immediately clear that the traditional sampling method in archaeology—that is, "find-the-biggest-cave-in-the-valley-and-throw-a-shovel-in-the-pickup-and-dig-it"—would not answer such questions. We needed to know how the sites in different microenvironments related to one another, so focus had to be on the archaeology of the *total* valley rather than at simply one or two "key" sites. For example, one often hears that prehistoric hunter-gatherers of the Desert West "preferred to live in caves." Actually, it's the archaeologists who seem to prefer the caves because that's where the stratigraphy is. The truth of the matter is that caves represent only a minor portion of the annual seasonal round in most desert areas.

The Reese River Valley is a big place, about 30 miles wide and over 125 miles long. So I arbitrarily isolated a smaller target area, a tract of land of about 300 square miles. This area seemed to approximate the territory used by a single Western Shoshoni family band, so it theoretically should contain the remains of subsistence practices from an entire annual cycle. The objective now became to survey this area and map every bit of historic and prehistoric cultural activity. Because of these objectives, the small sites became every bit as important as the large ones, and the research design had to consider the overall settlement pattern rather than just cultural chronology.

For purposely practical reasons, I chose to conduct my survey in 500-meter squares. The survey areas, roughly one-third of a mile on a side, became the elements of the survey (see Fig. 5.7). There are a total of 1400 of these survey tracts in the Reese River Valley. I soon realized that the total length of time required to survey all 1400 elements was prohibitive—something like 20 field seasons with a crew of 30 people! Since no right-thinking archaeological graduate student undertakes a project like that, I did the next best thing. I random-sampled. Figuring that I could probably muster field crews for two summers of fieldwork, I would have sufficient time to survey about 140 or so of the 500-meter square tracts. Thus, I needed a $140/1400 = 0.10$, or a 10 percent sample.

Look at Fig. 5.7 closely. There are actually three different areas within the overall grid. The large center area corresponds to the sagebrush-covered bottomlands of the Reese River Valley. This lifezone is called A in Fig. 5.7. Then on either side of A is a second lifezone, the piñon pine and juniper biotic community called B. Thus, the B zone consists of land on the east and west sides of Reese River Valley. Finally, the area adjacent to the piñon-juniper belt, the upper sagebrush comunity, has been labelled C. In other words, the total area has divided into grids of 500-meter squares and then partitioned by the three dominant plant communities. Partitioning a sample space like this is called *stratification*.[7] The density of archaeological sites within the lower sagebrush zone could be contrasted with site density in the piñon–juniper zone.

Now to the actual random sampling: Because the sample was divided into three sampling *strata*, I needed to select a 10 percent random sample from each stratum. Let us take stratum A first, which contains exactly 632 population elements. We must generate a 10 percent sample containing exactly 62 elements. To do so, the potential elements were numbered 1 through 632, and a table of random numbers was opened to any page. Only the first three digits of each column were considered. Whenever a random number fell within the range

---

[7]Stratification is a common sampling strategy in anthropology. Sample spaces are stratified basically for one of two reasons: (1) to decrease the variance of the samples (that is, to obtain relatively homogeneous subunits within the sample space) or (2) to delimit subpopulations which are themselves domains of study. In the Reese River design, macroenvironments are held relatively constant within strata in order to facilitate comparisons among the assemblages associated with each stratum. The strata are to be defined on anthropological, rather than statistical, grounds. According to Kish (1965: 100), "Neither objectivity nor regularity is needed for sorting sampling units into strata. On the contrary, subjective sorting may be superior to rigid procedures for creating homogeneous strata. In the entire selection procedure this is the area *par excellence* for the exercise of personal judgment based upon expert knowledge of the list (sample space) and the subject matter." Also see Blalock (1972: chapter 21) for a discussion of stratified random sampling in social science.

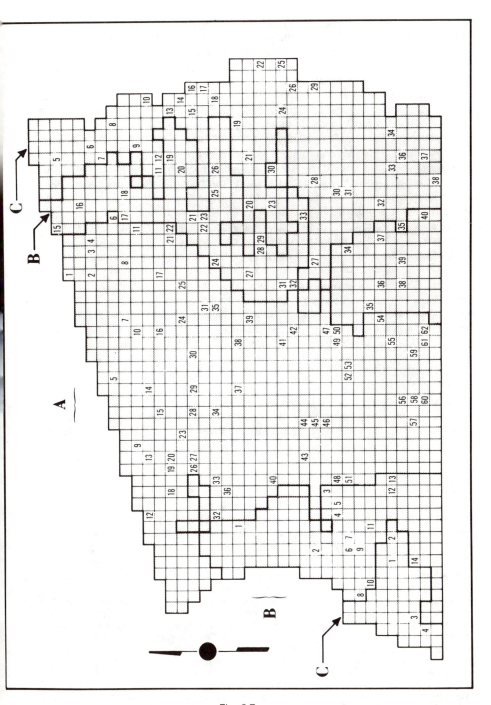

Fig. 5.7

1–632, the element corresponding to that number was included in the sample. Figure 5.7 shows how the random sampling of each stratum turned out.

In all candor, I was a bit skeptical about the random selection process at the time. Not only did I suffer the jitters common to most graduate students embarking upon their doctoral research, but when the Reese River sample was conceived (1968), random sampling was still considered an odd and unusual way for an archaeologist to spend his time.[8] So, partly to steel myself against the critics and also to provide plenty of accomplices, I threw the *First Annual Reese River Random Sample Party*. Faculty advisors and fellow graduate students were invited to witness the official Reese River sample. My "guests" were greeted at the door with the RAND table of random digits (all one million of them) and requested to "find 10 random numbers between one and 632— *quick.*" Not only were the 140 sample tracts generated in this fashion, but the veracity of the sample's "randomness" was witnessed by at least two dozen more or less "reliable" witnesses. Whatever the faults of the Reese River fieldwork, at least the integrity of the sample cannot be questioned.[9]

The Reese River fieldwork took two years to complete, as expected, and the results have been discussed in Thomas (1971a, 1973, and 1974). The ethnographic Western Shoshoni model was found to be remarkably accurate predictor of the prehistoric subsistence practices, which have an antiquity of at least 5000 years at Reese River. This is not to say that the Western Shoshoni model has been *proved*; the model has simply survived one empirical test and there could be other models which explain the data equally as well. But we now know that the prehistoric record holds nothing which is *inconsistent* with the ethnographies. This is standard scientific procedure: One really never proves anything in science—bad theories are simply rejected, one by one (a point considered in detail in Chapters 9 and 16).

Sampling in anthropology will be considered more fully in Chapter 15. For now, we must emphasize only the options involved. Every anthropologist worth his salt works with samples, whether he realizes this or not. Working with a complete population involves mere description, without relevance beyond the bare specifics at hand. Anthropological fieldwork almost always takes some set of data as "representative" or "typical" of some larger phenomenon. So, the real question is *not* whether to sample or not. Every anthropologist samples. The important question is how the sample is to be taken. Too often, samples arise from convenience or fancy or happenstance. Unfortunately, there is no way of assessing how well these "grab samples" represent their populations.

---

[8]In fact, some colleagues are still snickering about all the time I wasted, looking where "we all knew there weren't any sites anyway." Such are the times in which we labor.

[9]This raises an interesting point. Suppose a sample is *too good*? What if the random numbers for stratum *A* had turned out to be 1–62, within a possible range of 1–632? The entire sample would have been compressed into a small corner of the Reese River Valley. Although samples such as this may be "random" in the strict sense, they might fail miserably as "representative." For this reason, many sampling texts suggest *systematic* sampling, which ordinarily selects only the direct first element randomly and then systematically counts off the remainder of the sample at some established interval. A systematic sample of the Reese River Valley would have involved selecting a random digit between one and ten (for a 10 percent sample), and then counting off every tenth element on the map. Systematic sampling exchanges true randomness for a high degree of representation (see Kish 1965: chapter 4; and Blalock 1972: 514–516).

The real asset of random methods for generating our samples is that we eliminate the investigator's inevitable biases and prepare the way to let the data tell us what they have to say.

● *He who drinks from the Nile will return again to Egypt.*—Anon.

SUGGESTIONS FOR FURTHER READING

Gnedenko and Khinchin (1961).
Hays (1973: chapters 1, 2, 3, and 4).
Kemeny (1959: chapter 4).
Kerlinger (1973: part 3).
McFadden (1971).
Mendenhall (1971: chapter 4).

EXERCISES

5.1   Evaluate the following expressions:
       (a) 8!   (b) 7!/10!   (c) $C_{10,2}$ (d) $P_{2,2}$ (e) $P_{5,1}$ (f) $C_{8,3}$

5.2   There are 20 tags in an urn, and these tags are numbered from 1 to 20. If one tag is drawn at random, what is the probability that the number drawn
       (a) Is 19?
       (b) Is odd?
       (c) Is less than 13?
       (d) Can be evenly divided by 2?

5.3   A slot machine has three reels, each containing ten digits $(0, 1, 2, \cdots 8, 9)$ plus a bar. The three reels turn independently when a coin is inserted and the lever is pulled. What is the probability of getting
       (a) A jackpot (that is, all bars)?
       (b) A 5 on the first reel, a 6 on the second, and a 7 on the third?
       (c) 5, 6, and 7 in any order?
       (d) All even numbers?
       (e) No even numbers?
       (f) Exactly two bars?

5.4   What is the probability of throwing "craps" (that is, rolling a 2, 3, or 12 in a single toss of two dice)?

5.5   How many possible hands are there in five-card stud poker?[10]

5.6   What is the probability of being dealt a royal flush in spades (that is, the Ace, King, Queen, Jack, and ten of spades)?

5.7   What is the probability of being dealt any royal flush?

5.8   What is the probability of being dealt one pair, with the remaining three cards different?

[10]Following Hays (1973: 177–178), we adopt a simplified poker game: five cards are dealt to a single player from a well-shuffled deck of 52 cards.

5.9 What is the probability of being dealt a flush (that is, all cards of the same suit)?

5.10 From eight women and four men, how many committees can be selected consisting of
(a) Three women and two men?
(b) Six people of which at least four are women?

5.11 A linguist has a word list consisting of five verbs and ten nouns.
(a) How many possible arrangements of these 15 words are there?
(b) If the verbs are to be listed first, how many possible lists are there?

5.12 A certain department of Anthropology requires its graduate students to take four core courses:

Anthro. 512   Ethnology
Anthro. 519   Human Evolution
Anthro. 503   Anthropological Linguistics
Anthro. 510   New World Archaeology

(a) If these courses are taken one at a time, how many possible sequences are there?
(b) What is the probability of the following sequence?

Anthro. 503, 510, 512, 519

(c) Suppose that the graduate faculty instituted a new rule requiring all entering graduate students to take Human Evolution (Anthro. 519) first and then any other sequence of the remaining courses. Find the probability that a student would take the following sequence:

Human Evolution, Anthropological Linguistics, Ethnology, New World Archaeology

5.13 A graduate student has just written an article summarizing his Master's thesis and wishes to submit it for publication in a scholarly journal. He has assembled the following statistics on the acceptance rules of three major journals in this field:

Journal	Articles Received	Articles Accepted
Science	60	18
Nature	50	20
American Anthropologist	40	28

(a) On the basis of these previous rates of acceptance, which journal would be most likely to publish the article?
(b) Which journal is least likely to publish the paper?

5.14 One hospital has estimated that 60 percent of all male babies born there are bald, while only 45 percent of the female infants are bald. What are the chances that a particular bald child is a male?

5.15 A small museum in the United States is considering the purchase of a collection of 100 pots from a private collector, 20 of which the curator thinks were imported illegally. The collector's records show that half of the legal pots came from Mexico, and the curator suspects that 15 of the illegally imported pots also came from Mexico. What is the probability that one of the Mexican pots on display is illegally imported?

5.16 Three governmental agencies are accepting applications for grants to cover the cost of ethnological fieldwork. Last year, the first agency received 60 grant applications, and funded 50 percent of these. The second agency received 200 applications and funded only 20 percent, and the third agency funded 80 percent of the applications received. If all agencies continue last year's trend, which agency offers the best chance of an applicant's acceptance?

5.17 Three archaeologists have devoted their careers to finding remains of early man. The first archaeologist found a total of 12 sites, 4 of which had remains of early man. The second archaeologist found only 6 sites, but 5 of these were early man sites; the third archaeologist located 18 sites, only 2 of which contained artifacts of early man.
   (a) If you could give a grant to only one archaeologist, which would you judge had the greatest probability of finding the next early man site?
   (b) Given a particular early man site among the 36 sites mentioned above, what is the probability that the second archaeologist found it?
   (c) What is the probability that the second archaeologist *did not* find that particular site (compute this probability two ways)?

5.18 Consider the following data on the ability to taste PTC (from Kelso 1970: table 8–13):

Society	No. of Informants Tested	% Taster
Tamils	100	27
Negritos	50	18
Aborigines	50	4

What is the probability that a given taster is a Tamil?

5.19 The American Anthropological Association is having a presidential election, and the following figures have been released for the members' voting behavior in the past election:

	Subfield of Voter		
Voted for	Archaeologist, %	Physical Anthropologist, %	Ethnologist/ Linguist, %
Archaeologist	75	30	5
Physical Anthropologist	5	50	5
Ethnologist/ Linguist	20	20	90

(a) If an anthropologist is selected at random from the files of the American Anthropological Association and found to have voted for a physical anthropologist, what is the probability that he is an archaeologist?

(b) Who won the election?

5.20 During the summer of 1973, my field camp in central Nevada witnessed a rather severe outbreak of food poisoning. The incident followed a large party with another archaeological field crew, and we suspected that some (or perhaps all) of the salads had gone bad after exposure to the hot desert sun. A total of ten bowls of salad were served at the party: two bowls of potato salad, five bowls of macaroni salad, and three bowls of green salad. Samples of each salad were sent to a lab for analysis, and we were told that the chances of food poisoning from the potato and macaroni salads was 5 percent and only a 1 percent chance that the green salad had been spoiled.

(a) Given somebody suffering from food poisoning, what is the probability he ate macaroni salad?

(b) What is the probability this sick person ate either potato or macaroni salad?

6 The Binomial Distribution

● *He who has heard the same thing told by 12,000 eyewitnesses has only 12,000 probabilities, which are equal to one strong probability, which is far from certainty.*—Voltaire

6.1 DISCRETE RANDOM VARIABLES AND THEIR PROBABILITY DISTRIBUTIONS

The statistical experiments considered to this point assign numerical values (probabilities) to random events. For the elementary case of coin flipping, the probability of tossing a head was denoted as $p(H) = 1/2$. A slightly different notation can be used to express this same experiment. *Before* tossing our coin, let us define X as *whatever outcome might be obtained*. X can take only one of two possible states for any given toss: heads or tails. Similarly, rolling a single die can result in exactly six possible events, and X is free to assume only one of these six values. A genetic experiment with four possible phenotypes allows exactly four conceivable states for its X. In all cases, probabilities are assigned to the new symbol X just as before. If a die is rolled, for example, the probability of obtaining a 5 is symbolized as

$$p(A) = p(X = 5) = 1/6$$

This notation indicates that "the probability of event A is equal to the probability that X is equal to 5 which is equal to 1/6." X in this case symbolizes a random variable, conventionally expressed in terms of real numbers.[1] In an intuitive sense, the random variable X is the quantity which we wish to measure in a given experiment.

---

[1] The set of real numbers includes all integers, the ratios between nonzero integers, irrational numbers, and certain constants such as π.

Human birth rate can be a random variable. We might let $X = 1$ for a male birth and $X = 0$ for a female birth; or the numbers could be reversed. The mathematical results remain unchanged.

In a more formal sense,

X is called a *random variable on the sample space X* if X represents a function associating a real number with an event in some sample space S.

The mathematical term "function" refers to the rules which establish the exact correspondence between subsets of S—each subset is an event—and the actual numerical values of X. The rules for the random variable X are specified anew for each experiment. We must always be clear about just what X "means."

Chapter 2 distinguished between constants and variables. Variables were characterized as either discrete or continuous.

A random variable is *discrete* if X can assume only a *finite or countably infinite* range of values.

For instance, give this book to a friend and ask your friend to open it to any page. This statistical experiment involves the discrete random variable X. "Page number" is a *variable* because X is free to assume more than one value (otherwise X would be a constant). Selecting the page is *random* because there is absolutely no way of predicting beforehand which page will be selected. The random variable is *discrete* because X can assume only a limited (that is, finite) set of possible values; the range of X is limited to the numbers appearing in the corners of these pages. Although the exact number remains a mystery to us before the page is selected, we can be absolutely certain X will not equal 256.3 or 3.1516—these are impossible outcomes for a discrete variable. Even if a book has infinite pages, the outcome would still be a discrete random variable because these infinite pages are still countable, one at a time.

A *continuous* random variable can assume an infinitely large and uncountable range of values.

Continuous random variables do not involve neat intervals or intrinsic gaps of measurement. Quantities such as human stature and daily caloric intake are continuous random variables because they can assume any conceivable value along an infinitely large set of sample points. Although both continuous and discrete random variables are of anthropological interest, present discussion will center upon the discrete case, building a methodology to handle the distribution of continuous random variables (Chapter 7).

The random variable concept is a watershed in the statistical story. Two rather independent threads of reasoning have been developed so far. We considered techniques to analyze the data of anthropology: how to define operational variables, how to scale measurements, how to represent findings graphically and in frequency distributions, how to characterize samples and populations using quantitative measures. The second mode of inquiry developed the theory of probability: how probabilities are assigned to experimental events and what these probabilities mean. Now we can interlace these two somewhat disparate threads.

Chapter 5 emphasized that statistical experiments always result in well-defined outcomes. The random variable X is a numerical expression of this outcome. Event A has a probability assigned to it, and because the random variable X represents event A, the probability of A also applies to X. This simple correspondence provides our basis for statistical inference. Remember that a population was defined in Chapter 2 as any set of variates. The sample is some subset of the population. Statistical inference takes some known *sample* (characterized by a statistic) and generalizes about the *population* from which that sample was drawn. The sample is known; the population is unknown. Given knowledge only of a sample, any number of populations are possible. How to choose between these different populations?

The theory of probability comes to the rescue. We now suggest that the probability of an observable numerical event—that is, the variates of a sample—be calculated for a large set of possible populations. Each of the plausible populations thus receives a probability figure, indicating the likelihood that it could have produced the sample. We then choose the population having the highest associated probability of producing our observed sample (after Mendenhall 1971:100). This procedure amounts to an operational definition of statistical inference. Stated slightly differently:

Statistical inference involves finding the population with the highest probability of having produced the observed sample.

We will learn later how to compute these population probabilities. For now, it is sufficient to realize that associated population probabilities allow selection of the population "most likely" to have produced the sample.

The ideal dice can illustrate some basic properties of discrete random variables. Exactly 11 different outcomes exist when two dice are rolled simultaneously. Should both dice come up 1's (snake-eyes), the sum of the face values is 2; there is no smaller possibility. If both dice show six spots (boxcars), the sum is 12. Both 2 and 12 can occur in only one possible manner. The sum "3," however, can occur in two different ways:

First Die		Second Die		Sum
1	+	2	=	3
2	+	1	=	3

The sum "3" is therefore a "more likely" outcome than either snake-eyes or boxcars because there are more chances for success. A careful enumeration of all possibilities reveals that two dice can land in exactly 36 different configurations, and the sum of the two faces must range between 2 and 12.

Let us define X as "the sum of the two faces." In this context, X is a discrete random variable which must assume one of 11 possible values on every trial. Probabilities can now be assigned to each of the 11 outcomes.

This tabulation is called a *probability distribution* because it enumerates the total range of values for $p(X)$. The probability distribution is similar in many respects to the frequency distributions presented in Chapter 3. Like frequency tables, probability distributions are also divided into measurement classes. In both cases, these classes are nonoverlapping, and they enumerate the total possible range of values. The classes are both mutually exclusive and exhaus-

Random Variable, X	Probability of the Random Variable, $p(X)$
2	1/36
3	2/36
4	3/36
5	4/36
6	5/36
7	6/36
8	5/36
9	4/36
10	3/36
11	2/36
12	1/36
	36/36 = 1.0

tive. The major difference is that a frequency distribution involves the actual *observed* variates, whereas the probability distribution tabulates probabilities of *expected* occurrences. The frequencies must sum to N, and the probability distribution must sum to 1.0. We can therefore state two rather important properties for all probability distributions:

(1) $$0 \leq p(X_i) \leq 1$$

(2) $$\sum_{i=1}^{k} p(X_i) = 1$$

where k is the total number of measurement classes.

The probability distribution tabulated above tells us that the probability of a "6" on one roll of two dice is

$$p(X = 6) = 5/36$$

Probabilities for compound outcomes for the discrete random variable X can also be readily found from a probability distribution table. What is the probability, for example, of obtaining a number greater than 8 on a single trial? That is, what is the value of $p(X > 8)$?

The earlier discussion of probability showed that $p(X > 8)$ is equivalent to the union of 9, 10, 11, and 12. The Addition Rule (Section 5.8) for mutually exclusive events gives the total probability of $p(X > 8)$:

$$p(X > 8) = p(X > 9 \cup 10 \cup 11 \cup 12)$$
$$= p(X = 9) + p(X = 10) + p(X = 11) + p(X = 12)$$
$$= 4/36 + 3/36 + 2/36 + 1/36 = 10/36$$

The probability of the compound random variable ($X > 8$) is thus equal to 10/36.

Probability distributions will become extremely important to the subsequent development of statistical theory. In many cases, the probability distribution will provide the "theory" against which observed samples are tested.

6.2 MATHEMATICAL EXPECTATION OF A DISCRETE RANDOM VARIABLE

The probability distribution provides a useful model for the population. Two real dice should produce frequencies consistent with the probability distribution. Because this is so, the probability distribution should possess all of the parameters characteristically associated with a population—such as mean, variance, median, and so forth. For the moment, we will concentrate upon one particular parameter, the arithmetic mean. Assuming the probability distribution to be a satisfactory model of the theoretical population, this distribution should provide a clue (an *expectation*) of the unknown population mean.

Consider an example. Euphoria University charges tuition in direct proportion to the number of courses a student takes each semester. The tuition rate is $500 per course, with a maximum of three courses. The registrar's records show that over the past several years, roughly 10 percent of the students take a single course, 50 percent of the students enroll in two courses, and 40 percent take three courses.

The State of Euphoria has an upcoming gubernatorial election. The incumbent governor claims that because the "average" student takes two courses (and hence pays $1000), the tuition rates at Euphoria University are below the national average of $1100. To remedy this situation—and, incidentally, to keep subversive elements from infiltrating the University—the governor proposes a significant tuition increase. A student group has challenged the governor's figures, arguing that the average student at Euphoria really pays more than the $1100 national average. Who is correct?

Neither group has funds to make a complete survey of student tuition, so they must use approximate figures. If X denotes the fees paid per student, the probability distribution is as follows:

No. of Courses	Tuition, X	Probability, $p(X)$
1	$ 500	0.1
2	1000	0.5
3	1500	0.4

Let X be the discrete random variable and let N be the total enrollment at Euphoria U. Because N is large, we expect the event $(X = 500)$ to occur roughly 10 percent of the time, or about $0.1N$ times. The total fees for students taking a single course should be $500 (0.1N) = 50N$. The event $(X = \$1000)$ should occur about $0.5N$ times, giving rise to total tuition fees of $1000 (0.5N) = \$500N$. The event $(X = \$1500)$ occurs approximately $0.4N$ times, producing total fees of $1500(0.4N) = \$600N$. The total tuition generated in a single semester, therefore, is $50N + \$500N + \$600N = \$1150N$, and the average cost per student must be $1150N/N = \$1150$. This figure is $50 over the national average. The governor is incorrect.

Observe how this average was computed:

$$\frac{\$500(0.1N) + \$1000(0.5N) + \$1500(0.4N)}{N} = \$500(0.1) + \$1000(0.5) + \$1500(0.4)$$

$$= \$1150$$

In effect, this is the *weighted average* of all possible values of X, where the "weights" are the probabilities assigned to each state of variable X.

No sample was generated in this example. The average tuition per student, $1150, is a *theoretical* figure computed directly from the probability distribution. Average tuition can be interpreted in a couple of ways. It is, of course, the *weighted mean* of the theoretical probability distribution. The weighted mean is also called the *expected value* of the discrete random variable X, denoted as $E(X)$. In a more formal sense, the *expected value* of the discrete random variable X is

$$E(X) = \sum_{i=1}^{k} X_i p(X = X_i) \tag{6.1}$$

In the above example, X is the discrete random variable "tuition paid per semester," and $X_1 = \$500$, $X_2 = \$1000$, and $X_3 = \$1500$. As long as the probability distribution is an accurate model for the theoretical population, then the expected value is an estimator of the population mean μ. Therefore, $E(X) = \mu$. The expected value of the discrete random variable X will hereafter be assumed to be equal to μ and the terms will be used synonymously.

6.3 THE PROBABILITY DISTRIBUTION OF A BINOMIAL

● *A reasonable probability is the only certainty.*—E. Howe

Consider now how to construct the probability distribution for a discrete random variable. The simplest such distribution involves only two event classes, A and $\bar{A}$. Either event A occurs (a successful outcome) or A does not occur (the outcome is a failure). Statistical experiments of this sort, in which a given trial can result in one of only two possible outcomes, are called "Bernoulli processes." The venerable coin flipping experiment is probably the best known example of a Bernoulli process.

For simplicity, we adopt a slightly different notation for the Bernoulli process. The probability of event A in a Bernoulli trial will be called simply p, equivalent to the previous symbol $p(A)$. The probability of failure, $p(\bar{A})$, is denoted by q for a Bernoulli trial. The ground rules governing Bernoulli processes thus imply that the quantity $(p + q)$ must always equal unity. When dealing with equally likely outcomes, such as flipping a fair coin, then $p = q = 1/2$. If "4" is a success and "1, 2, 3, 5, 6" count as failures: $p = 1/6$ and $q = 5/6$.

Suppose that two parents have Type Oa blood. If they have six children, what is the probability that five of the children will have Type O blood? (This situation contrasts with examples from Chapter 5 because the outcome depends upon several repeated trials; in this case, six independent births.)

Both parents have the genotype O*a*, so their offspring can have only four possible genotypes, resulting in two phenotypes.

Genotype	Phenotype
OO	O
O*a*	*a*
*a*O	*a*
aa	*a*

Genetic combination is a random process and there is no method of predicting the outcome of any given trial. Predictions can be made only in terms of long-range probabilities. In the long run, three Type *a* offspring should be born for every Type O offspring.

We begin with the simplest case of a single child, building a methodology capable of handling six offspring (six trials). There are, of course, only two possible outcomes: O blood or *a* blood. The probability of success (that is, Type O blood) is $p = 0.25$ with $q = 0.75$. The chances of a success on the first birth are only 1:4. The second birth is totally independent of the first and also has two possible outcomes. *But, taken together*, the two initial births produce four (not two) different possible outcomes. The tree diagram in the table below demonstrates these four outcomes: both Type O, the first Type *a* and second O, the first Type O and the second Type *a*, and both Type *a*. The final column computes the probability for each of these distinct outcomes for two offspring. The probability of two Type O offspring, for example, is given by the *Multiplication Rule for Independent Events* (Section 5.8) to be $(p)(p) = (1/4)^2$.

First Child	Second Child	Outcome	Probability
	O	OO	$p^2 = \left(\frac{1}{4}\right)^2$
	a	O*a*	$pq = \left(\frac{1}{4}\right)\left(\frac{3}{4}\right)$
	O	*a*O	$qp = \left(\frac{3}{4}\right)\left(\frac{1}{4}\right)$
	a	*aa*	$q^2 = \left(\frac{3}{4}\right)^2$

The sum of the right-hand column in the table must equal 1.0:

$$p^2 + pq + qp + q^2 = 1.0$$

Exactly one of these mutually exclusive and exhaustive outcomes can occur. Their total probability must sum to unity (the probability of a certain event).

For the case of *three* offspring, the tree diagram becomes a bit more involved.

First Child	Second Child	Third Child	Outcome	Probability
		O	OOO	$p^3 = \left(\frac{1}{4}\right)^3$
	O	a	OOa	$p^2 q = \left(\frac{1}{4}\right)^2 \left(\frac{3}{4}\right)$
O		O	OaO	$pqp = \left(\frac{1}{4}\right)^2 \left(\frac{3}{4}\right)$
	a	a	Oaa	$pq^2 = \left(\frac{1}{4}\right)\left(\frac{3}{4}\right)^2$
		O	aOO	$qp^2 = \left(\frac{1}{4}\right)^2 \left(\frac{3}{4}\right)$
	O	a	aOa	$qpq = \left(\frac{1}{4}\right)\left(\frac{3}{4}\right)^2$
a		O	aaO	$q^2 p = \left(\frac{1}{4}\right)\left(\frac{3}{4}\right)^2$
	a	a	aaa	$q^3 = \left(\frac{3}{4}\right)^3$

The terms of the three offspring also sum to unity:

$$q^3 + 2q^2 p + 2qp^2 + p^3 = 1$$

If we were to continue constructing tree diagrams and summing the various probabilities, a pattern would eventually emerge among the probabilities.

For the case of a single birth ($n = 1$), the sum of the possibilities is

$$(q + p)^1 = q + p$$

For $n = 2$,

$$(q + p)^2 = q^2 + 2qp + p^2$$

For $n = 3$,

$$(q + p)^3 = q^3 + 3q^2 p + 3qp^2 + p^3$$

In all these cases, the proper probability values are given by the terms of the binomial expansion raised to the nth power. In Exercise 6.2 you are asked to prove by means of a tree diagram that the equation corresponding to $n = 4$ is

$$(q + p)^4 = q^4 + 4q^3 p + 6q^2 p^2 + 4qp^3 + p^4$$

The quantity $(q + p)$ is termed a "binomial."[2] Bernoulli processes which result in an expansion of this term are called *binomial experiments.*

Binomial experiments are therefore a special case of the Bernoulli process,

---

[2]A *binomial* is any mathematical expression consisting of at least one variable connected to any other term by a minus or a plus sign; for example, $(a + b)$, $(a + 7)$, $(b - X)$, $(ax + b)$.

having the following characteristics:

1. The Bernoulli trial must result in a success or a failure.
2. The binomial experiment consists of n identical and independent Bernoulli trials.
3. The probability of success of a single trial is

$$p(A) = p = \frac{s}{s+f}$$

4. The probability of failure of a single trial is

$$p(\bar{A}) = q = (1-p) = \frac{f}{s+f}$$

Experiments can be termed *binomial* whenever they satisfy these four conditions. Real-world circumstances seldom fulfill all prerequisites precisely, but the binomial model approximates many variables, often involving dichotomies such as rich–poor, Ego's generation–not Ego's generation, egalitarian–stratified, married–single, endogamous–exogamous.

Values of p and q can be explicitly established once a situation has been characterized as a binomial experiment. Sometimes these figures are obvious from the nature of the phenomenon ($p_{male\,birth} = 0.50$, Mendelian ratios, and so forth), but at other times probabilities must be estimated on the basis of previous studies. The probability of each particular outcome can then be determined from the *General Formula for the Binomial Expansion*, expressed as

$$(q+p)^n = q^n + C_{n,1}q^{n-1}p + C_{n,2}q^{n-2}p^2 + \cdots + p^n \tag{6.2}$$

The coefficient $C_{n,r}$ in the example represents the number of different ways in which n births could produce r offspring with Type O blood. Of course $(n-r)$ offspring will have Type a blood. The coefficient is omitted for the q^n and p^n cases because $C_{n,r} = 1$ in both events. The generalized binomial Expression (6.2) allows one to compute the more complex dichotomous probabilities.

The formula to find any *particular* term of the binomial expansion is

$$C_{n,r}q^{n-r}p^r \tag{6.3}$$

This formula provides a shortcut means of expressing any term in the expansion of the binomial $(q+p)$ to the nth power. Stated in words, Formulas (6.2) and (6.3) give us the following rules:

1. *Every term* in the binomial expansion comprises three parts:
   (a) a numerical coefficient ($C_{n,r}$)
   (b) a power of p
   (c) a power of q
2. The *first term* in the expansion always has a numerical coefficient of $C_{n,0} = 1$, in which the coefficient is understood and not written in the equation. The power of q is always n in the initial term of the expansion, and the power of p is hence zero. Since $p^0 = 1$, the term for p in the initial term is always dropped. Thus, the first term of the binomial expansion is always q^n.

3. In *each succeeding term*, the power of q is decreased by one in regular sequence, while the power of p is increased by one in regular order until the final term p^n is reached.

The binomial expansion can be used in the blood-type example to obtain specific probabilities under repeated trials.

1. Find the probability that no child among six children has Type O blood; that is, find $p(X = 0)$.

$$p(X = 0) = C_{n,r}q^{n-r}p^r = C_{6,0}\left(\frac{3}{4}\right)^6\left(\frac{1}{4}\right)^0$$

$$= \left(\frac{3}{4}\right)^6 = \frac{729}{4096} = 0.1780$$

where $C_{6,0} = 1$.

(Note that a computational step could have been saved, since the second rule for binomial expansions specified that the initial term is simply q^n.)

2. Find the probability that exactly one of six children has Type O blood; that is, $p(X = 1)$.

$$C_{n,r}q^{n-r}p^r = C_{6,1}\left(\frac{3}{4}\right)^5\left(\frac{1}{4}\right)^1$$

$$= 6\left(\frac{243}{4096}\right) = \frac{1458}{4096} = 0.3560$$

where

$$C_{6,1} = \frac{6!}{1!\,5!} = 6$$

3. Find the probability that exactly two of six children have Type O blood; that is, $p(X = 2)$.

$$C_{n,r}q^{n-r}p^r = C_{6,2}\left(\frac{3}{4}\right)^4\left(\frac{1}{4}\right)^2$$

$$= 15\left(\frac{81}{4096}\right) = \frac{1215}{4096} = 0.2966$$

where

$$C_{6,2} = \frac{6!}{2!\,4!} = 15$$

4. Find the probability that exactly three of six children have Type O blood; that is, $p(X = 3)$.

$$C_{n,r}q^{n-r}p^r = C_{6,3}\left(\frac{3}{4}\right)^3\left(\frac{1}{4}\right)^3$$

$$= 20\left(\frac{27}{4096}\right) = \frac{540}{4096} = 0.1318$$

where

$$C_{6,3} = \frac{6!}{3!\,3!} = 20$$

5. Find the probability that exactly four of six children have Type O blood; that is, $p(X = 4)$.

$$C_{n,r}q^{n-r}p^r = C_{6,4}\left(\frac{3}{4}\right)^2\left(\frac{1}{4}\right)^4$$

$$= 15\left(\frac{9}{4096}\right) = \frac{135}{4096} = 0.0330$$

where

$$C_{6,4} = \frac{6!}{2!\,4!} = 15$$

6. Find the probability that exactly five of six children have Type O blood; that is, $p(X = 5)$.

$$C_{n,r}q^{n-r}p^r = C_{6,5}\left(\frac{3}{4}\right)^1\left(\frac{1}{4}\right)^5$$

$$= 6\left(\frac{3}{4096}\right) = \frac{18}{4096} = 0.0044$$

where

$$C_{6,5} = \frac{6!}{1!\,5!} = 6$$

7. Find the probability that all six of six children have Type O blood; that is, $p(X = 6)$.

$$C_{n,r}q^{n-r}p^r = C_{6,6}\left(\frac{3}{4}\right)^0\left(\frac{1}{4}\right)^6$$

$$= \left(\frac{1}{4}\right)^6 = \frac{1}{4096} = 0.0002$$

where $C_{6,6} = 1$.

When all seven terms of this binomial expansion are summed, the result must equal unity:

$$(q + p)^6 = 0.1780 + 0.3560 + 0.2966 + 0.1318$$
$$+ 0.0330 + 0.0044 + 0.0002$$
$$= 1.0000$$

This example illustrates several important points regarding the binomial theorem. First of all, it should be clear that Expression (6.3) is merely a generalized formula for finding any individual term in the total expansion of a binomial given by Expression (6.2). Were we only concerned with a single specified outcome, such as the probability of exactly three of the six children having Type O blood, then Formula (6.3) could be used to compute that individual probability, $p(X = 3) = 0.1318$, ignoring the other six terms of the expansion.

The binomial theorem also facilitates computing the probability of compound events (which themselves comprise several possible outcomes). Suppose, for instance, that we wanted to know the probability of having four or more of six children with Type O blood. This involves the union of the individual probabilities of four, five, and six children. Since only one of these events can occur in a single family of six offspring, the events are mutually exclusive and the Addition Rule (Section 5.8) is applied.

$$p(X \geq 4) = p(X = 4) + p(X = 5) + p(X = 6)$$
$$= 0.0330 + 0.0044 + 0.0002 = 0.0376$$

The probability of any given combination of outcomes can be found in this fashion by simply adding the relevant probabilities determined by Formula (6.3).

Note finally that the summation of the component probabilities in all binomial expansions is exactly equal to unity, as demonstrated above for the case of $n = 6$ with $p = 0.25$ and $q = 0.75$. We know that the expansion of a binomial is exhaustive (that is, every possible outcome has been enumerated) and, since one of these mutually exclusive outcomes is sure to occur, the probability of a certain event must be 1.

Example 6.1

In seven consecutive tosses of a fair coin, what are the chances of obtaining:

(a) Exactly five heads?

$$p(X = 5) = C_{7,5} \left(\frac{1}{2}\right)^2 \left(\frac{1}{2}\right)^5 = \frac{21}{128} = 0.1641$$

where

$$C_{7,5} = \frac{7!}{5!\,2!} = 21$$

(b) Exactly seven heads?

$$p(X = 7) = C_{7,7} \left(\frac{1}{2}\right)^0 \left(\frac{1}{2}\right)^7 = \left(\frac{1}{2}\right)^7$$

$$= \frac{1}{128} = 0.0078$$

where

$$C_{7,7} = 1$$

(c) At least four heads?
In this case, the following events are all successes: 4 heads, 5 heads, 6 heads, 7 heads.

$$p(4 \leq X \leq 7) = C_{7,4} \left(\frac{1}{2}\right)^3 \left(\frac{1}{2}\right)^4 + C_{7,5} \left(\frac{1}{2}\right)^2 \left(\frac{1}{2}\right)^5$$

$$+ C_{7,6} \left(\frac{1}{2}\right)^1 \left(\frac{1}{2}\right)^6 + C_{7,7} \left(\frac{1}{2}\right)^0 \left(\frac{1}{2}\right)^7$$

$$= \frac{35}{128} + \frac{21}{128} + \frac{7}{128} + \frac{1}{128}$$

$$= \frac{64}{128} = 0.5000$$

(d) Less than two heads?

$$p(X < 2) = C_{7,0} \left(\frac{1}{2}\right)^7 + C_{7,1} \left(\frac{1}{2}\right)^6 \left(\frac{1}{2}\right)^1$$

$$= \frac{1}{128} + \frac{7}{128} = \frac{8}{128} = 0.0625$$

Example 6.2

A grave is known to contain eight human burials. What is the probability that exactly six of these burials are female?

To remain consistent with earlier notations, we define the probability of a *male* burial as p. But since $p = q$ in this case, we can rephrase the problem to consider the chances of discovering only two males among eight skeletons.

$$p(X = 2) = C_{8,2} \left(\frac{1}{2}\right)^6 \left(\frac{1}{2}\right)^2 = \frac{28}{256} = 0.1090$$

(Note that exactly the same result could be obtained by computing the probability for six of eight females.)

Example 6.3

Three dice are rolled simultaneously. What is the probability of obtaining
(a) Exactly two 4's?

In this case, we know that $p = 1/6$ and $q = 5/6$, so

$$p(X = 2) = C_{3,2} \left(\frac{5}{6}\right)^1 \left(\frac{1}{6}\right)^2$$

$$= 3 \left(\frac{5}{216}\right) = \frac{15}{216} = 0.0694$$

(b) At least two 4's?

$$p(X \geqslant 2) = C_{3,2} \left(\frac{5}{6}\right)^1 \left(\frac{1}{6}\right)^2 + C_{3,3} \left(\frac{1}{6}\right)^3$$

$$= \frac{15}{216} + \frac{1}{216} = \frac{16}{216} = 0.0741$$

6.4 PASCAL'S TRIANGLE

In the examples in Section 6.3 illustrating the binomial expansion, you undoubtedly noticed that many computations were repetitive. Time after time, for instance, it was necessary to compute the various powers of (1/2), especially $(1/2)^6$ and $(1/2)^8$. It would be advisable for you to compute these standardized constants only once. If you write these figures in some readily available place (such as the inside cover of this book), they will always be ready for immediate use. Not only will this save you time, but another possibility for error will be eliminated as well.

Expanding the binomial also requires computation of several combinations again and again, such as $C_{3,2} = C_{6,3} = 20$. There is a shortcut means for handling this problem too, by using *Pascal's triangle* (Table 6.1). In the 17th century, the French mathematician Blaise Pascal discovered this interesting phenomenon which now bears his name. Each number within this triangular graph can be found by adding the two numbers diagonally above (except along the margins). In the fifth row, for instance, the 5 can be found by adding together the 1 and the 4. Pascal's triangle can be expanded indefinitely merely by placing a 1 to start the new row and then adding the two numbers of the preceding row.

Among its other properties, Pascal's triangle provides the necessary coefficients for the binomial expansion. Remember that for $n = 4$ the proper binomial terms were found from Formula (6.2) to be

$$(q + p)^4 = q^4 + 4q^3p + 6q^2p^2 + 4qp^3 + p^4$$

Rather than having to recompute the coefficients from $C_{n,r}$ in each case, the same sequence of coefficients (namely, 1 4 6 4 1) can be read directly from the $n = 4$ row of Pascal's triangle. The coefficients of $(q + p)^{10}$ are found to be (1 10 45 120 210 252 210 120 45 10 1) without having to resort to combination calculations at all. When using Pascal's triangle as a shortcut to computing the binomial, be certain to remember just what these terms actually mean. That is, the first term remains the probability of zero successes and always has a coefficient of unity.

In addition, by taking the sum of the coefficients for any row of the triangle, the total number of equally possible outcomes can be found,[3] *provided p = q.* Adding the coefficients along the row $n = 4$, we find

$$1 + 4 + 6 + 4 + 1 = 16$$

Thus, when $n = 4$ (and $p = q = 1/2$), there are exactly 16 equally likely outcomes. If four coins were flipped, the probability of no head (that is, all tails) must be 1/16, since the left-hand coefficient in Table 6.1 is 1. Similarly, the probability of obtaining three heads in four tosses is 4/16 because the fourth coefficient of this row is 4. This result corresponds to the binomial term

$$p(X = 3) = C_{n,r}q^{n-r}p^r = C_{4,3}\left(\frac{1}{2}\right)\left(\frac{1}{2}\right)^3$$

---

[3]The restriction of $p = q = 1/2$ is necessary in this particular case because the numerator in the expression $q^{n-r}p^r$ will be something other than 1 for all other situations. If $p = 1/10$, for instance, then $q = 9/10$, so the expression will have a numerator equal to 9 rather than 1.

TABLE 6.1   Pascal's Triangle

$n=1$	1	1								
2	1	2	1							
3	1	3	3	1						
4	1	4	6	4	1					
5	1	5	10	10	5	1				
6	1	6	15	20	15	6	1			
7	1	7	21	35	35	21	7	1		
8	1	8	28	56	70	56	28	8	1	
9	1	9	36	84	126	126	84	36	9	1
10	1	10	45	120	210	252	210	120	45	10	1
. . .										

Example 6.4

Use Pascal's triangle to find the probability of obtaining more than seven heads in nine tosses of a coin.

For row $n = 9$,

$$1 + 9 + 36 + 84 + 126 + 126 + 84 + 36 + 9 + 1 = 512$$

There are thus exactly 512 equally likely outcomes, and since "more than seven heads" means that either eight or nine heads are successes,

$$p(X > 7) = \frac{9}{512} + \frac{1}{512} = \frac{10}{512} = 0.0195$$

6.5 THE BINOMIAL DISTRIBUTION

Let us return to the problem of predicting the sex of unborn offspring. Setting p = probability of a male birth = 0.50, there are only two possibilities[4] for a single birth ($n = 1$):

$$(q + p)^1 = \frac{1}{2} + \frac{1}{2} = 1.00$$

Each term in this Bernoulli process represents the probability of a mutually exclusive outcome. The sum of the probabilities equals unity, and both outcomes are shown on Fig. 6.1. The first bar of the histogram represents the probability of no male birth (that is, a female birth, since $n = 1$). The height of this bar represents its probability, which is 0.50. The second bar represents the probability of a single male birth. The total area enclosed by both bars represents the probability of 1. Note how Fig. 6.1 uses *area* to represent *probability*; in a sense, the probability distribution is a specialized form of the Venn diagram.

Similar histograms can be constructed for the cases of $n = 2$, $n = 3$, and $n = 4$. Each histogram is fixed for given values of n and p, and this shape is characteristic of the binomial distribution. In each case, the number of successes is a discrete random variable.

The histogram resulting from the expansion of a binomial to the nth power is called a *theoretical binomial probability distribution.*

The binomial probability distribution is symmetrical as long as $p = q = 1/2$. But the distribution becomes skewed when q and p are not equal. Figure 6.2 graphs the blood-type example discussed at the beginning of this chapter. The most probable outcome (the *mode*) is a single offspring with Type O blood, so the entire histogram is skewed to the right.

[4]Unless stated explicitly to the contrary, the expected sex ratios will be assumed to be 50:50, even though the true figure seems generally to be closer to $p = 0.515$.

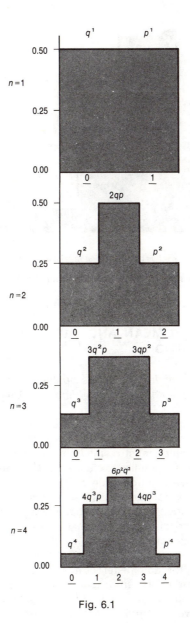

Fig. 6.1

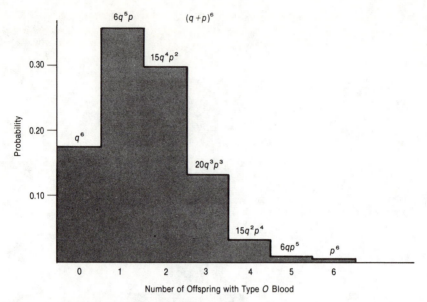

Fig. 6.2 Asymmetrical histogram for binomial probability distribution, with $p = 0.25$ and $n = 6$.

6.6 EXPECTED MEAN AND VARIANCE OF THE BINOMIAL DISTRIBUTION

● *The gambling known as business looks with disfavor on the business known as gambling.*—A. Bierce

Let me emphasize the critical point of Section 6.5: *The binomial theorem can be used to construct the complete probability distribution of a binomial.* Exactly $(n + 1)$ distinct probabilities must result from expanding the variable $(q + p)^n$. These terms are always mutually exclusive and exhaustive; so, when taken together, they cover every conceivable outcome of the binomial experiment. The individual terms therefore comprise the expected probability distribution of the discrete random variable X. This probability distribution will be helpful in assessing the likelihood of actual binomial processes. Now we can examine how to compute the expected mean and variance of this theoretical binomial distribution.

A crafty old instructor administered a surprise quiz of seven true-false questions to his introductory anthropology class. Because the exam was unexpected, the $N = 256$ students were totally unprepared and all were forced to guess at the answers. Some of the more mathematically sophisticated students were even observed surreptitiously flipping quarters. The probability of a correct answer is obviously a success. This probability is exactly equal to the probability of an incorrect guess: $p = q = 1/2$. Assuming that all students took the same exam and that there was no cheating (that is, that the exams were totally independent of each other), this situation satisfies criteria for a binomial experiment (Section 6.3). The probability distribution for the discrete random variable X, "the correct number of responses," is listed in Table 6.2, and the *expected curve* for the exam scores is represented in the histogram in Fig. 6.3(a).

But in computing the class grading curve, the instructor is not interested in expected probabilities; he is concerned with the *expected frequencies* of the test scores. This example has exactly eight possible values for X, ranging from $(X_1 = 0)$ to $(X_8 = 7)$; these are the total correct answers for each student. The expected probabilities of each score can be found by expanding the binomial, as explained earlier. The expected frequencies of each test score are equal to the product of $p(X = X_i)$ times N.[5]

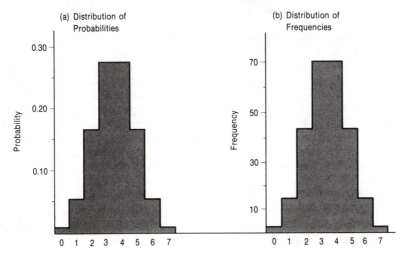

Fig. 6.3 Probability and frequency distributions for hypothetical test scores on seven true-false questions, $N = 256$ students: (a) Distribution of probabilities; (b) distribution of frequencies.

How many students are expected to receive 100 percent? These lucky students will have correctly guessed all seven questions. The probability of $(X = 7)$ is given by Expression (6.3):

$$C_{n,r}q^{n-r}p^r = C_{8,8}q^0p^8 = (1/2)^8$$
$$= 1/128$$

This expected probability is converted to an expected frequency by multiplying by $N = 256$. Therefore, the expected frequency of $(X = X_7)$ is equal to $p(X = 7)N = (256)(1/128) = 2$. Assuming all students guessed, only two students are expected to guess all seven questions correctly. The remaining expected frequencies are computed in Table 6.2.

---

[5]When considering the binomial distribution, be certain to distinguish between n, the number of independent trials, and N, the population size.

TABLE 6.2 Hypothetical Distribution of Test Scores on Seven True-False Questions, $N = 256$ Students.

Number of Correct Responses, X_i	Probability, P_i	Expectation, E_i	$X_i f_i$	X_i^2	$X_i^2 f_i$
0	1/128 = .0078	2	0	0	0
1	7/128 = .0547	14	14	1	14
2	21/128 = .1641	42	84	4	168
3	35/128 = .2734	70	210	9	630
4	35/128 = .2734	70	280	16	1120
5	21/128 = .1641	42	210	25	1050
6	7/128 = .0547	14	84	36	504
7	1/128 = .0078	2	14	49	98
		$N = 256$	$N = 896$		3584

These expected frequencies are plotted on the histogram in Fig. 6.3(b). Note the similarity between the frequency histogram and the probability distribution. In fact, the only difference between the two is the scale of the y-axis. The total area under the histogram for each diagram is found by summing the areas of the individual bars. The binomial probability distribution histogram has an area of $\Sigma p\,(X = X_i) = 1.00$ (the probability of a certain event). The area under the frequency distribution is $\Sigma p\,(X = X_i)N = 256$, the total aggregate of students. In one case, the area represents the entire population of students ($N = 256$), but the shapes of the distributions are identical.

In assigning grades to this exam, the instructor is forced to consider another problem: What is the expected mean score of this quiz? The mean of the theoretical frequency distribution is found from Table 6.2 in precisely the same manner as any other mean:

$$\mu = \frac{\sum_{i=1}^{k} X_i f_i}{n} = \frac{896}{256} = 3.50$$

This population mean corresponds to the exact center of the frequency histogram [Fig. 6.3(b)].

The standard deviation about the population mean can also be determined as before, using computing Formula (4.19):

$$\sigma = \sqrt{\frac{3584 - ((896)^2/256)}{256}} = 1.32$$

But even by using the shortcut computational methods, finding the population mean and standard deviation for a binomial distribution is a tedious (and often error-prone) operation. More than 20 individual multiplications are required.

Remember that Expression (6.1) defined the *expectation* of a random variable as

$$E(X) = \Sigma X_i p\,(X = X_i)$$

The value of $E(X)$ was said to estimate μ, the population mean. A glance at

Table 6.2 reveals that the population mean of the binomial distribution was computed in exactly this manner—that is, as the summation of the products between probabilities and outcomes of X (namely, the X_i). Fortunately, there is an easier method for finding the mean of a binomial distribution.

For all binomial distributions in which p is the probability of success and $(1-p) = q$ is the probability of failure, the population mean of the expected frequency of n trials is

$$\mu = np \qquad (6.4)$$

The population standard deviation of a binomial distribution is

$$\sigma = \sqrt{npq} \qquad (6.5)$$

Be certain to distinguish between the number of independent trials (n) and the population size (N).

For the distribution in Table 6.2, the binomial formulas produce the following values:

$$\mu = \frac{1}{2}(7) = 3.5$$

$$\sigma = \sqrt{7\left(\frac{1}{2}\right)\left(\frac{1}{2}\right)} = \sqrt{\frac{7}{4}} = 1.32$$

These results obtained from the binomial formulas are equal to those computed by standard methods (within a small rounding error). Not only are they easier to compute, but they are also more accurate. Values μ and σ represent the expected mean and variance of a binomial population.

One final point regarding the binomial distribution requires emphasis. This chapter is concerned strictly with *theoretical expectations* of a discrete random variable: theoretical probability distributions, theoretically expected frequencies, expected population means, expected population variances. All these expectations are parameters, specific to unknown populations. The binomial distribution has been examined in such detail in order to establish a mechanism for making predictions about future samples. There are no actual samples yet. The next chapter also deals only with theoretically expected values, but for a continuous random variable. Once the expected distribution has been fully developed, we will be in a position to confront actual samples of variates and to evaluate how they differ from our expectations. But along the way, be certain to keep in mind the distinction between what we expect in the ideal case from what we will eventually observe in the real world.

Example 6.5

If 10 coins are simultaneously tossed 49 times in succession, what is the expected mean and standard deviation of the distribution?

We define $p = q = 1/2$, with $n = 10$ and $N = 49$:

$$\mu = np = 10\left(\frac{1}{2}\right) = 5.0$$

$$\sigma = \sqrt{npq} = \sqrt{10\left(\frac{1}{2}\right)\left(\frac{1}{2}\right)} = \sqrt{\frac{10}{4}}.$$

$$= \sqrt{2.50} = 1.58$$

● *Man must go up or down, and the odds seem to be all in favor of his going down and out.*—H. G. Wells

SUGGESTIONS FOR FURTHER READING

Bliss (1967: chapter 2). Concentrates primarily upon biological and genetic applications.
Hays (1973: chapter 5).
Mendenhall (1971: chapter 6). More advanced treatment.
Sokal and Rohlf (1968: chapter 5).

EXERCISES

6.1 Name five anthropologically relevant variables which follow a binomial distribution. Name the dichotomous states of each variable.

6.2 Use a tree diagram to find the binomial expansion for $n = 4$.

6.3 What should Pascal's triangle read for $n = 12$?

6.4 A fair coin is tossed six times. "Tails" is a success.
(a) In how many ways can six tails be obtained?
(b) In how many ways can two tails be obtained?
(c) In how many ways can five tails be obtained?
(d) What is the probability of obtaining more than four tails?
(e) What is the probability of obtaining fewer than three but more than four tails?
(f) What is the probability of obtaining three or four tails?
(g) In what two ways could the answer to part (f) have been obtained?
(h) Construct the probability distribution histogram for this situation (similar to Fig. 6.1).

6.5 If $p = 1/2$ and $n = 8$,
(a) What is the mean number of successes in the population of all trials?
(b) What is the population standard deviation?
(c) What is the population variance?
(d) Draw the histogram representing the probability distribution.
(e) What can be said about the shape of this distribution?

6.6   Assume a binomial population with $p = 1/3$ and $q = 2/3$. If we were to draw a random sample of $n = 10$ observations from this population,
(a) In how many ways can we obtain a sample with exactly five successes?
(b) What is the probability of obtaining any one sample with five successes? (Do not multiply out the answer.)
(c) What is the probability of obtaining exactly five successes?

6.7   Yesterday I selected five catalogued artifacts for exhibition from the American Museum of Natural History collections. Assuming that the selection of each artifact involved an independent choice,
(a) What is the probability that all five catalogue numbers are even?
(b) What is the probability that the first artifact's catalogue number ends in 5?
(c) What is the probability that exactly two of the five artifacts have numbers ending in 5?

6.8   Over his past five decades on the bench, Judge Hangen has sentenced three of every four defendants to death. Eight new cases are pending.
(a) What is the probability that at least six defendants will be acquitted?
(b) What is the probability that the third defendant will be declared guilty?
(c) What is the probability that all will be declared guilty?

6.9   A physical anthropologist is testing among the Eskimo of northern Alaska for the ability to taste PTC (phenylthiocarbamide). Previous studies indicate that about 25 percent of all Eskimos are nontasters.
(a) If five informants are tested, what is the probability that precisely three are nontasters?
(b) What is the probability that all but one are nontasters?
(c) Suppose that 20 Eskimo villages were selected for more intensive study and that five informants were randomly chosen from each village. How many villages are expected to have exactly two nontasters?
(d) What is the expected average number of nontasters for the villages in part (c)?
(e) Construct the histogram representing the probability distribution in part (c).

6.10   A primatologist has been studying the behavior of the mountain gorilla in Albert National Park, Congo. Over a period of 60 study days, he has been able to successfully locate a foraging group of mountain gorilla only about two-thirds of the time. A group of visiting scientists have only nine days to spend in the study area.
(a) What are their chances of never seeing a mountain gorilla?
(b) What is the probability of seeing gorilla on exactly eight days?
(c) What is the probability of seeing gorilla at least seven of the nine days?

*6.11   A particularly ornery archaeologist has warned his field crew that in the past he has fired about 25 percent of his diggers within the first month. If ten people were hired initially,

(a) What is the probability that four people will be fired?
(b) Are the odds better than 2:1 that nobody will be fired?
(c) What is the probability that fewer than three people will be fired?
(d) What is the probability that everyone will be fired?
(e) What assumptions are being made in these calculations?

7 The Normal Distribution as a Continuous Random Variable

● *The physicians of the Middle Ages had developed many practical measures which they could not explain, but which had the merit of working. For example, they burned fresh wounds with a hot iron. At the time of the French Revolution all of these old practices were cast aside as being superstitious. Medicine attempted to be scientific, with awful results. Instead of cauterizing fresh wounds, they were bandaged in lint, which we know must have been bacteriologically filthy. Gangrene was the usual consequence.* —P. Sears

7.1 THE NORMAL CURVE

Chapter 6 introduced discrete random variables and their probability distributions. One example of a discrete random variable, the binomial, was developed in some detail. By expanding the binomial, one can find exact probabilities of any particular outcome of a multiple trial experiment, and since all these outcomes have been enumerated, a histogram can be constructed to represent this distribution. Regardless of n, these histograms array the probabilities of individual outcomes. In effect, the probabilities are represented by areas within the histogram. The binomial probability distribution can be summarized by a population mean and variance.

Because the binomial is a discrete random variable, individual outcomes are divided into rather neat and intrinsically distinct categories (one success, two successes, and so forth). Later on, this chapter introduces the notion of a *continuous* random variable involving an X totally without the neat categories of discrete random variables.

We can set the stage for the continuous random variable by returning once again to our ideal coins. The probability distributions for several coin-flipping

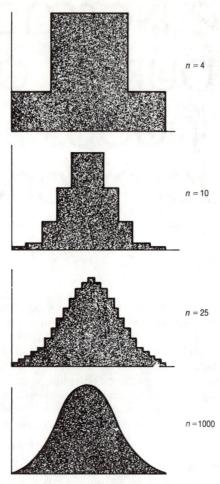

$n = 4$

$n = 10$

$n = 25$

$n = 1000$

Fig. 7.1 Binomial probability distributions for various values of n.

experiments are depicted in Fig. 7.1. These distributions must all be symmetrical because $p = q = 1/2$ in all cases.

When three coins are tossed, exactly four possible outcomes exist: X_i = no heads, $X_2 = 1$ head, $X_3 = 2$ heads, or $X_4 = 3$ heads. The probability distribution for this experiment assumes the characteristic stair-step shape which we associate with finite discrete random variables. If nine coins are tossed, a total of ten different outcomes become possible. The probabilities for both experiments are represented by histograms in Fig. 7.1. Although n differs, the *maximum* probability must still equal the sum of the mutually exclusive outcomes, and this sum is equal to unity: $\Sigma p(X = X_i) = 1$. So histograms for both $n = 4$ and $n = 10$ must contain exactly the same area—unity. The difference between the two distributions is that unity is divided into four discrete chunks for $n = 4$ and ten chunks for $n = 10$. Figure 7.1 illustrates this fact clearly; the stair steps are much smaller for $n = 10$. If 24 coins were tossed, the individual histogram bars would become smaller still. In general, the stair steps decrease as n increases.

Now, what would happen to the bars of the probability distribution histogram if 1000 coins were tossed? The total space is still unity, but now unity must be divided into 1000 chunks. The result of $n = 1000$ trials is that the individual bars will become so small that they virtually disappear.

The smooth curve suggested by expansion of the binomial (when n is large) is called the normal curve.

The case of $n = 1000$ is represented in Fig. 7.1; the individual stair steps are so small that we cannot see them. This is a normal curve. The term "normal" is used to describe this bell-shaped curve, but note that this is a specialized usage. Normal curves have nothing to do with "ordinary," "average," or "typical."

7.2 THE NORMAL CURVE AS AN APPROXIMATION OF THE BINOMIAL

● Get your facts first and then you can distort 'em as much as you please.—M. Twain

The shape of the normal curve is suggested by the binomial distribution. We introduce the normal curve in this intuitive fashion in order to emphasize the interrelationship between these two important distributions.

But a problem arises with the normal curve. Binomial distributions are relatively easy to manipulate because the frequencies are readily tabled by direct class. Every histogram bar represents an interval intrinsic to the data, and each interval has a known probability. But the normal curve is defined as continuous and lacks discrete divisions. How can probability intervals be computed for a continuous curve?

Consider a simple binomial exercise: What are the chances of obtaining less than three heads in seven tosses of a fair coin? From Formula (6.3) we know

$$p(X < 3) = \left(\frac{1}{2}\right)^7 + C_{7,1}\left(\frac{1}{2}\right)^6\left(\frac{1}{2}\right) + C_{7,2}\left(\frac{1}{2}\right)^5\left(\frac{1}{2}\right)^2$$

$$= \frac{1}{128} + \frac{7}{128} + \frac{21}{128} = 0.227$$

The histogram in Figure 7.2(a) represents the eight possible outcomes and the number of successes (two or fewer heads) are shaded. The mean and standard deviation of the population distribution for $n = 7$ are as before.

$$\mu = np = 3.5$$

$$\sigma = \sqrt{npq} = 1.32$$

The total area enclosed by the histogram must be equal to unity, and the area of the shaded portion represents the probability $p(X < 3) = 0.227$.

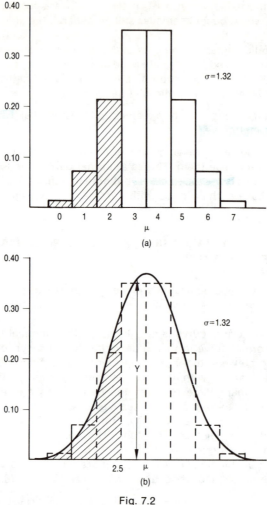

Fig. 7.2

The midpoint of each class interval of the histogram can be connected by a smooth curve as in Fig. 7.2(b). The normal curve can thus be used to *approximate* these same binomials. Although the discrete classes evaporate, the basic binomial properties are retained in the normal approximation. The total area under the curve remains equal to unity. The shaded area still represents the probability of two or fewer successes, and the population mean and standard deviation are unchanged.

But consider the rub. Continuous curves lack intervals, so how can we compute the discrete probabilities for two heads, one head, and no heads? To cope with this development, it will be necessary to look a bit deeper into the structure of the normal curve.

The normal curve has been operationally defined as the curve suggested by smoothing the binomial expansion. The classes simply disappear. But mathematical statisticians approach the normal curve in a more rigorous manner by deriving the *mathematical formula* of the normal curve. That formula is complex and beyond our current needs, but we can benefit from what the formula tells us. Four basic terms are involved [Fig. 7.2(b)]: μ, σ, X_i, and Y; μ is the x-axis value for the highest point on the normal curve (also corresponding to the median and the mode). As before, the variability of the curve is represented by σ. The x-axis is like that of a binomial distribution and any given point on that line can be indicated by X_i (just as the class midpoint in the binomial was called X_i). So, the only new term in the normal curve formula is Y. As long as discrete classes exist, probabilities can be represented by vertical bars; the probability of any given outcome is directly proportional to the area contained by that vertical rectangle. This area is obviously the product of the width (w) and the rectangle height (which we can call Y).

As the number of classes in the binomial expansion increases, the relative width of each rectangle decreases. When n is large, the rectangle width (w) becomes small; as n becomes very large, the "rectangle" approaches zero width. If n were to reach infinity, the histogram bar would be reduced merely to a line of length Y. It is no longer meaningful to ask the area (the probability) of these rectangles because lines have only height (Y) and no width ($w = 0$). Therefore, all individual probabilities are zero when $n \to \infty$. We have reached a dead end.

It is possible in such cases only to consider the *probabilities to either side* of the vertical line at X_i—probabilities more extreme, less extreme, or the exact probability between two X_i which are separated by some space. If this seems confusing, return to the simple binomial example of two or fewer successes in seven trials [Fig. 7.2(a)]. Under the normal approximation, we cannot compute $p(X = 0)$, $p(X = 1)$, or $p(X = 2)$ directly from the binomial probabilities because the class intervals disappeared when the normal curve was drawn. But it is possible to find the total area to the *left of two successes*: Two heads are a success and three heads are a failure. The midpoints of these classes are $X_1 = 2.00$ and $X_2 = 3.00$ [Fig. 7.2(b)]. Both classes extend beyond their midpoints, so their common boundary is the point at $X = 2.5$ on the x-axis. The question now becomes: *What is the probability (area) to the left of $X = 2.5$?*

Here is where the mathematical formula for the normal curve comes into play. That formula tells us that, given μ, σ, and X_i, Y can be calculated. That is, if the shape of the normal curve (defined by μ and σ) is known, then the height of the curve (Y) at point X_i is also known. But even more critical is the fact that once we know Y, *areas under the normal curve* associated with that particular Y can be determined. Given μ, σ, and X_i, the probability can be calculated. These computations are tedious and involve techniques beyond our present scope, so the corresponding areas under the normal curve have been compiled in Table A.3 (Appendix B).

Unfortunately, no single table can contain data for all possible normal curves. Infinitely many normal curves exist because the distribution changes with each shift in μ or σ. For this reason, Table A.3 provides the areas for a special normal curve characterized by $\mu = 0$ and $\sigma = 1$. These values are not particularly sacred; in fact, respective means and standard deviations of precisely zero and

1 almost never occur in the real world. But it is a simple matter to convert any empirically observed distribution into this conventional form through the use of the *standardized normal deviate*, denoted by *z*:

$$z = \frac{X_i - \mu}{\sigma} \tag{7.1}$$

This simple conversion allows any set of normally distributed variates to be transformed into a distribution with $\mu = 0$ and $\sigma = 1$.

The values for z are listed in the first column of Table A.3, and the three adjacent columns contain various expressions of the probabilities. Column A denotes the area between z (the standardized value of X_i) and μ. Column B indicates the area contained in the larger portion of the curve, and column C represents the probability associated with the smaller part of the curve. It is good policy to graph all such problems [as in Fig. 7.2(b)] and shade the desired area before using Table A.3. With this diagram at hand, the proper probability figure can be found with little difficulty.

Now we can determine the probability of rolling two or fewer heads by using the normal approximation. This probability is represented by the total area to the left of $X_i = 2.5$. But the X_i must first be converted to a z-score (that is, standardized to $\mu = 0$ and $\sigma = 1.0$):

$$z = \frac{X_i - \mu}{\sigma} = \frac{2.5 - 3.5}{1.32} = -0.76$$

The normal curve is always symmetrical, so the distance from any $+z$ to the distribution mean must be the same as the distance from the same $-z$ to μ. The sign of z is thus ignored in Table A.3. The area to the left of $z = -0.76$ is clearly the *smaller* portion under the curve [Fig. 7.2(b)], so the appropriate area is found in column C to be $p(X \leq 2) = 0.2236$. This probability can be interpreted precisely the same as those obtained earlier using the binomial expansion.

Keep in mind that the binomial method yields the *true* probability associated with a given outcome, while the normal curve method provides only an *approximation* of this true probability. Figure 7.3 shows why the normal curve is less accurate than the binomial computation. The normal curve passes only

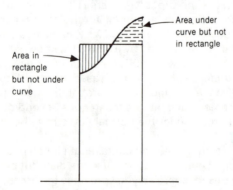

Fig. 7.3 Comparison of areas under smooth curve and under a binomial interval (after Blalock 1972: 95).

through the midpoints of the histogram rectangles. Part of each binomial interval is erroneously *excluded* from the curve and another portion of the rectangle is erroneously *included*. The sum of these two small areas for all histogram rectangles is termed the error of approximation. The above binomial probability is $p(X \leq 2) = 0.227$ and the probability computed by the normal approximation is $p(X \leq 2) = 0.224$. The error is due to the small value of $n = 7$. As the value of n increases, the histogram bars become relatively narrower, thereby decreasing the error of approximation. A general rule is that the normal approximation should be applied only when n is greater than about 20, and an n of 25 or 30 is preferable. For $n > 30$, the error of approximation becomes negligible.

Example 7.1

Use the normal approximation to determine the probability of obtaining between 8 and 12 tails when 20 coins are tossed.

A first necessary step in all problems relating to probability and the normal curve is to diagram the exact question under consideration (Fig. 7.4). In this case the shaded area represents the probability of obtaining

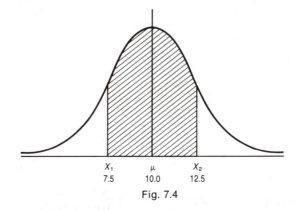

| X_1 | μ | X_2 |
| 7.5 | 10.0 | 12.5 |

Fig. 7.4

between 8 and 12 heads. Using the values along the x-axis as $X_1 = 7.5$ and $X_2 = 12.5$, the mean is

$$\mu = np = 20 \left(\frac{1}{2}\right) = 10.0$$

and the standard deviation is

$$\sigma = \sqrt{npq} = \sqrt{20 \left(\frac{1}{2}\right)\left(\frac{1}{2}\right)} = \sqrt{5}$$

$$= 2.24$$

Computing first the z-score between μ and X_1,

$$z_1 = \frac{7.5 - 10.0}{2.24} = -\frac{2.50}{2.24} = -1.12$$

and the area between μ and X_2 is

$$z_2 = \frac{12.5 - 10.0}{2.24} = \frac{2.50}{2.24} = 1.12$$

So the probability of obtaining 8 and 12 heads is the area contained between $z_1 = -1.12$ and $z_2 = 1.12$. Table A.3 (Appendix) indicates that the area between the mean and $\pm z$ is 0.3686. Therefore the total probability in question is

$$p(8 \leq X \leq 12) = 2(0.3686) = 0.7372$$

If you doubt the utility of the normal approximation, I invite you to find the binomial expansion for $n = 20$. Despite the amount of labor involved in computing the binomial, the discrepancy between the two methods is negligible.

Example 7.2

It is known that of the 2890 people in a given society, approximately 867 are over 60 years of age. If an anthropologist has taken a random sample of ten informants:

(a) What is the probability of having at least eight people over 60? (Use the binomial distribution.)

If drawing an informant over 60 years old is termed a success,

$$p = \frac{867}{2890} = 0.30$$

$$\mu = np = 10(0.30) = 3.0$$

$$\sigma = \sqrt{npq} = \sqrt{10(0.30)(0.70)} = 1.45$$

We need to find the probability of having eight, nine, or ten successes in a sample of ten informants:

8 successes: $C_{10,8}(0.70)^2(0.30)^8 = 45 \left(\dfrac{321,489}{10,000,000,000} \right)$

9 successes: $C_{10,9}(0.70)(0.30)^9 = 10 \left(\dfrac{137,781}{10,000,000,000} \right)$

10 successes: $C_{10,10}(0.30)^{10} \quad = 1 \left(\dfrac{59,049}{10,000,000,000} \right)$

$$p(8 \leq X \leq 10) = \frac{14,467,005 + 1,377,810 + 59,049}{10,000,000,000} = 0.0016$$

(b) Rework problem (a), using the normal approximation.

In this case, the probability in question is the z-score to the right of 7.5 on Fig. 7.5:

$$z = \frac{\mu - X_1}{\sigma} = \frac{7.5 - 3.0}{1.45} = 3.10$$

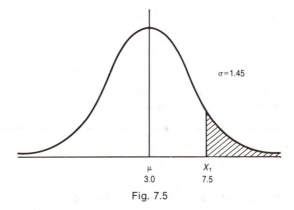

Fig. 7.5

From Table A.3 the area corresponding to $z = 3.10$ is

$$p(8 \leq X \leq 10) = 0.0010$$

The error of approximation is $0.0016 - 0.0010 = 0.0006 = 0.06$ percent. (As mentioned above, the normal approximation should really be used only in cases with $n \geq 15$, but this illustration serves to point out the relationship between binomial methods, and the normal approximation.)

(c) Using the normal approximation, what is the probability of selecting between two and five informants older than 60?

This case requires computation of two areas of probability (Fig. 7.6): area 1 from two informants (taken as $X_1 = 1.5$) to the mean, and area 2 from the

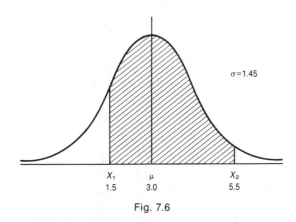

Fig. 7.6

mean to five informants (taken as $X_2 = 5.5$). The probability between X_1 and μ (area 1) is

$$z_1 = \frac{1.5 - 3.0}{1.45} = -1.03$$

$$= 0.3485$$

and the probability between μ and X_2 (area 2) is

$$z_2 = \frac{5.5 - 3.0}{1.45} = 1.72$$

$$= 0.4573$$

The total probability of obtaining between two and five successes is (area 1) + (area 2) = 0.3485 + 0.4573 = 0.8058.

Example 7.3

From late September into early October, the Copper Eskimos are almost exclusively dependent upon caribou for their food (Damas 1969:45). Caribou drives were organized such that the herds were stampeded between long rows of rocks, where they could be more effectively ambushed. Let us assume that during this one-month period, drives are attempted every other day; that is, there are generally 15 such drives attempted during this period. But, on the average, only about 20 percent of the drives are successful in ambushing the caribou herds.

If a local band of Copper Eskimos needs the protein from at least two successful drives during this critical one-month period, what is their probability of survival?

It is known from past experience that 20 percent of the $n = 15$ drives are successful: $p = 1/5$ and $q = 4/5$. The average number of successful drives per year is

$$\mu = np = 15\left(\frac{1}{5}\right) = 3.0$$

$$\sigma = \sqrt{npq} = \sqrt{15\left(\frac{1}{5}\right)\left(\frac{4}{5}\right)} = 1.55$$

Assuming that at least two successful drives are required for survival, the probability of survival is shown on Fig. 7.7. To find the probability

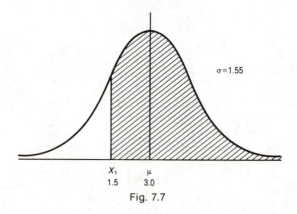

$\sigma = 1.55$

X_1 μ
1.5   3.0

Fig. 7.7

represented by two or more successes ($X_1 = 1.5$), we compute

$$z = \frac{1.5 - 3.0}{1.55} = -0.97$$

This value corresponds to a probability of $p(X \geq 1.5) = 0.8340$ (column B, Table A.3), which represents the probability of survival for any given year. Conversely, the probability of starvation is 0.1660.

Example 7.4

Solve Example 6.2 using the normal approximation.

Although the n is too small in this case for accurate use of the normal approximation, this example provides a useful illustration of the relationship between the binomial method and the normal approximation.

If $p = 1/2$ and $n = 8$, what is the probability that six of eight human burials are female? (Note here that a female burial has been defined as a success.)

$$\mu = np = 8\left(\frac{1}{2}\right) = 4.0$$

$$\sigma = \sqrt{npq} = \sqrt{8\left(\frac{1}{2}\right)\left(\frac{1}{2}\right)} = 1.41$$

From Fig. 7.8 the two values of z are

$$z_1 = \frac{5.5 - 4.0}{1.41} = 1.06$$

$$z_2 = \frac{6.5 - 4.0}{1.41} = 1.77$$

To determine the probability contained between the two values of z, we must first find the area between each z and μ.

$$\text{area 1} = 0.3554, \qquad \text{area 2} = 0.4616$$

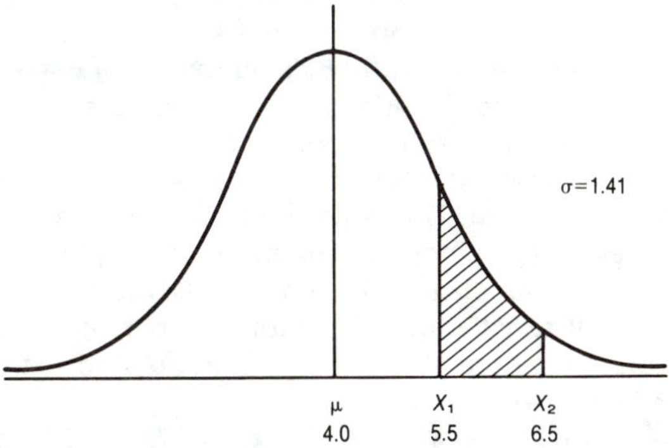

| μ | X_1 | X_2 |
| 4.0 | 5.5 | 6.5 |

Fig. 7.8

So the probability of exactly six female burials is the difference of the respective values of areas:

$$p(X = 6) = (\text{area 2}) - (\text{area 1}) = 0.4616 - 0.3554$$

The probability for this same outcome was determined by the binomial method to be

$$p(X = 6) = \frac{28}{256} = 0.1090$$

The error of approximation in this case is $0.1090 - 0.1062 = 0.0028$. Ordinarily, n should be greater than 30 or so.

7.3 SOME GENERAL PROPERTIES OF THE NORMAL DISTRIBUTION

1. *Normal curves are symmetrical*. Regardless of μ or σ, the left-hand tail of a normal curve is always the mirror image of the right-hand tail. Remember that binomial distributions were symmetrical *only* when $p = q = 1/2$, so it follows that the normal curve best approximates the binomial expansion when p and q are equal.

2. *Normal curves are asymptotic at both ends*. All binomial probability distributions with a finite n have abrupt end points corresponding to the observed range of the frequency distribution (Fig. 7.1). For $n = 3$, for instance, there is no chance of an observation landing outside the four charted outcomes because the binomial is totally self-contained between zero and 3. By contrast, the bell-shaped normal curve never actually touches the x-axis because (in theory) there is no limit to where the data points might fall. The probability of finding a variate under the normal curve becomes increasingly small as one travels farther from the midline, but that probability never equals zero.

3. *The maximum height of the normal curve is at the mean*. Because the normal curve is no more than a graphic statement of probabilities, this is just another way of stating that the most probable—hence in the long run, most frequent—position in the normal distribution is near the mean. The mean, median, and mode of an ideal normal curve are identical.

4. *Areas contained under the normal curve represent probabilities of events*. The various areas contained under any normal curve are readily calculated and tabulated. It should be clear that if the normal curve represents the probability of an event occurring, then the total area contained is equal to unity, the probability of a certain event. This is precisely the same as stating that the sum of the probabilities in the binomial expansion $(q + p)^n$ must equal 1. It also follows that since the normal curve is symmetrical, the area on each side of the mean must represent exactly half of the total probability. The *area* contained under any portion of the normal curve can be interpreted as the probability of a random variate falling within that area.

5. *Distribution of the means of repeated samples will tend to be normally distributed*. According to the Central Limit Theorem, as we will see in Chapter 8,

even if the *variates* of a particular variable are not exactly distributed in normal fashion, the distribution of the *means of repeated samples* of those variates will always be normally distributed (provided the sample sizes are of sufficient size). Because of this property, many sampling experiments can be effectively handled through statistics grounded in normal theory.

7.4 THE NORMAL CURVE AS A CONTINUOUS RANDOM VARIABLE

An interesting collection of fluted projectile points was found at the Witt site, in central California (Riddell and Olsen 1969). Because fluted points are generally found in contexts of extinct fauna (particularly mammoth and extinct bison), it is of interest to know how these projectile points were used in California. Were they attached to thrusting spears (implying large animals such as mammoth and mastodon); were they tips for javelins, perhaps used to dispatch bison; or could they be arrow points, such as were used to hunt bighorn sheep and antelope? No bones were found directly associated with the artifacts, so we will probably never know their exact function, but archaeologists are accustomed to hazarding quasi-educated guesses. In general, spears tend to be rather bulky and heavy, while arrow shafts are thinner and lighter. It is commonly assumed that "artifact width" is the variable which reflects the diameter of the original shaft. Once an archaeologist can determine the type of weapon, he can then limit the choice of possible prey involved. The fluted points from the Witt site have a mean width of $\mu = 2.0$ cm and $\sigma = 0.35$ cm (Riddell and Olsen 1969: table 1).

Suppose that a new fluted point was discovered nearby. Although the general morphology compares well with the Witt site points, the new artifact is only 1.6 cm wide, well below the mean of the artifacts from the Witt site. The width measurements of the original artifacts are variates of a statistical population. This population has a characteristic μ and σ. Is this artifact too narrow to have come from the Witt site?

The situation has been expressed graphically, using a normal probability curve (Fig. 7.9). Just as in the binomial cases, the total area under the curve

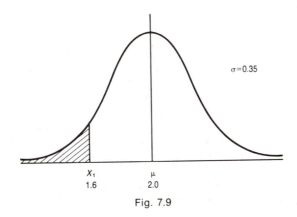

$\sigma = 0.35$

X_1
1.6

μ
2.0

Fig. 7.9

represents a probability of $\Sigma p\,(X = X_i) = 1.00$. We must find the probability that a new variate belongs to this population. The shaded area represents the chances of a $\leqslant 1.6$ cm width occurring. A somewhat similar binomial situation is the case of, say, tossing a coin 15 times. If 13 heads were obtained, should we question whether this is a fair coin (that is, $p \neq q$)? Both the binomial and the normal case ask for the probability of a particularly rare outcome.

But the data from the Witt site artifacts are quite definitely not binomial. Artifact width is not a discrete random variable, and the sampling conditions do not involve a Bernoulli process. Artifact width is a *continuous random variable*.

The random variable X is said to be continuous if the X_i can assume a continuum of values.

Continuous random variables assume a probability distribution which can serve as a model for unknown populations of variates just as do discrete variates. The basic difference between discrete and continuous variables lies in their underlying structure. Discrete variates must fall into countable intervals, as discussed in Chapter 6. But continuous variables lack such intervals (although sometimes crude instruments of measurement impose *artificial* intervals upon continuous data). A comprehensive discussion of the nature of continuous variables is beyond the present scope; to do so requires use of the calculus, which was ruled out of limits for this discussion. The point is that the normal curve per se (instead of an approximation to the binomial) involves a continuous rather than discrete variable. The underlying structure of discrete and continuous random variables is quite different. Fortunately, the calculations involving the normally distributed continuous random variable X are virtually identical to those already considered for the binomial approximation.

Let us continue discussing the Witt site artifacts, keeping in mind that random variable X is now continuously distributed. Since μ and σ are already known, it is only necessary to find the value for X_i in order to compute z. The normal approximation to the binomial required correction for the size of the class interval. The midpoint between three and four heads, for example, was $X_i = 3.5$. But continuous random variables lack such intervals and no correction is necessary. Therefore, $X_i = 1.6$ cm, the *exact* value of the variate in question. The value for z is now found as before:

$$z = \frac{1.6 - 2.0}{0.35} = -1.14$$

The probability corresponding to the smaller area for $z = 1.14$ is found in Table A.3 to be $p\,(X_i < 1.6) = 0.1271$. The statistical conclusion is as follows: If the population of projectile point widths from the Witt site is normally distributed with $\mu = 2.0$ cm and $\sigma = 0.35$, then a randomly selected artifact from that population is expected to have a width of $\leqslant 1.6$ cm fewer than 13 times in 100 trials. That is, a Witt site point will be $\leqslant 1.6$ cm only 12.7 percent of the time in the long run. This probability gives us a basis for judging the new specimen.

Thus, the normal curve is useful both in approximating the discrete binomial and in handling continuous random variables. In practice, the theory underlying each of the two applications is quite different, but the methods of computing the respective probabilities are virtually identical. Two points should be kept in mind:

1. Binomial formulas for mean and standard deviation *cannot be used* for continuous data. It is necessary to apply the general formulas from Chapter 4 to continuous random variables.
2. There is no need to correct the continuous random variate, X_i, for the class midpoint. The continuous random variate in question is always equal to X_i.

Example 7.5

Kelso (1970: 235) has estimated the mean stature of American Indians to be 163.7 cm, with a standard deviation of 5.79 cm.

What proportion of American Indians can be expected to be taller than 165.0 cm? The probability in question is represented by the shaded area in Fig. 7.10:

$$z = \frac{165.0 - 163.7}{5.79} = 0.23$$

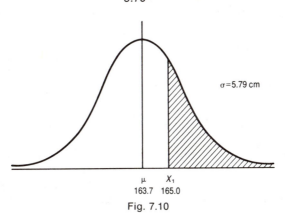

$\sigma = 5.79$ cm

μ X_1
163.7   165.0

Fig. 7.10

The probability in question is found in Table A.3 to be

$$p\,(X > 165) = 0.4090$$

Assuming Kelso's figures as representative, it can be concluded that about 41 percent of all adult American Indians should be taller than 165.0 cm.

Example 7.6

Archaeologists occasionally venture into ethnographic fieldwork in order to establish reliable quantitative estimates for use upon prehistoric data. In one such case, Steven LeBlanc (1971:210) investigated a series of houses in the village of Fasito'otai, western Samoa. LeBlanc found the average total roofed area per person to be $\mu = 13.2$ m^2, with a standard deviation of $\sigma = 6.9\,\mathrm{m}^2$ (Fig. 7.11). Let us assume that the people of Fatsito'otai can be taken as indicative of all people in general; that is, assume that all individuals in all cultures require a similar amount of living space (this is probably a false assumption). Danger Cave, an important archaeological site in western Utah, has a floor area of approximately $18.5 \times 36.5\,\mathrm{m}$ (Jennings 1957). What is the probability that more than 75 people lived simultaneously in Danger Cave?

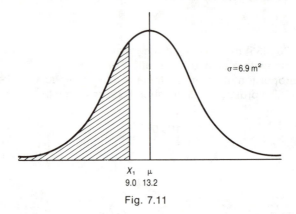

$$\sigma = 6.9\,\mathrm{m}^2$$

$$\begin{array}{cc} X_1 & \mu \\ 9.0 & 13.2 \end{array}$$

Fig. 7.11

The floor area of Danger Cave is $18.5 \times 36.5 = 675.25\,\mathrm{m}^2$. For 75 people to live in Danger Cave at one time, they would require $675.25/75 = 9.0\,\mathrm{m}^2$ per person. We wish to know the probability that the prehistoric Utah population lived with a personal space of $X_1 = 9.0\,\mathrm{m}^2$.

$$z = \frac{9.0 - 13.2}{6.9} = -0.61$$

Assuming the Samoan analogy to be valid, the probability that 75 or more people lived simultaneously in Danger Cave is only 0.2709.

7.5 RELATIONSHIP OF σ TO THE NORMAL CURVE

The standard deviation was said earlier to have a critical relationship to the normal curve. This is why σ is preferable to the mean deviation. We are now in a position to appreciate that importance of σ.

Chapter 4 suggested that two-thirds of all normally distributed variates could be expected to lie within one standard deviation ($\pm\sigma$) of the population mean and about 95 percent of these variates within two standard deviations ($\pm 2\sigma$). Specifically, for a perfectly normal distribution, these proportions are

$\mu \pm \sigma$ contains 68.26% of all variates
$\mu \pm 2\sigma$ contains 95.44% of all variates
$\mu \pm 3\sigma$ contains 99.74% of all variates

Similarly,

50% of all variates fall within $\mu \pm 0.674$
95% of all variates fall within $\mu \pm 1.960$
99% of all variates fall within $\mu \pm 2.575$

These are important proportions because they allow us to generalize about unknown properties or populations. Consider the first proposition in detail—that 68.26 percent of all variates in a normal distribution lie within a single standard deviation of the mean (Fig. 7.12). Normal distributions are always

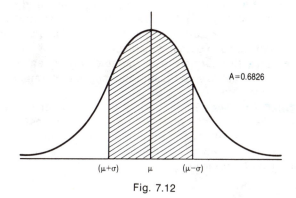

A=0.6826

$(\mu+\sigma)$ μ $(\mu-\sigma)$

Fig. 7.12

symmetrical. If 68.26 percent of the variates fall between $(\mu +\sigma)$ and $(\mu -\sigma)$, then 68.26/2 = 34.13 percent are expected to fall on either side of the mean. The area 0.3413 corresponds to $z = 1.00$ in Table A.3. We know that

$$z = \frac{X_i - \mu}{\sigma}$$

In this case, the quantity $(X_i - \mu)$ can be taken as equal to $z = \sigma/\sigma = 1.00$. This is the same value taken from Table A.3, and we have proved that exactly 68.26 percent of variates lie within $\pm 1\sigma$ of μ in a normally distributed population.

Similar computations establish that approximately 95 percent of the variates fall between $\mu \pm 2\sigma$. In this case, the quantity $(X_i - \mu) = 2$:

$$z = \frac{2\sigma}{\sigma} = 2.00$$

The area corresponding to $z = 2.00$ is found to be 0.4772. Hence, 2(0.4772) = 0.9544, or approximately 95 percent of the variates lie within $\mu \pm 2\sigma$.

7.6 REASONS FOR USING THE NORMAL DISTRIBUTION

This chapter began with the tale of how physicians in the Middle Ages cauterized open wounds with a hot iron. Even though the biological mechanisms were unknown at the time, this practice had the distinct virtue of saving lives. Like the cauterizing treatments during the Middle Ages, the mathematical mechanisms underlying the normal distribution are also poorly understood. The normal curve is a mathematical abstraction which furnishes a convenient probabilistic model to apply to real data; the normal curve model almost never describes the data perfectly. Despite this fact, there are compelling reasons why the normal curve remains critical to modern statistical theory (after Snedecor and Cochran 1967: 35):

1. *Convenience.* Tables of the normal distribution density function (such as Table A.3) are readily available, saving investigators the tedium of continually undertaking similar computations anew.
2. *Goodness of Fit.* Despite the fact that the normal distribution is a mathematical abstraction, many real-world variables are *approximately* normally distributed, including many common biological, demographic, ecological, and archaeological variables.
3. *Transformations.* Nonnormal linear variables can often be converted to approximately normal form by using common transformation procedures (see Chapter 14).
4. *Central Limit Theorem.* Even if variates are not themselves normally distributed, the *means of samples* from those variates do tend toward normality. Because of this important condition, many data involving samples can be efficiently handled using statistics based upon the normal distribution (see Chapter 8).

SUGGESTIONS FOR FURTHER READING

Dixon and Massey (1969: chapter 5). Excellent introduction to the normal curve as a continuous distribution, including discussion of the normal curve equation.

Hays (1973: chapters 7 and 8). Discussion of the properties of the normal curve, with especial attention to examples encountered in social science.

Sokal and Rohlf (1969: chapter 6).

EXERCISES

7.1 Use Table A.3 (Appendix B) to find the area under the normal curve between
   (a) $z = 0.10$ and $z = 0.55$ (b) $z = -0.1$ and $z = 0.1$
   (c) $z = 0.0$ and $z = 1.96$ (d) $z = -1.50$ and $z = 2.00$

7.2 Use the normal approximation to solve Exercise 6.8(a).
   (a) What is the discrepancy between the two answers?
   (b) Which answer is more accurate?

7.3 A random sample of ten adults in a given society is being interviewed by each of 150 ethnologists.
   (a) How many investigators would you expect to report that their sample contained two or fewer female informants? (Use an exact method.)
   (b) Recompute the answer to (a), using an approximation.
   (c) What assumptions are required for each method?

7.4   The frequency of sickle cell anemia in central Africa is known to be about 20 percent. If 20 informants are randomly selected from a village of 450 inhabitants,
   (a) How many different samples could possibly be selected?
   (b) What is the term of the binomial expansion for the probability that exactly 12 of the sampled informants have sickle cell anemia? (Take sickle cell anemia as a "success," as dubious as the procedure might intuitively sound.)
   (c) Use the normal approximation to determine the actual probability in (b).
   (d) What is the probability that 12 or more informants will have sickle cell anemia?
   (e) What is the probability that none of the informants will have sickle cell anemia?

7.5   A sample of three families is to be selected from a community of 13 families.
   (a) Give the number of different samples which could possibly be selected.
   (b) Assuming the sample to be random, what is the probability that a given family will be selected?

7.6   An archaeologist has determined over the years that the average student in an archaeological field course can excavate a 10 cm level in a 1 meter square test unit in about 1.3 hours, with a standard deviation of 15 minutes. What is the probability that a randomly selected student from a field course,
   (a) Takes longer than 1 hour to excavate a single level?
   (b) Takes less than 2 hours?
   (c) Works at least twice as fast as the average?

7.7   Some professors insist on retaining the archaic method of "grading on the curve." One common scheme is as follows:

   A if score exceeds $\mu + 1.5\sigma$
   B if score is between $\mu + 0.5\sigma$ and $\mu + 1.5\sigma$
   C if score is within $\mu \pm 0.5\sigma$
   D if score is between $\mu - 0.5\sigma$ and $\mu - 1.5\sigma$
   F if score is less than $\mu - 1.5\sigma$

   Suppose that this system is rigidly followed in a course of 200 students.
   (a) How many students should receive a "B"?
   (b) How many students should receive passing grades (that is, D or better)?

7.8   The cranial capacity of Olduvai hominid 7 (FLKNN 1) has been estimated from a biparietal endocast to be approximately 657 cc.
   (a) The average cranial capacity of *Homo africanus* is known to be roughly 521 cc, with a standard deviation of 67 (Wolpoff 1969: 183). What is the probability that any member of that population could have a cranial capacity at least as large as that of the Olduvai hominid 7?
   (b) Wolpoff has further estimated the cranial capacity of *Homo erectus* to be 935 cc, with a standard deviation of 132 cc. What is the probability

that a given *Homo erectus* cranium could have a cranial capacity as small as or smaller than FLKNN 1?

7.9 Mendelian genetic theory predicts that crossing two varieties of sweet peas should result in progeny with three times as many purple flowers as white flowers.
   (a) What is the probability that of 100 offspring, at least 85 will have purple flowers?
   (b) What is the probability of obtaining between 15 and 30 white-flowering plants in a sample of 100 progeny?

7.10 A population of 590 variates is known to be normally distributed with a mean of 100. If 300 of them lie between 90 and 110, what is the population standard deviation?

7.11 A normal distribution with mean 50 and standard deviation of 12 is known to have exactly 250 variates between 45 and 60. How large is this population?

7.12 Eveleth (1972) has found that the average stature of Nordestino males in northeastern Brazil is 161.57 cm, with a standard deviation of 6.5 cm.
   (a) What is the coefficient of variation? What does it mean?
   (b) What is the probability that a given informant is taller than 170 cm?

7.13 Wolpoff (1969) has computed that the cranial capacity of *Homo neander-thalensis* averages 1342 cc, with a standard deviation of 169 cc. If cranial capacity is normally distributed,
   (a) What is the probability of finding a Neanderthal cranium with a cranial capacity greater than 1500 cc?
   (b) What is the probability that a given Neanderthal skull has a cranial capacity between 1300 and 1400 cc?
   (c) How many newly discovered Neanderthal crania must be excavated before finding one having a cranial capacity of less than 1200 cc?
   (d) How many skulls must be found before the sample is expected to have three crania with cranial capacities greater than 1600 cc (using a 0.90 level of probability)?

8 Point and Interval Estimation of Means and Variances

● *There is always an easy solution to every human problem—neat, plausible and wrong.*—H. L. Mencken

8.1 INTRODUCTION

Inferential statistics operate by estimating the value of an unknown population parameter from a given sample statistic. Efficacy of particular statistical estimators is judged on two scores: stability and freedom from bias. By *stability* we mean that independent random samples should produce consistent statistics. Of course, since different variates are involved in each sample, the statistics will fluctuate somewhat between samples, but as the sample size increases, the statistics should become more consistent. That is, as n approaches N (the population size), the statistical estimator should approach the parametric value.

Adequate estimators should also be *unbiased.* When statistics are computed from the repeated sampling of a population, the *average* of these estimators should equal the parameter. A statistic is called a *biased estimator* whenever a consistent discrepancy appears between the average of the statistics and the parameter. Sometimes correction factors can satisfactorily compensate for bias in estimation.

These two criteria allow one to measure the performance of conventional statistics. Some statistics are better estimators than others.

8.1.1 Sample Mean

Repeated random sampling experiments have shown that the sample mean $\bar{X}$ is both a stable and an unbiased estimator of the population mean μ. As the sample size (n) approaches N, the probability that $\bar{X}$ differs substantially from μ

approaches zero. This follows from the earlier discussion in Chapter 6 of mathematical expectation of μ.

8.1.2 Sample Median

We intuitively expect the sample median to be the best estimator of the population median, and this is true. Unfortunately, we seldom wish to estimate the population median. Generally, more useful is to note that the sample median is also a good estimator of the population *mean* μ for symmetrical distributions. This is so because the mean, median, and mode must exactly correspond in a distributed normal population. But the sample median is a less efficient estimator of μ than is $\bar{X}$—that is, a relatively larger n is required for a stable estimate—so the sample median is never a first choice to estimate μ. The median is most commonly used in conjunction with *nonparametric* statistical methods (Chapter 12).

8.1.3 Sample Mode

The mode also coincides with the mean in symmetrical populations. But the sample mode is a rather unsavory statistic because of its capricious fluctuations under repeated random sampling. The parametric mode is best estimated by the equation in Theorem 8.1.

Theorem 8.1: Population mode $= \bar{X} - 3(\bar{X} - [\text{sample median}])$
$$= -3(\text{sample median}) - 2\bar{X}.$$

Theorem 8.1 reflects the tendency of medians to lie approximately one-third the distance between the sample mean and mode (see Simpson, Roe, and Lewontin 1960:73 for more discussion of this point). The sample mode is generally computed when only nominal level measurements are available, or when one needs a rapidly computed indicator of central tendency, such as in a preliminary summary of field or laboratory data. The mode is a *quick-and-dirty* estimator of central tendency.

8.1.4 Observed Range

The range of a population depends strictly on the two extreme variates. The probability of randomly selecting both extreme variates in a small sample is slight, so the observed (sample) range fluctuates a great deal under repeated sampling. The observed range is also biased because the two variates are generally less (they cannot be *more*) than the actual population extremes.

8.1.5 Sample Variance

Population variance was defined in Formula (4.8) as

$$\sigma^2 = \frac{\sum_{i=1}^{n} (X_i - \mu)^2}{N}$$

The most obvious estimator, σ^2, would *seem* to be[1]

$$\hat{S}^2 = \frac{\Sigma_{i=1}^{n}(X_i - \bar{X})^2}{n}$$

The estimator $\hat{S}^2$ is computed in a manner identical to the population variance except that sample values were substituted for parameters (that is, $\bar{X}$ replaced μ and n was substituted for N). Similar substitution was used when computing $\bar{X}$ to estimate μ.

Random sampling experiments show $\hat{S}^2$ to be a biased statistic, consistently underestimating the true σ^2. This bias can be corrected by substituting $(n-1)$ for n in the denominator, so the *best estimator of the population variance* is defined as

$$S^2 = \frac{\Sigma_{i=1}^{n}(X_i - \bar{X})^2}{n-1}$$

This expression, using $(n-1)$ in the denominator, was introduced earlier to define sample variance (Formula 4.9). As n increases, the difference between S^2 and $\hat{S}^2$ becomes negligible,[2] but Formula (4.9) is preferred to estimate σ^2 because it is unbiased, even in small samples. S^2 is referred to here as "sample variance," but remember that the formula differs slightly from population variance, since S^2 was derived to provide the best estimate of σ^2.

8.2 DISTRIBUTION OF THE SAMPLE MEAN

● *Plus Ultra* (translation: More Beyond)—Motto of King Charles V, Emperor of Holy Roman Empire

Section 8.1 suggested that statistical estimators can be rated in terms of overall stability and unbiased results. Let us illustrate this with scores from the Scholastic Aptitude Test (SAT), a standard college entrance examination. The SAT has been designed so that the population of student scores is normally distributed, with $\mu = 500$ and $\sigma = 100$. If the test scores for 1976 form a population, random samples of any size can be generated. The participating students could be sequentially numbered, for instance, and then a sample selected from a random-number table. Or each score could be recorded on

[1]The accent on $\hat{S}$ in the expression $\hat{S}^2$, called a *circumflex*, is often used in statistics to signify estimators. The expression $\hat{S}^2$ is generally read "S hat squared."

[2]Some statistics books do not correct the sample variance for unbiased estimation (S^2 is defined as $\hat{S}^2$). Although a good case can be made for either approach, the $(n-1)$ formula was selected here because it more closely follows the logic of statistical inference. In fact, only rarely are social scientists interested in sample values per se; rather, the emphasis is usually upon estimating parametric values. At any rate, sample variance computed as $\hat{S}^2$ (with n as the divisor) can readily be converted by the term $(n/(n-1))$:

$$\hat{S}^2 \left(\frac{n}{n-1}\right) = S^2$$

You should be sure, whenever computing a standard deviation, to explicitly state whether the denominator is n or $n-1$.

discs, placed in a large urn, well mixed, and then withdrawn one by one until the proper sample size is reached. This method is, of course, the technique by which random numbers are generated in the devastating *Keno* games of Reno and Las Vegas.[3]

Section 8.1.1 suggested that $\bar{X}$ is the best estimator of μ, but of course $\bar{X}$ will only rarely exactly equal μ. Neither will the sample variance exactly correspond to σ^2 because most populations have too much variability for such precise results. But as long as sample size is satisfactorily large, then we can expect both $\bar{X}$ and S^2 rather closely to *approximate* the parameters. The larger the sample size, the better the approximation.

Two distinct distributions are involved here. First there is the initial *distribution of variates within the population*. The original distribution in this case includes all individual SAT scores for 1976. These variates are normally distributed and characterized by μ and σ^2 [Fig. 8.1(a)]. But there is also the *distribution of variates within a single sample*, consisting of n randomly selected variates characterized by $\bar{X}$ and S^2 [Fig. 8.1(b)].

Suppose now that more than one sample is drawn from the population of SAT scores. Let us fix the sample size at, say, $n = 50$, and draw several different samples from the thousands of SAT scores in the original population. An infinite number of such samples could be selected from this population. Each individual sample mean can be assigned a subscripted symbol ($\bar{X}_1, \bar{X}_2, \bar{X}_3 \cdots$) and each sample variance could be similarly distinguished ($S_1^2, S_2^2, S_3^2 \cdots$). Because the population of SAT scores for 1976 consists of thousands of variates, repeated selection of random samples of size $n = 50$ undoubtedly involves different variates in each sample. The sample mean and variance will fluctuate somewhat from sample to sample. We can now construct a *third* distribution, using the independent sample means of size n as variates. This new population, called the *distribution of sample means*, is characterized by two new parameters: the mean of the sample means ($\mu_{\bar{x}}$) and the variance of the sample means ($\sigma_{\bar{x}}^2$). This third distribution is quite distinct from either (1) the original population of variates or (2) the distribution of individual variates within a sample of size n. The distribution of sample means no longer considers the original variates as such; the sample means are themselves variates. Figure 8.1 illustrates the configuration of the three distributions.

Consider a useful theorem about the distribution of sample means.[4]

Theorem 8.2: If random samples of size n are repeatedly drawn from a normally distributed population with mean μ and variance σ^2, then the sampling distribution of sample means will also be normal, with

$$\text{mean } \mu_{\bar{x}} = \mu \quad \text{ and } \quad \text{variance } \sigma_{\bar{x}}^2 = \sigma^2/n.$$

[3]Generating truly random samples is a tricky business. The most *expeditious* sample technique in the case of SAT scores would be simply to include all scores from a particular classroom or a given school, or perhaps from an entire school district. But such "ready made" samples have built into them serious biases of socioeconomic class, relative degree of preparation, and a general regional component. Only by true random sampling procedures can we expect to obtain a satisfactorily unbiased sample. The complex topic of sampling is considered in more detail in Chapter 15.

[4]The derivation and proof of this theorem are beyond the present scope, but the interested reader is referred to Hays (1973: 278–279).

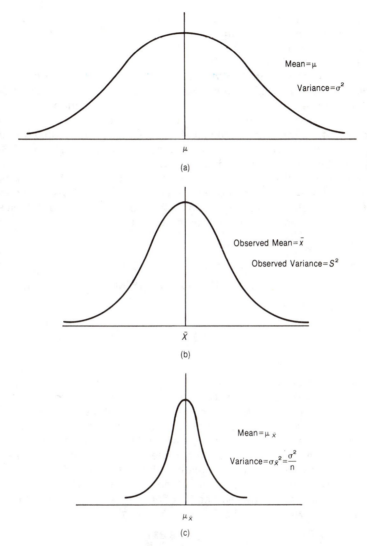

Fig. 8.1 (a) Population of initial variates; (b) variates within a single sample; (c) distribution of sample means.

Expression $\sigma_{\bar{x}}$ in Theorem 8.2 is called the *standard error of the mean.* In effect, the standard error is the standard deviation of the distribution of sample means.

This is an important generalization which tells us that means of random samples from a normal population form a *new* distribution which is itself normally distributed. Secondly, we know that the mean of the population of original variates is equal to mean of the population of sample means—that is, μ. Theorem 8.2 also validates our intuitive feeling that the larger the sample size, the better is the variance estimate. When only a single variate is selected (when the sample size is $n = 1$), the variance is($\sigma_{\bar{x}}^2 = \sigma^2/n = \sigma^2$). But increase the sample size to, say, $n = 3$, and the variance of the sampling distribution is decreased by one-third ($\sigma_{\bar{x}}^2 = \sigma^2/3$). If $n = 10$, then the variance becomes $\sigma_{\bar{x}}^2 = \sigma^2/10$. As the sample size increases until $n = N$, then $\sigma_{\bar{x}}^2 = 0$ and $\mu_{\bar{x}} = \mu$ for a finite population. The sample in this case is reduced to a single variate, $\bar{X} = \mu$, and single variates have no variance at all. We can better examine the implications of Theorem 8.2 and the distribution of sample means through an example.

Section 4.4.5 introduced a statistical population of $N = 99$ breadth measurements of the first lower molar of the pygmy chimpanzee (Table 4.7). Suppose that 26 students in a physical anthropology seminar were assigned to study the molars in this collection. Each student was instructed to randomly (and independently) select two skulls from the collection of 99 skulls, measure the breadth of the right M_1 and then compute the proper descriptive statistics for his sample. One student's worksheet might appear as follows:

Variates

Molar of skull 1: $X_1 = 8.7$ mm

Molar of skull 2: $X_2 = 9.1$ mm

Descriptive Statistics

$n = 2$

$\bar{X} = 8.9$ mm

$S^2 = 0.08$ mm²

The instructor then added subscripts to each student's worksheet in order to distinguish the work of student No. 1 from that of student No. 2, and so forth. Thus, with 26 students participating in the seminar, there would be a total of 26 sample means computed, each based upon independent samples of $n = 2$; $\bar{X}_1, \bar{X}_2, \bar{X}_3 \cdots \bar{X}_{25}, \bar{X}_{26}$. We can now ignore the 99 original variates (the X_i) and consider only these sample means computed by the seminar participants. The students have sampled a new population, the distribution of sample means of size $n = 2$. Theorem 8.2 tells us the mean of the original variates. Using the empirical results computed earlier (Section 4.4.5), we find the mean of the distribution of size $n = 2$ to be

$$\mu_{\bar{x}} = \mu = 8.83 \text{ mm}$$

Theorem 8.2 also indicates that the variance of the distribution of sample means decreases as the sample size increases. For $n = 2$,

$$\sigma_{\bar{x}}^2 = \frac{\sigma^2}{n} = \frac{0.230}{2} = 0.115 \text{ mm}^2$$

These parameters characterize the infinitely large distribution of sample means from samples of size $n = 2$.

The results of the seminar's laboratory exercise appear in Table 8.1.[5] Note

[5]These results were actually obtained by simple random-number simulation. Each of the original tooth measurements was assigned a number from 1 to 99. Twenty-six random samples of size $n = 2$ were then selected from a table of random digits. Simulations such as this are commonplace in

TABLE 8.1

mm	Distribution of Original Variates N = 99	Distribution of Sample Means n = 2	n = 5	n = 20
7.7	|			
7.8				
7.9	||			
8.0	||||			
8.1	|||	||		
8.2	⅃⅃|			
8.3	||			
8.4	||||	|||	|	
8.5	⅃⅃ |||	||	||	
8.6	||||	||||	|||	|
8.7	⅃⅃ |||	||	||	||
8.8	⅃⅃ |||		|||	⅃⅃ ||||
8.9	⅃⅃ |||	||||	|||	⅃⅃ |
9.0	⅃⅃	|	⅃⅃ |	⅃⅃ |
9.1	||||	|	||	||
9.2	⅃⅃ ||	|||	|||	
9.3	⅃⅃ |||| |	||	|	
9.4	⅃⅃	||		
9.5	||||			
9.6	||			
9.7	||			
9.8	|			

how the distribution of the sample means is less dispersed than the original distribution of variates, exactly as Theorem 8.2 predicts. The variance decreases as n increases. The observed value of $S_{\bar{x}}^2 = 0.148$ mm^2 falls reasonably close to the parametric value of $\sigma_{\bar{x}}^2 = 0.155$ mm^2. The mean of the 26-sample means is 8.80 mm, a reasonable estimate of the parametric mean $\mu_{\bar{x}} = 8.83$ mm.

Suppose now that each student is assigned to study five skulls rather than just two. The sample size has now been increased from $n = 2$ to $n = 5$. We know that the parametric mean is independent of sample size (Theorem 8.2), so the mean of the distribution of sample means for $n = 5$ must remain as before: $\mu_{\bar{x}} = \mu = 8.83$ mm. The variance of the new population is

$$\sigma_{\bar{x}}^2 = \frac{\sigma^2}{n} = \frac{0.230}{5} = 0.045 \text{ mm}^2$$

The results of this second sampling have been simulated and tabulated in Table

sampling experiments and provide us with an easy method of determining sample means and variances. The approximations would become better, of course, as the number of samples increased. Be certain to distinguish between the *number of samples* (in this case, the 26 seminar students) and *sample size*, which is $n = 2$.

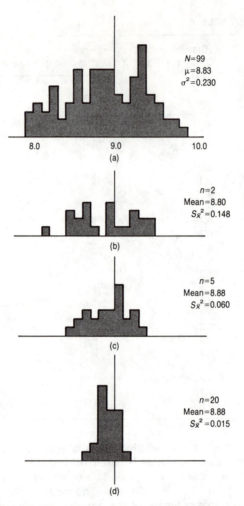

Fig. 8.2 Distribution of sample means for original population of 99 skull measurements.

8.1. The sample mean changes only slightly with an increase in sample size, but the variance of the sample means decreases significantly and falls quite close to the parameter ($S_{\bar{x}}^2 = 0.060$ mm^2). This smaller variance is expected because σ^2 is divided by 5 rather than by only 2.

Finally, each student was assigned to measure M$_1$ on 20 different skulls. The population mean again remains constant and the parametric variance decreases to

$$\sigma_{\bar{x}}^2 = \frac{\sigma^2}{n} = \frac{0.230}{20} = 0.012$$

The frequency distribution of size $n = 20$ for 26 students is presented in Table 8.1, and once again the sample mean and variance closely approximate their respective parameters.

The frequency histogram for the original 99 variates has been plotted in Fig. 8.2, along with the distributions of sample means of sizes 2, 5, and 20. Note how closely these three means correspond to the original population mean as predicted by Theorem 8.1. Note further that as n increases, the dispersion of the sample means about μ decreases. That is, the variability between the various measures of $\bar{X}$ decreases as the sample size becomes larger, and the sampling distribution appears more clumped. So, the larger the sample, the less likely are extreme values of the sample means. Theorem 8.2 tells us not only that $\sigma_{\bar{x}}^2$ becomes smaller as n increases, but also *how much smaller*: Since $\sigma_{\bar{x}}^2 = \sigma^2/n$, the variance decreases in a manner exactly and inversely proportional to the sample size.

The distribution of the sample means is important in statistics because it provides a new method for computing the probability of specific events. The z-values were used to this point only to determine the probabilities associated with selecting a single variate from a population. To find the probability of exactly 25 heads in 30 tosses of a coin, for instance, observations were first converted to z-scores, and the associated area was determined from Table A.3 (Appendix B). The distribution of sample means provides a similar technique for finding the probability of selecting an *entire sample*. But to do this, the standardized normal deviate requires slight redefinition:

$$z = \frac{\bar{X} - \mu}{\sigma_{\bar{x}}} \qquad (8.1)$$

The underlying structure of the z remains unchanged, but $\bar{X}$ (sample mean) has been substituted for X_i (the original variates) and $\sigma_{\bar{x}}$ inserted for σ, where $\sigma_{\bar{x}} = \sigma/\sqrt{n}$. This value of $\sigma_{\bar{x}}$ follows directly from Theorem 8.2. This modification of the z-statistic can be used to enter Table A.3 to find areas contained under specific portions of the normal curve. The normal curve in this case represents the distribution of the sample means.

The following examples illustrate in detail how Theorem 8.2 is useful in statistical hypothesis testing.

Example 8.1

We know that !Kung Bushmen adults work an average of 2.2 days per week, with a standard deviation of about 0.72 day per week (data from Lee 1969: table IV).

(a) What is the probability that a particular, randomly selected !Kung adult will work more than 2.5 days during a given week?

This probability involves a single variate. Let X (Fig. 8.3) represent the normally distributed random variable "individual work week." The probability of a single !Kung working more than 2.5 days is given by the area to the right of $X_i = 2.5$ days, assuming that the individual work week is normally distributed. The value of $X_i = 2.5$ is first standardized:

$$z = \frac{X_i - \mu}{\sigma} = \frac{2.5 - 2.2}{0.72} = 0.42$$

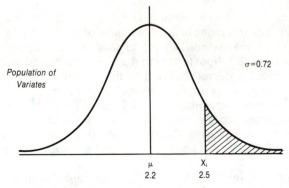

Fig. 8.3 Population of variates.

The probability associated with this event is found to be $p(X \geq 2.5) = 0.3372$. We can expect only about one !Kung in three to work 2.5 days or more in a given week. (Nothing in this procedure departs from methods discussed in Chapter 7.)

(b) A single waterhole has been randomly selected from the set of all !Kung waterholes. What is the probability that the 31 resident adults of this waterhole will, *as a group*, average more than 2.5 days of work on this given week?

This is a very different question from that considered in (a) above, in which a single variate (the work week) of one randomly selected adult was considered. But the present probability considers a *mean selected from the theoretical population of means of samples of size* $n = 31$, in Fig. 8.4.

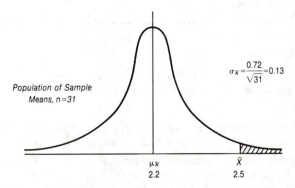

Fig. 8.4 Population of Sample Means, $n = 31$.

The mean of this theoretical population is as before, $\mu_{\bar{x}} = \mu = 2.2$, but the variance is now $\sigma_{\bar{x}}$.

The random variable is now $\bar{X} = 2.5$, which is standardized to z by

Expression (8.1):

$$z = \frac{\bar{X} - \mu_{\bar{x}}}{\sigma_{\bar{x}}} = \frac{2.5 - 2.2}{0.13} = 2.31$$

$$A = 0.0104$$

The curve for the distribution of sample means is markedly less dispersed than the curve for the distribution of raw variates. This is so because the standard deviation of the population of sample means has been divided by $\sqrt{n}$ (Theorem 8.2). The area for the region to the right of $\bar{X} = 2.5$ (and hence the associated probability) is notably smaller. In other words, a single variate, X, can be expected to fluctuate much more than a mean, $\bar{X}$, of a sample of size $n = 31$.

Example 8.2

At one archaeological site, projectile points are known to have a mean weight of 4.3 grams, with $\sigma = 1.44$ grams. These figures are based upon previous excavation.

What is the probability that a random sample of 50 points excavated the next year from this site will average less than 3.5 grams?

The weights of the original batch of artifacts from this site is considered a population. We assume that these variates are normally distributed. We are asked to consider a subsequent random sample of size $n = 50$, for which $\bar{X} \leq 3.5$ grams (Fig. 8.5). The random variate $\bar{X} = 3.5$ is first stan-

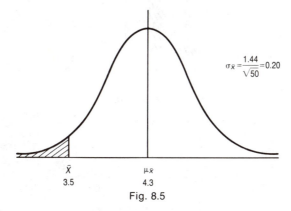

$$\sigma_{\bar{x}} = \frac{1.44}{\sqrt{50}} = 0.20$$

$$\begin{array}{cc} \bar{X} & \mu_{\bar{x}} \\ 3.5 & 4.3 \end{array}$$

Fig. 8.5

dardized to a z-score:

$$z = \frac{\bar{X} - \mu_{\bar{x}}}{\sigma_{\bar{x}}} = \frac{3.5 - 4.3}{0.20} = -4.00$$

From Table A.3 we find the probability of this event to be $p(\bar{X} \leq 3.5) < 0.0001$. The chances of getting a new sample weighing this little are virtually nil.

Example 8.3

The mean stature of Eskimos is known to be 162.80 cm, with $\sigma = 3.04$ cm (from Kelso 1970:237).

(a) What are the chances that a certain band of 35 adult Central Eskimos average between 162.0 and 163.0 cm tall? We assume the band represents a random pick from all Eskimo bands of size 35 and that stature is normally distributed.

Given the parameters for all Eskimo bands, Theorem 8.2 leads us to expect that stature for a single band of size $n = 35$ is

$$\mu_{\bar{X}} = \mu = 162.80 \text{ cm}$$

$$\sigma_{\bar{X}} = \frac{3.04}{\sqrt{35}} = 0.51$$

The problem is to determine the likelihood of a random $\bar{X}$ falling between $\bar{X}_1 = 162.0$ cm and $\bar{X}_2 = 163.0$ cm (Fig. 8.6). These two sample means must

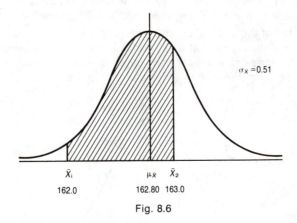

$\sigma_{\bar{X}} = 0.51$

$\bar{X}_1$ $\mu_{\bar{X}}$ $\bar{X}_2$

162.0   162.80   163.0

Fig. 8.6

first be standardized:

$$z_1 = \frac{\bar{X}_1 - \mu}{\sigma_{\bar{X}}} = \frac{162.0 - 162.80}{0.51} = \frac{-0.80}{0.51} = -1.57$$

$$z_2 = \frac{\bar{X}_2 - \mu}{\sigma_{\bar{X}}} = \frac{163.0 - 162.80}{0.51} = \frac{0.20}{0.51} = 0.39$$

From Table A.3 we find the area between μ and standardized $\bar{X}_1$ to be 0.4418 and the area between standardized $\bar{X}_2$ and μ to be 0.1517. Hence, the probability of a mean stature falling between 162.0 and 163.0 cm is

$$p(162 \le X \le 163) = (\text{area 1}) + (\text{area 2})$$

$$= 0.4418 + 0.1517 = 0.5935$$

(b) For the population of all Eskimos, how large a sample must be taken if the standard error of the mean height is to be 0.20 cm?

Remembering that the standard error was defined as $\sigma_{\bar{x}} = \sigma/\sqrt{n}$, we find

$$n = \left(\frac{\sigma}{\sigma_{\bar{x}}}\right)^2 = \left(\frac{3.04}{0.20}\right)^2 = 231 \text{ Eskimos}$$

8.3 THE CENTRAL LIMIT THEOREM

Theorem 8.2 is a potent tool for assessing the probability that a given sample could have been drawn from a certain statistical population. Theorem 8.2 made two critical assumptions:

1. The original variates must be randomly selected (and hence independent of one another).
2. The population of original variates (the X_i) must be normally distributed.

Note that these assumptions were explicitly stated in each application in Section 8.2.

Now that you are familiar with Theorem 8.2, *forget it*. We have to consider an even more important proposition, which surpasses Theorem 8.2 altogether.

Theorem 8.3—The Central Limit Theorem. If random samples are repeatedly drawn from a population with finite mean μ and variance σ^2, the sampling distribution of the standardized sample means will be normally distributed with $\mu_{\bar{x}} = \mu$ and variance $\sigma_{\bar{x}}^2 = \sigma^2/n$. The approximation becomes more accurate as n becomes larger.

It is difficult to overestimate the usefulness of the Central Limit Theorem (CLT) in statistical inference. Although the wording of the CLT appears superficially similar to that of Theorem 8.2, there is one important difference: Nowhere does the Central Limit Theorem specify that the original population of X_i variates must be normally distributed. The theorem refers to standardized means, the distribution of $(\bar{X} - \mu_x)/\sigma_{\bar{x}}$ being approximately normal. *Regardless of the shape or form of a population distribution, the distribution of the randomly selected sample means approaches a normal distribution as n increases.* We therefore behave as if $\bar{X}$ is approximately normal with mean μ_x and variance $\sigma_{\bar{x}}^2$, as long as n is large. This remarkable property of samples was first recognized by the French mathematician Laplace in 1812, and normal distributions are often called *Laplace distributions*.

● *You can learn more from the dead than from the living, if only because there are so many more of them.* —A. Gingrich

Proof of the CLT is far beyond the scope of this discussion, but a simple sampling experiment should illustrate both the properties and the significance

194

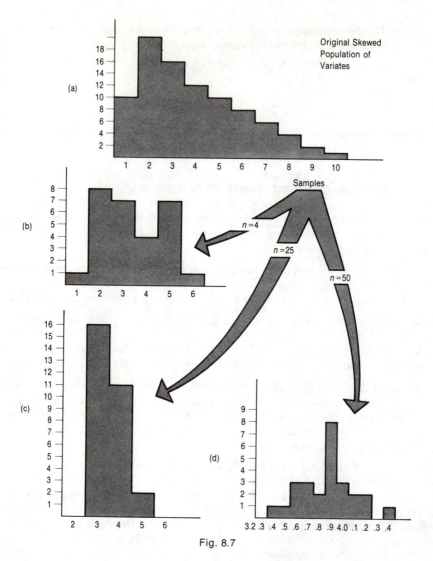

Fig. 8.7

of the Central Limit Theorem.[6] Consider the population of 88 variates [Fig. 8.7(a)] with $\mu = 3.90$ and $\sigma = 2.2106$. The CLT tells us that repeated random sampling should produce standardized sample means which are normally distributed even though the distribution is obviously skewed to the right (and therefore not normal). The parametric mean of all possible sample means of size n is known to be $\mu_{\bar{x}} = \mu$, and the variance[7] is $\sigma_{\bar{x}}^2 = \sigma^2/n$.

[6]Proof of the Central Limit Theorem can be found in Cramér (1946: 213–218).
[7]Since the distribution of Fig. 8.7(a) is taken as a population, σ^2 is computed with N rather than $(N-1)$ in the denominator, as suggested earlier. The difference between σ^2 and S^2 is rather slight $(4.9431 - 4.8869 = 0.0562)$ because N is 88. For smaller populations, this difference becomes more serious.

A sampling experiment will illustrate how Theorem 8.3 works on a nonnormal population of variates. Each of the $N = 88$ variates was written on a small metal-rimmed archaeological specimen tag, placed in a large bowl, and well stirred. Students from my introductory course on quantitative methods at The City College of New York drew random samples of these tags and recorded their results. Each tag was then returned to the bowl and the contents well mixed prior to the next selection.

The first student drew samples of size $n = 4$ and the results appear on the histogram of Fig. 8.7(b). Each of the 28 different samples is characterized by a mean ($\bar{X}_1, \bar{X}_2 \cdots \bar{X}_{25}$) which becomes, in effect, a variate of the random variable X. The mean and standard deviation of the means can be compared with the parametric value predicted by Theorem 8.3.

Parameter (expected)	Statistic (observed)
$\mu_{\bar{x}} = \mu = 3.90$	$\dfrac{\sum_{i=1}^{25} X_i}{25} = 3.73$
$\sigma_{\bar{x}} = \dfrac{\sigma}{\sqrt{n}} = \dfrac{2.21}{\sqrt{4}}$	$S_{\bar{x}} = 1.27$
$= 1.11$	

While the resulting histogram is not normal, the radical skewness of the original population has disappeared even with the small sample size of $n = 4$.

The CLT tells us that an increased sample size should render the frequency histogram even more normal. A second student was then asked to select samples of size $n = 25$ from the bowl of 88 variates.

Parameter (expected)	Statistic (observed)
$\mu_{\bar{x}} = \mu = 3.90$	$\dfrac{\sum_{i=1}^{25} \bar{X}_i}{25} = 3.93$
$\sigma_{\bar{x}} = \dfrac{2.21}{\sqrt{25}} = 0.44$	$S_{\bar{x}} = 0.55$

Note that the histogram for $n = 25$ [Fig. 8.7(c)] has become considerably more symmetrical.

Finally, a third student was asked to draw samples of size $n = 50$:

Parameter (expected)	Statistic (observed)
$\mu_{\bar{x}} = \mu = 3.90$	$\dfrac{\sum_{i=1}^{25} \bar{X}_i}{25} = 3.87$
$\sigma_{\bar{x}} = \dfrac{2.21}{\sqrt{50}} = 0.31$	$S_{\bar{x}} = 0.23$

Note once again [Fig. 8.7(d)] the close correspondence between the randomly generated sample values and those parameters implied by the Central Limit Theorem. Even with the relatively small number of samples drawn, the distribution of sample means rapidly approaches normality in these experiments, and the sample statistics estimate the appropriate parameters quite respectably (be certain not to confuse the number of samples, 25 in this case, with the sample size *n*).

A similar sampling experiment was conducted with a *rectangular* distribution of variates (Fig. 8.8). Students selected sample sizes of 4, 25, and 50 as before, and these samples again illustrate the validity of the CLT on remarkably nonnormal distributions. As expected, an increase in sample size produces a decreased variance and a progressive normality in the frequency histogram.

The overall significance of the CLT is really twofold. For one thing, Theorem 8.3 applies to *all sums*, not just the sample means (which are really themselves

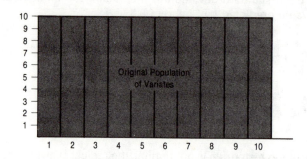

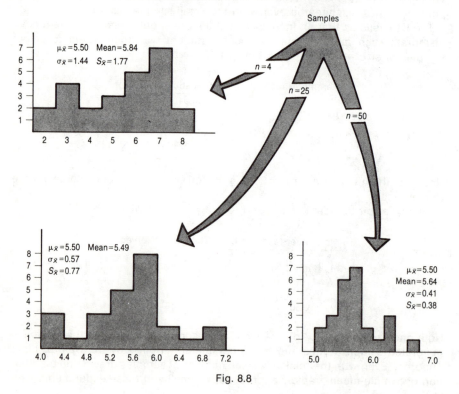

Fig. 8.8

sums, divided by n). This seems to explain in part why so many real-world measurements tend to be distributed in normal fashion (Mendenhall 1971: 154). *Human stature* is one example of a common anthropological variable known to follow a normal distribution.

It is possible to imagine that any particular informant's stature comprises hundreds of smaller, related measurements—cranial height, cervical vertebral height, length of femur, and so forth, each of which is itself subject to variability and has its own sampling distribution. Therefore, since human stature is really the sum of hundreds of individual random variables, stature should be subject to the conditions set forth in the Central Limit Theorem. The fact that the CLT holds for all sums explains in large measure why many of the common anthropological variables (such as time, distance, weight, temperature, and brightness) tend to exhibit an approximately normal distribution.

A second more significant aspect of the CLT is that many common *statistics* are themselves sums or simple averages. When this is the case, and when sample size is sufficiently large, Theorem 8.3 allows one to proceed, using the mechanics of the normal distribution. Thus the CLT tells us that we need not be overly concerned whether X is normally distributed as long as we are directly involved with the distribution of $\bar{X}$ or similar statistics. It is the tremendous versatility of the CLT that justifies the efforts expended upon the normal distribution by mathematical statisticians.

> ● *It's a little like the story that ran around the Viennese coffeehouses about Freud's great success with the man who was a bedwetter. What, he cured him of that? Well, no, the man still wet the bed. But he stopped feeling guilty about it.—* A. Gingrich

8.4 SAMPLING DISTRIBUTION OF THE DIFFERENCE BETWEEN SAMPLE MEANS

Practical situations often require comparison between two population means, when *neither* is known. To this point, we have assumed that at least *one* of the two means is known. Suppose that we wish to test for a difference in stature between two skeletal series. This comparison must be based upon an estimation of two parametric means because each series represents a single sample selected from a hypothetical population of similar samples. The two population means can be denoted by μ_X and μ_Y and the variances by σ_X^2 and σ_Y^2. The sample sizes are n_X and n_Y, respectively. In computing the statures of the two samples, we are actually testing the hypothesis that $\mu_X - \mu_Y = 0$. We are testing, in effect, whether or not these two samples could have been selected from the same statistical population.

We know from Theorem 8.3 that the mean of the sample means for each population is

$$\mu_{\bar{x}} = \mu_X \quad \text{and} \quad \mu_{\bar{y}} = \mu_Y$$

But we are now dealing with a new population, the population consisting of the *difference between the two sample means.* It can be established that the population mean of the difference between sample means is

$$\mu_{X-Y} = \mu_{\bar{X}} - \mu_{\bar{Y}} = \mu_X - \mu_Y \qquad (8.2)$$

Formula 8.2 tells us that the difference between two statistical populations can be estimated by the difference in stature between the individual population means.

Estimating the *variance* of this new distribution is a more difficult situation. It would seem intuitively that combining two varying populations would create a new population which is more variable than either of the original populations. That is, each of the original populations contributes a portion of its variability to the new population's variance. A theorem of mathematical statistics confirms this intuitive suspicion: The variance of either the *sum* or the *difference* of two independent random variables is equal to the *sum of their respective variances*:

$$\sigma^2_{X+Y} = \sigma_X^2 + \sigma_Y^2$$
$$\sigma^2_{X-Y} = \sigma_X^2 + \sigma_Y^2$$

The variance of the resulting population is the sum of the original variances, regardless of whether the two original variables are added or subtracted. It follows that the variance of the difference between means is the sum of the variances of the two sample means:

$$\sigma_{\bar{X}-\bar{Y}}^2 = \sigma_{\bar{X}}^2 + \sigma_{\bar{Y}}^2 \qquad (8.3)$$

where

$$\sigma_{\bar{X}}^2 = \sigma_X^2/n_X \qquad \text{and} \qquad \sigma_{\bar{Y}}^2 = \sigma_Y^2/n_Y$$

There has been no stipulation that the samples be of the same size. All that is required is that the two samples be statistically independent.[8] Furthermore, the Central Limit Theorem tells us that the difference between means approaches a normal distribution as n becomes sufficiently large. This is true even if the original populations are not themselves normally distributed.

In order to utilize the distribution of the difference of sample means for hypothesis-testing, the standardized normal deviate must again be redefined. By substituting Expressions (8.2) and (8.3),

$$z = \frac{(\bar{X} - \bar{Y}) - \mu_{\bar{X}-\bar{Y}}}{\sigma_{\bar{X}-\bar{Y}}}$$

Expression (8.4) is illustrated in the following examples.

Example 8.4

It is known that Indians of the American Southwest tend on the average to be taller than Eskimos, and Kelso (1970: 237) reports that the southwest-

---

[8]Although these expressions are given in terms of *variances*, it is often necessary to use the *standard deviation* form in computation, which is simply the square root of Expression 8.3.

$$\sigma_{\bar{X}-\bar{Y}} = \sqrt{\sigma_{\bar{X}}^2 + \sigma_{\bar{Y}}^2}$$

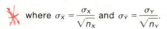 where $\sigma_{\bar{X}} = \dfrac{\sigma_X}{\sqrt{n_X}}$ and $\sigma_{\bar{Y}} = \dfrac{\sigma_Y}{\sqrt{n_Y}}$.

ern groups have a mean stature of 168.87 cm with a standard deviation of 3.80 cm.

What is the probability that the sample mean of a random sample of 50 southwestern Indians is at least 8.0 cm taller than the sample mean of an independent random sample of 35 Eskimos?

We know from Example 8.3 that the mean stature for Eskimos is 162.80 cm, with a standard deviation of 3.04 cm. Denoting the random variable "Eskimo stature" as X and "southwestern stature" as Y, the difference between the two population means, $\mu_{\bar{X}-\bar{Y}}$, is estimated by $(\bar{X} - \bar{Y})$:

$$\bar{X} - \bar{Y} = 162.80 - 168.87 = -6.07 \; cm$$

This figure represents the expected difference between the means of the two populations. Finding the standard deviation of this mean is a bit more tedious. We know that

$$\sigma_X = 3.04, \qquad \sigma_Y = 3.80, \qquad n_X = 35, \qquad n_Y = 50$$

The standard errors can be then computed:

$$\sigma_{\bar{X}} = \frac{\sigma_X}{\sqrt{n_X}} = \frac{3.04}{\sqrt{35}} = 0.51 \; cm$$

$$\sigma_{\bar{Y}} = \frac{\sigma_Y}{\sqrt{n_Y}} = \frac{3.80}{\sqrt{50}} = 0.54 \; cm$$

The standard error of the difference between the means is

$$\sqrt{\frac{x\sigma^2}{n} + \frac{y\sigma^2}{m}} \; \eqsim \qquad \sigma_{\bar{X}-\bar{Y}} = \sqrt{\sigma_{\bar{X}}^2 + \sigma_{\bar{Y}}^2} = \sqrt{0.51^2 + 0.54^2}$$

$$= \sqrt{0.5517} = 0.743$$

The observed difference between sample means (Fig. 8.9) can now be standardized:

$$z = \frac{(\bar{X} - \bar{Y}) - \mu_{\bar{X}-\bar{Y}}}{\sigma_{\bar{X}-\bar{Y}}} = \frac{-8.00 - (-6.07)}{0.743}$$

$$= -2.60$$

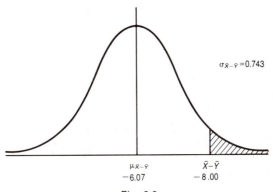

$\sigma_{\bar{X}-\bar{Y}} = 0.743$

$\mu_{\bar{X}-\bar{Y}}$
-6.07

$\bar{X}-\bar{Y}$
-8.00

Fig. 8.9

From Table A.3 we find that $p([\bar{X} - \bar{Y}] \geq 8.0) = 0.0049$. There are fewer than 5 in 1000 chances that the difference in stature between the Eskimo and southwestern samples will be 8.00 cm or more. Because of Theorem 8.3, there has been no need to assume normality.

Example 8.5

A large eastern university reported the following IQ scores for 1976:

Physical Science majors: $\mu_x = 126.0$, $\sigma_x = 20.0$
Social Science majors: $\mu_y = 120.0$, $\sigma_y = 25.0$

If an introductory anthropology course has 35 physical science majors and 70 social science majors, what is the probability that the average IQ for social science students is at least five points below the average for the physical scientists? (We must assume here that the anthropology class contains independent random samples of physical and social science majors.)

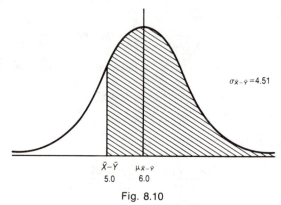

Fig. 8.10

The standard error in the difference between means (Fig. 8.10) is

$$\sigma_{\bar{X}-\bar{Y}} = \sqrt{\frac{20^2}{35} + \frac{25^2}{70}} = \sqrt{20.36} = 4.51$$

The difference between sample means is standardized to a z-score:

$$z = \frac{5.0 - 6.0}{4.51} = 0.22$$

Table A.3 indicates that the area corresponding to $z = 0.22$ is 0.0871. The overall probability that the social science sample will score at least five points below the sample of physical scientists is

$$p([\bar{X} - \bar{Y}] > 5.0) = 0.0871 + 0.5000 = 0.5871$$

8.5 CONFIDENCE INTERVALS ABOUT THE SAMPLE MEAN

Analysis of the normal distribution can thus indicate whether or not a given sample mean is appropriate for estimating the population mean. A statistic will rarely equal the parameter which it estimates because sampling is always subject to error. The sample mean estimates the most likely point (on the x-axis) for μ. But sometimes we need to measure the range over which the $\bar{X}$'s can be expected to vary. That is, we sometimes need an *interval estimation* in addition to a *point estimation*. This interval specifies the limits beyond which μ is not likely to fall. This range is termed the *confidence interval* of the mean and the end points are called *confidence limits*.[9]

We first begin with the desired level of probability; simply decide how confident you wish to be—50, 80, or 95 percent, or whatever. How great a probability do you wish to assign to your estimate? Suppose you decide to operate at the level of 95 percent confidence. You are really asking: What are the empirical limits within which an unknown μ can be expected to occur about 95 percent of the time? Once again, the results must be standardized for $\mu = 0$ and $\sigma = 1$. If we denote the standardized 95 percent confidence limit on the x-axis as $z_{0.95}$, then the z conversion can be solved for μ.

$$\mu = \bar{X} \pm z_{0.95}\sigma_{\bar{x}} \qquad (8.5)$$

This new expression tells us that the probability is 0.95 that the true value of μ lies between $\bar{X} + [z_{0.95}\sigma_{\bar{x}}]$ and $\bar{X} - [z_{0.95}\sigma_{\bar{x}}]$. These limits are occasionally expressed as a "plus-minus," since a normal distribution must be symmetrical about its mean.

How are these confidence limits to be interpreted? Suppose one were to draw repeated samples of size n from a population of N variates (where n is naturally less than N) and from each sample establish a 95 percent confidence interval on μ. In the long run, about 95 percent of these intervals would actually contain μ and about 5 percent would not (assuming that $C_{N,n}$ is a large number). Of course the true mean for any sample lies either within the interval or outside it. The confidence limits simply express the likelihood of such an event. There is, of course, nothing sacred about the 95 percent confidence limits. Any other figure might prove more suitable, depending upon the practical situation involved.

Statistical confidence limits provide us with a band of probability within which we can usually expect μ to occur. We generally wish that this confidence

---

[9]"Probable error" is an archaic term which occasionally crops up in the anthropological literature in lieu of "confidence interval." The probable error is defined as

probable error = standard error × 0.675

The rationale behind the *probable error* is that exactly 50 percent of the variates under a normal curve are known to lie within ±0.675 standard error of the mean. So the *probable error* is supposed to indicate the empirical limits within which 50 percent of the sample means should lie. Unfortunately, this implication is incorrect. We know that for a small n, the t distribution departs markedly from its normal counterpart. The actual 50 percent limits for a sample of size $n = 10$ are ±0.703 standard error, rather than the ±0.675 standard error suggested by the *probable error*. So, for comparative purposes, the *probable error* is worse than useless and I join Simpson, Roe, and Lewontin (1960: 161) in urging you *never* to bother computing this dubious statistic.

interval be as small as possible, but the smaller the probability band, the larger is the probability that a sample mean will fall outside that limit.

Suppose, given that $\sigma = 3.70$ cm, that a random sample of 55 adults have an average stature of 166.64 cm. Operating at a probability level of 0.95, what are the empirical limits within which we expect the population stature, μ, to be?

The standard error of the mean for samples of size $n = 55$ is

$$\sigma_{\bar{X}} = \frac{\sigma}{\sqrt{n}} = \frac{3.70}{\sqrt{55}} = 0.499 \text{ cm}$$

For 95 percent confidence limits, we know that $0.05/2 = 0.0250$ of the area under the normal curve must lie outside each limit of confidence. Looking down column C in Table A.3 we see that 0.0250 corresponds to $z = 1.96$. From Formula (8.5) the 95 percent confidence limits of the mean are

$$\bar{X} + z_{0.95}\sigma_{\bar{X}} = 166.64 + 1.96(0.499) = 167.62 \text{ cm}$$
$$\bar{X} - z_{0.95}\sigma_{\bar{X}} = 166.64 - 1.96(0.499) = 165.66 \text{ cm}$$

These figures indicate that the chances are 95 percent that the true parametric mean for adult stature lies between 165.66 and 167.62 cm.

Some of the z values for common confidence intervals are

Confidence Interval, %	α	z
90	0.10	1.64
95	0.05	1.96
99	0.01	2.57
99.9	0.001	3.30

● *Que la siguiessen y no pidiessen mas cuenta*. (translation: Follow me and ask no questions!)—F. Magellan

---

Example 8.6

Kelso (1970: table 7–9) gives the mean cephalic index for a sample of 11 Polynesian informants to be $\bar{X} = 80.66$ percent. Assume the sample to be random, and $\sigma = 3.0$ percent.

(a) What are the 95 percent confidence limits?

The standard error of the mean is found as before:

$$\sigma_{\bar{X}} = \sigma_X / \sqrt{n} = \frac{3.0}{\sqrt{11}} = 0.90$$

Substituting $z_{0.95} = 1.96$ into Expression (8.5),

$$\mu = \bar{X} \pm z_{0.95}\sigma_{\bar{X}}$$
$$= 80.66\% \pm 1.96(0.90) = 80.66\% \pm 1.76$$

the 95 percent confidence limits are 78.89 and 82.42 percent.

(b) What are the 99 percent confidence limits?

In this case, $z_{0.99} = 2.57$.

$$\mu = \bar{X} \pm z_{0.99}\sigma_{\bar{x}} = 80.66\% \pm 2.56(0.90)$$

The confidence interval is from 78.36 to 82.96 percent.

SUGGESTIONS FOR FURTHER READING

Blalock (1972: chapter 11). Brisk but helpful introduction to the sampling distribution of means and the Central Limit Theorem.

Mood and Graybill (1963: chapter 7). A calculus approach to the Central Limit Theorem as a moment-generating function.

Sokal and Rohlf (1969: chapter 9). Comparison of two sample means introduced as a simplified variant of one-way analysis of variance.

EXERCISES

8.1 Wolpoff (1969) estimates the following parameters for fossil hominid cranial capacity:

	Mean, cc	Standard Deviation, cc
Homo africanus	521	67
Homo erectus	935	132
Homo neanderthalensis	1342	169

(a) Which of the taxa demonstrates the least variability in cranial capacity? (Support your answer.)

(b) Suppose a cave is found to contain 30 roughly contemporary hominids which average 1000 cc in cranial capacity (with a standard deviation of 149 cc). What is the probability that these fossils are Homo erectus on the basis of cranial capacity alone?

(c) What are the chances of finding a sample of 64 Neanderthal skulls with an average cranial capacity less than 1300 cc?

(d) How likely is it that a sample of 100 H. africanus crania will average between 500 and 550 cc?

(e) How large a sample of H. erectus skulls would be required to be 90 percent confident that they would average greater than 920 cc in cranial capacity?

(f) If 30 H. africanus crania are being compared with 45 Neanderthal crania, what is the probability that the average cranial capacity of the Neanderthal sample exceeds the H. africanus sample by at least 850 cc?

8.2 Nordestino males of northeastern Brazil are known to have an average facial height of 11.57 cm, with $\sigma = 0.84$ cm (Eveleth 1972: table 1).

(a) What is the probability that a single randomly selected Nordestino male will have a facial height greater than 12 cm?

(b) What is the probability that a sample of 36 Nordestino males will average a facial height greater than 12 cm?

(c) What are the assumptions involved in parts (a) and (b)?

(d) What is the probability that a single, randomly selected Nordestino informant will have a facial height between 11 and 12 cm?

(e) What is the probability that the sample in part (b) averages between 11 and 12 cm?

8.3 The crown height of the first maxillary premolar averages as follows (data from Moss, Chase, and Howes 1967: table 1):

	Mean, mm	Standard Deviation, mm
American white	8.9	0.89
American black	8.7	0.80

If a sample of 50 informants were measured from each population,

(a) What is the probability that the sample of American whites would average at least 0.3 mm higher than the American black sample?

(b) What is the probability that the American black sample would exceed the American white sample in crown height of the first premolar?

8.4 McKenzie (1970: table 1) has demonstrated that fluted points from the state of Ohio average 67.04 mm in length, with a standard deviation of 21.87 mm.

(a) What are the chances that a new sample of 55 fluted points will average shorter than 6.5 cm?

(b) Suppose that a new Paleo-Indian site is under excavation in Ohio. How large a sample is necessary to be 90 percent certain that the sample mean does not deviate from the population mean (as determined by McKenzie) by more than 2 mm?

(c) If there are a total of 5000 fluted points from Ohio, about how many are shorter than 70 mm?

8.5 French males are known to average 337.76 months of age when they marry, while French females average only 284.43 months at marriage, with standard deviations of 11.03 and 14.25 months, respectively (J. A. Harris 1930: table 4). If these ages are distributed normally and random samples of 50 French males and 50 French females are drawn,

(a) What is the probability that the males will exceed the females in age at marriage by less than four years?

(b) Is the age at marriage more variable for men or women?

8.6 Suppose that two normally distributed and independent populations have identical means and standard deviations of 5.5 and 7.5, respectively. If 36 variates are drawn from each population, what is the probability that the difference between the sample means exceeds 1.0 in absolute value?

8.7 If a random sample of 64 variates is drawn from a population, how many variates should be taken in a second sample from that population to insure that the standard error of the mean of the second sample is one-half of the standard error of the mean of the first sample?

9 Introduction to Hypothesis Testing

● *He understood* how; *he did not understand* why.—G. Orwell

9.1 PROBABILITIES: SO WHAT

Over half of the discussion thus far has been concerned with *probabilities*: the general nature of probabilistic statements, how independent and dependent probabilities are combined, how to compute probabilities of various rare events, and how to find the odds in common gambling situations. Chapter 8 went to great lengths in discussing how statistics are used to estimate parameters of unknown populations. The binomial theorem was applied to some discrete random variables. The normal distribution can be used both to estimate this discrete binomial and to compute probabilities for certain continuous random variables. Each procedure culminates in an explicit statement of probability: "the chances of throwing three heads in a row are one in eight"; "there are fewer than five chances in 1000 of finding so large a difference between means"; $p(X \geq 10) = 0.143$. But with the exception of weathermen and bookmakers, few of us have much to do with probability statements. Realistic anthropological situations are very rarely expressed directly in probabilistic terms.

So, having dutifully assimilated the machinations of probabilities, you are ad libitum entitled to question: *Probabilities: So what*?

We observed earlier that a statistic assumes the *exact value* of a parameter only by rare accident. Nobody realistically expects to obtain *exactly* 500 heads and 500 tails in 1000 tosses of a coin. This outcome would be a rare event, expected to occur only a couple of times in 1000 trials. Most populations are so variable that statistics tend only to oscillate about the parametric value, but rarely will they exactly equal that parameter. Although obtaining exactly 500 heads in 1000 tosses is unlikely, we know that roughly 95 percent of our attempts should produce between 470 and 530 heads if we use a fair coin. Working with samples invariably involves an element of chance and some margin of error, and statistical procedures provide the empirical methods necessary to assess the degree of error involved.

We are left with a rather obtuse statement: Large probabilities denote common events while small probabilities indicate rarer events. But just how large a probability is required before an event is "common," and how small must a probability be before it's considered "rare"? Is 26 chances in 100 "rare" enough, or is one chance in 100 truly "rare"? Or one chance in 1000? Should an event occurring 50 percent of the time be considered "common," or must "common" events happen 95 or 99 percent of the time? Although a method is available for assigning probabilities, a workable decision-making technique is still lacking. *Probabilities: So what?*

An anthropological example should clarify this need for a decision-making apparatus. Early in the history of cross-cultural studies, fieldworkers reported a custom among many nonwestern societies in which infants and children were occasionally killed by their own parents. Particularly prevalent was the practice of *female infanticide*—killing female infants—and a century of anthropologists have offered explanations for the custom. Some nineteenth-century ethnologists associated female infanticide with exogamy. Theorist John McLennan held, for example, that the primal human social unit must have once been a tightly knit, warlike group of brothers, who were locked into constant and fierce competition with their equally warlike neighbors. To maintain military strength and to conserve their scarce economic resources, these bands preferred to rear more male than female offspring. This decision obliged them to eliminate the unwanted female children. Other anthropologists contend that infanticide contributes to a proper quantitative balance between sexes. When mortality among males increases as a result of raiding, warfare or hazardous hunting, female infanticide keeps the sex ratio in balance. Some argue that infanticide is directly subsistence-linked. Whenever twins are born—or successive births too closely spaced—the second (or sometimes the female) child is killed for the good of the other infant.

Infanticide is generally studied by directly questioning informants: Do you kill female infants? The response to this question is neatly tallied into a cultural inventory:

Society practices female infanticide   Yes _____
                                                         No _____

After hundreds of societies were surveyed in this manner, ethnologists began to evaluate the tabulations searching for cross-cultural regularities.

Do patrilocal societies tend to practice female infanticide more than matrilocal societies?
Do hunter-gatherers practice female infanticide more often than agricultural peoples?
Do societies at war tend to practice female infanticide less than societies at peace?

The search for cause can be narrowed as patterns begin to emerge.

But recently, anthropologists have begun to worry about the degree to which informants give accurate appraisals of on-the-ground behavior. After all, ethnographers are interlopers in a society and many culturally sensitive subjects are not readily discussed with strangers. Often a critical disparity appears between the spoken word and the actual deed. The selfsame informants who deny practice *X* can sometimes be observed performing exactly that same practice, although perhaps in latent fashion. Marvin Harris suggests that this situation holds for female infanticide. In times of ecological stress, the simple neglect of babies can become a significant form of infanticide. Mothers, already burdened with a difficult workload, become somewhat less responsive to the demands of their children, and infants are left unattended for longer periods and are nursed less effectively. Harris (1972: 18) suggests that "in an ecological perspective, the line separating infant neglect from infanticide is extremely thin." So, in addition to other problems facing ethnographers, informant testimony regarding infanticide can be questioned. This articulation between the informant's cognitive viewpoint (the *emic*) and actual on-the-ground behavior observable by the fieldworker (the *etic*) has become a focus of much current anthropological research.

Fortunately, there is another method by which female infanticide can be examined without relying upon informant testimony. In general, we expect the juvenile sex ratio to be equal. If female infanticide occurs, then an excess of male children ought to occur. In one such study, R. W. Dunning conducted an age-sex census among the Pekangekum band of Ojibwa living in central Ontario. The census revealed a curiously asymmetrical sex ratio: 42 male children under six years of age to only 32 females of a corresponding age (Dunning 1959: 68). Dunning inquired about the practice of female infanticide, and the Ojibwa recounted only four episodes of infanticide between 1947 and 1955; apparently there was no sexual preference to account for the preponderance of male children. Could the relative scarcity of female children be due to unreported (perhaps covert) female infanticide? Or was this asymmetrical ratio due merely to the vicissitudes of chance fluctuation in birthrate?

Here is a concrete situation in which one must confront the role of chance. The question of female infanticide would not have arisen had the sex ratio been roughly equal, but the 42:32 sex ratio creates some doubt.

It is important to distinguish between biological and cultural phenomena. The sex ratio at birth is a biological phenomenon, and we generally assume an equal rate of birth for males and females. But here we are concerned only with the incidence of infanticide, a cultural event. Let p denote the proportion of female children reaching adolescence and q represent the proportion of male children surviving childhood. If no infanticide is involved, then we expect males and females to survive childhood in roughly the same proportion, $p = q = 1/2$. By applying the normal approximation to the binomial theorem, the situation can be expressed as follows: Given a random sample of 74 Ojibwa children, what is the probability that 32 or fewer would be female by chance alone? The statistical population is a large set of Bernoulli variates: The sex of all Ojibwa children under six years. The sample consists of the sex of those informants involved in Dunning's census. The parameters of this theoretical binomial sampling dis-

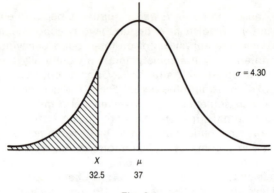

Fig. 9.1

tribution are μ and σ:

$$\mu = np = 74(\tfrac{1}{2}) = 37$$

$$\sigma = \sqrt{npq} = 4.30$$

The area of the normal curve in question (Fig. 9.1) lies to the left of $X = 32.5$. In this case, X is a discrete random variable denoting the number of successes in 74 trials, where a female child is defined as a success.

The variate $X = 32.5$ is first standardized to a z-score:

$$z = \frac{X - \mu}{\sigma} = \frac{32.5 - 37}{4.30} = -1.05$$

This z-value corresponds to a probability of $p(X \leq 32.5) = 0.1469$. In other words, an asymmetrical sex ratio with so few females out of a sample of 74 could be expected to occur roughly 15 times in 100 cases. This assumes the sex ratio to be symmetrical.

But, here again, the gap must be bridged between numbers and people. What does the cold number $p(X \leq 32.5) = 0.1469$ tell us about Ojibwa infanticide? *Probabilities: So what?*

Sex ratio figures are also available for the Kutchin of northern Alaska. The Hudson's Bay Company records for 1858 indicate the following population figures for children:

	Male	Female
Yukon Kutchin	218	137
Peel River Kutchin	83	53

The Hudson's Bay census also shows a preponderance of male children. The sex ratios are standardized as before:

$$Z_{\text{Yukon}} = \frac{137.5 - 355(1/2)}{\sqrt{355(1/2)(1/2)}} = \frac{137.5 - 177.5}{9.42} = 4.25$$

$$Z_{\text{Peel R.}} = \frac{53.5 - 136(1/2)}{\sqrt{136(1/2)(1/2)}} = 2.48$$

The corresponding probabilities are $p(X \leq 137.5) < 0.0001$ and $p(X \leq 53.5) = 0.007$. Once again an inquiry about sociocultural practices is answered by a number. *Probabilities: So what?*

We have reached another crossroads, a point at which a firm decision is necessary. The dilemma of projecting behavior from numbers can be simplified into a dichotomous pair of conclusions.

EITHER

H_0 1. Males and females have an equal chance of reaching adulthood. The observed census is an unlikely deviation from 50:50, and hence a rare event has occurred.

OR

H_1 2. Females actually have a lower probability of surviving preadulthood than males ($p < 0.50$).

The choice between these two options lies at the very heart of statistical reasoning. The statistical procedures of inferring from sample to population are designed precisely to provide such a decision-making apparatus.

9.2 DEFINING A PROCEDURE TO TEST HYPOTHESES

● *Definitions would be good things if we did not use words to make them.*—J. Rousseau

The following six steps provide a framework for "testing" a research hypothesis against the theory of probability and statistics.

    I. State the statistical hypotheses.
    II. Select a level of statistical significance.
    III. Select an appropriate statistical model.
    IV. Define the region of rejection.
    V. Perform the computations and make the statistical decision.
    VI. State this decision in nonstatistical terms.

These operations are relatively straightforward and, when applied correctly, they will provide repeatable results (repeatedly).

9.2.1 Step I: State the Statistical Hypotheses

The initial step in testing a statistical hypothesis requires that the substantive research propositions be translated into specific statistical statements. Just as variables must be operationally defined, so must we operationally define statistical hypotheses. In considering whether or not the sex ratios in three separate bands are out of balance, two alternative interpretations of the data were suggested: (1) *either females have an equal probability of surviving preadulthood and the disparities in the census are due to chance fluctuations*, or (2) *the sex ratios have been culturally altered.* These mutually exclusive propositions accurately reflect the reality under consideration. But statements (1) and (2) are anthropological propositions, not statistical propositions.

Statistical hypotheses are statements about population parameters. We assumed at the outset that males and females had an equal probability of surviving to adulthood: $p = q = 1/2$. This proposition amounts to a statistical hypothesis because something is inferred about a population parameter. The hypothesis that male–female sex ratios are equal can be called a *null hypothesis* (H_o) and expressed symbolically as

$$H_o: \quad p = q$$

The hypothesis which competes with H_o is that the sex ratios have been culturally altered. The research hypothesis can be also converted to a statistical statement, called the *alternative hypothesis* and denoted as H_1.

$$H_1: \quad p \neq q$$

These two competing statistical statements hypothesize about the underlying proportions of the population from which samples have been drawn. The statistical decision-making process enables us to assess the census data—one of the two competing hypotheses must be rejected.

The null hypothesis concept was initially suggested by Sir Ronald A. Fisher, who applied the term "null" to any statistical hypothesis which one wishes to disprove. In this sense, the term "null" meant to *nullify*. In many situations, one seeks to establish a difference between populations, where one has not been previously recognized: *Homo erectus* is *taller* than *Homo habilis*; the IQ of rural children is *higher* than that of urban children; Clovis points are *older* than Folsom points. The research experience often involves a refinement and splitting of previously existing categories. According to this model, research begins with a null hypothesis stating that two populations are equivalent and tries to disprove (to *nullify*) this equivalence. Progress amounts to revealing differences where none were previously recognized.

Many null hypotheses set a given parameter equal to zero. The expression H_o: $\mu = 0$ denotes symbolically the null hypothesis that the parametric mean is equal to zero. Null hypotheses may also specify the proposition that two given populations have identical means:

$$H_o: \quad \mu_X - \mu_Y = 0$$

Null hypotheses also often express nonzero differences between populations:

$$H_o: \quad \mu_X - \mu_Y = 2$$

Nonzero null hypotheses are usually more difficult to frame because previous experimentation is required to establish the specific difference predicted. Null hypotheses may even stipulate that certain critical relationships should hold between ratios, as in the case of Mendelian genetics.

As Simpson, Roe, and Lewontin (1960: 175) note, the null hypothesis is similar to the assumption of innocence in a court of law. An arbitrary assumption is made until the evidence weighs "beyond a reasonable doubt" against that assumption. Assumptions are initially specified and evidence is examined to determine the tenability of the initial assumption. Some null hypotheses survive scrutiny; others fall. Fred Kerlinger expresses this same sentiment in somewhat more attractive form: "The null hypothesis taunts us 'You're wrong, there is no relation; disprove me if you can'" (1973: 202).

The alternative statistical hypothesis (H_1) provides the counterpoint to the null hypothesis. If H_o suggests that an event is *so*, then H_1 argues the event is *not so*. Each alternative hypothesis is therefore closely paired to a null hypothesis. The simplest pair is *nondirectional*: If H_o suggests that two quantities are equal, then H_1 automatically asserts that they are not equal. Taking μ, the population mean of the continuous random variable "adult stature," a nondirectional pair of hypotheses would be

$$H_o: \quad \mu = 165 \text{ cm} \qquad H_1: \quad \mu \neq 165 \text{ cm}$$

The null hypothesis projects that the average adult stature for a given population is about 165 cm. The alternative proposition asserts that H_o is false. Sample values can be compared to both hypotheses. Which hypothesis best accounts for the observed evidence? The null hypothesis looks good if the sample mean is roughly equal to 165 cm. If a sample mean (estimating μ) is either significantly higher or lower than 165 cm, then H_1 seems preferable. Nondirectional H_1 are often called *two-tailed* because values from either end of the frequency distribution can potentially negate H_o. That is, $\bar{X}$ can be either *too large* or *too small* to match H_o.

Alternative hypotheses may also be expressed in *directional* format. Suppose that H_o projects that stature is greater than or equal to 165 cm. The corresponding alternative hypothesis asserts simply that the average height is significantly shorter than 165 cm.

$$H_o: \quad \mu \geq 165 \text{ cm} \qquad H_1: \quad \mu < 165 \text{ cm}$$

The sample statistic is again compared to μ, and one hypothesis is rejected. Directional alternative hypotheses are termed *one-tailed* because only one end of the frequency distribution can potentially negate H_o. In this case, only $\bar{X}$'s significantly smaller than 165 cm mitigate against H_o.

The infanticide example may be expressed in either directional or nondirectional terms. If interest is strictly in infanticide—regardless of whether male or female children are involved—these proportions should be expressed in *nondirectional* format (because both ends of the frequency distribution are relevant):

$$H_o: \quad p = q \qquad H_1: \quad p \neq q$$

Significant deviations from $p = 0.50$ *in either direction* would result in the rejection of the null hypothesis.

But if the research interest is strictly in female infanticide as suggested above, then a directional pair of hypotheses is required.

$$H_o: \quad p \geq q \qquad H_1: \quad p < q$$

where p is the proportion of females surviving childhood.

This directional H_o is vulnerable only to a preponderance of male offspring. An equal sex ratio, or one indicating an abundance of females, would not precipitate rejection of H_o.

Some examples will illustrate how anthropological propositions are translated into operational pairs of statistical hypotheses.

Anthropological proposition: Asians tend to have broader heads than Europeans.

Continuous Random Variable:

$$\text{Cephalic index} = \frac{\text{head breadth}}{\text{head length}} \times 100$$

Statistical Hypotheses:

$$H_0: \quad \mu_{Asia} \leq \mu_{Europe}$$
$$H_1: \quad \mu_{Asia} > \mu_{Europe}$$

Anthropological proposition: Pueblo III sites are larger than those of Pueblo II.

Continuous Random Variable: "Large" is defined as "μ = average rooms per site."

Statistical Hypotheses:

$$H_0: \quad \mu_{PIII} \leq \mu_{PII}$$
$$H_1: \quad \mu_{PIII} > \mu_{PII}$$

Anthropological proposition: Agricultural peoples work at a different rate than do hunter-gatherers.

Continuous Random Variable: "Work" is defined as "μ = average days per week spent in economic pursuits."

Statistical Hypotheses:

$$H_0: \quad \mu_{ag} = \mu_{h\text{-}g}$$
$$H_1: \quad \mu_{ag} \neq \mu_{h\text{-}g}$$

Anthropological proposition: Agricultural peoples work harder than do hunter-gatherers.

Continuous Random Variable: Same as above

Statistical Hypotheses:

$$H_0: \quad \mu_{ag} \leq \mu_{h\text{-}g}$$
$$H_1: \quad \mu_{ag} > \mu_{h\text{-}g}$$

9.2.2. Step II: Select a Level of Statistical Significance

● *Granted that one can never tell from which direction the angel of light will descend, we share the obligation of making ourselves responsible for strategic guesses.*—M. Harris

Beware! The innocent word "significance" is about to acquire a very specialized definition. *Significant* will become a Big Word. The concept of statistical significance must not be confused with significance of any other sort: Should you become tempted to equate *statistically significant* with generally positive adjectives such as "important," "momentous," "weighty," or "trenchant," kindly resist this temptation. A "statistically significant" finding can sometimes be patently meaningless in an anthropological sense, and the reverse is also true.

To this point, an operational pair of statistical hypotheses have been defined. Our statistical decision can take one of only two potential forms: (1) reject H_o, or (2) do not reject H_o. This decision will be based upon information contained within a sample. Because a "statistic" always implies inference based upon incomplete information from samples, statistical decisions will always contain an unavoidable margin of built-in error. The larger the sample, the less dangerous is this error. But uncertainty nevertheless remains a component of all statistical inference, and therefore inferences can never constitute *proof* in the strict sense. The statistical hypothesis testing procedure is really just an aid toward making our guesses as educated as possible.

When making actual statistical decisions, the true population characteristics are unknown, and we never know whether the decision is actually valid. But, if the actual truth about the populations is known, then inferences based upon samples can be judged for accuracy. A correct decision can take two forms. If the null hypothesis is really true for the population—and one can never know this simply by inspecting a sample—then a correct decision is made when H_o is retained. Similarly, another correct decision is rendered whenever a false H_o is rejected. Only these two possibilities exist for correct statistical inference: reject the false null hypotheses and do not reject the true ones.

Two possibilities also exist for error. The incorrect rejection of a true null hypothesis is termed a *Type I error*, and the incorrect acceptance of a false H_o is called a *Type II error*. These possibilities are presented in tabular form as follows:

Research Decision	The null hypothesis is actually	
	False	True
Reject H_o	OK *Correct decision*	Type I error, α
Accept H_o	Type II error, β	OK *Correct decision*

The probability of committing a Type I error is conventionally symbolized by α (Greek *alpha*), and the probability of committing a Type II error is designated by β (Greek *beta*). Given the unappetizing prospect that some degree of error is always possible, the task facing statistical inference is to maximize the probability of correct decisions and minimize the probability of the two incorrect options.

The probability α denotes the likelihood of rejecting a true hypothesis. Suppose one were to toss a coin 1000 times in order to decide if $p = q$ for that coin. A Type I error in this case would be declaring the coin to be "unfair" ($p \neq q$) when in fact the coin is fair ($p = q$). Alpha is the probability of making such an error. Say we predetermine $\alpha = 0.01$. We will only incorrectly reject H_o about once in 100 times, not a bad rate of error. But nobody likes to be wrong, so why not set α even smaller? A level $\alpha = 0.001$ or even $\alpha = 0.00000001$ virtually eliminates the possibility of our committing a Type I error on any single trial.

But every silver lining has its cloud. In this case, for every *decrease* in α there is a corresponding *increase* in β. That is, if the sample size is fixed, the probabilities α and β are inversely related. As the probability of incorrectly rejecting a true null hypothesis becomes smaller, the chances of accepting a false H_o becomes increasingly larger.

Thus, the attempt to reduce Type I errors by decreasing α will automatically make Type II errors more likely. The reverse is also true. An abhorrence of Type II errors might convince you to set β at a minuscule level, but as β becomes smaller, and hence less likely, the Type I error becomes increasingly probable. The only effective manner to combat this seesaw effect and to minimize both α and β is to change the design of the experiment itself. An increase in n will simultaneously decrease α and β, as long as more samples can be collected. Or perhaps the investigator can restructure the research hypotheses into a directional (one-tailed) format, thereby increasing the ability of the statistical model to avoid both Type I and Type II errors.

There are times, of course, when the actual nature of the situation dictates which type of error is more costly. The difference between Type I and II errors is perhaps most graphic in medical research. Suppose that in one laboratory, researchers are attempting to find a cure for glaucoma, a disease of the eye characterized by an increase of pressure within the eyeball. Glaucoma ultimately damages the optic disk, thereby producing blindness. A number of different drugs have been tested to find a method for relieving the pressure on the inner eye. The null hypotheses in these experiments is that a drug D produces no effect upon the disease. The alternative hypothesis holds that drug D causes a significant improvement in the diseased condition. Which error is more important in this case: rejecting a true H_o or accepting a false null hypothesis?

The answer is dictated by the nature of the situation. As long as the drug produces no harmful side effects, the probability of a Type II error, β, should be minimized. Patients are daily going blind while researchers search for a cure, and no stone can be left unturned for fear of overlooking a potentially viable cure. A few true H_o can be erroneously rejected—that is, a few H_1 incorrectly accepted—as long as a potential cure is not allowed to pass unnoticed. There is clearly more danger in overlooking an effective cure (false H_o–true H_1) than in accepting a useless treatment (true H_o–false H_1). The ineffective treatments will gradually be winnowed out by further testing and experimentation. A rather high level of α (coupled with a stringent β) would be permissible in this case to avoid overlooking a viable treatment.

	The Drug D is Actually	
Research Decision	Effective (false H_o)	Ineffective (true H_o)
Reject H_o	CURE *Correct decision*	Type I error, α
Accept H_o	Type II error, β	Useless Drug *Correct decision*

But suppose that the potential cure has dangerous side effects which could injure a patient's health. Priorities must change. Suppose a drug prevents advanced blindness, but the treatment itself introduces a high risk of brain damage, or the drug places an undue strain on the heart, or becomes addictive with prolonged usage. In these cases, the danger clearly lies in a Type II error, in accepting a false H_o. If the null hypothesis is in fact true and drug D has no significant effect in curing glaucoma, then the dangerous side effects put a premium on the incorrect rejection of H_o. The probability of a Type I error, α, should be set rather low in order to avoid the danger of prescribing an ineffective yet dangerous drug.

Conflicts between levels of α and β also occur in modern industrial quality controls. The null hypotheses in an automobile factory are the safety or environmental specifications imposed upon industry by regulatory agencies. The profit motive on these production lines sets the level of α to be small. As few automobiles are rejected as possible. Less concern is demonstrated here for β, which represents the probability of accepting a false H_o. From the profit standpoint, there is obviously more concern with cost control than the risk of passing a few defective or substandard automobiles through the inspection. The consumer, on the other hand, could not care less about how many lemons are rejected from an assembly line; the buyer wants only to be assured that *his* automobile is a safe one. So the level of β is of paramount interest to the consumer while α is clearly more important to the producer. For this reason, the probability of a Type I error is sometimes known as the "producer's risk" and β is the "consumer's risk."

Rarely do Type I or Type II errors have intrinsic values in social science. Commonly, the anthropologist is concerned with minimizing all kinds of errors. While the specter of neither error is appalling—nobody's life hangs in the balance—social scientists still wish their decisions to be as correct as possible. Only an increase in n or a change in the research design can simultaneously minimize both α and β, so how can we be as correct as possible under the circumstances?

Research statisticians traditionally focus upon α, the probability of committing a Type I error. The calculations involving α are somewhat less complex than those for β and, once α and n are set, β is predetermined. Establishing the exact value for α forces us to operationally define a "small" probability. If the probability associated with a particular outcome is "small," then the decision is vastly simplified: either (1) an exceptionally rare event has just occurred, or (2) the null hypothesis is false.

Common statistical procedure rejects the first alternative that a rare event has occurred. As statisticians, we will proceed under the rosy assumption that rare events rarely happen to "us." Statistical hypothesis testing really involves an empirical playing of odds, and statisticians always bet against the rare event. The belief is that the correct decision will have been made in the long run, and we will have been wrong only the predetermined "small" number of times.

This is a very critical point. An arbitrary cut off point must be selected before we can interpret our data: if the probability is less than this arbitrary level (α), then H_o is judged incorrect. We will always bet against the other alternative, that a rare event has occurred. Therefore the statistician is usually correct *in the long run*. This arbitrary cutoff point for α is called the *level of statistical significance*. Any probability smaller than α is called *statistically significant*. Events with probabilities smaller than α are *significant departures* from H_o. Rather than admit that a rare event has occurred, we choose to throw out H_o.

Therefore, setting α is critical because this definition of "small" dictates which hypotheses will be accepted and which will be rejected. But guidelines for setting α are difficult to set out. The significance level is a statement of just how willing one is to be wrong in the long run. I cannot dictate how willing you are to be wrong. The Radiocarbon Laboratory at the University of Pennsylvania, for example, always sets the significance level at $\alpha = 0.10$ (Ralph 1971: 18). This means that in the long run the laboratory is willing to reject a correct H_o about once in ten times. On the other hand, many psychologists are much less tolerant of incorrect decisions. In fact, some psychological journals refuse to publish research results which are not at least significant at $\alpha = 0.01$. This means that they will tolerate only one incorrect decision in 100 experiments; some journals even insist on the 0.001 level, one incorrect decision in 1000. Fortunately, anthropologists have refrained from imposing these silly standards upon one another. In fact, when I took my first statistics course, the professor (an archaeologist, incidentally) urged us to make up our own minds about the α level: "Just take a walk in the park until you find an alpha you're comfortable with—then nobody can tell you you're wrong."

Despite this appeal to free will, social science has adopted a *traditional level* of statistical significance. By this convention, a probability is considered "small" if it is less than 0.05. Why $\alpha = 0.05$? There are no good reasons other than tradition and the warm, intuitive feeling that "one error in 20 ain't bad." The convention dictates that results can be called "statistically significant" if the probability is ≤ 0.05. Similarly, results are "highly significant" if their probability is less than 0.01. The 0.05 level is commonly used for illustrative purposes throughout this book, and 0.05 is indeed the most common level in anthropological literature. *But there is nothing sacred about the 0.05 level*, or any other level for that matter.

The level of statistical significance is nothing more than a statement about willingness to commit a Type I error. The statement may be expressed either as probability (such as $\alpha = 0.01$) or as percentage (such as the 5 percent level of significance). The normal approximation to the binomial told us earlier that the probability of a sex ratio as extreme as that for the Ojibwa was $p(X \leq 32.5) = 0.1539$. We therefore estimate that the probability of observing a sex ratio for this deviant by random sampling is about 15 in 100. Is 15 percent so small that we doubt H_o: $p = q$?

Here again we encounter a personal problem. How willing are we to be wrong? Had we set $\alpha = 0.05$, then we could conclude: The chances of obtaining the Ojibwa sex ratios are not small enough for us to doubt H_o. Maintaining the 0.05 level of statistical significance, one would further conclude that both Peel River and Yukon Kutchin sex ratios are "indeed too small" ($p_{Yukon} < 0.0001$ and $p_{Peel R.} = 0.007$). H_o would be rejected because both Kutchin samples are "significant deviations" from expectation under the null hypothesis.[1]

[1]An allied statistical concept is that of *power*, defined as: Power $= 1 - \beta$. As the complement of β, power refers to the ability of a statistical test to reject H_o when in fact the null hypothesis is false. Because of the intimate relationship between Type I and II errors, the power of a test is determined by α and the sample size. It is with reluctance that I exclude a discussion of power in this section. Comments will be made from time to time about the relative power (or efficiency) of various statistical tests discussed in subsequent chapters. Often one test is judged superior to another on the basis of power considerations, but the computations are excluded from this presentation.

Any level of α can be applied, whatever seems appropriate to the investigator. The null hypothesis is rejected in the Ojibwa case for all levels of α greater than or equal to 0.1539. Should alpha be established at *greater* than $\alpha = 0.1539$—and this is usually considered too high a probability for a Type I error—then H_o would not be rejected. The decision depends entirely upon the level established for alpha.

In actual practice, α and β are not single numbers, but rather are critical values which define *regions* within the probability distribution. H_o will be rejected for all probabilities less than or equal to α. Alpha is thus the boundary beyond which events are defined as "rare," and hence unacceptable under H_o.

9.2.3 Step III: Select an Appropriate Statistical Model

The research proposals have been suitably translated into statistical hypotheses and "improbable" has been operationally defined as α. The next step is to select the appropriate statistical model for computing the probability statement. A special caution is required to be sure that samples satisfy all assumptions of the statistical test selected. There are really two kinds of assumptions involved here.[2] First of all, there is that important assumption called the *null hypothesis*. You didn't realize that H_o is an assumption? Well, it is—and a very important assumption at that! We assume the null hypothesis to be true until the empirical evidence convinces us otherwise. Once H_o becomes untenable, then H_1 is assumed to hold. H_o and H_1 are defined as mutually exclusive and exhaustive alternatives, so we always assume one or the other to be true.

The second kind of assumption is more positive. These assumptions comprise the *model* of the statistical test. One selects the statistical test appropriate to some problem and then assumes that the conditions of the model hold for the conditions at hand. A number of statistical models will be considered in later chapters. To this point, only the binomial model and the normal distribution model have been considered; both models involve important assumptions discussed earlier. These assumptions must be considered one by one for each application of a statistical test. If conditions seem to fulfill the assumptions, then the model holds for this application. If the assumptions are violated, then a more appropriate statistic should be found.

Taken together, the null hypothesis and the statistical model provide a decision-making apparatus. Empirical data are compared to the expectation under all these assumptions. If the sample agrees with expectation, then there is no reason to doubt any of the assumptions. The null hypothesis, just one of several assumptions, survives the empirical evidence.

But what if the sample fails to agree with expectation, given α? In this case, you know that something is amiss with one of your assumptions, but which one? Each of the assumptions has the same logical status, and the null hypothesis assumption is no more logically vulnerable than any other assumption. Here is where careful design of the statistical test is important and why the assumptions of the model must be satisfied. This is your only choice, if you have selected the appropriate statistical model. The model's assumptions *must* be valid—otherwise you would have chosen another model—so you are left with only one possibility, the null hypothesis. *As long as the assumptions of the*

[2]This section follows Blalock (1972: 156–159) in some respects.

statistical model are valid, then the null hypothesis must be your incorrect assumption.

All that remains is to move from the abstract statistical model to precise statements which predict specific properties of samples. The bridge between model and sample is provided by the *sampling distribution* of the statistical model. Probability distributions, such as those considered in Chapters 6 and 7, tell us the likelihood of all possible outcomes in an experiment. These sampling distributions hold only as long as all of the assumptions (including H_o) are true.

9.2.4 Step IV: Define the Region of Rejection

A fixed level of statistical significance declares to the world a willingness to reject a correct H_o about 100α times in every 100 trials. By so doing, one admits that chance factors will cause statistics to deviate from the expected parameters. But depending upon σ and n, there is a limit (100α percent) beyond which chance differences will almost never occur. The level of significance operationally establishes this boundary between acceptable and unacceptable results. Whenever a difference exceeds this preestablished limit, then we must question the underlying assumption. As long as the statistical model rests upon valid assumptions, then the null hypothesis is singled out as the faulty assumption and must be rejected. When the difference between expected and observed falls within the acceptable range of variability, then the null hypothesis is not rejected (that is, no assumptions need to be questioned).

One final translating task remains before a statistical hypothesis can be considered "tested." Just as research hypotheses must be transformed into operational statistical hypotheses, so must the probability distribution of the test statistic be converted into empirical units. The specific empirical correlate of the level of significance is known as the *region of rejection*, or the *critical level.* The region of rejection contains all possible empirical values in the sampling distribution which have been judged to be incompatible with a true H_o, given α. The level of significance is a probability, but the region of rejection is a statement in the direct units of analysis, such as centimeters, number of sites per square mile, kilocalories per day, and so forth.

The null hypotheses in the case of Pekangekum Ojibwa female infanticide were

$$H_o: \quad p \geq q \qquad H_1: \quad p < q$$

These hypotheses are *one-tailed* because concern is strictly with *female* infanticide. Let us set $\alpha = 0.05$. What observations require us to reject H_o, given α?

The critical region comprises that 5 percent area under the normal curve which contains unacceptable deviations from $H_o: p \leq q$. We find from Table A.3 (Appendix) that exactly 5 percent of the sampling distribution lies outside $z = 1.64$ (Fig. 9.2).

Dunning's original Ojibwa sample involved 74 preadults, so the region of rejection contains the number of extreme cases in the sampling distribution which fall into the unacceptable 5 percent area beyond $z = 1.64$.

This probabilistic statement must now be translated into the actual number of

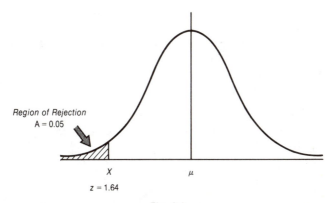

Fig. 9.2

preadult females in the sample. Solving the z equation for X,

$$z = \frac{\mu - X}{\sigma}$$

$$X = \mu - z\sigma$$

$$= 37 - 1.64(4.30) = 30 \text{ female children}$$

The region of rejection (Fig. 9.3) is thus 30 or fewer females in a sample of 74 preadults.

The critical region supplies the operational criteria necessary to test hypotheses. Given a significance level of $\alpha = 0.05$, any random sample of 74 Ojibwa children having *30 or fewer* females will tell us to reject H_o. Similarly, any sample with *31 or more* will tell us not to doubt H_o. In other words, samples falling within the region of rejection always favor H_1, while samples falling outside the critical region will favor H_o. The region of rejection is defined by alpha and by the sampling distribution of the appropriate statistical model. This is the classical theory of hypothesis testing.

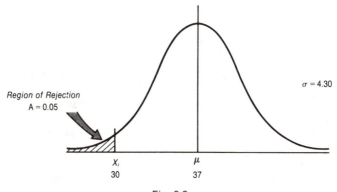

Fig. 9.3

By a similar procedure, the directional (one-tailed) region of rejection for the Yukon Kutchin example is 162 or fewer female children. Suppose that interest is shifted from the occurrence of female infanticide among the Ojibwa to the case of Ojibwa infanticide in general. The statistical hypotheses now become nondirectional (two-tailed).

$$H_o: \quad p = q \qquad H_1: \quad p \neq q$$

Let us retain the 0.05 level of statistical significance. The region of rejection must shift, however, because *both* ends of the normal curve contain unacceptable extremes (Fig. 9.4).

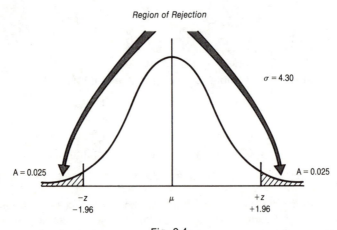

Fig. 9.4

The probability of a Type I error remains constant at 5 percent, but now the area representing that probability must be divided between the left- and right-hand tails of the normal curve. *Each tail now contains only $\alpha/2$ of the total area.* For $\alpha = 0.05$, Table A.3 shows that $0.05/2 = 0.025$ of the area lies outside $z = +1.96$, and 0.025 lies outside $z = -1.96$; therefore, a total area of 0.05 lies more extreme from $z = \pm 1.96$. Solving the z-equation for X_i, the critical boundaries for the two-tailed region of rejection are

$$X_i = \mu \pm z\sigma = 37 \pm 8.4$$
$$= 28.6 \text{ and } 45.4$$

The region of rejection (Fig. 9.5) consists of *fewer than 29 females or more than 45 females* in a random sample of 74 Ojibwa children. These extreme cases favor H_1, while all samples containing between 29 and 45 females favor the null hypothesis, given $\alpha = 0.05$ and the assumptions of the normal approximation to the binomial.

The two-tailed testing format reduces the single-tail region of rejection by half and represents that $\alpha/2$ area on the opposite end of the sampling distribution. Obviously, statistical hypotheses expressed in one-tailed form are more likely to reject H_o than are their two-tailed counterparts, assuming that the direction of

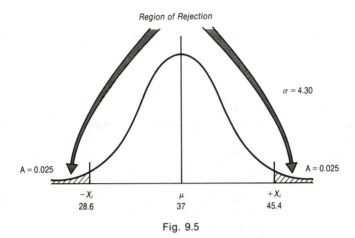

Fig. 9.5

deviation can be predicted beforehand (Chapter 16 considers one-tailed and two-tailed strategies in more detail).

Especial caution is in order when dealing with the region of rejection for discrete random variables. Any census will obviously result in whole numbers. There could not possibly be 21.6 female preadults. But note that the normal approximation to the binomial sampling distribution assigns continuous limits to the critical region. Thus, a census with exactly 29 Ojibwa females would fall *outside* the region of rejection, while the case of 28 female offspring would fall *inside* the critical region.

9.2.5 Step V: Perform Computations and Make Statistical Decision

With the critical region it becomes a simple matter to compare these a priori limits on the sampling distribution to the empirical sample. For the one-tailed Ojibwa case, we know that 30 or fewer female children fall within the region of rejection. Dunning's 1954 census disclosed exactly 32 female children. This sample does not fall into the critical region, and the statistical decision is not to reject H_o. Note that the same census data also fall outside the two-tailed critical areas, and H_o is likewise retained.

This statistical decision has taken the normal approximation to the binomial as a model against which to compare an actual sample. As long as the model holds (that is, as long as the model assumptions are valid), we reject or accept the H_o assumption on the basis of the sample. Be certain to note that the model involved is the hypothetical sampling distribution or a random variate. The model is not the data.

The one-tailed region for the Yukon Kutchin was found previously to be 162 or fewer females. The Hudson's Bay Company figures show only 137 female preadults in 1858. This result falls well into the $\alpha = 0.05$ critical area, and the null hypothesis must be rejected. Would the two-tailed alternative have changed this statistical decision?

222

9.2.6 Step VI: State the Decision in Nonstatistical Terms

It is not sufficient merely to examine a body of data and declare that either "the null hypothesis is rejected" or "H_o is not rejected." The goal of anthropological research is never a statement of statistics, but is rather a statement about people.

Dunning's sample did not allow us to reject the null hypothesis of equivalent sex ratios. H_o survived an actual sample. In an anthropological sense, this means that there was not enough evidence in this one sample to require us to question an equal rate of survival for male and female children. Dunning's sample contains no support for infanticide of any sort, whether male or female. The null hypothesis was rejected, however, for both Yukon and Peel River Kutchin, on the basis of the Hudson's Bay Company samples. The census revealed a statistically significant preponderance of male over female children. There is too great a difference in the sex ratios to be attributed to chance alone, given $\alpha = 0.05$. But note that the conclusion does not state that female infanticide was actually operative among the nineteenth-century Kutchin. Statistical association must never be confused with a causal sequence. There could be any number of rival anthropological theories to explain the prevalence of male over female children; infanticide is but one substantive explanation. The implications of these restrictions are considered in more detail in Section 9.3 and also in Chapter 16.

Example 9.1

Previous research indicates that the prehistoric Basketmaker populations of the American Southwest averaged about 169.0 cm in stature, with $\sigma = 3.55$ cm. An archaeologist has just excavated several burials from a dry cave, and the physical anthropologist finds that the average stature for 45 of these newly recovered specimens is 167.9 cm. Are these individuals too short to be Basketmakers (at the 0.05 level)?

I. *Statistical hypotheses:* Let μ be adult stature.

$$H_o: \quad \mu \geq 169.0 \text{ cm}$$
$$H_1: \quad \mu < 169.0 \text{ cm}$$

II. *Level of significance:* $\alpha = 0.05$ for a one-tailed test.
III. *Statistical model:* The normal curve model
IV. *Region of rejection* (Fig. 9.6): The empirical limit of the directional region of rejection is

$$X = \mu - z\sigma_{\bar{x}} = 169.0 - 1.64(0.53)$$
$$= 168.13 \text{ cm}$$

V. *Statistical decision:* The observed value of $X = 167.9$ falls within the region of rejection. H_o is rejected at $\alpha = 0.05$.
VI. *Nonstatistical decision:* The 45 burials appear to be too short to belong to the Basketmaker human population.

Note that had a level of significance been set initially at $\alpha = 0.01$, the

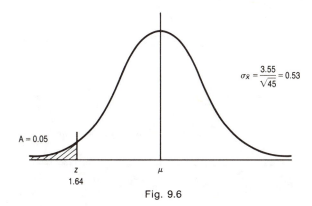

$$\sigma_{\bar{x}} = \frac{3.55}{\sqrt{45}} = 0.53$$

A = 0.05

z
1.64

μ

Fig. 9.6

region of rejection would be

$$X = \mu - z\sigma_{\bar{x}} = 169.0 - 2.33\,(0.53)$$
$$= 167.77$$

The null hypothesis would not have been rejected at the 0.01 level. As long as all the statistical calculations are presented, the reader is free to assign his own alpha level and make a different statistical decision, if warranted.

Example 9.2

A genetic experiment involves *Drosophila*, the common fruit fly. Mendelian genetic theory predicts that normal and truncated wings should appear in offspring in a ratio of 1:1. The final count reveals 67 pairs of normal wings and 73 sets of truncated wings. Does this observed ratio represent a significant deviation from expectation under genetic theory?

    I. *Statistical hypotheses:* Let p = probability of truncated wings and q = probability of normal wings.

$$H_o:\ \ p = q \qquad H_1:\ \ p \ne q$$

   II. *Level of significance:* $\alpha = 0.05$ for a two-tailed test.
 III. *Statistical model:* The normal approximation to the binomial sampling distribution.
 IV. *Region of rejection* (Fig. 9.7): The appropriate value of z corresponding to $A = \alpha/2 = 0.025$ is found from Table A.3 to be $z = 1.96$. The parameters of the binomial sampling distribution are

$$p = q = \frac{1}{2}$$

$$\mu = np = 140\left(\frac{1}{2}\right) = 70.0$$

$$\sigma = \sqrt{140\left(\frac{1}{2}\right)\left(\frac{1}{2}\right)} = 5.92$$

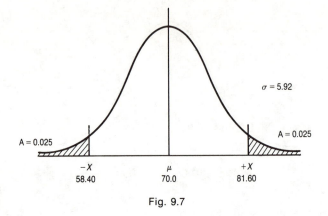

Fig. 9.7

The empirical region of rejection is bound by

$$X = \mu \pm z\sigma = 70 \pm 1.69(5.92)$$
$$= 60 \text{ and } 80$$

V. *Statistical decision:* The probability of truncated wings is p, so the actual count of 73 pairs of truncated wings does not fall within the region of rejection. H_o is not rejected.

VI. *Nonstatistical decision:* The experiment on *Drosophila* wing form is consistent with established genetic principles. (Note that in this case the research hypothesis was identified with H_o rather than with H_1, as is often the case.)

9.3 WHAT DOES A STATISTICALLY SIGNIFICANT RESULT MEAN?

● *Only one thing's a cinch—that's the strap that holds the saddle on.*—B. Jones

If you read Section 9.2 carefully, you noted that the results of statistical hypothesis testing were stated in very precise English. The wording was almost painstakingly deliberate. When the statistic fell into the critical region, the null hypothesis was unequivocally "rejected." But how was the alternative decision worded? When the test statistic failed to fall within the region of rejection, the null hypothesis was "not rejected." The null hypothesis was not "accepted," as one might expect. Why is this so?

The hypothesis-testing episode began with the question: Do the results at hand differ from those expected by chance alone? More specifically: How often would we expect to get so great a difference because of random sampling error? An appropriate statistical model was selected, the research hypotheses were translated into operational hypotheses and the critical region was defined as containing all possible samples which would be unacceptable (given α), and the statistical model was described. The sample was then compared to the critical region. The final decision declares whether or not the observed deviation is "significantly" different from those expected under H_o. In this manner, we concluded that the Hudson's Bay census of 1858 contained sex ratios "significantly different" from those expected by chance deviations at $\alpha = 0.05$. In this sense, "every experiment may be said to exist only in order to give the facts a chance of disproving the null hypothesis" (Fisher 1935: 16).

Recently, Raoul Naroll has suggested we approach statistical inference from the opposite direction. Rather than search for results which are "significant at the α level," we might rename our statistical machinery "insignificance testing" (Naroll 1971). The burden of proof is thereby shifted. Using Naroll's terminology, we could say that the Peel River Kutchin census data have "passed an insignificance test at the 0.05 level." The phrasing emphasizes the fact that this result *may or may not* have merit, depending upon the substantive explanations. But had the data "failed" the insignificance test, as did the Ojibwa census, we could justifiably conclude that the alternative hypothesis is a worthless explanation of the findings. "Significance tests" do not establish significance at all. *Significance testing establishes only which hypotheses are worthless.*

Thus, the actual nature of statistics is negative rather than positive. Scientific research in anthropology will never prove that a theory is *right*; anthropologists can prove only that rival theories are *wrong*. This skepticism, endemic to science, results directly from the elusive nature of causality, a topic to be considered later.

Because of the skeptical structure of statistics, we should always be more confident in negative findings than in positive assertions. At the conclusion of an episode of hypothesis testing, either we firmly reject the null hypothesis— only implying the tenability of H_1—or withhold judgment on the grounds that the data are insufficiently deviant to allow rejection of H_o. The null hypothesis is not *accepted* because too many complicating factors are involved.

● *Science? The Savage frowned. He knew the word. But what it exactly signified he could not say. Shakespeare and the old men of the pueblo had never mentioned science... science was something you made helicopters with, something that caused you to laugh at the Corn Dances, something that prevented you from being wrinkled and losing your teeth.—* A. Huxley

SUGGESTIONS FOR FURTHER READING

Brim and Spain (1974)
Kemeny (1959: chapters 5–7)
Kerlinger (1973: chapters 2, 12, 17–21)
Morrison and Henkel (1970)
Pelto (1970: chapter 7)
Siegel (1956: chapters 2, 3)
Thomas (1974: chapter 7)

10 The Student's t-Distribution

I ask for more information because I am unable to unscrew the unscrutable.—S. Ervin

10.1 INTRODUCTION

Now we know how to translate research hypotheses into the language of statistical inference and how to test some of the more elementary propositions. The null hypothesis, you will remember, posits an expected value of some population parameter, and the alternative hypothesis covers the other potential values of that parameter. Once the variability of the sampling distribution is determined from the Central Limit Theorem, the z-value is compared with a predetermined level of statistical significance. In this manner decisions can be rendered regarding the credibility of null hypotheses based upon the sample at hand.

But here we encounter yet another snag. It seems that all the examples considered thus far have assumed that σ is known. At the time, of course, I did not explain just how we came to know σ; I just stated an arbitrary value. Unfortunately, such is rarely the case in actual research, and we must now face the practical difficulty of modifying what we have already learned to account for a more realistic application. Specifically, we must assess the impact of substituting S for σ in computing the standardized normal deviate z.

10.2 THE t-DISTRIBUTION

Chapter 8 established that the standard error is really just the standard deviation of the sampling distribution of sample means:

$$\sigma_{\bar{x}} = \frac{\sigma_x}{\sqrt{n}}$$

227

So $\sigma_{\bar{x}}$ applies to the theoretically infinite population of sample means. But when σ is unknown, then the standard error must be estimated from the sample data at hand. The best *estimate of the standard error of the mean* is

$$S_{\bar{x}} = \frac{S_x}{\sqrt{n}} \tag{10.1}$$

$S_{\bar{x}}$ is generally called simply the *standard error of the mean*, but keep in mind that $S_{\bar{x}}$ functions as a statistic whose job is to estimate $\sigma_{\bar{x}}$ (and, by extension, σ). The standard error tells us that any difference between the population mean and the sample mean drawn from the population is an "error" which has been spawned by the vicissitudes of sampling. Were there no errors, then all the $\bar{X}_i$ would be identical, regardless of how many samples had been drawn. In this case, the standard error would drop to zero. But a standard error of zero is impossible for any real run of data because of the omnipresent errors of sampling.

$S_{\bar{x}}$, therefore, estimates $\sigma_{\bar{x}}$ when σ is unknown. We know that the quantity $z = (\bar{X} - \mu)/\sigma_{\bar{x}}$ is a random variable with a mean of zero and a variance of 1. If the X_i are normally distributed, these quantities are exact; otherwise, the result is only approximate. Table A.3 (Appendix) provides the probabilities associated with various areas contained under this z-distribution. What effect does the substitution of $S_{\bar{x}}$ for $\sigma_{\bar{x}}$ have upon the distribution of z?

In the early days of statistical theory, the estimated standard error of the mean, $S_{\bar{x}}$, was simply substituted forthwith into the formula for z, a• though no estimation was involved at all. But we now know that substituting $S_{\bar{x}}$ for $\sigma_{\bar{x}}$ produces a different, rather distinctive, mathematical entity called t:

$$t = \frac{\bar{X} - \mu}{S_{\bar{x}}} \tag{10.2}$$

Despite the superficial similarity of z and t, a couple of critical differences distinguish the behavior of each.

The numerator of the familiar z-score depends upon two quantities: The sample mean and the population mean. Sample means are always random variables, but the population mean is a parameter and hence is constant for a given population. Thus, for a particular population, the numerator of z depends strictly upon $\bar{X}$, and μ is constant. The denominator of z is also invariant because $\sigma_{\bar{x}}$ is constant for a sample size n. The specific value of any z depends strictly upon the value of the sample mean.

The distribution of the t-ratio is more complex. As with z, the numerator of t is a random variable, dependent upon $\bar{X}$. But unlike z, the denominator of t is not constant; $S_{\bar{x}}$ is a statistic varying from sample to sample. The value of any particular t depends upon *both* the sample mean and the sample variance. The t-ratio has become a function of sample size, since $S_{\bar{x}} = S/\sqrt{n}$, and herein lies the salient difference between z and t. If the same population were repeatedly sampled, a given value of $\bar{X}_i$ would always produce exactly the same value of z. But any given value of $\bar{X}_i$ can produce widely different values of t because $S_{\bar{x}}$ is computed from the specific sample at hand.

The t-ratio is thus more variable than z, and the extreme variates create longer tails for a t-distribution than for a normal distribution. The probability distribu-

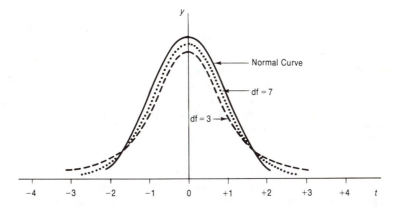

Fig. 10.1   Comparison of two *t*-distributions with the normal curve (after Alder and Roessler 1972: 156).

tion function of *t* becomes flatter than the normal curve, especially when small values of *n* are involved (see Fig. 10.1); the smaller the sample size, the "flatter" becomes the *t*-distribution relative to the normal curve. Conversely, as *n* increases, the distribution of *t* tends toward normality. In fact, for samples of size *n* = 30 and larger, the normal distribution and the *t*-distribution are virtually identical.

The problem of defining a probability distribution for *t* when σ is unknown remained a puzzle throughout the nineteenth century, despite other notable advances in statistical theory. The precise mathematical distribution of *t* was finally established by William S. Gosset, a statistician employed by the Guinness brewery in Dublin. The Guinness people had a strict rule prohibiting their employees from publishing their discoveries, but due to the importance of Gosset's computation, the company granted him the "privilege" of publishing his findings, provided he remain anonymous.

Gosset published his classic paper "The probable error of the mean" in 1908 under the pseudonym of "Student," and many feel that this single article laid the foundation for modern statistical theory. Curiously, the name "Student" has remained permanently affixed to the *t*-distribution even though Gosset's real name was publicly released shortly thereafter. Gosset's mathematical findings are beyond the present scope,[1] but his derivation of the equation for *t* allowed others to tabulate the various probabilities contained under the probability distribution of *t* (see Table A.4). The *t*-tables are quite simple to operate and allow ready computation for practical research problems when σ is unknown.

Assigning a probability figure to *t* requires only two simple quantities: the level of significance and the sample size. Probability values ranging from $\alpha = 0.450$ to $\alpha = 0.005$ are listed across the top of Table A.4. This table has been constructed for testing two-tailed hypotheses, so each probability includes the area under *both* tails of the *t*-distribution. The appropriate significance level for

[1]The equation for the Student's *t*-distribution is given by Mood and Graybill (1963: 233) and discussed in detail by Hays (1973: 392–399).

a one-tailed case is found by consulting the figure listed under $p = 2\alpha$. If a one-tailed hypothesis were to be tested at the 0.01 level, the appropriate column of Table A.4 is $p = 2\alpha = 2(0.01) = 0.02$.

The sample size is also necessary to enter Table A.4, but note that the rows are labelled "df" rather than the familiar n. The abbreviation df stands for *degrees of freedom*, a most important statistical concept. For now, we must settle for a relatively general explanation of this concept. The number of degrees of freedom in a sample is the number of freely varying quantities. Suppose you wished to find four integers which sum to 20:

$$a + b + c + d = 20$$

You could assign any possible value for any three digits; say, a, b, and c. But because the sum must equal 20, the last digit to be selected (d in this case) is *not* free to vary. The value of the final digit is "fixed," predetermined, because there is only a single value which will still produce a sum of 20. Suppose you selected the following integers:

$$a = 42 \qquad b = 26 \qquad c = -96$$

The d can take only one possible value: $d = -48$. The total number of integers involved in this example is $n = 4$. But the *total number of independent choices* is only $(n - 1) = 3$. The number of independent choices is termed the number of *degrees of freedom*. We have lost one degree of freedom by imposing the condition that the numbers must sum to 20. The number of degrees of freedom are given by n minus the number of conditions imposed upon the variates.

Although you may not have realized it, a condition has been imposed on the sample being tested against the t-distribution: The sample variates must have a mean of $\bar{X}$. Every sample has exactly n variates, but only $(n - 1)$ of these variates are free to vary independently of one another. The last value is predetermined by the equation $\bar{X} = \Sigma X_i / n$. Hence, *for the t-distribution, the number of degrees of freedom is always* $(n - 1)$.

10.3 COMPARING A SAMPLE TO A POPULATION WHEN σ IS UNKNOWN

We now possess a distribution which facilitates hypothesis testing, regardless of whether or not σ is unknown. We can now approach realistic data without making unrealistic assumptions. The t-test is not without assumptions, of course, and these are discussed in Section 10.9.

One common application of the t-distribution often involves comparing a sample mean with some parametric mean. For two-tailed testing, the statistical hypotheses are

$$H_o: \quad \mu = A \qquad H_1: \quad \mu \neq A$$

where A is some hypothetical value. The directional versions of these hypotheses are

$$H_o: \quad \mu \geq A \qquad (\text{or } \mu \leq A)$$
$$H_1: \quad \mu < A \qquad (\text{or } \mu > A)$$

The constant A is zero in many cases, but A is free to assume any a priori value. The equation for t has already been introduced as Formula (10.2)

$$t = \frac{\overline{X} - \mu}{S_{\bar{x}}} \quad \cdot \text{ with df} = (n - 1)$$

where $S_{\bar{x}} = S/\sqrt{n}$. A couple of simple examples should suffice to illustrate this application of the *t*-distribution.

Example 10.1

Consider the following generalization: Hunter-gatherers tend to have an average population density of about 10 square miles per person. Test this hypothesis upon the following data taken from Steward (1938: 48–49) for the Northern Paiute of the western United States.

Owens Valley	2.1 square miles per person
Deep Springs	10.7
Fish Lake Valley	9.9
Saline Valley	16.6
Death Valley	30.0

Let μ be the population mean for the continuous random variable "population density." The statistical hypotheses are

$H_o:$ $\mu = 10$ square miles per person

$H_i:$ $\mu \neq 10$ square miles per person

Because σ, the standard deviation of the random variable X, is unknown, the *t*-test must be used instead of the familiar model of the normal distribution. This is a two-tailed test, with $\alpha = 0.05$. With df $= 5 - 1 = 4$, the boundary of the critical region for t is $t_{0.05} = 2.776$. The critical region itself is actually a set of *t*-values such that $|t| > 2.776$.

The sample size is $n = 5$ and the descriptive statistics are

$$\overline{X} = \frac{69.3}{5} = 13.86 \text{ square miles per person}$$

$$S = \sqrt{\frac{431.97}{4}} = \sqrt{107.99}$$

The standard error of the mean is estimated by

$$S_{\bar{x}} = \frac{\sqrt{107.97}}{\sqrt{5}} = 4.65 \text{ square miles per person}$$

The *t*-ratio in this case is

$$t = \frac{13.86 - 10.0}{4.65} = 0.83$$

232

Since this computed t-statistic does not fall within the critical region, H_o is not rejected. We conclude that the Northern Paiute data are consistent with the generalization that hunter-gatherers have an average population density of 10 square miles per person.

Suppose that one erroneously applied the normal distribution model instead. The sample standard deviation must be taken to estimate σ, despite the small sample size of $n = 5$:

$$z = \frac{\bar{X} - \mu}{\sigma_{\bar{x}}} = \frac{13.86 - 10.0}{10.39/\sqrt{5}} = 0.83$$

We find the associated probability to be $p = 0.2005$. Since we know that the true probability ($t = 0.83$) lies between 0.4 and 0.5, the incorrect application of the normal distribution model would cause us to underestimate the true probability by more than 50 percent.

Example 10.2

Clovis projectile points tend, on the average, to be about 7.5 cm long (Wormington 1957: 263). The Lehner Ranch site in southern Arizona yielded 13 projectile points associated with the butchered remains of mammoth, horse, bison, and tapir. The excavators (Haury, Sayles, and Wasley 1959: table 1) list the following length measurements for these artifacts (numbers in parentheses are estimates):

Point	Length, cm	Point	Length, cm
1	(8.7)	8	4.7
2	7.9	9	5.6
3	8.3	10	3.1
4	7.4	11	7.8
5	(3.6)	12	9.7
6	6.2	13	5.2
7	8.1		

Since the average length of these 13 points is less than 6.7 cm, are these points significantly shorter than most Clovis points (at the 0.05 level)?

Let μ be the population mean of the random variable "total length." σ is unknown.

Statistical hypotheses:

$$H_o: \quad \mu \geq 7.5 \text{ cm}$$
$$H_1: \quad \mu < 7.5 \text{ cm}$$

Critical region: With df $= (13 - 1) = 12$ and a one-tailed test:

$$t_{2\alpha} = t_{0.10} = 1.782$$

Sample statistics:

$$\bar{X} = \frac{86.3}{13} = 6.64 \text{ cm}$$

$$S = 2.06 \text{ cm}$$

$$S_{\bar{x}} = \frac{2.06}{\sqrt{13}} = 0.57 \text{ cm}$$

t-ratio:

$$t = \frac{6.64 - 7.5}{0.57} = -1.51$$

Statistical decision: Since the computed value does not fall within the region of rejection, H_o is not rejected.

Research decision: The sample of 13 projectile points from the Lehner Ranch are not significantly shorter than typical Clovis points.

As an aside, let us examine the computation of the sample standard deviation. The above value of S was computed by Formula (4.13):

$$S = \sqrt{\frac{\Sigma(X_i - \bar{X})^2}{n-1}} = \sqrt{\frac{50.88}{12}} = 2.06 \text{ cm}$$

But suppose that the formula with divisor of n had erroneously been applied. Then

$$\hat{S} = \sqrt{\frac{\Sigma(X_i - \bar{X})^2}{n}} = \sqrt{\frac{50.88}{13}} = 1.98 \text{ cm}$$

This value of S can readily be corrected by using the correction factor presented earlier:

$$S = \sqrt{\frac{n}{n-1}} \, \hat{S}$$

$$= \sqrt{\frac{13}{12}} (1.98) = 2.06 \text{ cm}$$

This correction is often necessary when dealing with standard deviations computed on a computer.

10.4 CONFIDENCE INTERVALS FOR μ WHEN σ IS UNKNOWN

The earlier discussion of confidence intervals for the population mean (Section 8.5) assumed that σ was known. Substituting $S_{\bar{x}}$ for $\sigma_{\bar{x}}$ vitiates use of the normal distribution, upon which Expression (8.6) was based.

The *t*-distribution allows us to derive a new expression which is applicable even though σ is unknown. Solving Expression (10.2) for μ, we find the *confidence limits for μ when σ is unknown* to be

$$\mu = \bar{X} \pm tS_x \qquad (10.3)$$

The *t*-distribution is symmetrical, so the confidence limits fall equidistant from $\bar{X}$. Confidence intervals are computed in a manner identical to those of the normal distribution except that the tabled value of *t* is substituted for *z* and $S_{\bar{x}}$ is involved rather than $\sigma_{\bar{x}}$.

Example 10.3

Find the 99 percent confidence limits for the 13 Clovis points from the Lehner Ranch site (Example 10.2).

The appropriate value of *t* with 12 degrees of freedom is $t_{0.01} = 3.055$. Substituting into Expression (10.3):

$$\text{Confidence limits} = 6.64 \pm 3.055 \left(\frac{2.06}{\sqrt{13}} \right) \text{cm}$$

$$= 6.64 \pm 1.74 \text{ cm}$$

We conclude with 99 percent confidence that the true parametric length of these Clovis points lies between 4.90 and 8.38 cm.

Example 10.4

Five skulls were excavated from a large Pleistocene cave in mainland China:

Skull	Cranial Capacity, cc
1	1225
2	1135
3	1055
4	1225
5	1030

Find the 95 percent confidence interval for this population.

We compute $\bar{X} = 1134.0$ cc with $S = 91.68$ cc. The appropriate value of *t* with four degrees of freedom is found from Table A.4 to be $t_{0.05} = 2.776$. Substituting into Equation (10.3):

$$\text{Confidence limits} = 1143.0 \pm 2.776 \left(\frac{91.68}{\sqrt{5}} \right) \text{cc}$$

$$= 1134.0 \pm 113.63 \text{ cc}$$

We can conclude that the probability is 0.95 that the true population mean lies between 1020.4 and 1247.7 cc.

10.5 COMPARING TWO SAMPLE MEANS WHEN σ IS UNKNOWN

Section 10.3 presented a method for evaluating statistical hypotheses about the mean of a single population. Some value for μ (which we called A) was compared to the sample value. But sometimes it is impossible to frame a hypothesis specific enough to predict exact values for μ. Anthropologists are often interested in comparisons which evaluate differences between two sample means without reference to specific values for μ. Not only are comparative studies important in themselves in anthropology, but relational hypotheses (as opposed to absolute hypotheses) also sidestep the task of predicting exact values for μ. It is almost impossible, for example, to predict an absolute value for the cranial capacity of a sample of *Australopithecus* skulls. But it is a relatively easy matter to predict that *Australopithecus* skulls should have a smaller cranial capacity than a sample of Neanderthal skulls. Similarly, we can guess that hunters such as the Eskimo will have a higher per capita protein intake than a largely plant-gathering group such as the Western Shoshoni, even though the precise value of the protein intake for either group is unknown.

Only rarely will a sample mean ever exactly equal the population mean. This is because of sampling error. Similarly, two populations with identical means $(\mu_1 = \mu_2)$ will almost always yield samples with different means ($\bar{X}_1 \neq \bar{X}_2$), once again because of sampling error. So the question must arise when comparing two sample means as to whether the difference is due to a real difference between the populations or whether the disparity between the samples should be attributed to chance alone.

Consider the archaeologist attempting to infer prehistoric population dynamics from a settlement pattern survey. He might suspect that one plant community supported a denser population than did the adjacent biotic community, even though he cannot accurately predict the population densities of two areas. Valley floor biota might, for instance, be expected to support a greater population density than the neighboring hilly mountain flanks. Accepting the "number of rooms per building" in an archaeological site as an operational indicator of population density, the hypotheses would appear

$$H_o: \quad \mu_X \leq \mu_Y \qquad H_1: \quad \mu_X > \mu_Y$$

We are predicting an ordinal relationship ("greater than") rather than a metric hypothesis ("*how much* greater than"). Suppose that a sample of nine contemporary sites were excavated to test this proposition:

Valley Floor, Site	No. of Rooms
1	9
2	10
3	7
4	10

$\bar{X} = 9.0$ rooms per site; $S_x = 1.41$ rooms per site.

Mountain Flanks, Site	No. of Rooms
1	6
2	5
3	7
4	4
5	5

$\bar{Y} = 5.4$ rooms per site; $S_Y = 1.14$ rooms per site.

The descriptive statistics tell us that the valley floor sites tend to have more rooms than sites on the mountain flanks ($\bar{X} = 9.0 > \bar{Y} = 5.4$). The research hypothesis would appear to be correct (at least the direction is right). But the size difference is not overwhelming and might well be due to mere sampling error rather than a true difference in site size.

That is, we must consider the *standard error* of this difference because the larger the standard error, the less chance there is of a true population difference. But if the standard error is relatively small, the *population* of valley floor sites probably has more rooms than the mountain sites, as suggested in the research hypothesis.

This situation is analogous to that encountered in Chapter 8, when two samples were compared. If the population variances were known, then Expression (8.5) could have been used to determine the standardized normal deviate. But as in so many problems of this sort, we must deal with the results at hand.

The first difficulty is to estimate these unknown population variances. We must assume that the two populations have identical variances. By so doing, we can argue that any discrepancy between the samples relates only to differences in central tendency rather than differences in *shape* of the distribution of variates about the mean.

All statistical estimates improve as n increases, so the best possible estimate of either population variance will include the relevant variates. There are two distinct samples involved here, but because we assume the population variances to be equal, we can combine the deviations about the respective sample standard deviation. The individual variances are *pooled* into one single, best estimate of population variance:

$$S_p = \sqrt{\frac{\Sigma(X_i - \bar{X})^2 + \Sigma(Y_i - \bar{Y})^2}{n_x + n_y - 2}} \tag{10.4}$$

This new expression is called the *pooled estimate of the standard deviation*. S_p combines the total amount of deviation about $\bar{X}$ in the first sample with the amount of deviation about $\bar{Y}$ in the second sample and then averages this by dividing by the combined number of degrees of freedom. Two degrees of freedom are lost because two independent means were computed. S_p is an unbiased estimator of σ only as long as the individual population variances are assumed to be equal.

Let us see how the pooled estimate of σ works on the archaeological data at hand. Each sample has a known standard deviation: S_x estimates the variability in the number of rooms per site on the valley floor (σ_X) and S_Y estimates the variability in the mountain sites (σ_Y). By assuming that $\sigma_X = \sigma_Y$, S_X and S_Y are combined (*pooled*) into a single estimator, S_p.

$$S_p = \sqrt{\frac{6.00 + 5.20}{4 + 5 - 2}} = \sqrt{1.60} = 1.26$$

Thus, S_p estimates that the population standard deviation of rooms per site on the valley floor—and by assumption, also on the mountain slopes—is $\sigma_X = \sigma_Y = 1.26$ rooms per site.

With this new estimate of total variability firmly in hand, it becomes possible to define an appropriate expression of the *t*-ratio to test for a difference between two samples:

$$t = \frac{(\bar{X} - \bar{Y}) - \mu_{\bar{X}-\bar{Y}}}{S_{\bar{X}-\bar{Y}}} \tag{10.5}$$

where df $= n_X + n_Y - 2$. In this expression,

$$\mu_{\bar{X}-\bar{Y}} = \mu_X - \mu_Y$$

and

$$S_{\bar{X}-\bar{Y}} = \sqrt{\frac{S_p^{\,2}}{n_X} + \frac{S_p^{\,2}}{n_Y}}$$

Note that S_p^2/n_X corresponds to $S_{\bar{X}}^2$. The general configuration of the *t*-ratio remains as before. A parametric mean (in this case $\mu_{\bar{X}-\bar{Y}}$) is subtracted from the sample estimate of this mean, $\bar{X} - \bar{Y}$, and is then divided by an estimate of the standard error of the difference between the sample means ($S_{\bar{X}-\bar{Y}}$).

We can now statistically assess the difference between two small sample means. $S_{\bar{X}-\bar{Y}}$ is found in the archaeological example to be

$$S_{\bar{X}} = \sqrt{\frac{1.60}{4}} = \sqrt{0.40}; \qquad S_{\bar{Y}} = \sqrt{\frac{1.60}{5}} = \sqrt{0.32}$$

$$S_{\bar{X}-\bar{Y}} = \sqrt{0.40 + 0.32} = \sqrt{0.72} = 0.85 \text{ room per site}$$

Note there is no need to take the square root when computing $S_{\bar{X}}$ and $S_{\bar{Y}}$. The radicals will automatically cancel when $S_{\bar{X}}$ and $S_{\bar{Y}}$ are substituted into $S_{\bar{X}-\bar{Y}}$.

The value of *t* in the example is

$$t = \frac{3.6 - 0}{0.85} = 4.24$$

with df $= 4 + 5 - 2 = 7$. This observed *t* is highly signficant since $t_{0.02} = 2.998$ with 7 degrees of freedom. Hence, the archaeological samples allow rejection of H_0, and we may justifiably conclude that valley sites tend to have more rooms than do the mountain sites. (Whether the index of "rooms per archaeological site" is a relevant indicator of prehistoric population density, of course, remains an archaeological rather than a statistical matter.)

An understandable degree of confusion can arise from the several variance estimates involved in comparing two samples. To <mark>summarize:</mark>

S_x = standard deviation of sample X (estimates σ_x).

S_Y = standard deviation of sample Y (estimates σ_Y).

S_P = pooled standard deviation of both sample X and Y (best estimate of both σ_x and σ_Y, which are assumed to be equal).

$S_{\bar{x}} = S_p/\sqrt{n_x}$ is the standard error of sample X.

$S_{\bar{y}} = S_p/\sqrt{n_Y}$ is the standard error of sample Y.

$S_{\bar{x}-\bar{y}}$ = standard error of the difference between the two sample means (estimates $\sigma_{\bar{x}-\bar{y}}$).

Example 10.5

In Example 10.1, a sample of five Northern Paiute bands were found to have an average population density of $\bar{X} = 13.86$ square miles per person, with $S_x = 10.39$. The following sample of 11 Western Shoshoni bands (the Northern Paiute and Western Shoshoni are neighbors in the Great Basin) shows an average population density of $\bar{Y} = 7.91$ square miles per person. Can the Western Shoshoni be said to have a higher population density than the Northern Paiute at the 0.05 level (data from Steward 1938: 48–49)?

Band	Population Density, square miles per person
Reese River	3.6
Railroad Valley	9.0
Antelope Valley	11.0
Gosiute	12.5
Diamond Valley	3.8
Ruby Valley	2.8
Palisade	3.3
Halleck	4.0
Battle Mountain	2.5
Kawich	17.0
Little Smoky Valley	17.5

Statistical hypotheses:

$$H_o: \quad \mu_x \geq \mu_Y \qquad H_1: \quad \mu_x < \mu_Y$$

Region of rejection: For a one-tailed test with $(5 + 11 - 2) = 14$ degrees of freedom, $t_{0.10} = 1.761$.

To find $S_{\bar{x}-\bar{y}}$, we must first find S_p, the pooled estimate:

$$S_p = \sqrt{\frac{431.8 - 334.1}{5 + 11 - 2}} = \sqrt{6.98}$$

$$S_{\bar{x}-\bar{y}} = \sqrt{\frac{6.98}{5} + \frac{6.98}{11}} = \sqrt{2.03} = 1.43$$

Note that the sample standard deviation per se (S_x and S_Y) is not needed in finding $S_{\bar{X}-\bar{Y}}$, since $\Sigma(X_i - \bar{X})^2$ and $\Sigma(Y_i - \bar{Y})^2$ are the appropriate terms for finding S_p, which in turn is substituted into $S_{\bar{X}-\bar{Y}}$.

The *t*-ratio is found to be

$$t = \frac{(13.86 - 7.91)}{1.43} = 4.16$$

The computed value of *t* far exceeds the critical region, so H_o is rejected. On the basis of the two samples at hand, Western Shoshoni can be said to have a higher population density than Northern Paiute. Another way of stating this conclusion is that Northern Paiute and Western Shoshoni samples do not appear to have been selected from the same statistical population.

Example 10.6

A paradox in the evolution of culture is how consistently man's technological advances seem to backfire; Marvin Harris (1971: 216) has called such advances the "labor-saving devices that increase work." It can be said, for example, that advanced agricultural techniques have *increased* (rather than decreased) the per capita amount of work required for survival. To test this hypothesis, fieldwork was carried out among the Bushmen (a hunter-gatherer people) and a group of West African subsistence farmers. This sample of 26 Bushmen indicated that each works an average of 805 hours per year, with $S = 10.3$. The 16 West Africans in the sample spent an average of 820 hours per year, with $S = 12.9$ hours. Do these results support the hypothesis that hunter-gatherer groups tend to work less than agriculturalists (at the 0.01 level)?

Let us term the Bushmen as group X and the farmers as group Y.

Statistical hypotheses:

$$H_o: \quad \mu_X \geq \mu_Y \qquad H_1: \quad \mu_X < \mu_Y$$

Region of rejection: For a one-tailed test with $(26 + 16 - 2) = 40$ degrees of freedom, $t_{0.02} = 2.423$.

We know the two sample standard deviations, $S_X = 10.3$ and $S_Y = 12.9$, so it is necessary to work back to find the sum of the squared deviations:

$$S_X = \sqrt{\frac{\Sigma(X_i - \bar{X})^2}{n - 1}}$$

$$\Sigma(X_i - \bar{X})^2 = S_X^2(n_X - 1) = (10.3)^2(25) = 2652.25$$
$$\Sigma(Y_i - \bar{Y})^2 = S_Y^2(n_Y - 1) = (12.9)^2(15) = 2496.15$$

The pooled estimate of the standard deviation is

$$S_p = \sqrt{\frac{2652.25 + 2496.15}{40}} = 11.35$$

The standard error of the difference is

$$S_{\bar{x}-\bar{y}} = \sqrt{\frac{128.71}{26} + \frac{128.71}{16}} = \sqrt{4.95 + 8.04}$$

$$= \sqrt{12.99} = 3.60$$

The t-ratio is found to be

$$t = \frac{(805 - 820) - 0}{3.60} = -4.17$$

Since $|t| = 4.17 > t_{0=02} = 2.423$, the results are judged to be statistically significant and H_0 is rejected. These two samples lead us to conclude that Bushmen seem to work significantly less than West African agriculturalists. Further generalization—to all hunter-gatherers and agriculturalists—becomes an anthropological rather than a statistical matter.

10.6 COMPARING A SINGLE VARIATE TO A SAMPLE

The following formula can be used to determine the probability that a single isolated variate belongs to the same population as a given sample:

$$t = \frac{(\bar{X} - X_i)\sqrt{n/(n+1)}}{S_x} \tag{10.6}$$

where S_x is the standard deviation of the sample. The number of degrees of freedom are equal to $df = (n - 1)$. This formula is derived from a simplification of Expression (10.5) which compared the means of two independent samples: One "sample" in this case consists of a single variate. Note that had two "samples," each containing only a single variate, been compared, then $df = n_x + n_y - 2 = 0$. Two isolated variates cannot be compared.

Example 10.7

Paleoanthropologist Bryan Patterson found a fragment of human mandible at Kangatotha, west of Lake Rudolf, Kenya. A radiocarbon analysis determined a probable age of 2835 B.C. ± 100. The crown area of M_1 on the Kangatotha mandible is 139.2 mm^2 (data from Coon 1971b: table 2). By contrast, Shaw measured a series of 73 South African Bantu informants and found the crown area of M_1 to be only 115.5 mm^2 (assume $S = 11.0$ mm). Is the Kangatotha molar too large to be Bantu at the 0.01 level of significance?

Statistical hypotheses:

$$H_0: \quad \mu \leq 115.5 \text{ mm} \qquad H_1: \quad \mu > 115.5 \text{ mm}$$

Region of rejection: For a one-tailed test with $\alpha = 0.01$, and df $= 72 - 1 = 71$, $t_{0.02} = 2.390$. (The tabled value for 60 df is sufficient in this case.)

The *t*-ratio is computed to be

$$t = \frac{(115.5 - 139.2)\sqrt{73/74}}{11.0} = -2.14$$

This value of t is less than the critical value, so H_o is not rejected. Thus, the crown area of the Kangatotha molar is not significantly different from the Bantu sample. They could represent the same statistical population. You should note, however, that this conclusion does *not* have taxonomic implications.

10.7 SPECIAL CASE: STATISTICAL INFERENCE IN RADIOCARBON DATING

Radiocarbon dates are the final product of a fascinating collaboration between nuclear physicists, statisticians, and archaeologists. Radioactive decay is a random process. Beta emissions are produced as C^{14} atoms decay to N^{14} (nitrogen), and these emissions can be detected by sensitive Geiger counters. The underlying principle of this complex technique is simple—the fewer emissions, the older the carbon. Although the average number of emissions can be predicted over a given span of time, nobody can ever predict precisely which atoms will decay at any particular time. The radiocarbon laboratory employs Geiger counters to measure the number of beta particles emitted over a 1000-minute interval. Because radioactive decay is a random process, the sample variability must be taken into account, and samples are always counted twice. If the counts from the two runs are in "statistical agreement," further counting is unnecessary.

The "radiocarbon date" itself consists of two parts, a mean and a standard deviation: $\bar{X} \pm S$. For example, an archaeologist might receive the following radiocarbon determination from the laboratory:

950 ± 40 radiocarbon years B.P. (before present)

In this case, $\bar{X} = 950$, which estimates the true age of the sample (μ). The degree of variability between counting runs is expressed by S, the sample standard deviation. The population standard deviation is unknown and estimated by S. The larger the S, the more variability was observed between counting runs, and the less reliable is $\bar{X}$ in estimating μ. From what we already know about the nature of the normal curve, this means that there is a 68.26 percent chance that the true age falls within the range of $\bar{X} \pm S$, that is, between 910 and 990 radiocarbon years ago. The average age of any sample is only an *estimate* of the true age, so the plus-minus factor should never be omitted from radiocarbon determinations.

An example should clarify these elementary statistical aspects of radiocarbon dating. During the 600-year Classic period, the Maya erected carved stone monuments (stelae) bearing "Long Count" dates. The dates seem often to denote the date of dedication of a temple or other ceremonial structure, although the exact meaning of the inscriptions is still unknown. Mayan epigraphers have struggled for decades trying to correlate the Mayan Long Count system with the Christian calendar.[2] The search was finally narrowed to a series of discrete choices.

Any given katun (Maya period of 20 years, each consisting of 366 days) can recur in the Maya system only once every 260 years. As a result, scholars have correlated given Maya dates to several intervals along the Christian calendar, depending upon the zero point chosen for the Maya system. The Maya date 9.15.10.0.0 3 Ahau 8 Mol, for example, dedicated Temple IV at the Classic Maya site of Tikal, Guatemala. George Spinden correlated this date to August 29, A.D. 481. A second reckoning, the Goodman–Thompson–Martinez correlation, sets this same Maya dedicatory date exactly 13 katuns (260 years) later, at June 28, A.D. 741. A solid case was made for both correlations, based upon historic records of the Maya calendar, and a stalemate resulted. Fortunately, some of the inscriptions at Temple IV were upon wooden lintels, so the radiocarbon laboratory at the University of Pennsylvania ran a series of tests upon the lintel itself in an effort to resolve the correlation problem. The hope was that the C^{14} dates would correspond to one of the two likely correlations, setting the dispute to rest.

Although dozens of radiocarbon determinations were processed on the Tikal beams, consider for the moment the implications of a single date (from Satterthwaite and Ralph 1960: table 1).

Laboratory Number	Beam Number	Age, years B.P.	Age, years A.D.
P-236	Room 2, VB2	1262 ± 38	697 ± 38

Each "radiocarbon date" is assigned a laboratory number. If subsequent runs were made on the same sample, a new number would be assigned to keep the independent determinations separate. Date P-236 (the 236th determination run by the Pennsylvania Laboratory) has an average age of $\bar{X} = 697$ radiocarbon years,[3] with a sample standard deviation of $S = 38$ years. Remembering that $\bar{X}$ is only an estimate of the true age of the Tikal lintel, the standard deviation can be used to compute the same limits of confidence for the true age (μ). There is, for example, a 0.6826 probability that the true age lies between A.D. 659 and A.D. 735 (see Fig. 10.2). There is also a probability of 95 percent that the true age falls between A.D. 622 and A.D. 771 ($\bar{X} \pm 1.96S$). While these reliability estimates place the true age of the sample within a known error factor, the data do not directly tell us about the correlation problem.

By inspection, we can see that the sample mean of P-236 is 44 years younger

[2]See the discussion earlier in Section 2.4.3 for a consideration of this problem in terms of levels of measurement.

[3]By convention, all C^{14} dates are computed as years before 1950.

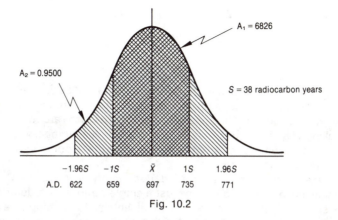

Fig. 10.2

than the Goodman–Thompson–Martinez correlation, but is 216 years too old for the date predicted from the Spinden correlation? Can we therefore say that date P-236 supports the Goodman–Thompson–Martinez correlation? Is the date close enough, or is the 54-year discrepancy too large a difference? Could the error of dating be so great as to support *both* correlations? Or does P-236 suggest that both correlations are wrong? Because radiocarbon dating is a random process, and because of the error introduced in the counting process itself, all radiocarbon dates involve such variability. The solution to the correlation problem will not be absolutely clear-cut. The answer must be expressed in terms of probability.

Figure 10.3 includes both correlation dates for the Maya calendar. We are now dealing with sample statistics (rather than population parameters), so the expressions on the normal curve are denoted by $\bar{X}$ rather than μ, as before. The point X_1 is A.D. 741, the date predicted by the Goodman–Thompson–Martinez correlation. The probability that the true age of sample P-236 is A.D. 741 or older corresponds to

$$z_1 = \frac{X_1 - \bar{X}}{S} = \frac{741 - 697}{38} = 1.16$$

$$p(X \geq 741) > 0.12$$

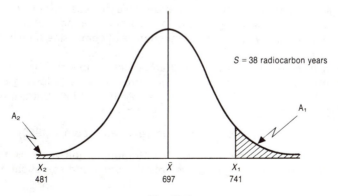

Fig. 10.3

The probability that sample P-236 dates the event to A.D. 481 or younger is

$$z_2 = \frac{X_2 - \bar{X}}{S} = \frac{481 - 697}{38} = -5.68$$

$$p(X \le 481) < 0.0001$$

These results tell us that while the probability that P-236 actually dates the Spinden correlation is virtually nil, the chances of this single sample corresponding to the Goodman-Thompson-Martinez correlation are more than 12 percent. Taking only the results from P-236, the Spinden correlation seems to be eliminated. There remains a good chance that the Goodman–Thompson–Martinez correlation is correct.

But because of the randomness and uncertainty involved in C^{14} dating, archaeologists have learned never to trust a single radiocarbon determination. The large series of dates run for the Tikal lintels, for example, eventually confirmed the Goodman–Thompson–Martinez correlation by an overwhelming margin. The methods for comparing C^{14} dates to see whether they date a single episode will be considered later in this chapter.

> ● *What we seek in any realm of human thought is not absolute certainty, for that is denied us as men, but rather the more modest path of those who find dependable ways of discerning different degrees of probability.*—E. Trueblood

10.7.1 Computing the Radiocarbon Estimates

The radiocarbon age estimate—really a sample mean—is merely the adjusted mean of Geiger counts on ancient charcoal-bearing samples. But the statistical deviation is a more complex statistic, reflecting three major sources of variability: variation in

1. The ancient sample
2. Environmental radiation striking the Geiger counter
3. The known-age calibration sample.

Let us examine how these independent sources of variation are integrated into a single estimate of standard deviation. This discussion not only provides added insight into the workings of the radiocarbon method, but also furnishes an excellent opportunity to review the mechanics of computing (and combining) standard errors.

We begin from scratch by following an actual sample through the various manipulations involved in the radiocarbon process. The following data were obtained from vault beam 2, room 3 in Temple IV at Tikal (Satterthwaite and Ralph 1960: table 1):

(P-243) 1223 ± 46 radiocarbon years B.P. (before 1950)

P-243 can also be expressed as A.D. 727 ± 46 radiocarbon years. But this final age estimate results only after a series of laboratory and statistical manipulations.

Once the beam was removed from the temple, a small sample of zapote wood was cleaned manually to remove termite remains and then soaked in hydrochloric acid to dissolve inorganic carbon compounds. The sample was then placed in a combustion tube with pure oxygen gas and the mixture was ignited to convert the ancient solid carbon into carbon dioxide gas. This gas was filtered to remove contaminants, and then piped into a Geiger counter. We know that a beta particle is emitted each time a C^{14} atom decays back into N^{14}. The actual radiocarbon analysis counts the number of beta emissions—and by extension, the number of C^{14} decays—with a Geiger counter. The length of the counting interval depends both upon the material being dated and also the age of the sample; most laboratories count their samples overnight for a standard interval of 1000 minutes, and every sample is counted at least twice.

The laboratory worksheet for the Tikal date P-243 appears as follows:

Date Counted	Total Count, X_t
3/15/59	37,069
3/16/59	36,918

The total count, X_t, is the exact number of beta emissions recorded in a single 1000-minute counting run. P-243 was counted on both 15 and 16 March. As long as these two net counts are found to be in statistical agreement—by a chi-square test (discussed in Chapter 11)—no further counting runs are necessary. The average of the two total counts is

$$\bar{X}_t = \frac{37,069 + 36,918}{2} = 36,993 \text{ counts}$$

But the University of Pennsylvania radiocarbon laboratory, like every other place on this planet, is subject to atmospheric radioactivity which registers on laboratory Geiger counters along with the ancient sample emissions. The amount of this background radiation, called b, must be determined for each radiocarbon laboratory and then periodically rechecked for fluctuation. During March 1959, the University of Pennsylvania radiocarbon laboratory was bombarded by an average of $b = 9416$ radioactive emissions per 1000-minute counting interval. The net number of emissions, $\bar{X}_n$, from sample P-243 is thus found by subtracting b from each of the total counts. The average net count for both counting runs is

$$\bar{X}_n = \frac{(37,069 - 9416) + (36,918 - 9416)}{2}$$

$$= \frac{(27,653 + 27,502)}{2} = 27,578 \text{ counts}$$

So the average net count, $\bar{X}_n$, is actually a sample mean. More precisely, $\bar{X}_n$ is the mean number of beta emissions per 1000-minute counting interval. The standard error (the standard deviation of the mean) is given by

$$S_{\bar{x}} = \frac{\sqrt{(X_t + b)n}}{n}$$

where n is the number of counting runs.[4] This rather unusual expression is different from the previous standard errors we have encountered because radiocarbon emissions follow the *Poisson distribution*, a variant of the binomial distribution.

The standard error of the net counting rate for sample P-243 is

$$S_{\bar{x}} = \frac{\sqrt{(36{,}993 + 9416)2}}{2} = 152.3 \text{ counts per 1000 minutes}$$

The *net rate per minute*, called I, is then found by dividing by the standard counting interval, 1000 minutes:

$$I = \frac{27{,}578}{1000} = 27.578 \text{ counts per minute}$$

with a standard error of

$$S_I = \frac{S_{\bar{x}}}{1000 \text{ minutes}} = 0.152 \text{ counts per minute}$$

The net counting rate is then converted to an age estimate by comparing the amount of decay in the ancient sample relative to a modern sample. To find this relative amount of decay, it is necessary to know the existing radioactivity of modern samples. The University of Pennsylvania laboratory measured the beta emissions in a number of recent oak tree samples and found the average zero-age counting rate, I_0, to be

$$I_0 = 32.146 \pm 0.040 \text{ counts per minute}$$

The standard error of the difference between the average zero-age rate of emission (I_0) and the emission rate of the ancient Tikal sample (I) is found, as before, as the square root of the sum of the squared individual standard errors:

$$S_t = \sqrt{(0.152)^2 + (0.040)^2} = 0.157 \text{ counts per minute}$$

The value of S_t thus reflects the total combined variability due to fluctuations in (1) the ancient sample, (2) the background, and (3) the zero-age sample. The results of the radiocarbon analysis are hence summarized as

$$\bar{X}_n \pm S_t \text{ counts per minute}$$

Translating the figures from "counts per minute" to "radiocarbon years ago" is accomplished by substitution into the routine formula for age computation (based upon a half-life of 5568 years):

$$\text{absolute time} = \log (I_0/I) \times 18.5 \times 10^3$$

S_t is added to and subtracted from $\bar{X}_n$ to compute the range of one standard error from the mean. These "minimum" and "maximum" ages (± 1 standard error) are substituted into the conversion formula:

---

[4]The symbolism employed here departs somewhat from that generally used by radiocarbon laboratories (for example, Ralph 1971), to remain consistent with the present discussion.

Maximum age:

$$\bar{X}_n - S_t = 27{,}578 - 0.157$$
$$= 27.421 \text{ counts per minute}$$

Maximum time:

$$\log\left(\frac{27.421}{32.146}\right) \times 18.5 \times 10^3 = \log(0.85301) \times 18.5 \times 10^3$$
$$= 1277 \text{ radiocarbon years ago}$$

Minimum age:

$$\bar{X}_n - S_t = 27.578 + 0.157 = 27.735$$

Minimum time:

$$\log\left(\frac{27.735}{32.146}\right) \times 18.5 \times 10^3 = 1186 \text{ radiocarbon years ago}$$

The average of the minimum and maximum ages of this sample provides the best estimate of the true age of the sample: $(1277 + 1186)/2 = 1232$ radiocarbon years ago. The standard error (expressed in years ago rather than in counts per minute) is found as simply half the difference between the "minimum" and "maximum" ages: $(1277 - 1186)/2 = 46$ radiocarbon years ago.

All that remains is to convert the date to "years before 1950." Since the counting runs took place in 1959, the date is converted to $1232 - 9 = 1223$. The final report from the radiocarbon laboratory is

(P-243) 1223 ± 46 radiocarbon years B.P.

Thus, the plus-minus factor appended to radiocarbon dates is really a standard error (the standard deviation of the sample mean).

But a couple of critical assumptions are necessary before the procedures of statistical inference can be applied to radiocarbon dates. We must initially assume that the large number of counts recorded on each run renders the distribution of means (or the distribution of the difference between sample means, if two dates are being compared) practically indistinguishable from that expected for a normally distributed population (Spaulding 1958). That is, the *t*-distribution with an infinitely large number of degrees of freedom is assumed to hold for radiocarbon determinations. We also assume that the rounding of published standard errors does not introduce any significant inaccuracy.

In addition, we are using the standard error derived from averaging the "maximum" and "minimum" ages when it is actually known that the true standard error (expressed in years) always has a plus error somewhat greater than the minus error. But for dates of moderate age, this discrepancy is not marked. For these reasons, comparing radiocarbon ages using the *t*-distribution is only an approximation which becomes less accurate as the age of the sample increases. When greater accuracy is required, it will be necessary to work with the actual counting runs rather than with the dates as expressed in absolute years (see Satterthwaite and Ralph 1960, for a more detailed discussion of these points).

10.7.2 Comparing a Radiocarbon Date to a Fixed Age

Let us return to the Maya Long Count problem. The t-distribution is useful in determining which, if any, of the standard correlations is consistent with the Tikal radiocarbon dates. Although only two of the correlations were mentioned earlier, the Temple IV dates at Tikal were actually tested against five different Maya-Christian correlations (Satterthwaite and Ralph 1960: tables 15 and 17).

Correlation	Estimated Age of Temple IV, Tikal
Spinden	A.D. 481
Dinsmoor	A.D. 504
Goodman–Thompson–Martinez	A.D. 741
Kreichgauer	A.D. 858
Escalona Ramon	A.D. 1001

We can see from inspection that P-243 (A.D. 727) is remarkably close to the Goodman–Thompson–Martinez (GTM) reckoning, but a test of statistical significance will show us just how close the GTM date and P-243 really are.

Statistical hypotheses[5]:

$$H_o: \quad \mu = \text{A.D. } 741 \qquad H_1: \quad \mu \neq \text{A.D. } 741$$

Region of rejection: For a two-tailed test at $\alpha = 0.05$ with df $= \infty$, $t_{0.05} = 1.96$.

Observed t-ratio:

$$t = \frac{\bar{X} - \mu}{S_{\bar{x}}} = \frac{727 - 741}{46} = -0.30$$

The null hypothesis cannot be rejected in this case because $t = 0.30 < t_{0.05} = 1.96$. We conclude that Tikal sample P-243 is consistent with the Goodman–Thompson–Martinez hypothesis.

Note that this conclusion in no way confirms the GTM correlation because other correlations might also account for a C^{14} date of A.D. 727 at Tikal. Each of the other population correlations can be tested against P-243 in precisely the same manner:

$$H_o: \quad \mu = \text{A.D. } 481 \qquad t_{\text{Spinden}} = \frac{727 - 481}{46} = 5.35$$

$$H_o: \quad \mu = \text{A.D. } 504 \qquad t_{\text{Dinsmoor}} = \frac{727 - 504}{46} = 4.85$$

$$H_o: \quad \mu = \text{A.D. } 858 \qquad t_{\text{Kreichgauer}} = \frac{727 - 858}{46} = -2.85$$

$$H_o: \quad \mu = \text{A.D. } 1001 \qquad t_{\text{Escalona Ramon}} = \frac{727 - 1001}{46} = -5.96$$

[5]It matters little whether radiocarbon samples are expressed in years A.D., B.C., or years ago. Only the difference between the dates appears in the numerator of the t-ratio.

Every observed *t* falls well within the critical region and the null hypothesis for each of the four correlations must be rejected. We reject the Spinden, Dinsmoor, Kreichgauer, and Escalona Ramon correlations as untenable, in light of date P-243 from Tikal.[6]

Note how carefully both the statistical findings and the substantive implications have been expressed. Scientific theories such as these are never actually proved *correct*; practical research is directed only toward proving the competing theories *wrong*. Radiocarbon evidence from Tikal allows rejection of the four prevalent hypotheses competing with the Goodman–Thompson–Martinez correlation. But the GTM correlation has by no means been *proved correct*, since there could always be additional hypotheses which are likewise consistent with the C[14] evidence. After a thorough and well-designed attempt at refutation such as this has failed, a theory can only *tentatively* be presumed to be correct. It can never be proved so (see Naroll and Cohen 1970: 26).

● *No study, whether a true experiment or not, ever proves a theory; it merely probes it.*—R. Winch and D. Campbell

Confidence Limits of a Radiocarbon Date   Because there might be other hypotheses to explain the Tikal dates, a further step can be taken toward a final solution to the correlation problem by computing the limits within which other acceptable hypotheses must fall. The 95 percent confidence interval for date P-243 is

$$\mu = \bar{X} \pm t_{0.05} S_{\bar{x}}$$

$$\mu = \text{A.D. } 727 \pm 1.96 \, (46)$$

$$\mu = \text{A.D. } 727 \pm 90.2 \text{ radiocarbon years}$$

Thus, at a 0.95 level of probability, any acceptable correlation must place the dedicatory date of Temple IV at Tikal no earlier than A.D. 637 and no later than A.D. 817. None of the seriously proposed correlations fall within this interval, so we are still left with a provisional acceptance of the Goodman–Thompson–Martinez reckoning. Note that computing the confidence interval is a superior method (in this case) of decision making.

Comparing Two Radiocarbon Dates   Sometimes one needs to apply statistical logic inference when two radiocarbon dates are compared. Consider the dating of the Lehner Ranch site in southern Arizona, where Paleo-Indian artifacts were found in clear-cut association with the remains of nine butchered mammoths. A firehearth was discovered nearby and charcoal samples were submitted to the University of Arizona radiocarbon laboratory, with the following results:

(A-40a)	10,900 ± 450 years ago
(A-40b)	12,000 ± 450 years ago

---

[6]Of course no right-thinking archaeologist would rely upon a single radiocarbon date for so bold a conclusion; Satterthwaite and Ralph ran a total of ten C[14] dates on beams and lintels from Temple IV alone.

The means of these two samples differ by some 1100 years, even though the charcoal came from a single firehearth. Does this 1100-year gap represent a true difference or can this discrepancy more readily be accounted for by statistical error?

Statistical hypotheses:

$$H_0: \quad \mu_{A\text{-}40a} = \mu_{A\text{-}40b}$$
$$H_1: \quad \mu_{A\text{-}40a} \neq \mu_{A\text{-}40b}$$

Region of rejection: For a two-tailed test at $\alpha = 0.05$, and with infinite degrees of freedom, $t_{0.05} = 1.96$.

The standard error of the difference between sample means is found as before:

$$S_{\bar{X}-\bar{Y}} = \sqrt{S_{\bar{X}}^2 + S_{\bar{Y}}^2} = \sqrt{450^2 + 450^2} = 636 \text{ years}$$

The t-ratio is

$$t = \frac{(\bar{X} - \bar{Y}) - \mu_{\bar{X}-\bar{Y}}}{S_{\bar{X}-\bar{Y}}} = \frac{(10{,}900 - 12{,}000) - 0}{636} = -1.73$$

Since $t = 1.73 < t_{0.05} = 1.96$, H_0 is not rejected, and we conclude that the difference between dates A-40a and A-40b is not significant. The two dates could well date a contemporary event at the Lehner Ranch site.

What should we conclude when a significant difference emerges, indicating that two dates are really "different?" Statistically, this decision tells us that the two radioactive samples have probably been selected from different statistical populations, but the archaeological ramifications are more difficult to assess. Archaeologists generally assume that, all else being equal, a difference in radiocarbon dates results from a true age difference between the samples. But this remains only an assumption because several other factors could cause contemporaneous samples to "date" differently: impure CO_2, radon in counter, electronic circuit breakdowns, Geiger counter failure, cosmic ray showers, even atmospheric fallout. In the Tikal study alone, Satterthwaite and Ralph rejected over 40 percent (34 of 83) of their counting runs as spurious. There is also the danger of contaminating the sample itself by sloppy excavation, by percolating groundwater, by rodent burrowing, by rootlets, or even by insects.

It is always possible to introduce significant error into the samples and hence create a spurious radiocarbon date. There are even cases when several dates on the same log have produced widely different age determinations, although the samples must be of exactly identical age. There seems to be many a "slip 'twixt the cup and the lip" in radiocarbon dating, and statistical inference establishes whether or not a significant discrepancy exists between dates. Only nonstatistical considerations can *explain* that discrepancy.

Problems may also arise when structuring the research hypotheses into statistical hypotheses. If the Lehner Ranch null hypothesis had been directional (one-tailed), the region of rejection would have been $t_{0.10} = 1.65$, and the observed difference between the dates would have been declared "significant." The two-tailed alternative was selected in this case because no prior hypotheses existed to suggest *which* sample should be older than the other. It simply turned out that the determination for A-40b was older than that for A-40a. But had there been some specific reason to suggest that A-40b would be older *before the actual results were known*, then a one-tailed test would have been in order.

● *Ours is the age which is proud of machines that think, and suspicious of men who try to.*—H. Jones

10.8 THE CASE OF PAIRED VARIATES

The data considered thus far were purposely selected so that each variate was totally uneffected by the other sample variates. The assumption of independent variates follows from our earlier definition of random sampling. But there are some hypotheses of interest involving data which are not independent of one another; the variates are "paired" with each other. Consider the following hypotheses:

Right-handed individuals tend to have larger right arms than left arms.
First-born individuals are usually stronger than their second-born siblings.
Students are rarely smarter than their professors.
Wives tend to be more motivated than their husbands.

These variates are linked into naturally occurring dyads (right-left, male-female, older-younger), and such linkage vitiates any usage of the *t*-test discussed so far.

Pairing of variates has an importance far greater than simple convenience because pairing is a tactic in the general strategy of efficient research design. The idea behind a purposeful pairing of variates is to increase the basis of comparison on a desired effect. Extraneous factors ("noise") can sometimes produce a significant difference even when there is no difference resulting from the phenomenon under study. Conversely, these same extraneous factors can sometimes mask a true difference, resulting in an incorrect acceptance of the null hypothesis. Errors of this sort can never be totally eliminated, but cautious design of experiments can purge a great deal of noise from the data.

A basic rule in designing experiments is to control what can be controlled and to randomize the uncontrollable. Pairing controls extraneous factors by grouping variates which are alike in all respects save the condition under study. In learning experiments, for instance, subjects are often paired by IQ scores so that variable degrees of intelligence will not mask the actual rates of learning or retention. Pairs are also commonly constructed to control for bias by sex, age, generation, socioeconomic background, motivation, or achievement. Acculturation studies often involve the natural pairings produced in "before-after" observations. Such variates are termed *self-pairing* when a single variable is measured on two occasions under different conditions.

But the use of paired variates destroys the assumption of statistical independence and necessitates an alteration in *t*-testing methods. The following example illustrates this simple modification.

A controversial topic in anthropology has been the so-called nature-nurture problem: To what extent is behavior conditioned by environmental as opposed to genetic factors? Identical (monozygotic) twins are a common tool in this dialogue, especially when an investigator can study pairs of twins who have been raised separately, under different environmental conditions. If the performance of the twins varies, this difference is probably due to environmental factors, since the twins have inherited identical genetical material. Below are the actual performance scores of 11 pairs of identical twins. Each twin was rated on the quality of his or her educational background, and then each was tested on the Stanford–Binet IQ test (data from Newman, Freeman, and Holzinger 1937: chapter 10). Does a superior educational background produce a highly significant difference in IQ?

Pair	Superior Education	Inferior Education
I	97	85
II	78	66
III	101	99
IV	106	89
V	93	89
IX	102	96
X	127	122
XI	116	92
XII	109	116
XVII	115	105
XVIII	96	77

By inspection we see that in nearly all cases (10 of 11), the individual from the superior educational background also exhibits a higher score on the IQ test. But we also know that such results might occur by chance alone. Let us find just how likely (or unlikely) these findings really are.

The population standard deviation $(\sigma_{\bar{x}-\bar{y}})$ is unknown and the sample size is too small to use the sample standard deviation $(S_{\bar{x}-\bar{y}})$ to estimate that parameter. Because two distinct samples are involved, one might be tempted to apply the t-test to compare the two samples (Section 10.5). The hypotheses would be

$$H_o: \quad \mu_X \leq \mu_Y \qquad H_1: \quad \mu_X > \mu_Y$$

where μ_X represents the average IQ score of the twin raised in the superior educational environment.

But such a test would be incorrect because a basic assumption has been violated. Not only must the population variances be equal and both populations follow a normal distribution, but the two populations must also be *statistically independent of one another*. The standard t-test requires that the selection of variates in the first sample be logically independent from selection of the second sample. But since each individual in the first sample has a corresponding individual (its twin) in the second sample, neither samples nor populations are independent.

We must introduce a new variable in order to test for differences in paired data:

$$D = (X_i - Y_i)$$

The paired scores are subtracted and their difference produces a new variable, called D ("the pair differences"). In effect, D recasts the pairs into a single sample. Sample statistics can then be found in the conventional manner, except that the values of D_i are substituted for the X_i:

$$\bar{D} = \frac{\Sigma D_i}{n}$$

$$S_d = \sqrt{\frac{\Sigma(D_i - \bar{D})^2}{n-1}}$$

$$S_{\bar{d}} = \frac{S_d}{\sqrt{n}}$$

where n is the number of pairs. To determine the sampling distribution, t is computed as

$$t = \frac{\bar{D} - \mu_{\bar{d}}}{S_{\bar{d}}} \tag{10.7}$$

where $\mu_{\bar{d}}$ is the population value of the mean difference. The number of degrees of freedom are df $= (n-1)$.

The data in the example are analyzed as follows:

Statistical hypotheses:

$$H_0: \quad \mu_{\bar{d}} = 0 \qquad H_1: \quad \mu_{\bar{d}} \neq 0$$

Region of rejection: For a significance level of 0.01 in a two-tailed test with df $= (11-1) = 10$, $t_{0.01} = 3.169$.

The t-ratio is most easily found by using the following table.

Pair	Superior Ed., X	Inferior Ed., Y	D	$(D - \bar{D})$	$(D - \bar{D})^2$
I	97	85	+12	+ 2.5	6.25
II	78	66	+12	+ 2.5	6.25
III	101	99	+ 2	− 7.5	56.25
IV	106	89	+17	+ 7.5	56.25
V	93	89	+ 4	− 5.5	30.25
IX	102	96	+ 6	− 3.5	12.25
X	127	122	+ 5	− 4.5	20.25
XI	116	92	+24	+14.5	210.25
XII	109	116	− 7	−16.5	272.25
XVII	115	105	+10	+ 0.5	0.25
XVIII	96	77	+19	+ 9.5	90.25
			+104		760.75

$$\bar{D} = \frac{104}{11} = 9.5$$

$$S_d = \sqrt{\frac{760.75}{10}} = 8.72$$

$$S_{\bar{d}} = \frac{8.72}{\sqrt{11}} = 2.63$$

Substituting into Expression (10.7) to find t with 10 degrees of freedom,

$$t = \frac{9.5 - 0}{2.63} = 3.61$$

The computed value of t is sufficiently large to fall within the region of rejection. We conclude that a superior educational environment does seem to influence IQ scores when hereditary factors are held constant.

Example 10.8

Early twentieth century anthropology attempted to combat the prevalent racist theories of the time by demonstrating how environmental factors often overshadow the influence of heredity (that is, race). Franz Boas, himself a member of an immigrant minority, argued that the better nutritional and health care available in the United States caused far-reaching physical effects on the offspring of recent immigrants. Boas collected an incredible volume of data on physical changes occurring in immigrants and their children so that he could monitor the relationship between environmental and hereditary factors. The data in the following table are stature measurements for American-born and foreign-born Bohemian males (data from Boas 1912: table 1, appendix). Informants are paired to eliminate age effects. Do the American-born Bohemians appear to be larger than their foreign-born counterparts, as Boas suggested?

These data cannot be compared by the simple t-test for the difference between sample means because the informants have been purposely paired into age grades. But we can test the hypothesis that the average difference between the American-born and foreign-born informants is significantly different from zero. That is

$$H_o: \quad \mu_d \leq 0 \qquad H_1: \quad \mu_d > 0$$

Age	American-born Males, cm	Foreign-born Males, cm	D	$(D - \bar{D})$	$(D - \bar{D})^2$
4	99.4	98.0	+1.4	−0.5	0.25
5	105.7	101.0	+4.7	+2.8	7.84
6	110.7	110.6	+0.1	−1.8	3.24
7	116.0	111.7	+4.3	+2.4	5.76
8	122.5	118.2	+4.3	+2.4	5.76
9	128.5	128.1	+0.4	−1.5	2.25

Age	American-born Males, cm	Foreign-born Males, cm	D	$(D - \bar{D})$	$(D - \bar{D})^2$
10	132.7	135.1	− 2.4	− 4.3	18.49
11	137.7	134.7	+ 3.0	+ 1.1	1.21
12	141.1	140.0	+ 1.1	− 0.8	0.64
13	147.9	148.1	− 0.2	− 2.1	4.41
14	152.3	150.4	+ 1.9	0.0	0.0
15	155.5	155.2	+ 0.3	− 1.6	2.56
16	162.7	160.7	+ 2.0	+ 0.1	0.01
17	167.6	165.0	+ 2.6	+ 0.7	0.49
18	175.0	167.7	+ 7.3	+ 5.4	29.16
19	171.2	167.0	+ 4.2	+ 2.3	5.29
20	168.6	171.0	− 2.4	− 4.3	18.49
			+ 32.6		105.85

$\bar{D} = 32.6/17 = 1.9$ cm; $S_d = \sqrt{105.85}/16 = 2.57$; $S_{\bar{d}} = 2.57/\sqrt{17} = 0.62$.

These values are substituted into the *t*-ratio:

$$t = \frac{1.9 - 0}{0.62} = 3.06$$

The critical region in this case is defined for a one-tailed test with df = (17 − 1) = 16 and a significance level of 0.01. From Table A.4 we find $t_{0.02} = 2.583$. The computed *t*-ratio exceeds this value, so we reject H_o and conclude that the sample of American-born Bohemians are significantly taller than those of foreign birth. Note again how a careful pairing of the data permits us to control for age in this experiment.

10.9 ASSUMPTIONS OF THE *t*-TEST

Once statistical hypotheses are formulated, more than one statistical test method is often available to test the propositions. Exactly which test is appropriate depends upon the underlying models and assumptions. There is a real danger in applying tests to data which violate critical assumptions, since false assumptions lead to the rejection of H_o just as surely as can the legitimate properties of the data. The null hypothesis of a particular test might be concerned with comparing two sample means. For instance: Should the underlying assumptions of the test model not be met, the results can appear "significant" whether or not there is any true difference between the two means. As long as there is doubt about the validity of the assumptions, one cannot be certain that H_o has been properly rejected or whether the rejection results from a spurious assumption.

Four explicit assumptions accompany the application of Student's *t*-test: interval scale of measurement, independent errors, normally distributed population, and homogeneity of variance. Let us consider each of the prerequisites in more detail.

1. *The variable is measurable on an interval scale.* Level of measurement is really more a procedural matter than an assumption of the *t*-test. The sample mean and variance appear in the *t*-ratio, and these statistics can be computed only upon interval (or ratio) level variates. Nonparametric alternatives to the *t*-test are readily available whenever the level of measurement fails to reach an interval scale (see Chapter 12).

2. *The variables must exhibit independent errors (except for paired variates).* This second assumption requires that the selection of any single variate in no way influences the probability of selection of any other variate from the population. This requirement rarely poses a problem in disciplines such as psychology, where research usually centers about closely controlled experiments. The psychologist usually establishes purposeful pairing, control groups, repetitive testing, or some other technique to maintain the independent errors of observation. But too little attention has been paid in anthropology to the problems of research design, especially by archaeologists and paleoanthropologists. Sampling in anthropology is a distressingly complex subject and will be considered in more detail in Chapter 15.

3. *The sample variates are randomly selected from a normally distributed population.* It was necessary to assume that the basic population distribution was originally normal in order to find the exact probability distribution of the *t*-ratio. This is due to a theorem of mathematical statistics which states that, given random and independent observation, the sample mean and variance are independent of one another *if and only if* the population distribution is normal (see Mood and Graybill 1963: 228–231). Only for normal distributions can we be certain that the random variables necessary for the *t*-ratio (the sample mean and standard deviation) are statistically independent.

Unfortunately, we can seldom justify this assumption in practical application. Faced with the problem of analyzing obviously nonnormal data, one could attempt to transform the data into a form which does meet this assumption (by methods discussed in Chapter 14) or look elsewhere for another statistical test. The distribution-free (nonparametric) family of statistics are particularly useful in this regard (Chapters 11 and 12). But even nonparametric statistics exact a price because we lose some available information in exchange for freedom from restrictive assumptions.

There is, fortunately, another alternative. Now that the assumption of normality has been clearly stated and justified on mathematical grounds, it becomes my pleasure to inform you that normality can be ignored in most applications of the *t*-test. Mechanical sampling experiments by investigators in the early 1930s and recent computer simulations have shown that nonnormality has only a slight effect on the *t*-test as long as (1) the sample sizes are fairly large and (2) the test is not directional. The only error introduced into two-tailed testing is a slight modification in the true level of probability. If, for example, one operates within a tabled significance level of 0.05, the actual probability of a nonnormal population will really lie somewhere between 0.04 and 0.07, depending upon the degree of skewness. Thus, the overall effect of ignoring the normal assumption is that the table value of *t* will lead us to report slightly too many significant findings (Cochran 1947). With this in mind, one should attempt to use larger samples when the underlying normality of the variates is in question.

More serious errors result from one-tailed testing because highly skewed distributions can seriously alter the tabled values of *t*, seriously over- or underestimating the true probability figures. A larger sample should be taken when one suspects a departure from normality in a directional hypothesis. Some techniques for detecting such departures from normality are discussed in Chapters 11 and 14.

4. *When comparing two samples, the two parent populations must have homogeneous variances.* Although the *t*-test does not directly involve the population variances, σ_X^2 and σ_Y^2, these two parameters must still be assumed to be equal. This is necessary so that observed differences between samples can be ascribed strictly to differences in the *central tendencies* rather than to differing *shapes* of the distributions about the mean. This important assumption, sometimes termed *homoscedasticity*, is a concept we will encounter again in the discussion of correlation.

Note that the assumption about homogeneity of variances applies only when two small samples are being compared. There is no assumption about σ when testing a single sample because *S* is obtained empirically and substituted directly into the *t*-ratio.

But what if this assumption is violated? Although the assumption of homogeneity of variance is more critical than that of normality, sampling experiments also indicate that (1) as long as the sample sizes are roughly equal and (2) the parent populations have distributions of approximately the same shape, the two population variances can deviate substantially from one another without introducing undue error into the level of probability. As long as these conditions are met (no matter what the variances may be) samples as small as $n = 5$ will produce acceptable results. The only difficulty is that a tabled probability value of 0.05 will only be within ±0.03 of the true level. For samples larger than 15, the true probability will most likely be within ±0.01 of the true value. When one has strong reason to suspect that the variances are truly unequal and the distributions are also of different shapes, then one should explore the possibility of applying the *Behrens test*, described in Bliss (1967: 215–218).

● *Sanity is not statistical.*—G. Orwell

SUGGESTIONS FOR FURTHER READING

Statistical Aspects of Radiocarbon Dating

Long and Rippeteau (1974)

Raoph (1971). A beginner's introduction to the laboratory and statistical methods involved in radiocarbon dating; Ralph takes a single charcoal sample through the dating process at the University of Pennsylvania laboratory.

Spaulding (1958)

EXERCISES

10.1 The average pithecanthropine cranial capacity is generally estimated to be about 1000 cc. Based upon cranial capacity alone, could the skulls discussed in Example 10.4 be pithecanthropine ($\alpha = 0.01$)?

10.2 A group of ten male skeletons has just arrived at a large eastern museum. Unfortunately, they have been improperly catalogued, and their place of origin is uncertain. Based upon the inadequate records available with the collection, the museum staff has guessed that these are North American Indian skeletons. The physical anthropologist in charge computes that the average stature of the ten specimens is 161.3 cm with $S = 10$ cm. Judging strictly from stature, is there sufficient reason to doubt that these skeletons are American Indian? (Kelso 1970: 235, gives 163.7 cm as the average Amerind stature.)

10.3 The following two radiocarbon dates were obtained for level DI at Danger Cave, Utah (Jennings 1957: table 11):

$$10{,}270 \pm 650 \quad \text{(M-204)}$$
$$11{,}151 \pm 570 \quad \text{(C-610)}$$

(a) What are the two-thirds limits of confidence for the Michigan date?
(b) What are the 95 percent limits for the true age of the Chicago sample?
(c) What is the probability that the true age of M-204 is actually older than 10,800 years?
(d) What is the probability that the true age of M-204 lies between 10,000 and 11,000 years old?
(e) What is the probability that C-610 is actually 10,800 years or younger?
(f) Suppose that the true age of both samples was known to be 10,715 years. Which sample came closer (in terms of probability) to estimating the true age? (*Hint:* Be certain to consider the relative standard deviations.)

10.4 In a study designed to determine the relationship between climate and facial structure, Koertvelyessy (1972) obtained the following figures for frontal sinus surface area in Eskimo males:

	Mean, cm^2	Standard Deviation, cm^2	n
$\bar{X}$ Colder habitat	2.076	1.974	33
$\bar{Y}$ Warmer habitat	3.794	2.866	29

(a) Do the Eskimo from the colder environment tend to have significantly smaller frontal sinuses?
(b) Would an Eskimo with a frontal sinus area of 5.0 cm^2 be considered "aberrant" in the colder habitat?

10.5   A team of investigators measured the root length of the first mandibular premolar in a sample of American Whites and American Blacks (data from Moss, Chase, and Howes 1967: table 4):

	American Whites, mm	American Blacks, mm
Mean	14.8	14.4
Standard deviation	0.97	1.97
n	15	7

(a) Is there a significant difference in root length?
(b) Could the American White population average a root length longer than 15 mm?
(c) Could the American Black population average less than 12 mm?

10.6   Two kinds of rooms are often found in the pueblos of the American Southwest: large rooms, probably involved in day-to-day living, and smaller rooms, most probably used for storage (Hill 1970). One useful indicator of the prehistoric function of these rooms involves the kinds of pottery sherds they contain. Since modern pueblo families generally take their meals in the habitation rooms, we can expect to find more pottery from food plates and bowls in the habitation areas than in the storage rooms. Similarly, large storage jars should be more common in the storage rooms. Unfortunately, several other variables—such as family size, methods of food preparation and storage, differential hygiene (some families sweeping their floors cleaner than others), and time of occupation—also enter into the recovery of pottery sherds, hence obscuring room function.

In order to minimize the effects of these extraneous factors and concentrate strictly upon room function, an experiment was designed to test for differences in pottery frequency. In a particular pueblo, it became apparent that each large room was directly connected by a doorway to a smaller room. The inference is that a single family used both rooms, one for storage and the other for habitation. By pairing the large and small rooms on the basis of a shared doorway, many of the extraneous variables, such as family size, sanitary practices, and so forth, can be controlled. After excavation, the density of cooking sherds was computed as follows:

	Sherds per Cubic Meter	
Doorway	Large Room	Small Room
A	23	11
B	42	36
C	12	10
D	15	17
E	62	49
F	39	28

Assuming that these sherds reflect only food-preparation vessels and not food storage, can we conclude at the 0.05 level that more cooking took place in the large rooms?

*10.7 The Grasshopper site is a rather large masonry ruin located in Arizona. In an attempt to infer changes in prehistoric social organization, excavators have carefully recorded the dimensions of each room, and also of the fire hearths associated with rooms (data from Ciolek-Torello and Reid 1974: table 1):

Room	Room Size, m²	Firehearth Size, cm²
Later rooms		
3	18.6	838
5	13.7	589
6	15.8	1860
7	21.3	1440
11	12.9	1456
13	14.4	800
205	17.7	1004
216	17.5	761
218	22.4	1435
319	23.4	1444
349	16.1	1386
359	25.9	1140
371	15.3	1013
398	12.4	870
425	12.6	1534
Earlier rooms		
1	17.3	1864
2	16.4	1350
18	22.0	2937
28	18.1	1564
146	15.7	1665

(a) Is there a significant difference in room size between early and late rooms?

(b) Do these data support the hypothesis that the earlier rooms had larger firehearths?

(c) Is the firehearth size more variable in the earlier rooms?

11 Nonparametric Statistics: Nominal Scales

● *THE LAW OF NATURAL PERVERSITY: You cannot successfully determine beforehand which side of bread to butter.* —L. Peter

11.1 INTRODUCTION TO NONPARAMETRIC STATISTICS

The theoretical models underlying the t- and z-statistics are grounded in a few explicit and rather important assumptions. By way of review, the following is assumed by the simple test for a difference between two means (see Section 10.9):

1. The variable is defined on an interval or ratio scale.
2. The samples exhibit independent errors.
3. The sample variates have been randomly selected from a normally distributed population.

These conditions are rarely tested outright. They are usually just *assumed* to hold for the case at hand. As long as these requirements are reasonably satisfied, the parametric model remains a powerful tool, enabling us to test hypotheses and to establish confidence limits.

But must we set aside our elaborate parametric machinery when these conditions cannot be assumed? Section 10.9 discussed one aspect of this problem, noting that some degree of violation is permissible, *as long as the sample sizes are sufficiently large and the hypotheses are nondirectional.* That is, parametric methods are valid as long as the assumptions are at least *approximately* true. The t-test, for example, requires only that (1) the population is *approximately* normal, (2) the variables exhibit *largely* independent errors, and (3) the scale is *close enough* to an interval scale. Normality need not be assumed for the t-test as long as the sample size is sufficiently large that the

261

Central Limit Theorem comes into play. Fudge factors such as this allow analysts to proceed under the parametric model, even though the specifics are something less than ideal.

But real data often place unacceptable constraints upon parametric assumptions, constraints so severe that the model simply does not apply, regardless of how inclined one might be to fudge the assumptions. It is precisely in samples of smaller size that the normal distribution is most likely to be violated, and about which one is forced to make an assumption of normality. When the sample is small, the Central Limit Theorem is of no assistance. Once the basic conditions underlying the parametric model prove untenable, the statistical inferences based upon these false assumptions become likewise suspect. When one's assumptions do not hold, the computed levels of probability no longer bear a credible relationship to true probability values. Although a t-test can physically be computed on a nonnormal population or upon ordinal variables, the resulting levels of significance are worse than incorrect. They are downright misleading and confounding. The parametric model has a built-in gray zone which permits a certain flexibility regarding assumptions. But there is a point beyond which assumptions should not be stretched, a point at which parametric methods must be scrapped in favor of a more realistic model.

This chapter introduces a sorely needed alternative to normal theory statistics, since both the t-test and the standardized normal deviate assume (1) interval or better measurement and (2) a normal distribution. The *nonparametric* family of statistical methods assumes neither condition. Nonparametric statistics comprise a large battery of techniques derived to free us from unrealistic and restrictive assumptions. There was surprisingly little interest in nonparametric methods until the mid-1940s when Frank Wilcoxon proposed a test distinguished by its simplicity. Wilcoxon's test assumed neither interval measurement nor normal distribution of population variates, yet produced excellent results when compared to the common t-test (Wilcoxon's test is presented in Chapter 12). Over the past three decades, literally dozens of nonparametric devices have been derived to cope with the social science problems. Unfortunately, most nonparametric methods lack the efficiency of Wilcoxon's test. In fact, some tests extract a dear price indeed in terms of information lost, but at least they offer a viable alternative to the parametric assumptions.

A statistic is *nonparametric* if any *one* of the following conditions applies (after Conover 1971: 94):

1. The statistic can be used on *nominal* scale data; *or*
2. The statistic can be used on *ordinal* scale data; *or*
3. The statistic can be used on a random variable of unspecified distribution.

The first two conditions allow the valid analyses of nominal and ordinal variables. This is especially important for anthropologists, who are often forced to deal with rather crude scales of observation. The third condition, that data can arise from a distribution of unspecified shape, has led some statisticians to call these tests *distribution-free.*

Nonparametric statistics have several advantages beyond mere freedom from unrealistic assumption. For one thing, nonparametrics usually require fewer computations than their parametric counterparts. Some nonparametric tests require only one operation to count plus and minus signs. Thus, the theory underlying nonparametric tests is usually easier for the beginner to follow. Do not be misled by this simplicity. Parametric methods can produce elegant results in the hands of the skilled statisticians, but to the uninitiated these more advanced methods can prove disastrous. The normal theory of statistics has been compared to an expensive camera, equipped with dozens of complex options. Trained photographers use such costly equipment to produce results worthy of the lofty price tag. But to the beginner, just learning the fundamentals of photography, a new Honeywell Pentax ESII with a 50 mm f/1.4 Super-Multi-Coated Takumar lens, self-timer, FP and X sync, battery checker, PC terminal, hot shoe, and shutter-release lock produces more confusion than well-exposed negatives. There are times when a small Brownie box camera is preferable to a more expensive model costing 20 times the price. Nonparametric statistics have much in common with the modest, yet dependable, Brownie camera. Both are cheap and easy to understand, difficult to abuse, and rather easy to explain to one's friends. Small wonder that the term "quick-and-dirty" is lovingly bestowed upon the nonparametric statistics.

Nonparametric analysis can also facilitate a more efficient collection of data. If one strongly suspects that a given population is asymmetrical or otherwise nonnormally distributed, then ordinal or even presence–absence methods of recording data might be just as useful as measurements accurate to 0.01 mm. Normal theory should not be applied to extremely nonnormal populations, regardless of how precise are one's measurements. The nonparametric methods also allow one to use smaller samples, sometimes saving additional costly fieldwork. And the resulting probabilities from nonparametric computations are often exact, avoiding the arbitrary cutoff points (critical regions) necessary with the z- and t-statistics.

But all these obvious virtues of the nonparametric approach must not detract from its role as a second-best substitute for normal theory. When information exists on the population distribution, and when level of measurement is satisfactory, the normal theory should be used forthwith. To apply nonparametric methods to such situations is an ill-advised waste of information. Furthermore, the comforting phrases "nonparametric" and "distribution-free" must not be misread to imply "assumption-free." Nonparametric methods make a couple of rather critical assumptions which cannot be ignored.

Although you might not have realized it, a nonparametric statistical test has already been introduced. The *binomial test* (Chapter 6) assumed neither a normal distribution nor an interval level of measurement. Hence, the binomial test qualifies as nonparametric on two counts. Binomials such as heads–tails, male–female, or blood type are only nominal level variates, and a moment's reflection reveals that a Bernoulli variable could not be distributed normally because only two possibilities exist for each variable.[1]

Several additional nominal-level nonparametric tests are presented in this chapter, including the ubiquitous chi-square test. Chapter 12 considers further

---

[1] Be careful here not to confuse the binomial statistic with the variables themselves. The binomial *statistic* becomes distributed in normal fashion as the sample size increases (in fact, this is a characteristic common to many nonparametric statistics), but this is a very different matter indeed from assuming that the variates themselves distribute normally.

nonparametric methods which are suitable for ordinal level variates. More advanced nonparametric methods of correlation are presented in conjunction with their parametric counterparts.

● *General Grant only knew two songs—one was* Yankee Doodle *and the other wasn't.*—A. Gingrich

11.2 THE CHI-SQUARE TEST

Chi-square gets my vote as anthropology's most used (and abused) statistic. The technique is flexible, and the computations are elementary and easily carried out without computational machinery. As long as certain limitations and assumptions are satisfied, the chi-square techniques can play a pivotal role in quantitative anthropology.

Recall how useful the binomial distribution was when a given trial had but two possible outcomes—success or failure. Several examples from Mendelian genetics were discussed earlier. One of Mendel's experiments considered round and wrinkled peas (see Example 11.1), which were expected to occur in the ratio of 3:1. Outcomes of this sort were characterized as simply R (success) or W (failure). Mendel's breeding experiments involved a simple null hypothesis: H_o: $p = 0.75$, where p is the probability of a round seed on a given trial. The associated probabilities were computed and compared with the theoretical binomial probability.

Viewed another way, binomial experiments compare empirically derived observed (O) values with theoretically expected (E) figures. The normal approximation to the binomial can also be used to test H_o, provided n is sufficiently large (n being the total number of seeds observed).

But suppose there are more than two possible outcomes. Many genetic situations involve several significant phenotypes, too many outcomes to be succinctly characterized as success or failure. There are, for instance, *four* equally likely blood types for the offspring of a heterozygous A and a heterozygous B.

	Offspring	
Parents	Genotype	Phenotype
ao	ab ao	AB A
bo	bo oo	B O

Mendelian theory tells us that, in the long run, unions of this sort should produce offspring with blood types AB:A:B:O in approximately the ratios of 1:1:1:1. The *expected frequencies* for a sample of $n = 100$ such offspring would be ($E = np$).

Type AB: $E_1 = 100(0.25) = 25$
Type A: $E_2 = 100(0.25) = 25$
Type B: $E_3 = 100(0.25) = 25$
Type O: $E_4 = 100(0.25) = 25$

These expected figures can then be tested upon an actual sample of 100 such offspring. Suppose the empirical data consist of the following observed (O_i) values:

Type AB: $O_1 = 32$
Type A: $O_2 = 13$
Type B: $O_3 = 24$
Type O: $O_4 = 31$

The observed values are not equal to exactly 25 for each blood type, but random sampling theory predicts that some degree of deviation is likely. We must decide whether these observations conform to the expected Mendelian frequencies or whether the deviation is too great for the theory to hold.

Had this situation been expressed in terms of success and failure—such as the probability of obtaining Type AB blood as opposed to all other types—then p and q could have been defined as before and the binomial theorem used to compare the expected with the observed values. But introducing more than two possible alternatives (E_k with $k > 2$) vitiates the binomial theorem as we know it.

Fortunately, the χ^2 (to be read "chi-square") test was designed for just such situations:

$$\sum_{i=1}^{k} \frac{(O_i - E_i)^2}{E_i} \qquad (11.1)$$

where O_i are the experimentally observed values and the E_i are the theoretically expected frequencies for the kth class. There is no limit to the magnitude of k in the χ^2 distribution,[2] as there was in the case of the binomial (where $k = 2$).

The chi-square statistic sums the deviations for each class in the frequency distribution. The ($O_i - E_i$) differences are squared to produce a nonzero sum. The squared deviations are then divided by the expected number of cases in each measurement class. This standardizes the chi-square statistic, just as the variates in a normal distribution were standardized into z-scores. Dividing by E_i weights the contribution of each class so that the biggest proportion of the chi-square sum does not always come from the most numerous class.

The value of the χ^2 statistic is best computed from the following conventional tabular format (χ^2 in this case is 9.20).

---

[2]Some introductory textbooks label the chi-square statistic X^2 rather than χ^2 and, in a strict sense, this procedure is more accurate. The values listed in chi-square tables are really *statistical estimations* of true chi-square parameters. The computed values of the chi-square estimator can vary somewhat because it is sometimes necessary to "correct for continuity" (Section 11.4). While these considerations are germane to a truly exhaustive consideration of this technique, such rigor is beyond the current scope. The symbol χ^2 is used here to indicate both the estimates obtained from computation and the tabled values of the chi-square statistic. By so doing, we can avoid any confusion between χ^2 and the symbol for the common variable X.

Blood Type	O_i	E_i	$(O_i - E_i)$	$(O_i - E_i)^2$	$(O_i - E_i)^2 / E_i$
AB	32	25	7	49	1.96
A	13	25	-12	144	5.76
B	24	25	-1	1	0.04
O	31	25	6	36	1.44
	100	100	0		$\chi^2 = 9.20$

But computing a chi-square statistic is only half the battle. So far, no decision can be made about the *probability* of any observed value of chi-square. That is, a sampling distribution for the chi-square statistic is necessary so that we can judge the acceptability of a null hypothesis. Just as with the normal distribution, the probability of obtaining *exactly* the expected outcome is zero for a continuous random variable. A certain amount of variability is expected in the chi-square statistic, just as variability was expected in the ABO blood type experiment itself.

But how much variability should we expect? To answer this question, statisticians have repeated randomized experiments literally hundreds of times and then constructed histograms of the chi-square sampling distribution. Two variables are involved in the sample chi-square experiments: the number of experimental cases (n) and the number of observed-expected comparisons (k). As long as n is kept above critical minimum values, the frequency distribution of χ^2 stabilizes within each level of k. But instead of dealing directly with k, we must follow a procedure similar to that of the t-test (Chapter 10), and instead consider the number of *degrees of freedom*, where df $= (k - 1)$. Degrees of freedom in this case refers to the number of classes within a chi-square table, which may be filled arbitrarily without altering the expectations.

Note that degrees of freedom for the χ^2 distribution is determined by k, the number of independent observed-expected comparisons, rather than by sample size (n). For the ABO blood-type experiment,

$$n = 100, \quad k = 4, \quad df = (4 - 1) = 3$$

The chi-square distribution for 3 degrees of freedom is known to follow the distribution given in Fig. 11.1.[3] The x-axis represents the range of possible χ^2 values; chi-square cannot drop below zero and the right-hand tail asymptotes toward positive infinity. The ordinate, scaled in probabilities, ranges between zero and unity. Although chi-square distributions are generally quite asymmetrical, there exists a close parallel between normal and chi-square distributions. Both curves represent probabilities. The higher the curve, the more probable is the interval represented. As χ^2 becomes larger and larger, the probability of observing this or larger values diminishes. Figure 11.1 indicates that 50 percent of all observed χ^2 (with df $= 3$) are expected to exceed 2.4. Only 5 percent of the χ^2 variates should exceed about 7.8 and only 1 percent of the χ^2 values should be greater than about 9.21. But because there is a different graph for each

[3] The actual derivation of this curve, and its formula, are beyond the scope of the present text (see Hays 1973: 432–436).

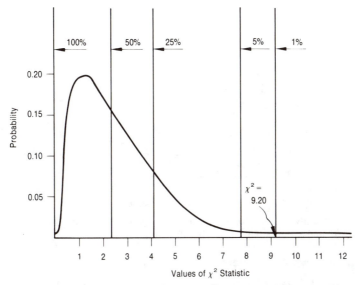

Fig. 11.1 Probability distribution function of χ^2 values with 3 degrees of freedom.

change in the number of degrees of freedom, these figures have been recorded on Table A.5 (Appendix).

Figure 11.1 enables us to evaluate the results obtained in the ABO blood group experiment. Chi-square was computed to be $\chi^2 = 9.20$, but until now we had no way of relating this figure to a probability statement. We could not tell whether this value represented a significant departure from expectation or whether the observed deviations were likely by chance alone. Figure 11.1 shows that an observed $\chi^2 = 9.20$ or greater can be expected to occur less than 5 percent of the time. Actually, Table A.5 shows this figure more accurately to be $\chi^2_{0.05} = 7.81473$. The probability of any particular χ^2 value is zero, as with any continuous random variable. It is the probability of *exceeding* the given value that is of interest in the chi-square test.

A different chi-square probability distribution curve results for each change in degrees of freedom. Several of these curves appear in Fig. 11.2. Each curve is asymmetrical, commencing at zero and tailing off toward positive infinity. Table A.5 presents the probability functions for the common significance levels and for degrees of freedom up to 100.

Now we are in a position to use the chi-square statistic as a hypothesis-testing device. Consider χ^2 in terms of the six steps of hypothesis testing presented in Section 9.2.

Step I. *Statistical hypotheses:* Mendelian theory predicted that blood types AB, A, B, and O should occur in the ratio of 1 : 1 : 1 : 1. The null hypothesis for $n = 100$ trials is therefore

$$H_o: \quad E_1 = 100(0.25) = 25$$
$$E_2 = 100(0.25) = 25$$
$$E_3 = 100(0.25) = 25$$
$$E_4 = 100(0.25) = 25$$

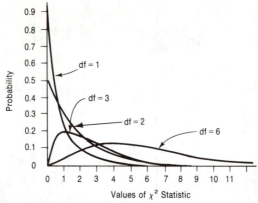

Fig. 11.2 Probability distribution functions for values of χ^2 with several degrees of freedom (after Sokal and Rohlf 1969: fig. 7.12).

The alternative hypothesis states that H_o is false:

$$H_1:\quad E_1 \neq 25;\qquad E_2 \neq 25;\qquad E_3 \neq 25;\qquad E_4 \neq 25$$

Chi-square deals only with generalized deviation and the alternative hypothesis in the chi-square test does not specify just which class (or classes) will deviate from expectation. Any observed value with a large deviation from expectation is sufficient to reject H_o.

Another phrasing of the statistical hypotheses expresses *probabilities* rather than *expectations*. There are four classes in this example, $k = 4$. The probability of class 1 occurring on a given trial is $p_1 = 0.25$; this is the probability of a given offspring having Type AB blood. The probability of Type A blood—class 2—is $p_2 = 0.25$, and so forth. The statistical hypotheses can be expressed in terms of these theoretical relative frequencies (for any sample of size n).

$$H_o:\quad p_1 = p_2 = p_3 = p_4 \qquad H_1:\quad p_1 \neq p_2 \neq p_3 \neq p_4$$

This second version is usually easier to frame when the various probabilities are equal, but in many cases (such as Example 11.2), the expected frequency null hypothesis is easier to visualize.

Once again we should mention the relationship between the chi-square and the binomial distributions. So long as $k = 2$, then the binomial distribution is identical to the chi-square distribution (see Example 11.1).

Step II. *The statistical model:* The chi-square probability distributions (such as those of Fig. 11.2) provide us with a statistical model. This model changes with every level of degree of freedom, so a number of different curves are necessary; Table A.5 summarizes several of the appropriate curves. Thus, our statistical model consists of the χ^2 probability distribution when all assumptions (including H_o) are met. A region of rejection for observed values of the chi-square statistic can be defined, just as with the t-statistic and the standardized normal deviate z. If the observed χ^2 does not deviate from expectation, then we have no reason to question any of our assumptions, and H_o survives. But when an observed chi-square falls into the critical region under the probability distribution, we must search for an invalid assumption. The chi-square statistic is a *nonparametric* statistic, as defined earlier in Section 11.1. The assumptions of the chi-square test are discussed in Section 11.5. As long as these simple assumptions are intact—and a statistical test should not be applied if the assumptions are not valid—then our faulty assumption must be the null hypothesis. All statistical tests operate in this manner.

Step III. *Level of statistical significance:* The alpha level is chosen as before. Although the same general principles for selecting the alpha level apply to chi-square testing, some confusion seems to arise regarding one- and two-tailed alternatives. These difficulties will be discussed in Section 11.9.

Step IV. *Region of rejection:* The critical region is that area under the chi-square sampling distribution which contains unacceptable deviations, given alpha. In the example at hand, with df $= 4 - 1 = 3$, the 0.05 critical region is given by Table A.5 to be $\chi^2_{0.05} = 7.815$. This means that any observed chi-square *greater than or equal to* 7.815 is unacceptably large, given a significance level of 0.05. This is the statistical model against which the actual data are juxtaposed.

Step V. *Calculations and statistical decision:* Formula (11.1) is used to compute the actual observed sample value of the chi-square statistic. In this case, $\chi^2 = 9.20$, a value falling into the region of rejection. Thus, the sample tends to favor H_1 over H_0, given α.

Step VI. *Nonstatistical decision:* As before, these quantitative findings must be rephrased in terms of the research situation. The hypothetical random sample of $n = 100$ offspring has contradicted Mendelian theory. Because such a large deviation will occur by chance fewer than 5 in 100 times of such experiments, we reject the Mendelian theory in this case and search for alternative genetic explanations for our deviant results.

Example 11.1

In 1859, Gregor Mendel conducted a genetic experiment with pea plants (*Pisum*) which were all known to be heterozygous for wrinkled seeds. Mendel found that upon plant maturation, 5474 seeds from his experimental plants were round, while only 1850 seeds were wrinkled. Do these results support Mendel's theory that round seeds should outnumber wrinkled seeds in a 3:1 ratio?

Step I. *Statistical hypotheses:*

$$H_0: \quad p = 0.75 \qquad H_1: \quad p \neq 0.75$$

where p is the relative frequency of round seeds.

Step II. *Statistical model:* The chi-square method is appropriate for comparing these two discrete classes (round versus wrinkled seeds). The assumptions of nominal nonparametric tests apply (discussed at the end of Chapter 12).

Step III. *Significance level:* Let $\alpha = 0.05$ for a two-tailed (nondirectional) test.

Step IV. *Region of rejection:* Table A.5 provides the sampling distribution of the chi-square statistic. The degrees of freedom in this case are $df = k - 1 = 2 - 1 = 1$. The critical region thus contains all values of the chi-square statistic greater than or equal to $\chi^2_{0.05} = 3.841$.

Step V. *Calculations and statistical decision:* The standard chi-square format is as follows:

Outcome	Observed value O_i	Expected value E_i	$(O_i - E_i)$	$(O_i - E_i)^2$	$(O_i - E_i)^2 / E_i$
Round	5474	$7324(0.75) = 5493$	-19	361	0.066
Wrinkled	1850	$7324(0.25) = 1831$	19	361	0.197
	7324	7324			$\chi^2 = 0.263$

The observed chi-square statistic does not fall into the critical region. The sample results hence favor H_o at $\alpha = 0.05$.

Step VI. *Nonstatistical decision:* This experiment does not represent a significant departure from the predicted $3:1$ Mendelian ratios at $\alpha = 0.05$.

For the simple case of $k = 2$, the chi-square and binomial methods produce identical results. For illustration, the same Mendelian sample can be tested using the normal approximation to the binomial distribution.

Step I. *Statistical hypotheses:*

$$H_o: \quad \mu = np = 7324(0.75) = 5493 \qquad H_1: \quad \mu \neq np \neq 5493$$

where p is the relative frequency of round seeds, and n is the total number of seeds.

Step II. *Statistical model:* The normal approximation to the binomial distribution. Assumptions of nominal level nonparametric tests apply.

Step III. *Significance level:* Let $\alpha = 0.05$ for a two-tailed (nondirectional) test.

Step IV. *Region of rejection:* Any value of $z \geq 1.96$ will fall into the critical region for $\alpha = 0.05$.

Step V. *Calculation and statistical decision:* The experimentally observed results must first be standardized:

$$z = \frac{X_i - \mu}{\sigma} = \frac{5475 - 5493}{37} = 0.49$$

where $\mu = np = 7324(0.75) = 5493$ and $\sigma = \sqrt{npq} = \sqrt{7324(0.75)(0.25)} = 37$.

The observed value of z does not fall within the region of rejection and H_o is retained.

Step VI. *Nonstatistical decision:* This experiment does not represent a significant departure from the expected 3:1 Mendelian ratio, at $\alpha = 0.05$.

Example 11.2

Suppose that a particular theory predicts that, in the long run, hunter-gatherer marriages tend to occur in the following percentage proportions:

Spouse from own village,   25
Spouse's village within 50 miles,   25
Spouse's village more than 50 miles, 50

Julian Steward (1938: 67) collected the following data for the Northern Paiute of the Fish Lake Valley of eastern California:

Spouse from own village,   4
Spouse within valley,   15
Spouse from another valley,   13

Assuming that the radius of the Fish Lake Valley is about 50 miles, are these data consistent with the above theory?

Step I. *Statistical hypotheses:* The expectations arise from preexisting theory: Marriages are predicted to occur in a 1:1:2 ratio for spouse from own village, nearby village, and distant village. In other words, there are three different groups ($k = 3$), each with a distinct probability: $p_1 = 0.25$, $p_2 = 0.25$, $p_3 = 0.50$.

$$H_o: \quad E_1 = np_1 = 32(0.25) = 8$$
$$E_2 = np_2 = 32(0.25) = 8$$
$$E_3 = np_3 = 32(0.50) = 16$$
$$H_1: \quad E_1 \neq 8; \ E_2 \neq 8; \ E_3 \neq 16$$

Note here how the alternative hypothesis is composite. H_i simply states that one or more propositions of H_o are false.

Step II. *Statistical model:* The binomial model is no longer applicable because more than two discrete classes are involved ($k > 2$). This is why H_o is expressed as p_1, p_2, and p_3; the p versus q notation of the binomial applies only when $k = 2$. The chi-square sampling distribution is relevant here and nominal level nonparametric assumptions apply.

Step III. *Significance level:* Let $\alpha = 0.05$ for a nondirectional test. Note that we do not specify which of the E_i classes is deviant. Any significant deviation will reject H_o.

Step IV. *Region of rejection:* This example has df $= k - 1 = 3 - 1 = 2$. The critical region thus contains all chi-square statistics $\geq \chi^2_{0.05} = 5.99147$.

Step V. *Calculations and statistical decision:*

Outcome	O_i	E_i	$(O_i - E_i)$	$(O_i - E_i)^2$	$(O_i - E_i)^2/E_i$
Own village	4	8	−4	16	2.000
Within valley	15	8	7	49	6.125
Another valley	13	16	−3	9	0.563
	32	32			$\chi^2 = 8.688$

This χ^2 exceeds the critical value of $\chi^2_{0.05} = 5.99147$ and falls into the region of rejection. The sample data favor H_1, so we reject H_o.

Step VI. *Nonstatistical decision:* The Fish Lake Paiute data depart significantly from the marriage theory at $\alpha = 0.05$. Be sure to note here that chi-square tells us only about the *overall* agreement with theory. By examining the actual data, we see that the Fish Lake Paiute have a much higher rate of spouses from within the valley than the theory predicted.

11.3 TWO-BY-TWO CONTINGENCY TABLES

Section 11.2 introduced the logic for the chi-square statistic, but we have considered only the *univariate* case. As the name implies, the univariate chi-square test treats a single dimension, such as blood type, marriage practices, or seed shape in pea plants. Although univariate chi-squares can ultimately handle an infinity of variables, each dimension must be considered *one at a time*. We will now examine the *bivariate* form of the chi-square test, beginning with the simplest application, the *2 × 2 contingency table.*

In their study of urbanization and its impact upon family structure, Stanley Freed and Ruth Freed collected data in Shanti Nagar, a small village in northern India (Freed and Freed 1969). The Freeds were particularly concerned with the response of traditional family organization to increasing industrialization. They interviewed a random sample of 107 families to determine precisely how the introduction of wage labor influenced traditional family structure.

Family head, 39 years and younger		
Traditional job	26	
Nontraditional cash income	15	41
Family head, 40 years and older		
Traditional job	59	
Nontraditional cash income	7	66
		107

Their field data clearly suggest a trend. The younger men tend to follow nontraditional employment, while the older, more conservative family heads tend to remain within traditional occupational roles. Can these data be said to represent a significant socioeconomic trend within the entire village, or is this apparent tendency specious, due merely to chance errors of sampling?

The research objective is concerned with the articulation between two distinct variables: age of family head and type of employment. These field data can be rearranged into the concise tabular format of a 2×2 contingency table, as follows:

	Occupation		
Family Head	Nontraditional Job, Cash Income	Traditional Job	Total
39 years and younger	15	26	41
40 years and older	7	59	66
Total	22	85	107

This conventional format presents two-way classification in each of two dimensions and shows at a glance both variables, their relative contributions to the total counts, and the precise articulation between the states of each variable. The various quarters (or cells) of the 2×2 table are commonly represented by letters as shown in the next table, where the variable states in this general case have been labelled plus and minus. While this designation applies strictly only to presence/absence data, the notation can apply to any true dichotomy (male–female, traditional–nontraditional, and so on).

	First Variable		
Second Variable	+	−	Total
+	a	b	$(a + b)$
−	c	d	$(c + d)$
Total	$(a + c)$	$(b + d)$	n

The chi-square statistic always compares empirically observed values to theoretically expected frequencies. Sometimes the expected values are predicted from a "theory," as with the Paiute marriage example, but the expected frequencies are more often simply those expected by chance alone. If there were, for example, no functional relationship between informant age and his occupation, then the two states of the variables could be expected to sort independently (and hence randomly). Finding the random expectation is simple when all column and row totals are equal $(a + b) = (c + d) = (a + c) = (b + d) = n/4$. Each cell should contain exactly one-quarter of the observations, if the results have been randomly distributed. Only rarely do real data turn out to be equally distributed, so we must devise a method of producing the expected frequencies of chance association. We begin with the fact that expectation = np. Since n, the total number of counts in the table is already known, it remains only to find the value for p, the probability of a single observation falling into a given cell by chance. Only when the row and column totals are equal will $p = 0.25$.

Let us find the frequency of cell a using the Shanti Nagar data as an example. Ignoring the row distinction for the moment, the probability of randomly selecting a Shanti Nagar informant with a nontraditional occupation is

$$p_{C1} = \frac{22}{107} = \frac{a+c}{n} = 0.206$$

p_{C1} is the probability given by the total of the first column in the contingency table. Similarly, the probability of an informant's holding a traditional job is estimated by

$$p_{C2} = \frac{85}{107} = \frac{b+d}{n} = 0.794$$

These two probabilities taken together represent certainty, and their sum must exactly equal unity.

The row probabilities are fashioned in an identical manner. The chance that a randomly selected informant is younger than 40 is

$$p_{R1} = \frac{41}{107} = 0.383$$

and the probability of choosing an informant 40 or older is

$$p_{R2} = \frac{66}{107} = 1.00 - 0.383 = 0.617$$

But the four figures represent *total probabilities* for rows or columns, not probabilities for individual cells. We must find, for example, $(p_{C1,R1})$, the probability of a random variate falling into row cell a. The individual row and column probabilities are independent of one another, and hence must be *multiplied*. The probability associated with cell a is

$$p_{C1,R1} = p_{C1} \times p_{R1} = (0.206)(0.383) = 0.079$$

Now the expected frequency for cell a is readily found to be

$$E_a = n(p_{C1,R1}) = 107(0.079) = 8.45$$

Probability Rule II (Section 5.8) can be used in the same way to find the other expected values.

$$E_b = n(p_{C2,R1}) = 107\left(\frac{85}{107}\right)\left(\frac{41}{107}\right) = 32.55$$

$$E_c = n(p_{C1,R2}) = 107\left(\frac{66}{107}\right)\left(\frac{22}{107}\right) = 13.55$$

$$E_d = n(p_{C2,R2}) = 107\left(\frac{66}{107}\right)\left(\frac{85}{107}\right) = 52.45$$

In general, the expected probabilities for a contingency table can be found by the simple formula

$$E_i = \frac{(\text{row total})(\text{column total})}{\text{grand total}}$$ (11.2)

Row and column totals of the expected frequencies are always fixed in a 2×2 contingency table. It is therefore necessary only to compute a single cell frequency, using Formula (11.2). Once E_a (or any other cell) is known, the other expected frequencies can be obtained by subtraction.

With both observed and expected values available, the chi-square statistic is easily computed, as shown in the following table. Note that all $(O_i - E_i)$ computations are equal. This fact, true for all 2×2 tables, provides a useful check for possible error in computing the expected frequencies.

Outcome	O_i	E_i	$(O_i - E_i)$	$(O_i - E_i)^2$	$(O_i - E_i)^2/E_i$
a	15	8.45	6.55	42.90	5.077
b	26	32.55	−6.55	42.90	1.318
c	7	13.55	−6.55	42.90	3.166
d	59	52.45	6.55	42.90	0.818
	107	107.00	0.00		$\chi^2 = 10.379$

In order to assess the statistical significance of $\chi^2 = 10.379$ we must first determine the number of degrees of freedom. Degrees of freedom were defined for the univariate version of chi-square as the number of independent $(O_i - E_i)$ comparisons, given by $(k - 1)$, but the bivariate case involves overlapping and intersecting $(O_i - E_i)$ comparisons. The degrees of freedom are defined for all contingency tables (not just the special 2×2 case) as

$$df = (R - 1)(C - 1)$$ (11.3)

A single degree of freedom is lost in both rows and columns. Since the row and column frequencies are independent, the two individual degrees of freedom are multiplied. In 2×2 tables, the number of degrees of freedom is always 1.

The 2×2 table generally tests the hypothesis that two variables are independent, that the states of one variable sort independently from the states of the other variable. In the present example, the tabled value of χ^2 for a single degree of freedom and $\alpha = 0.01$ is 6.63490. The observed χ^2 value exceeds the tabled value. The result falls into the region of rejection, and therefore the null hypothesis of independence is rejected. On the basis of this test, the Freeds concluded that "family heads of Shanti Nagar less than 40 years of age are more likely to be employed for cash at nontraditional jobs than older men" (Freed and Freed 1969: 352).

Thus, the χ^2 statistic operates rather differently from t and z because the chi-square statistic sums the squares of all deviations. Hence, the results cannot be negative. Chi-square tables are computed only for two-tailed tests and ignore directionality. Whenever directionality is required by an alternative hypothesis, it is necessary to halve the tabled significance level. A 2×2 table was used to test the above two-tailed test of independence, and the appropriate region of rejection was given by Table A.5 as $\chi^2_{0.01} = 6.63490$. But if the same situation had

Don't have to go out as far with V^2 crit to reject H_0

~~wrong~~

been tested with a directional alternative hypothesis, the situation would have become one-tailed, and the appropriate region of <u>rejection</u> would be $\chi^2_{0.01} = 7.87944$ (the χ^2 value actually tabled for $\chi^2_{0.005}$). In other words, all nondirectional hypotheses significant at the 0.01 level would be significant at the $0.01/2 = 0.005$ level had direction been specified beforehand. H_o is always rejected more readily in a one-tailed format.

Since all 2×2 tables have a single degree of freedom (and hence all the $(O_i - E_i)$ comparisons are identical), the computations can be made much simpler than for the general chi-square case. The *computational formula for 2×2 contingency* tables is

$$\chi^2 = \frac{(ad - bc)^2 n}{(a + b)(c + d)(a + c)(b + d)} \tag{11.4}$$

Results obtained from Formula (11.4) will, of course, always have a single degree of freedom.

Example 11.3

Use the computing formula for 2×2 contingency tables [Expression (11.4)] to test for independence in the data on page 273.

The hypothesis-testing format should clarify the exact steps involved in chi-square testing of 2×2 tables.

Step I. *Statistical hypotheses:*

H_o: Age is independent from occupation

H_1: Occupation varies in proportion to age

The null hypothesis holds that the first variable (age) should have no effect upon the second variable (occupation). In effect, the expected values (the E_i) constitute this null hypothesis because these values should occur only when the row and columns sort independently. But because the computing formula is to be used, the actual E_i values need not be computed.

Step II. *Statistical model:* The model in this case is the chi-square sampling distribution with a single degree of freedom.

Step III. *Level of significance:* Let $\alpha = 0.01$ for a nondirectional test.

Step IV. *Region of rejection:* From Table A.5, we find that any observed value of chi-square greater than or equal to $\chi^2_{0.01} = 6.63490$ falls into the region of rejection.

Step V. *Calculation and statistical decision:* Using Formula (11.4), we find the observed chi-square value to be

$$\chi^2 = \frac{[(15)(59) - (26)(7)]^2 107}{(41)(66)(22)(85)} = \frac{(703)^2 107}{5,060,220}$$

$$= 10.450$$

The discrepancy between this result and that obtained previously ($\chi^2 =$ 10.449) is due to errors of rounding.

The observed value falls into the critical region, and thus the results appear to favor H_1.

Step VI. *Nonstatistical decision:* Based upon the Freeds' data, we conclude that occupation of family head and age appear to be interrelated in the village of Shanti Nagar.

The 2×2 contingency table is a rather special application of the *row by column* ("R $\times$ C") *contingency table*. χ^2 statistics can be computed for any cross-cutting pair of variables, involving any number of states with the appropriate number of degrees of freedom, once again given by df $= (R - 1)(C - 1)$. There is (in theory) no limit to the number of cells which can be considered in an R $\times$ C table, although in practice these tables are rarely larger than six rows by six columns.

Let us return to the Island of Tikopia and examine how chi-square is computed for a large R $\times$ C table. Early in his study of Tikopian kinship, ethnographer Raymond Firth attempted to determine the nature of social force. He detected initially the *local association*, village solidarity, created by common coresidence in the same community. Local associations were fostered by activities such as fishing, dancing, ordinary communication, and daily interpersonal interaction (Firth 1957: 66). The *ties of descent* also exert a strong social force, manifested largely through membership in inherited clans. Although descent and coresidence should theoretically crosscut one another, Firth knew that most villages tended to be dominated by a single clan. Firth noted a "native attitude which regards a village as being primarily under the aegis of one group [that is, one clan]," even though minority descent groups possess full legal and land rights. Firth attempted to test this attitude in practice by conducting a census of relating clan membership to village membership (Table 11.1). Do these data support Firth's hypothesis that villages tend to be dominated by certain clans?

The research proposal can be phrased as a null hypothesis: Clan membership and village residence are independent variables in Tikopia. The alternative hypothesis is nondirectional (two-tailed) and a significance level $\alpha = 0.01$ is

TABLE 11.1   Clan distribution in Tikopian villages (after Firth 1957: table 1).

4×3

Village	Clan			Total
	Ravena	Namo	Faea	
Kafika	31	2	43	76
Tafua	4	16	46	66
Taumako	39	6	16	61
Fanarere	10	3	2	15
Total	84	27	107	218 = n

judged sufficient. A χ^2 statistic should enable us to determine whether clan membership and village residence are independent.

Table 11.1 has four rows and three columns, so there are $(4-1)(3-1) = 6$ degrees of freedom. Chi-square can be computed precisely as in Section 11.2 for all of the $R \times C = 12$ $(O_i - E_i)$ cells.

From Expression (11.2), the expected value of cell CI,RI (Ravena clan in the Kafika village) is

$$\frac{(76)(84)}{218} = 29.28$$

The other expected frequencies could be found in this manner, but one really needs only to compute a few expected values, obtaining the remainder by subtraction. Because these data have 6 degrees of freedom, only six values are truly independent; the remaining six can be determined by subtraction.

The actual chi-square statistic for Table 11.1 follows.

O_i	E_i	$(O_i - E_i)$	$(O_i - E_i)^2$	$(O_i - E_i)^2/E_i$
31	29.28	1.71	2.96	0.100
2	9.41	-7.41	54.91	5.835
43	37.30	5.70	32.49	0.871
4	25.43	-21.43	459.24	18.059
16	8.17	7.83	61.25	7.504
46	32.40	13.60	184.96	5.709
39	23.50	15.50	240.25	10.223
6	7.56	-1.56	2.43	0.322
16	29.94	-13.94	194.32	6.490
10	5.78	4.22	17.81	3.081
3	1.86	1.14	1.30	0.699
2	7.36	-5.36	28.73	3.904
218	217.97	0.00		$\chi^2 = 62.797$

The observed value of chi-square is found to be $\chi^2 = 62.797$, far exceeding the tabled value of $\chi^2_{0.01} = 16.8119$. The null hypothesis of no association is rejected. We conclude that the data of Table 11.1 do indeed support the hypothesis that clan membership and village residence are not independent in Tikopia. Perhaps this is a causal relationship, or perhaps these two variables are functionally linked to a third variable. We cannot decide causality on the basis of a chi-square (or any other statistical) test.

Example 11.4

A large cache of chert bifaces was recovered at the Pomranky site in Michigan. Does the blade shape appear to be nonrandomly associated with the stone type (data from Binford 1963: 158)?

Blade Shape	Stone Type		
	White Chert	Dark-gray to Brownish Chert	Total
Expanding ovate	23	0	23
Excurvate	86	50	136
Ovate	108	81	189
Parallel ovate	12	6	18
Total	229	137	366

In this case, $df = (4 - 1)(2 - 1) = 3$, and the region of rejection begins at $\chi^2_{0.05} = 7.81473$ for this two-tailed test.

O_i	E_i	$(O_i - E_i)$	$(O_i - E_i)^2$	$(O_i - E_i)^2/E_i$
23	14.39	8.61	74.13	5.151
0	8.61	− 8.61	74.13	8.610
86	85.09	0.91	0.83	0.010
50	50.91	− 0.91	0.83	0.016
108	118.25	−10.25	105.06	0.888
81	70.75	10.25	105.06	1.485
12	11.26	0.74	0.55	0.049
6	6.74	− 0.74	0.55	0.081
366	366.00	0.00		$\chi^2 = 16.290$

Since the observed value of χ^2 is far greater than $\chi^2_{0.05}$ for 3 degrees of freedom, one is justified in concluding that stone type is significantly associated with blade form in this particular cache. Especially important in this association is the lack of dark-gray to brownish chert blades in an expanding ovate form (since all were of white chert), and also the tendency for ovate blades to be made of white rather than colored chert.

11.4 YATES' CORRECTION FOR CONTINUITY

Let us perform an elementary sampling experiment to see just how the chi-square distribution operates. Suppose that the observed frequencies had exactly agreed with the expected frequencies in the ABO blood type experiment at the beginning of this chapter:

$$\chi^2 = 4\frac{(25 - 25)^2}{25} = 0.000$$

χ^2 will equal zero in all cases of perfect agreement. The next smallest value of chi-square is found when a single blood type—say, AB—has one more case than expected ($25 + 1 = 26$). Because sample size, n, is constant, some other cell must lose a count, dropping its frequency to $25 - 1 = 24$ cases. Now

$$\chi^2 = 2\frac{(25 - 25)^2}{25} - \frac{(26 - 25)^2}{25} - \frac{(24 - 25)^2}{25}$$

$$= 0.000 + 0.040 + 0.040 = 0.080$$

These are the two lowest possible values for χ^2 in this univariate case: $\chi^2 = 0.000$ and $\chi^2 = 0.080$. No intermediate value can possibly fall between zero and 0.080, as long as k, n, and the expected values are held constant. In other words, the actual sampling distribution of chi-square varies only in discrete steps. The frequency diagram representing the true chi-square distribution is a histogram, with a stair-step profile rather than a smooth, continuous curve such as that given for the normal curve.

These discrete results for chi-square can be derived only through lengthy sampling experiments, such as that with the ABO blood groups. Because of the tedium involved in this process for each value of degrees of freedom, it has proved helpful to approximate the actual discrete chi-square distribution with a continuous curve. The chi-square distribution can be approximated much in the manner that approximates a binomial histogram. The formula for the chi-square approximation is not of interest here, but Fig. 11.1 shows this continuous approximation for df = 3. All the chi-square values in Table A.5 were computed from the continuous curve approximation rather than the actual discrete chi-square histograms. The error resulting from this approximation is negligible as long as the expected frequencies remain relatively large. But data in social sciences are often quite scarce, and one must often rely upon relatively small samples. It is thus necessary to adjust the computed chi-square statistic for small samples in order to conform to the theoretical distribution.

Yates' correction for continuity performs this adjustment, and is a relatively simple matter. Yates' correction subtracts 0.5 from the absolute value of the difference between the observed and the expected:

$$\chi_c^2 = \sum \frac{(|O_i - E_i| - 0.5)^2}{E_i} \tag{11.5}$$

The corrected chi-square statistic is often denoted by χ_c^2 to distinguish the value from the uncorrected figure. The correction effect reduces the computed chi-square value and hence minimizes the discrepancy between the observed and the expected tallies.

The following shortcut computational formula corrects for continuity for 2×2 contingency tables:

$$\chi_c^2 = \frac{n[(ad - bc) - (n/2)]^2}{(a + b)(c + d)(a + c)(b + d)} \tag{11.6}$$

The number of degrees of freedom remains unaffected.

Unfortunately, there is remarkably little agreement among statisticians as to exactly when the Yates' correction for continuity should be applied. Alder and Roessler (1972: 239) recommend that chi-square be corrected whenever df = 1, while Adkins (1964: 343) suggests correction only when one or more E_i fall below 5. Recent work on this situation by Grizzle (1967) indicates that the Yates' correction generally overcompensates for differences in continuity. The calculated values are overly depressed and the probability of a Type I error is lowered below the stipulated value. Although this evidence is not definitive, it would seem adequate to apply the correction for continuity only when (1) one or more of the E_i fall below 10 in a 2×2 contingency table, or (2) more than two of the E_i fall below 5 in a larger $R \times C$ table (Blalock 1972:286). Note that the chi-square computations on page 273 and Exercise 11.3 should have been corrected for continuity.

Example 11.5

Use computational Formula (11.6) to correct Freed's data for continuity.

Chi-square should be corrected in this case because the expected value of cell a falls below 10:

$$\chi_c^2 = \frac{107[(15 \cdot 59 - 26 \cdot 7) - (107/2)]^2}{(41)(66)(22)(85)}$$

$$= \frac{45,137,976}{5,060,220} = 8.920$$

The correction for continuity has lowered the computed chi-square value by nearly 15 percent in this case, but the result still remains significant.

Example 11.6

When trying to explain why different cultures practice various modes of marital residence pattern, anthropologists have often suggested that the division of labor by sex determines in large part where a couple will reside after marriage. According to this theory, in societies where the male predominates in the division of labor (that is, where men do more work), then the residence should be patrilocal; where the females predominate, residence should tend to be matrilocal. To test this theory, Carol and Melvin Ember (1971) examined the relevant data for North American societies as listed in the *Ethnographic Atlas* (Murdock 1967):

Division of Labor	Pattern of Residence		
	Patrilocal	Other	Total
Men do more work than women	21	22	43
Other	6	15	21
Total	27	37	64

Are these results consistent with the theory that division of labor determines the pattern of marital residence (at the 0.05 level)?

Since the expected frequency of cell c is less than 10, ($E_c = (21)$ $(27)/64 = 8.86$), the chi-square computation should be corrected for continuity.

O_i	E_i	$(O_i - E_i)$	$[|O_i - E_i| - (1/2)]$	$[|O_i - E_i| - (1/2)]^2$	$\dfrac{[|O_i - E_i| - (1/2)]}{E_i}$
21	18.14	2.86	2.36	5.57	0.307
22	24.86	−2.86	2.36	5.57	0.224
6	8.86	−2.86	2.36	5.57	0.629
15	12.14	2.86	2.36	5.57	0.459
64	64.00	0.00			$\chi_c^2 = 1.619$

The alternative hypothesis in this case is *directional* ($ad > bc$), so the proper region of rejection is given by $\chi^2 = 2.70554$ with a single degree of freedom. Since the observed chi-square statistic fails to exceed the predetermined value, the null hypothesis cannot be rejected. In other words, these data fail to support the proposition that societies in which men do more work should be patrilocal. Note that had chi-square been computed *without* correcting for continuity, the resulting value ($\chi_c^2 = 2.377$) would still have failed to be significant at $\alpha = 0.05$.

11.5 ASSUMPTIONS OF THE CHI-SQUARE TEST

1. Nominal level of measurement. There is no minimal level of measurement required by the χ^2 test other than simple categorization (nominal scale). Ordinal or better data must be reduced into categories for chi-square testing. When such data are available, it is wise to attempt to use a more efficient test, such as rank-ordering tests (Chapter 12) or the *t*-test. Sometimes one scale in a bivariate contingency table will be metric (or ordinal) while the other scale is only nominal. Statistical testing is limited in such cases by the *lowest* rank of measurement. The more advanced scale must be reduced to categories (as, for example, in the Freeds' data used in the beginning of this chapter).

2. Independent random sampling. Variates must be randomly selected such that variates are selected independently, each with an equal chance for inclusion in the sample. Furthermore, in the bivariate case, the distribution of one variable cannot be allowed to influence the distribution of the other variable. Chi-square cannot be used to test "before–after" or paired variates, for instance, because the two conditions are clearly related to one another. They are not independent. Chi-square would also be invalid in the situation in which $n = 200$ for 10 informants who have responded to the same 20 questions. The responses to each question presumably depend upon question content and will therefore be interrelated. The McNemar test is appropriate for testing two related samples on the nominal level of measurement.

3. Appropriate sample size. The n must be suitably large for the chi-square approximation to hold. Section 11.11 provides some general guidelines regarding sample size. Note that the minimum values are determined by the *expected* frequencies rather than by the actual observed counts. Also note that there is no assumption that the samples have been selected from a normally distributed population. Chi-square is a nonparametric test.

11.6 SOME COMMON ERRORS IN APPLYING THE CHI-SQUARE TEST

● *A device that explains everything explains nothing.*—L. White

At the outset, I nominated chi-square for anthropology's most abused statistic. Many of these errors involve arithmetic mistakes, expected frequencies which are too small, or misapplication of chi-square when some other statistical method is more appropriate. Some hints for avoiding such more-or-less mechanical errors are presented in Section 11.11.

More serious difficulties involve the underlying logic and interpretation of the chi-square statistic. It is difficult to overemphasize the importance of stating a hypothesis prior to computing a chi-square. The a priori null hypothesis directly determines how the observations are to be evaluated—not the other way around.

Consider the following example:

Settlement Pattern	Post-Marital Residence		
	Patrilocal	Matrilocal	Neolocal
Nonsedentary	18	20	25
Sedentary	13	30	43

Do these data indicate a significant relationship between residence pattern and settlement type?

The computed chi-square statistic for this 2×3 contingency table is $\chi^2 = 4.127$, with 2 degrees of freedom. Because chi-square is less than the tabled value of $\chi^2_{0.05} = 5.99147$, the null hypothesis of no relationship cannot reasonably be rejected. By this interpretation, there is no reason to suspect a functional relationship between residence and settlement pattern.

But these data could be examined in another frame of reference. Suppose we had specifically postulated a functional relationship between *patrilocal* residence and *nonsedentary* residence. The data can now be compressed into a 2×2 contingency table. The chi-square for this 2×2 table is $\chi^2 = 3.841$. Now the null hypothesis is rejected and the possibility of a functional relationship remains.

Settlement Pattern	Post-Marital Residence	
	Patrilocal	Other than Patrilocal
Nonsedentary	18	45
Sedentary	13	73

These conflicting results illustrate the critical importance of stating one's research hypothesis *prior* to evaluating the data at hand. In the first instance, the null hypothesis took the three post-marital residence categories as equal in substantive importance, and the results were insignificant. But in the second case, a more specific null hypothesis focused directly upon patrilocal residence and the two residual categories were pooled. A degree of freedom was lost by combining matrilocal and neolocal residence, and the results emerged as significant on precisely the same probability sample of $n = 149$ societies.

It requires no great imagination to realize that a "pet" hypothesis (usually phrased as H_1) can fare better when the data are scanned prior to the statement of H_o, so that residual categories can be pooled. But this sneaky procedure intermingles data with theory, violating both the letter and the spirit of statistical inference.

Let me also emphasize that chi-square is *not* designed to measure the *degree of association* between two variables. Chi-square only tests whether the observed departure from expectation is more than random chance would suggest. Chi-square is computed as the *summation* (not the average) of the squared deviations. The magnitude of χ^2 is clearly a function of sample size: the larger the sample, the greater the chance for significant results. Obviously, an association might well appear significant for a large sample, but insignificant on a small one.

Furthermore, it is important to remember that chi-square can be judged significant only on the basis of a *previously decided* level of significance. In general, it is irrelevant whether the computed value is equal to $p = 0.001$ or $p = 0.000,000,000,01$. Alpha had been set in advance to reflect one's willingness to commit a Type I error. Either this alpha level was exceeded or it was not. The *amount* of discrepancy between expected and observed values of chi-square is irrelevant. For this reason, statistical measures other than chi-square should be used when one is interested in the *strength* of association rather than actual *existence* of association (this point is developed in more detail in Chapter 12).

11.7 TESTING INTERNAL HYPOTHESES WITH CHI-SQUARE

Chi-square was used in earlier examples to assess the discrepancy between observed and expected values. All the null hypotheses were generated on the basis of considerations other than on those directly inherent in the sample at hand. Established Mendelian genetic theory, for instance, generated null hypotheses for the genetic experiments. Similarly, the Freeds' null hypothesis— that traditional family leadership is independent of urbanization—resulted from previously held ideas of culture change rather than from the actual sample data. Situations such as this, in which H_o is derived without direct knowledge of the sample, involve *extrinsic hypotheses*. The null hypothesis is *external* to the sample.

But the χ^2 can also test for deviations when expected values arise from the sample itself. Known as *intrinsic hypotheses*, these propositions have been derived (or estimated) directly from the actual observations at hand. Suppose an investigator is interested in determining whether particular observed variates conform to an a priori distribution—say, a normal distribution. He is testing an intrinsic null hypothesis because the parametric μ and σ must be estimated directly from the sample statistics $\bar{X}$ and S. Put another way, there are infinite normal distributions from which a sample could have been drawn, but the investigator is interested only in the one population with mean μ and standard deviation σ. This information is available only *after* the sample has been drawn.

The major procedural difference between intrinsic and extrinsic hypotheses involves the number of degrees of freedom. The number of degrees of freedom in the univariate case was determined by subtracting 1 from the total number of k classes (df $= k - 1$). This single degree of freedom was lost because of the fixed sum of n. One degree of freedom was lost in contingency tables for each variable for the same reason [df $= (R - 1)(C - 1)$]. But for intrinsic hypotheses, one *additional* degree of freedom is lost for every parameter estimated from the sample. In testing for normality, one degree of freedom is lost, as before, because of the fixed sum of n. Two *additional* degrees of freedom are also lost because μ and σ must be estimated from $\bar{X}$ and S. So, when testing a sample against the expected normal distribution, df $= k - 3$. Testing for a binomial distribution requires only the estimation of μ (since σ is fixed, given μ), so df $= k - 2$. Keep in mind the distinction between intrinsic and extrinsic hypotheses as we consider how to test for goodness of fit to the normal distribution.

11.8 GOODNESS OF FIT TO A NORMAL DISTRIBUTION

In Chapter 4 we considered a set of measurements on the lower first molar of pygmy chimpanzee. We simply assumed that these data came from a normally distributed population, but now we can apply the chi-square statistic to test for normality. For convenience, a frequency distribution containing these data has been reproduced in Table 11.2.

In asking whether or not these data are normally distributed, we are testing the null hypothesis that the sample data (with $n = 99$, in this case) have been selected from a normally distributed population. The alternative hypothesis is nondirectional because we do not care in which direction the deviation might occur.

In order to determine precisely *which* normal population is being considered, the parametric mean and standard deviation must be estimated from sample values. The population mean, μ, is estimated by $\bar{X} = 8.83$ mm, and $S = 0.479$ mm estimates sigma, the population standard deviation. Because of this estimation, testing for normality always requires a rather large sample size (generally in excess of 100 or so). Contingency cell frequencies should be combined in the manner set forth in Section 11.11. Try to keep all cell frequencies greater than 5.

The expected frequencies under the normal distribution are easily generated from the z-distribution. Starting with the lowest class interval, z is

$$z_1 = \frac{X_1 - \bar{X}}{S} = \frac{8.0 - 8.83}{0.479} = 1.73$$

The area to the left of $z_1 = 1.73$ is found from Table A.3 to be $A_1 = 0.0418$. This

TABLE 11.2 Chi-square test for goodness of fit for normality. Data are 99 breadth measurements on the first lower molar of pygmy chimpanzee (see Table 4.3).

Class Interval, mm	O_i	E_i	$(O_i - E_i)$	$(O_i - E_i)^2$	$(O_i - E_i)^2/E_i$
<7.9	3	4.14	1.14	1.30	0.314
8.0–8.1	7	5.28	1.72	2.96	0.056
8.2–8.3	8	9.07	1.07	1.14	0.126
8.4–8.5	12	12.76	0.76	0.58	0.045
8.6–8.7	12	15.89	3.89	15.13	0.952
8.8–8.9	16	15.91	0.11	0.01	0.001
9.0–9.1	9	14.12	5.12	26.21	1.857
9.2–9.3	18	10.26	7.74	59.91	5.839
9.4–9.5	9	6.27	1.26	1.59	0.253
>9.6	5	5.32	0.32	0.10	0.019
	99	99.02			$\chi^2 = 9.462$

$df = 7$; $\chi^2_{0.05} = 14.0671$.

area corresponds to the probability of a randomly selected variate being smaller than 8.0 mm. The expected frequency for $n = 99$ is

$$E_1 = np_1 = 99(0.0418) = 4.1$$

The expected frequency of class "8.0–8.1" is determined in a similar manner:

$$z_2 = \frac{X_2 - \bar{X}}{S} = \frac{8.2 - 8.83}{0.479} = 1.31$$

$$A_2 = 0.4582 - 0.4049 = 0.0533$$

The second expected frequency is

$$E_2 = np_2 = 99(0.0533) = 5.3$$

Expected frequencies can be similarly computed for the remaining classes in Table 11.2. As a final check upon these calculations, the summation of the expected values must be equal to n within a small rounding error.

Both expected and observed frequencies are now available. Chi-square can be computed to determine whether the observed deviations are of significant magnitude to reject the null hypothesis.

As mentioned earlier, testing for normality always involves a loss of 3 degrees of freedom because both μ and σ must be estimated from sample statistics. Assuming a significance level of 0.05, Table A.5 indicates that since $\chi^2 = 9.461 < \chi^2_{0.05} = 14.067$. The results are not significant, which means that this sample of 99 variates could easily have been from a normally distributed population of variates.

Example 11.7

In Exercise 3.5, the sample mean and standard deviation were computed for a series of 256 fluted projectile points from Virginia. Before performing a detailed attribute analysis on these data, archaeologist James Fitting tested the variates for normality (Fitting 1965: table 1). Do these length measurements sufficiently follow a normal distribution at the 0.05 level?

In order to keep all cell frequencies above 5, the first two categories (less than 2.9 cm) and the last two divisions (longer than 10.0 cm) were pooled, thereby leaving nine categories ($k = 9$). The mean and standard deviation of the sample are known to be $\bar{X} = 5.8$ cm and $S = 2.07$ cm. The probability of any randomly selected variate from the population with $\mu = \bar{X} = 5.8$ and $\sigma = S = 2.07$ falling into the first category ("less than 2.9 cm") is the area to the left of $X_1 = 3.0$ cm in the z-distribution:

$$z_1 = \frac{3.0 - 5.8}{2.07} = 1.35 \qquad A_1 = 0.0885$$

The expected frequency of this class is

$$E_1 = 256(0.0885) = 22.66$$

Other expectations are found in a similar manner.

Length, cm	O_i	E_i	$(O_i - E_i)$	$(O_i - E_i)^2$	$(O_i - E_i)^2/E_i$
<2.9	8	22.66	−14.66	214.92	9.484
3.0–3.9	30	26.68	3.32	11.02	0.413
4.0–4.9	56	39.99	16.01	256.32	6.410
5.0–5.9	60	49.02	10.98	120.56	2.459
6.0–6.9	35	45.88	−10.88	118.37	2.580
7.0–7.9	33	34.92	− 1.92	3.69	0.106
8.0–8.9	12	21.50	− 9.50	90.25	4.198
9.0–9.9	13	10.09	2.91	8.47	0.839
>10.0	9	5.43	3.57	12.74	2.347
	256	256.17			$\chi^2 = 28.836$

The degrees of freedom in this case are given by df $= (k - 3) = 6$, and the critical value of chi-square is $\chi^2_{0.05} = 12.5916$. Since the observed value is over twice this expected value, we can conclude that the fluted projectile point lengths were probably not drawn from a normally distributed population. Specifically, this significant departure is caused by the absence of very large points (that is, larger than 10.0 cm) and also by the lack of points shorter than 2.9 cm. There also seems to be an overabundance of points between about 4.0 and 7.0 cm.

11.9 SMALL VALUES OF χ^2: THE STRANGE CASE OF MENDEL'S PEAS

The chi-square variants discussed so far involved only the right-hand tail of the chi-square distribution (Fig. 11.1). The reason for this is that the χ^2 statistic is computed by summing the squares of the deviations. All these deviations from the expected values are positive; therefore, the larger the summed deviations, the greater the chi-square statistic. Only the right-hand tail of the distribution is thus involved.

We have also stressed the importance of directionality in the alternative hypothesis for 2×2 tables. Directionality in this case is not identical to one- or two-tailed hypothesis testing of the normal curve. The significance testing of the chi-square distribution involves only the right-hand tail (regardless of directionality). As long as a priori directions were specified in 2×2 tables (either $ad > bc$ or $ad < bc$), the alpha level must be halved. A directional result significant at the tabled 0.10 value, for example, is in fact known to be significant at $\alpha = 0.05$.

But do not conclude from all this that χ^2 methods must *always* be concerned with only the right-hand tail of the distribution. There are some unusual instances when one might wish to determine whether the sum of the squared deviations (as reflected in the χ^2 statistic) could be *too small* to be attributed to chance alone. Suppose that an experiment with 10 degrees of freedom produced a chi-square of, say, 3.00. Table A.5 indicates a probability of greater than 0.975, corresponding to $\chi^2 = 3.00$. That is, there is more than a 97.5 percent chance of a randomly generated chi-square statistic occurring to the *right* of 3.00. However, this situation can also be reversed: There is less than 2.5 percent chance of a randomly generated chi-square value falling to the left of $\chi^2 = 3.00$. Very small chi-squares are themselves rare events, with a known probability of occurrence. In a strictly probabilistic sense, an extremely small chi-square disproves the null hypothesis just as surely as would a very large chi-square value. But within the conventional hypothesis-testing format discussed in Chapter 9, chi-squares with associated probabilities of $p = 0.975$ or larger (while still a rare occurrence) do not allow the rejection of H_o. In fact, the null hypothesis appears to be strongly supported by such results. To resolve this problem, it is necessary to stress again that statistical hypothesis testing must be problem-oriented. Procedures must be designed to answer specific questions at hand rather than merely to blindly follow rigid formats of inquiry.

The problem of the small χ^2 is well illustrated by the classic genetic experiments of Gregor Mendel. Every beginning anthropology student has been subjected to the traditional tale of how Gregor Mendel, an obscure monk, discovered the laws of inheritance. His work was relegated to obscurity until 16 years after his death, when it was miraculously rediscovered by no fewer than three independent scientists. This parable is taken as a tribute to the self-correcting nature of science (the truth will out), and the tale also seems to support the doctrine of independent invention. Independent cultural trajectories can be parallel and often repetitive.

At any rate, statistician Sir Ronald Fisher has posed a highly heretical question. Should we take Mendel literally? Fisher, himself an accomplished geneticist, reconstructed Mendel's famous experiments from various contemporary notes and reports. According to Fisher's reconstruction, Mendel took eight years to complete his experiments. Mendel apparently discovered the critical 3:1 phenotypic ratio rather early in the experimentation, and Fisher wondered aloud whether the actual published experiments represented a true *discovery* or a staged *demonstration* to illustrate previous findings.

Fisher analyzed Mendel's later results, using the chi-square test to scrutinize the role of chance in the genetic experiments. One of Mendel's experiments, for instance, was designed to illustrate the independent segregation of genetic factors—in this case, seed shape and color. In Mendel's notation, the following conditions were involved:

Seed Shape	Seed Color
AA Round (homozygous)	BB Yellow (homozygous)
Aa Round (heterozygous)	Bb Yellow (heterozygous)
aA Round (heterozygous)	bB Yellow (heterozygous)
aa Wrinkled (homozygous)	bb Green (homozygous)

Mendel's theory predicts that if the two traits truly segregate randomly in the same plants, then the progeny should appear in a fixed ratio 9:3:3:1, as follows:

(round, yellow) : (round, green) : (wrinkled, yellow) : (wrinkled, green)

$$9 \quad : \quad 3 \quad : \quad 3 \quad : \quad 1$$

In 1862, Mendel harvested the seeds of 15 plants known to be heterozygous on both seed shape and color. The offspring seeds were harvested the following year with the following results:

	Seed Shape			
Seed Color	AA	Aa	aa	Total
BB	38	60	28	126
Bb	65	138	68	271
bb	35	67	30	132
Total	138	265	126	529

The predicted ratios (9:3:3:1) were found in the 1863 experiment to be 9.1:3.1:2.9:0.9. When Mendel published these and other findings, he did not analyze the element of chance in experimentation. (The chi-square distribution was unknown at the time, but enough was known about the binomial distribution to estimate the probability of obtaining such satisfactory results.) Mendel ignored random effects and declared that the experimentally devised ratios overwhelmingly confirmed his predictions. These experiments eventually established the independent segregation of genetic traits.

As science progressed throughout the early twentieth century, the role of chance became an important criterion in experimental design. Writing in 1936, Fisher wondered if, given the normal exigencies of genetic experimentation, Mendel's results could be *too good*? In effect, Fisher tested the *left-hand* side of the chi-square distribution to see if there was *less* deviation (that is, too low a χ^2 value) than one should expect under chance conditions. Fisher's actual computations (Fisher 1936) were quite similar to the bivariate R×C tables considered in Section 11.3. But in this case, the expected probabilities were computed from Mendel's theoretically predicted ratios rather than from marginal totals.

Genotype	Phenotype	O_i	$E_i = np$	$(O_i - E_i)$	$(O_i - E_i)^2$	$(O_i - E_i)^2/E_i$
BB–AA	Round, yellow	38	529 (1/16) = 33.06	4.94	24.40	0.7380
BB–Aa	Round, yellow	60	529 (2/16) = 66.12	6.12	37.45	0.5565
Bb–AA	Round, yellow	65	529 (2/16) = 66.12	1.12	1.25	0.0190
Bb–Aa	Round, yellow	138	529 (4/16) = 132.24	5.76	33.18	0.2510
bb–AA	Round, green	67	529 (2/16) = 66.12	0.88	0.77	0.0120
bb–Aa	Round, green	35	529 (1/16) = 33.06	1.94	3.76	0.1140
BB–aa	Wrinkled, yellow	28	529 (1/16) = 33.06	5.06	25.60	0.7740
Bb–aa	Wrinkled, yellow	68	529 (2/16) = 66.12	1.88	3.53	0.0530
bb–aa	Wrinkled, green	30	529 (1/16) = 33.06	3.06	9.36	0.2830
		529	528.96			$\chi^2 = 2.8005$

These calculations produce a chi-square value of $\chi^2 = 2.8005$, with df = $(k - 1) = 8$. Table A.5 indicates that almost 95 percent of all chi-square values (with 8 degrees of freedom) are expected to fall to the right of $\chi^2 = 2.73264$. In other words, we expect such a low chi-square only about one time in every twenty independent experiments.

So, in this particular bifactorial genetic experiment, Mendel obtained results which were uncommonly close to expectation. Fisher went on to investigate the remainder of Mendel's experiments conducted during this eight-year interval. When all these experiments are combined into a single chi-square figure, the computed value of $\chi^2 = 41.606$ with 84 degrees of freedom, a figure corresponding to a probability of $p = 0.9993$. Remembering that chi-square tables refer only to the right-hand tail of the chi-square distribution, the actual probability associated with Mendel's complete results is only $p = 1.000 - 0.9993 = 0.0007$. That is, Fisher demonstrated that there are fewer than 7 in 1,000 chances of obtaining Mendel's results by chance alone.

How do we account for Mendel's near-perfect findings? The early experiments (probably in 1858) may have come as such a revelation to Mendel that he knew enough at that time essentially to frame his entire theory of genetic factor and gametic segregation. His confidence in his early discovery can be seen in several ways: He conducted no further experiments directly to test the 3:1 ratio, since he had already established this to his satisfaction; he ignored the then-current body of statistical inference, through which he could have "tested" his results; he conducted no tests to establish the equivalence of contribution from each parent, preferring simply to assume the 3:1 ratio once again. While it is unfair to accuse Mendel of directly doctoring his results, Fisher contended that chi-square analysis clearly indicates that most (if not all) of Mendel's experiments must have been falsified to agree with expectation. Perhaps Mendel's figures were intended only to illustrate his general principles. Perhaps the results were not to be taken seriously. Mendel could have purposely modified the counts, in order to support a principle he knew to be correct. It is even possible that Mendel was deceived by overly loyal assistants who knew all too well what results the good monk Mendel expected.

Whatever the ultimate explanation, the point is not to deride Mendel's contribution to genetic theory. His insights alone qualify him for plaudits, regardless of the experimental evidence. This intriguing case merely illustrates another application of the chi-square statistic, the situation in which χ^2 is too small to allow for a normal amount of randomness. Mendel's experiments seem to illustrate Fisher's generalization that "fictitious data can seldom survive a careful scrutiny, as, since most men underestimate the frequency of large deviation arising by chance, such data may be expected to agree more closely with expectation than genuine data would" (Fisher 1936).

11.10 FISHER'S EXACT TEST

It was mentioned earlier that although the chi-square distribution is estimated by a continuous curve, observed frequencies are always compared with expected frequencies along discrete intervals. All chi-square statistics therefore only approximate the chi-square continuous curve. These approximations are suitable for most purposes, as long as n is kept suitably large, but in many anthropological cases the frequencies of interest are simply too small to be tested for significance by chi-square methods. Ronald Fisher, the same Fisher who investigated Mendel's genetic experiments, derived a technique for computing the *exact probability* of contingency tables. The approximations are thereby avoided altogether, and this procedure is known as *Fisher's Exact Test*.

Consider again the generalized 2×2 contingency table:

Second Variable	First Variable		
	$+$	$-$	Total
$+$	a	b	$(a+b)$
$-$	c	d	$(c+d)$
Total	$(a+c)$	$(b+d)$	n

To determine whether a particular set of results is too rare to have arisen by chance alone, it is necessary to find the probability of obtaining these frequencies in a random experiment. One proceeds in such cases as though this sample were really a population, so the statistical situation can be rephrased: Given the observed marginal totals (which are regarded as fixed), what is the probability of getting random observations within a contingency table as extreme as the observed a, b, c, and d, or results even more extreme?

The number of "successes" for a 2×2 contingency table is defined as the number of possible ways in which the observed cell frequencies could have been randomly selected. Although the derivation of the formula is beyond the scope of this text,[4] it is known that

$$\text{number of successes} = \frac{n!}{a!\,b!\,c!\,d!}$$

[4]This formula has been derived from the coefficients of the *multinomial distribution*, which is analogous to the binomial situation except that the possible outcomes are not limited strictly to success and failure. In this case, there are four possible outcomes for each trial, namely, a, b, c, or d.

The probability fraction associated with this event, the number of successes, becomes the numerator. The denominator in this case is the total number of ways in which a 2×2 table could be constructed with the same marginal totals. Beginning with the row totals, $(a + b)$ and $(c + d)$, how many ways can n items be randomly selected such that $(a + b)$ is a success?

Because the order of selection is irrelevant to the probability fraction, the number of randomly selected successes is given by $C_{n,(a+b)}$. Similarly for the column totals, there are exactly $C_{n,(a+c)}$ possible successes. You should convince yourself that identical results would be obtained had either $(c + d)$ been selected for the rows, or $(b + c)$ for the columns. To obtain the total possible combinations between rows and columns, it is necessary to multiply the individual outcomes. Hence, the total numerator of the probability is given by

$$C_{n(a+b)} \cdot C_{n(a+c)} = \frac{n!}{(a + b)!\,(c + d)!} \cdot \frac{n!}{(a + c)!\,(b + d)!}$$

From the coefficients of the multinomial distribution it can be shown that there are

$$\frac{n!}{a!\,b!\,c!\,d!}$$

ways of obtaining the observed cell frequencies. Thus, the probability of obtaining a contingency table with cell frequencies $a, b, c,$ and d can be computed as the ratio of the two quantities given above. This can be simplified to

$$= \frac{(a + b)!\,(c + d)!\,(a + c)!\,(b + d)!}{n!\,a!\,b!\,c!\,d!} \tag{11.7}$$

This equation facilitates computation of the exact probability of obtaining the frequencies observed in the 2×2 table. But we need to test a null hypothesis which considers not only the frequencies observed but also results to be potentially *more extreme* than those actually obtained. It becomes necessary to compute each individual probability associated with the more extreme results. The summation of all these exact probabilities comprises Fisher's Exact Test.

Consider the following example, which illustrates the computational procedures involved. Suppose that 14 mummies (6 males and 8 females) were discovered in a prehistoric habitation cave in western Nevada. Of these burials, 9 were found to be lacking heads (a frequent custom in this area). From the data at hand, is it justifiable to conclude that males were more frequently decapitated than females (at the 0.05 level)?

Burials	With Skulls	Without Skulls	Total
Male	0	6	6
Female	5	3	8
Total	5	9	14 burials

Specifically, we are interested in whether the two sets of dichotomous categories (sex and burial condition) sort independently of one another. Had this sample been larger, the question could have readily been resolved by the chi-square test, but because $n = 14$ and there seems to be no chance of increasing the sample size, chi-square must be ruled out (for precise statements on the minimum sizes recommended for the chi-square test, see Section 11.11). It is precisely this sort of situation in which Fisher's Exact Test proves to be valuable.

Fisher's test is designed to answer one question: What are the chances of obtaining observed results as extreme (or more extreme) as those obtained in the experiment? The null hypothesis here is that males are just as likely to be decapitated as females. The alternative hypothesis considered the probability that males are *more frequently* decapitated. Specifically, under the alternative hypothesis, we expect:

Few males with skulls (cell *a*)
Several males without skulls (cell *b*)
Several females with skulls (cell *c*)
Few females without skulls (cell *d*)

So, in this case, the alternative hypothesis is directional.[5]

$$H_1: \quad ad < bc$$

We can see by inspection that indeed $ad < bc$, as expected, but we need further to determine whether this could occur by chance alone. (Had the reverse situation occurred in the observed data ($ad > bc$), then H_1 is obviously wrong and no test of statistical significance is required.)

The level of significance must be halved because the alternative hypothesis is directional (are more males decapitated?). In order to reach significance at $\alpha = 0.05$, the exact probability must be less than or equal to $p = 0.025$. This is the region of rejection for Fisher's test.

The exact probability is found by substituting the observed archaeological frequencies into Formula (11.7):

$$p = \frac{6!\,8!\,5!\,9!}{14!\,0!\,6!\,5!\,3!}$$

$$= \frac{4}{143} = 0.028$$

Remember that the final probability in Fisher's Exact Test refers to the observed arrangement, or *more extreme arrangements*. Since H_1 predicts that $ad < bc$, there can be no more extreme arrangement than having a zero in cell *a*. In fact, whenever a zero occurs in any cell of a 2×2 table, the single probability computation covers the most extreme case because no frequency can be more extreme than zero.

---

[5]When cells *a* and *d* are predicted to be common, a "positive" association is said to exist. Conversely, when the variables are inversely proportional, with cells *b* and *c* more common, then a "negative" association exists. The terms "negative" and "positive" are arbitrarily assigned to distinguish the two sorts of directional alternative hypotheses which might exist in 2×2 contingency tables (Coult 1965).

The computed value of $p = 0.028 > p$, $\alpha = 0.025$, an observed figure falling outside the region of rejection, and the results are judged not to be a significant departure from randomness. The excavator cannot justifiably conclude that men within this particular cave site tended to be decapitated more frequently than women.

Suppose that the data occurred in the following configuration:

Burials	With Skulls	Without Skulls	Total
Male	8	2	10
Female	3	5	8
Total	11	7	18

The alternative hypothesis in this case is that $bc < ad$. The probability of obtaining exactly such an arrangement is

$$p_2 = \frac{10!\,8!\,11!\,7!}{18!\,8!\,2!\,3!\,5!} = 0.079$$

Fisher's test is also concerned with more extreme probabilities, so we must also consider all cases in which the product of bc is lower than the observed case; that is, when $bc < 3(2) = 6$. The overall probability of occurrence is given by

$$p = p_0 + p_1 + \cdots + p_r$$

where r = frequency of the rarest cell + 1.

In other words, the overall probability is the sum of the individual observed frequencies plus all other less likely probabilities, given constant marginal totals.

These additional probabilities can be determined by subtracting 1 from both b and c (and, of course, adding 1 to a and d in order to keep the row and column totals constant). The second most extreme arrangement is

$$bc = (2 - 1)(3 - 1) = 2$$

and the third most extreme arrangement is

$$bc = (1 - 1)(2 - 1) = 0$$

Cell b is empty in the third case, so there can be no more extreme arrangements along the diagonal bc.

For the present example, p_2 has already been computed to be 0.079.

$$p_1 = \frac{10!\,8!\,11!\,7!}{18!\,9!\,1!\,2!\,6!} = 0.0088$$

$$p_0 = \frac{10!\,8!\,11!\,7!}{18!\,10!\,0!\,1!\,7!} = 0.00025$$

The total probability of the observed frequency or those more extreme is

$$p = p_2 + p_1 + p_0 = 0.079 + 0.0088 + 0.00025 = 0.167$$

This final probability figure of $p = 0.167$ is sufficiently greater than $p_\alpha = 0.025$ assigned so that the null hypothesis cannot be rejected. The observed frequency of this second example could well have arisen simply by chance.

So far, we have used Fisher's Exact Test only to examine the directional alternative hypothesis; in the strict sense, this test should be reserved for directional cases. But there are times when an alternative hypothesis can be stated only about the *existence* of an association rather than its direction. The alternative hypothesis in such cases is simply

$$H_1: \quad ad \neq bc$$

In addition to the probability of obtaining the observed frequency, one must also compute the more extreme positions of positive ($ad > bc$) and negative ($ad < bc$) associations.

Suppose that the last problem had been expressed differently? Does decapitation appear to have any association with sex? No direction is expressed in this statement, so both positive and negative associations must be considered. The probability of more positive associations was computed above, so all that remains to solve the nondirectional hypothesis is to determine the probability of the more extreme negative associations.

The most extreme negative association would be when cell d is empty, rendering $ad = 0$. The probability for this case is

$$p_{0\,(negative)} = \frac{10!\,8!\,11!\,7!}{18!\,3!\,7!\,8!\,0!} = 0.0038$$

The next smallest extreme negative association (with a 1 in cell d) has the probability of

$$p_{1\,(negative)} = \frac{10!\,8!\,11!\,7!}{18!\,4!\,7!\,6!\,1!} = 0.0528$$

Both cases are "more extreme" than the observed arrangement of frequencies because their probabilities are smaller than the observed frequencies:

$$p_{0\,(negative)} = 0.0038 \qquad p_2 = 0.079$$
$$p_{1\,(negative)} = 0.0528 \qquad p_2 = 0.079$$

The next largest negative association (with a 2 in cell d) has a probability of

$$p_{2\,(negative)} = \frac{10!\,8!\,11!\,7!}{18!\,5!\,5!\,6!\,2!} = 0.2217$$

This probability is not "more extreme" than that of the observed arrangement ($p_2 = 0.079$), and the value of $p_{2\,(negative)} = 0.2217$ should not be included in the summary probability statement.

The total probability of the two-tailed alternative is given as the sum of (1) the probability of the observed case, (2) the probabilities of more extreme positive associations, and (3) the probabilities of more extreme negative associations:

$$p = p_2 + p_1 + p_0 + p_{0\,(negative)} + p_{1\,(negative)}$$
$$= 0.079 + 0.0088 + 0.00025 + 0.0038 + 0.0528$$
$$= 0.145$$

Because this final probability $p = 0.145 > p_\alpha = 0.05$, the null hypothesis cannot be rejected for the nondirectional case.

Fisher's Exact Test involves a prodigious amount of calculation when the smallest cell frequency on the relevant diagonal is much greater than about 3. In such cases, one is well advised to process these data upon a computer, and adequate programs are readily available (for example, Sokal and Rohlf 1969: 702–703). There are also tables to cover some of the values for Fisher's Exact Test (Siegel 1956: tables; row and column totals smaller than 15). Unfortunately, these tables partially vitiate the precision of the "exact" test, since one reads only significance levels rather than the exact probabilities. But for most hypothesis-testing purposes, these levels of significance are adequate.

Example 11.8

Noncommercial societies often practice a unilocal residential pattern in which the newly married couple moves to a prescribed setting: patrilocal, matrilocal, or avunculocal. Both societies may also simultaneously practice two or more patterns of consanguinal residence, in a situation termed *multilocal*. Carol Ember and Melvin Ember (1972) conducted a cross-cultural study to test several explanations of the multilocal residential pattern. One theory holds that multilocal societies tend to have undergone recent depopulation so that choice of spouses is limited to a survival population. For purposes of this test, the Embers operationally defined a population as depopulated if the population had dropped more than 25 percent in the 30-year period prior to fieldwork.

Do the following 27 cases, randomly selected from the Human Relations Area Files, support the depopulation hypothesis at the 0.05 level?

Data of this sort are commonly presented in a special form of the 2×2 contingency table, in which the actual society name rather than simply the cell frequency is entered into the cell. Presentation in this fashion allows investigators to examine the sample societies for other variables of interest, such as geographic area, subsistence base, or linguistic stock.

Depopulation	Multilocal Residence		Total
	Present	Absent	
Present	Chukchee	Crow	
	Comanche	Kaska	
	Ila	Tapirape	
	Lau	Tehuelche	
	Mandan	Tlingit	
	Nambicuara		
	Yaruro		12

Depopulation	Multilocal		Total
	Present	Absent	
Absent	Burmese	Annamese	
		Aymara	
		Bikinians	
		Burusho	
		Cuna	
		Kikuyu	
		Kol	
		Lepcha	
		Pukapukans	
		Seri	
		Somali	
		Tikopia	
		Toda	
		Wogeo	15
Total	8	19	27

The directional alternative hypothesis (do multilocal societies tend to be depopulated?) involves a "positive" association:

$$H_1: \quad ad > bc$$

For these results to be significant, the observed probability must exceed $\alpha/2 = 0.05/2 = 0.025$.

Fisher's Exact Test is appropriate in this case because of the low expected frequency in cell d: ($E_d = 15(8)/27 = 4.44$). Two separate probabilities are computed: the observed case in which cell c contains one case, and the more extreme instance in which cell c would have been empty (but with the row and column totals fixed).

The probability associated with the observed frequencies is

$$p_1 = \frac{12! \, 15! \, 19! \, 8!}{27! \, 5! \, 7! \, 14! \, 1!} = 0.00535$$

and the probability of the more extreme case on the ad diagonal is

$$p_0 = \frac{12! \, 15! \, 19! \, 8!}{27! \, 4! \, 8! \, 15! \, 1!} = 0.00022$$

So the total probability of observing data this extreme or more extreme by chance alone is

$$p = p_1 + p_0 = 0.00535 + 0.00022$$
$$= 0.00557$$

Since $p = 0.006 < p = 0.025$, the null hypothesis is rejected, and the conclusion is that the Embers' cross-cultural test supports an association between residence and recent depopulation.

11.11 GENERAL SIZE CONSIDERATIONS

The following size recommendations can serve as guidelines for applying the chi-square and Fisher's Exact tests (Cochran 1954; Grizzle 1967).

Guideline I. *Two-by-two contingency tables.*
    A. Use *Fisher's Exact Test* if
        1. n is less than 20; or
        2. n is between 20 and 40, and the smallest E_i is less than 5.
    B. Use the chi-square test if
        1. n is greater than 40; *or*
        2. n is between 20 and 40, and the smallest E_i is greater than 5.
        3. Yates' Correction for Continuity is necessary only when the smallest E_i is less than 10.

Guideline II. $R \times C$ *contingency tables* (*where* $R > 2$ *or* $C > 2$). Chi-square is permissible if
    A. All E_i are greater than 5; *or*
    B. No more than about 20 percent of the cells have E_i less than 5 *and* no E_i is less than 1; *or*
    C. More than about 20 percent of the cells have E_i less than 5 *and* no E_i is less than 2.

11.12 THE McNEMAR TEST FOR CORRELATED PROPORTIONS

The chi-square and Fisher's Exact tests are the most common methods for examining relationships between two variables in the 2×2 format. Both tests assume two conditions: (1) the sample has been randomly selected from its population, and (2) the two samples are *mutually independent*. All previous 2×2 tables have implicitly conformed to these assumptions. The null hypothesis has been that all cell frequencies should be in relative proportion to their corresponding row and column totals. Any disproportionate cell will inflate the sample statistic and hence cast doubt upon H_o.

But suppose that the second assumption has been violated and that the samples lack mutual independence. Are the chi-square and Fisher's Exact tests then invalid? Quite simply: yes, they are. Because these standard contingency tests cannot be used when the variables are mutually dependent, an alternative is recommended.

What specifically is meant by *mutual independence* within a contingency table? Two variables are dependent when the frequencies of one variable logically influence the values of the second variable. A prime example of this relationship is the familiar "before–after" research design of psychological or educational experiments. Suppose that 150 college sophomores are questioned whether or not they think marijuana should be legalized. Each subject is then shown a recorded television segment in which a number of heroin addicts testify that marijuana led them directly into abuse of hard drugs. Graphic examples of suicides "under the influence of marijuana" are presented along with clinical discussions of the links between marijuana usage, lung cancer, and chromosome damage. These same 150 subjects are then questioned again: "Do you now believe that marijuana should be legalized?"

Some students who formerly favored legalization will probably change their attitudes because of the potential hazards. But others who were originally opposed to legalization will undoubtedly resent the biased television presentation as "brainwashing" and will favor legalization largely as a means of protest. The results from the experiment can be arrayed in the familiar 2×2 format.

	After Television Segment	
Before TV Segment	Favor Legalization	Oppose Legalization
Favor legalization	a	b
Oppose legalization	c	d

Is there a significant change in attitude due to the television program?

Meaningless chi-square or Fisher's Exact statistics could easily be computed from these data. This experiment violates the assumption of mutual independence between samples, and hence both tests are invalid. The *same* subjects have been asked the *same* questions, so the "before" variable influences the "after" variable.

The *McNemar Test for Correlated Proportions* is specifically designed to assess the significance of change between dependent variables. The chi-square test is sensitive to changes in *all four cells*; any major deviation from expectation inflates chi-square. But in the above cases, interest is only in those cells denoting change, that is, the number of students who have changed their attitudes toward legalization of marijuana. Cells *a* and *d* represent continuity, those individuals who declined to alter their opinions regarding legalization. Only cells *b* and *c* represent changes in attitude, and the McNemar test provides a statistical method for assessing the relative significance of change. The null hypothesis of *no change* states simply that the frequencies of cells *b* and *c* should be roughly similar. The larger the discrepancy between cells *b* and *c*, the less tenable is the null hypothesis. As long as the sample remains relatively large, any particular probability can be approximated by the chi-square distribution where

$$\chi^2 = \frac{(|b - c| - 1)^2}{b + c} \tag{11.8}$$

with a single degree of freedom.[6]

Consider an archaeological application of the McNemar statistic. Three archaeologists—Tom, Dick, and Harriet— have convened to discuss the prehistoric cultural sequence of the Yahoo Basin. A total of 75 archaeological sites are known from this area, and the session begins with Dick and Harriet comparing their analyses of these sites. Harriet classifies 50 of the 75 sites into the Early

---

[6]Note that although the *chi-square distribution* is used to find the probability of the McNemar statistic, the assumptions and methods of the McNemar test are quite distinct from those of the 2×2 χ^2 test.

Period, and the remaining 25 sites into the Late Period; Dick classifies these same sites as 47 Early and 28 Late. Because of this surprising amount of disagreement, they tabulate their findings for site-by-site comparisons. Of the 50 sites that Harriet has called Early, Dick has agreed with only 40, calling the remaining 10 sites Late. Harriet has classified 25 sites Late, while Dick has listed 28 Late sites. In other words, Harriet and Dick have agreed on only 40 Early sites and 18 Late sites, and they have disagreed on the temporal affinity of the remaining 17 sites.

		Harriet	
Dick	Early	Late	Total
Early	40	7	47
Late	10	18	28
Total	50	25	75

Most archaeologists realize how much subjectivity is involved in such cases, and error will never be eliminated. Random errors are of less concern, since they tend to cancel one another in the long run, but systematic errors of classification are more serious and can disrupt entire cultural sequences. Harriet and Dick disagree on 17 sites. How much disagreement is due to random errors of classification and how much to a systematic bias resulting from differing conceptions of Early and Late phases?

The McNemar test is useful here because only cells b and c of the contingency table are involved; these are the cells of disagreement. Clearly, the typology lacks precision, but do systematic errors appear? The McNemar statistic is computed from Formula (11.8),

$$\chi^2 = \frac{(|7 - 10| - 1)^2}{10 + 7} = 0.364$$

This small value of chi-square (with a single degree of freedom) does not approach the significant values in Table A.5, so the null hypothesis is not in danger. Harriet and Dick do not appear to be classifying the sites in significantly different ways. Their differences are due simply to random errors, and future research will surely reduce this random component.

The situation is somewhat different when Harriet's typology is compared with Tom's list. Tom and Harriet likewise disagree on the temporal placement of 17 sites. The percentage disagreement is exactly the same as that between Dick and Harriet (23%). But take a closer look at the nature of the disagreement.

		Harriet	
Tom	Early	Late	Total
Early	36	3	39
Late	14	22	36
Total	50	25	75

Harriet has classified only three of Tom's Late sites as Early, and Tom has classified 14 of Harriet's Early sites as Late. The McNemar comparison is as follows:

$$\chi^2 = \frac{(|14 - 3| - 1)^2}{17} = 5.88$$

This value of chi-square is significant past the 0.05 level.

The peculiar situation illustrated above needs to be considered in a bit more detail because an important concept is at stake. Two comparisons were made based upon a single sample of 75 sites. Harriet's classifications agreed with Dick's by 58/75 = 77 percent, and Harriet's also agreed with Tom's by 77 percent. The two situations were identical in overall agreement. The character of disagreement is quite different. Harriet and Dick essentially split their differences in half. They disagreed randomly. The McNemar test evaluated the cell frequencies for b and c (7 and 10, respectively) and concluded that these proportions could readily be due to random error. Harriet and Tom likewise disagreed on 17 of the sites, but the proportion of cases between the critical cells seems to be out of line, with $b = 3$ and $c = 14$. The McNemar test concluded that this disproportionate outcome will occur by chance in fewer than 5 in 100 random samples. Some systematic source of error is probably at work here: Either Tom consistently calls Harriet's Early sites as Late, or Harriet consistently classifies Tom's Late sites Early. The difference cannot be distinguished on these data alone. Although both comparisons involved an error of 23 percent, the errors between Harriet's and Tom's typology seem more grievous because a systematic bias results.

● *Statistical thinking will one day be as necessary for efficient citizenship as the ability to read and write.*—H. G. Wells

Example 11.9

A matrilocal residence system is one in which a newly married couple takes up residence in the village of the bride's mother. Anthropologists have attempted to explain the origin of specific matrilocal systems for well over a decade, but few have devised a set of specific causes which can explain *all* matrilocal systems. A recent study by Divale (1974) attempts just such a universal explanation.

Divale's argument goes as follows: When a population migrates into an already inhabited region, warfare usually results, and the society best equipped to fight such battles will have an adaptive advantage. Matrilocal residence selects for more efficient warfare because the agnatically related males are scattered over several communities; patrilocal systems do not fare so well because the females rather than the male warriors are scattered. Thus, matrilocality is caused by migration and is an adaptation to the resulting disequilibrium. Does the following cross-cultural sample support Divale's contention that recently migrated societies tend to change to matrilineality?

Before Migration	After Migration		
	Matrilocal	Patrilocal	Total
Matrilocal	39	12	51
Patrilocal	35	32	67
Total	74	44	118

The sample consists of 118 societies which are known to have recently migrated. The post-marital residential pattern remains unchanged in 71 of these societies, while 47 societies have changed their patterns (12 from matrilocal to patrilocal and 35 in the other direction).

This contingency table cannot be tested using the chi-square statistic because the same variable (residence) has been measured twice on each society. McNemar's test is the appropriate statistic to test the significance of the residential change:

$$\chi^2 = \frac{(|35 - 12| - 1)^2}{35 + 12} = 10.298$$

with a single degree of freedom. The result is significant beyond the 0.01 level. Chance phenomena do not seem sufficient to explain this change, and the data from these 118 societies do not conflict with Divale's hypothesis of matrilocal residence patterns.

SUGGESTIONS FOR FURTHER READING

Conover (1971: chapter 4)
Hays (1973: chapter 11)
Morrison and Henkel (1970). A collection documenting abuses of chi-square and other significance tests in the social sciences.
Siegel (1956: chapters 4, 6, 8)

EXERCISES

11.1 The following figures reveal the cross-cultural prevalence of riddles in 137 societies (data from Roberts and Forman 1971):

	Level of Political Integration			
	Absent	Autonomous Local	Minimal State	State
Riddles absent	9	40	16	31
Riddles present	0	8	10	23

(a) Is there a significant difference in riddling behavior between societies with autonomous local political organization and societies with the state? (Use a chi-square statistic.)
(b) Recompute part (a) using the binomial distribution.
(c) Is there a significant association between presence of riddles and higher political organization?

11.2   Investigators from the Government Hospital Tel-Hashomer, Israel, conducted a long-range study on colorblindness among Jews and Arabs living in Israel. The following cases of red–green blindness were noted in a large sample of informants living in central Israel (data from Adam, Doron, and Modan 1967):

	Normal Vision	Red/Green Blindness
Arabs	638	75
Jews	1085	43

Does this study indicate a significant difference in the frequency of colorblindness?

11.3   In a study on the cultural patterning of sexual beliefs and behavior, Minturn et al. (1969) generated a cross-cultural sample of 135 societies using the Human Relations Area File.
(a) Do the following data, extracted from their survey, support the hypothesis that divorce is more difficult in societies in which the nuclear family is the primary social unit?

	Ease of Divorce	
Family Organization	Difficult	Easy
Extended	12	25
Nuclear	7	3

(b) Why did you select the coefficient you did?

11.4   The Graduate Division of the University of California, Berkeley, processed a total of 12,763 applications for graduate study for the fall of 1973 (data from Bickel, Hammel, and O'Connell 1975: table 1).

	Outcome	
Applicants	Admit	Deny
Men	3738	4704
Women	1494	2827

(a) Do these data indicate that sexual bias is operative in the admission process?

(b) What is the danger of applying the chi-square statistic in this case?

*11.5 Some social anthropologists have hypothesized a functional relationship between Hawaiian kinship terminology and prohibition of cross-cousin marriage. Do these data from the *Ethnographic Atlas* support such a hypothesis (data from Goody 1970: table 6)?

Hawaiian Kin Terms	Prohibition on Cross-Cousin Marriage	
	Present	Absent
Present	200	39
Absent	219	206

11.6 The following data characterize phenotypic frequencies of the *ABO* blood system among three Macro-Maya speaking societies in southern Mexico (data from Cordova, Lisker, and Loria 1967: 59)?

	ABO System Phenotype			
	A	*B*	*O*	*AB*
Chol	16	1	135	0
Chontol	10	3	88	0
Totonac	9	0	70	0

(a) Is there a significant difference in *ABO* phenotypes among the three groups?

(b) In the above calculation, which phenotypes (if any) must be excluded from the chi-square calculation? Why?

11.7 The acculturational study of rural Buganda discussed earlier (Chapter 2) generated the following data (Robbins and Pollnac 1969: table 5).

	Beverage Choice		
Age	Traditional	Mixed	Modern
17–40	13	16	11
40+	29	7	2

Do these data support the notion that the younger members of Buganda society prefer nontraditional alcoholic beverages?

11.8 Based upon a sample from the *Ethnographic Atlas*, Ember and Ember (1971) determined the following relationship between warfare and residence:

	Pattern of Residence	
Warfare	Matrilocal	Patrilocal
External	Callinago Cherokee Creek Kaska Navaho Miskito	
Internal	Mataco Yao	Azande Ganda Jivaro Kapauku Murngin Nama Nootka Nuer Tallensi Tiv

Is there a significant relationship between warfare and residence?

11.9   As part of a study on blood-group frequencies in the higher primates, a team of scientists tested the chimpanzees at the Edinburgh Zoo for the ability to taste PTC. A total of 27 chimps were tested (data from Fisher, Ford, and Huxley 1939).

	Males	Females
Taster	11	9
Nontaster	3	4

(a) Do the male chimps seem to have a greater ability to taste PTC than the females?

(b) Why is the chi-square statistic an invalid measure in this case?

*11.10   The following mortality figures come from three North American archaeological sites. The archaic population is from Indian Knoll, Kentucky; the Hopewellian series is from the Pete Klunk Mounds in southwestern Illinois; and the Middle Mississippian sample is from the Dickson Mounds, also in Illinois (data from Blakely 1971: table 3).

	Age at Death		
	0–19	20–39	40+
Archaic	60	18	23
Hopewell	106	80	108
Middle Mississippian	215	150	114

(a) Is the mortality rate significantly different between the archaic and Hopewellian samples?

(b) Is the age at death different between Hopewell and Middle Mississippian samples?

(c) Are the three samples significantly different from one another?

(d) What levels of measurement are involved?

12 Nonparametric Statistics: Ordinal Scales

● *It is better to be ignorant than to know what ain't so.*—S. Ervin

12.1 RANK-ORDER STATISTICS

Chapter 11 considered some statistics relevant to nominal scale data. These statistics were called *nonparametric* because no minimal level of measurement was stipulated—and nominal is as low as one can go—or because no assumptions were necessary regarding the population distribution. This chapter presents further nonparametric methods by considering statistics appropriate to the ordinal level of measurement. These techniques are sometimes called *rank-order statistics* because variates are usually arrayed along an ordered scale rather than being actually measured.

12.2 THE WILCOXON TWO-SAMPLE TEST

The Wilcoxon test examines two samples to see whether their respective populations have different central locations. The *t*-test did this by looking at the sample means. After considering the variances, the *t*-test assessed whether the two samples represented the "same" population mean, or "different" population means, given alpha. The Wilcoxon test also serves this function, but on a different sort of data. The *t*-test required an interval scale of measurement, while the Wilcoxon test is designed for ordinal-level data. As discussed in Chapter 2, ordinal-level samples have no "measurements" in the strict sense. Because variates are simply placed into a relevant order (or *ranking*), ordinal samples cannot be characterized by means. The *median* must suffice for ordinal variates. Thus, the *t*-test examines for a difference between population means, and the Wilcoxon test looks for different population medians.

Suppose that two prehistoric cemeteries were excavated. The stature of each individual could be estimated by measuring the relevant bones, and a t-test could tell whether the first population was taller than the second. But suppose that the cemeteries had been disturbed by pothunters, and too few bones were available for the physical anthropologist to make reliable stature estimates. In this case, the burials could be ordered only in a sequence from relatively short to relatively tall, based upon relative robusticity of the bones. The t-test would be useless here because no sample means can be computed. The best we could do, given the ranked nature of the skeletal information, would be to find the median (or halfway point) in each skeletal series. The Wilcoxon test could then be used to look for stature differences between the cemeteries.

The initial step in all ordinal testing is to place the variates in a numbered sequence (called a *rank order*). The skeletons from cemetery A would be lined up by increasing stature next to those from cemetery B. Find the shortest skeleton in either collection, and give this specimen the rank 1. The second shortest gets a 2 and so forth until all skeletons have been numbered. Now sum the ranks for the first cemetery and call this sum W_1. The sum of the rankings for the second sample is called W_2. The Wilcoxon test provides a method to tell whether the first samples tend to rank higher overall than the second sample. This would mean that the individuals in the first cemetery tended to be taller. The null hypothesis of the Wilcoxon test holds that W_1 should be greater than W_2 only about half the time (assuming the samples to have the same number of variates). If the sum of ranks for the two samples is roughly the same, there is no reason to doubt H_o. That is, there is no reason to suspect a difference between the medians. But the larger the difference between W_1 and W_2, the less likely it becomes that the samples will be random samples from populations with identical medians. The directional alternative hypothesis suggests either that W_1 in fact exceeds W_2, or perhaps vice versa. The Wilcoxon statistic enables us to see whether significant differences exist between W_1 and W_2.

Another example will illustrate these computations. Anthropologists often assume that there is some advantage for hunting societies to keep the related males within the same residential group throughout their life. Not only do hunters cooperate and share more readily with kinsmen, but they are also more effective when hunting in familiar home territories. So, it is hypothesized that hunting groups should tend to be patrilocal, and this hypothesis can be tested against a random sample of North American societies selected from the *Ethnographic Atlas*. Societies in the *Atlas* can be characterized as either *patrilocal* or *matrilocal*, and can also be rated on the relative importance of hunting in the overall economy. If the above hypothesis is correct, then patrilocal societies should tend to be more dependent upon hunting than are matrilocal groups. The following eight societies were randomly selected:

	Atlas Code	Relative Dependence upon Hunting, %
Matrilocal		
Huron	1	6-15
S. Ute	6	56-65

	Atlas Code	Relative Dependence upon Hunting, %
Matrilocal (contd)		
W. Apache	4	36–45
Antarianunts	3	26–35
Patrilocal		
Slave	5	46–55
Gros Ventre	8	76–85
Santee	7	66–75
Kiowa	9	86–100

Had the relative importance of hunting been expressed in precise percentages, conventional parametric methods could have been used to test for a significant difference. But since the relative importance of hunting is estimated in only rather gross intervals, the exact methods of the *t*-test are inapplicable. To repeat, the *t*-test requires at least an interval scale, but these data are only ordinal.

These subsistence data can easily be rank-ordered according to the relative dependence upon hunting and the numerical rankings assigned to each society. The matrilocal societies and their associated ranks have been underlined.

Scale of hunting importance, %.

Slight Dependence ← ─────────────────────────────── → Strong Dependence

Huron	Antarianunts	W. Apache	Slave	S. Ute	Santee	Gros Ventre	Kiowa
0–5	26–35	36–45	46–55	56–65	66–75	76–85	86–100
(1)	(2)	(3)	(4)	(5)	(6)	(7)	(8)

The sum of the ranks for the matrilocal societies is

$$W_1 = 1 + 2 + 3 + 5 = 11$$

The sum of the ranks for the patrilocal societies is

$$W_2 = 4 + 6 + 7 + 8 = 25$$

The grand total for all ranks is

$$1 + 2 + 3 + 4 + 5 + 6 + 7 + 8 = W_1 + W_2 = 36$$

Note that the sum $W_1 + W_2$ is a constant for all situations containing exactly eight outcomes, regardless of the specifics of the samples.

The research hypothesis suggests that the matrilocal societies (sample 1) should have had less dependence upon hunting than had the patrilocal sample. Thus, the sum of ranks for the patrilocal societies is greater than the sum of ranks for the matrilocal societies: $W_2 > W_1$. Is the result $(W_2 - W_1) = 14$ a sufficient deviation for the result to be considered statistically significant?

In probabilistic terms, there are eight independent trials in this experiment, so the probability must be found that a sample of $n_1 = 4$ such outcomes will have ranks which sum to less than or equal to the observed value of $W_1 = 11$. That is, the situation requires the number of combinations of eight items taken four at a time:

$$C_{8,4} = \frac{8!}{4!\,4!} = 70$$

By trial and error it is found that only two possible ways exist to obtain a sum of ranks less than or equal to $W_1 = 11$:

$$W_1 = 1 + 2 + 3 + 4 = 10$$

$$W_2 = 1 + 2 + 3 + 5 = 11$$

There are no other possibilities which sum to 11 or less. Thus the total probability of obtaining $W_1 \leq 11$ if H_o is true is

$$p = \frac{2}{70} = 0.0286$$

The statistical hypotheses were one-tailed, so the results are significant beyond $\alpha = 0.05$, and H_o is rejected. This sample is thus consistent with the notion that hunting societies in North America tend to be patrilocal.

To clarify just how the Wilcoxon test is used for statistical inference, this example can be recast into the six steps of hypothesis testing.

Step I. *Statistical hypotheses:* The research hypotheses are as follows:

H_o: Postmarital residence is independent of dependence upon hunting (*or* matrilocal societies tend to hunt more than patrilocal societies).

H_1: Patrilocal societies tend to hunt more than matrilocal societies.

These statements now must be translated into specific statistical hypotheses. If W_1 is the sum of ranks for matrilocal societies,

$$H_o: \quad p(W_1 = W_2) \geq 1/2$$

$$H_1: \quad p(W_1 = W_2) < 1/2$$

The two propositions actually reflect the relationships between the respective population medians.

Step II. *Statistical model:* The distribution of the Wilcoxon statistic provides a statistical model against which to judge the specific sample values. The Wilcoxon two-sample test assumes (1) both samples are randomly selected, (2) the samples are independent, (3) at least ordinal measurement, and (4) both samples are variates of continuous random variables (see Section 12.7).

Step III. *Significance level:* Let $\alpha = 0.05$ for a directional test.

Step IV. *Region of rejection:* The Wilcoxon test is called an *exact test* because the result is a specific *point* rather than an *area*. The "region of rejection" for this case is defined directly from the level of significance. Any probability for the sample difference smaller than $p = 0.05$ exceeds the critical value. That is, the critical value is alpha itself.

Step V. *Calculations and statistical decision:* The test statistic for this sample has been previously computed to be $p = 0.0286$. Because this observed value is smaller (less likely) than the critical value of $p = 0.05$, the null hypothesis is rejected.

Step VI. *Nonstatistical decision:* These data are consistent with the hypothesis that patrilocal societies tend to hunt more than matrilocal societies, for all alpha ≥ 0.0286.

This example was purposely made quite simple, with W_1 kept small. But for larger values of W_1, the trial-and-error enumeration of possible outcomes becomes overly tedious. Fortunately, there is an easier method of finding the exact probability of rankings by using Table A.6. To enter this table, one needs only the values of n_1, n_2, and a statistic called the *Wilcoxon U:*

$$U = W_1 - \frac{n_1(n_1 + 1)}{2}$$
(12.1)

For the above example,

$$U = 11 - \frac{4(4 + 1)}{2} = 1$$

Table A.6 indicates that the numerator (found under the column labelled $U = 1$) is 2, and that $C_{n,n_1} = 70$. Hence, the probability is found to be precisely that value computed by longhand:

$$p = \frac{2}{70} = 0.0286$$

The Wilcoxon test has a twin cousin known as the *Mann–Whitney U test.* Although the tests are computationally rather distinct, the actual statistic employed is identical. The Mann–Whitney phrasing of this test is sometimes used in the anthropological literature, so the reader is referred to discussions in Blalock (1972: 255–260), Conover (1971: 224–236) and Hays (1973: 778–780).

Example 12.1

Two schools of thought seem to exist among counselors regarding the best preparation for graduate study in anthropology. Most graduate students in anthropology come from a strong anthropological background, with the bulk of them having the B.A. degree in anthropology. But there is a strong minority who come to graduate school with a training in some field other than anthropology. Some advantages exist, for example, to a geological undergraduate training for the professional archaeologist, for psychology or economics for the ethnologist, and for the under-graduate study of biology or genetics for the physical anthropologist. The following census of 12 graduate students was taken at Couvade University.

Do the graduate students coming to anthropology from other backgrounds seem to do better on their qualifying examinations than do graduate students with the B.A. degree in anthropology?

Performance on qualifying examinations.

Undergraduate Training	Best ←————————————————————————→ Worst											
Anthropology	A		E	G H I						L	
Not Anthropology	B C D	F			J K						
	1 2 3	4 5 6	7	8 9	10 11	12						

The students with nonanthropological backgrounds have been underlined and denoted by W_1 because the sum is the smallest.

$$n_1 = 6 \qquad W_1 = 2 + 3 + 4 + 6 + 10 + 11 = 36$$
$$n_2 = 6 \qquad W_2 = 1 + 5 + 7 + 8 + 9 + 12 = 42$$

The value of U is computed to be

$$U = W_1 - \frac{n_1(n_1 + 1)}{2} = 36 - \frac{6(7)}{2} = 15$$

The numerator corresponding to $U = 15$ with $n_1 = n_2 = 6$ is given in Table A.6 (Appendix) to be 323, with a denominator of $C_{6,6} = 924$. The probability of finding a sum of ranks, W_1, is thus

$$p = \frac{323}{924} = 0.3496$$

Had this test been two-tailed, this probability would have been doubled. These findings indicate no reason to suspect that undergraduate training influences performance on graduate school qualifying examinations if $\alpha \leq 0.2940$.

12.2.1 The Wilcoxen Two-Sample Test with Tied Variates

A slight problem arises when ties in ranking occur, and such cases require a modification in the Wilcoxon test, as illustrated below.

Because the post-cranial skeletons of *Homo erectus* and Neanderthal are virtually identical, the most significant taxonomic criteria involve cranial differences. *Homo erectus* had a smaller cranial capacity, more angular brow ridges and more developed facial prognathism than did Neanderthal. Minor differences also occur in the relative cranial proportions. Table 12.1 presents some cranial

TABLE 12.1 Maximum cranial length measurements (in millimeters) from two series of fossil men (data from Coon 1971a: table 37).

Homo erectus		Neanderthals and Skhūl	
Pithecanthropus 4	199?	La Ferrassie	209
Pithecanthropus 1	183?	Neanderthal	199
Solo 11	200	Spy 1	201
Sinanthropus 3 (*)	188	Circeo 1	204
Sinanthropus 10	199	Le Moustier Y	196
Sinanthropus 12	185.5	Tabun 5	206
Saldanha	200	Skhūl 5	192
Broken Hill	208	Skhūl 9	213

(*) Young, subadult; all others are adult.

length measurements which would seem to indicate that *Homo erectus* had a shorter head than Neanderthal. But is this rather small difference in head length statistically significant?

Upon initial inspection of the data, one might be tempted to use a simple *t*-test, but a closer look indicates that the measurements lack the accuracy implied by the *t*-test. The measurements for both Pithecanthropus skulls, for instance, are little more than guesses, while Sinanthropus 12 was accurately measured to 0.1 mm. In addition, the Sinanthropus 3 skull is not a mature individual, so the cranial length is probably somewhat less than that of the adult form. When dealing with specimens as rare as complete fossil crania, one simply cannot control the errors of measurement with much precision; often, inconsistent measurements such as these must suffice. To avoid implying spurious accuracy, the length measurements in Table 12.1 have been reduced to ordinal relationships; the relative rank ordering is thus maintained without implying true interval accuracy.

Considering the *Homo erectus* specimens as sample 1, the following rank ordering is achieved (sample 1 underlined).

Original Data	Rank Number	Original Data	Rank Number
183	1	200	9.5
185.5	2	200	9.5
188	3	201	11
192	4	204	12
196	5	206	13
199	7	208	14
199	7	209	15
199	7	213	16

Note that in two cases (199 and 200 mm), the variates were tied. The rank number is assigned in such instances by using the *average ranking* for that score; it is thus necessary to sum the tied ranks and divide by the number of ties involved.

$$\text{Rank}_{199} = \frac{6+7+8}{3} = 7$$

$$\text{Rank}_{200} = \frac{9+10}{2} = 9.5$$

The sum of the ranks is found to be

$$W_1 = 1 + 2 + 3 + 7 + 7 + 9.5 + 9.5 + 14 = 53$$
$$W_2 = 4 + 5 + 7 + 11 + 12 + 14 + 15 + 16 = 84$$

The value of U is found in the usual manner:

$$U = 53 - \frac{1}{2}8(8+1) = 17$$

Table A.6 indicates that $C_{16,8} = 12,870$ and the corresponding value of $U = 17$ is 879, so the two-tailed probability in this case is

$$p = \frac{2(879)}{12,870} = 0.1366$$

Because of the relatively large probability figure, we conclude that this sample provides insufficient evidence to reject H_0, assuming $\alpha \leq 0.1366$. We can demonstrate no significant difference between cranial lengths of *Homo erectus* and Neanderthal.

This section has tacitly introduced a slightly different mode of statistical inference. Because the probability values computed by the Wilcoxon test are *exact*, they can be directly used for statistical inference without bothering with a region of rejection. Thus, the value of $p = 0.1366$ will be insufficient to reject H_0 for any alpha level *less than or equal to* 0.1366. This interval includes most common significance levels (that is, 0.05, 0.01, 0.001), and we can safely assume that almost all investigators would retain H_0. The real advantage of exact tests is that the alpha level need not be specified. A current trend in social science applications of statistics is to forego the actual hypothesis-testing procedure and simply state exact levels of probability. This leaves the decision "reject or not reject" to the reader. This trend is perfectly healthy, as long as we understand the procedures of statistical inference *when we finally do wish to make a decision*. Sometimes specifying the six steps helps insure that the statistical model and its assumptions have actually been met.

Example 12.2

The Midland site in west Texas yielded one of the oldest human skulls in the Americas. The artifact inventory included some rather conventional Folsom projectile points and also an artifact called a *Midland* point. The Midland points are identical in every way to the Folsom finds except that Midland points lack the diagnostic channel flute. Since their discovery, Midland points have been found in a number of localities in the American Southwest, but archaeologists are still hard-pressed to explain the curious absence of the channel flute. Some suggest that the Midland points were originally manufactured on a very thin flake, and therefore the blank was too thin to channel. This argument makes a certain amount of sense if the channel flake was executed to thin the artifact; then artifacts already quite thin would not need to be fluted. The measurements below are for artifacts found at the original Midland site.

Are the Folsom points significantly thicker than the Midland points?

For demonstration purposes, these thickness measurements will be reduced to rank orderings, and the Wilcoxon two-sample test will be used to compare the two samples statistically.

Thickness measurements for artifacts from the Midland site (data from Wendorf, Krieger, Albritton and Stewart 1955).

Folsom		Midland (unfluted Folsom)	
Catalog No.	Thickness, inches	Catalog No.	Thickness, inches
16	0.14	19	0.13
17	0.08	24	0.12
18	0.14	25	0.11
55	0.19	27	0.19
74	0.19	29	0.10
		30	0.09
		31	0.11
		32	0.10

The variates must first be rank-ordered:

Folsom	.08								.14	.14		.19	.19
Midland		.09	.10	.10	.11	.11	.12	.13			.19		
Ranking	1	2	3.5	3.5	5.5	5.5	7	8	9.5	9.5	12	12	12

The sum of ranks can be computed next:

$n_1 = 5$ $W_1 = 1 + 9.5 + 9.5 + 12 + 12 = 44$

$n_2 = 8$ $W_2 = 2 + 3.5 + 3.5 + 5.5 + 5.5 + 7 + 8 + 12 = 47$

The Wilcoxon statistic can now be computed:

$$U = 44 - \frac{5(5+1)}{2} = 44 - 15 = 29$$

$$C_{13,5} = \frac{13!}{5!8!} = \frac{13 \cdot \cancel{12} \cdot 11 \cdot \cancel{10} \cdot 9}{\cancel{5} \cdot \cancel{4} \cdot 3 \cdot 2} = 1287$$

This value of U exceeds the tabled frequencies, so H_o is not rejected. We can conclude that these data do not support the suggestion that Folsom points tend to be thicker than Midland points.

A two-sample t-test of these same data produces a test statistic of $t = 1.465$ with 11 degrees of freedom. This value of t is not significant at even the $\alpha = 0.1$ level. In general, the t-test and the Wilcoxon two-sample test will produce almost identical results.

12.2.2 Normal Approximation to the Wilcoxon Two-Sample Test

As long as neither n_1 nor n_2 exceeds 8, Table A.6 can be used to find the appropriate probability values associated with the Wilcoxon statistic. But ordinal scales are so widespread in the social sciences that problems commonly arise which are appropriate to the Wilcoxon test, but which exceed the tabled values of n_1 and n_2. As an alternative to computing additional—and more cumbersome—probability tables to accommodate these larger samples, it has been shown that as long as the samples are large enough, the distribution of W_1 approaches a normal distribution with the following parameters[1]:

$$\mu_W = \frac{n_1(n+1)}{2}$$

$$\sigma_W = \sqrt{\frac{n_1 n_2(n+1)}{12}} \tag{12.2}$$

where $n = n_1 + n_2$. These formulas assume that no ties are present.

The following example approximates the Wilcoxon test through use of the normal distribution. Phyllis Jay Dolhinow made extensive observations on the dominance behavior of female langurs in Northern India. Dolhinow hypothesized that social position is largely a function of the individual female's status as a mother and also her phase in the reproductive cycle (Dolhinow 1972: 220). As field studies progressed, individual females became identifiable on sight, and Dolhinow was able to establish the female dominance hierarchy for the Kaukori langur troop (see Table 12.2). Assuming that all females suspected of pregnancy were in fact pregnant, do these data support the hypothesis that reproductive status is associated with position in the dominance hierarchy?

This comparison involves two groups, pregnant and not pregnant langurs, each of which has been ranked for dominance; hence, the Wilcoxon test is clearly in order. The rank ordering can be recast.

Original Data	Rank Ordering	Original Data	Rank Ordering
A	1	J	10
B	2	K	11
C	3	L	12
D	4	M	13
E	5	N	14
F	6	O	15
G	7	P	16
H	8	Q	17
I	9	S	18

The ranks of the pregnant females have been underlined. In this case, $n_1 = 7$ and $n_2 = 11$, values which are too large for Table A.6. The normal approximation to the Wilcoxon statistic will be used to derive a probability value for this event.

[1]For verification and discussion of these Wilcoxon parameters, see Wilcoxon (1947) and Alder and Roessler (1972: 179).

TABLE 12.2 Female dominance hierarchy of the Kaukori langur troop (modified slightly from Dolhinow 1972: tables 5–7). Individual "A" is most dominant, and "S" is most dominated.

Female	Reproductive Status	Female	Reproductive Status
A	Not pregnant	J	Pregnant
B	Pregnant	K	Not pregnant
C	Pregnant	L	Pregnant
D	Not pregnant	M	Pregnant
E	Pregnant	N	Not pregnant
F	Not pregnant	O	Not pregnant
G	Pregnant	P	Not pregnant
H	Not pregnant	Q	Not pregnant
I	Not pregnant	S	Not pregnant

The sum of the ranks in the first sample is

$$W_1 = 2 + 3 + 5 + 7 + 10 + 12 + 13 = 52$$

Because the sample size is relatively large, W_1 should be distributed roughly in normal fashion, with parameters given by Expression (12.2).

$$\mu_W = \frac{7(18+1)}{2} = 66.5$$

$$\sigma_W = \sqrt{\frac{7(12)(19)}{12}} = 11.53$$

The question now concerns the probability of obtaining results as deviant as $W_1 = 52$, where $\mu_W = 66.5$ and $\sigma_W = 11.53$. This is accomplished by using the normal approximation:

$$z = \frac{52 - 66.5}{11.53} = -1.26$$

which corresponds to an area of 0.1038. The two-tailed probability for the case of female langur domination is thus

$$p = 2(0.500 - 0.3962) = 0.2076$$

H_0 must be retained for all $\alpha < 2(0.1038) = 0.2076$.

The research conclusion is that this sample indicates no association between reproductive status and an individual's position in the female dominance hierarchy.

The normal approximation for the Wilcoxon test also holds when ties are present, but the following corrected formula must be used to compute the standard deviation:

$$\sigma_W = \sqrt{\frac{n_1 n_2 [n(n^2 - 1) - \Sigma T_i]}{12n(n-1)}} \tag{12.3}$$

318

where $n = n_1 + n_2$, and $T_i = (t_i - 1)t_i(t_i + 1)$ in which t_i = number of ties at rank i. This computation is illustrated in Example 12.4.

Example 12.3

In a classic study of the ecology of the American Southwest, Julian Steward (1937) demonstrated how ethnographic and archaeological data could jointly be focussed upon problems of general anthropological interest. Steward felt that the matrilineal clans of the Southwest could better be expressed as an adjustment to ecological pressures than through mere diffusion from neighboring areas. Steward argued that localized exogamous lineages had once been crowded during prehistoric times into large multilineage communities, probably due to increased population density. The unilateral groups devised ceremonies, totems, and other cultural devices which fostered group solidarity, thereby maintaining corporate identities. In time, the lineages thus evolved into clans. To support this thesis that small villages had once aggregated into large communities, Steward cited archaeological data showing that the number of habitation rooms increased through time in relation to ceremonial kivas. The data for the last two periods of Southwestern archaeology are presented below.

Do these archaeological data support Steward's hypothesis of a significant increase in the room:kiva ratio between Pueblo IV period (A.D. 1300–1700) and historic times?

Pueblo village growth (data from Steward 1955: 165–167).

Period	Site	House:Kiva Ratio
Pueblo IV	Tshirege, Rio Grande	60:1
PIV	Tsankawi, Rio Grande	30:1
PIV	Otowi, Rio Grande	90:1 (?)
PIV	Yapashi, Rio Grande	92:1 (?)
PIV	Kotyiti, Rio Grande	240:1 (?)
Pueblo V	Oraibi, Hopi	35.4:1
PV	Walpi, Hopi	34.2:1
PV	Sichumovi, Hopi	36:1
PV	Shipaulovi, Hopi	33.3:1
PV	Mishongnovi, Hopi	31.8:1
PV	Hano, Hopi	52.5:1
PV	Zuni	95.4:1
PV	Zuni	289.8:1

Although the data tabulated are expressed as ratios, the actual measurements are quite inconsistent: The Pueblo V figures are derived from known family counts, while the Pueblo IV ratios consist of counts from archaeological excavations. To avoid misleading feelings of concreteness, the ratios have been reduced into rank orderings:

Original Data	Rank Ordering	Original Data	Rank Ordering
30	1	60	8
31.8	2	90	9
33.3	3	92	10
34.2	4	95.4	11
35.4	5	240	12
36.0	6	289.8	13
52.5	7		

The Pueblo IV data have been underlined, so $n_1 = 5$ and $n_2 = 8$. The sum of ranks is found to be

$$W_1 = 1 + 8 + 9 + 10 + 12 = 40$$
$$W_2 = 2 + 3 + 4 + 5 + 6 + 7 + 11 + 13 = 51$$

Because n_1 and n_2 are relatively small, Table A.6 could be consulted for the associated probability level. $C_{13,5}$ is found to be 1287, but there is no probability value listed for $U = 25$. This is because the probability is too large to bother listing. Nevertheless, let us find the exact probability by using the normal approximation to the Wilcoxon statistic:

$$\mu_W = \frac{5(14)}{2} = 35$$

$$\sigma_W = \sqrt{\frac{5(8)(14)}{12}} = 6.83$$

The standardized normal deviate is found to be

$$z = \frac{40 - 35}{6.83} = 0.73$$

The probability for a one-tailed alternative is

$$p = 0.5000 - 0.2673 = 0.2327$$

The result is not significant and H_0 is not rejected for $\alpha < 0.2327$. These data fail to lend support to the ecological hypothesis advocated by Steward. (In all fairness to Steward, however, he was interested primarily in a possible increase *before* Pueblo IV times, which turns out to be highly significant.)

Example 12.4

In their investigation of the relationship between child training practices and subsistence economy, Barry, Child, and Bacon (1959) hypothesized that child rearing among pastoral societies—in which food is extensively accumulated and stored—tends to value personality traits such as compliance and conservation. On the other extreme, societies with relatively little accumulation of food resources, particularly hunters and fishermen, were expected to reward individualism, assertiveness, and a venturesome attitude in youth. The authors selected a large cross-cultural sample to test their hypothesis, and the societies were scored on the relevant personality traits. Positive scores were awarded to groups with a relatively high degree of compliance, while assertion was rated negatively.

Do these cross-cultural findings support their hypothesis at the 0.01 level?

Because of the relatively large size of the samples, it becomes necessary to apply the normal approximation to the Wilcoxon two-sample test. The rank ordering appears as follows:

Animal Husbandry		Hunting, Fishing	
+ 13.5	Aymara	+ 4	Teton
+ 13.5	Tepoztlan	+ 1	Tahgan
+ 11.5	Lepcha	+ 0.5	Hupa
+ 8.5	Swazi	0	Chiricahua
+ 8.5	Tswana	0	Murngin
+ 8	Nyakyusa	0	Paiute
+ 8	Sotho	− 2	Arapaho
+ 7	Nuer	− 2	Kwakiutl
+ 7	Tallensi	− 2.5	Cheyenne
+ 6.5	Lovedu	− 2.5	Kaska
+ 6.5	Mbundu	− 2.5	Klamath
+ 6.5	Venda	− 2.5	Ojibwa
+ 6	Kikuyu	− 3	Ona
+ 6	Zulu	− 4	Aleut
+ 4.5	Pondo	− 6.5	Jicarilla
+ 4	Chagga	−10	Western Apache
+ 3	Ganda	−10.5	Siriono
+ 2.5	Chamorro	−11	West Greenland Eskimo
+ 2.5	Masai	−12	Aranda
+ 1	Chukchee	−12	Comanche
0	Tanala	−13.5	Crow
− 2.5	Thonga	−15	Manus
− 3	Araucanian		
− 3	Balinese		

Original data	Ranks	Original Data	Ranks
$\overline{-15}$	$\overline{1}$	1	25.5
$\overline{-13.5}$	$\overline{2}$	2.5	27.5
$\overline{-12}$	$\overline{3.5}$	2.5	27.5
$\overline{-12}$	$\overline{3.5}$	3	29
$\overline{-11}$	$\overline{5}$	4	30.5
$\overline{-10.5}$	$\overline{6}$	4	30.5
$\overline{-10}$	$\overline{7}$	4.5	32
$-\ \overline{6.5}$	$\overline{8}$	6	34
$-\ \overline{4}$	$\overline{9}$	6	34
$-\ \overline{3}$	$\overline{11}$	6	34
$-\ \overline{3}$	$\overline{11}$	6.5	36
$-\ \overline{3}$	11	6.5	36
$-\ \overline{2.5}$	15	6.5	36
$-\ \overline{2.5}$	15	7	38.5
$-\ \overline{2.5}$	15	7	38.5
$-\ \overline{2.5}$	15	8	40.5
$-\ \overline{2.5}$	15	8	40.5
$-\ \overline{2}$	18.5	8.5	42.5
$-\ \overline{2}$	$\overline{18.5}$	8.5	42.5
$\overline{0}$	$\overline{21.5}$	11.5	44
$\overline{0}$	$\overline{21.5}$	13.5	45.5
$\overline{0}$	$\overline{21.5}$	13.5	45.5
$\overline{0}$	$\overline{21.5}$		
0.5	24		
$\overline{1}$	$\overline{25.5}$		

The sum of ranks for the hunting-fishing groups is

$$W_1 = 1 + 2 + 3.5 + 3.5 + 5 + 6 + 7 + 8 + 9 + 11 + 15 + 15 + 15 + 15 + 18.5 + 18.5$$
$$\qquad + 21.5 + 21.5 + 21.5 + 24 + 25.5 + 30.5$$
$$= 297.5$$

The parameters of the U distribution are

$$\mu_w = \frac{22(46+1)}{2} = 517$$

Because of the presence of ties, the standard deviation must be computed from Formula (12.3). The values of t_i are listed below.

Rank	No. of Ties	$(t_i - 1)t_i(t_i + 1) = T_i$	
-12	2	$1 \cdot 2 \cdot 3$	6
$-\ 3$	3	$2 \cdot 3 \cdot 4$	24
$-\ 2.5$	5	$4 \cdot 5 \cdot 6$	120
$-\ 2$	2	$1 \cdot 2 \cdot 3$	6
0	4	$3 \cdot 4 \cdot 5$	60
1	2	$1 \cdot 2 \cdot 3$	6
2.5	2	$1 \cdot 2 \cdot 3$	6
4	2	$1 \cdot 2 \cdot 3$	6

Rank	No. of Ties	$(t_i - 1)t_i(t_i + 1) = T_i$	
6	2	$1 \cdot 2 \cdot 3$	6
6.5	3	$2 \cdot 3 \cdot 4$	24
7	2	$1 \cdot 2 \cdot 3$	6
8	2	$1 \cdot 2 \cdot 3$	6
8.5	2	$1 \cdot 2 \cdot 3$	6
13.5	2	$1 \cdot 2 \cdot 3$	6
			$\Sigma T_i = 288$

The standard deviation is thus

$$\sigma_W = \sqrt{\frac{22 \cdot 24[46 \cdot (2116 - 1) - 288]}{12 \cdot 46 \cdot 45}}$$

$$= \sqrt{2058.9} = 45.38$$

The standardized normal deviate is thus

$$z = \frac{297.5 - 517}{45.38} = -4.84$$

The area associated with this extremely high value of z is too small to even appear in Table A.3, so the results are judged to be highly significant and H_o is rejected. This sample supports the hypothesis advanced by Barry, Child, and Bacon: that societies which rely upon stored food will tend to teach compliance while hunting–fishing groups tend to train their children toward more assertive behavior.

12.3 KOLMOGOROV–SMIRNOV TWO-SAMPLE TEST

Like the Wilcoxon procedure, the Kolmogorov-Smirnov test examines differences between two samples which have been measured into ordinal categories. Although the Wilcoxon test is still feasible with tied variates, the corrections for ties create considerable computational difficulties. The Kolmogorov–Smirnov test readily facilitates analysis of scales where many ties occur, yet avoids reducing the data to nominal relations, as does a conventional chi-square statistic.

The Kolmogorov–Smirnov test involves a rather simple underlying theory. Two ordinal level samples are involved, as in the Wilcoxon test. These two samples are arranged into a set of cumulative proportions; the procedure here is identical to that discussed in Section 3.3.4 when the cumulative curve (or *ogive*) was constructed. The null hypothesis of the Kolmogorov–Smirnov test asserts that the cumulative proportions of the first sample shall be essentially similar to those of the second sample. The larger the maximum absolute differences between the cumulative proportions, the less likely becomes H_o. The distribution of the Kolmogorov–Smirnov statistic, D, is known and the critical values for the two-tailed Kolmogorov-Smirnov test are listed in Table A.8(b).

One of anthropology's thorniest problems is how to construct cross-cultural samples, an issue considered in detail in Chapter 15. The problem is whether the samples should be selected in a purely random fashion, or whether the universe should be "stratified" initially by continent (or culture area) and then sampled within the strata. Simple random sampling has certain statistical virtues, while careful stratification tends to eliminate the undesirable effects of cultural diffusion. Greenbaum (1970) has recently attempted to shed some light on this problem by statistically comparing samples generated through both methods. A simple random sample of 69 African societies was first selected from the total list of African cultures contained in the *Ethnographic Atlas* (Murdock 1967). Each society was rated on the variable *dependence upon agriculture*; these results appear in Table 12.3.

The 863 societies listed in the *Atlas* were then divided into 412 *cultural clusters*, each of which represents a grouping of highly similar societies which are known to have had extensive contact. So, each of the societies within a cluster are quite similar, and each cluster is dissimilar from its neighbors. A *stratified random sample* was then constructed of 69 African societies, with only one society permitted from each cluster (no clusters closer than 200 miles were permitted). This statistical method is designed to screen contamination due to proximity or diffusion, yet still produce a random sample. The stratified sample was also rated in Table 12.3 according to *dependence upon agriculture*.

Do these samples contain significant differences at the 0.01 level?

A nondirectional Kolmogorov–Smirnov two-sample test is relevant here, thus preserving the ordinal nature of the variable under study. The critical values of the two-tailed D statistic are given by Table A.8(b) to be

$$0.05\ level: \quad 1.36\ \sqrt{\frac{n_1 + n_2}{n_1 n_2}}$$

$$0.01\ level: \quad 1.63\ \sqrt{\frac{n_1 + n_2}{n_1 n_2}}$$

(12.4)

TABLE 12.3   Comparison of simple random and stratified random samples for 69 African societies (data from Greenbaum 1970).

Dependence upon Agriculture, %	Random Sample		Stratified Sample		Difference
	Raw	Cum., %	Raw	Cum., %	
0–25	4	0.058	4	0.058	0.0
26–45	11	0.217	6	0.145	0.072
46–75	49	0.928	55	0.942	0.014
76–100	5	1.0	4		0.0
	69		69		

The *cumulative proportions* of each measurement class must first be computed. In the random sample given in Table 12.3, the proportion of societies depending less than 25 percent on agriculture is given by $4/69 = 0.058$. The proportion depending less than 45 percent on agriculture is $(4 + 11)/69 = 0.217$ and so forth. Similar computations are performed on the stratified sample, and the D statistic is simply the maximum deviation between the various pairwise comparisons. In this case, $D = 0.072$, the observed difference for the cumulative proportion for 0–45 percent dependence on agriculture.

The critical value of D at $\alpha = 0.01$ is computed from Expression (12.4) to be

$$D = 1.63 \sqrt{\frac{69 + 69}{69(69)}} = 0.277$$

The observed value of D falls short of the critical value, so the null hypothesis is not rejected. This experiment fails to show a significant difference between the two sampling schemes for the African continent.

To summarize the steps in using the Kolmogorov–Smirnov test:

Step I. *Statistical hypotheses:*

H_o: There is no difference in dependence on agriculture between random sampling and the stratified sampling.

H_1: There is a difference between the two sampling methods.

In a more rigorous sense, H_o holds that D should be about equal to zero, while H_1 suggests that D will be significantly greater than zero.

Step II. *Statistical model:* The Kolmogorov–Smirnov model deals only with cumulative proportions. Under a true H_o, the respective unknown cumulative distributions should be identical, such that $D = 0$. The test assumes: (1) random sampling, (2) independent samples, (3) at least ordinal scale measurements, and (4) underlying continuous distribution of the variables.

Step III. *Significance level:* Let $\alpha = 0.01$ for a two-tailed test.

Step IV. *Region of rejection:* From Expression (12.4), any observed value of $D \geq 0.277$ falls into the critical area of the sampling distribution.

Step V. *Calculations and statistical decision:* The computed value of $D = 0.072$ does not exceed the critical value, so the samples appear to favor H_o at $\alpha = 0.01$.

Step VI. *Nonstatistical decision:* The experiment demonstrated no significant difference between the sampling methods for African societies.

The Kolmogorov–Smirnov test can also be phrased in one-tailed fashion, and the significance of such tests is determined by converting the D statistic to chi-square, distributed with 2 degrees of freedom,

$$\chi^2 = 4D^2 \frac{n_1 n_2}{n_1 + n_2} \tag{12.5}$$

The standard chi-square tables can then be used to determine the critical value of χ^2 for the directional Kolmogorov–Smirnov test. Keep in mind, however, that although D has been converted to a chi-square distribution, the Kolmogorov–Smirnov procedure examined a quite different relationship among variables than did the chi-square test considered in Chapter 11.

An application of the directional version of the Kolmogorov–Smirnov test involves cross-cultural comparisons of *riddles*. Riddling behavior has a rather uneven distribution throughout the world, and a recent study by Roberts and Forman (1971) attempted to account for this unusual distribution. Among other hypotheses considered, Roberts and Forman examined the relationship between the presence of riddles and the level of political organization. A cross-cultural survey was conducted in which societies were rated on the presence/absence of riddling, and political integration was ranked along a seven-step ordinal scale ranging from "lack of political integration" to the "state" level (Table 12.4). Is riddling associated with a high level of political integration?

The Kolmogorov-Smirnov statistic preserves the ordinal ranking in the level of political integration, yet handles a case which contains too many ties for the Wilcoxon test. For a directional application at $\alpha = 0.01$ (df = 2), the critical value of the chi-square statistic is found to be $\chi^2 = 9.210$ (Table A.5).

The two samples are presented in Table 12.4 along with their cumulative proportions. The maximum deviation between ranks is found in the second category, in which $D = 0.307$. The chi-square statistic conversion for this value is given by Formula (12.5):

$$\chi^2 = 4(0.307)^2 \frac{45(101)}{45 + 101} = 11.730$$

This observed value of χ^2 exceeds the critical value of 9.210; hence, H_o is rejected. Based upon these data, Roberts and Forman concluded that riddles appear to be associated with a high level of political organization.

TABLE 12.4   Cross-cultural comparison of riddling and the level of political integration (data from Roberts and Forman 1971).

Level of Political Integration	Riddles		
	+	−	D
Absent	0 (0.0)	9 (0.089)	−0.089
Autonomous local	8 (0.178)	40 (0.485)	−0.307
Peace groups	2 (0.222)	2 (0.505)	−0.283
Dependent	2 (0.267)	3 (0.535)	−0.268
Minimal state	10 (0.489)	16 (0.693)	−0.204
Little state	7 (0.644)	6 (0.752)	−0.108
State	16 (1.0)	25 (1.0)	0.0
	45	101	

The rationale behind the Kolmogorov–Smirnov statistic depends upon the continuous distribution function and is beyond the present scope. The interested reader is referred to Conover (1971: chapter 6).

Example 12.5

When administering final examinations, I have often wondered whether the better students tend to work more quickly or more slowly than the poorer students. A good case can be made for either position. I often advise students to stick with their first hunch; "You either know it or you don't," I sagely counsel. But I have also seen unprepared students simply scan an examination, make some cursory guesses, and leave the classroom prematurely. I once kept track of the order in which students turned in their exams in an introductory anthropology course. Do the better students (those receiving A, B, or C grades) work at different rates than the poorer students?

Time, minutes	Good Students f	cum.	Poor Students f	cum.	D
0–40	5	0.179	3	0.143	0.036
41–45	3	0.286	0	0.143	0.143
46–50	9	0.607	4	0.333	0.274
51–55	6	0.821	8	0.714	0.107
56–60	5	1.0	6	1.0	0.0
	28		21		

The largest deviation between the cumulative proportions is found between 46 and 50 minutes, so $D = 0.274$.

This is a two-tailed test and the 0.01 critical value of D is given by Expression (12.4):

$$D = 1.63 \sqrt{\frac{28 + 21}{28(21)}} = 0.470$$

The computed value of D falls short of this critical value, so H_o is not rejected. These data indicate that there is apparently no relationship between the time a student spends on an exam and the grade received.

12.4 TWO RELATED SAMPLES

Both the Wilcoxon and Kolmogorov-Smirnov two-sample tests tacitly assume that each sample is selected independently. That is, the selection for variate i in the first sample can in no way influence selection of variate i in the second sample. But many situations occur in which two variates are *paired* to one another, as considered earlier in Section 10.8. As long as the paired *p*-variates are normally distributed, and both variables are measurable on a metric scale, then the *t*-test can be used to test the relationships. But when these conditions are not fulfilled, the following nonparametric alternatives to the paired *t*-test can be helpful.

12.4.1 The Sign Test

The *sign test* is probably the least complicated member of the nonparametric family of statistical tests. As the name implies, this test considers only the direction (that is, the *sign*) of differences and ignores the magnitude of these differences. The sign tests involves a "paired" research design in which the variates have not been selected independently; rather they are grouped a priori into pairs by criteria such as before–after, male–female, left–right, first born–second born, and so forth. Because only the direction of difference is considered by the sign test, variables can be measured only on an ordinal scale. The only assumption of the sign test, aside from random selection, is that, regardless of the level of measurement, the variable must have an underlying continuous distribution. Thus, we assume that should ties occur between scores, these ties will have resulted from errors of measurement rather than from any inherent equalities within the actual phenomena; this is a common assumption for rank-order statistics. An anthropological example will illustrate the computations involved in the sign test.

Archaeologists frequently employ some rather loose analogies to the ethnographic record. Some well-documented modern primitives are often considered to be "living fossils," functioning analogies which can be used to infer practices of prehistoric technology, division of labor, economics, and kinship structures. But these analogies can never be strictly assumed without first establishing some firm relationships within the ethnographic record itself. Archaeologists occasionally assume, for instance, that females are responsible for the pottery of the archaeological sites. This assumption has led to some rather sophisticated attempts to study ceramic design elements as clues to prehistoric patterns of postmarital residence, inheritance, and even corporate lineality.

The ubiquity of female potters in the ethnographic record serves as an illustration of how the sign test simplifies statistical analysis. A random sample of 22 societies was selected from the *Ethnographic Atlas*. The statistical population was operationally limited to pottery-making societies within aboriginal North America. The *Atlas* codes this variable into the following categories:

F: Females alone perform the activity, male participation being negligible.
G: Both sexes participate, but females do appreciably more than males.
E: Equal participation by both sexes without marked or reported differentiation in specific tasks.
N: Both sexes participate, but males do appreciably more than females.
M: Males alone perform the activity, female participation being negligible.

This scale of measurement is ordinal when applied to pottery making, but the actual degree of participation is clearly a continuous phenomenon which could be measured in metric fashion if the data were of high enough quality. But because we are interested only in whether males or females make the pottery, the data can be reduced into simply dichotomous categories:

+   females participate more than males (categories $F + G$)
−   males participate more than females (categories $N + M$)

There is no significance to the symbols + and −, for any other set of binary symbols would have served equally well. These data are listed in Table 12.5 (note that had the original five-step ranking been retained, one of the two-sample tests would have been appropriate). When cases of equal dependence (*Atlas* coding E) occur in the sign test, these cases are dropped, so the original sample size has been reduced from 22 to only 20 societies.

The results of the survey indicate that 16 of the 20 societies have female potters. We wish now to determine the probability that such extreme results could be due to mere chance association. If these results were to prove statistically significant, then the ethnographic analogy might well hold for archaeological cases as well. Alternatively, one could argue that the four societies with male potters represents too large a deviation from expectation. This phrasing should strike a familiar bell, since this precise situation was discussed earlier in connection with the binomial theorem (Chapter 6). In fact, *the sign test is no more than a nonparametric application of the binomial theorem.* The sign test involves dichotomous relationships, so it is clear that the arithmetic mean is not a suitable measure of central tendency. The null hypothesis holds that if the two categories are independent, then roughly half of the signs should be minus and half should be plus. Female potters have been designated as plus, so a prevalence of female potters should result in a positive value of the *median*. This proposition could be tested using the normal approximation to the binomial distribution, although $n = 20$ makes the approximation somewhat questionable. Operating at a significance level of 0.01, the region of rejection in this sign test becomes that area under the normal curve which represents the extreme cases of the plus sign. Thus, the region of rejection is set at $p \leq 0.01$.

TABLE 12.5 **Twenty randomly selected North American societies. A plus sign denotes female potters (data from *Ethnographic Atlas*, Murdock 1967).**

Society	Potter	Society	Potter
Nunivak	+	Zapotec	−
Baffinland	−	Cochiti	+
Yokuts	+	Ponca	+
S. Ute	+	Klamath	−
Shivwits	+	Sanpoil	+
Kaibab	−	White Knife	+
Walapai	+	Chemehuevi	+
Oto	+	Arikara	+
Hano	+	Hidatsa	+
Tewa	+	Mixe	+

If H_o is true, then the mean and standard deviation under the binomial should be

$$\mu = np = \frac{1}{2}(20) = 10$$

$$\sigma = \sqrt{npq} = \sqrt{5} = 2.24$$

The sample of 20 cases produced 16 societies with positive signs, so it becomes necessary to find the area under the normal curve to the right of 15.5, as shown in Fig. 12.1.

The appropriate value of z is

$$z = \frac{15.5 - 10.0}{2.24} = 2.45$$

From Table A.3, the associated probability value is found to be

$$p = 0.50 - 0.4929 = 0.0071$$

This probability falls well within the region of rejection, so the null hypothesis is rejected. At the 0.01 level, these findings are consistent with the hypothesis that females tend to be potters in North America. But since 20 percent of the sample societies had male potters, one cannot unequivocally assume that all prehistoric potters were in fact female. The analogy remains probabilistic.

To summarize the sign test:

Step I. *Statistical hypotheses:*

$$H_o: \quad p \le q \qquad H_1: \quad p > q$$

Step II. *Statistical model:* The normal approximation to the binomial distribution is applied under the following assumptions: (1) the sampling is random, (2) the Bernoulli random variables are independent, (3) the measurement scale is at least ordinal.

Step III. *Level of significance:* Let $\alpha = 0.01$ for a directional test.

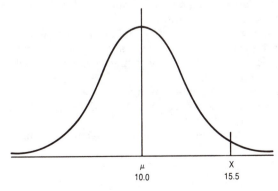

Fig. 12.1

Step IV. *Region of rejection:* The sign test is an exact test, so the critical probability value is defined directly by α. All probabilities ≤ 0.01 will reject H_o.

Step V. *Calculations and statistical decision:* The sample value was computed earlier to be $p = 0.0071$, so H_o is rejected.

Step VI. *Nonstatistical decision:* This sample is consistent with the hypothesis that prehistoric potters tended to be female.

Caution is in order when small samples are used in the sign test. When n is very small, the most extreme possible probability might still not fall within the region of rejection. Consider, for example, the case in which $n = 4$. The probability of obtaining all pluses is $(½)^4 = 0.0625$. Of course this value will never exceed any conventional alpha level. The sample size must be at least larger than about 6, and larger values are desirable.

Because the sign test ignores the quantitative differences between variates, it is clear that the *t*-test utilizes more information and hence is more efficient. That is, the sign test will often fail to detect a difference which the *t*-test would have declared significant. Using the sign test thus increases the probability of a Type II error, and "power" is decreased. Thus, the parametric *t*-test is preferable *as long as the assumptions can be justified.* On the other hand, once results are judged significant by the sign test, these findings will generally be replicated by the more powerful tests.

The sign test is particularly well suited to cases involving *paired* variates. It is well known in social psychology, for example, that IQ scores can be strongly influenced by the environment during early childhood. Let us consider the hypothesis that urban-raised children will, on the average, fare better on IQ tests than children raised in a rural setting. To eliminate as many genetic (inherited) factors as possible, nine pairs of monozygotic twins were located; in each pair one twin was raised in the city, while the other was reared in rural conditions. The IQ scores are reproduced in Table 12.6.

A similar situation was investigated in Chapter 10 (Section 10.8) using the *t*-test for paired variates. But because of the vagaries of IQ testing, the investigator felt uneasy about the validity of using the raw IQ scores, so he elected to consider only the *absolute differences* between scores rather than consider the *magnitude,* which might be spurious. The data are now reduced to a form no longer applicable to the *t*-test.

The null hypothesis in this situation holds that the number of pluses and minuses should be roughly equal. This test is one-tailed because H_1 predicts that the city-reared children will receive superior IQ scores to the rural children. Alpha has been fixed at 0.05.

The data in Table 12.6 indicate that in six of the nine pairs, the urban-raised child received superior IQ scores. Are these findings significant enough to justify the research hypothesis?

If H_o is true, then the mean and standard deviations should be

$$\mu = np = \frac{1}{2}(9) = 4.5$$

$$\sigma = \sqrt{npq} = 1.5$$

TABLE 12.6   IQ scores from monozygotic twins raised in urban and rural environments.

Twin Code No.	IQ Scores		Differences	
	Rural	Urban	Raw	Sign
A	84	92	− 6	−
B	87	86	1	+
C	100	104	− 4	−
D	78	76	2	+
E	89	102	−13	−
F	96	92	4	+
G	115	123	− 8	−
H	108	112	− 4	−
I	72	76	− 4	−

Then z is found to be $(5.5 - 4.5)/1.5 = 0.67$ and Table A.3 indicates that $A = 0.2486$. The resulting probability value thus is $p = 0.2514$, a figure which is obviously not significant, and H_0 cannot be rejected. These results thus fail to support the research hypothesis that city and rural upbringing has a significantly positive effect upon IQ scores.

Example 12.6

In his monograph *Descendants of Immigrants* (1912), Franz Boas collected a wealth of comparative data, in addition to the stature information considered earlier. Boas was particularly interested in *hair color* because of its visibility and widespread significance as a racial indicator. Unfortunately, the modern techniques of physical anthropology for determining hair color (using standardized samples and reflectance spectrophotometry) were unavailable in 1908 when Boas was commissioned by the U.S. Immigration Commission to investigate the physical changes of immigrants. So Boas devised a method of measuring whereby the hair immediately over the forehead was ranked along an ordinal scale ranging from black to flaxen. Each color grade was assigned a number from 1 to 17. One set of Boas' data compared hair color of American-born and foreign-born Sicilian males (listed below) paired in age-graded classes. Is there a significant difference in hair color?

This example raises some interesting problems of measurement. Because the hair-color categories consist of discrete ordered categories, the level of measurement is only ordinal, thereby negating use of the t-test for paired variates. The sign test allows comparison of two samples without assuming anything about the level of measurement, other than that Boas properly ranked hair color from dark to light.

Hair color of Sicilian males (data from Boas 1912: table IX).

Age Class, years	American-born	Foreign-born	Difference
5	10	9	+
6	10	12	–
7	10	10	0
8	11	9	+
9	8	8	0
10	8	10	–
11	8	9	–
12	8	8	0
13	7	8	–
14	8	8	0
15	7	7	0
16	5	8	–
17	6	6	0

The original set of 13 pairs is reduced to only $n = 7$, once the tied scores are removed. If H_o is true, the binomial parameters are

$$\mu = \frac{1}{2}(7) = 3.5$$

$$\sigma = \sqrt{7\left(\frac{1}{2}\right)\left(\frac{1}{2}\right)} = 1.32$$

The standardized normal deviate is computed as usual.

$$z = \frac{2.5 - 3.5}{1.32} = 0.76$$

The corresponding area under the normal curve is $C = 0.2236$ and, because the test is two-tailed, $p = 2(C) = 0.4472$. Clearly, the null hypothesis remains inviolate. We conclude that Boas' data indicates no particular modification in hair color between American-born and foreign-born Sicilians.

12.4.2 The Wilcoxon Signed-Ranks Test

The sign test is useful when the assumptions of the paired t-test are untenable, but the sign test utilized only the directional relationships within a set of data, ignoring the magnitude of difference in every case. The *Wilcoxon Signed-Ranks Test* is a more powerful nonparametric tool which maintains the relative magnitude of difference between the ranked pair. The Wilcoxon method gives more weight to greater differences than to smaller ones, while the sign test records only which variate is larger, but not *how much* larger.

Let us examine the workings of the Wilcoxon test in another example involving monozygotic twins. Some subtle physical differences sometimes are known to exist between first- and second-born twins; a first-born child, for instance, is often more dolichocephalic (roundheaded) than its twin, probably due to the fetal posture at birth. Some investigators likewise have noted a size difference between monozygotic twins. Since monozygotic twins are known to share an identical heritage and to be exactly of the same age, this difference in size can be ascribed only to some aspect of intrauterine conditions. An apparent factor seems to be the structure of the prenatal blood circulation because there is a "third circulation"—in addition to parental and fetal—by which blood actually passes from one twin to the other through the placenta. Other prenatal environmental factors could be due to variability in the uterine mucosa, and also variability in the size of placental vessels themselves. Any of these sources could result in one fetus receiving better nourishment than its twin.

With these factors in mind, it is possible to posit, following Gunnar Dahlberg, that the first-born twin tends to be larger than the second-born twin. Table 12.7 contains a sample of 16 sets of stature measurements collected by Dahlberg (1926). Do these data support the hypothesis that first-born twins tend to be larger?

The relations within these data could be tested by the t-test, as long as one is willing to assume an underlying normal distribution. But if we wish to handle these data in nonparametric fashion, then either the sign or Wilcoxon Signed-Ranks Test could be used. The Wilcoxon test is preferable here in order to preserve the magnitude of size differences between twins.

The one-tailed situation produces the following statistical hypotheses for the Wilcoxon Signed-Ranks test:

$$H_o: \quad \text{Median difference} \leq 0 \qquad H_1: \quad \text{Median difference} > 0$$

These hypotheses are comparable with those of the t- and sign tests, but each statistical test is based upon rather different assumptions and procedures.

The Wilcoxon test statistic is called T, defined as *the sum of differences of ranks with the least frequent sign*. Let X_i represent variates in the first sample and Y_i variates in the second sample. If fewer differences exist between $(X_i - Y_i)$, T is defined as the sum of these negative differences; otherwise the positive differences are summed to yield T.

The initial step in computing the Wilcoxon Signed-Ranks Test is to list the differences in stature within each pair, hence reducing the 16 pairs of variates in Table 12.7 to only 16 values of D. Whereas the sign test expressed these differences only in present/absent categories, the Wilcoxon paired test preserves the *ranks* of the differences (and, of course, the t-test preserves the actual quantitative magnitude). Two pairs of twins were exactly the same size, so these pairs are excluded from further consideration, and the sample size is reduced to $n = 14$. The absolute value of the remaining differences are then assigned rank orderings, with the smallest difference receiving the assigned rank of 1. Ties are handled as before by assigning the average of the tied ranks to each tied case.

Two different methods are available for determining the statistical significance of these pairwise ranks. As long as the number of cases are fewer than 50, Table A.7 can be used directly to define the critical region of rejection. In this case, with $n = 14$, the critical level at the 0.05 level is found to be 25. This means that any observed sum of ranks less than or equal to 25 will be considered significant. Had this test been two-tailed, then the critical value of T would be found under $\alpha/2 = 0.025$; for $n = 14$, this critical value of $T = 21$.

The observed value of T is found in Table 12.7 to be 23, which is *less* than the critical value of $T = 25$; the critical number indicates "the maximum number of aberrant cases," so values less than or equal to the critical value are significant. H_o is rejected, and we conclude that Dahlberg's data on monozygotic twins are consistent with random fluctuations: that first-born twins do not appear to be significantly larger than the second-born.

Wilcoxon's T statistic is approximately distributed in normal fashion for samples of greater than about $n = 20$, so the results of the *Wilcoxon Signed-Ranks Test* can be evaluated using a slightly modified version of the standardized normal deviate:

$$z = \frac{T - \mu}{\sigma} \tag{12.6}$$

where the parametric mean and standard deviation for $N = n$ cases are defined as

$$\mu = \frac{N(N + 1)}{4}$$

$$\sigma = \sqrt{\frac{N(N + 1)(2N + 1)}{24}}$$

TABLE 12.7 Stature differences (in millimeters) between first- and second-born monozygotic twins (data from Dahlberg 1926: appendix I, table 1).

Stature, First Born X_i, mm	Stature, Second Born Y_i, mm	Difference $D = X_i - Y_i$	Rank $X_i > Y_i$	Rank $X_i < Y_i$
1014	1019	− 5		3.5
1186	1179	7	6	
1348	1334	14	10	
1357	1340	17	12	
1704	1709	− 5		3.5
1454	1434	20	13	
1592	1534	58	14	
1245	1261	− 16		11
1380	1377	3	2	
1052	1058	− 6		5
1273	1262	11	9	
1426	1417	9	7.5	
1409	1400	9	7.5	
1253	1252	1	1	
1396	1396	0		
1219	1219	0		
			Σ of ranks = 82	$T = 23$

These parameters allow evaluation of the deviation of T relative to the familiar normal curve.

This large-sample method can be illustrated by returning to Boas' data on the physical changes of immigrants to the United States. These data were already analyzed by the paired version of the t-test (Example 10.8) in which a sample of American-born Bohemians were found to be significantly taller than those of foreign birth. The informants were paired in age grades for ages 4 through 20. These data are rank-ordered in Table 12.8, in which we find the value of the Wilcoxon statistic to be $T = 21$.

The parametric mean and standard deviation for a population of $N = n = 17$ pairs are

$$\mu = \frac{17(18)}{4} = 76.5$$

$$\sigma = \sqrt{\frac{17(18)(34+1)}{24}} = 21.12$$

The value of z can be computed from Expression (12.6) as

$$z = \frac{21 - 76.5}{21.12} = -2.63$$

The value of $z = -2.63$ corresponds to a probability figure of $p = 0.0043$ in Table A.3, a figure which is highly significant. H_o is rejected and we conclude that American-born Bohemians seem to be notably taller than foreign-born Bohemians of the same racial stock. These findings agree with those of the t-test

TABLE 12.8 Comparison of stature between American- and foreign-born Bohemians (data from Boas 1912).

Age	American-born, cm	Foreign-born, cm	D	Ranks $X_i > Y_i$	Ranks $X_i < Y_i$
4	99.4	98.0	+1.4	6	
5	105.7	101.0	+4.7	16	
6	110.7	110.6	+0.1	1	
7	116.0	111.7	+4.3	14.5	
8	122.5	118.2	+4.3	14.5	
9	128.5	128.1	+0.4	4	
10	132.7	135.1	−2.4		9.5
11	137.7	134.7	+3.0	12	
12	141.1	140.0	+1.1	5	
13	147.9	148.1	−0.2		2
14	152.3	150.4	+1.9	7	
15	155.5	155.2	+0.3	3	
16	162.7	160.7	+2.0	8	
17	167.6	165.0	+2.6	11	
18	175.0	167.7	+7.3	17	
19	171.2	167.0	+4.2	13	
20	168.6	171.0	−2.4		9.5
				Σ ranks = 132	$T = 21$

performed earlier, and the Wilcoxen Signed-Rank Test requires fewer procedural assumptions. Note further that since $n = 17$, Table A.7 could also have been used to compute an associated probability of $p < 0.005$.

12.5 THE KOLMOGOROV–SMIRNOV ONE-SAMPLE TEST

The Kolmogorov–Smirnov test compares observed and expected frequencies in a manner quite similar to the $R \times C$ chi-square test (Section 11.8). Both tests consider the "goodness of fit" between an expected distribution and the distribution of an actual random sample. The Kolmogorov–Smirnov test is preferable to χ^2 when the samples are small because the Kolmogorov–Smirnov method always provides an exact probability, regardless of n. Remember that chi-square assumes a sample size sufficient to satisfy the approximation to a continuous distribution of the χ^2 statistic.

This simple notion behind the Kolmogorov–Smirnov One-Sample Test can readily be illustrated using an archaeological example. Small quantities of Early Woodland (Black Sand phase) pottery sherds were found at the Macoupin site in the lower Illinois Valley (Rackerby 1973). Because the bulk of the cultural materials at Macoupin are Middle Woodland (Havana phase) in age, the excavators wanted to know whether these rare Early Woodland materials were associated with a particular stratigraphic level at the site or whether the aberrant sherds were simply strewn randomly throughout the site midden. The later Havana phase materials ran consistently from the surface to a depth of about 24 inches, while the Black Sand sherds seemed to concentrate in the upper levels: 0–6 inches, 11 sherds; 6–12 inches, 13 sherds; 12–18 inches, 11 sherds; 18–24 inches, 3 sherds. Can we justify the conclusion that the Black Sand sherds are uniformly distributed throughout the midden at the Macoupin site?

The Kolmogorov–Smirnov One-Sample Test can readily answer this question. The first step is to plot the observed sherd frequencies (labelled f in Table 12.9) by stratigraphic unit. Then the *cumulative* proportions of each stratigraphic unit are computed. The 0 to 6 inch level contained $11/38 \times 100 = 28.9$ percent of all the Black Sand sherds. The top *two* levels (0 to 6 and 6 to 12 inches) contained $(11 + 13)/38 \times 100 = 63.2$ percent of all these sherds, and so forth. Because we know that the Havana phase sherds were uniformly dispersed throughout the

TABLE 12.9 Stratigraphic placement of Black Sand pottery sherds at the Macoupin site (data from Rackerby 1973).

Stratigraphic Unit, inches	Frequency, f	Cumulative Frequency	Cumulative Proportion	Expected Proportion	Difference
0–6	11	11	$11/38 = 0.289$	0.250	0.039
6–12	13	24	$24/38 = 0.632$	0.500	0.132
12–18	11	35	$35/38 = 0.921$	0.750	0.171
18–24	3	38	$38/38 = 1.0$	1.0	0.0
	$n = 38$				

deposit, the null hypothesis states that the Black Sand should also distribute randomly throughout the levels of the site. So the expected cumulative proportion of the first stratum is $1/4 = 0.25$, the expected cumulative proportion of the first two strata is $1/2 = 0.50$, and so on. The main difference between this procedure and that of the familiar chi-square test is how the expected frequencies have been computed. The Kolomogorov–Smirnov method deals with expected cumulative proportions, while the χ^2 projects deal with expected absolute frequencies.

The final operation is to find the absolute differences between the observed and expected proportions (final column of Table 12.9). The Kolmogorov–Smirnov statistic, D, is merely the *maximum difference* between expected and observed proportions. In the example from the Macoupin site, D is found in the third row, the stratum consisting of 12 to 18 inches below the surface:

$$D = 0.171$$

The distribution of the Kolmogorov–Smirnov D statistic has been compiled in Table A.9. For the case of the 38 Black Sand potsherds, the critical value of D at the 0.05 level is

$$D = \frac{1.36}{\sqrt{38}} = 0.221$$

The observed D falls short of the critical level, so H_o is not rejected. Use of the Kolmogorov–Smirnov One-Sample Test allowed the excavator to conclude that "these data do not demonstrate stratigraphically that the Havana deposits are superimposed on the Black Sand deposit, but rather that there is considerable admixture of earlier material in later levels" (Rackerby 1973: 99).

Only the two-tailed version of the Kolmogorov–Smirnov One-Sample Test has been discussed here. The critical regions for the one-tailed option are poorly understood and have been omitted (see Siegel 1956:49) for appropriate references).

12.6 RUNS TEST

When a coin is tossed ten times, a "run" of ten heads is obviously a quite unlikely outcome.

HHHHHHHHHH

Whether this succession represents good or evil luck depends only on where one has placed his money, and Chapter 5 has considered methods to evaluate precisely the probabilities of such outcomes. But a second kind of departure from randomness has yet to be considered, a departure dealing only with *successions of events* rather than with their *relative frequency*. This section will consider a test to determine randomness in successive events.

Everyone has heard the riverboat gambler's expression "a run of luck." This sequence can consist of good luck—"Stick with me, baby, I can't lose!!"—or, more commonly, bad luck—"Somebody up there hates me." But in either case, a run of luck involves a sequence of events which deviates from expectation under randomness.

One possible outcome from tossing a coin ten times is

HHHHHTTTTT

In terms of strict frequency, the overall ratio 50 : 50 is the most likely outcome for a fair coin. But the occurrence of precisely five heads followed by exactly five tails is not a very likely event in terms of succession. In each of the ten independent trials, there are only two "runs": The sequence of five heads comprises the first run, followed by a second run of five tails. This is a very rare outcome. In fact, when we concentrate strictly upon sequence, there is only one more extreme outcome—a single run of all heads or all tails. These sequences have many fewer runs than are expected from chance phenomena.

At the other extreme, it is possible to have *too many* runs in a random sequence:

HTHTHTHTHT

The alternating head–tail sequence is a very unlikely event; in this case, a total of ten runs occurred. Clearly, the number of possible runs varies from one to n for any dichotomous variable. But the most likely number of runs is somewhere intermediate between the two extremes.

The *runs test* uses this simple concept of sequence to test for randomness. The more extreme (that is, the less frequent) the number of runs, the less likely it is that the sample is actually a random mix. The null hypothesis in this case is that the two dichotomous states are well mixed, that independent events should exhibit no tendency either to clump or to rigidly alternate. The computations of the runs tests can be illustrated by a simple example.

One particularly prolific family has spawned 12 children. While the frequencies are as expected, six boys and six girls, the order of birth seems rather odd, since the boys were born almost in sequence, followed by most of the female offspring.

MFMMMMMFFFFF

Does this sequence depart from randomness so far that we are entitled to question that the order of birth is randomly determined?

First it is necessary to find the total number of runs in the $(n_1 + n_2)$ births:

M   F   MMMMM   FFFFF
1   2   3   4

There are only four runs in this sequence of 12 seemingly random events. The statistical dilemma is to decide whether four runs in 12 events is a rare event.

For small runs as this, the critical values have been compiled in Table A.10. Whenever an observed number of runs is less than or equal to the appropriate tabled value, then H_o can be rejected at the 0.05 level. Strictly speaking, this is a test for *too few* runs, so the result is one-tailed. Tables for the alternative (*too many* runs) can be found in Siegel (1956).[2]

---

[2]As Blalock (1972: 252) has pointed out, this situation might cause some confusion unless care is taken with terminology. The runs test is one-tailed because we are considering only the possibility of *too few* runs. But, unlike most one-tailed tests, the direction has not been predicted, since either the variable *X* or *Y* could occur first. The sign test is a one-tailed test in which direction is not specified.

Table A.10 indicates that for $n_1 = 6$ and $n_2 = 6$, the critical region for the 0.05 level is three or fewer runs. Because four runs were observed in the birth sequence above, H_o is not rejected at the 0.05 level. No doubt arises that the order of birth departs from a random sequence.

When either sample size exceeds 20, then Table A.10 is no longer applicable. But as the sample sizes increase, the distribution of r (the number of runs) approaches normality with mean and standard deviation as follows

$$\mu_r = \frac{2n_1 n_2}{n_1 + n_2} + 1$$

$$\sigma_r = \sqrt{\frac{2n_1 n_2(2n_1 n_2 - n_1 - n_2)}{(n_1 + n_2)^2(n_1 + n_2 - 1)}}$$

(12.7)

where $n = n_1 + n_2$. This handy, yet slightly less cumbersome, computational procedure is illustrated in Example 12.7.

It is interesting to note that although the number of runs, r, approaches normality in the larger samples, the runs test remains nonparametric because the normal distribution still need not be assumed for the population of variates.

Example 12.7

The table below contains the annual rainfall tabulation for the period 1901–1950 for Sante Fe, New Mexico. If we operationally define "dry year" as one receiving 13 inches or less rainfall, can we say that wet and dry years appear to cluster (data from Schulman 1956: table 19A)?

Year	Rainfall, inches	Year	Rainfall, inches
1901	15.61	1920	18.56
1902	15.53	1921	14.37
1903	15.77	1922	13.67
1904	5.49	1923	10.75
1905	19.34	1924	13.63
1906	14.06	1925	8.14
1907	19.42	1926	15.83
1908	13.23	1927	13.20
1909	9.71	1928	14.70
1910	12.54	1929	13.60
1911	10.66	1930	17.14
1912	17.78	1931	15.47
1913	12.72	1932	16.90
1914	12.75	1933	14.23
1915	20.36	1934	12.88
1916	16.16	1935	13.71
1917	10.98	1936	12.32
1918	9.58	1937	19.48
1919	17.92	1938	11.49

Year	Rainfall, inches	Year	Rainfall, inches
1939	15.00	1946	11.30
1940	15.62	1947	14.17
1941	17.96	1948	16.06
1942	12.63	1949	15.41
1943	12.00	1950	12.31
1944	6.79	Mean	14.27
1945	13.03		

There are a total of 22 runs, with the number of dry years $n_1 = 17$ and the number of wet years $n_2 = 33$. The mean of the distribution of r is

$$\mu_r = \frac{2(17)(33)}{50} + 1 = 23.44$$

and the standard deviation is

$$\sigma_r = \sqrt{\frac{2(17)(33)(2 \cdot 17 \cdot 33 - 17 - 33)}{50^2(49)}}$$

$$= 3.12$$

The standardized deviate is thus

$$z = \frac{22 - 23.44}{3.12} = -0.46$$

This value is obviously not significant and we can conclude that these precipitation figures do not tend to cluster in wet and dry years.

12.7 SOME ASSUMPTIONS OF NONPARAMETRIC STATISTICS

The preceding nonparametric statistical techniques were considered in an almost negative fashion: The "Jones test for circular asymmetry" is useful because we don't have to assume X, Y, or even Z. But let us not be misled by the terms "nonparametric" or "distribution-free" to the erroneous conclusion that these techniques are somehow *nonassuming* or *assumption-free*. Nonparametric statistical tests make some very important assumptions which should not be ignored.

First of all, all nonparametric techniques of statistical inference assume that the sample was constructed through random sampling. Specifically, each element in the population must have had an *equal* and *independent* chance for selection.

In addition, many of the distribution-free tests involve comparing two samples, such as the chi-square test of a 2×2 table, Fisher's Exact Test, the Wilcoxon Signed-Ranks Test, and the Kolmogorov-Smirnov Two-Sample Test.

These two samples are assumed to be mutually independent in that the controls for selection of the first sample can in no way influence selection of the second sample. Violation of this independence can seriously change the computed levels of significance unless the test is specifically constructed to handle such dependence (as with the McNemar test).

Finally, the ordinal level tests assume that the underlying scales of measurement are actually continuous in nature. The units of observation are discrete because of the relative crude scales used for measurement: Either men or women make the pottery; either a group is heavily reliant upon fishing, or hardly dependent upon fishing, or they don't fish at all; either langur A dominates langur B or otherwise. Because of these crude categories of measurements, independent variates will occasionally be rated into the same category. The *Ethnographic Atlas*, for instance, rates both the Copper Eskimo and the Kaska as 36 to 45 percent dependent upon hunting. But even though these two societies are operationally considered to be "equal," we still must assume that there is really some slight difference which has simply gone undetected. This tie in ranking occurred because of our gross scale of measurement; given a suitably accurate measuring system, presumably we could detect a difference between the Copper Eskimo and the Kaska. Thus, in nonparametric testing, all ties are assumed to result from a gross system of measurement. So a moderate number of ties are permitted in the ordinal-level testing as long as ties are corrected by suitable formulas. Such is the conventional thinking about ties (for example, Siegel 1956).

But it must be mentioned that recent work on the problems of ties indicates that even when a high degree of agreement occurs in ordinal scales, there is almost no effect upon the computed level of significance (Conover 1971 and Noether 1972). Of course some nonparametric tests are more appropriate than others in the presence of ties. The Wilcoxon Two-Sample Test, for instance, becomes computationally undesirable as the ties increase, so one would do well to switch to an alternative rank-order test. The assumption of continuity is mentioned here only to warn prospective users that although one is commonly cautioned to assume an underlying continuity of measurement, such guidelines have little practical effect upon modern application of the rank-order statistics.

SUGGESTIONS FOR FURTHER READING

Blalock (1972: chapter 14)
Conover (1971: chapters 5, 6)
Siegel (1956)

EXERCISES

12.1   The male adults in two contiguous bands of hunter-gatherers were measured for stature (in centimeters):

Band A:	152	159	163	149	164
Band B:	156	167	169	155	172

Is there a significant difference in stature between these two bands (use the Wilcoxon Two-Sample Test)?

12.2 Five radiocarbon dates are available for each of two archaeological sites:

Site A:	A.D. 520	A.D. 490	A.D. 525	A.D. 540	A.D. 690
Site B:	A.D. 590	400 B.C.	A.D. 740	A.D. 730	A.D. 820

(a) Use the *t*-test to see whether site A is significantly older than site B.
(b) Use the Wilcoxon Two-Sample Test to test the same hypothesis.
(c) Which method is preferable? Why?

12.3 A census revealed the following mortality figures for two societies:

Age at Death

Society A:	62	54	78	56	45	58	64	63	63	34	53	45
Society B:	54	78	67	45	68	69	39	83	78	68	71	69

Does society B appear to be longer-lived than society A?

12.4 Two neighboring archaeological sites have been excavated and the projectile points from each analyzed.

Total Weight, grams	Site A	Site B
<1.0	2	0
1.0–1.9	15	6
2.0–2.9	10	13
3.0–3.9	3	6
4.0–4.9	5	5
5.0–5.9	2	6
≥6.0	0	3

In this area, points become lighter through time. Is site A later than site B? (Use the Kolmogorov-Smirnov Two-Sample Test.)

12.5 The following grades were assigned in a freshman anthropology course:

Grade	Total	Eventually Graduated	Did Not Graduate
A	35	28	7
B	130	82	48
C	90	62	28
D	52	38	14
F	18	3	15

Use the appropriate nonparametric method to determine whether those students with higher grades in this freshman course tended to graduate more frequently than those students receiving lower grades.

12.6   Fluted points are important time markers of the big-game hunting tradition in North America. McKenzie (1970) compiled the following data on the number of individual flutes per projectile points for two early types in Ohio.

Number of Flutes	Cumberland Points	Holcombe Points
0	11	10
1	22	8
2	4	0
3	1	4
4	0	0
>4	0	1

Is there a significant difference in the number of flutes between Cumberland and Holcombe points?

12.7   The following figures were obtained in a study of work habits among married couples.

	Hours Worked per Week	
Couple	Males	Females
A	39	41
B	51	42
C	23	35
D	45	39
E	67	54
F	39	43
G	42	46
H	51	51
I	32	36
J	40	42
K	56	53
L	41	41
M	43	45
N	37	39
O	40	41

Do these findings indicate that females tend to work more hours per week than males? (Use the sign test.)

12.8   Use the Wilcoxon Signed-Ranks Test to solve Exercise 12.7.

12.9 Use the Wilcoxon Signed-Ranks Test to reanalyze the educational data on monozygotic twins in Section 10.8.

12.10 Section 12.3 and Exercise 11.1 have tested the same set of empirical data. How do the test assumptions differ between the two approaches?

12.11 The following figures are observations on a series of housepits on the lower Snake and mid-Columbia River drainages in the northwestern United States (data from Southard 1973).

Plan-Outline	Site	Age	Size, m²	Depth, cm
Rectangular	45 KL 5/3	Pre-2110 ± 100 BP	10.5	20
	45 KL 5/3	2110 ± 100 BP	16.0	40
	45 KL /53	Pre-2110 ± 100 BP	20.0	25
	45 KL 5/3	Pre-2110 ± 100 BP	25.0	40
	35 UM 35	2420 ± 120 BP	15.5	40
	35 GM 15/13	· · ·	11.0	30
	35 GM 3	1170 ± 160 BP	10.0	40
Circular	35 GM 9/5	Post-940 ± 280 BP	10.0	40
	35 UM 17	early historic	15.4	35
	35 GM 9/5	· · ·	15.0	60
	35 GM 15/13	390 ± 140 BP	15.0	30
	35 GM 15/13	Pre-390 ± 140 BP	17.0	30
	45 BN 6	Late prehistoric, early historic	18.5	60
	35 GM 22	Late prehistoric, early historic	19.5	30
	45 KL 5/3	Pre-2140 ± 210 BP	24.5	40
	35 GM 22	Late historic	28.0	30

Use appropriate nonparametric techniques to test the following hypotheses. (Be certain to explain why you chose a particular statistic.)
(a) Rectangular houses tend to have a smaller floor area than circular.
(b) Rectangular houses tend to be more ancient than circular houses.
(c) Sites in Oregon (that is, those prefaced by "35") tend to be later than those in Washington.

12.12 Use a nonparametric method to reanalyze the data from Franz Boas' study on Bohemian stature (Example 10.8).
(a) How do the nonparametric results differ from those obtained earlier with the t-test?
(b) Which of the statistics methods seems to be most appropriate? Why?

12.13 Return to the data from the Grasshopper Ruin (Exercise 10.7):
(a) Use an appropriate nonparametric method to test for a significant size difference between early and late rooms.
(b) Retest the hypothesis concerning firehearth size, using nonparametric methods.
(c) What are the advantages and disadvantages of each approach to these data?

13 Linear Regression

13.1 THE LINEAR RELATIONSHIP

Throughout the past few chapters, we have assigned rather specific definitions
to commonplace terms such as *variable*, *constant*, *random*, *population*, and
significance. Time has come to consider another Big Word, and that word is
function. When the value of a random variable Y changes in response to a
corresponding change in random variable X, then Y is said to be a function of X.
The nature of this dependency is presently irrelevant. Regardless of whether the
dependency is specific or generalized, causal or coincidental, all such relationships can be symbolized as

$$Y = f(X)$$

to be read as "Y is a function of X."

Some elementary relationships between random variables were encountered
in the discussion of the chi-square statistic, but we must now consider the
generalized bivariate relationship in more detail. Specifically, there are two
common methods for expressing the relationship between two variables—
mathematical equations and graphs.

The most elementary function between two random variables is simply

$$Y = f(X) = X$$

This function tells us that the value of Y must always exactly equal the value of
X. This simple function is that assumed in tree-ring dating (dendrochronology)
for example. A perfect one-to-one relationship exists between the age of a living

345

tree and the number of *annual rings*: One ring represents one year.

number of annual rings = age in years

$$Y = X$$

Because $Y = f(X) = X$, the number of annual rings (Y) is a *function* of X, the age of the tree. This function predicts that a ten-year-old tree should have exactly ten growth rings. A 1000-year-old tree must have 1000 rings.

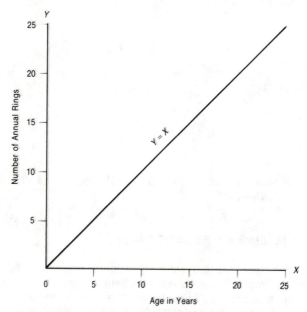

Fig. 13.1   Relationship between age of tree and number of annual growth rings.

Functional relationships can also be graphed. Figure 13.1 shows the graph for the function $Y = X$. The vertical axis (the *ordinate*) generally is taken to denote Y and the horizontal X-axis (the *abscissa*) plots the values of the X variable. The Y-axis in this case depicts the number of growth rings per tree and the abscissa scales the tree's age in years. The ordinate meets the abscissa at the *origin* of the graph, so the origin of Fig. 13.1 represents zero on both the X and Y scales. Zero age predicts zero annual rings.

The appropriate curve for Fig. 13.1 was found by plotting the various values satisfying the equation $Y = X$.

When X is:	0	1	2	4	7	28	99	$\cdots$
Then Y is:	0	1	2	4	7	28	99	$\cdots$

This curve is "linear" because all of these potential values can be described by a single straight line. This "curve" commences at the *origin* because both scales truncate at zero; a negative age or a minus count of rings is patently impossible.

Convention dictates that the X variable be called the *predictor* (or *indepen-*

dent) variable and that *Y* be the *predicted* or *dependent* variable. Both terms follow from the general function $Y = f(X)$. Because the *X* variable can often be controlled in experimental situations, a change in *X* is said to induce a shift in *Y*. Sometimes these terms reflect a causal sequence in which *X* is said to cause *Y*, but care must be taken to avoid confusing a *causality* with simple *prediction*. Fire engines are excellent indicators of fires, ambulances associate with automobile accidents, and police officers invariably occur at the scene of a crime.

Age is the independent variable in dendrochronology because we happen to know from plant physiology that age *causes* trees to produce annual rings. Age (*X*) accurately predicts the number of rings (*Y*); in this case, a causal relationship exists. But prediction equations may often be written in the reverse form. The number of rings predicts age. A living tree with ten rings must be exactly ten years of age. This reasoning sets the foundation for the science of dendrochronology.

Tree-ring samples can be counted in living trees by careful use of an increment borer. The tree is not harmed. Edmond Schulman, a dendrochronologist from the University of Arizona, took literally hundreds of borings from a bristlecone forest located at an elevation over 10,000 feet in eastern California. Using the simple function $Y = X$, Schulman discovered the oldest living thing in the world. One bristlecone—lovingly christened *Pine Alpha*— dated back to 2194 B.C. And Pine Alpha still lives! In this case, *Y* is the tree's age, predicted by *X*, the number of annual rings. Obviously, the decision of which variable is *X* (the *predictor*) depends strictly upon what one wishes to predict, age or number of rings.

At the risk of repetition, let me underscore once again a canon of statistical inference: Association must never be confused with causality. The predictive relationship implicit in $Y = f(X)$ may represent a true causal linkage, or it may not. The issue is determined by substantive rather than statistical considerations. The common statistical labels *independent* and *dependent* must not be allowed to cloud the causal issue because these terms are often assigned merely for convenience. The choice of independent variables lies with the specific empirical intent or the perspective of the investigator. For this reason, the *X* variable will be termed the *predictor* variable, to avoid any confusion of true dependence or independence.

Let us now move to a bit more complicated function:

$$Y = f(X) = \beta X$$

where β represents any constant.[1] The expression $Y = \beta X$ is another specific example of the general function $Y = f(X)$. In the previous example of a function, $Y = X$, the multiplicative constant (β) was equal to unity, $\beta = 1$. The function $Y = X$ tells us that an increase in a single unit of *X* corresponds to an increase in precisely one unit of *Y*. The more general case of $Y = \beta X$ implies a change in one unit of *X* for every β units of change in *Y*. If $Y = 10X$, then one unit change in *X* produces +10 units of change in *Y*. The constant β can likewise be negative, in which case *Y* decreases with an increase in *X*.

[1] Be careful here not to confuse the regression β with the probability of committing a Type II error.

An elementary example of the $Y = \beta X$ function is the rate of exchange between international monetary systems. Although these rates tend to fluctuate daily, the relationship between any two currencies is fixed at any given point in time. On March 4, 1974, the *New York Times* reported the commercial selling rate between currencies of the United States and Spain to be 1.72. Translated into functional notation, this relationship becomes $Y = 1.72X$, where X is the value of the Spanish *peseta* and Y is the value of the U.S. penny (0.01 U.S. dollars). In other words, one U.S. penny is equal to 1.72 pesetas. This relationship is diagrammed in Fig. 13.2. The functional line once again commences at the origin (zero U.S. pennies = zero *pesetas*) and extends indefinitely upward.

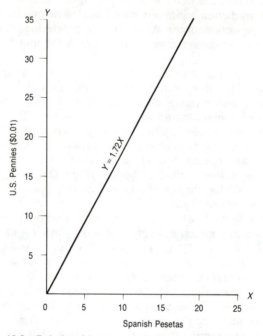

Fig. 13.2 Relationship between U.S. and Spanish currency.

All monetary rates can be expressed in this simple form. Only the absolute value of β changes to fit the particular circumstance. Note also how X is arbitrarily assigned to the Spanish currency. There is no causal linkage in any of the currency exchanges; X is simply a convenient point of reference.

Using the multiplicative constant β requires us to introduce another new term, the *slope*. The multiplicative constant β represents the slope of a line. The slope of the line in Fig. 13.1, for instance, is $\beta = 1$. One unit of change in X creates one unit shift in Y. Similarly, in Fig. 13.2, a unit shift in the value of X creates a 1.72 unit shift in Y. The magnitude of Y changes more relative to X in the second case because the line is *steeper*. That is, the slope of the line in Fig. 13.2 is greater than that of Fig. 13.1. Consider the two equations

$$Y = 1X \qquad Y = 1.72X$$

The only difference between these two functions is the value of the multiplicative constant. In the tree-ring example, β must equal unity, while the exchange rate had been fixed at $\beta = 1.72$. So, clearly, *the slope of any line depends only upon the value of β.* The lines will become steeper as β increases. Furthermore, a positive value of β means that the function line slopes in a positive direction (Y increasing with X); a negative β denotes a negative slope (Y decreasing as X increases). Mathematically speaking, the slope of a line is given by the tangent of the angle formed by the function line and the X-axis, but this derivation is not important to our purposes. The meaning of β is also apparent simply from plotting values of Y for given X.

The lines of Figs. 13.1 and 13.2 pass through the origins of their respective graphs. This is reasonable: Trees of zero age have no annual rings, and all monetary rates of exchange must commence with zero money. But one final statistical phrase is required to completely generalize this discussion of the linear relationship. Several lines are graphed in Fig. 13.3, each of which shares a slope of $\beta = 1$. These lines are all parallel, and differ only in their position relative to the axes. Only line A passes through the origin. The equations for all

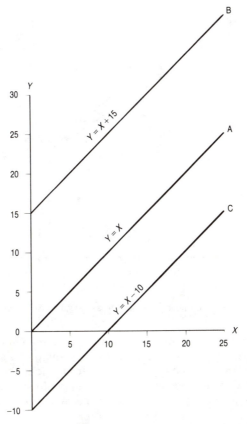

Fig. 13.3   Equations with identical slope but different Y-intercepts.

350

other lines involve a new constant. For line *B*, this constant is $\alpha = 15$ and for line *C*, the constant takes the value of $\alpha = -10$. This new term is called the *additive* constant and is symbolized by α.[2] The general formula for all linear relationships can now be given:

$$Y = f(X) = \alpha + \beta X$$

The term α is also known as the *Y-intercept*, since its value is the precise point at which the function line intercepts the *Y*-axis. When $X = 0$, then $Y = \alpha$. Only when $\alpha = 0$ will the line intersect the origin; note that $\alpha = 0$ in Figs. 13.1 and 13.2.

The additive constant can be illustrated by *Bergmann's rule*, that biological principle which relates an animal's size to the temperature of the habitat (see Birdsell 1972:465–467). Bergmann's rule predicts that polar animals should have a greater body size than animals living near the equator. In general, a larger body mass will tend to retard heat loss in colder climates, so less energy is expended by larger bodies. This relationship is expressed in Fig. 13.4. For

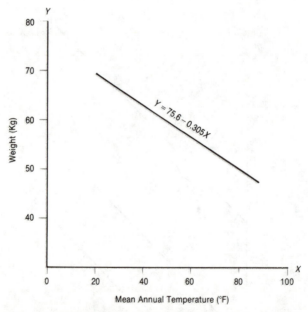

Fig. 13.4   Graph illustrating Bergmann's rule (after Roberts 1953).

those readers who seem comforted by the belief that man has little in common with other animals, Fig. 13.4 might come as something of a shock. This graph has been derived from *human* populations throughout the world, and size clearly decreases with an increase in temperature. Bergmann's rule predicts human size as well as that of the lower beasts. This expression can be

[2]Once again, do not confuse the regression α with the probability of committing a Type I error.

summarized as

$$Y = 75.6 - 0.305X$$

where X is measured in degrees Fahrenheit and human weight (Y) is given in kilograms. This function tells us a great deal about the interrelationship between temperature and size. For every additional degree of temperature, the average weight of a human population can be expected to decrease about 0.305 kg. Bergmann's rule indicates that environmental factors tend to operate on mankind regardless of culture. Even in a mild climate such as southern California, between 80 and 90 percent of the food consumed is required to maintain a body temperature of 98.6F; quite obviously, the situation is much worse in an Arctic environment. Despite the fact that igloos are heated to a balmy 75 degrees, the true limiting factor upon human populations appears to be the $-60°F$ temperatures encountered outside (Birdsell 1972:467).

To summarize, any *linear* relationship can be described by the simple equation

$$Y = \alpha + \beta X \tag{13.1}$$

where X is the *predictor* variable, Y is the *predicted* variable, α is the Y-intercept, and β is the slope of the line.

13.2 LEAST SQUARES REGRESSION (MODEL I REGRESSION)

With the formal properties of the linear relationship at hand, we arrive at the major topic of this chapter—the concept of *regression*. The actual word "regression" sometimes causes a bit of confusion, but this distraction is unnecessary once one realizes the genesis of the concept. The pioneering effort on the study of linear relationships was made by Sir Francis Galton, a nineteenth-century scholar of rather amazing breadth. Galton was an accomplished statistician, whose early studies of heredity were among the vanguard of pre-Mendelian genetics. He was also a prominent anthropologist (in the original sense of the term), contributing to such diverse fields as dermatoglyphics (fingerprinting), anthropometry, evolution, and eugenics. (Sir Francis is, incidentally, the same Galton whose infamous "problem" has bemused anthropologists for the past 80 years, as discussed in Chapter 15.)

Of immediate interest is Galton's paper entitled "REGRESSION *towards* MEDIOCRITY *in* HEREDITARY STATURE," published by *The Journal of the Anthropological Institute of Great Britain and Ireland* in 1885. In this classic paper, Galton advanced his "Law of Regression." He hypothesized as a result of genetic experiments upon peas that "offspring did not tend to resemble their parent seeds in size—but to be always more mediocre than they—to be smaller than the parents if the parents were large; to be larger than the parents, if the parents were very small" (1885:246). Galton felt that offspring tend to "regress" toward the population average; hence his title "Regression towards Mediocrity...." To generalize this relationship, Sir Francis compiled hundreds of measurements of human stature and plotted these points on the familiar X-Y coordinate axis, similar to those already considered. Parent's stature was plotted against the stature of the offspring, and a marked linear relationship emerged. Galton called the line describing this positive relationship a *line of regression* because it demonstrated how offspring "regressed" toward mediocrity. Statisticians subsequently modified Galton's idea to apply to all lines predicting values of one random variable (*Y*) from knowledge of the other random variable (*X*). Therefore, the line in Fig. 13.4 is a *regression line* because it predicts human size (*Y*), given mean annual temperature (*X*). Similarly, the lines in Section 13.1 predicted a tree's age (given the number of annual tree rings) and the U.S. dollar equivalent to any particular sum of Spanish *pesetas*. Later in this chapter we will even be able to rather accurately predict temperature by counting the number of chirps from crickets. But it is first necessary to examine just how regression lines are computed.

No explanation was offered in Section 13.1 as to how the regression lines were derived. The lines were simply offered as inalterable truth. Closer examination shows that actually two rather different kinds of regressions were considered. The tree-ring example is an *exact* fit, plotted without error. A ten-year-old tree must have exactly ten growth rings, not nine or eleven or any other number. The relationship between the U.S. dollar and the Spanish *peseta* is likewise exact, without any inherent error.

But the equations for Bergmann's rule represent a rather different sort of regression. The line in Fig. 13.4 is not an exact relationship at all, but rather an *estimate* roughly describing some data points. This particular graph was derived by D. F. Roberts of the Anthropology Laboratory at Oxford University. Roberts first surveyed the anthropometric literature and then selected a series of 116 societies from around the world (Roberts 1953). The relationship between these body weights and the mean annual temperature was plotted point by point on the coordinate system shown in Fig. 13.5. Each symbol in Fig. 13.5, represents one society. This method of graphical representation in which *N* pairs of values for *X* and *Y* are arranged into a coordinate system is called a *scatter diagram*, or simply a *scattergram*, so these points represent the actual data relevant to Bergmann's rule. The problem now becomes how to describe these 116 independent points by one simple line.

Unfortunately, any number of lines could be drawn through the points swarming about Fig. 13.5. If ten people were asked to "eyeball" a line to describe the points, ten different regression lines would undoubtedly result. But ten lines describing one phenomenon are not succinct summaries of data, and the problem becomes: How to choose?

A regression line is a linear function, and the direction of that line is completely determined by the values of α and β in the equation $Y = \alpha + \beta X$. Thus, the problem of *fitting a line to scattergram points reduces simply to determining values for α and β such that the N points lie as closely as possible to the regression line.* Remember that regression lines predict the values of *Y*, given values of *X*. Then this equation must be derived from a scattergram, and the resulting predictions are subject to error precisely because the points tend to scatter. One way to minimize this error would be to draw a line such that exactly half the points would fall above the line and half below. The errors could then be said to "cancel out." But this definition is still unsuitable because many such lines exist and would bisect a swarm of points. A truly satisfactory line of regression must be unique.

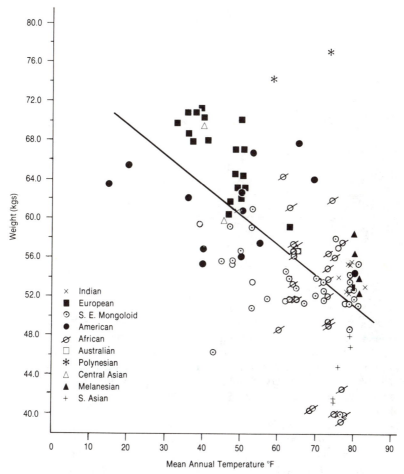

Fig. 13.5   Scattergram used to generate equation for Bergmann's rule in Fig. 13.4 (after Roberts 1953: fig. 7).

In practice, the most suitable fit for a regression line is given by the *criterion of least squares*. Simply defined, the least squares fit places a line such that the *sum of squares of the vertical deviations from this line is minimized*. Consider the graph in Fig. 13.6. Each point has two coordinates, the specific value of random variable X (denoted by X_i) and the specific value of the random variable Y (called Y_i). The duty of the regression line is to estimate Y_i, given X_i. There is no error associated with X_i because this figure is arbitrarily selected. Given X_i, find Y_i. Hence, the total error of estimate in least squares linear regression relates only to the random variable Y. This is an important point.

A glance at Fig. 13.6 reveals that there must actually be *two values* of the random variable Y associated with a given X_i. First there are the actual observed values of Y. These are the Y_i which comprise the empirical data, such as the 116 societies plotted on Fig. 13.5. But there is also a second meaning of Y implied on all scattergrams, and that is the value of Y *estimated* by the least squares

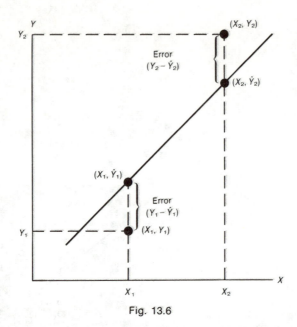

Fig. 13.6

line. Let us call these estimated values the $\hat{Y}_i$. The estimated $\hat{Y}_i$ are computed from the least squares regression equation $Y = \alpha + \beta$ (we will see in a moment how to find these values for α and β). Because the $\hat{Y}_i$ are given by the regression equation, it follows that all $\hat{Y}_i$ must lie directly upon the least squares line. To reiterate: The *observed* data are represented by the Y_i of a scattergram. The *expected* values of Y, all of which lie directly on the regression line, are denoted by $\hat{Y}_i$.

The two distinct sets of coordinates are plotted for each datum point on Fig. 13.6. The first set represents the actual *observed* values, (X_i, Y_i). Also present is the estimated value of each point, predicted by the regression line. The coordinates of the estimated position are $(X_i, \hat{Y}_i)$. Only the Y_i values have been estimated (by $\hat{Y}_i$); the X_i are known and hence error-free. The accuracy of estimation for the least squares line of regression can be judged by the distance between the observed and expected positions, given by $|Y_i - \hat{Y}_i|$. If the regression line (a prediction) passed directly through every observed point, then no error is involved because $\Sigma |Y_i - \hat{Y}_i| = 0$.

But few estimates are that accurate. Most data will have points lying some distance from the regression line. The error for the first datum point on Fig. 13.6 is given by $|Y_1 - \hat{Y}_1|$. This is a measure of how far the actual point lies away from its expected location in the least squares line. The error for the second point is $|Y_2 - \hat{Y}_2|$ and that for the Nth point is $|Y_N - \hat{Y}_N|$. The least squares method places a line of regression such that the *sum of squares* of the differences between observed and expected values of Y is kept at the smallest possible level. This is the "least squares" criterion:

$$\Sigma(Y_i - \hat{Y}_i)^2 = (Y_1 - \hat{Y}_1)^2 + (Y_2 - \hat{Y}_2)^2 + \cdots + (Y_N - \hat{Y}_N)^2$$
$$= minimum$$

Because all the X_i are "fixed" by arbitrary decision, the total error of estimation is restricted to the vertical (Y) dimension. The least squares fit minimizes these vertical distances between the swarm of points and the regression line describing them.

The issue now becomes relatively straightforward: Given a swarm of points (that is, N observed pairs of Y_i and X_i), find the constants α and β such that $\Sigma(Y_i - \hat{Y}_i)^2$ is a minimum. This problem is solved only by methods beyond the present scope—the formula is derived in Hays (1973:622–623) and Cramér (1946:271–272)—and β is given by the following formula:

$$\beta = \frac{\Sigma(X - \mu_X)(Y - \mu_Y)}{\Sigma(X - \mu_X)^2}$$

$$= \frac{\Sigma XY - N\mu_X\mu_Y}{\Sigma X^2 - N\mu_X^2} \tag{13.2}$$

As before, the constant β represents the slope of the regression line. Equation (13.2) might look somewhat forbidding at first, but closer inspection reveals that the computations are really quite straightforward. Only a few readily determined values are necessary: N (the number of pairs), μ_X, and μ_Y (the means of both variables), ΣX^2 and ΣXY (the sum of the cross products). (This expression is actually a *computing* formula, similar to those introduced earlier for finding the variance.)

Once β has been computed, it remains only to find α. Although not discussed here, the derivation of least squares regression stipulates that the line must always pass through the means of both dimensions, μ_X and μ_Y. (These means are, of course, computed from the observed datum points rather than the $\hat{Y}_i$, the estimated values of Y.) By substituting the mean values into Formula (13.1) and solving this formula for the constant α,

$$\alpha = \mu_Y - \beta\mu_X \tag{13.3}$$

Constants α and β now define the least squares estimate of the regression equation. The resulting line of regression is the "best fit" because the squared deviations for Y_i from $\hat{Y}_i$ have been minimized. Whenever the least squares method is used, it is customary to denote the regression equation as

$$\hat{Y} = \alpha + \beta X \tag{13.4}$$

The circumflex indicates that values of $\hat{Y}_i$ are *estimated*, but not known. These new methods are illustrated by a simplified example.

We know that body weight increases with height, but what is the exact nature of this relationship? The students in a small physical anthropology seminar were grouped by height into 2 inch intervals. One student was then randomly selected from each group and measured. In this manner, a simple sample was obtained for weight within each arbitrary height increment.

These measurements are plotted on Fig. 13.7. The X variates are graphed on the abscissa as usual. X is "fixed" in this case because each 2 inch height class has been purposely selected rather than randomly sampled. There is no sampling error on X because students were simply assigned to the correct group. The weights become the Y variates in this study, and are plotted on the vertical axis. Each Y_i is a random sample of weight from within a particular

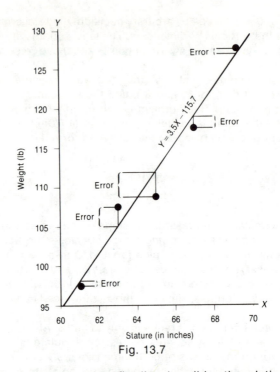

Fig. 13.7

height class. The problem now is to fit a line describing the relationship between these five datum points. The equation of this line can then be used as a loose analogy to estimate the unknown weights for fossil material.

Five quantities are necessary for the least squares method of regression: ΣX, ΣX^2, ΣY, ΣXY, and N. These values are found in Table 13.1, so the constant β is found from Expression (13.2):

$$\beta = \frac{36{,}475 - 5(65)(111.8)}{21{,}165 - 5(65^2)} = +3.5$$

α is found from Formula (13.3):

$$\alpha = 111.8 - 3.5(65) = -115.7$$

TABLE 13.1

Height Class, inches	X, Class Midpoint inches	Y, Weight, lb	XY	X₂
60–62	61	98	5,978	3,721
62–64	63	107	6,741	3,969
64–66	65	109	7,085	4,225
66–68	67	117	7,839	4,489
68–70	69	128	8,832	4,761
	$\Sigma X = 325$	$\Sigma Y = 559$	36,475	21,165

$\mu_X = 325/5 = 65.0$ in.; $\mu_Y = 559/5 = 111.8$ lb.; $N = 5$.

The final regression equation describing these data is given by Expression (13.4):

$$\hat{Y} = \alpha + \beta X$$
$$= -115.7 + 3.5X$$
$$= 3.5X - 115.7$$

This line can now be fitted to the datum points by substituting some arbitrarily selected sample values. Take the hypothetical value of $X_i = 60$. By substituting into the regression Equation (13.4), we find that when X_i is 60 in., then $\hat{Y}_i = 94.3$ lb. This point must lie on the regression line. Similarly, when $X_i = 70$ in., the least squares equation tells us that $\hat{Y}_i = 129.3$ lb. We now have two points which must lie on the line of regression. Because two points always define a line, the new regression line describing the population of five datum points can be drawn on Fig. 13.7.

To summarize: The least squares criterion is a method of computing values of α and β. This is simple statistical description. The least squares regression equation, $\hat{Y} = \alpha + \beta X$, is thus equivalent to other descriptive measures such as the mean, the median, or the variance. As do all descriptive statistics, the data being described may represent either a sample or a population. If the data constitute a statistical population, then the descriptive summary is called a parameter. If the data are sampled from a sample, then the descriptive measure is a statistic. No statistical inference has taken place so far.

Example 13.1

The table below presents some blood pressure data from a sample of American Indians of the Trio and Wajana tribes of Surinam. These figures were collected by Glanville and Geerdink in 1967 and 1968 on the Upper Courantyne, Lawa, and Tapanahony rivers where missions had recently been established (Glanville and Geerdink 1972).

Find the regression equation which best describes this statistical population.

Age Group (midpoint), X	Diastolic Blood Pressure, Y	X^2	XY	Y^2
5	60	25	300	3,600
7	63	49	441	3,969
9	69	81	621	4,761
11	74	121	814	5,476
13	75	169	975	5,625
15	71	225	1,065	5,041
17	77	289	1,309	5,929
19	85	361	1,615	7,225
21	78	441	1,638	6,084
117	652	1,761	8,778	47,710

$\mu_X = 13.0$ years; $\mu_Y = 72.4$ mm; $N = 9$.

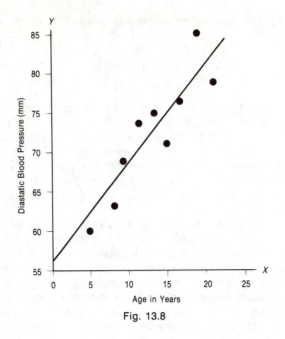

Fig. 13.8

The first step in all problems of linear regression is to plot the scattergram (Fig. 13.8). This helps to determine whether a linear solution is applicable. The data in this case appear to fall in roughly linear fashion, so computation of the regression equation can be attempted.

The multiplicative constant is found to be

$$\beta = \frac{8778 - 9(13.0)(72.4)}{1761 - 9(13.0)^2} = \frac{307.2}{240}$$

$$= 1.28$$

By substitution, the Y-intercept is

$$\alpha = 72.4 - 1.28(13.0) = 55.76$$

The regression equation for the relationship is thus

$$\hat{Y} = 55.8 + 1.28X$$

This line can now be plotted by solving the equation for several arbitrary values of X.

When X is $\cdots$	then $\hat{Y}$ must be
6	63.4
10	68.6
20	81.40

This line has been added to the scattergram. Note that the line of regression must pass through both μ_X and μ_Y.

Example 13.2

Use Kroeber's data (Kroeber 1925: 891) on California Indian populations (Table 3.1) to find the line of regression best describing the depopulation in California between 1835 and 1860.

In this case, *time* is the *predictor* variable (X) and *population* is the *predicted* variable (Y). The scattergram indicates that these data plot on a relatively straight line, but the standard regression procedures are complicated by the large numbers involved (Fig. 13.9). Each variable will be

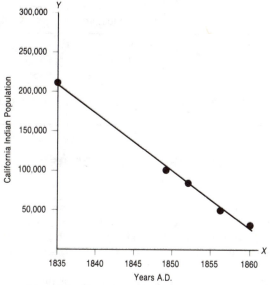

Fig. 13.9   (Data from Kroeber 1925: 891).

coded for easier computations. *Time* can be coded by subtracting 1800 from each variate; since time is relatively distributed, this coding simply takes A.D. 1800 as point zero rather than the year A.D./B.C. Population will be coded as $0.0001Y$. The computations are as follows:

Time		Population			
Raw Data	Coded Data, X	Raw Data	Coded Data, $\hat{Y}$	X^2	XY
1,835	35	210,000	21.0	1,225	735.0
1,849	49	100,000	10.0	2,401	490.0
1,852	52	85,000	8.5	2,704	442.0
1,856	56	50,000	5.0	3,136	280.0
1,860	60	35,000	3.5	3,600	210.0
	252		48.0	13,066	2157.0

$\mu_X = 50.4$ years; $\mu_Y = 9.6$ people; $N = 5$.

The regression constants are computed as usual

$$\beta = \frac{2157 - 5(50.4)(9.6)}{13066 - 5(50.4)^2} = -0.718$$

$$\alpha = 9.6 + 0.718(50.4) = 45.79$$

Thus, the *coded* regression equation is

$$\hat{Y} = 45.79 - 0.718X$$

Sample values can now be computed, decoded by reversing the coding procedure, and the regression line plotted.

When (coded) X is $\cdots$	then (coded) Y must be	Decoded X	Decoded $\hat{Y}$
40	17.07	1840	170,700
50	9.89	1850	96,900
55	6.30	1855	63,000

The resulting line of regression has been plotted on the scattergram.

13.3 ESTIMATING THE ERRORS OF REGRESSION FOR POPULATIONS

So far we have simply assumed that a linear relationship exists between the random variable X and Y. But the least squares procedure can be applied to *any* array of N points, whether or not a linear relationship holds; so, it becomes necessary to determine whether or not the regression equation is meaningful to a specific set of data. Consider the following example.

Clinical researchers have developed a number of methods to determine a child's age, based strictly upon skeletal evidence. One common source of data is the *Greulich–Pyle Atlas*, which presents standardized X-rays of wrist and hand ossification. The X-rays of any living child can be assigned a "skeletal age" by comparison with the standards from this Atlas. Data on 52 subadult males were collected by the Denver Child Research Council in order to assess the accuracy of skeletal age, and the least squares method was used to fit a line to these points. Consider these $N = 52$ observations to be a statistical population. Are the expected values, the $\hat{Y}_i$, on a straight line?

The first important measure of linearity in a population is known as the *standard error of estimate.* So far, we have explicitly assumed that no errors are involved on the X random variable. All the errors of estimation are due to deviations in a vertical (Y) direction. The chronological ages plotted on Fig. 13.10 qualify under this model because there are no errors in finding chronological age; we know this from birth records. The total deviation between the 52 points and the regression line must be due to errors involved in reading the wrist X-rays. This error is given by $\Sigma(Y_i - \hat{Y}_i)^2$. The *average error* for each point is found simply by dividing the summed squared deviations by $N = 52$, the number

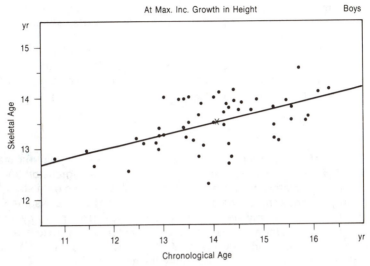

Fig. 13.10   Scattergram of skeletal age against chronological age at the time of maximum increment of growth for 52 boys (after Maresh 1971: fig. 5).

TABLE 13.2   Computations for Fig. 13.10.

$\Sigma X = 730.20$ years; $\Sigma X^2 = 10,334.98$ years^2

$\Sigma Y = 701.60$ years; $\Sigma Y^2 = 9,480.44$ years^2

$\Sigma XY = 9,870.39$ years^2; $N = 52$

$$\mu_x = \frac{730.20}{52} = 14.0423 \text{ years}$$

$$\mu_Y = \frac{701.60}{52} = 13.4923 \text{ years}$$

$$\beta = \frac{9870.39 - 52(14.0423)(13.4923)}{10,334.98 - 52(14.0423)^2} = 0.225$$

$$\alpha = 13.4923 - 0.225(14.0423) = 10.33 \text{ years}$$

of independent variates in the population. This new index of average deviation is known as the (*population*) *mean squared error of estimate*, denoted by $\sigma^2_{Y \cdot x}$:

$$\sigma^2_{Y \cdot x} = \frac{\Sigma (Y_i - \hat{Y}_i)^2}{N} \tag{13.5}$$

The mean squared error indicates the variance for Y, given X. The mean squared error of estimate for Fig. 13.10 is $\sigma^2_{Y \cdot x} = 0.194$ years^2. This measure denotes the degree of variation between the actual population of $N = 52$ points and the least square estimates of the regression line, $\hat{Y} = 10.33 + 0.225 X$. If all the population points were to fall exactly on the regression line, then the relationship would be perfectly linear and $\sigma^2_{Y \cdot x} = 0.0$. The larger the mean squared error, the greater is the deviation from linearity. A strong analogy exists between the mean square error of estimate and the population variance: Whereas σ^2 accounts for the variability about a single *point* (μ), $\sigma^2_{Y \cdot X}$ considers the variability about a single *line*, determined by $\hat{Y} = \alpha + \beta$.

Unfortunately, $\sigma^2_{Y \cdot X}$ is expressed in *squared units*, such as years², cm², or grams². This shortcoming, encountered with the population variance, is remedied by taking the square root of the parameter. Hence, the (*population*) *standard error of estimate* is defined as

$$\sigma_{Y \cdot X} = \sqrt{\frac{\Sigma(Y_i - \hat{Y}_i)^2}{N}}$$

(13.6)

The meaning of $\sigma_{Y \cdot X}$ is really quite close to that of the population standard deviation. The predictions resulting from a least squares regression line with a small $\sigma_{Y \cdot X}$ will be relatively accurate. That is, the $\hat{Y}_i$, which lie on a straight line, satisfactorily describe the observed Y_i. A large standard error of estimate warns that the relationship is only weakly linear, and hence description by a straight line lacks accuracy. When $\sigma_{Y \cdot X}$ is small, a knowledge of any X_i tells us a great deal about the corresponding value of Y_i. When $\sigma_{Y \cdot X} = 0$, then $\hat{Y}_i = Y_i$, and the relationship between X and Y is perfectly linear.

As with the standard deviation, a useful shortcut computing formula simplifies calculation of the population standard error of estimate for regression. Not only are the computations involved in Equation (13.6) too laborious, but the numerous subtractions tend to introduce considerable errors of rounding. The following computational formula is always preferred for finding the standard error of estimate:

$$\sigma_{Y \cdot X} = \sqrt{\frac{\Sigma Y^2 - \alpha \Sigma Y - B \Sigma X Y}{N}}$$

(13.7)

The only new quantity required by the computing formula is ΣY^2; all the remaining sums are required to find the regression constants α and β. The regression of skeletal age on chronological age is found to have a population standard error of estimate of

$$\sigma_{Y \cdot X} = \sqrt{\frac{9480.44 - 10.33(701.60) - 0.225(9870.39)}{52}}$$

$$= 0.482 \text{ year}$$

Measuring goodness of fit for regression can be approached in an alternative method. The average skeletal age of the population of $N = 52$ pre-adults plotted in Fig. 13.8 is known to be $\mu_Y = 13.49$ years. The variability about μ_Y is customarily denoted by the population standard deviation, as

$$\sigma_Y = \sqrt{\frac{\Sigma(Y_i - \mu_Y)^2}{N}}$$

Using computing Formula (4.18), we find that the population standard deviation for skeletal age is

$$\sigma_Y = \sqrt{\frac{\Sigma Y_i^2 - [(\Sigma Y_i)^2/N]}{N}} = \sqrt{\frac{9480 - (701.6^2/52)}{52}}$$

$$= 0.515 \text{ year}$$

Two estimates of variability in the Y_i are thus available: The population standard error of estimate, $\sigma_{Y \cdot x} = 0.482$ year, and the population standard deviation, $\sigma_Y = 0.515$ year. It is clear that the least squares regression line provides a more accurate estimator of the Y_i than does the mere standard deviation of Y. The *improvement in estimation* of the linear estimate over the point estimate can be expressed as the ratio of the mean squared standard error of estimate, $\sigma_{Y \cdot x}^2$, to the population variance, σ_Y^2:

$$k^2 = \frac{\sigma_{Y \cdot x}^2}{\sigma_Y^2} \tag{13.8}$$

The expression k^2 is known as the *Coefficient of Nondetermination*, and its meaning should be obvious: k^2 represents the proportion of variability in the Y variable which remains *unexplained* after the nature of the X and Y articulation has been assessed by $\sigma_{Y \cdot x}^2$. That is, k^2 tells us how much variability the regression equation does not "account for." When k^2 is equal to zero (that is, $\sigma_{Y \cdot x} = 0.0$), then a perfect correspondence between X and Y must exist because all the variability in Y can be accounted for by a knowledge of X. This means that $\hat{Y}_i = Y_i$ for all i. Conversely, when k^2 equals unity, no relationship exists at all: X tells us exactly nothing about Y. The Coefficient of Nondetermination for the example of skeletal versus chronological age is

$$k^2 = \frac{0.482^2}{0.515^2} = \frac{0.2323}{0.2652} = 0.876$$

This value of k^2 tells us that the regression of the Y_i on X *fails to account* for about 88 percent of the total variability known to exist in Y_i. We could also reverse this coin and concentrate upon the amount of variance *explained* by regression, as expressed by the *Coefficient of Determination* (ρ^2):

$$\rho^2 = 1 - k^2 = 1 - \frac{\sigma_{Y \cdot x}^2}{\sigma_Y^2} \tag{13.9}$$

The Coefficient of Determination, denoted by the Greek letter ρ^2, is merely the complement of k^2. The above value of $k^2 = 0.876$ must have $\rho^2 = 1.0 - 0.876 = 0.124$. The Coefficient of Determination indicates that the regression equation accounts for only about 12 percent of the variability in skeletal age. The choice between k^2 and ρ^2 reflects only one's philosophy: optimistic (percent explained by ρ^2) or pessimistic (percent unexplained by k^2).

One further index of interest is the square root of the Coefficient of Determination:

$$\rho = \sqrt{\rho^2} = \sqrt{1 - \frac{\sigma_{Y \cdot x}^2}{\sigma_Y^2}} \tag{13.10}$$

The symbol ρ is also known as the *population correlation coefficient*. This measure, an extremely important index of the bivariate relationships between two normally distributed populations, is used in practice considerably more often than either coefficients of determination or nondetermination. So important is rho that Chapter 14 is devoted to discussion of the correlation coefficient.

13.4 LEAST SQUARES REGRESSION AS STATISTICAL INFERENCE

Hubert Blalock (1972: 364) calls regression lines the *laws* of social science: All else being equal, a knowledge of X sufficiently predicts the behavior of Y. But anthropologists are accustomed to accepting some rather loosely constructed "laws," not only because of the crude measurements, but also because of the general variability of human behavior. Most social scientists freely acknowledge that while the laws of the physical scientists are quite exact, social and behavioral laws must always remain less precise, more fluid, only actuarial in nature. It seems that the laws of social science have a built-in degree of variability. So, if social scientists indeed seek the "underlying laws" governing human behavior, and if regression equations can serve as one expression of these laws, *how then is the sampling variability in regression to be handled*?

Regression lines have been treated simply as descriptive devices used to summarize populations of bivariate points. The equation $\hat{Y} = 7179.6X - 13,189,132$ *describes* the quantitative depopulation of California Indians between 1835 and 1860; the expression $\hat{Y} = 3.5X - 115.7$ *describes* the relationship between stature and weight in a certain physical anthropology seminar; the equation $\hat{Y} = 10.33 + 0.225X$ *describes* the relationship between chronological age and skeletal age in 52 subadults from the Denver area. Used in this manner, regression is a tool which allows anthropologists to fit descriptive lines to known populations of points.

Accordingly, the indices derived in Section 13.3 were all based upon *populations* of variates, and Greek letters were used to denote the population parameters. But regression fulfills a more critical niche in anthropology than does mere description. Regression lines computed for *samples of variates* and the least squares equations used in statistical inference to predict an unknown parameter seem an observed sample. Regression equations have functioned to this point only in the limited capacity of descriptive devices. Regression can now be treated as a tool for inferential statistics.

Figure 13.11 illustrates the sampling distribution for the regression equation. For every value of X there exists a *distribution* of Y_i values. The regression equation estimates one single value ($\hat{Y}_i$) of these values. The prediction $\hat{Y}_i$ occurs on the regression line directly above the preselected value on the X-axis. But the actual observed values of the Y variable—denoted simply by Y_i—could lie anywhere on the vertical axis above the given X value, as illustrated in Fig. 13.9. The predicted value Y_i resulting from the least squares equation is thus taken as an estimator of the theoretical mean of the distribution of Y_i at point X_i. A different normal distribution holds for every interval along the X-axis. The scatter of such points depends not only upon the value of $\hat{Y}_i$ (the estimated mean above X_i) but also upon the shape of the population about the line of regression. If the population of points lies close to the line, then the observed sample of points should also land rather close to the line of regression.

Section 13.3 introduced the concept of the population standard error of estimate due to regression. The average error was determined for every Y_i in a population by dividing the sum of squared deviations by the number of points. $\sigma_{Y \cdot X}$ is a population parameter, applicable whenever an entire population of

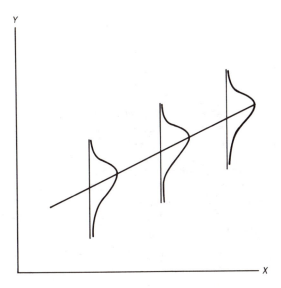

Fig. 13.11

variates can be observed, but when this complete population is only partly visible—when this population has been *sampled*—then the parameter $\sigma_{Y \cdot x}$ can be *estimated* only by an appropriate sample statistic. Let us denote the (*sample*) *standard error of estimate* as $S_{Y \cdot x}$:

$$S_{Y \cdot x} = (\text{estimate of } \sigma_{Y \cdot x}) = \sqrt{\frac{\Sigma(Y_i - \hat{Y}_i)^2}{n - 2}} \qquad (13.11)$$

$S_{Y \cdot x}$ is a sample statistic which functions as do other statistics considered earlier. The sample standard deviation, for example, was used as an estimator of the population standard deviation whenever only a sample of size $n < N$ was available. The population standard deviation, σ_x, was computed with a denominator of simply N, thereby providing average variability for each variate within the population. But a slight modification in S_x was computed with a denominator of $(n - k)$, where k denoted the number of degrees of freedom lost in the act of computing the standard deviation. Because $\bar{X}$ was required before S_x could be computed, exactly one degree of freedom was lost, so S_x was computed with a denominator of $(n - 1)$.

A parallel situation holds when the standard error is estimated for regression. The population parameter was computed strictly as the average squared deviation per variate pair, with a denominator of N. But to obtain an estimate of $\sigma_{Y \cdot x}$, one must consider the number of degrees of freedom lost due to computations. In this case, $k = 2$, which means that two previously computed quantities are necessary: the regression coefficients α and β. So it is that the denominator of Expression (13.11) contains $(n - 2)$, whereas the denominator of $\sigma_{Y \cdot x}$ is simply N.

The population standard error of estimate was computed earlier to be $\sigma_{Y \cdot x} = \sqrt{12.074/52} = 0.482$ year. $\sigma_{Y \cdot x}$ is a parameter describing a population of

52 variates. If the 52 subjects had been considered to be a *sample* of size $n = 52$ (rather than a *population* of size $N = 52$), then the sample standard error of estimation would properly be

$$S_{Y \cdot X} = \sqrt{\frac{12.074}{52 - 2}} = 0.491 \text{ year}$$

The difference in value between parameter and statistic in this case is virtually nil because of the large sample size. But in the blood pressure example (Example 13.1) with $N = 9$, the difference is rather large: $S_{Y \cdot X} - \sigma_{Y \cdot X} = 4.117 - 3.631 = 0.486$ mm. This discrepancy, apparent in all small samples, causes certain sampling difficulties which will be subsequently considered.

As with most estimators of variability, the standard error of regression is based upon deviations about means. But a *computing formula* is available which enables computation of standard error of estimate without the necessity of finding each individual deviation:

$$S_{Y \cdot X} = \sqrt{\frac{\Sigma Y^2 - a \Sigma Y - b \Sigma XY}{n - 2}} \qquad (13.12)$$

This formula is generally preferable to (13.11) because errors of rounding are minimized.

The confidence limits about a specific regression prediction are given as

$$\text{confidence limits} = \hat{Y} \pm t S_{\hat{Y}} \qquad (13.13)$$

where

$$S_{\hat{Y}} = S_{Y \cdot X} \sqrt{\frac{1}{n} + \frac{(X - \bar{X})^2}{(\Sigma X_i^2 - (\Sigma X_i)^2 / n)}}$$

for a specific value of X and $(n - 2)$ degrees of freedom. The general format of Expression (13.13) should be familiar: Confidence limits are defined as some critical region on either side of some mean, this interval being defined by t and $S_{\hat{Y}}$. The t-value is determined as before from Table A.4 by the appropriate level of significance (95 percent confidence interval, 99 percent confidence interval, etc.) and also by the number of degrees of freedom, in this case $(n - 2)$ degrees of freedom. The measure of variability, $S_{\hat{Y}}$, is the direct analog of $S_{\bar{X}}$ which was used in earlier confidence limits computations. Just as $S_{\bar{X}}$ is the standard error of the mean $\bar{X}$, so is $S_{\hat{Y}}$ the standard error of the estimate $\hat{Y}$. Remember that these confidence limits apply only to the specified value of X and not to the entire regression equation.

We are now in a position to use the least squares estimate as an inferential statistic. Let us return to the case of blood pressure among the Surinamese (Example 13.1). Remember that the informants were considered earlier to constitute a population of $N = 9$ variates. The relationship between age (X) and blood pressure (Y) was described by the standard regression equation:

$$Y = \alpha + \beta X = 55.8 + 1.28X$$

Suppose now that these same informants are taken to represent a sample of size $n = 9$, which was randomly selected from the biological population of all

Surinamese. (To accomplish such sampling, it would be necessary to independently draw a single informant from each age group.) The population parameters are unknown in this situation, and must be estimated by sample statistics. To keep this new distinction straight, it is necessary to redefine the regression equation. The regression coefficients α and β are now unknown parameters, which must be estimated by sample statistics, which we denote as a and b. The *least squares regression equation for samples* is thus

$$\hat{Y} = a + bX \qquad\qquad (13.14)$$

The new statistics a and b are defined identically to α and β except that all parameters have been replaced by statistics:

$$b = \frac{\Sigma(X - \bar{X})(Y - \bar{Y})}{\Sigma(X - \bar{X})^2} = \frac{\Sigma\,XY - n\bar{X}\bar{Y}}{\Sigma\,X^2 - n\bar{X}^2} \qquad (13.15)$$

$$a = \bar{Y} - b\bar{X} \qquad\qquad (13.16)$$

The symbolism of regression might seem a bit excessive, but this is really necessary in order to keep the descriptive functions of least squares regression from its inferential function.

The least squares equation describing the *sample* of $n = 9$ Surinam informants is therefore

$$\hat{Y} = a + bX = 55.8 + 1.28X$$

The numbers here remain unchanged from Example 13.1, although now a is taken to estimate α and b estimates β.

How is this regression expression used as an inferential statistic? Suppose that we wish to predict the blood pressure of a ten-year-old Surinamese. The regression equation for $X = 10$ yields $\hat{Y}$:

$$\hat{Y} = 55.8 + 1.28(10) = 68.6 \text{ mm}$$

Of course nobody should expect that all ten-year-old Surinam informants will have exactly this blood pressure, but $\hat{Y}$ serves as an estimate for the average blood pressure of ten-year-olds. The sample standard error of regression was computed previously to be $S_{Y \cdot X} = 4.117$ mm, so the 95 percent confidence limits are given by Formula (13.13):

$$\text{confidence limits} = \hat{Y} \pm t_{0.05} S_{\hat{Y}}$$

$$= 68.6 \pm 2.365(4.117) \sqrt{\frac{1}{9} + \frac{(10.0 - 13.0)^2}{1761 - 117^2/9}}$$

$$= 68.6 \pm 2.365(1.587)$$

$$= 68.6 \pm 3.753 \text{ mm}$$

The value of $t_{0.05}$ was found from Table A.4 listed under $(9 - 2) = 7$ degrees of freedom. At the 95 percent confidence level, we expect a randomly selected ten-year-old Surinam male to have a blood pressure reading greater than 64.85 mm but less than 72.35.

Select another age, say, $X = 6$ years. The regression prediction is $\hat{Y} =$

63.44 mm, with the following 95 percent confidence interval:

$$\text{confidence limits} = 63.4 \pm 2.365(4.117)\sqrt{\frac{1}{9} + \frac{(6.0-13.0)^2}{1761-117^2/9}}$$

$$= 63.4 \pm 2.365(2.311)$$

$$= 63.4 \pm 5.466 \text{ mm}\cdot$$

Similarly, the 95 percent confidence interval for $X = 20$ years is

$$\text{confidence limits} = 81.4 \pm 2.365(4.117)\sqrt{\frac{1}{9} + \frac{(20.0-13.0)^2}{1761-117^2/9}}$$

$$= 81.4 \pm 5.466 \text{ mm}$$

Note that these confidence intervals about every Y_i are *specific for a given X.* The confidence interval for $\hat{Y} = 68.6$ mm (corresponding to $X = 10$) are ± 3.753 mm, while those for an age of $X = 6$ are ± 5.466 mm. The closer the samples fall to the mean of X (in this case, $\bar{X} = 13.0$ years), the smaller will be the confidence interval about $\hat{Y}$. That is, the predictions become less accurate as the given X deviates from $\bar{X}$. Note further that because $X = 6$ and $X = 20$ are equidistant from the mean age of $\bar{X} = 13.0$ years, the confidence intervals are identical.

These three confidence intervals have been plotted on Fig. 13.12. The enclosed

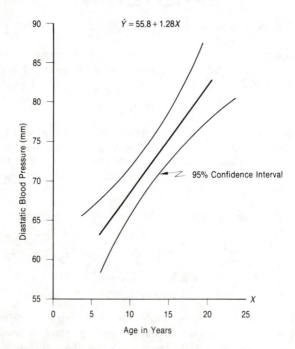

Fig. 13.12 Regression of blood pressure and age for Surinam informants (data from Glanville and Geerdink 1972: table 2).

area represents the approximate 95 percent confidence band for the total regression equation. This band does not parallel the line of regression; rather it pinches in toward the mean and fans out as one deviates from the mean because predictions about the mean of X are known to be more accurate than those some distance from $\bar{X}$. Furthermore, note that the confidence band about the regression line does not extend beyond the observed range of the sample variates.

Example 13.3

Determine the standard error of estimate for the stature-weight data in Fig. 13.7.

The sample standard error of estimate can be found using Formula (13.12), a method which entails actually computing the deviations between observed and predicted variates.

X	Y	$\hat{Y} = a + bX$	$\|Y - \hat{Y}\|$	$\|Y - \hat{Y}\|^2$
61	98	$3.5(61) - 115.7 = 97.8$	0.2	0.04
63	107	$3.5(63) - 115.7 = 104.8$	2.2	4.84
65	109	$3.5(65) - 115.7 = 111.8$	2.8	7.84
67	117	$3.5(67) - 115.7 = 118.8$	1.8	3.24
69	128	$3.5(69) - 115.7 = 125.8$	2.2	4.84
				20.80

Substituting into (13.11),

$$S_{Y \cdot X} = \sqrt{\frac{20.80}{3}} = 2.63 \text{ lb}$$

The computing formula allows much easier computation, however, because the sums involved are the same as those used in Table 13.1 to find a and b.

$$S_{Y \cdot X} = \sqrt{\frac{63,007 - (-115.7)559 - 3.5(36,475)}{3}}$$

$$= \sqrt{\frac{20.80}{3}} = 2.63 \text{ lb}$$

The only new quantity required is Y^2. Whenever tables of computations are framed, one should usually include a column for Y^2. Even though Y^2 is not directly involved in finding the regression equation, this sum is handy when assessing errors of regression.

13.5 ASSUMPTIONS OF LEAST SQUARES REGRESSION

The least squares method has been used for two distinct purposes in this chapter: Description and inference. As long as the objective is simply to describe a swarm of points, the assumptions need not trouble us. It is not necessary to assume anything about the form of the distribution or the variability of the Y_i over the X_i, or even to worry about the level of measurement implied (Hays 1973: 636). All a least squares description does is treat N distinct cases *as if* they were linear. The regression equation describes the population of points in terms of their tendency to associate in a linear fashion. This description is tenable only for the exact N points considered.

But when the least squares method is used to generate inferences about unknown values of $\hat{Y}$, then some important assumptions are required:

1. The predictor variable, X, is measured without error. The levels of X_i are to be arbitrarily selected beforehand by the investigator and do not result from any sort of sampling operation. There is only one special situation, however (the so-called *Berkson case*), which permits a special sort of error to creep into the X_i. As long as the errors on X are strictly resultant from inaccuracies of measurement or the lack of suitable experimental precision, then least squares regression can still be valid. That is, if informants are selected for age, a certain amount of error might result among nonliterate subjects who are truly ignorant of their age. Or when students are grouped into classes of increasing stature, there may be some small error due to using a 1 meter tape. Errors of this kind can be permitted only as long as their magnitude is totally unrelated to the magnitude of the variate (see Sokal and Rohlf 1969: 482–483). This sort of error occurs on Fig. 13.5. With only this exception, random fluctuation of X is not permitted in least squares procedure.

2. The samples along the regression line are homoscedastic. Each of the normally distributed populations of Y_i above each X must have the same variance. That is, the $\sigma_{Y \cdot x}$ for all X are assumed to be equal.

3. A linear relationship must exist between X and Y (or a suitable transformation must be applied; discussed in Chapter 14).

4. Both X and Y are measurable on at least an interval scale.

5. The line of regression applies only within the observed range of the X_i.

6. The Y_i for any given level of X must be independently and randomly selected from a normally distributed population above X (see Fig. 13.11).

13.6 LEAST SQUARES REGRESSION THROUGH THE ORIGIN

Situations sometimes demand that specific regression lines must commence, or pass through, the origin of the coordinate graph, and the previous example (Section 13.1) relating age to the number of annual growth rings serves as a case in point. The discussion was presented *as if* one year will always produce *precisely* one ring, but this assumption holds true only in the long run. Specific trees are known to fail to add rings in some years, or the rings are too indistinct for detection by dendrochronologists. In trees such as the bristlecone pine, several trunks often exist. Some of these trunks might be dormant at any one time, thereby failing to add rings over sometimes lengthy intervals. But despite the exigencies which introduce error into the simple $Y = X$ relationship, the regression line should still logically commence at the origin of the graph and then progress outward (as in Fig. 13.1). When the age is zero, there must be zero tree rings, regardless of what random errors are introduced by climatic and physiological factors.

It becomes useful in many such cases to fit a special line of regression which automatically begins at the origin $(0, 0)$. This is a limited case of the general regression situation $Y = a + bX$, in which the Y-intercept is a priori defined to be $a = 0.0$. That is, this line of regression is required to intercept the Y-axis at point zero. So, the formula for the *regression through the origin* reduces simply to

$$\hat{Y} = b''X \qquad (13.17)$$

where $b'' = \Sigma XY / \Sigma X^2$. The superscript b'' distinguishes the slope computed from Expression (13.15) for the common slope b.

This simplified least squares estimate can be illustrated in the case of germinating plant seeds. When planted, a seed has zero height, and time of growth is also zero. The stalk then progresses steadily through both time and height, in its inexorable climb upward. Height measurements were taken at odd intervals on a single stalk of corn which was growing near Davis, California (Table 13.3). A regression line can be fitted to these data, using the standard $\hat{Y} = a + bX$ method (see Table 13.3), with the following result:

$$\hat{Y} = 15.3 \text{ cm} + 8.23X$$

where Y is measured in centimeters and X is age in weeks. A series of sample points can be readily generated from this expression, and the line has been fitted to the actual data in Fig. 13.11. But note that this conventional approach to regression produces a line intersecting the Y-axis at $a = 15.3$ cm. Even the rankest urbanite must surely recognize that no hybrid, regardless of its vigor, could possibly begin growth with a height of 15 cm! Although the least squares fit has adequately minimized $\Sigma(Y_i - \hat{Y}_i)^2$, the resulting equation produces substantively ridiculous results.

A more appropriate regression line would commence at the origin, thereby denoting zero height to a newly planted corn kernel. Taking the Y-intercept a priori to be $a = 0.0$, the regression Formula (13.17) is readily applicable. From the data in Table 13.3, the proper slope is found to be

$$b'' = \frac{\Sigma XY}{\Sigma X^2} = \frac{14,600}{1593} = 9.17$$

The new regression equation is thus

$$\hat{Y} = b''X = 9.17X$$

Sample values have been computed from this new equation and plotted in Fig. 13.13. The two lines of regression are nearly parallel, the difference in slope amounting to only $(b'' - b) = 9.17 - 8.23 = 0.94$ cm increase per week. But the

TABLE 13.3   Observations on one stalk of corn near Davis, California.

Age, weeks X	Height, cm Y	X^2	XY
4	56	16	224
8	81	64	648
12	110	144	1,320
14	130	196	1,820
17	150	289	2,550
20	172	400	3,440
22	209	484	4,598
97	908	1,593	14,600

$\bar{X} = 13.9$ weeks; $\bar{Y} = 129.7$ cm; $n = 7$.

Regression by standard least squares methods:

$$b = \frac{14,600 - 7(13.9)(129.7)}{1593 - 7(13.9)^2} = 8.23$$

$$a = 129.7 - 8.23(13.9) = 15.3$$

Then

$$\hat{Y} = 15.3 + 8.23X$$

Regression through the origin:

$$b = \frac{14,600}{1593} = 9.17X$$

$$\hat{Y} = 9.17X$$

15.3 cm difference in the Y-intercept causes a rather wide difference between the actual paths of the lines.

	X, Age in weeks			
Y, Height in cm	5	10	15	25
$\hat{Y} = 15.3 + 8.23X$	56.5	97.6	138.8	221.1
$\hat{Y} = 9.17X$	49.9	91.7	137.6	229.3
Difference	6.5	5.9	1.2	8.2

The difference between the two methods of regression can also be illustrated by comparing the sample values from each equation. Both regression lines pass through the sample means, so the discrepancy between predictions becomes worse as the samples diverge from the mean values.

Each prediction method possesses certain advantages. The initial equation of least squares is more accurate, providing the exact minimum value of the total error of estimate. So, when predicting a single occurrence of Y from an X—How tall will the corn be in 15 weeks?—the standard least squares method will provide superior results. But, while introducing a somewhat higher total error of

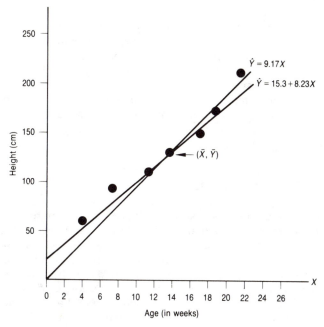

Fig. 13.13   Regression of corn height and age, plotted by least squares and through-the-origin

estimate, the regression through the origin produces a graphic solution which is more acceptable in terms of overall substantive implications. The decision as to which method is best will depend only upon the situation at hand rather than upon abstract mathematical properties.

13.7 LEAST SQUARES REGRESSION OF Y ON X VERSUS REGRESSION OF X ON Y

Care has been taken to restrict discussion to the "regression of Y on X." The X values have been taken as the *predictor* variates, fixed at predetermined values. Y has been the *predicted* variable, presumably randomly selected from the population of points above each X_i. Thus, both the mode of sampling and the substantive predictive interest serve to distinguish X from Y in the regression model considered so far. But circumstances will arise occasionally in which it becomes necessary to reverse the relationship and attempt to predict values of X, given the Y_i. A new regression equation would thus be involved:

$$\hat{X} = c + dY \tag{13.18}$$

These new regression coefficients correspond to the X-intercept and slope, except that the quantity $\Sigma(X_i - \hat{X}_i)^2$ has been minimized.

When the resulting line for Equation (13.18) is plotted, it will almost never correspond exactly to the line produced by $\hat{Y} = a + bX$. In fact, as long as error is present on *either* variable, different lines will always result. Only when all points lie exactly on their lines of regression will the two lines coincide. That is, only when $\Sigma(X_i - \hat{X}_i)^2 = \Sigma(Y_i - \hat{Y}_i)^2 = 0$ will a single regression equation apply for both X on Y and Y on X. Extreme caution is in order whenever one attempts to tamper with the predictor-predicted relationship in regression. Sokal and Rohlf (1969:446–448) have discussed methods for predicting X from a given Y, including a method to compute a confidence interval for this inverse prediction. But more often, however, the assumptions of least squares regression will not be satisfied in such cases, and a second regression method will prove a more effective means of prediction.

13.8 MODEL II REGRESSION

The regression method discussed so far has been based upon the assumptions listed in Section 13.5. Least squares methods are especially well suited for controlled experimental conditions in which the predictor values—the X_i—can be artificially "fixed" by the investigator. Errors on the X variable are thereby eliminated. Now we must consider a second method of fitting a regression line, called *Model II*. Under *Model II the X variable is no longer fixed*. The X_i are randomly selected in a manner identical to selection of the Y_i variates. In fact, the assignment of the labels "predictor" and "predicted" in Model II regression is merely for convenience because no intrinsic difference is necessary to regress X on Y or Y on X under the Model II method of regression.

When using the least squares procedure for estimation, it was necessary to assume that the Y_i were normally distributed for every X_i. No assumptions were necessary regarding X except that the level of measurement was interval scale. The sampling distribution of Model I (least squares regression, Section 13.2) was depicted in Fig. 13.11. But Model II methods of regression consider X and Y to be equivalent variables. The Y_i must be normally distributed above the X, and the X_i must likewise be normally distributed across the Y. Because both X and Y are assumed to be independent and normally distributed, the population distribution is known as *bivariate normal*. To visualize this configuration, it is necessary to conceive of a very large number of datum points stacked about the intersection of μ_X and μ_Y. Of course not all points will land exactly on the two means, so random errors will distribute the points farther and farther from this intersection. The greater these random errors, the more dispersed are the datum points. The computer-generated diagram in Fig. 13.14(a) shows that, in three dimensions, the bivariate normal distribution is bell-shaped. As long as the X and Y are measured on identical scales, the bivariate normal mound tends to be symmetrical. When differing scales of measurement are involved, or whenever correlation between X and Y is strong, the bell-shape becomes distorted into a more elliptical shape [see Fig. 13.14(b)]. Both the Model II regression and the correlation coefficient r (to be considered in detail in Chapter 14) assume that the X_i and Y_i are randomly sampled from such a bivariate normal population distribution.

Least squares models can, of course, be used to fit a line describing a bivariate normal distribution, but because of the errors on X, inferences from that line are not valid. Probably the best technique for fitting a line to random

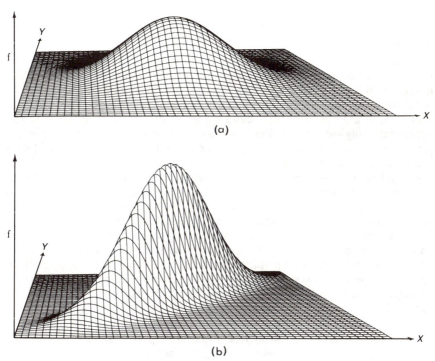

Fig. 13.14 Computer generated frequency diagrams illustrating the bivariate normal distribution. The parametric correlation between variables X and Y in Fig. 13.14(a) is equal to zero, while in Fig. 13.14(b), $\rho = 0.9$ (after Sokal and Rohlf 1969: figs. 15.1 and 15.2).

samples of X and Y is *Bartlett's Three-Group Method*. The estimates of the parametric regression coefficients are quite accurate, but an even greater advantage is that Bartlett's method is extremely easy to compute.

Originally introduced by Bartlett in 1949, this regression technique involves a few simple steps:

1. Rank the variates into descending order on one of the variables; since both variables have been randomly sampled, assignment of X and Y is arbitrary.
2. Divide the ordered array into thirds. Should the number of (X_i, Y_i) pairs not be a multiple of 3, then arrange the categories so that the first and third groups are of the same size.
3. Compute the grand means $\bar{X}$ and $\bar{Y}$ as usual, and then also find the subgroup means for the first and third groups ($\bar{X}_1$, $\bar{Y}_1$, $\bar{X}_3$, $\bar{Y}_3$).
4. The slope of the Model II regression equation is given by

$$b' = \frac{\bar{Y}_3 - \bar{Y}_1}{\bar{X}_3 - \bar{X}_1} \qquad (13.19)$$

Following Sokal and Rohlf (1969), the regression coefficients for Model II will be denoted as a' and b' to distinguish them from their Model I counterparts.

5. The Y-intercept is given by

$$a' = \bar{Y} - b'\bar{X} \qquad (13.20)$$

The resulting equation provides the "best fit" when both variables have been randomly sampled. This is not a least squares regression, so special methods are required for significance testing and confidence interval computations. The following example illustrates Bartlett's method of regression.

Like many anthropologists, I spend a good deal of my time doing fieldwork, which generally entails camping in some fairly remote spot for months on end. One summer, when I was excavating Gatecliff Shelter in central Nevada, I found myself lolling about the evening campfire, listening to the crickets and watching the sagebrush grow. The crickets reminded me that I read somewhere that crickets chirp in response to the temperature: The colder the night, the less the crickets chirp, until they finally refuse to sound off at all in freezing temperatures. I mentioned this astounding little piece of trivia to my crew members, and they must have been as desperate for entertainment as I was, because we all commenced counting cricket chirps to see how cold it was. Of course none of us knew the magic formula for converting chirps to temperature, so we decided to derive our own formula.[3] We performed the counts off and on throughout the night and the following morning, and our results are tabulated in Table 13.4.

TABLE 13.4   Field Data for cricket chirps from Monitor Valley, central Nevada.

Number of Chirps per Minute X	Temperature, °F Y	
47	50	
61	56	$\bar{X}_1 = \dfrac{180}{3} = 60.00$
72	57	$\bar{Y}_1 = \dfrac{163}{3} = 54.33$
78	57	
93	63	
106	67	
110	68	
122	73	$\bar{X}_3 = \dfrac{364}{3} = 121.33$
132	70	$\bar{Y}_3 = \dfrac{211}{3} = 70.33$

$\bar{X} = 821/9 = 91.22$; $\bar{Y} = 561/9 = 62.33$.

[3]For the uninitiated, counting cricket chirps is not as easy as it might sound. Some of the critters are boldly sounding off for all to hear, but others—perhaps the younger crickets—are squeaky and difficult to hear. We finally devised a method to reduce the error in our counts: three of us counted the same chirps for 15 sec, but the episode was recorded only if two of us agreed on our count.

The problem was this: Given the number of cricket chirps per minute (X), find the equation which will predict temperature in degrees Fahrenheit (Y). In this case, both the Y_i and the X_i have been sampled rather than arbitrarily selected; thus, the least squares approximation is invalidated. As long as the populations of cricket chirps and temperature are distributed in bivariate normal fashion, Bartlett's method of regression is appropriate. The first step in finding the magic formula for using the cricket's "vocal thermometer" is to reorder the data into ascending order of X, and divide this array into thirds. The necessary means are computed in Table 13.4, so a' and b' are computed as follows:

$$b' = \frac{\bar{Y}_3 - \bar{Y}_1}{\bar{X}_3 - \bar{X}_1} = \frac{70.33 - 54.33}{121.33 - 60.00} = 0.2609$$

$$a' = \bar{Y} - b'\bar{X} = 62.33 - (0.26)91.22 = 38.61$$

Rounding the computed values of a' and b' to quantities more suitable for field usage, the final prediction equation is thus

$$\hat{Y} = 39 + 0.26X$$

A few sample points must be computed in order to fit this line to the scattergram:

Chirps per minute (X):	50	100	150
Temperature °F (Y):	52	65	78

The data and the best fit line appear in Fig. 13.15. Note that the line determined by Bartlett's Best Fit Method not only passes through the subgroup means, but also through the grand means $\bar{X}$ and $\bar{Y}$.

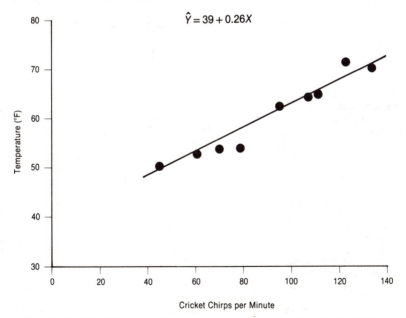

Fig. 13.15   Magic formula for connecting cricket chirps to temperature.

Because Bartlett's method does not assume fixed effects on X, the prediction equation for X from Y is simply the reverse of Y from X. If we had wished to predict the number of chirps for any particular temperature, the equation would be readily found as follows:

$$b' = \frac{\bar{X}_3 - \bar{X}_1}{\bar{Y}_3 - \bar{Y}_1} = \frac{121.33 - 60.00}{70.33 - 54.33} = 3.833$$
$$a' = \bar{X} - b'Y = 91.22 - 3.833(62.33) = -147.7$$
$$\hat{X} = 3.7Y - 148$$

Note that this revised equation will still predict the above sample values.

We noted above that Bartlett's method of finding the best-fit line has the distinct advantage of considerably easier computations than the least squares method. Unfortunately, this computational ease is more than offset by the difficulties in finding the confidence limits to Bartlett's line of regression. The interested reader is referred to discussions in Simpson, Roe, and Lewontin (1960:233–235) and Sokal and Rohlf (1969:483–486) for the appropriate methods.

The standard error of estimate is also invalid when Bartlett's Three-Group Method is used. The best measure of strength of linearity is the correlation coefficient r, which is discussed in Chapter 14.

Inference from Model II regression makes the following assumptions[4]:

1. *Variables X and Y are assumed to be in bivariate normal distribution* (see Fig. 13.12).
2. *A linear relationship must exist between X and Y.*
3. *Both X and Y are measurable on at least an interval scale.*
4. *The line of regression applies only within the observed range of the X_i.*

[4]Some confusion seems to exist about the topic of inference from linear regression, not only among the users of the technique but also among mathematical statisticians as to just which methods of regression are applicable to which empirical situations. The advocates of a *hard line* approach to regression restrict the true least squares method (Model I regression) to cases in which the values of X_i have been rigidly predetermined, as in laboratory situations or agricultural field experiments. Although a certain degree of error might creep into X through faulty observation, the variable X can still be considered to be "fixed" as long as it has not been *sampled* in the conventional sense. Some less rigorous techniques of regression are available for use whenever the variable X has been sampled rather than selected. Examples of this *hard* approach to regression are found in Sokal and Rohlf (1969), Hays (1973), Bliss (1967), and Dixon and Massey (1969).

A second perspective—I hesitate to term the *soft line*—holds that the mathematically valid distinction between fixed and random effects on X has little relevance to actual application of regression methods. To paraphrase one such advocate, the hard approach makes good mathematical statistics but rather poor science. This view is held by Simpson, Roe, and Lewontin (1960), who argue that the Model I regression techniques can be applied to X variables of any sort (fixed or random), as long as measurement is interval scale or better. The distinction is often made between the predictive (functional) and the descriptive (structural) purposes of regression equations.

Finding myself at the crossroads of this dilemma, I have opted for the hard-line approach to the related topics of regression and correlation. Models I and II regression methods are presented in a format following Sokal and Rohlf (1969), among others. Both extreme positions are represented in the recent literature of anthropology. I personally remain undecided about the efficacy of totally ignoring the mathematical strictures for fixed effects on X; and, in addition, once the more rigorous methods of regression have been mastered, then one is in excellent position to select a *hard* or *soft* posture at will, depending upon the particular applications at hand. That is, once the two models of regression are understood, then one is free to select methods from a position of strength and knowledge rather than by mere dogma. The *soft* position—at least at an introductory level—lacks this flexibility.

Example 13.4

While analyzing the archaeological findings at Fort Michilmackinac, Lewis Binford made the interesting observation that kaolin pipestems can be used to date historic archaeological sites. It seems that during the seventeenth and eighteenth centuries, the average diameter of these pipestems decreased in a remarkably consistent fashion. The relationship between site age and stem-bore diameter has been assembled by Heighton and Deagan (1971: fig. 1) for the 12 colonial archaeological sites tabulated below.

Site	Age, A.D.	Pipestem Diameter; 1/64 in.
Williamsburg (Coke Garret I)	1757	4.62
Clay Bank	1695	6.11
Tutter's Neck, Va. (Pit A)	1706	5.82
Silver Bluff, S.C.	1748	4.91
Ft. Frederica, Ga.	1743	4.91
Archer Cottage, Yorktown	1769	4.31
Ft. Michilmackinak	1768	4.55
Ft. Michilmackinak Barracks	1775	4.07
Warrasqueoi	1688	6.50
Brunswick Town	1751	4.88
Ft. Necessity	1754	4.4
Spaulding's Lower Store	1770	4.63

Find the line of regression which allows age predictions of an archaeological site from its mean stem–bore diameter.

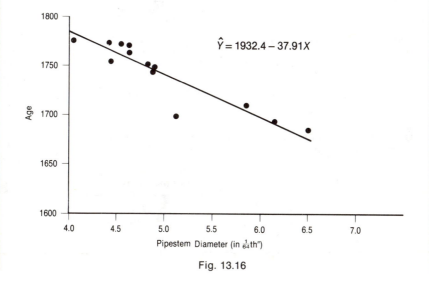

$$\hat{Y} = 1932.4 - 37.91X$$

Fig. 13.16

The least squares approximation does not apply to this case because neither variable is "fixed" in a statistical sense. Specifically, we wish to predict the age of archaeological sites (Y) from knowledge of the pipestem diameters (X), but both X and Y are random variables. The data must first be plotted to determine whether a linear description makes sense. Since these variables appear to be roughly linear in fashion, Bartlett's Model II regression can be used to estimate the best fit.

X	Y	X^2	Y^2	XY
4.07	1,775	16.56	3,150,625	7,224.25
4.31	1,769	18.58	3,129,361	7,624.39
4.4	1,754	19.36	3,076,516	7,717.60
4.55	1,768	20.70	3,125,824	8,044.40
4.62	1,757	21.34	3,087,049	8,117.34
4.62	1,770	21.44	3,132,900	8,134.91
4.88	1,751	23.81	3,066,001	8,544.88
4.91	1,743	24.11	3,038,049	8,558.13
4.91	1,748	24.11	3,055,504	8,582.68
5.82	1,706	33.87	2,910,436	9,928.92
6.11	1,695	37.33	2,873,025	10,356.45
6.50	1,688	42.25	2,849,344	10,972.00

The grand mean and group means must be computed:

$$\bar{X} = \frac{59.71}{12} = 4.98 \qquad \bar{Y} = \frac{20,924}{12} = 1743.67$$

$$\bar{X}_1 = \frac{17.33}{4} = 4.33 \qquad \bar{X}_3 = \frac{23.34}{4} = 5.84$$

$$\bar{Y}_1 = \frac{7066}{4} = 1766.50 \qquad \bar{Y}_3 = \frac{6837}{4} = 1709.25$$

The Model II regression equation constants are thus

$$b' = \frac{1709.25 - 1766.50}{5.84 - 4.33} = -37.91$$

$$a' = 1743.67 - (-37.91)(4.98) = 1932.4$$

$$\hat{Y} = 1932.4 - 37.91X$$

The following sample values indicate how this regression equation can be used by the historic archaeologist.

When the mean bore diameter is $\cdots$	The estimated age of the site is
4.25	A.D. 1771
5.00	A.D. 1743
6.00	A.D. 1705

SUGGESTIONS FOR FURTHER READING

Bliss (1967: chapter 13)
Simpson, Roe, and Lewontin (1960: chapter 11)
Sokal and Rohlf (1969: chapter 14)

EXERCISES

13.1 Given the following data:

X	Y
−2	0
1	3
3	7
4	10
7	16

(a) Find the equation of the least squares line describing these five points.
(b) Draw the scattergram and fit the regression line.
(c) What is Y when $X = 2$?
(d) Find the population standard error of estimate.

13.2 Given the following data:

X	Y
2	18
4	15
5	12
9	7
10	2

(a) Find the least squares equation describing these data.
(b) Draw the scattergram and regression line.
(c) Find the population standard error of estimate.

*13.3 Given the following variates:

X	Y
10	12
17	26
20	42
16	22
18	26
23	45
29	50
8	6
13	20

(a) Find the least squares line describing these points.

    (b) Use Model II techniques to determine the regression equation.

    (c) Plot both equations on a scattergram.

    (d) What assumptions are necessary for each method?

13.4 By studying radiographs of the fetus, McKim, Hutchinson, and Gavan (1972) derived the following regression equation projecting prenatal age from the length of the femur in the unborn rhesus monkey:

$$\hat{Y} = 50 - 0.35X$$

where $\hat{Y}$ is "days prior to birth" and X is "femoral length in millimeters."

    (a) Graph this equation.

    (b) When the femur is 20 mm in length, about how many days prior to birth is the fetus?

    (c) How old is a fetus with a 40 mm femur?

*13.5 Return to the data from the Grasshopper Ruin (Exercise 10.7).

    (a) Find the equation which allows prediction of hearth size from a knowledge of room size for the early rooms.

    (b) If another room from the early rooms is found to be 20 m^2, how large would you predict its firehearth to be?

    (c) What measure can we use to determine the accuracy of this prediction?

14 Correlation Coefficients

● *If experimentation is the Queen of the Sciences, surely statistical methods must be regarded as the Guardian of the Royal Virtue.*—M. Tribus

14.1 CORRELATION IN A SAMPLE

The notion of correlation was briefly introduced in Section 13.3. The population correlation coefficient ρ was defined as the square root of the Coefficient of Determination. But ρ applies only to correlation within a population. When a sample is involved, a new statistic, called r, must be considered. Therefore, r estimates ρ from a sample of variates. Originally derived by biometrist Karl Pearson, the sample correlation coefficient is also commonly called the *Pearson Product-Moment Coefficient*. The correlation coefficient (and its nonparametric equivalents) plays such a critical role in bivariate statistical analysis that correlation must be given especial attention in this chapter.

Consider the scattergram in Fig. 14.1. Coordinate systems can help in assessing the degree of scatter in a swarm of points. The coordinates describe four equal quadrants, labelled A, B, C, and D. If the swarm of points is randomly distributed about their sample means—in this case, about the origin of the graph—then the number of points should be roughly distributed throughout all the quadrants. But if a linear relationship is present, then the points will be distributed unequally among the four quadrants. A *positive linear relationship* produces a distribution in which quadrants A and C contain more points than would quadrants B and D. Similarly, a *negative linear relationship* places an excess of points in quadrants B and D. So the relative abundance of points among the four quadrants can serve as a rough indicator of linearity; Fig. 14.1 illustrates this simple principle.

Now consider the scattergram in Fig. 14.2, and assume that these datum

384

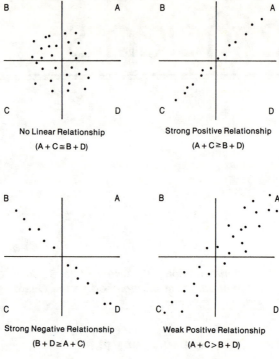

Fig. 14.1

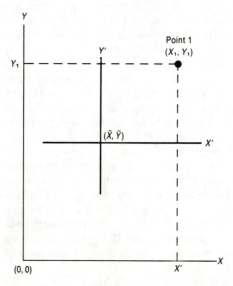

Fig. 14.2

points (X_i, Y_i) represent random samples from a homoscedastic bivariate normal population. If the intention were to describe merely the *form* of the relationship between X and Y, then a *descriptive* line could be fit to these points, using Model II regression (Section 13.8). But let us set aside the question of form for the moment and consider only the *strength* of the linear relationship between X and Y. Following convention, the origin of the X–Y coordinate system is set at $(0, 0)$; any point can be located on Fig. 14.2 merely by describing its vertical and horizontal relationship to the zero origin. This coordinate system can be redefined (as in Fig. 14.3) such that the origin is placed at the two sample means, $\bar{X}$ and $\bar{Y}$. Each of these new axes can be labelled X' and Y' to distinguish them from the original axes X and Y which originated at $(0, 0)$.

Any individual datum point can now be located precisely on the coordinate system by measuring its horizontal and vertical distance from the origin. When the origin was taken as zero, then any point is exactly $(X_i - 0) = X_i$ horizontal units from the origin and $(Y_i - 0) = Y_i$ vertical units above the origin. With the origin redefined as $\bar{X}$ and $\bar{Y}$, the distance to the origin becomes $(X_i - \bar{X})$ horizontal units and $(Y_i - \bar{Y})$ vertical units. The values of the product between these two distances, $(X_i - \bar{X})(Y_i - \bar{Y})$, provides a general distance figure from the point to the graph origin. When a point falls within quadrant A, then the product $(X_i - \bar{X})(Y_i - \bar{Y})$ must be a positive number (Fig. 14.3). Similarly, points in quadrant C must also have a positive product, while the points in B and D must always produce a negative product of deviations.

This reasoning can be generalized from a single point to the entire swarm of points on a scattergram. A strong, positive linear relationship produces a positive value of the *sum of products*, which is $\Sigma(X_i - \bar{X})(Y_i - \bar{Y})$, because most of the points must lie within quadrants A and C. The larger this sum, the stronger must be the positive linearity between X and Y. Similarly, a negative linearity produces a larger negative value for $\Sigma(X_i - \bar{X})(Y_i - \bar{Y})$. No linear trend is

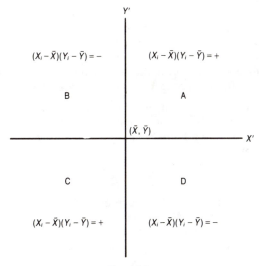

Fig. 14.3

evident whenever the sum of the products of the deviations from $\bar{X}$ and $\bar{Y}$ is zero.

So, clearly, the sum of deviations is a serviceable indicator of the strength of a bivariate linear relationship, but this index is hampered by a couple of limitations. The sum obviously increases as the number of points, n, increases, and therefore the sum of deviations is useful only as long as samples of identical size are to be compared. Moreover, the sum is expressed in the units of analysis— that is, the diverse units of the scales of X and Y—rather than in simple absolute units. The initial difficulty is remedied simply by dividing the sum by n: $\Sigma(X_i - \bar{X})(Y_i - \bar{Y})/n$ expresses the *average* deviation about $\bar{X}$ and $\bar{Y}$, thereby stabilizing the sum against fluctuations in sample size. Each individual deviation can then be divided by the sample standard deviation in order to cancel the actual units of analysis; a similar procedure was used to derive z, the standardized normal deviate. This modified indicator measures the dispersion of a bivariate normal sample about its individual means $\bar{X}$ and $\bar{Y}$,[1] as follows:

$$r = \frac{1}{n}\Sigma \frac{(X_i - \bar{X})}{S_x} \cdot \frac{(Y_i - \bar{Y})}{S_Y}$$

$$r = \frac{\Sigma(X_i - \bar{X})(Y_i - \bar{Y})/n}{\sqrt{\Sigma(X_i - \bar{X})^2(Y_i - \bar{Y})^2/(n-1)}}$$

(14.1)

The sample correlation coefficient r is simply an alternative algebraic form for estimating ρ, derived in Section 13.3. This form in Equation (14.1) is preferable because it illustrates just how affinity can be computed over a series of bivariate pairs.

The correlation coefficient has a number of desirable properties:

1. A value of $\rho = 0$ (estimated by r) indicates that no linear relationship exists between two variables. They are *linearly unrelated*.
2. The *magnitude of ρ* (estimated by r) denotes the *strength* of the linear relationship. Large absolute values of ρ indicate a close relationship, while smaller absolute values of ρ indicate that X and Y are only weakly related.
3. The *sign of ρ* denotes the *direction* of the relationship.
4. The maximum value of $\rho = +1.00$ indicates a perfect positive correlation (larger X means larger Y) and the maximum negative value of $\rho = -1.00$ indicates a perfect negative correlation (larger X means smaller Y).

The sample correlation coefficient is very closely related to the sample regression constants in a mathematical sense. The correlation coefficient is simply the slope constant b multiplied by the ratio of the sample standard deviations of X and Y:

$$r = b_{Y \cdot X} \frac{S_X}{S_Y}$$

(14.2)

Because the regression constant b is expressed in the specific units of analysis ("so many unit changes in Y for every unit change in X"), multiplication by the standard deviations will "standardize" the slope into a dimensionless statement of correlation. But this intimate relationship between r and b should not be

---

[1]For large samples, the difference between n and $n - 1$ becomes negligible, so they simply "cancel" in Expression 14.1.

taken as meaning that they are equivalent expressions, to be interchanged at will. They rely upon some rather different assumptions, and the methods of correlation and regression fulfill rather different needs in social science.

14.2 COMPUTING THE CORRELATION COEFFICIENT

A "computing" method for finding r is given in the following computing formula:

$$r = \frac{\Sigma XY - n\bar{X}\bar{Y}}{\sqrt{(\Sigma X^2 - n\bar{X}^2)(\Sigma Y^2 - n\bar{Y}^2)}} \tag{14.3}$$

Like most of the computing formulas, Expression (14.3) avoids the difficulties of actually determining the individual deviations about the sample mean. Some examples should clarify the meaning and computation of the correlation coefficient.

I employ a number of students in the archaeological lab of the American Museum of Natural History in New York City. The bulk of their duties consists of measuring and classifying archaeological artifacts. One task, for instance, involves taking ten measurements on all of the projectile points processed through the laboratory. Aside from the general grousing I have come to expect from such vacuous duties, a couple of students made a seemingly legitimate protest. "Why do we have to measure *length*, *thickness*, and *weight* for each artifact," they asked, "when we all *know* that the three variables are functions of but a single variable—*size*. Because most of the artifacts are broken, only thickness can be measured with accuracy; both weight and length are generally only estimates from broken artifacts. Why must length and weight be determined when we already know thickness?"

The question set me thinking just how closely thickness, weight, and length were really related in these artifacts. This is an issue of correlation: If length, thickness, and weight are highly correlated, then they are also redundant, and one measurement will serve just as well as three. So I told the students that if they could demonstrate adequate correlation, they could junk the redundant measurements.

They began first with the thickness and weight variates for eight Elko Eared projectile points (Table 14.1). Their first step was to plot the data on a scattergram (Fig. 14.4). The symbols X and Y have been assigned arbitrarily in this case because no predictions are involved. A linear trend appears to be evident, but there is also a good deal of scatter. How correlated are weight and thickness?

All the necessary terms have been computed in Table 14.1, and from Formula (14.3) the coefficient of correlation is found to be

$$r = \frac{155.49 - 8(5.10)(3.76)}{\sqrt{[(212.80 - 8(5.10)^2][(114.61 - 8(3.76)^2]}}$$
$$= +0.78$$

The value of $r = +0.78$ is a rather high value, demonstrating a certain validity of the students' complaints. Weight and thickness are indeed quite redundant, and should produce quite similar results in any typological scheme.

388

TABLE 14.1 Comparison of weight and thickness measurements for eight Elko Eared projectile points from Reese River, central Nevada (Thomas 1971a)

Thickness, cm X	Weight, grams Y	XY	X^2	Y^2
5.0	3.3	16.50	25.00	10.89
4.6	3.5	16.10	21.16	12.25
4.8	4.0	19.20	23.04	16.00
5.8	3.8	22.04	33.64	14.44
5.3	4.2	22.26	28.09	17.64
4.3	3.5	15.05	18.49	12.25
6.7	4.5	30.15	44.89	20.25
4.3	3.3	14.19	18.49	10.89
40.8	30.1	155.49	212.80	114.61

$\bar{X} = 40.8/8 = 5.10;\ \bar{Y} = 30.1/8 = 3.76.$

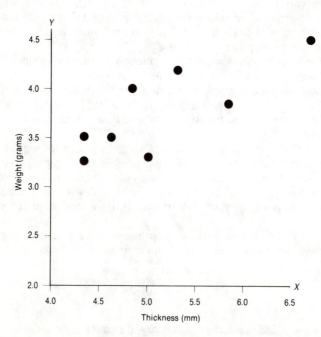

Fig. 14.4 Thickness versus weight of eight Elko Eared points from Reese River, Nevada (data from Thomas 1971a).

Example 14.1

According to population ecologist Paul Ehrlich, "the single most important factor in a country's reproductive rate is the motivation of the people
toward the regulation of family size . . . if a couple is determined not to
have more than two children, they usually will not, regardless of whether
there is a birth control clinic down the street" (Ehrlich and Ehrlich 1972:
318).

Do the following data from seven Latin American cities support Ehrlich's
contention that the actual birth rate is correlated with social norms
regarding ideal family size?

Desired family sizes of women in seven Latin American cities.

Latin American Cities	Average Number of Children Wanted	1971 Birth Rate of Country
Bogota, Columbia	3.6	44
Buenos Aires, Argentina	2.9	22
Caracas, Venezuela	3.5	41
Mexico City, Mexico	4.2	42
Panama City, Panama	3.5	41
Rio de Janeiro, Brazil	2.7	38
San Jose, Costa Rica	3.6	45

As in all correlation cases, assignment of X and Y is totally arbitrary:
The number of desired children is assigned to X and the 1971 birth rate is
Y.

X	Y	X^2	Y^2	XY
3.6	44	12.96	1,936	158.40
2.9	22	8.41	484	63.80
3.5	41	12.25	1,681	143.50
4.2	42	17.64	1,764	176.40
3.5	41	12.25	1,681	143.50
2.7	38	7.29	1,444	102.60
3.6	45	12.96	2,025	162.00
24.0	273	83.76	11,015	950.20

$$\bar{X} = \frac{24.0}{7} = 3.43 \qquad \bar{Y} = \frac{273}{7} = 39.00$$

$$r = \frac{950.20 - 7(3.43)(39)}{\sqrt{[(83.76 - 7(3.43)^2][(11,015) - 7(39)^2]}}$$

$$= +0.610$$

These data clearly support Ehrlich's contention that norms are positively related to actual birth rate, at least in Latin America.

14.3 THE MEANING OF CORRELATION AND REGRESSION: USE AND ABUSE

Many practicing anthropologists feel perfectly at home with most statistical techniques, yet they experience a certain trepidation when faced with the issues of correlation and regression. The computations are so closely related arithmetically that one is often tempted to compute both r and the regression equation for all sets of bivariate data, in hopes of covering all the bases. But these two techniques are hardly interchangeable, and their misuse is notoriously common throughout the literature of anthropology. It is difficult to know which statistic is more abused, the chi-square test or the regression-correlation duo. Neither misuse is particularly amusing.

It seems that relatively few problems arise when the regression and correlation statistics are employed in purely descriptive fashion. The population regression coefficients readily describe the *form* of the linear relationship, while the parametric correlation coefficient ρ measures the *degree of dispersion* about this regression axis. But difficulties seem to arise when samples are generated and then inferences extended back to the parent population. Two intersecting criteria must be considered whenever such bivariate samples are to be analyzed: (1) the precise objective of analysis, and (2) the exact nature of the variables which were sampled. Table 14.2 summarizes the following discussion.

Both regression and correlation assume at least interval scales of measurement. When either X or Y fails to qualify as fully interval, then one must turn to one of the nonparametric techniques considered later in this chapter. As long as the values of X are fixed—that is, whenever the levels of the predictor variable are under the control of the experimenter—the least squares approximation of regression should be used to describe the precise relationship between X and Y. Least square regression permits the analyst to predict the probabilistic outcomes of Y, given information about the predetermined levels of X. This agreeable situation occurs most frequently in disciplines such as psychological experimentation, educational testing, and agricultural field studies. The investigator predetermines a value of X and then measures the attendant responses on Y_i. The X variable really has no "distribution" in the strict sense, so

TABLE 14.2 Relationship between correlation and regression (after Sokal and Rohlf 1969: 497).

Nature of Selecting X_i and Y_i	Purpose of Investigation	
	Determine dependence relationship (*prediction*)	Establish strength of association (*interdependence*)
X fixed, Y random	Model I regression (least squares)	*Meaningless*, except as measure of goodness of fit between data and line of regression (use r^2)
Both X and Y random	Model II regression (Bartlett's method)	Correlation coefficient

assumptions are not required about the variance of X. X has been selected rather than sampled.

How secure are these predictions based upon Model I regression? To determine the variability of Y about an arbitrary X, the amount of variance "accounted for" by X must be compared with the total variability in Y. There is no variability in X. The Coefficient of Nondetermination was previously defined as

$$k^2 = 1 - \frac{\text{variability in } Y \text{ not accounted for by } X}{\text{total variability in } Y}$$

$$= 1 - \frac{S_{X \cdot Y}^2}{S_Y^2}$$

When $k^2 = 0$, then the variability in Y is completely determined from a knowledge of X.

The accuracy of Model I regressions can alternatively be expressed as the Coefficient of Dispersion, defined earlier as $r^2 = (1 - k^2)$. Whenever $r^2 = 1$, the X variability is said to account for the total variability observed in Y. *But the correlation coefficient r is meaningless in the contexts of Model I regression.* The sample correlation always assumes a bivariate normal distribution, which is clearly never the case when levels of X are fixed. Lacking the bivariate normal distribution, one cannot infer ρ from r. Thus, although the correlation coefficient is computationally related to r^2, r is merely the square root of the Coefficient of Determination—these two statistics are grounded in very different assumptions. The statistics r and r^2 are not interchangeable for Model I regression; r^2 has meaning only when X has been fixed. Furthermore, regression is a predictive technique for guessing the value of Y given X, while the Coefficient of Determination provides an estimate of goodness of fit for these predictions.

A rather different statistical situation exists whenever both X and Y represent random variables. In general, sampling from bivariate normal populations implies an interest more in the strength of relationships than in their form. So bivariate populations are more generally involved with correlation as the basic analytical tool. The correlation approach applies to the sampling situation, whereas the (Model I) regression approach implies a more closely controlled experimental study. Should one actually need to *predict* one random variable from another, then Bartlett's method (Section 13.8) for curve fitting can be used to describe the observed form of articulation between random X and Y. The labels *predictor* and *predicted* are assigned arbitrarily in Model II because there is no structural difference between the distributions of the two variables.

14.4 TESTING r FOR STATISTICAL SIGNIFICANCE

Extreme values of r are relatively easy to interpret. As long as r hovers about zero, then one can feel quite assured that no substantial degree of correlation exists between the X and Y populations. That is, r is almost certainly near zero. Similarly, as r approaches the maximum values of $r = \pm 1.00$, then linear correlation seems a virtual certainty. But because r is merely a statistical estimator of ρ, the sampling errors cannot be ignored. Whenever r assumes an intermediate value between zero and unity, the correlation coefficient should be assessed for *statistically significant deviations by chance*. A number of null hypotheses can be considered, depending upon the precise research objective.

14.4.1 Testing against a Specific ρ

The most common statistical test for the significance of the sample correlation coefficient is to determine whether ρ differs from zero. Are the two variables correlated?

$$H_o: \quad \rho = 0 \qquad H_o: \quad \rho \geq 0 \qquad H_o: \quad \rho \leq 0$$
$$H_1: \quad \rho \neq 0 \qquad H_1: \quad \rho < 0 \qquad H_1: \quad \rho > 0$$

This test attempts to determine if the observed deviation of r from zero is sufficiently large to represent a rare sampling event. The test can be phrased in either one- or two-tailed forms.

Observed values of r can be converted to the familiar t-statistic as follows:

$$t = \frac{r - \rho}{\sqrt{(1 - r^2)/(n - 2)}} \tag{14.4}$$

Two degrees of freedom are lost in computing Expression (14.4), so for any r, df $= (n - 2)$.

The significance of r can also be tested by using simple distribution tables. The sampling distribution of r is known to vary, depending both upon ρ and n. For the special case of $H_o: \rho = 0$, the probability values have been compiled in Table A.11 (Appendix). Entering this table with $(n - 2)$ degrees of freedom, one can readily determine the *critical values* of r at the common levels of statistical significance. This table applies only to the two-tailed case, so the sign of r is ignored. Whenever direction has been specified—that is, one predicts either positive or negative correlation—the one-tailed probabilities can be found as simply twice those listed in Table A.11. So the critical value for a directional test with $(n - 2)$ degrees of freedom at $\alpha = 0.05$ is found under $\alpha = 0.10$.

Special circumstances sometimes arise in which one wishes to test whether ρ is equal to some value other than zero, such as $\rho = 0.90$ or $\rho = -0.75$. Such testing requires a conversion of r to z (discussed in Section 14.4.2). The interested reader is referred to discussions in Alder and Roessler (1972: 214–215) or Sokal and Rohlf (1969: 519) for the specifics.

Example 14.2

It was determined in Example 14.1 that the correlation between actual birth rate in Latin America and the ideal family size is $r = +0.610$. Does this coefficient indicate that ρ is significantly different from zero?

We must first assume that the seven examples were randomly generated from the Latin American population; if Ehrlich arbitrarily selected the best cases, a significance test is unwarranted. The number of degrees of freedom in this case are equal to $(n - 2) = (7 - 2) = 5$. Table A.11 indicates that the critical value for $\alpha = 0.01$ is $r = 0.8745$. We must conclude that no significant difference exists between the coefficient $r = +0.610$ and $\rho = 0.0$ at the 0.01 level.

Note: Here is a case in which a strict, insensitive dependence upon conventional statistical levels could be misleading. If more cases had been employed in the study, the results almost surely would have been significant. But even granting the small sample size and the lack of significance, one should probably not ignore so large a value as $r = +0.610$, even though it falls short of the tabled value. Ehrlich's example simply has too few cases to demonstrate a correlation which is probabilistically significant.

14.4.2 Confidence Limits of r

The statistical confidence limits about an observed correlation coefficient are sometimes more useful than testing for significance against specific values of ρ. Finding the interval about r is complicated by the fact that ρ must be known prior to finding the standard error of r. This unrealistic procedure led Sir Ronald Fisher to derive a second index of correlation, known as Z.[2]

$$Z = \frac{1}{2} \log_e \frac{1+r}{1-r} \tag{14.5}$$

where $\log_e$ is the natural logarithm based upon the constant base $e = 2.718$. As before, this conversion need not be accomplished every time because the values of Table A.12 provide ready access to the conversion of r to Z, so the computations in (14.5) can usually be avoided.

The sampling distribution of Z is known to be approximately normal, with a standard error approximated by

$$\sigma_z \simeq S_z = \frac{1}{\sqrt{n-3}} \tag{14.6}$$

How these two quantities are used to determine confidence limits about r is illustrated by a worldwide study of cultural patterns of child rearing made by Barry and Paxson (1971). They reported that the correlation between general indulgence during childhood and the use of carrying devices for infants (such as cradleboards) to be $r = +0.65$ for a sample of 42 societies. What are the 95 percent limits for ρ?

From Table A.12 we find that the observed value of $r = +0.65$ converts to $Z = 0.775$; an identical value of Z is found by using Formula (14.5). The standard error of this Z is found from (14.6):

$$\sigma_z = \frac{1}{\sqrt{42-3}} = 0.160$$

[2]Once again the statistical terminology conspires against us. Although the log conversion of r is denoted by Z, do not confuse this "zee" with z, the symbol used here for the standardized normal deviate. These two "zee's" have nothing in common.

The confidence interval about Z is given by standard methods, using the normal curve:

$$\text{confidence interval} = Z \pm 1.96\sigma_z$$
$$= 0.775 \pm 1.96(0.160)$$
$$= 0.775 \pm 0.314$$

So the 95 percent confidence intervals run from $+0.461$ to $+1.089$. But these intervals are still in values of Z and must be converted back to values of r. Again using Table A.12, we find the confidence intervals of r to run between $r = +0.43$ and $r = +0.80$. Clearly, this correlation between carrying devices and the indulgence of infants is positively correlated in the worldwide population. That is, we can be almost certain that ρ lies between $r = +0.43$ and $r = +0.80$. In this case, the confidence interval seems to provide more useful results than would the t-test against H_o: $\rho = 0$.

The question arises: Since the 95 percent confidence interval does not include $\rho = 0$, is this equivalent to rejecting H_o: $\rho = 0$ versus H_1: $\rho \neq 0$ at the 0.05 level, using (14.4)? The answer is yes. This confidence interval tells us that in the long run, we can expect to obtain intervals which will contain the (unknown) ρ about 95 percent of the time. As with all confidence intervals, an entire range of hypotheses has been implicitly tested. All null hypotheses suggesting values of ρ outside the interval $+0.43$ and $+0.80$ are implicitly rejected. Null hypotheses with $+0.43 \leq \rho \leq +0.80$ are not rejected.

Note further that the confidence limits are not symmetrical about $r = +0.65$, since the general distribution of ρ produces a diminishing effect upon the confidence limits for the positive values of r. When the correlation coefficient is negative, the lower confidence limits will be closer to r than will the upper limit.

14.4.3 Testing for a Difference between Two ρ

Two independent correlation coefficients can be statistically compared by transforming the r into standardized normal deviates. The raw r must first be converted to Z by using Table A.12. The standard error of the difference between two Z is given by

$$\sigma_{z_1-z_2} = S_{z_1-z_2} = \sqrt{\frac{1}{n_1-3} + \frac{1}{n_2-3}} \tag{14.7}$$

The statistical difference between the two Z can be computed as in earlier tests for differences. Another example from population ecology will illustrate the computations.

Paul Ehrlich contends that the families of a DC (developed country) generally come closer to their ideal size than those of the UDC (underdeveloped country). Ehrlich contends that the UDC generally exceed their desired family size, due to socioeconomic, religious, and political factors. Example 14.1 determined that the correlation between number of children wanted and the Latin American birth rate is $r = +0.610$. It is also known that the correlation is $r = +0.818$ for nine European countries. Assuming the European countries to be DC and the Latin American countries to be UDC, is the difference in correlations large enough to support Ehrlich's hypothesis?

Let us term the correlation for Europe as r_1, with $n_1 = 9$. The statistical hypotheses in this one-tailed test are

$$H_0: \quad \rho_1 \leq \rho_2 \qquad H_1: \quad \rho_1 > \rho_2$$

The one-tailed critical value of the standardized normal deviate, z, is found in Table A.3 to be 1.64.

The log conversion values of r are found from Table A.12 to be $Z_1 = 1.157$ and $Z_2 = 0.709$. Let me caution you once again not to confuse the meaning of the standardized normal deviate (z) with the log conversion of the correlation coefficient (Z). The standard error for the difference between the two Z conversions is found from Expression (14.7):

$$\sigma_{Z_1 - Z_2} = \sqrt{\frac{1}{9-3} + \frac{1}{7-3}} = 0.645$$

The standardized normal deviate for the difference is

$$z = \frac{(Z_1 - Z_2) - 0}{\sigma_{Z_1 - Z_2}} = \frac{1.157 - 0.709}{0.645}$$
$$= 0.695$$

The computed figure for z fails to exceed the critical value of $z = 1.64$, so the null hypothesis cannot be rejected. The census data from Latin America and Europe fail to support Ehrlich's contention that developed countries come closer to their ideal family size than do the underdeveloped countries.

14.5 RANK-ORDER CORRELATION

Measures of statistical correlation always involve *pairs* of observations; each of the pairs represents a bivariate random sample of size n. The correlation coefficient is but one measure of linear correlation, and r is the appropriate measure of affinity between X and Y *only* as long as three criteria are met:

1. Both X and Y are at least interval-scale variables.
2. The distribution of Y and X is bivariate normal.
3. Variables X and Y are related in linear fashion.

Use of r becomes suspect when any of these conditions is not met, and this section discusses two important nonparametric alternatives to the parametric correlation coefficient. Specifically, these nonparametric alternatives apply when conditions (1) and/or (2) are not met; the nonparametric methods still assume a linear relationship. As we will see, the nonparametric methods of correlation are particularly helpful in analyzing cross-cultural samples which are so common in today's ethnology.

14.5.1 Spearman's Rank-Order Correlation Coefficient

Data from the *Ethnographic Atlas* (Murdock 1967) have been used from time to time to illustrate various of the statistical techniques. Another source of easily retrievable ethnographic data is Human Relations Area Files (HRAF) with central headquarters in New Haven, Connecticut; the HRAF records are made available on a subscription basis to over two hundred universities and museums throughout the world.

The physical process of coding requires the analyst to decide whether or not a given trait is present within a society. Sometimes these decisions are quite easy to code:

(Col. 1) *Regional Identity*:
   Africa
   Circum-Mediterranean
   East Eurasian
   Insular Pacific
   North America
   South America
(Col. 39) *Type of Animal Husbandry*:
   bovine animals
   camels
   deer
   equine
   pigs
   other

But many interesting cultural variables are by their nature judgmental in character, such as *degree of anxiety, kind of family organization, intensity of agriculture* or *frequency of warfare*. Variables of this sort require the coder to make rather subjective decisions, decisions which tend to vary between analysts. A common control in coding ethnographic data is to employ multiple judges, who are unaware of the hypothesis and each of whom independently codes the same literature. The scores can then be compared to determine the relative objectivity of the categories.

In one such study, Bacon and others (1965) attempted a rather ambitious study of drinking behavior throughout the world. Ethnographic literature was assembled for a large sample of societies, and then raters independently coded these data into comparable cross-cultural categories. One variable under investigation in this study was *hostility and resentment of males while drinking*, which was categorized into the following divisions (Bacon and others 1965: 340):

A. Little or no expressions of resentment
B. Verbal expression of mild resentment such as slight impoliteness
C. Moderate quarreling
D. Serious quarreling
E. Quarreling frequently accompanied by physical fighting
F. Serious physical combat
G. Physical combat involving frequent injury to other persons

Every society in the sample was then independently scored by two investigators (Barry and Buchwald). When their ratings agreed, then the scale was considered to be relatively objective and hence acceptable. But if the judges disagreed on a number of cases, then they knew that the coding scheme lacked the necessary objectivity and required redefinition.

Suppose that the two judges obtained the following codes for the *hostility and resentment* variable:

	Judges	
Society	1st	2d
Ainu	B	B
Cayapo	D	D
Chukchee	G	G
Cuna	E	E
Ifugao	F	F
Maori	A	C

The two judges agreed in all cases except the New Zealand Maori. Is this single deviation to be expected by chance, or does there appear to be an inordinate amount of disagreement on the *hostility and resentment* scale?

The *Spearman Rank-Order Correlation Coefficient*, designated by r_s, is an index derived to analyze exactly this sort of situation. Originally defined in 1904, this measure is the earliest of the family of nonparametric statistics based upon ordinal ranking.[3] The statistic r_s compares the overall similarity of two ordinal rankings. The two judges' rankings can be considered as rank orderings: Each society is ranked relative to the others in terms of hostility and aggression.

Spearman's Rank-Order Correlation Coefficient is defined as

$$r_s = 1 - \frac{6\Sigma d_i^2}{n^3 - n} \tag{14.8}$$

where d_i is the raw difference between rankings of variate pair i, and n is the total number of such pairings.[4] Like r, Spearman's r_s ranges from $+1.0$ for a perfect positive correlation to -1.0 for absolute negative correlation.

To compute r_s, the societies must first be placed in rank-order for each scale. Judge A rated the six societies in the following order: (1) Maori, (2) Ainu, (3) Cayapo, (4) Cuna, (5) Ifugao, and (6) Chukchee. Judge B's results are similar, except that the Maori and Ainu are placed in reverse order, with Ainu receiving the rank of 1. The d_i are then found by subtracting rankings of judges. These scales are presented in Table 14.3. The sum of the deviations must always equal zero, a fact which provides a handy check for errors in either adding or subtracting the deviations. The d_i are then squared and summed, providing Σd_i^2. Formula (14.8) can now be applied to the results of Table 14.3:

$$r_s = 1 - \frac{6(2)}{6^3 - 6} = 1 - \frac{12}{210}$$

$$= +0.94$$

[3]Spearman's index is sometimes designated as rho, but the simpler r_s is used here to avoid confusion with the population parameter of the parametric correlation coefficient ρ.

[4]The derivation of r_s can be found in Siegel (1956: 203–204).

Society	Judge's Rankings			
	A	B	d_i	d_i^2
Maori	1	2	−1	1
Ainu	2	1	+1	1
Cayapo	3	3	0	0
Cuna	4	4	0	0
Ifugao	5	5	0	0
Chukchee	6	6	0	0
				$\Sigma d_i = 2$

Spearman's r_s is interpreted in a manner similar to r, so we see that the two ranking scales are indeed quite closely correlated. A second, more complicated example will further illustrate the versatility of r_s.

Villages of northern India generally host representatives from some 5 to 25 endogamous social groupings known as *castes*. Villagers regard each caste as higher (or lower) than another in terms of prestige and esteem. The result is a tightly structured social hierarchy. But a certain amount of disagreement generally exists as to the exact social ranking of particular castes. Stanley Freed, of the American Museum of Natural History, collected an interesting series of data from the small village of Shanti Nagar, northern India (Freed 1963). Freed interviewed a series of randomly selected male informants. Each informant was given a set of movable cards, upon each of which was written the name of a single caste. Informants were requested to arrange the caste cards in their appropriate social ordering. One informant, of the *Brahman* (priest) caste, arranged his cards into the following order: *Brahman* (priest), *Baniya* (merchant), *Jat* (farmer), *Baigari* (beggar), *Mali* (gardener), *Gola Kumhar* (potter), *Lohar* (blacksmith), *Jhinvar* (water carrier), *Maher Kumhar* (potter), *Nai* (barber), *Chamar* (leather worker), *Chuhra* (sweeper). A second informant, a member of the sweeper (*Chuhra*) caste, produced the following social ranking using the same deck of cards: *Brahman*, *Baniya*, *Jat*, *Jhinvar*, *Lohar*, *Mali*, *Bairagi*, *Nai*, *Gola Kumhar*, *Mahar Kumhar*, *Chamar*, *Chuhra*. The two rankings clearly contain many similarities—both place *Brahman* at the highest end of the hierarchy and the *Chuhra* at the bottom, for example, but the order of some intermediate ranks differs. How similar are the two social rankings?

This is obviously a problem in correlation: How closely does the *Brahman*'s ordering correlate with that of the sweeper? The standard correlation coefficient is irrelevant in this context because the caste rankings achieve only ordinal status. But Spearman's coefficient is readily applicable.

The data must first be assigned numerical rank orderings. The *Brahman*'s sequence has been numbered in order from the highest (1) to the lowest caste (12) on Table 14.4. The *Chuhra*'s ordering was then assigned the numbers according to the first sequence. Identical results will result if the *Chuhra*'s ordering is used as the first reference sequence; the *Brahman*'s ordering was arbitrarily selected. In this manner, the two rank orders can be compared simply by subtracting the two columns, with the absolute result tabulated in the difference (d_i) column. The differences are then squared and summed as before, and Σd_i^2 is substituted into Formula (14.8):

$$r_S = 1 - \frac{6(44)}{12^3 - 12} = +0.85$$

The rather high value of 0.85 indicates a very large degree of correspondence between the two orderings. Despite the fact that informants came from the very extremes of the caste spectrum, both agreed on their relative social standing. Freed went on to use r_S to compare the pairwise results for 23 other randomly selected informants to produce a median ranking scale for an entire village (Freed 1963: table 4). In this manner, an objective means of determining caste ranking was devised.

TABLE 14.4

	Social Rankings				d_i	d_i^2
	Brahman			Chuhra		
1	Brahman		1	Brahman	0	0
2	Baniya		2	Baniya	0	0
3	Jat		3	Jat	0	0
4	Baigari		8	Jhinvar	−4	16
5	Mali		7	Lohar	−2	4
6	Gola Kumhar		5	Mali	1	1
7	Lohar		4	Baigari	3	9
8	Jhinvar		10	Nai	−2	4
9	Mohar Kumhar		6	Gola Kumhar	3	9
10	Nai		9	Mahar Kumhar	1	1
11	Chamar		11	Chamar	0	0
12	Chuhra		12	Chuhra	0	0
					0	44

The case of Indian social castes is particularly useful to illustrate just how r_S functions, since castes are a perfect example of rank orderings which occur in social contexts. Suppose that two informants from Shanti Nagar produced exactly identical orderings as shown in Table 14.5.

Because the informants have agreed, the Σd_i^2 must equal zero, producing the following r_S of unity:

$$r_S = 1 - \frac{6(0)}{12^3 - 12} = 1 - \frac{0}{1710}$$

$$= +1.00$$

The opposite case would be an unlikely situation in which informants produce exactly reverse orderings, as in Table 14.6.

TABLE 14.5.

Social Rankings

A	B	d_i	d_i^2
1	1	0	0
2	2	0	0
3	3	0	0
4	4	0	0
5	5	0	0
6	6	0	0
7	7	0	0
8	8	0	0
9	9	0	0
10	10	0	0
11	11	0	0
12	12	0	0
		0	0

TABLE 14.6

Social Rankings

A	B	d_i	d_i^2
1	12	−11	121
2	11	− 9	81
3	10	− 7	49
4	9	− 5	25
5	8	− 3	9
6	7	− 1	1
7	6	1	1
8	5	3	9
9	4	5	25
10	3	7	49
11	2	9	81
12	1	11	121
		0	572

Spearman's coefficient for perfect disagreement is found to be

$$r_s = 1 - \frac{6(572)}{1716} = 1 - \frac{3432}{1716} = 1 - 2.00$$
$$= -1.00$$

Thus, the theoretically maximum value of $\Sigma d_i^2 = 572$ produces a perfectly correlated coefficient of $r_s = -1.00$. Of course no two informants could be expected to disagree in such extreme fashion.

Testing Spearman's r_s for statistical significance. Many applications of correlation require little more than relative measures of covariation (or the lack of it):

1. Do two *Brahman* informants tend to agree on caste ranking more closely than a *Brahman* and a *Chuhra*?
2. Does method A of coding ethnographic data produce more agreement among coders than does method B?

Answers to inquiries such as this can be directly provided by the r_s coefficients.

But cases sometimes arise in which one must generalize beyond the samples at hand to larger populations. The null hypothesis is that the variables lack true association, and only by chance has r_s deviated from zero. Two procedures are presented below which allow us to apply the hypothesis-testing procedures to r_s. But before considering these techniques, be certain to recognize one important sampling stricture. As long as the r_s coefficient is used strictly as *description*, then there are no restrictions on sampling. But if the r_s is interpreted to infer population characteristics from incomplete samples, then sampling must be random. That is, *addition of a test for statistical significance presupposes randomly generated variates from a specific population.*

The sampling distribution of r_s has been compiled in Table A.13.[5] These critical values refer to the one-tailed case in which the direction of association has been clearly specified. Positive values of r_s predict that large X should be paired with large Y, while a negative relationship pairs large X with small Y.

Table A.13 makes quick work of assessing the statistical significance of r_s. Spearman's rank-order coefficient was computed in the earlier cross-cultural drinking study to be $r_s = +0.94$. The critical value of r_s at $\alpha = 0.05$ with $n = 6$ is found from Table A.13 to be $r_s = 0.829$. We are justified in rejecting the null hypothesis in this case because the observed correlation is more extreme than this critical figure. We conclude that the two judges do not differ significantly in their scaling of drinking behavior in these six societies. Similarly, Table A.13 indicates that the correlation between the two Indian informants is significant beyond the 0.01 level. Positive associations were expected in both cases, so each test is one-tailed.

A second method for testing the significance of r_s is available when ten or more pairs are involved. The r_s distribution approaches normality as n increases, and the following approximation holds when $n \geq 10$:

$$t = \frac{r_s\sqrt{n-2}}{\sqrt{1-r_s^2}}$$

(14.9)

with $(n-2)$ degrees of freedom.

The caste data in the last section can be used as an example of the normal approximation of r_s:

$$t = \frac{0.85\sqrt{12-2}}{\sqrt{1-0.85^2}} = \frac{2.69}{0.5260}$$

$$= 5.11$$

[5]See Siegel (1956: 210–211) for a derivation of the r_s distribution.

A one-tailed test is involved, so at the 0.01 level with $(12-2) = 10$ degrees of freedom, Table A.4 indicates that the critical value is $t_{0.02} = 2.764$. The observed t statistic for r_s far exceeds this critical value, and the result is declared to be statistically significant. The correlation between *Brahman* and *Chuhra* informants is significantly distinct from zero, so the null hypothesis is rejected. Note that this significance test should not be attempted if the informants had not been selected in some random manner.

r_s *with tied observations.* Spearman's rank-order coefficient compares two ordinal scales to determine the degree of similarity between rankings. The computations assumed an underlying continuous scale for both variates, so ties should not occur between the observations. But in practice, ties are known to occur rather frequently within anthropological scaling, and it becomes necessary to correct the computations of r_s to compensate for tied ranks.

The presence of ties tends to lower the computed value of r_s. A correction factor for tied variates is

$$T = \frac{t^3 - t}{12} \tag{14.10}$$

If three scores were tied at the same rank, for example, then the correction is $T = 3^3 - 3/12 = 2$. This computation is to be performed for all sets of tied variates within the X variable. The quantity ΣT_x is the sum of the corrections on the X variable. Similar computations are performed on the Y ranking, to produce ΣT_Y.[6]

The following formula should be used for r_s whenever ties are present:

$$r_s = \frac{\Sigma X^2 + \Sigma Y^2 - \Sigma d^2}{2\sqrt{\Sigma X^2 \Sigma Y^2}} \tag{14.11}$$

where

$$\Sigma X^2 = \frac{n^3 - n}{12} - \Sigma T_x \quad \text{and} \quad \Sigma Y^2 = \frac{n^3 - n}{12} - \Sigma T_Y$$

This correction for ties admittedly complicates the computations somewhat, but many of the correction factors turn out to be redundant; once computed, these terms often recur in the same formula, thereby simplifying the arithmetic. An example should clarify the computation of r_s with ties.

Few students of anthropology would question that economic and political development are functionally related in modern industrial societies. But the cognate notion that this relation holds for *nonindustrial* societies has been the subject of long debate in anthropology. Melvin Ember attempted to test the relationship between political and economic factors in a cross-cultural analysis (Ember 1963). A random sample of 24 societies was drawn from the 565 contemporary and historical cultures in the "World Ethnographic Sample" (see Table 14.7). Each society was then ranked according to its relative economic and political development. Economic specialization is known to be quite closely correlated with the maximum community size, so *economic development* was operationally defined as the "upper limit of community size." Ember defined

---

[6]Confusion sometimes arises as to just which tied scores are "corrected." We are concerned here only with ties occurring *within ranks* of each variable. Ties between pairs of variates simply reduce to $d_i = 0$.

political authority as "the number of different political officials who participate in all levels of government" (for example, clan chief and head of an extended family). Table 14.7 contains the rankings of these economic and political indicators for the 24 sample societies. Can we say that economic and political development are positively correlated in nonindustrial societies?

TABLE 14.7 Relationship between upper limit of community size and differentiation of political authority (data from Ember 1963: table 5)

Rank Order of Societies	Community Size	Political Authority	d_i	d_i^2
Kaska	1	6	−5	25.00
Caribou Eskimo	2	2.5	−0.5	0.25
Kutubu	3	10	−7	49.00
Xam	5	2.5	2.5	6.25
Naron	5	6	−1	1.00
Mataco	5	6	−1	1.00
Tiwi	8.5	2.5	6	36.00
Ojibwa	8.5	10	−1.5	2.25
Bacairi	8.5	10	−1.5	2.25
Acholi	8.5	17	−8.5	72.25
Guahibo	11.5	2.5	9.0	81.00
Timucua	11.5	15	−3.5	12.25
Ontong Java	13	15	−2	4.00
Chamarro	15	10	5	25.00
Lango	15	10	5	25.00
Samoa	15	18.5	−3.5	12.25
Cuna	17	21	−4	16.00
Omaha	19	20	−1	1.00
Teton	19	13	6	36.00
Didinga	19	18.5	0.5	0.25
Huron	21	15	6	36.00
Tswana	22.5	22	0.5	0.25
Ashanti	22.5	23	−0.5	0.25
Thai	24	24	0	0.00
			0.0	444.50

As before, Spearman's coefficient judges the relationship between these two ordinal scales, but the computations differ somewhat from previous cases because of the tied scores. The sum of squared deviations is found as before; then the correction for ties must be applied. The community size rankings are tied into three sets: The score 8.5 occurs four times, and both 12.5 and 22.5 occur twice each:

$$\Sigma X^2 = \frac{n^3 - n}{12} - \Sigma T_x$$

$$= \frac{24^3 - 24}{12} - \left[\left(\frac{4^3 - 4}{12} \right) + 2 \left(\frac{2^3 - 2}{12} \right) \right]$$

$$= 1150 - 6 = 1144$$

A similar procedure is followed to correct for ties on the political authority scale:

$$\Sigma Y^2 = \frac{24^3 - 24}{12} - \left[2 \left(\frac{3^3 - 3}{12} \right) + \frac{2^3 - 2}{12} + \frac{4^3 - 4}{12} + \frac{5^3 - 5}{12} \right]$$

$$= 1152 - \left[2 \left(\frac{3^3 - 3}{12} \right) + \frac{2^3 - 2}{12} + \frac{4^3 - 4}{12} + \frac{5^3 - 5}{12} \right]$$

$$= 1152 - (4.0 + 0.67 + 5.33 + 10.42) = 1152 - 20.42$$

$$= 1131.6$$

These figures can now be substituted into computing Formula (14.11) for r_s when ties are present.

$$r_s = \frac{1136 + 1130.5 - 444.5}{2\sqrt{1146(1132.08)}} = 0.80$$

Using the normal approximation to Spearman's rank-order coefficient, the value of t is found to be

$$t = \frac{0.80\sqrt{22}}{\sqrt{1 - 0.80^2}} = 6.25$$

This figure is highly significant at $df = (n - 2) = 22$. The conclusion is that Ember's random sample strongly supports the hypothesis that economic and political development are positively associated in nonindustrial societies.

Had we failed to correct for the ties, the computed value of r_s would have been

$$r_s = 1 - \frac{6(444.5)}{24^3 - 24} = 1 - \frac{2,667}{13,800}$$

$$= 0.81$$

Although the difference proves slight in this case, an inordinate number of ties can cause r_s to seriously overestimate the actual correlation if the correction for ties has not been applied.

Example 14.3

Grammatical sex gender is known to correlate with a number of semantic categories which include Freudian sexual symbols, metaphorical extension, and sex role attributes such as beauty and masculinity. But such findings generally relate to a single language, or a few norms over several languages. Robert Munroe and Ruth Munroe have attempted to generalize these findings by examining the underlying relationships between sexual grammar and social structural factors in a cross-cultural study (Munroe and Munroe 1969). A sample of nine languages was selected from those discussed in the *Ethnographic Atlas* and then coded for (1) structural bias toward sex and (2) the prevalence of male-gendered nouns. Male cultural bias was considered to be present under *any one* of the following conditions: patrilocal residence (col. 16 in the *Atlas*), patrilineal kin groups (col. 20 in the *Atlas*), or patri-inheritance (cols. 74 and 76 in the *Atlas*). Each item present is assigned one positive point, and each item rated for "female bias present" receives one negative. Thus, a scale has been devised which ranges from +3 for strong structural bias toward males to −3 for strong structural bias for females; zero indicates the lack of structural sexual bias. The frequency of male and/or female nouns was expressed as "percent of male gender nouns" and words assigned to neuter gender were not recorded. The data for these societies are presented below.

Does this sample support the hypothesis that societies with a tendency toward male bias in social structure also manifest a bias toward male-gendered nouns in their grammar?

Society	Structural Sex Bias		Male-Gender Nouns		d_i	d_i^2
	raw	rank	raw, %	rank		
Lebanese (Arabic)	+3	7.5	64	9	−1.5	2.25
Kanawa (Hausa)	+3	7.5	63	7	0.5	0.25
Nama Hottentots	+3	7.5	63	7	0.5	0.25
Gujarati	+3	7.5	52	5	2.5	6.25
Irish	+2	5	63	7	−2.0	4.00
French Canadians	+1	3	48	4	−1.0	1.00
Byelorussians	+1	3	44	2	1.0	1.00
Greeks	+1	3	35	1	2.0	4.00
Dutch	0	1	45	3	−2.0	4.00
					0.0	23.00

The correction factors for ties are first computed.

$$\Sigma X^2 = \frac{9^3 - 9}{12} - \left[\left(\frac{4^3 - 4}{12}\right) + \left(\frac{3^3 - 3}{12}\right)\right]$$

$$= 60.75 - (5 + 2)$$

$$= 53.75$$

Spearman's coefficient is computed to be

$$r_s = \frac{34 + 54 - 23}{2\sqrt{34(54)}} = +0.76$$

For $n = 9$, this value of r_s is found to be significant at the 0.05 level, but not at 0.01.

Note that had the correction for ties not been applied, the following value would have been obtained:

$$r_s = 1 - \frac{6(23)}{9^3 - 9} = 1 - \left(\frac{138}{720}\right)$$

$$= +0.81$$

This uncorrected value is significant at beyond the 0.01 level, but the ties make this significance spurious.

14.5.2 Kendall's Tau

Spearman's coefficient of rank-order correlation compares two ordinal rankings in terms of their relative association; r_s is based upon the magnitude of the squared differences between the ranks. The same sets of data can be viewed from a rather different statistical perspective, and a second index of rank-order correlation emerges.

This new method can be illustrated using Freed's data on caste ranking in northern India. Two informants, a *Brahman* and a *Chuhra*, rated the 12 castes into appropriate orders. Although their overall conception of the social order was quite similar, the specific rankings were by no means identical, and *Kendall's tau* provides a new method for assessing this correlation.

The Kendall's tau statistic, τ, can be computed by either of two rather different methods. The first technique requires pair-by-pair enumeration such as completed in Table 14.8. Note that the *Brahman*'s responses (termed the X_i) have been placed into sequence and assigned ranks as before. The Y_i are also ranked, but each caste in Y_i receives the corresponding rank number from the X ordering. Thus, even though the *Chuhra* ranked the *Jhinvar* caste fourth, *Jhinvar* receives rank 8 to correspond with its placement in the *Brahman* ranking. The second step requires that we determine the exact number of *larger ranks* for every Y_i. Beginning with rank Y_1 (*Brahman*), we find there are precisely 11 larger rankings (Y_2 through Y_{12} are all larger). The rank Y_2 (*Baniya*) has ten larger subsequent ranks, and so forth. The fourth ranking, Y_4 (*Jhinvar*) has an assigned rank of 8, so only four subsequent ranks (10, 9, 11, and 12) are greater. After all ranks on Y have been enumerated, the total counts, ΣC_i, are summed to 56.

Kendall's tau can now be found through the enumeration method. First the *numerator* must be determined by the following formula:

$$\text{numerator} = 4\Sigma C_i - n(n-1) \tag{14.12}$$

TABLE 14.8

	X_i		Y_i	Subsequent Ranks Larger than Y_i	Counts, C_i
1	Brahman	1	Brahman	2,3,8,7,5,4,10,6,9,11,12	11
2	Baniya	2	Baniya	3,8,7,5,4,19,6,9,11,12	10
3	Jat	3	Jat	8,7,5,4,10,6,9,11,12	9
4	Baigari	8	Jhinvar	10 9,11,12	4
5	Mali	7	Lohar	10 9,11,12	4
6	Gola Kumhar	5	Mali	10,6,9,11,12	5
7	Lohar	4	Baigari	10,6,9,11,12	5
8	Jhinvar	10	Nai	11,12	2
9	Mahar Kumhar	6	Gola Kumhar	9,11,12	3
10	Nai	9	Mahar Kumhar	11,12	2
11	Chamar	11	Chamar	12	1
12	Chuhra	12	Chuhra		0
					$\Sigma C_i = 56$

where n is the number of variate pairs. In the example,

$$\text{numerator} = 4(56) - 12(11) = 92$$

The entire Kendall's tau statistic is defined to be

$$\tau = \frac{\text{numerator}}{\sqrt{[n(n-1) - \Sigma T_x][n(n-1) - \Sigma T_Y]}} \qquad (14.13)$$

where the numerator is computed from Expression (14.12). This formula for tau includes an automatic correction term for ties within rankings. For every set of ties within a ranking, the individual correction term is given by $t(t-1)$. If, for example, five variates were tied at a single rank, then $t(t-1) = 5(4) = 20$. The sum ΣT_x represents the total of the $t(t-1)$ corrections for the X scale, and ΣT_Y sums corrections over the Y ranks. When no ties are present, then $\Sigma T_x = \Sigma T_Y = 0$. Use of this correction will be illustrated in the examples to follow.[7]

The value of tau in the caste stratification example is computed from Formulas (14.12) and (14.13) to be

$$\tau = \frac{92}{\sqrt{[12(11) - 0][12(11) - 0]}} = \frac{92}{132}$$
$$= +0.697$$

Because the maximum of tau is ± 1.00, this measure clearly indicates that the agreement is close between the two informants. We know that the same data produced a value of $r_s = +0.85$ in the last section, so it becomes clear that τ and r_s measure somewhat different conceptions of correlation. Tau has certain intrinsic advantages over r_s as a measure of correlation, but τ unfortunately involves a bit of rather tedious computation.

Some of this computational burden is alleviated by using a *graphical solution* for finding the numerator of tau. The initial step in the graphic method is to list the sets of ranks as before. Then like ranks are connected by straight lines, as in Fig. 14.5. The number of intersections of these lines, termed ΣI, are then counted. If the ranks were ordered in identical fashion, then all connecting lines would be exactly parallel, with no intersections occurring at all. The sum ΣI increases as the rankings become more dissimilar. The two caste rankings produce lines which cross a total of $\Sigma I = 10$ times. This sum can be converted to the numerator of tau by the following expression:

$$\text{numerator} = n(n-1) - 4\Sigma I - \Sigma T_Y \qquad (14.14)$$

where ΣI is the number of crossings on the graph and ΣT_Y is the sum of the $t(t-1)$ factors for the second (Y) ranking. For the caste rankings on Table 14.8,

$$\text{numerator} = 12(11) - 4(10) - 0 = 132 - 40 = 92$$

---

[7]It becomes necessary to confess once again that the statistical notation lacks consistency. Throughout this book, Greek letters have generally denoted parameters and italic letters refer to statistics. But the system has broken down: Kendall's tau is clearly a statistic and not a parameter, but the statistic is called τ. The problem is obvious, of course, since t has already been assigned to Student's test. But the distinction between statistic and parameter should be kept firmly in mind by this point, so the devious terminology ought not cause undue conceptual difficulty.

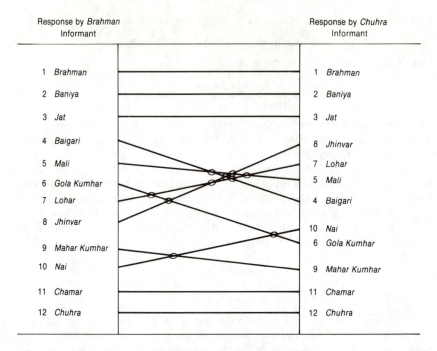

Fig. 14.5 Graphical solution for Kendall's τ.

This same numerator was computed by the enumeration methods, so the resulting values of τ are identical. Whenever ties occur, the lines should be drawn such that lines for tied variates do not cross. The graphical solution generally works better when only a moderate number of ties occurs.

The statistical significance of Kendall's τ can be tested in two ways, assuming that the samples were randomly generated. Whenever $n \leq 10$, the two critical values of the numerator of τ are given as follows (after Sokal and Rohlf 1969: 537):

	Numerator	
n	$\alpha = 0.05$	$\alpha = 0.01$
5	20	—
6	26	30
7	30	38
8	36	44
9	40	52
10	46	58

These critical values are exact only when no ties occur. A table of small n corrected for ties can be found in Burr (1960).

If the sample size exceeds 10, then the distribution of Kendall's tau can be approximated by a normal distribution. The null hypothesis of $H_o: \tau = 0$ can be tested by using a form of the standardized normal deviate:

$$z = \frac{\tau_{observed} - 0}{\sqrt{2(2n+5)/9n(n-1)}} \qquad (14.15)$$

The probability of such large differences between the observed tau and the null value of $\tau = 0$ can be found as usual from Table A.3.

The normal approximation method indicates that for the caste example,

$$z = \frac{0.697}{\sqrt{2(24+5)/108(11)}} = \frac{0.697}{\sqrt{0.0488}}$$

$$= 3.154$$

Table A.3 indicates a value of only $A = 0.0008$ corresponding to so small a z, so the probability that the obtained τ would deviate from $\tau = 0$ (in either direction) by chance alone is only $p = 0.0016$. The null hypothesis is rejected, and we conclude that the *Brahman* and *Chuhra* indeed rank the castes in a statistically indistinguishable manner.

An exact test of significance for Kendall's tau is also given by Naroll (1974), but the computations are so tedious as to require a computer for any large-scale application.

Example 14.4

Let us test the hypothesis that the more a society depends upon hunting, the more nomadic (that is, the less sedentary) will be that society. A sample of seven societies was randomly selected from the *Ethnographic Atlas*, and these societies were coded for the *dependence upon hunting* variable (col. 8) and the *settlement pattern* variable (col. 30).

Society	Hunting, percent dependence	Settlement Pattern
Copper Eskimo	36–45	Seminomadic communities
Djafun	0–5	Nomadic bands
Fox	36–45	Seminomadic communities
Gros Ventre	76–85	Nomadic bands
Makin	6-15	Complex settlements
Shasta	26–35	Semisedentary communities
Wishram	16-25	Semisedentary communities

Do these data support the hypothesis?

Kendall's tau coefficient is useful in this case, and τ will be computed by both methods. To find τ by enumeration, the variates must first be ranked in descending order of X (hunting), and then the ΣC_i can be computed.

Society	Hunting Rank	Settlement Rank	Subsequent Ranks	Total
Gros Ventre	1	1.5	3.5,3.5,5.5,5.5,7,(1.5)	5.5
Fox	2.5	3.5	(3.5),5.5,5.5,7	3.5
Copper Eskimo	2.5	3.5	5.5,5.5,7	3
Shasta	4	5.5	(5.5),7	1.5
Wishram	5.5	5.5	7	1
Makin	5.5	7		0
Djafun	7	1.5		0
				$\Sigma C_i = 14.5$

Note that the score "0.5" has been added to the C_i if the subsequent ranking is tied with the reference rank; these cases are enclosed in parentheses:

$$\text{numerator} = 4(14.5) - 7(6) = 58 - 42 = 16$$

Kendall's tau is thus

$$\tau = \frac{\text{numerator}}{\sqrt{[42-2][42-6]}} = \frac{16}{\sqrt{40(36)}}$$
$$= 0.422$$

Because n is less than 10, the tabled values indicate that the numerator (16) does not reach the critical value of 30; this sample has insufficient evidence to cause rejection of the null hypothesis. There is no reason to suspect a correlation between hunting and settlement pattern, based upon this limited sample.

The numerator of τ can also be found using the graphic method:

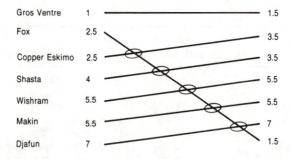

There are a total of five crossings, so the

$$\text{numerator} = 7(6) - 4(5) - 6 = 16$$

This is the same value of the numerator as found earlier, so the same value of tau must result.

Example 14.5

Spearman's r_s was applied earlier to Ember's cross-cultural study of community size and political authority (Table 14.7). Kendall's tau can also determine the relationship between these two variables.

Rank Order of Societies	Community Size	Political Authority	Sum of Larger Subsequent Ranks
Kaska	1	6	18
Caribou Eskimo	2	2.5	20.5
Kutubu	3	10	14
Xam	5	2.5	19
Naron	5	6	16.5
Mataco	5	6	16
Tiwi	8.5	2.5	16.5
Ojibwa	8.5	10	13.5
Bacairi	8.5	10	13
Acholi	8.5	17	7
Guahibo	11.5	2.5	13
Timucua	11.5	15	8
Ontong Java	13	15	7.5
Chamarro	15	10	9.5
Lango	15	10	9
Samoa	15	18.5	5.5
Cuna	17	21	3
Omaha	19	20	3
Teton	19	13	5
Didinga	19	18.5	3
Huron	21	15	3
Tswana	22.5	22	2
Ashanti	22.5	23	1
Thai	24	24	0
			$\Sigma C_i = 226.5$

The following ties exist on the X variable: Rank 5 (tied three times), rank 8.5 (tied four times), rank 11.5 (tied twice), rank 15 (tied three times), rank 19 (tied three times), and rank 22.5 (tied twice). The correction for ties on X is

$$T_x = 3(3-1) + 4(4-1) + 2(2-1) + 3(3-1) + 3(3-1) + 2(2-1)$$
$$= 34$$

Be certain to note here that t represents the *number of ties* in each rank rather than the *value* of the tied ranks. The correction for ties on the Y variable is

$$T_Y = 4(4-1) + 3(3-1) + 5(5-1) + 3(3-1) + 2(2-1)$$
$$= 46$$

The numerator of τ can then be computed:

$$\text{numerator} = 4(226.5) = 24(23) = 906 - 552$$
$$= 354$$

Tau is then computed to be

$$\tau = \frac{354}{\sqrt{[24(23) - 34][24(23) - 46]}}$$
$$= 0.69$$

The graphical method can also be used to determine the numerator of tau. In the diagram below, exactly 38 crossings occur. Thus,

$$\text{numerator} = 24(23) - 4(38) - 46$$
$$= 354$$

Rank Order of Societies	Community Size		Political Authority
Kaska	1		6
Caribou Eskimo	2		2.5
Kutubu	3		10
Xam	5		2.5
Naron	5		6
Mataco	5		6
Tiwi	8.5		2.5
Ojibwa	8.5		10
Bacairi	8.5		10
Acholi	8.5		17
Guahibo	11.5		2.5
Timucua	11.5		15
Ontong Java	13		15
Chamarro	15		10
Lango	15		10
Samoa	15		18.5
Cuna	17		21
Omaha	19		20
Teton	19		13
Didinga	19		18.5
Huron	21		15
Tswana	22.5		22
Ashanti	22.5		23
Thai	24		24

Thus, the same numerator is found by both methods and of course the values of tau are identical.

Formula (14.15) can be used to test the significance of this value of tau:

$$z = \frac{0.69}{\sqrt{2(2 \cdot 24 + 5)/9 \cdot 24(23)}}$$
$$= 4.72$$

Table A.3 indicates that this result is clearly significant.

14.5.3 Comparison of Spearman's r_s and Kendall's τ

τ and r_s have been computed for the same data, and the values of the two nonparametric correlation coefficients were found to differ. The reason for this is that the two coefficients are based upon rather different underlying models, and hence they do not measure "correlation" in exactly the same manner. But it turns out that r_s and τ utilize exactly the same amount of information, so they have identical *power*. This means that tests of significance based upon either τ or r_s will reject a false H_o at exactly the same level of statistical significance (see Siegel 1956:chapter 9). But several properties of τ have led to a general preference of Kendall's τ over r_s.

Probably the chief advantage of Kendall's statistic is that the distribution of τ approaches the normal more rapidly than does r_s. In fact, the distribution of τ is virtually identical to the normal in samples as small as $n = 9$. So τ seems generally more accurate than r_s in testing for statistical independence between ranked variables, especially when small or moderately sized samples are involved.

The direct and simple interpretation of τ also renders Kendall's tau generally more suitable for use in anthropology. The probability of any value of τ is defined simply in terms of concordant and discordant pairs which, while sometimes tedious to compute, present few conceptual difficulties. But the Spearman's r_s is based upon the squared sums of differences and becomes meaningful only through tortuous analogy with the parametric correlation coefficient r.

Kendall's τ seems also to produce a more meaningful result when a large number of ties are present. As would be expected, Spearman's r_s rather closely follows the Pearson Correlation Coefficient when the underlying distribution is more-or-less continuous, that is, when relatively few ties occur in ranking. But τ is often more accurate when a large number of cases must be classified into a relatively few ordinal classes.

τ has the final advantage over r_s in that tau can be generalized into a *partial correlation coefficient*. This statistic, called $\tau_{xy \cdot z}$ is particularly useful when observations upon two variables might in fact result from a causal connection with a third related variable. As Siegel (1956) has pointed out, a strong correlation of stature and vocabulary among school children might well be due to an important interrelationship with a third variable, such as age. Kendall's partial correlation is a close relative of Kendall's τ, and these statistics can be helpful in sorting out a number of related variables (see Siegel 1956: 223–229 and Conover 1971:253–255 for a discussion of the techniques of partial correlation).

All of these reasons seem to have convinced anthropologists to rely more upon τ than upon r_s. The main disadvantage of Kendall's tau is, of course, the somewhat tedious computations required whenever n is large. The graphic solution is of some help, especially when few ties are present. But an even greater boon has been the recent availability of computer programs to compute both r_s and τ with little effort (see, for example, the NONPAR CORR program available in the SPSS system devised by Nie, Bent, and Hull 1970).

The most important point to remember when working with rank-order correlation is that whichever coefficient is employed, the resulting value is specific only to that particular coefficient. It is quite improper to compute r_s for one data set, Kendall's τ on a second set, and then compare the values to determine relative degree of intercorrelation. For reasons detailed above, the coefficients measure correlation on different scales, and they are expected to produce different results.

14.5.4 Gamma

Regardless of whether τ or r_s is used, the question of excessive ties within ranks can become a serious problem. Although both τ and r_s can be corrected for ties, difficulties often arise when computing the cumbersome corrections. The normal approximation also becomes less valid as the number of ties increases. The correlation procedure can be simplified somewhat by grouping the ordinal variates into a few ranked categories. In effect, the data can thus be reduced into two tight ordinal sequences (A and B) within the standard R × C format (Blalock 1972: 421). For example, for case A:

Variable 2	Variable 1			
	Low	Medium	High	Total
High	0	0	30	30
Medium	0	30	0	30
Low	30	0	0	30
Total	30	30	30	90

A chi-square test for independence within an R × C table is commonly applied to analyze the relationship between two variables such as these, but as Naroll (1970c:163) has correctly pointed out, this practice has a major shortcoming. Compare case A with this second example, case B:

Variable 2	Variable 1			
	Low	Medium	High	Total
High	0	30	0	30
Medium	30	0	0	30
Low	0	0	30	30
Total	30	30	30	

The chi-square test will tell us that the two cases are identical. The variables in case A are arranged into a definite monotonic trend: Low variates predict low variates and high variates predict high variates. Case B lacks this notable trend. Unfortunately, a chi-square test for independence is blind to this difference because the test is not sensitive to changes on an ordinal scale. Chi-square must not be used in such cases.

The gamma coefficient has been designed for precisely those cases in which chi-square falters. Gamma (γ) requires that *both scales be ordinal*, and yet the data are grouped into the conventional R × C format; hence, gamma is particularly effective when so many ties occur that neither τ nor r_s can be used in comparing two ordinal rankings. The value of gamma is given by

$$\gamma = \frac{\text{no. of concordant pairs } minus \text{ no. of discordant pairs}}{\text{no. of concordant pairs } plus \text{ no. of discordant pairs}}$$

$$= \frac{\Sigma C_i}{\Sigma D_i} \tag{14.16}$$

A pair is termed *concordant* if they are ordered into the proper sequence and *discordant* if the sequencing is reversed. The first method used to find Kendall's tau in fact involved counting the number of concordant pairs (ΣC_i). The following (hypothetical) example shows how the pairs can be enumerated to find the gamma coefficient.

A study has been initiated to test the hypothesis that premarital sexual promiscuity is more prevalent among "primitive" than among "civilized" societies. A cross-cultural survey resulted in a random sample of 232 societies, each of which can be rated on (1) the level of sociopolitical complexity and (2) norms of premarital sexual behavior. Is there a relationship between the two variables?

These data are assembled in Table 14.9. Both scales are ordinal, but because the number of ties is excessive, neither τ nor r_s will serve as a suitable indicator of correlation. The chi-square statistic would adequately handle the format of the data, but χ^2 reduces such data to nominal form, thereby ignoring the important ordinal relationship.

To apply *gamma*, it is first necessary to determine the number of concordant pairs within the sample data. The levels of sociopolitical complexity have been ranked into five ordered categories, running from relatively low to very high levels of integration. Similarly, the norms of premarital sexual behavior have been scaled into three categories from high to low promiscuity. The upper left-hand cell (cell$_{1,1}$) contains six societies—those at the *state* level of complexity with a high degree of premarital sexual promiscuity. All six societies are "ties" in the earlier sense of τ and r_s. Furthermore, all societies listed on the first row ("state") are also tied with respect to the level of integration with cell$_{1,1}$. That is, all the societies on the first row are tied with respect to sociocultural

TABLE 14.9

Level of Sociocultural Complexity	Premarital Sexual Promiscuity			
	Weakly Prohibited	Prohibited	Strongly Prohibited	Total
State	6	8	19	33
City	7	15	20	42
Town	18	4	2	24
Village	36	18	19	73
Band	52	6	2	60
Total	119	51	62	232

integration, and all the cells in the first column are tied with regard to "high sexual promiscuity." For such tables, societies are termed *concordant* if they rank lower than those grouped in $\text{cell}_{1,1}$. Since row 1 and column 1 contain only societies tied with those in $\text{cell}_{1,1}$, none of these societies could possibly either agree (concur) or disagree (demur) with the theoretical ranking. But all the societies *down one row* ("city" or below) and *over one column* (the "moderate" and "low" columns) agree with the rankings of $\text{cell}_{1,1}$, and hence are termed *concordant societies*. The total number of these cases is given by the sum of the societies in $\text{cell}_{2,2}$ (15 societies), plus the total in $\text{cell}_{2,3}$ (four societies) and so forth:

$$15 + 20 + 4 + 2 + 18 + 19 + 6 + 2 = 86 \text{ societies}$$

Thus, 86 societies are concordant with the six societies in $\text{cell}_{1,1}$. The total number of *concordant pairs* (as distinct from *concordant societies*) is thus

$$6(86) = 516 \text{ pairs}$$

The concordant pairs must then be computed for the remaining cells in a similar manner. Moving to the second row of column 1 ($\text{cell}_{2,1}$), the cell contains 7 societies. Again, societies in the first column and second row represent "ties," so the concordant pairs involve only those groups below and to the right of $\text{cell}_{2,1}$:

$$7(4 + 2 + 18 + 19 + 6 + 2) = 7(51) = 357 \text{ pairs}$$

This process of enumeration continues down the first row—note that the last row of the first column will produce no concordant pairs—and then onto the second column, and so forth. The total number of *concordant pairs* for Table 14.9 is thus

$$\Sigma C_i = 6(86) + 7(51) + 18(45) + 36(8) + 8(43)$$
$$+ 15(23) + 4(21) + 18(2)$$
$$= 2780 \text{ pairs}$$

The total number of *discordant pairs* is found in a manner reverse to that described above. A discordant pair matches a selected reference case with all societies known to rank lower on either scale. So, the procedure begins with the upper right-hand cell ($\text{cell}_{1,3}$) and proceeds to enumerate *down and to the left*. The total number of pairs discordant with $\text{cell}_{1,3}$ are

$$19(15 + 7 + 4 + 18 + 36 + 6 + 52) = 19(138) \text{ pairs}$$

The next count is obtained from $\text{cell}_{2,3}$:

$$20(4 + 18 + 18 + 36 + 6 + 52) = 20(134) = 2680 \text{ pairs}$$

The total number of *discordant pairs* for the entire table is

$$\Sigma D_i = 19(138) + 20(134) + 2(112) + 19(58)$$
$$+ 8(113) + 15(106) + 4(88) + 18(52)$$
$$= 10{,}410 \text{ pairs}$$

We now have both quantities necessary to compute gamma from (14.16):

$$\gamma = \frac{2780 - 10{,}410}{2780 + 10{,}410} = -0.579$$

This rather strong negative value of gamma moderately supports the hypothesis that premarital sexual promiscuity is correlated with the less advanced levels of sociopolitical organization. That is, a low level of sociocultural complexity is found to occur with high promiscuity, and high complexity predicts a lower level of promiscuity. This is why the value of gamma is negative. Naroll's (1974) exact test of significance applies to gamma as well as Kendall's tau.

Example 14.6

In Chapter 11, Divale's hypothesis for the evolution of matrilocality was discussed (Example 11.9). In addition to predicting the gross change toward matrilocality upon warfare and migration, Divale also predicted a definite cycle of residence patterns, beginning with patrilocality and evolving into uxorilocality.

Do the three *descent* types appear to correlate with Divale's evolutionary sequence of *residence* types (data from Divale 1974)?

Residence	Descent Types			
	Matrilineal	Ambilineal	Patrilineal	Total
Uxorilocal	1	5	1	7
Matrilocal	52	0	0	52
Matrilocal/ avunculocal	5	0	0	5
Avunculocal	50	0	0	50
Avunculocal/ virilocal	7	2	0	9
Virilocal	26	29	21	76
Patrilocal	4	2	542	548
Total	145	38	564	747

Gamma is an appropriate coefficient with which to assess the relationship between these two ordinal pairs. The number of *concordant pairs* is found as follows:

$5(21 + 542) = 2815$ pairs
$52(2 + 29 + 21 + 2 + 542) = 52(596) = 30,992$ pairs
$5(2 + 29 + 21 + 2 + 542) = 5(596) = 2,980$ pairs
$50(2 + 29 + 21 + 2 + 542) = 50(596) = 29,800$ pairs
$7(29 + 21 + 2 + 542) = 4,158$ pairs
$26(2 + 542) = 14,144$ pairs
$2(21 + 542) = 1,126$ pairs
$29(542) = 15,718$ pairs
$1(2 + 29 + 21 + 542) = 596$ pairs
$$\Sigma C_i = 102,329$$

Similarly, the number of *discordant pairs* is

$1(52 + 5 + 50 + 7 + 2 + 26 + 29 + 4 + 2) = 177$ pairs
$21(4 + 2) = 126$ pairs
$5(52 + 5 + 50 + 7 + 26 + 4) = 720$ pairs
$2(26 + 4) = 60$ pairs
$29(4) = 116$ pairs

$$\Sigma D_i = 1199$$

From Formula (14.16), the gamma coefficient is found to be

$$\gamma = \frac{102,329 - 1,199}{102,329 + 1,199} = 0.977$$

This strong value of $\gamma = 0.976$ leaves little doubt of a positive association between residence and descent, in the order hypothesized by Divale (1974).

14.6 CORRELATION ON THE NOMINAL SCALE

Probably the most common measure of statistical correlation—perhaps better termed *association*—between nominal variables is the chi-square statistic, considered in detail in Chapter 11. But one major difficulty with chi-square is that its value depends upon the size of sample, n. To see that this is so, examine the following contingency table:

25	35	60
35	25	60
60	60	120

The value of the χ^2 statistic can be readily computed to be 3.32, with a single degree of freedom. Because this value is not significant at the 0.05 level, the null hypothesis of no association would generally not be rejected.

Let us now modify the frequencies slightly by *doubling* the figures in the above contingency table:

50	70	120
70	35	120
120	120	240

A single degree of freedom remains, but the chi-square statistic is now inflated to $\chi^2 = 6.68$. The results are now found to be significant beyond the 0.01 level, and H_o would be rejected.

What has happened here? Although the actual numbers of the two tables differ—the second is exactly twice the first—the *relationships of the cells to one another remains constant*. The chi-square statistic is a direction function of sample size, and hence chi-square can never be used as an indicator of the *strength* of a relationship. The two tables above are identical in terms of their percentage relationship, and such proportional similarity is often of interest to the social scientist. If one merely reports a chi-square test as (1) significant or (2) not significant, then the analysis of contingency tables would be totally obfuscated.

A number of coefficients have been proposed from time to time to measure the strength of relationship within a contingency table. No attempt will be made to cover the range of such coefficients. Every statistic is designed to fit specific needs, and only a couple of the most important measures of association will be introduced.

14.6.1 The Phi Coefficient

Look carefully again at the two contingency tables presented above. As the cell frequency increased, the chi-square statistic simultaneously increased and eventually made the grade as "statistically significant," even though the relationship between the two variables was absolutely unchanged. In fact, χ^2 increased not only with n, but also exactly in proportion to n; the second value of χ^2 is about twice the first (within a small rounding error). When n doubles, so does χ^2; when n triples, χ^2 also triples. This same difficulty has been encountered a number of times before, as in Chapter 4, when we needed a measure of sample dispersion. You will remember that the sum of squared deviations about the mean, $\Sigma(X_i - \bar{X})^2$ increased in exact proportion to sample size. This difficulty was solved by dividing the squared deviations by n; the *sample variance*, S^2, was the resultant statistic. Because S^2 is an average of the squared deviations, the statistic is independent of sample size. A similar strategy will enable us to "salvage" the chi-square statistic for assessing the strength of nominal associations. The process of simply dividing by n will free the chi-square statistic from the undesirable inflation due to increasing sample size:

$$\frac{\chi^2}{n} = \phi^2 \qquad (14.17)$$

This new expression is known as *phi squared* (pronounced "fee squared"). Here, ϕ^2 is simply a variant of χ^2, which has been rendered independent of sample size. The most commonly encountered form is simply ϕ ("fee"), the square root of Expression (14.17). Because ϕ applies only to the 2×2 contingency format, the following computational formula is helpful:

$$\phi = \frac{ad - bc}{\sqrt{(a + b)(a + c)(b + d)(c + d)}} \qquad (14.18)$$

where a, b, c, and d represent the various cell frequencies defined earlier for Fisher's Exact Test [Formula (11.10)]. Note that ϕ consists merely of the difference between the diagonals ($ad - bc$), divided by the square root of the product of the row and column totals.

Unlike its cousin the chi-square statistic, the phi coefficient has some definite limits: ϕ ranges only between $+1$ and -1. This range readily follows from the definition of ϕ. The following contingency table indicates the extreme of

420

absolute positive association:

50	0	50
0	50	50
50	50	100

The phi coefficient is found to be

$$\phi = \frac{(50)(50) - (0)(0)}{\sqrt{(50)(50)(50)(50)}} = \frac{2500}{2500} = +1.00$$

As expected, a perfect positive association produces a value of $\phi = +1.00$. Such situations will occur whenever every instance of variable 1 occurs with every instance of variable 2, and an absence of variable 1 invariably denotes the absence of variable 2.

The opposite extreme arises whenever variables 1 and 2 *never* co-occur (that is, when cells a and d are empty), which produces the case of *absolute negative association*:

0	50	50
50	0	50
50	50	100

The phi coefficient for this case is

$$\phi = \frac{(0)(0) - (50)(50)}{\sqrt{(50)(50)(50)(50)}} = \frac{-2500}{2500} = -1.00$$

Perfect negative association will always produce $\phi = -1.00$.

Finally, there is the situation in which variables 1 and 2 have no association at all:

25	25	50
25	25	50
50	50	100

$$\phi = \frac{(25)(25) - (25)(25)}{\sqrt{(50)(50)(50)(50)}} = \frac{0}{2500} = 0.00$$

These simple examples provide an intuitive understanding to the meaning of various values of ϕ.

Example 14.7

O'Nell and Selby (1968) have postulated that Zapotec culture allows men more opportunity for escape than females. Community pressure, for instance, effectively bars most females—especially younger women—from using alcohol as an escape from reality. If this notion is correct, then one expects to find relatively more males than females attending socially sanctioned fiestas.

To test this hypothesis, O'Nell and Selby conducted a census at one cuelga ("a drunken fiesta lasting from three to five days, customarily celebrated in honor of a person's Saint's day") in the village of Santo Tomas Mazaltepec, a Zapotec pueblo near Oaxaca, Mexico.

Reported attendance at Cuelgas in Santo Tomas Mazaltepec: Differential response by sex.

	Attend	Do Not Attend	Total
Men	26	4	30
Women	12	13	25
Total	38	17	55

Does there appear to be a strong association between sex and attendance at the cuelga? Is this difference significant at the 0.01 level?

The first question is one of strength of association, so the ϕ coefficient must be computed:

$$\phi = \frac{26(13) - 4(12)}{\sqrt{30(25)(38)(17)}} = \frac{290}{696.1} = 0.42$$

The phi coefficient indicates a positive association of moderate strength in the predicted direction.

The statistical significance of this association can be found by using the standard chi-square statistic (corrected for continuity).

O_i	E_i	$|O_i - E_i|$	$|O_i - E_i| - \frac{1}{2}$	$[O_i - E_i - \frac{1}{2}]^2$	$[O_i - E_i - \frac{1}{2}]^2 / E_i$
26	20.7	5.3	4.8	23.04	1.11
4	9.3	5.3	4.8	23.04	2.48
12	17.3	5.3	4.8	23.04	1.33
13	7.7	5.3	4.8	23.04	2.99
					$\chi^2 = 7.91$

This value of χ^2 is significant beyond the 0.01 level, but the moderate value of ϕ should sound a note of caution against undue preoccupation with the high level of statistical significance.

Example 14.8

In his study of the southern Yanomamö, Chagnon (1967) suggested that warlike tribes tend to emphasize a cultural norm of ferocity—the more ferocious the warrior, the higher is his prestige. A cultural manifestation of this ferocity is a strong tendency for one group to attack the neighboring peoples in an attempt to expand its social territory. The following data have been extracted from Otterbein (1970: 130–149, appendices C and D).

	Territory Constant or Contracting	Territory Expanding
Attacking continual or frequent	Amara Fox Ila Mossi Nandi Papago Saramacca Tibetans Wishram	Abipon Aztec Egyptians Jivaro Mundurucu Plains Cree Sema Somali Thai Timbira Tiva
Infrequent	Albanians Amba Ambo Andamanese Copper Eskimo Dorobo Gisu Hawaiians Lau Marshallese Monachi Motilon Mutair Orokaiva Santa Ana Tikopia Tiwi Toda Trumai	Japanese

Do these results support the hypothesis that a strong relationship exists between cultural "ferocity" and the tendency for a society to expand its territory? Is this difference statistically significant?

The chi-square statistic for this 2×2 table is as follows:

O_i	E_i	$(O_i - E_i)$	$(O_i - E_i)^2$	$(O_i - E_i)^2/E_i$
9	14	−5	25	1.786
11	6	5	25	4.167
19	14	5	25	1.786
1	6	−5	25	4.167
				$\chi^2 = 11.9060$

This value is significant beyond the 0.01 level. To measure the strength of this association, the ϕ coefficient can be computed from Formula (14.18):

$$\phi = \frac{9(1) - 11(19)}{\sqrt{(20)(20)(28)(12)}} = -0.546$$

Phi could also be computed directly from χ^2 using (14.17):

$$\phi^2 = \frac{\chi^2}{n}$$

$$= \frac{11.906}{40} = 0.298$$

which corresponds closely with the value $\phi^2 = -0.546^2 = 0.2981$ computed from (14.18). Although the χ^2 is statistically significant, the value of $n = 40$ and $\phi = -0.546$ warns that the relationship is not totally overwhelming.

14.6.2 Tau-b

The ϕ coefficient is clearly restricted to the 2×2 nominal format, but another related measure, called tau-b (or τ_b) expands ϕ to the general $R \times C$ contingency table. Like ϕ, τ_b assumes only a nominal level of measurement. Tau-b was initially defined in an important series of articles by Goodman and Kruskal (1954, 1959, and 1963); also see Blalock (1972: 300–302).

To illustrate how τ_b operates, let us return to Example 14.7. Remember that O'Nell and Selby investigated the relationship between sex roles and participation in the Zapotecan *cuelga*. We found earlier that the ϕ coefficient for this contingency table was $\phi = 0.42$. Chi-square indicates this to be significant beyond the 0.01 level.

Now we can examine this same situation using a different probabilistic approach. Suppose that the ethnographer had missed the actual *cuelga*, but was told that 38 of the 55 people in the village attended.

Attend *cuelga* (B_1)	38
Did not attend	
cuelga (B_2)	17
	55 residents of Santo Tomas Mazaltepec

Given only this limited census, how well could an ethnographer guess which individuals attended, and which stayed away? We could, for example, line up the 55 villagers and form them into two groups: One group of 38 who we thought attended and the remaining 17 people who we figured stayed away.

Since we have no outside information, these two groups could be assigned randomly. How many people are incorrectly classified? The probability that any single informant is *incorrectly* placed into group B_1, those who attended the *cuelga*, is clearly $p(B_2) = 17/55$. Because 38 individuals must be independently assigned into group B_1, in the long run, we expect to make only $38 - 11.7 = 26.3$ correct assignments to the group which attended the *cuelga*. Similarly, the error of *incorrectly* assigning informants to the second group is $p(B_1) = 38/55$. Since 17 such assignments are made, we expect that again there will be $17(38/55) = 11.7$ errors. (There is only 1 degree of freedom here, so an error in group B_1 automatically implies a corresponding error in group B_2.) Thus, we estimate a total of $11.7 + 11.7 = 23.4$ errors if the informants are randomly assigned to groups B_1 and B_2.

These errors were made by blind chance. What would happen if we were given additional information about the *cuelga*? Suppose somebody told the ethnographer that, of the 38 villagers attending, exactly 26 were males. Now we could reconstruct the 2×2 contingency table considered earlier in Example 14.7.

	Men A_1	Women A_2	Total
Attend *cuelga* (B_1)	26	12	38
Did not attend *cuelga* (B_2)	4	13	17
Total	30	25	55

Does a knowledge of the sex ratio at the *cuelga* help in deciding whether or not individual informants attended? Let's see.

We know that 26 of 30 males in Santo Tomas Mazaltepec attended the *cuelga*. Thus, the probability that any particular male *did not attend* is only $p(A_1B_2) = 4/30$. We must now guess at which 26 attended, so we can expect to make about $26(4/30) = 3.5$ errors of assignment. We also expect to make about $4(26/30) = 3.5$ errors when guessing which males did not attend (again, note the single degree of freedom). The probability that a randomly selected woman did not attend the *cuelga* is $p(A_2B_2) = 13/25$. A total of $12(13/25) = 6.2$ errors are likely in deciding which women attended, and $13(12/25) = 6.2$ errors are expected among those who did not attend. Therefore, a total of four kinds of errors exist when we try to reconstruct the cells of the contingency table: $3.5 + 3.5 + 6.2 + 6.2 = 19.4$. These errors are expected when guessing attendance, once sex is known.

So how much does a knowledge of this second variable improve our estimate of who attended the *cuelga*? The proportional diminution of errors is defined as

$$\tau_b = \frac{(\text{no. of errors when } A \text{ is not known}) - (\text{no. of errors when } A \text{ is known})}{\text{no. of errors when } A \text{ is not known}}$$

$$(14.19)$$

For the example at hand,

$$\tau_b = \frac{23.4 - 19.4}{23.4} = 0.17$$

We can say that a knowledge of the sex distribution saves us about $23.4 - 19.4 = 4.0$ errors in the long run.

So τ_b is a measure of just how well one variable predicts a second. In this example we attempted to predict *cuelga* attendance based upon a knowledge of the sex ratio at the festival. That makes *cuelga* attendance (B) the *dependent* (or predicted) variable and sex ratio (A) the *independent* (or predictor) variable. If A and B are statistically independent, then a knowledge of A should have no effect whatsoever on the outcome of B. Tau-b measures the strength of association of A, given B.

This same positive association was assessed in Example 14.7, using another coefficient, ϕ. The coefficients ϕ and τ_b are rather closely related: $\tau_b = \phi^2$. In this example, $\phi = 0.42$ and $\tau_b = 0.18$. Tau-b is often more meaningful than ϕ because of the intuitively obvious meaning of τ_b.

But τ_b has a second and more important advantage over ϕ. Remember that ϕ can be computed only for 2×2 contingency tables. Tau-b has no such restrictions and is applicable to any R $\times$ C table. As an illustration of this, let us once again consider Raymond Firth's kinship and residence cross-tabulation for Tikopia (from Table 11.1).

Village	Clan			Total
	A_1 Ravena	A_2 Namo	A_3 Faea	
B_1: Kafika	31	2	43	76
B_2: Tafua	4	16	46	66
B_3: Taumako	39	6	16	61
B_4: Fanarere	10	3	2	15
Total	84	27	107	$218 = n$

The chi-square statistic computed earlier indicates that the null hypothesis of no association must be rejected. That is, that residence and kinship are not statistically independent on Tikopia. The τ_b coefficient now permits us to assess just *how much association* exists between kinship and residence in this sample.

First consider this question: What does a knowledge of kinship (A) tell us about residence (B)? Kinship is taken here to be the independent variable, and we wish to assess its impact upon residence. If there were no association, the τ_b should be zero, and a knowledge of A would not reduce the errors of assigning informants to residences. τ_b is computed as before. First we find the number of errors resulting in B when A is unknown. A total of 76 Tikopians live in the village of Kafika. The probability of error in randomly assigning an informant to Kafika is $p(\bar{B}_1) = (218 - 76)/218 = 142/218$. In the long run, we can expect to commit about $76(142/218) = 49.5$ errors in assigning informants to Kafika. The other three villages are handled in a similar fashion: For Tafua, we expect $66(152/218) = 46.0$ errors; for Taumako, $61(157/218) = 43.9$ errors; for Fanarere, $15(203/218) = 14.0$ errors. A total of $49.5 + 46.0 + 43.9 + 14.0 = 153.4$ errors are thus estimated for assigning villagers without a knowledge of their kinship. Now we must find what improvement, if any, there is when clan affinities of the villages are known. We know that 31 Tikopians of the Ravena clan live at Kafika, so a total of $31(53/84) = 19.6$ errors is likely. The errors for the other cells are found in a similar manner:

Ravena	Namo	Faea
31(53/84) = 19.6	2(25/27) = 1.9	43(64/107) = 25.7
4(80/84) = 3.8	16(11/27) = 6.5	46(61/107) = 26.2
39(45/84) = 20.9	6(21/27) = 4.7	16(91/107) = 13.6
10(74/84) = 8.8	3(24/27) = 2.7	2(105/107) = 2.0
53.1	15.8	67.5

Total errors in B, when A is known, are $53.1 + 15.8 + 67.5 = 136.4$. The relative improvement in estimating B from a knowledge of clan affiliation is thus

$$\tau_b = \frac{153.4 - 136.4}{153.4} = \frac{17.0}{153.4} = 0.11$$

This is a rather low value, indicating only a weak association between kinship and residence at Tikopia. χ^2 and τ_b tell us rather different things about the same sample. The chi-square statistic was quite large, suggesting that we reject H_o and conclude that kinship and residence are not independent at Tikopia. But τ_b warns us that this relationship, while significant, is not a very strong one. Even relatively weak associations can prove statistically significant, provided a large enough sample is involved (discussed further in Chapter 16).

Thus, τ_b provides an analog to ϕ, and τ_b is applicable to the general R × C case. But the conditions for τ_b must be rather carefully defined. Remember the question asked of the Tikopian sample: What does kinship imply about residence? Residence was the dependent variable. Another question remains unanswered by τ_b: What does residence (B) tell us about kinship (A)? Kinship is now put in the dependent position, and this is a rather different situation. A second coefficient must be defined to assess the impact of B on A.

$$\tau_a = \frac{\text{(no. of errors in } A \text{ when } B \text{ is unknown)} - \text{(no. of errors when } B \text{ is known)}}{\text{no. of errors when } B \text{ is unknown}}$$

(14.20)

The value for the Tikopian sample is $\tau_a = 0.17$, indicating a slightly stronger value than for τ_b. In general $\tau_a \neq \tau_b$.

14.7 CURVILINEAR REGRESSION AND CORRELATION

● *We didn't know we was poor until we went to town.*—R. Cash Hancock

This consideration of correlation has stressed repeatedly that the techniques apply only to situations in which *linear relationships* are suspected between predictor and predicted variables. A host of other mathematical techniques exist which consider nonlinear (that is, *curvilinear*) relationships. Unfortunately, once the linear approximation is known to be invalid, then a bewildering variety of nonlinear regression possibilities jump forth: exponential growth or decay, asymptotic, logistic growth, polynomials of various orders, and so on. The strategy of curvilinear regression consists of sorting through the numerous possibilities at hand in hopes of finding a single curve which best fits the data. Most of these techniques are more advanced than the present scope, and some rather sophisticated analyses of variance designs are often required to determine just which line produces the "best fit." For these reasons, a detailed discussion of curvilinear regression is not attempted here, and the interested reader is referred to Hays (1973: chapter 16) and Sokal and Rohlf (1969: 468–476). Computer programs for fitting curvilinear regression are also available in most comprehensive statistical packages for computers.

There is one technique of curvilinear correlation and regression, however, which deserves mention, for it is not only indeed critical to many anthropological situations, but is also relevant to the current approach. The technique is *logarithmic transformation* and the principle is quite simple: Nonlinear relationships are mathematically converted into linear proportions, and then the standard linear models of correlations and regression can be applied as before. The logarithmic transformation is thus really a device whereby the tedious techniques of curvilinear regression can be avoided. There is a clear analogy between the logarithmic transformation in regression and the transformations considered earlier to approximate the normal distribution.

The simplest logarithmic relationship is the *geometric series*: Growing populations of any species tend to expand geometrically until increase is slowed by extraneous factors.[8] Let us consider the hypothetical situation in which a lifeboat is washed ashore on the deserted island of Malthus. Coincidentally enough, the boat contains two compatible strangers, one male and one female. Upon landing and realizing they have no hope of escape, the strangers decide first to be friends and second to attempt colonization of the island. The population must increase rapidly so that the offspring can survive in this hostile land, so they make an informal pact, agreeing that the rate of growth must be exactly double: two children for every adult. Thus, while the first generation of Malthusians number only two individuals—the original refugees—the second generation will jump to a population of four (two children for each original Malthusian). Once the second generation ceases reproducing, the third generation will number eight people. The fourth generation jumps to sixteen people, and so on. This situation of geometric population increase is graphed in Fig. 14.6. The actual quantitative increase skyrockets as the generations go by, but the basic rate of reproduction remains constant—two offspring for each adult. This characteristic situation cannot be described by the linear regression and correlation techniques considered thus far because the quantitative increase obviously is not linear. But a very simple transformation will allow analysis of this increase *as if it were* linear.

Let us take the common logarithm of the population within each generation and plot these transformed population figures. The population of the first

[8]These extraneous influences constitute the "checks to increase" discussed by Charles Darwin. Whether these influences originate from factors intrinsic within the population or from extrinsic forces, such as food or weather, remains an open issue among population ecologists.

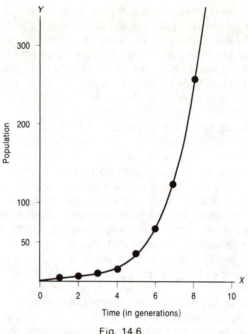

Fig. 14.6

generation is known to be 2, so log(population) is $\log_{10} 2 = 0.301$. The log of the population of generation 2 is $\log 4 = 0.602$ (exactly *twice* that of the first generation). The log of population in generation 3 is $\log 8 = 0.903$, exactly *three* times that of generation 1, and so forth. When log(population) is plotted against time (in generations), a perfectly linear relationship results (Fig. 14.7). Bartlett's method of regression determines the best fit to describe this line as

$$\log \hat{Y} = bX = 0.301X$$

Few should be surprised that the slope of this line is $\log 2 = 0.301$, and that the Y-intercept is through the origin. The correlation coefficient obviously must be $r = +1.00$. Although only ten generations were used in this computation, the equation $Y = 0.301X$ allows projection for the population of any given generation. The projected population for generation 15, for example, is

$$\log \hat{Y} = 0.301(15) = 4.5150$$
$$\hat{Y} = \text{antilog}(4.5150) = 32,734$$

Assuming constant conditions, the population of generation 95 is estimated to be 3.935×10^{28} individuals, obviously time for Zero Population Growth.

This simple logarithmic transformation of Y converts a clearly curvilinear relationship into a straight line, and the methods of regression and correlation can be applied to these transformed scores with impunity. An even easier method of analysis is available whenever only a best-fit regression line is necessary.

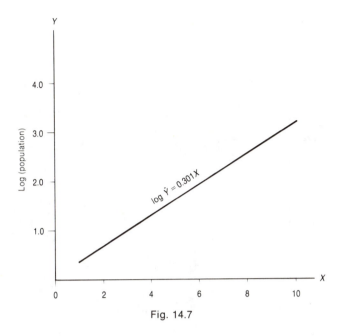

Fig. 14.7

Especially constructed graph paper (*semilog paper*) automatically performs the logarithmic transformation on a set of raw Y_i scores (Fig. 14.8). The X-axis remains on the common arithmetic scale, but the Y-axis is graduated along a logarithmic progression. That is, the distance between 1 and 10 is exactly equal to the distance between 10 and 100, which is exactly equal to that between 100 and 1000. The Y units are thus scaled in exponential fashion, just as one would progress mechanically by using a table of common logarithms. The generational times are plotted on the horizontal axis as before, but the population figures are plotted along the logarithmic divisions of Y. The Malthusian data in Fig. 14.8 has been plotted on *semilog* paper, producing results identical to those of Fig. 14.7, but without the bother of resorting to the logarithmic tables. *Semilog* paper is handy whenever one variable must be transformed and when only an estimate of the regression line is needed. Once the descriptive line of best fit is drawn, the graph can be used in a fashion similar to an actual regression equation, in order to predict interim values of Y from X. When the points tend to scatter—that is, when $\rho \neq \pm 1.00$—the graphic method provides a useful first step in deciding whether or not a semilogarithmic relationship in fact exists. If so, then the individual logs can be found in the tables, and the more rigorous regression and correlation coefficients can be computed. If the points turn out not to be linear, then little effort has been wasted on the preliminary graphics.

A second sort of logarithmic transformation is available when *both* variables must be converted from arithmetic to logarithmic scales. To illustrate the *allometric* or *log–log transformation*, let us examine the relationship which has come to be called *Naroll's constant*. Raoul Naroll correctly realized that the relationship between human population and the floor areas they inhabit would

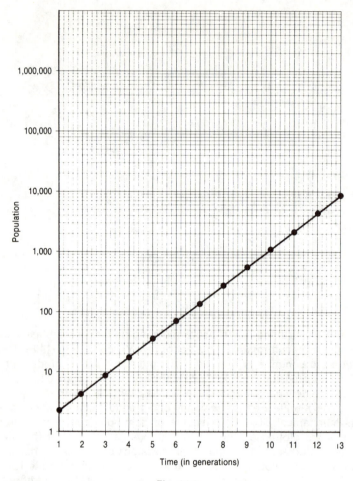

Fig. 14.8

be of interest to prehistoric archaeologists. Specifically, if a systematic relationship could be demonstrated between population and floor area by using a cross-cultural survey technique, then archaeologists would be able to estimate prehistoric population size simply from a knowledge of site size. Naroll (1962a: table 1) constructed a cross-cultural sample of 18 societies: 6 each come from North America and Oceania, 3 from South America, 2 from Africa, and 1 from Eurasia. This sample has been reproduced in Table 14.10. Does there appear to be a systematic relationship between the size of a community and the physical area it occupies?

This is clearly a problem amenable to regression analysis, and a scattergram of the data has been constructed in Fig. 14.9. A Model II regression provides the best linear fit to be

$$\hat{Y} = 939.3 + 0.487X$$

**TABLE 14.10   Cross-cultural data relating floor area to population size
(after Naroll 1962a: table 1).**

Society	Largest Settlement (L.S.)	Estimated Population of L.S.	Estimated Floor Area of L.S.
Vanua Levu	Nakaroka	75	412.8
Eyak	Algonik	120	836
Kapauku	Botekubo	181	362
Wintun	?	200	900
Klallam	Port Angeles	200	2,420
Hupa	Tsewenalding?	200	2,490
Haluk	Ifaluk	252	3,024
Ramkokamekra	Ponto	298	6,075
Bella Coola	Bella Coola	400	16,320
Kiwai	Oromosapua	400	1,432.2
Tikopia	Tikopia	1,260	8,570
Cuna	Ustupu	1,800	5,460
Iroquois	?	3,000	13,370
Kazak	?	3,000	63,000
Ila	Kasenga	3,000	47,000
Tonga	Nukualofa	5,000	111,500
Zula	?	15,000	65,612
Inca	Cuzco	200,000	167,220

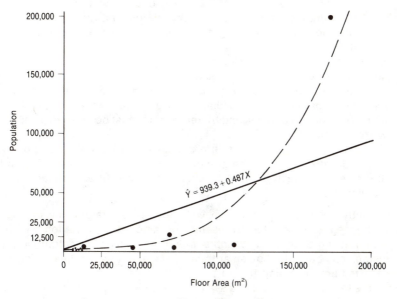

Fig. 14.9

This line has been fitted to the data, but the difficulties with this approach should be obvious. The linear correlation for these data is $r = +0.776$, denoting that only about 60 percent of the variability in Y can be accounted for by X. The scattergram indicates that because the bulk of Naroll's cases have a site size (X_i) somewhat smaller than about 10,000 m^2, the data points are hopelessly bunched into the lower left of the scattergram while the point representing the Inca of Cuzco lies isolated in the upper extreme. The common linear regression derived above has little relevance to the empirical scatter of points because *this relationship is obviously not linear.* In fact, it has been difficult to represent all the data on a single graph: When the Inca are included, the bulk of the cases becomes blurred. Predictions emanating from a linear description of nonlinear phenomena area are generally found to be spurious and misleading.

But the data on Fig. 14.9 look suspiciously like an *allometric* function, as estimated by the dashed line. If floor area and settlement size are indeed allometric pairs, then a log–log transformation of the scales should provide a more suitable procedure of estimation. Before attempting the transformation, it is a good idea to see how well the allometric function fits the actual data.

Standard log–log paper provides a quick-and-dirty method for determining whether or not an allometric curve sufficiently describes a set of data. To plot data on log–log paper, follow these steps:

1. *Determine the number of "cycles" present in the data.* The number of logarithmic cycles within a data set refers to the number of meaningful decimal places. The population figures on Table 14.10 range between 75 and 200,000 people, encompassing the following decimal digits: tens, hundreds, thousands, ten thousands, and hundred thousands. At least five logarithmic cycles will be required to describe the populations. The floor areas range from 412.8 to 167,220 m^2, so at least four log cycles are involved (hundreds, thousands, ten thousands, and hundred thousands). Thus, the appropriate log–log paper must contain at least four or five logarithmic cycles.
2. *Establish arithmetic scales on the log–log graph.* Following the conventions of regression, the horizontal axis will depict X, so the X-axis is divided into floor areas (expressed in square meters) and Y-axis is divided to represent population. The scalar intervals follow an exponential rather than arithmetic frequency, and therefore care must be taken to avoid errors in transcription.
3. *Plot the data points on the scattergram.* If more than 50 or so points are involved, the data should be grouped into a frequency distribution so that the means of each frequency class can be plotted instead of each individual point.

A perfectly allometric relationship will produce a straight line on log–log paper; the degree of scatter represents the amount of deviation within the sample. If log–log paper is unavailable, then the common (or natural) log table conversions can be plotted on an arithmetic scale, but use of the log–log paper saves the tedium of finding the $2n$ logs.

Once the log–log scattergram is available, one can readily determine whether computing allometric regression is worthwhile. Figure 14.10 indicates that

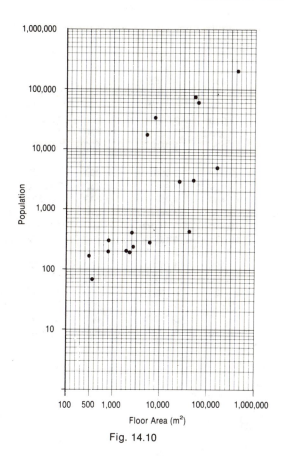

Fig. 14.10

although a good deal of dispersion remains, a log–log transformation does indeed render the points much more linear than merely the raw variates would indicate. Thus, the graph indicates that log–log regression would be a suitable technique to apply to Naroll's data.

The general allometric formula is expressed as

$$\log \hat{Y} = \log a + b \log X \qquad (14.21)$$

where a and b are the common coefficients of linear regression. As mentioned earlier, the log–log transformation is not technically a method of curvilinear regression; the variates are merely converted from a curvilinear (geometric) to a linear (arithmetic) scale of measurement and then treated *as if they were linear*.

Table 14.11 shows the computations necessary to find the proper regression line for Naroll's population data. All raw scores are initially converted into common logarithms; then the standard computations are used to find the value of the two regression constants. The Model II method of fitting the regression line has been employed here because the X variable, the *estimated floor area of largest settlement*, is a random variable, subject to errors of sampling. The final

TABLE 14.11 Log–log transformation of Naroll's data on Table 14.10.

Society	X	log X	Y	log Y	
Kapauku	362	2.55871	181	2.25768	
Vanua Levu	412.8	2.61574	75	1.87506	
Eyak	836	2.92221	120	2.07918	log $\bar{X}_1 = 2.93178$
Wintun	900	2.95424	200	2.30103	log $\bar{Y}_1 = 2.23601$
Kiwai	1,432.2	3.15594	400	2.60206	
Klallam	2,420	3.38382	200	2.30103	
Hupa	2,490	3.39620	200	2.30103	
Ifaluk	3,024	3.49471	252	2.40140	
Cuna	5,460	3.73719	1,800	3.25527	
Ramkokamekra	6,075	3.78355	298	2.47422	
Tikopia	8,570	3.94792	1,260	3.10037	
Iroquois	13,370	4.12613	3,000	3.47712	
Bella Coola	16,320	4.21272	400	2.60206	
Ila	47,000	4.67210	3,000	3.47712	
Kazak	63,000	4.79934	3,000	3.47712	log $\bar{X}_3 = 4.79527$
Zulu	65,612	4.81697	15,000	4.17609	log $\bar{Y}_3 = 3.78873$
Tonga	111,500	5.04727	5,000	3.69897	
Inca	167,220	5.22324	200,000	5.30103	

$$\bar{X} = \frac{68.84800}{18} = 3.82500; \quad \bar{Y} = \frac{53.15784}{18} = 3.12000$$

$$b' = \frac{3.78873 - 2.23601}{4.79527 - 2.93178} = 0.833$$

$$a' = 3.120 - 0.833(3.825) = 0.066$$

$$\log \hat{Y} = 0.833 \log X - 0.07$$

allometric line of regression is given by

$$\log Y = 0.833 \log X - 0.07$$

Sample values from this equation have been computed on Table 14.11, and the line of regression has been fitted to the datum points of Fig. 14.11. Note how much closer the data cluster around the log–log approximation than did the same data about the simple arithmetic regression. The linear correlation coefficient for the allometric plot is $r = +0.878$, accounting for over 77 percent of the variance in Y. Thus, the log–log transformation represents 77% − 60% = 17% improvement over the simple, untransformed method.

So, the mechanics of allometric correlation and regression offer few additional computational challenges. But unexplained so far is just why the log–log transformation works so handily and just what an allometric relationship really signifies. One even hears occasional grumblings that transformations smack of "cooking one's data" in order to obtain more successful results. The fact is that this general suspicion of data transformations is grounded in an interesting ethnocentric fallacy. Many of our mathematically naive colleagues seem to feel

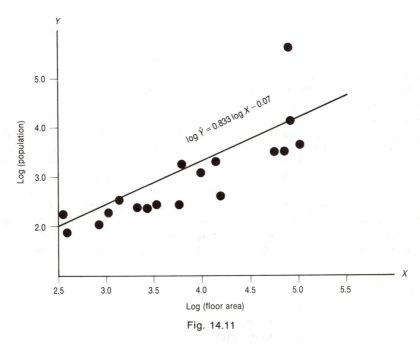

Fig. 14.11

that the common decimal scale is somehow more "natural," that arithmetic scales are somehow better equipped to reflect the characteristics of man and nature. Until recently, Western schooling has inflated the importance of the arithmetic relationship (largely by default) until we are led to look with suspicion at any deviation from the commonplace decimal system. Recent developments such as the "New Math" and talk of the United States converting to metric equivalents has fortunately undermined some of this suspicion, but many social scientists still seem to look askance at nonarithmetic scales. I should think, however, that anthropologists, of all the social scientists, should be most sensitive toward regarding one's own system as somehow "most natural" or "better" than other systems; this is simply an ethnocentric viewpoint.

Specifically with reference to the log–log transformation, there are solid reasons why the allometric relationship provides a more valid measuring scale in some contexts. The allometric formula was originally introduced in 1881 by Snell to express the relationship between brain size and body mass in mammals, and allometric relationships have since been discovered to operate in a number of social and biological circumstances. Specifically, the allometric equation holds that the *ratio* between two variables is roughly constant. For example, adult human weight is known to range roughly between 67 and 89 kg, over a range of about 22 kg. In *Macaca mulatta*, however, the adult weight varies from about 5.7 to 12.0 kg, a range of only 6.3 kg. Thus, it could be stated that the weight of *Homo sapiens* is vastly more variable than that of the *Macaca*. But such a facile pronouncement suffers from the fallacy of using observed range of variability as a point of comparison. Such a measure is clearly unfair. A more suitable method of comparison involves the relative *proportion* of variability, such as the ration between the greatest and the least values. For man, this ratio is about $89/67 = 1.33$, while for the macaque the ration is $12/5.7 = 2.10$. Clearly, the macaque is somewhat more variable than man, and this relationship has been obscured by using the common arithmetic scaling procedure.

The concept of *proportionate range* can best be expressed in logarithmic form. If X_1 is the largest variate and X_2 is the smallest, then the logarithm of the ratio $(X_1/X_2) = \log X_1 - \log X_2$. For man, this ratio was determined previously to be about $X_1/X_2 = 1.328$. But alternatively, one can state that, for *Homo sapiens*, $\log X_1 - \log X_2 = \log 1.328 = 0.51587$. Because $\log X_1$ is the logarithm of the heaviest human and $\log X_2$ is the log of the lightest adult, then $\log X_1 - X_2$ is the range of logarithms for modern human mass. That is, because few humans weigh more than 89 kg ($\log 89.0 = 1.94939$) and few weigh less than 67 kg ($\log = 1.82607$), the range of log weights can be determined by subtraction: $1.94939 - 1.82607 = 0.12332$, or about 0.12. This basic logarithmic, or *allometric*, difference is roughly constant over most human measurements, although sometimes variability may be exceedingly wide or narrow for specific characteristics. The logarithmic range for human *stature*, for example, is known to be only about 0.17. Thus, the ratios are roughly constant, even though the individual arithmetic measurements vary widely. Thus, the logarithmic transformations help isolate the fundamental principles underlying the jumble of observable phenomena.

Allometric relationships have been recognized in a wide variety of biological and social phenomena. Demographers often apply the log–log formula to analyze the growth of urban centers, and allometrics have been used to describe changing word frequencies in languages. The size of the human cranium is known to change allometrically with respect to body height as the individual grows from childhood to maturity. Naroll has recently established a log–log relationship between the number of occupational specialities and the absolute population size. The interested reader is referred to the excellent review article by Naroll and Bertalanffy (1965), in which the principle of allometry is considered throughout the biological and social sciences. Simpson, Roe, and Lewontin (1960: chapter 15) also treat the mathematical aspects of the allometric constant, with specific reference to animal growth.

SUGGESTIONS FOR FURTHER READING

Adkins (1964: chapters 12–14)
Blalock (1972: chapters 17, 18)
Siegel (1956)
Sokal and Rohlf (1969: chapter 15)

EXERCISES

14.1 Return to the variates in Exercise 13.1.
    (a) Find the correlation coefficient for these data.
    (b) Is this correlation significantly different from zero (at 0.05)?

(c) Find the 95 percent confidence limits for this r.

(d) What percent of the variance in Y is explained by the linear relationship existing between X and Y?

*14.2 Return to the data of Exercise 13.3.

(a) Compute the correlation coefficient.

(b) Is this correlation significantly different from zero (at 0.05)?

(c) Compute the 95 percent confidence limits for r.

14.3 A correlation coefficient of 0.60 is found in a sample of 25 pairs. Is this significantly different from zero at the 0.05 level of significance?

14.4 How large a correlation coefficient is needed from a sample of size 15 to justify the claim that the variables are linearly related (at the 0.05 level)?

14.5 A sample of 95 pairs has a correlation coefficient 0.80. Is this significantly different from $\rho = 0.50$ at the 0.05 level?

14.6 Use Spearman's r_s to test the hypothesis that the upper limit of community size is directly proportional to the degree of economic specialization (data from Ember 1963: table 1).

Relationship between upper limit of community size and number of types of economic specialist.

Rank Order of Societies	Community Size	Economic Specialization
Yagua	1	6.5
Naron	2	1.5
Ulithi	3	11
Hupa	4	11
Ainu	5	1.5
Lesu	6	11
Egedesminde	7	11
Moken	8	11
Ramkokamekra	9	3.5
Bella Coola	10.5	3.5
Kiwai	10.5	14.5
Tikopia	12	22
Ona	14	6.5
Nuer	14	16
Samoa	14	17.5
Flathead	16	6.5
Hopi	17	20
Crow	18	14.5
Cuna	19	17.5
Nama	20	6.5
Dahomey	21	20
Zululand	22	20
Nupe	23	23
Inca	24	24
Aztec	25	25

14.7 Test the hypothesis in Exercise 14.6, using Kendall's tau. Which coefficient seems more appropriate? What are the strengths and weaknesses of each?

14.8 The following data have been extracted from Ember (1963: table 2):

Relationship between relative importance of agriculture and number of types of economic specialist.

	Types of Economic Specialist	
Agriculture	2–5	6 or more
Relatively unimportant	8	1
Relatively important	3	10

(a) Use an appropriate test to determine whether there is a statistically significant relationship between agriculture and the types of economic specialists (at 0.05).
(b) What is the *strength* of this relationship?

14.9 Ember also compared the importance of agriculture with the number of types of political officials (1963: table 6).

	Number of Types of Political Officials	
Agriculture	Fewer than 5	5 or more
Relatively unimportant	8	1
Relatively important	4	11

(a) Is this a statistically significant association (at 0.05)?
(b) Which association is stronger, that between agriculture and economic specialization (Exercise 14.8) or the present example?

14.10 In Exercise 11.4, how strong is the association between the sex of applicant and admission to graduate school? Which statistical measure (correlation or significance) seems more appropriate here? Why?

14.11 In Exercise 11.7, how strong is the relationship between Bugandan drinking patterns and age?

15 Sampling Problems in Anthropology

● *MORISON'S MUSING: No theory is valid that makes nonsense of what follows.*

15.1 THE NATURE OF ANTHROPOLOGICAL SAMPLES

The time has come to backtrack somewhat and examine an issue glossed over in previous discussions. Raymond Firth's census of Tikopian kinship was considered earlier to illustrate use of the chi-square statistic (Section 11.3). Membership in three Tikopian clans was cross-tabulated against residential village, and the chi-square statistic computed for this 4×3 table resulted in a rejection of H_o; clan membership is significantly associated with residential area in Tikopia. A chi-square statistic was also applied to the Freeds' data from northern India; in this case the age of the family head was significantly associated with occupation. These examples were considered only as illustrations of the specific computing procedure. The logic and rationale for such testing now require close inspection.

The objective of statistical inference is to generalize about true characteristics of a population based upon limited sample information. Chi-square told us that Tikopian clan membership associates with the residential unit. Specifically, the chi-square statistic indicated that the probability of finding so strong an association between two truly independent variables by chance alone is less than 1 in 100. The null hypothesis—that kinship and residence are statistically independent—was rejected on the basis of a seemingly aberrant sample. Although kinship and residence cannot be framed into an immediate causal relationship on the basis of chi-square, these findings seem to suggest at least a functional linkage between the two factors.

The difficulty should be obvious. Statistical inference generalizes from sample

439

to population. The sample consisted of observations on all 218 informants who live in the four primary villages of Tikopia. But what is the population from which this sample was selected? The residents of the Island of Tikopia surely cannot be the population, since Firth completely enumerated all residents of the large villages for his "sample." Perhaps the true population is the Solomon Islands, which are politically allied with Tikopia into the British Solomon Islands Protectorate. But Tikopia was not randomly selected from within the Protectorate; moreover, Tikopia is known to have stronger cultural ties with Samoa and Tonga than with the Solomons. Perhaps the true population consists of the islands comprising the "Polynesian fringe" in Melanesia. Or perhaps the population includes all of Polynesia. Could it be that Tikopia represents all of the smaller islands of the Pacific? Would the real population please stand up!

How could this problem have arisen? All statistical methods require random sampling, and a random sample can result only from a random selection procedure. Each variate within a population must have had an *equal and independent* probability of inclusion in the sample. Was Tikopia selected for fieldwork from a table of random digits or by repeated coin flipping? Hardly. Raymond Firth chose to work where he did because Tikopia was one of the few islands remaining with minimal outside contact in 1928. "Primitive Polynesians are rare nowadays," Firth tells us. "Most of the islanders have taken to farming, to cricket, to politics and even a few to anthropology." No random sampling here. Firth selected Tikopia by default.

But I don't intend to demean Raymond Firth; his field methods actually stand him in the best twentieth-century tradition of ethnographic fieldwork. In fact, like Firth's work on Tikopia, most fieldwork in anthropology reflects a curious blend of scientific foresight, logistical planning, and happenstance. Consider another example—how Margaret Mead came to work among the Arapesh of Highland New Guinea:

> The long climb into the mountains on slippery trails, sometimes up almost perpendicular cliffs and sometimes in riverbeds, was slow and difficult, particularly as I had to be carried, but there was no other way into the interior. When we were part way there, the accident of Reo's success in attracting carriers from farther inland boomeranged. Our carriers left us stranded with all our gear in a village on a mountaintop with no one to move our six months' supplies in either direction—into the interior or back to the coast. So we had no means of reaching the people we had intended to study and no choice but to settle down, build a house, and work with the simple, impoverished Mountain Arapesh, who had little ritual and less art, among whom we now found ourselves. Earlier, when Reo had made his brief trip into the interior to organize carriers, he had found out, as he put it, that "these people haven't any culture worth speaking of—sisters-in-law are friends!" Now that we were stuck in the mountain village, Alitoa, he decided that he would study the language—(Mead 1972:194–195)

Mead's Arapesh experience is probably more typical than not for ethnological fieldwork, and similar expediencies influence the rest of anthropology's samples as well. Archaeological sites are selected for excavations for a wide variety of reasons: A site will soon be destroyed by a high rise or a highway contractor, or by erosion, or by pothunting vandals; a site has just been discovered and excites the excavator; a handy site is needed for a Saturday "dig" class at nearby Utopian University. The fact is that relatively few (archaeological) sites have been excavated by previous design.

Consider the reasoning which led me to select the Reese River Valley of central Nevada for some of my own archaeological fieldwork. The Reese River area was very carefully chosen for a number of reasons:

(a) it is accessible, yet only by dirt road, so it is relatively free of "pothunting" activity; (b) good maps (15' and Reese River Survey, both U.S.G.S.) are available for the entire valley; (c) most land is federally owned, thus obviating the problem of uncooperative landowners; (d) the slopes have abundant piñon trees, which have yet to be successfully related to archaeological activities, in spite of their ethnographic importance; and (e) the area has not been subjected to archaeological research to date, so its resources are completely at our disposal—(Thomas 1969:94).

Yet this published account only tells part of the story. There were additional compelling factors about the Reese River Valley which were (quite properly) omitted from the scholarly publication. For one thing, the Reese River is a beautiful place—I liked the land and it seemed like a nice place to spend my summers. Because much of the actual archaeology was to be performed by students enrolled in my University of California summer courses, I also made *physical comfort* another major concern. One sterling lesson shone through from my own undergraduate archaeology days: uncomfortable students are grumpy students, and grumpy students are inefficient fieldworkers. The work schedule and the budget were both too rigid to allow for student inefficiency due to sunburn, heat stroke, dehydration, fatigue, or mutiny. So physical living conditions and outright personal preference were prime factors in my deciding to spend three field seasons in the Reese River Valley. I doubt that my reasons are much different from many other (candid) archaeologists'.

Dozens of comparable examples could be trotted forth to illustrate the vagaries and vicissitudes of anthropological fieldwork. But these cases should illustrate my point: Anthropologists select the sites of their fieldwork for a number of diverse—and sometimes colorful—reasons, and *random selection is rarely one of these reasons.*

Random sampling is itself a rare event in anthropology, an assertion which should startle nobody. I don't mean to imply that random sampling is not a worthwhile procedure. It is. But a realistic approach to quantitative methods demands that we see just what violence is wrought by the failures and deficiencies of sampling in anthropology.

15.2 THE HYPOTHETICAL SAMPLING UNIVERSE

● *OCCAM'S RAZOR: Entia non sunt multiplicanda praeter necessitatem.* (*translation:* In explaining obscure matters, imaginary things should never be postulated as existing.)

If misery enjoys company, then anthropologists are indeed a comfortable lot. Anthropology's sampling difficulties are shared among a wide range of other sciences. Many of the techniques we know as "inferential statistics" evolved from practiced statistical applications to agricultural field studies. These experiments were designed to answer some pragmatic questions regarding levels and rates of fertilization, efficacy of hybrid grains, dietary requirements of livestock, and so forth. Agricultural experiments are commonly repeated year after year, under a wide variety of soil and climatic conditions, to insure that diverse experimental conditions are represented. But the suitability of these experimental conditions varies a great deal, in direct proportion to the doggedness and insight of the investigators. The difficulty here, as with anthropological fieldwork, is that statistical inference allows only generalization from a sample to the population from which that sample was randomly selected. How can an agricultural experiment qualify as a "random sample from specified population?"

The sampling problem is thus not a new one. W. S. Gosset began his classic 1908 paper (this paper defined the basics of the Student's *t*-test) with the statement:

Any experiment can be regarded as forming an individual from a "population" of experiments which might be performed under the same conditions. A series of experiments is a sample drawn from this population—(Student 1908:1).

Gosset's programmatic statement defines a new sort of population. The most important characteristic of Student's population is that it is *hypothetical*. This is a population of all possible experiments which *could* have taken place. Experimental findings are thus said to represent a *random sample* generated from the total population of all hypothetically possible samples. Why a *random* sample? Why not—it's only a hypothetical population, so we can "sample" it in any way we please. This hypothetical population is infinite for the "hard" sciences, as long as experimental replications can theoretically continue indefinitely. But for disciplines with a historical dimension, such as prehistoric archaeology and human paleontology, experimentation is restricted to a large, yet finite, universe of possibilities. A finite number of Pueblo IV sites exist today; there will never be any more. We can never hope to create more specimens of *Australopithecus robustus*. New finds will still be made, of course, but our study will forever remain restricted to those materials now buried.

The key phrase in Student's statement is "under the same conditions." The hypothetical universe consists of all experiments which could have taken place *under similar conditions*. The physical scientist has relatively little trouble specifying these standard conditions. Whenever a chemist compresses two gasses, he always specifies STP, which means *standard temperature of 0°C* and *standard pressure at 760 mm of mercury*. But what constitutes "similar conditions" for cultural events?

I mentioned my motives in selecting the Reese River Valley for three seasons of archaeological fieldwork, motives neither statistical nor random. I was more concerned with the practicalities of performing archaeological field investigation. The specific objective of this fieldwork was to reconstruct the prehistoric settlement patterns of this area. But the Reese River Valley is over 100 miles long, and the financial resources were not sufficient to examine so large an area. A 15-mile-long cross section of the valley was thus selected for intensive settlement pattern survey. A 500 meter grid system was imposed over this restricted test area, and a 10 percent random sample of 1400 of the 500 m^2 squares was generated. I knew beforehand that this area had been occupied since about 2500 B.C., so the specific objective was to reconstruct the settlement patterns for this 4500 span of prehistoric time within this specific area. Fieldwork took three summers with a crew ranging in size from 23 to 45 people, and the settlement patterns were ultimately reconstructed (see Thomas 1973). Because I was very careful to collect a 10 percent *random sample* from *within* the study area, I felt quite safe about generalizing the results to the entire 15 by 20-mile area originally sampled. I had statistics on my side when inferring from a randomly generated sample to the population from whence the sample was selected.

But the ultimate objective was an *anthropological* statement rather than a *statistical* statement, and the problem arose as to *how far can this pattern be generalized beyond the 1400 square tracts in the initial population?* After all, three years is a considerable investment in fieldwork, and merely describing 300 square miles hardly seems worth the effort. Could I legitimately extend the observed settlement pattern to the entire 100 miles of the Reese River Valley? Or what about generalizing to the entire central Nevada region? Or perhaps across the entire Great Basin? Have I found *the* settlement pattern for western North America? Could I crow that my three years' fieldwork laid bare the settlement patterns of all hunter-gatherers, regardless of time or space? What is the population against which I can project my sample results?

In a purely statistical perspective, the only valid generalization is the first statement: A 10 percent random sample indicates that patterns *X*, *Y*, and *Z* hold for the entire 100 percent of the population. These inferences emanate from a sample and extend to the exact population from which that sample was randomly selected. This is as far as I can go on *statistical* grounds. All statements beyond this rock-bottom level deal with a *hypothetical population* such as that suggested by Student. As an anthropologist, I am entitled to extend my findings as far as I wish, provided Student's caveat *under similar conditions* can be defined. The Reese River sample comes from a very large hypothetical population of *similar samples which exist under similar conditions.* The boundaries of this hypothetical population are defined on nonstatistical grounds and must be justified as such. Suppose I decide to make the following case: Since the critical resources of the survey area are virtually constant for the entire 100-mile length of the Reese River Valley, the aboriginal settlement pattern was probably identical throughout the entire valley. That is, I could assert that all prehistoric occupants of the Reese River Valley lived *under similar conditions.* If you wish to assume the role of skeptic, you are free to challenge my assertion of *similar conditions.* You might point out that the Reese River actually flows underground for a distance, and this lack of water must have influenced the prehistoric settlement pattern. Or you might observe that local drainage patterns create a large *playa* in the middle of the valley; the fish and waterfowl associated with this playa must surely have affected the settlement pattern. The anthropological literature is littered with concrete (and heated) examples of this sort of debate regarding similar conditions or the lack of similar conditions.

The point is that two distinct levels of inference are operating. As long as my inferences at Reese River dealt with a randomly generated sample from an explicitly defined population, I was on firm statistical grounds. The results were grounded in probability theory and as such were relatively robust to challenge. But once I shifted reference, from the *concrete population* to the *hypothetical population*, my arguments lost steam because of the difficulties in defining "similar conditions." Resorting to the hypothetical population opens the door to challenges based upon substantive anthropological and demographic evidence. Statistical inference based upon the true population was free from such challenges.

And yet, when applied properly, the hypothetical population construct remains a valid tool. Strictly speaking, Firth's Tikopian census is a statistical population, not a statistical sample. Applying a chi-square statistic to a statistical population is meaningless. But if Firth's census is viewed as a random sample from the hypothetical population of all such samples which exist *under similar conditions*, then the situation is framed in a probabilistic light. Here it does not matter one whit that Firth's sample is not random. Nobody said it was. The sample statistic of $\chi^2 = 62.786$ tells us that *if* Firth's sample had been random, such findings would occur fewer than one time in one thousand trials. Firth's census differs a great deal from that expected by chance alone. The critical difference between *actual* sampled populations and *hypothetical* populations existing under similar conditions enables the anthropologist to do a great deal of meaningful inference, *even though the sample is not random*.

There are, of course, difficulties in using the concept of the hypothetical universe, and one of the most important difficulties involves the potential abuse of the concept of randomness. Statistical results emerge as "significant" because of three kinds of factors: (1) There could be a real discrepancy between the values posited under H_o and those observed in the sample; (2) extraneous variables, uncontrolled in the experimental design, could have intervened to inflate the sample statistic; or (3) random factors could have occurred. This third vector, the influence of chance events, is relied upon to explain a good many deviations from the expected values. Random events are generally considered to be small, independent conditions which conspire to upset expectation. We know that coins will almost never produce exactly 50 percent heads because minor events influence each toss of the coin: small breezes, variability in the way an individual tosses the coin, coins dropping different distances at different rates. If all these random factors could simultaneously be controlled—perhaps by some marvelous error-free coin-flipping machine—then the results should be predictable with total certainty. Only the laws of physics would control each outcome.

Similar random errors operate within anthropological data to confound the results. Three basic sources of random error seem to be involved: errors of sampling, errors of content, and errors of analysis. A *sampling error* occurs when a sample poorly represents the population from which it was drawn. All but the most uniform populations have a few variates falling on the extremes of the distribution; whenever these extreme variates are included in the sample, that sample becomes slightly less representative of its population. I am reminded of the time I demonstrated the "laws of chance" to some skeptical anthropology students in an introductory statistics course. Mysterious forces operate in the real world, I told them, which make chance phenomena operate in a highly predictable manner. I pointed out how well the unknown can be predicted from probabilities of past performances, citing baseball averages and human sex ratios as supportive evidence. I showed them how radiocarbon dating is based upon random decay of the C^{14} molecule (and we all know how scientific radiocarbon dates are!). Then I launched my gambling examples, which I figured should clinch the argument. I expansively asked one skeptical student to flip a quarter 20 times. We would let that quarter demonstrate the simple case of $p = q = 1/2$. When the experiment resulted in 19 tails and but a single head, I could do little but sheepishly plead sampling error.

This case involved a sample which was probably a poor indicator of the population. One wonders how many "randomly generated" samples have been rejected—tossed out, ignored, recomputed—because they seemed too unbelievable. Cross-cultural ethnographic samples constantly run the risk of unrepresentative random samples, as do archaeological surveys in which the randomly generated samples poorly reflect the actual population from whence they sprang.

Errors of content arise whenever the anthropologist records faulty data. The first chapter of Naroll's *Data Quality Control* (1962b) discusses many cases in which errors can creep into the ethnographer's notes. Archaeologists seem especially vulnerable to errors of this sort, perhaps because of the large crews necessary on most excavations: level bags are mislabelled or misplaced; radiocarbon or pollen samples are easily contaminated; housefloors are destroyed before they have been recognized; vertical stratigraphy is overlooked by hasty or incompetent excavators. The archaeological laboratory is a chamber of horrors where random errors arise as if by orthogenesis. Artifacts are miscatalogued and catalogue numbers disappear or become illegible. The detailed measurements of physical anthropology and archaeology are in error due to the faulty calibration of balances, inexperienced personnel reading the vernier scales of calipers, and a host of allied difficulties. There is also the serious danger of systematic error whenever measurements must be estimated from incomplete or damaged specimens. But sometimes one must make strategic guesses or else diminish one's sample beyond practical utility.

Errors of this sort are the nemesis of anthropology. Fortunately, we know from the celebrated Heisenberg uncertainty principle that there is an absolute limit to the precision in any set of data. If a physicist were to measure the velocity of an electron to, say, within 10 percent, that measurement would still be greatly in error. Even though the error in position is miniscule, a 10 percent error is as great in this case as an error of one mile in a human stature estimate. The Heisenberg principle assures us that errors of content will *always* be present. There is always an absolute limit to precision of measurement, although anthropologists are a long way from approaching this limit. At least Heisenberg has spared us the goose-chasing search for the ultimate anthropometric device which will forever eliminate errors and lead us to the land of blissful numeration.

Finally, there are *errors of analysis*, a category including phenomena as diverse as keypunch errors, arithmetic mistakes in finding descriptive statistics, misidentification due to illegible field notes, computer malfunctions, and so on.

I am reminded of the time as a graduate student when I personally (and laboriously) keypunched over 8000 cards of artifact measurements. The cards were carefully machine-verified and reverified to eliminate all possible error. When I was finally satisfied, the bulky boxes of cards were temporarily stored in a closet. Once I was finally ready to actually analyze these data, I discovered that a steam heater had so badly warped and deformed the cards that they produced "garbage" when processed by the computer. Fortunately, the magnitude of error was so great that I quickly discovered the problem and threw away the entire batch of cards. Presumably, errors of this sort plague the unfortunate processor of quantitative data, and there are times when computers qualify under Marvin Harris' appellation "labor saving devices which increase work."

The point is that significance testing techniques cannot distinguish these random errors from (1) actual differences and (2) uncontrolled systematic factors. Inferential statistics merely compute the probability that random influences in general could have conspired to produce a given result. A problem thus arises with the hypothetical universe of possibilities. What are the potential sources of random error in Firth's Tikopian kinship data? Sample error as such cannot exist because the sample consists of *all* available informants. Sampling occurs only in a hypothetical sense, so errors cannot possibly arise. It is impossible to draw a nonrepresentative sample from our hypothetical population. Errors of analysis also seem rather remote. Only 218 informants were queried and there were no keypunching or laboratory measurements to introduce error. It is possible, though I think unlikely, that errors were made in the hand tabulation of the census data. Possibly some of the Tikopians were misclassified as to clan or village, or possibly the same informant was counted twice.

The point is that when entire populations are treated *as if* they were samples, a good deal of potential "sampling error" is lost as explanation for deviant results due to "chance factors." Furthermore, the meticulous transcription, labelling, and processing of field data greatly minimizes the likelihood of errors of content and analysis. So, it is possible when dealing with hypothetical populations to "dry up" the potential sources for random error. If such errors cannot possibly have operated, isn't it meaningless to measure the probability that they *could have* occurred?

One alternative to this awkward situation is simply to perform sloppy fieldwork and shoddy analysis. We could thus go forth confidently computing our probabilities, secure in the knowledge that we have introduced plenty of error into our data. Perhaps a wiser course of action is simply to recognize the problem of diminishing sources of random error when dealing with the hypothetical universe: The fewer errors we can possibly have, the less heavily we should rely upon chance to explain the observed results. In reality, data are probably never totally free from error. Even if such were the case, how would we know it?

Regardless of the difficulties in application, it is clear that many anthropologists, whether or not they are aware of it, rely upon the hypothetical universe of possible samples. This elusive population is admittedly an artificial construct, designed in part to ease the social scientist over a difficult methodological hurdle. Some mathematical statisticians reject this construct out of hand. "The onus lies on the exponent of statistical theory," argues Hogben (1968), "to furnish irresistible reasons for adopting procedures which have still to prove their worth against a background of three centuries of progress in scientific discovery accomplished without their aid." In fact, even aggressive advocates of the hypothetical universe concept advise caution; Hagood (1941: 304, 425), for instance, admits that the construct is "relatively new and not too well defined . . . it is therefore only an imagined possibility and whether or not one wishes to utilize the concept is still at the discretion of the individual research worker." More to the point, anthropologists *do* use the construct, whether or not they wish to defend it.

I personally think that anthropologists are justified in using many of the "softer" statistical concepts (such as the hypothetical universe of possibilities) on the grounds that we remain a primitive science. All legitimate attempts to truly advance the state of our art must be encouraged. In addition, anthropologists do not seem quite so readily enamored with statistical elegance per se as many of our more quantitatively sophisticated colleagues in social science. That is, we don't have as much to lose from bending the rules of statistics, since most anthropologists probably only half-believe their statistics anyway. The true efficacy of concepts such as the hypothetical universe of possibilities for anthropology should probably be judged not strictly upon abstruse theoretical grounds, but rather upon the quality of the solid results which spring therefrom. At least we must judge success, or lack of it, upon anthropological rather than purely statistical criteria.

15.3 SIR FRANCIS AND HIS PROBLEM

● *MURPHY'S LAW:*
(1) Nothing is as easy as it looks.
(2) Everything takes longer than you think.
(3) If anything can go wrong, it will.

The origins of cross-cultural ethnology are generally traced back to the work of E. B. Tylor. Tylor, a professor at Oxford, pioneered anthropological thinking, particularly in the field of cultural evolution. In 1888, Tylor presented a paper entitled "On a Method of Investigating the Development of Institutions," in which he considered the functional relationship between patterns of postmarital residence and ritual avoidance of one's in-laws. Tylor assembled a massive worldwide corpus of data in the hope of demonstrating that "the development of institutions may be investigated on the basis of tabulation and classification." Although his data consisted largely of hearsay reports from adventurers, missionaries, and soldiers of fortune, Tylor was convinced that anthropology could be systematized. Using what he called "social arithmetic," Tylor commenced with a rather modest beginning to an ambitious project. "The point I chose was a quaint and somewhat comic custom as to the barbaric etiquette between husbands and their wives' relatives," explained Tylor, "They may not look at one another, much less speak, and even then, avoid mentioning one another's names." Tylor tabulated data on 282 societies to determine just how the "comic custom" of kin avoidance related to postmarital residence. If Tylor were alive today, he would doubtless judge the significance of association with a chi-square statistic, hopefully coupled with a coefficient such as ϕ to assess the strength of association. But the mathematical statistics of Tylor's day had no measures of correlation or significance, so Tylor did his best to compute the "probable closeness of causal connection." He figured that such extreme associations "would show their concurrence only once or twice by chance in so large a sample of societies." Tylor presented his findings orally to the Royal Anthropological Institute of London in 1888. The minutes of that meeting record that Tylor's work was generally well received, especially his efforts to compile comprehensive files of primitive customs throughout the world. In fact, the 1889 Tylor paper is now considered a classic of anthropological research, and was reprinted by Moore (1961).

As was the custom, the president of the Royal Anthropological Institute commented at length on the paper at hand. The president of the Institute at the time happened to be Sir Francis Galton, master of topics as diverse as genetics, human evolution, and biostatistics; in fact, this is the same Galton who coined the term *regression*, discussed in Section 13.2. Galton expressed deep concern over Tylor's "social arithmetic." In today's idiom, Galton questioned Tylor's contingency tables. Galton feared that the trait tallies might be inflated because the same trait could be counted several times—once for each closely related society. The islands of the Malay region were a case in point. They were tallied as individual cases, even though the common cultural heritage of all these islands is indisputable. Is each island an independent case, or should the entire Malay region as a whole be taken as one case? When related societies are taken as independent, these "duplicate copies" of the same phenomenon will ruin any probability calculation, and Galton wondered just how many of Tylor's 282 societies could be considered truly independent. In other words, Galton was chiding Tylor for not using independent events. Historically related cultures may not be independent because of diffusion, and the probability of a given trait can be seriously inflated by such duplication.

Interestingly enough, the difficulty of assessing the independence of cases in cross-cultural samples has become known as *Galton's problem*, a misnomer. In fact, Galton simply made an insightful observation; the real problem was Tylor's. The implications of Galton's problem have had a strange impact upon the trajectory of anthropology. The influence of statistical methods upon Franz Boas, acknowledged dean of early twentieth-century anthropology, is a case in point. Boas was himself an accomplished statistician who ingeniously applied some advanced statistical methods to the study of living racial types, to genetics, and also to ethnological data. In fact, Boas later credited himself with being the first anthropologist after Tylor's 1888 discussion to apply statistics to the field of mythology in his *Indianische Sagen*. In retrospect, Boas commented (Boas 1940:309) that, "I might have established some nice coefficients of correlation for elements of mythology" [had such coefficients been available at the time]. Shortly after his study of mythology, Boas travelled to the interior of British Columbia, where he discovered clanless tribes with family organization and patrilineal trend clearly adopted from their coastal neighbors. Boas quickly became convinced that the complexities of cultural diffusion will negate effective statistical handling of ethnological data such as Tylor advocated (and Boas defended in the 1890s). Boas later confided to Robert Lowie, a former student, that the overall gravity of Galton's problem will always prevent the useful statistical analysis of ethnological data (Lowie 1946: 229). To what degree the objections of Galton ultimately influenced Boas is uncertain, but once Boas became disillusioned with Tylor's statistical methods, he flatly denied the validity of statistical analysis of any ethnological data. As a direct result, the statistical methods lay dormant in ethnology for decades until their revival by A. L. Kroeber and his students at Berkeley during the mid-1930s. Even with today's more sophisticated statistical methods at our disposal, ethnologists must still wrestle with the problem Galton first recognized over 85 years ago.

15.3.1 Solving Galton's Problem

Two general strategies have been followed in the attempt to compensate for the lack of statistical independence among societies of the world.[1] Naroll (1970b:977) terms the first approach the *sifting method*. Quite simply, the ethnologist attempts mechanically to rid the sample of duplicates. Beatrice Whiting's monograph on Paiute sorcery is a good example of this sifting procedure in practice (Whiting 1950). After a lengthy period of fieldwork among the Northern Paiute of southern Oregon, Whiting determined that social control was exerted largely through ties within the extended family. Wrongs were often adjudicated by social relationships, frequently taking the form of physical violence and sorcery. When one person wronged another, he feared not only assault but also sickness induced by sorcery. Based upon her experience among the Northern Paiute, Whiting hypothesized that sorcery and coordinate social action must be functionally linked, and she tested her hypothesis using cross-cultural methods. A sample of 50 societies was selected from the Cross-Cultural Survey files (now renamed the Human Relations Area Files) and each sample society was rated on (1) importance of sorcery and (2) methods of social control.

   Whiting scored the importance of sorcery by determining the degree to which people believed that sorcery was responsible for sickness. Social control was assessed by determining the society's treatment of murder. If murder was generally settled by retaliation, then the social control was classified as *coordinate*; but when murder cases were solved by a specifically delegated authority, the society was considered to have *superordinate* control. Whiting's hypothesis predicted that sorcery should be most highly developed in societies with coordinate control and will be virtually absent where superordinate control is present. Table 15.1 shows the contingency table for Whiting's 50 sample societies. These results show a rather strong relationship between coordinate control and sorcery—$\phi = +0.57$ and $p < 0.01$ by chi-square—thus supporting the Whiting hypothesis of sorcery.

   But Whiting admitted that the results were open to criticism from two major sources. There is the initial question of whether or not she had accurately coded

---

[1]This section on Galton's problem relies heavily upon the work of Raoul Naroll, particularly Naroll (1970b).

TABLE 15.1 The 50 randomly selected societies used to test Whiting's hypothesis on sorcery (adapted from Whiting 1950: table I).

Status of Sorcery	No Superordinate Justice (coordinate control)			Superordinate Justice	
Important	Arunta	Apache	Barama Caribs	Ashanti	Hill Maria Gonds
	Buka	Chuckchee	Delaware	Azande	Kwakiutl
	Dieri	Copper Eskimo	Jivaro	Chagga	Lamba
	Dobu	Ifugao	Witoto	Fiji	Sanpoil
	Kiwai	Kutchin		Kamilaroi	
	Kwoma	Mala		Tiv	
	Lesu	Maori		Venda	
	Murngin	Paiute			
	Orokaiva	Yurok			
	Trobriands	Zuni			
Unimportant	Lango			Bali	Cayapa
				Japan	Cheyenne
				Kazak	Crow
				Lepcha	Samoa
				Masai	Tikopia
				Ontong Java	Tonga
				Riff	
				Tanala	

the importance of sorcery and social control. Under ideal conditions, such coding should be performed by at least two independent judges who are unaware of the hypothesis being tested. She was unable to arrange such coding, but attempted to verify her evaluations against other independent studies.

Whiting noted further that a more critical point could be made "on the grounds that in selecting the tribes used in the correlation no allowance was made for historical connections and diffusions" (1950:88). Perhaps the Australian tribes (the Dieri, Arunta, Murngin, and Kamilaroi) share so many traits in common that they are really duplicate cases, and hence lack statistical independence. The New Guinea groups (Kwoma, Orokaiva, and Kiwai) could produce similar biasing effects. Although Whiting did not use the term, she was concerned about the magnitude of Galton's problem. The difficulty was controlled by filtering (or sifting) these interdependent societies. Whiting operationally defined *interrelated* as sharing "an area which is generally recognized as having cultural unity." Only a single society from each cultural area was retained, and the sample was reduced from the original 50 societies to only 26 cases, each of which belongs to a distinct cultural area. This filtered sample (Table 15.2) still supports the research hypothesis ($\phi = +0.73$ and $p = 0.00019$ by Fisher's Exact method).

Interestingly enough, the relationship appears to be stronger in the filtered sample than among the raw data. If Galton's problem were truly operative in the initial sample, then one should expect a *decrease* in association once the redundant cases are removed. Either Galton's problem was not such a problem after all, or else Whiting's sifting techniques failed to solve the difficulties of intercorrelation. Naroll (1970b: 978) has pointed out that Whiting's solution to Galton's problem is vulnerable because diffusion cannot legitimately be assumed to stop at culture areas or even at continental boundaries. The triad

TABLE 15.2   The 26 remaining societies after sample has been *sifted* for historical contact and common origin (adapted from Whiting 1950: table III).

Status of Sorcery	No Superordinate Justice		Superordinate Justice	
Important	Arunta	Barama Caribs	Ashanti	
	Chuckchee	Kwoma	Azandi	
	Copper Eskimo	Trobriands	Hill Maria Gonds	
	Delaware	Tupinamba	Kwakiutl	
	Ifugao	Witoto		
	Paiute			
	Zuni			
Unimportant			Cheyenne	Bali
			Japan	Cayapa
			Lepcha	Kazak
			Masai	Samoa
			Riff	
			Tanala	

of domesticated maize-beans-squash is known, for example, to have diffused throughout most of the Western hemisphere.

A second, more successful strategy of attacking Galton's problem is known collectively as the *propinquity method*. Although there are at least seven different propinquity solutions, all the methods begin with the assumption that diffusion can be measured as a function of geographical proximity (propinquity). Using various probabilistic models, similarities between neighbors are taken to reflect diffusion, whereas similarity between more distant peoples more probably reflects a functional relationship rather than a simple historical or diffusionary contact. The propinquity methods are relatively simple to understand and inexpensive to operate, but lack of space precludes detailed summary of the methodology. See Naroll (1970b) for a cogent review of both mechanics and logic of the propinquity solutions to Galton's problem.

15.3.2 Expanding Galton's Problem

Most anthropologists think of Galton's problem only in the context of cross-cultural research, and the attempts to vitiate this difficulty are concerned only with the contaminated samples of worldwide cultural groups. But in the broader perspective, Galton's problem extends far beyond the focus of cross-cultural ethnology. Galton cited a rather specific instance of the more general difficulty known as *spatial autocorrelation* (Loflin 1972). Whenever observations are known to be interdependent, such results will conspire to produce inconsistent and unreliable statistical estimators of the true population characteristics. When the usual statistical tests are computed for such redundant data, serious overestimation of reliability will often result.

These problems are by no means restricted to conventional cross-cultural studies. Consider the difficulties arising in obtaining samples of fossil primates. Obtaining paleontological samples is a rather different matter from taking samples from among living primate populations, and most paleontological field collections cannot meet the rigid specifications of random-sampling theory: Fossil samples are more heterogeneous than samples from living populations because many specifications such as age, sex, and diet cannot be adequately controlled; prehistoric biotic communities (*facies*) influence such samples, so the paleontologist can never assume that he has animals from a single community, or whether the fossils represent several different biota; the agencies of burial and fossilization make some critters more likely candidates for survival into modern times; natural agencies of exposure make some fossils more readily available than others to the modern scientist; differential weathering introduces bias; the collector himself introduces skewing effects because entire depositions of fossils are rarely retrieved—more commonly, expeditions return only with "exhibition quality" specimens, or selected "target species," or the more portable bones, leaving the unwieldy specimens in the field; some invertebrate fossils such as the brachiopods, gastropods, and trilobites are collected simply because of their intrinsic appeal to the human eye. Literally dozens of factors are known to influence the sampling bias of paleontology.

But I wish to point out that *Galton's problem* also operates to obfuscate the samples of human paleontologists. Between 1929 and 1934, for instance, Tabun and Skhūl caves were excavated on Mt. Carmel (in what is now Israel). Between the two sites, an extraordinary series of fossils was unearthed, representing a dozen or so individuals. The archaeological contexts are virtually identical, and it appears that the two caves were occupied at roughly the same time period, about 36,000 years ago. The Mt. Carmel fossils are extraordinary because their physical type differs from both the Classic Neanderthal form of Europe and from later *Homo sapiens sapiens* morphology. The Mt. Carmel brow ridges are large, but not as large as Classic Neanderthal; the faces are somewhat reduced in size and lack the "inflated" look of Classic Neanderthal; the limb bones seem slender and more moderate of proportion than the Neanderthals. These important skeletons have convinced some modern paleontologists that the Mt. Carmel fossils represent a true *hybridization* between the earlier Classic Neanderthals and contemporary populations of the modern *sapiens* forms who were living to the northeast on the Russian steppes. Other paleoanthropologists interpret the Mt. Carmel material as simply an intermediate stage in the rather orderly evolution from Classic Neanderthal to modern man. Depending upon one's perspective, the Mt. Carmel finds can support either the theory that Neanderthal was in the direct line of human evolution or that the Neanderthals represent a side branch, a dead-end which became extinct during the Pleistocene.

The present point does not concern whether or not Neanderthal stands in our direct family tree, but rather to what extent our interpretation of the fossil evidence has been colored by a version of Galton's problem. How does spatial autocorrelation influence paleontological samples? Nobody knows to what extent the Mt. Carmel finds could have been related. The skeletons might possibly represent a single group of very close relatives. If so, then the "atypical" cranial form could represent nothing more than a family resemblance (restricted gene pool) rather than the far-reaching evolutionary implications that paleoanthropologists have assigned to them. That is, if the Mt. Carmel people were closely related, then they represent only *one* independent case, rather than *one dozen* cases. How far would modern genetic inferences take us if our sample were restricted to a single family from the Little Italy section of New York City? Or Hell's Kitchen? Or Harlem? Or Taos Pueblo? Or Hyannis Port?

Although it seems rather unlikely that the dozen Mt. Carmel skeletons form a single close-knit family, can we deny that they might represent members of a large extended family, who perhaps buried their dead at a shrine sacred to the family? And if this were true, then the skeletons represent only a minuscule fraction of the gene pool operating in the circum-Mediterranean area about 36,000 years ago.

The fact is that a dangerously large proportion of the human fossil record is based upon a few significant clusters of finds. Consider this: Our total sample of pithecanthropine (*H. erectus*) fossils number fewer than a hundred well-documented specimens (Buettner–Janusch 1973: table 8.3). But over 40 of these individuals are "Peking Men" from the single cave of Chou Kou Tien in northeastern China, and ten additional *Homo erectus* specimens are "Solo Men" from the Ngangdon site on Java. In other words, *over half of the known Homo erectus specimens in the world come from only two sites.* Nobody knows to what extent the Peking specimens are interrelated, but who can deny the possibility? Galton's problem of autocorrelation between individual cases might even prove more devastating in the paleontological context than in the cross-cultural matrix. Whether or not specific inferential statistics are computed for *Homo erectus* or the Mt. Carmel finds is irrelevant. The evidence of paleontology comes from samples, and these samples consist of intercorrelated observations. Do we consider the Peking men to be 40 percent of the *Homo erectus* material because 40 skeletons were found, or should we consider them as only a single case because the skeletons are likely to be closely related? There have been no attempts to compensate for Galton's problem in the study of human evolution; none of the cross-cultural solutions seem relevant to this case, and the magnitude of error remains undetermined.

Nor do archaeologists escape the legacy of Sir Francis. A number of prehistorians have recently pointed out the fact that archaeological inference is directly conditioned by the methods of sampling (for example, Thomas 1973), and archaeologists face an unusual variant of the general Galton's problem. To date, few archaeologists analyze their prehistoric data using the methods and logic of cross-cultural analysis. How would an archaeological cross-cultural analysis operate? Although the following scenario is admittedly conjectural, recent studies by McNett (1967, 1970) suggest that methods of this nature might not be far away.

A massive compilation of archaeological data would first have to be synthesized into a central data bank; present archaeologists are probably operating at the level of Tylor in 1888. Perhaps some dogged archaeologist will pattern these files after HRAF (Human Relations Area Files). In fact, archaeologists could even dream up a catchy acronym such as the ARF (Archaeological Relations File), or perhaps WARP (World Archaeological Recording Project), or maybe even SHARD (Sample of Holocultural Archaeological Research Data). The major prehistoric cultures of the world could then be coded into objective categories for future statistical analysis. Consider the Cochise culture, for example. *Cochise*, a prehistoric manifestation of the generalized Desert culture, flourished in southern Arizona from about 7000 B.C. to about 1 A.D. The Cochise peoples could be treated as any society of the *Ethnographic Atlas*, and coded upon many of the *Atlas'* variables. The Cochise culture, for example, practiced little or no agriculture (col. 12), hunted a great deal (col. 8), lived in seminomadic bands (col. 30), lived in communities of less than 50 people (col. 31), lacked metallurgy (col. 42), lacked pottery manufacture (col. 48), and lacked class stratification (col. 68). Although some of the *Atlas* codings could not be applied to archaeological cultures—especially categories of kinship terminology, religion, sexual practices, and linguistic affiliation—these variables are more than compensated by relevant ecological and material cultural categories. Many problems will arise with specific codings, of course, but ethnographic cross-cultural coding is at present still not without such difficulty.

Once the data files had been established, investigators could follow the lead of their current cross-cultural brethren and test a variety of hypotheses upon randomly selected prehistoric societies. Specific aspects of interest could be the role of ecological factors in shaping cultural practices, the relationship between population size and productivity, the reasons for migration and warfare, the evolution of the state. In fact, many of the objectives of modern cross-cultural analysis could fruitfully be explored upon the archaeological samples, since only archaeological data possess suitable time depth to test many of the underlying mechanisms of cultural change and social process. But the introduction of time depth brings us up short. *Time* is at once archaeology's greatest asset and its most significant handicap. Here we must confront Galton's problem. In conventional cross-cultural studies, Galton's problem is just an instance of spatial autocorrelation, in which neighboring or historically related societies interact. Obviously, the Cochise culture did not exist in a vacuum, and Cochise is quite similar to the neighboring, contemporary cultures such as "Lovelock" in western Nevada, the "Oak Grove" and "Topanga" cultures of coastal southern California, and the "Amargosa" culture of the Mohave desert. Is this basic similarity due to similar adaptations to similar environments (parallel cultural process) or due to diffusion of traits through direct and indirect cultural contact (diffusion)? Galton's problem strikes again! Probably the diffusionary and adaptational processes of the past operated similarly to those of the ethnographic present, and Galton's problem is just as large a factor in archaeological as in ethnographic sampling. Perhaps some version of the "sifting" or "propinquity" solutions will be adapted for archaeological sampling. But one obvious difference is that the ethnographic culture area concept remains a constant for historical groups, while archaeological culture areas (area co-traditions) are known to fluctuate through time, making the propinquity methods more tricky to apply.

Even assuming that the problems of prehistoric areal covariation can be adequately solved, we also encounter a more nettlesome version of intercorrelation. Galton objected that Tylor failed to consider the *spatial autocorrelation* between societies. But when archaeologists (inevitably) turn to a hologeistic consideration of their data, they will also be plagued with *temporal autocorrelation*. Societies are interrelated not only through space but also through time. Galton's problem, as stated in 1889, refers only to the contemporary (or horizontal) cultural contact. But archaeological interactions can also involve genetic (or vertical) contact. The Cochise culture illustrates this difficulty quite clearly. Although I discussed Cochise as a single prehistoric society, Cochise has actually been divided into three chronological *phases*:

Sulphur Spring Cochise (ca. 7000 B.C.–5000 B.C.)
Chiricahua Cochise (5000 B.C.–1900 B.C.)
San Pedro Cochise (1900 B.C.–1 A.D.)

All three phases of Cochise show a number of overriding similarities: sparse population, nonsedentary seasonal round, use of sandals (with moccasins rare), ground stone implements, use of *atlatl*, no pottery, and so forth. Yet each phase has some quite diagnostic attributes. The Sulphur Spring phase contains a sparse artifact inventory, including thin, flat milling stones and percussion-flaked, plano-convex tools for chopping and scraping (and little else). The Chiricahua phase introduces a number of new stone-tool types and basketry, and the San Pedro Cochise adds the use of pressure flaking, a new type of steep-beveled end scraper, and the occasional use of the bow and arrow. In addition, the San Pedro peoples began harvesting primitive corn as early as 3000 B.C., with squash and beans available by at least 1000 B.C. Although all three Cochise phases maintain a tradition which lasts for 7000 years, each phase reflects in situ adaptation and evolution.

For purposes of coding and cross-cultural analysis, do we have *one case* or *three cases*? If the Cochise culture is a single unit, how can the internal time phasing be handled? Or if the three phases must be considered as individual cases, then an alarming degree of temporal autocorrelation will exist. This is a problem not generally encountered with ethnographic surveys, where internal change is a relatively minor proposition. There is presently no name for the bias due to temporal and/or genetic relationships. Presumably some day in the future, an enterprising archaeologist (X) will present a pioneering paper analogous to the 1889 Tylor paper, illustrating the holocultural analysis of archaeological samples. Then an equally insightful critic will arise from the audience to point out the hazards of temporal-genetic autocorrelation. Following tradition, this unfortunate critic's name will inextricably be wed to the problem of temporal interrelationships (X's problem). Until the day when genetic interdependence is reified into X's problem, this brief scenario must stand as warning.

It seems that no subdiscipline of anthropology will be totally immune from the wrath of Galton, although, to date, only the cross-cultural specialists have come to grips with the intercorrelation problem. The remaining anthropological subfields will doubtless someday follow suit.

● *There once was a little girl who wrote a thank-you note to her grandmother for giving her a book about penguins for Christmas: "Dear Grandmother, Thank you very much for the nice book you sent me for Christmas. This book gives me more information about penguins than I care to have."*—H. Smith

16 A Parting Word of Caution

● *Ritual or ceremonial is a fixed set of solemn observances. It need not be tied up with religion but develops whenever behavior is taken seriously*—R. Lowie

16.1 STATISTICAL PRACTICES AS RITUAL BEHAVIOR

Some skeptics suggest that the application of statistical methods by social scientists amounts to little more than conventionalized ritual behavior. Taken in its proper anthropological perspective, this statement does indeed contain a kernel of truth.

Item: Emile Durkheim viewed ritual as "rules of conduct" prescribing appropriate behavior in the presence of "sacred objects."

Item: Ecclesiastical rituals generally employ a professional clergy or priesthood, often under the control of the central temple. Members of this select priesthood have acquired intricate ritual knowledge which is dispensed to the proletariat only under tightly specified circumstances.

Item: The magician believes that he *controls* supernatural power under restricted ritualized conditions. That is, he is confident that he possesses a tested formula. If he carries out the ritual exactly as prescribed by the formula, he will obtain the guaranteed results. The supernatural power has no volition of its own. It must respond because the enlightened magician has power over power.

Item: A. R. Radcliffe-Browne suggested that the performance of significant rituals, such as the Trobriand Islanders' *kula* ring, raises sentiments in the actors which are beneficial to the society in general. These "rites of solidarity" tend to enhance the sense of group identity by coordinating the action of individual members for group benefit.

Some limited parallels between ritual behavior and statistical behavior seem unavoidable. In fact, the very terms "ritual" and "rite" derive directly from the Latin *ritus* and recall the Greek *arithmos* meaning "number." The common phrase "do it by the numbers" further links the concepts of rite and number. The six steps of hypothesis testing introduced in Chapter 9 appear distressingly similar to Durkheim's "rules of conduct," and anybody who has ever witnessed an orientation tour to a local computer center should have little difficulty recognizing the "sacred objects" of statistics. Furthermore, most computer centers, and even some Anthropology Departments, employ "professional statistical consultants" who dispense information about the steps which must be followed if the statistical formulas are to respond in the guaranteed fashion. A "cult of the computer" has even arisen recently within anthropology, complete with sacred texts, omnipotent deities, and a host of ritual paraphernalia. But like the Trobriand *kula* ring, this cult has ramifications far transcending the immediate details of ritual. The current statistical awareness in the social sciences has fostered a far-reaching reexamination of the nature of scientific explanation, the quality of acceptable evidence, and the degree of bias introduced during anthropological fieldwork.

The point here is that statistical procedures can indeed function as mere ritual if we so desire. We could easily develop a false sense of security toward our conclusions and a static attitude of self-righteousness, content merely to utter prescribed phrases at prescribed times in prescribed places. The following guidelines are designed to keep anthropological statistics from slipping into the mystical realm of myth and ritual.

> ● *ART, SCIENCE—you seem to have paid a fairly high price for your happiness said the Savage.—A. Huxley*

16.2 THE TEN COMMANDMENTS OF STATISTICS

Some years ago, a discontented tribe of Social Scientists known as the Anthropologists left their homeland on the bleak Plateau of Impressionistic Groping, settling first here, then there, yet never finding true contentment. They tarried for a time amidst the Temples of Anthropometry. But they soon moved on, dissatisfied with weaving tapestries from meaningless cranial measurements. Their journeys were fraught with hazards: First they tottered above the precipice of Racial Determinism and Social Darwinism; then they navigated through the circular eddies of nineteenth-century Cultural Evolutionism, only to be trapped for decades in the box canyons of Historical Particularism.

But their wandering at last appeared to end when they came upon the new land—the lush Valley of Quantification. The Valley appeared to be a land of plenty: plenty of numbers, plenty of formulas, and plenty of computers. The Anthropologists surged forth brandishing their computer programs, their Munsell Color Charts, their random digit tables, and all the other implements necessary to exploit this rich new environment. Then amidst their revelries, they heard a voice. At first a murmur, the sound grew louder and louder, until they recognized the voice of The Science: "Ye must proceed with care. I can offer potent weapons to smite the antagonistic hordes of Small Samples and Probabilistic Uncertainty, but understand and accept the adherent responsibilities. Learn and keep the Covenant of Statistics. If ye steadfastly keep this Covenant, then ye shall be a special treasure unto me, for only you the Anthropologists, of all the tribes of Social Science, do indeed embrace all Peoples of the Earth. But if ye choose to disobey the Commandments of the Covenant and rape the resources of the valley of Quantification, I shall surely banish ye every one to the vapid hinterlands of pseudo-Science. Ye shall be derided and ridiculed by the Tribes of Biometrists, Econometrists, Psychometrists, and—yes indeed—even your close neighbors, the Sociologists."

And it came to pass on the third day, that there were thunders and lightnings. A dense cloud arose surrounding the Machine of Computing, and all the Anthropologists trembled.

And when the voice of the trumpet sounded long, and waxed louder and louder, the Science belched twice from deep within the 64K memory of the Machine of Computing, and the CalComp plotter slowly scribed the following lines:

● *If you fall in love with a machine there is something wrong with your lovelife. If you worship a machine there is something wrong with your religion.*—L. Mumford

COMMANDMENT I. Thou shalt not worship the 0.05 level.

Few cows seem more sacred in the pantheon of statistics than the conventional 0.05, 0.01, and 0.001 levels of statistical significance. Of these, surely the 0.05 level is the most revered. The popularity of these particular levels results no doubt from simple convenience and tradition, but anthropologists have come to rely heavily upon them to the virtual exclusion of other levels of probability. The question must arise as to whether most people really understand what levels of significance are all about. The alpha level deals only with one's willingness to commit a Type I error (that is, to reject a true H_o). The smaller the alpha, the larger becomes the probability of committing a Type II error (unless the sample size is increased). It is a sin to read more into the significance level than this.

Alpha should be chosen, whenever possible, after the sample size has been established because significant results are known to emerge more readily in large samples. Meehl (1967) once tested 55,000 Minnesota high school students for such diverse factors as sex, order of birth, religion, club participation, hobbies, and so on. Significant relationships emerged in fully 90 percent of all cases. "Meehl's paradox" illustrates that the research hypothesis is bound to be confirmed in very large samples in over half the cases by chance alone, whether or not the hypothesis is actually true. Pelto (1970) and Benfer (1968) have also urged caution in evaluating statistical results from large anthropological samples. A rigorous level of significance (say, 0.01 or less) should generally accompany such large samples, while a greater rate of Type I error ($\alpha = 0.05$ or even larger) is often permissible when n is small.

The best advice regarding the levels of statistical significance is simply to use common sense. Weigh the consequences of committing both Type I and Type II errors. Would one error exact a higher price than the other? Search for ancillary sources of information—previous studies, existing theory, similar conditions in allied disciplines—to provide clues (see for example, Labovitz 1968; Skipper, Guenther, and Nass 1967). But above all, do not select the 0.05 level as a comfortable ritual.

> ● *This teacher went into her classroom about fifteen minutes before the class was supposed to begin work and caught a bunch of her boys down in a huddle on their knees in the corner of the room. She demanded of them what they were doing, and one of them hollered back and said, "We were shooting craps." She said, "That's all right, I was afraid you were praying."*—S. Ervin

COMMANDMENT II. Thou shalt not infer a causal relationship from statistical significance.

Science attempts to isolate "universals" or "laws" from the seemingly incoherent tangle of reality; the successful quest for laws ultimately leads to clarification of specific causes known to produce predictable effects. The biological and physical sciences generally design laboratory or field experiments in which all causal factors save one are held constant; in this manner, the complex causal nexus is reduced to manageable proportions. But anthropology is rarely blessed with tightly designed experiments employing built-in controls. Anthropologists must accept circumstances largely as they exist in the real world, usually without the luxury of holding selected factors constant. Because social phenomena generally involve multiple causality, anthropologists often must rely upon analysis of extant associations. The judicious use of statistical techniques can be of great help in sorting out the patterned cultural responses from chance occurrences, but anthropologists must explicitly recognize that some phenomena are better explained by statistics than others. Sometimes statistics don't fit.

Anthropologists employ two classes of statistics: (1) *descriptive statistics* characterize central tendency, dispersion, correlation, and regression; and (2) *inferential statistics* infer unknown population parameters from incomplete sample data.

Descriptive generalizations of social phenomena are commonplace in anthropology.

Ninety percent of societies with Crow/Omaha kin terms have some form of unilineal descent.

Horticulturalists have a significantly higher degree of matrilocal residence than do hunter-gatherers.

The prehistoric Basketmaker II people hunted with the *atlatl* rather than bow and arrow.

The potlatch of the prehistoric Kwakiutl closely resembled the redistributive feasts of New Guinea and Melanesia.

Anthropology is also committed to unravelling relationships at a higher level of analysis. If X, then Y.

Unilineal descent *causes* Crow/Omaha kinship terminology.

Increased population pressure *caused* Mesolithic peoples to turn to an alternative subsistence base.

The principal *cause* of warfare among slash-and-burn horticulturalists is the limited availability of secondary forest growth.

Three important steps are necessary to establish the validity of such causal statements: (1) identify the important factors; (2) determine the predictor-predicted relationship among these factors; (3) establish and test the causal mechanism. Statistical methods greatly facilitate the first two steps, but difficulties are encountered on the third level. Associational statements (step 2) illustrate only that a significant relationship exists between variables X and Y. *Nothing in the framework of statistical inference justifies the automatic assertion that Y is causally related to X.* Statistics only establish that X serves as a predictor of Y. The causal arrow must be supplied by considerations extending beyond commonplace statements of statistical significance and association. Marvin Harris (1968: 621) has underscored this warning in *The Rise of Anthropological Theory:*

> *The difference between causal factors and mere predictive ones is not to be taken lightly. It is the difference in knowing whether wounds cause gunshots or gunshots cause wounds. Bullet holes are excellent predictors of gunshots. As all devotees of Hercule Poirot know, there is a high correlation between gunshots and bullet holes, but no murder has yet admitted of the possibility that it was the fatal wound which caused the gun to discharge its contents. Along the same lines, one might note how reliably rain predicts clouds, or how frequently fire engines are found near burning buildings. If any additional examples are needed, they are available to anyone who has a movie projector which can be run in reverse.*

This is not, of course, to assert that deft anthropologists should avoid causal inference. Quite to the contrary. Statistical methods can even be appropriate to such studies, particularly the judicious use of advanced correlation and regression techniques as discussed by Blalock (1964) and Boudon (1965). But causal statements never directly follow from statistical association.

A comprehensive discussion of causal analysis of cultural phenomena is beyond the present scope. The interested reader is referred to Pelto (1970: chapter 9), Harris (1968: chapter 21), and Köbben (1970). Other discussions can be found in Cohen and Naroll (1970: 5); Murdock (1949: chapter 7); Watson, LeBlanc, and Redman (1971: 140–150); and Clarke (1968: chapter 12).

COMMANDMENT III. Thou shalt not confuse statistical significance with substantive significance.

The initial step in hypothesis testing translates a research hypothesis into operational statistical statements. The next four steps are directed toward testing these statistical hypotheses: H_o either survives the test or is rejected. The final step translates the numerical findings back into substantive, anthropologically relevant statements. The translation and subsequent decoding from the numerical jargon of statistics to the everyday discourse of anthropology creates a potential chasm of confusion for the unwary.

A bridge between the substantive and the statistical can be seen in the familiar "If A, then B" perspective of the logician. B is a logical consequent of A. Let us call theory A the anthropological hypothesis and B the logical consequent having certain statistical implications. The statement that the Mousterian culture was practiced by European Neanderthals is a plausible theory. Certain consequences must logically follow if this theory is correct. We suspect, for instance, that only Neanderthal skeletons should appear in Mousterian contexts, and Neanderthals should appear *only* in Mousterian sites. *If* the Mousterian culture was practiced only by Neanderthals, *then* only Neanderthal skeletons should appear in Mousterian sites: If A, then B. The B proposition is a substantive proposal easily translated into a statistical contingency table.

	Neanderthal Skeletons	
Mousterian artifacts	+	−
+	a	b
−	c	d

The operational statistical hypotheses which follow are:

$$H_o: \quad ad \leq bc \qquad H_1: \quad ad > bc$$

A decision can be made regarding the tenability of the null hypothesis by tabulating inventories of major Middle Paleolithic sites. Suppose that the evidence weighs strongly against H_o—cells a and d are heavily loaded—and these results are declared significant at 0.01. The statistical decision rejects the null hypothesis in favor of H_1. The substantive conclusion is that Neanderthal skeletons are indeed associated with artifacts of the Mousterian culture.

Several cautions must be entered. First of all, the level of statistical probability applies only to the statistical conclusion, *not to the substantive decision*. The testing procedure *does not* warrant the statement that "there's less than a 0.01 chance that Neanderthals were not Mousterians." This conclusion grossly confuses the statistical with the substantive (see also Commandment VIII).

Second, an appropriate measure of association such as phi or gamma should accompany the level of significance. It is an error to weigh the level of significance more heavily than the actual size of a difference or the magnitude of association. Anthropological literature often considers only the p value as a "measure of association" without noting the actual size of the observed difference. The general goal of high predictability in social science is a laudable one, but this goal must not be confused with a high level of statistical significance. A 1 percent difference will prove statistically significant with a large enough sample, but in a practical sense such small differences are meaningless in modern social science (Selvin 1957).

Finally, one must avoid committing the *fallacy of affirming the consequent* (Blalock 1972: chapter 8). Proposition *B* appears to be correct in our example because Neanderthal skulls generally co-occur with Mousterian artifacts. But we cannot conclude from this finding that *A must* also be true, that Neanderthals in fact made those tools or that Neanderthals necessarily carried the Mousterian cognitive set about in their heads. We can only be certain that *A* is true by absolutely establishing that *no other statements* could predict *B*, such as: If *C*, then *B*, or if *D*, then *B*. This task is generally impossible because there seem to always be alternative explanations for the *B* phenomena. If Neanderthal were a relic collector, for example, then the Mousterian artifacts associated with Neanderthal burials could be heirlooms or antiques rather than the actual cultural remains of Neanderthals. Or perhaps Neanderthal's European successor, Cro-Magnon, was the pothunter. The Mousterian sites could conceivably represent prehistoric "museums," set up by a history-conscious Cro-Magnon. You can probably think of equally *possible*, although implausible, explanations for the fact that Mousterian tools and Neanderthal bones co-occur at archaeological sites. Because this is so, one can never prove that theory *A* must be true. In fact, infinitely many theories exist to explain any set of facts, as long as one is willing to discard enough other theories (see Kemeny 1959: chapter 5 on this point).

The term *significance test* can be a culprit creating problems with statistical results. As mentioned earlier, Naroll urges us to call our statistical tools *insignificance tests*, emphasizing that only irrelevant relationships can be established with statistical authority. Kish (1959: 139) suggests scrapping the term "significance" altogether and proposes that we speak of "tests against the null hypothesis." Either H_o survives these tests or not. Hays (1973: 384) regards the value of statistical results in terms of their "surprisal value." When the results appear likely under H_o, then their "surprisal value" is quite low. But the surprisal value is high when results appear unlikely under H_o, and we can direct actions accordingly. Keep in mind that many cases exist when statistical tests are inappropriate in the first place. Some results should simply be presented with appropriate confidence intervals, and the matter of "significant or not" be left to the reader.

This brief discussion considers only some of the severe problems arising when statistical significance is confused with substantive importance. Suitably alerted, the reader is urged to consider the growing body of literature on the misuse of statistical machinery in the social sciences. Some of the more relevant articles have been compiled by Morrison and Henkel (1970) and Steger (1971); see also Naroll's (1971) review of the problem.

● *If fifty million people say a foolish thing, it is still a foolish thing.*—B. Russell

COMMANDMENT IV. Thou shalt not confuse statistical significance with strength of association.

An alarming example from psychology illustrates the prevalence of this fourth sin in the social sciences. The results of a hypothetical statistical analysis were presented to a department of psychologists at a well-known American university. Nine faculty members, each with a Ph.D., and ten graduate students were asked to determine the credibility of findings in two sets of experiments. The first experiment used sample sizes of $n = 10$ and the second involved $n = 100$. Both samples produced significant results. The alarming upshot was that the psychologists felt more confident with the *large* sample results than with significant results derived from the small samples *at the same alpha level*! Not only did they confuse the relationship of n and p, but they were also guilty of sins VIII (using p as a measure of significance) and IV (confusing statistical significance with strength of association). This is particularly poignant, since the average psychologist is surely more statistically aware than the average anthropologist. Rosenthal and Gaito (1963) and Bakan (1967: chapter 1) consider further implications of the above study.

The point is that knowledge of *only* the level of statistical significance tells us precious little about the true magnitude of relationship under study. Several other factors, particularly sample size and the power of the given test, are known to influence probability levels in a manner quite independent from the magnitude of association. A linear correlation coefficient of $r = 0.11$, for example, can be the basis for rejecting H_o in one study, while $r = 0.25$ will fail to reject the null hypothesis in a second study, provided the sample sizes are large enough (300) and small enough (50), respectively (Morrison and Henkel 1969). A complete description of one's statistical analysis should include a statement of statistical significance (if relevant), an appropriate measure of associational strength, and the absolute magnitude of the observed differences.

COMMANDMENT V. Thou shalt not modify a priori hypotheses or the level of significance in light of specific sample data.

It is considered *cheating* to modify one's hypothesis to conform with a previously examined set of data. Once a hypothesis has been developed from a set of data, it becomes farcical to "test" for statistical independence within those same data. Of course they're related! That's what made you suspect the relationship in the first place! When hypotheses are "tested" upon the data that originally suggested them, and statistical significance levels are computed, a spurious sense of validity results. The computed levels of significance may have almost no relation to the true level (Selvin 1957 provides a quantitative example of this sin).

Alpha is only a statement of willingness to commit a Type I error. This willingness should be based upon a general familiarity with the empirical situation, but *not* upon the data contained in a specific sample. Like the statistical hypotheses, the level of significance is an a priori value set in advance of data manipulation and remaining intact throughout the testing episode.

● *I begin to smell a rat.* —M. de Cervantes

But there is the argument that "logic is timeless....," and it matters little whether a theory is conceived before, after, or during collection of data. In fact, very few investigators actually set significance levels or define all statistical hypotheses prior to beginning actual fieldwork. This is acceptable because of the special definition of *data*, discussed in Chapter 2. Data are not objects, but rather are empirical observations *made on* those objects. Thus, collection of data is more an analytical process than something one does "in the field." The important concept here is that formation of hypotheses be kept *logically* independent from the data used to test them; temporal order is only a side issue (see LeBlanc 1973, and Williams, Thomas, and Bettinger 1973 for conflicting sentiments on this point).

● *Some people, unfortunately, are lightning bugs; they carry their illumination behind them.*—S. Ervin

COMMANDMENT VI. Thou shalt not collapse contingency tables to generate significant results.

This sin was discussed earlier in Section 11.6. An attribute or ordinal scale, such as postmarital residence pattern or mode of settlement, can generally be dichotomized (or trichotomized) in a number of different ways. Obviously, one's "pet" hypothesis can be favored by the surreptitious manipulating of the cutting points on an ordinal scale. In fact, a judicious adjustment of categories can even change the directionality of a contingency table.

In a manner of speaking, the after-the-fact collapsing of contingency tables is actually a specialized example of the sin warned against in Commandment V (modifying hypotheses after inspecting the data). Contingency tables can legitimately be collapsed only for reasons which are clearly independent of the relations under investigation, such as inadequate data within certain cells (see Yule and Kendall 1937).

● *Don't pull the crime if you can't pull the time.*—Anonymous

COMMANDMENT VII. Thou shalt not test hypotheses with a shotgun.

This book has discussed how to test statistical hypotheses. It must be pointed out, however, that the actual *testing* of hypotheses is but one component in the overall scheme of science. It is equally important to realize just how hypotheses are derived in the first place.

There is no magic formula for generating good ideas. In fact, more than one brilliant scientific notion has arisen from what most people consider most "unscientific" circumstances. Take the case of the chemist Kekule, who had been wrestling with devising an appropriate structural formula to account for the behavior of the benzene molecule (as described by Hempel 1966: 16). One evening in 1865, Kekule was dozing before his fireplace, gazing into the fire. As the flames danced about, one flame seemed to whirl and catch its own tail. Kekule awoke with a start, suddenly realizing he just had solved the problem of benzene structure: The molecule is a hexagonal ring, originally suggested by the flame's dancing shape. Flashes of insight such as this are rare, and it has been said that the true role of genius in science is to suggest new hypotheses, to create order out of seeming chaos. It matters little how this insight occurs.

Once the creative hunches have been generated, deciding which of them best explains the data becomes a purely mechanical process. Research hypotheses are translated into operational statistical hypotheses which are then probed for their ability to explain phenomena of the real world. The null hypothesis either survives this test or perishes, depending upon its performance relative to the data.

These well-known canons of science are mentioned here to reinforce one very simple point. Significance testing is relevant only to scientific validation, not to scientific exploration. Good ideas can come from anywhere and dredging through a mass of unsorted data can be an illuminating procedure. In fact, computing preliminary statistics of description can be helpful in looking for insights. But tests of statistical significance can be misleading when applied in such preliminary studies. The *fishing expedition approach*—applying tests of significance to huge bodies of data in the hope of coming up with meaningful comparisons—seriously undermines the assumptions of significance testing. The results are much too lenient with respect to Type I errors (Kish 1959). It is possible only to test statistically an existing hypothesis. Such tests cannot explain *why* the hypothesis is true nor can they ferret out that hypothesis in the first place. An anthropological example should underscore this difficulty.

In 1966, Robert Textor published a volume entitled simply *A Cross-Cultural Summary*. Textor's "book" actually consists of 20,000 statistical intercorrelations of cultural traits. The 536 pages consist largely of computer printout, weighing a whopping eight (!) pounds. The objective behind tabulating this mass of data is twofold: (1) to allow the anthropologists to test a wide variety of already existing hypotheses, and (2) to generate new hypotheses and hunches. Of the literally tens of thousands of intercorrelations calculated by the computer, only the "best" 20,000 were included in the volume. The "weak" or "less supportable" correlations were winnowed out, using a cutoff point of $\alpha = 0.10$.

Textor's motives are surely worthy, but as Marvin Harris (1968: 621) has suggested, the 20,000 computer correlations "may actually be . . . a source of ignorance and confusion as well as of correlation." There is always a danger that the uninitiated will confuse correlation with causality (Commandment II) and judge a particular relationship as *confirmed* by its mere presence in the printout. One might argue, for example, that:

> *Cultures where male genital mutilation is present tend to be those where metal working is present because the computer showed that results will occur by chance fewer than one time in 10,000 cases.*

Or one could assert that:

> *Cultures where the plow is present tilt more toward being those where a high god is present, with p = 0.012.*

This statement is a direct quote from the Textor printout. One's argument could be further buttressed by the rationalization that the probabilities must be right—aren't they computed using Fisher's Exact Test?

Assertions of this sort impress only the statistically naive. These "laws" are merely the catch of a massive fishing trip. Lacking the interconnecting causal nexus, the "statistical significance" becomes irrelevant because the alpha level has been undermined by repetitive testing. *By chance alone*, we expect about 10 percent (for $\alpha = 0.10$) of the correlations to the spurious.

The point is not to discredit or make light of Textor's massive contribution. Obviously, the effort summarizes a mountain of quantitative cultural data. If simplistic errors in interpretation arise from *A Cross-Cultural Summary*, the fault will certainly *not* lie with the author, Robert Textor. I simply wish to caution the reader, yet again, against any unwarranted reverence for quantitative data in general and the levels of statistical significance in particular.

● *Anthropologists as a group do not know what they know; they do not know the questions to which they have accumulated the answers.*—D. French

COMMANDMENT VIII. Thou shalt not take *p* as a measure of significance.

A common error in the anthropological literature is to take the *p*-value (or alpha level) as a quantitative "measure" of significance for a total population. One encounters statements to the effect that a probability of $p < 0.05$ means "there's less than 5 percent probability that my field results could be due to chance," or "we can be 95 percent confident in our findings," or "we can predict the future outcomes with 95 percent accuracy." Unfortunately, none of these statements is consistent with the inference model employed in statistical hypothesis testing. "*p*" is merely an *inference* about a specific *sample* rather than a concrete measure of a population characteristic. The probability value is just an a priori condition allowing the researcher to determine whether or not H_o should be rejected. That decision will be incorrect a projected number of times per hundred such trials (assuming the assumptions hold). Conditions inferred from large samples—such as differences in means, correlations, associations, and so forth—may well hold true for the total population, but they nevertheless remain inferences.

COMMANDMENT IX. Thou shalt not take the assumptions of statistical models in vain.

Honor these assumptions and hold them inviolate. Better to use a less powerful test or a nonparametric alternative than to rape the underlying model.

COMMANDMENT X. It is a sin to place mathematical elegance before anthropological relevance.

Do not covet the mathematical rigor of neighboring disciplines, nor their infinite replicability, nor their level of predictability, nor anything that is of physical science. The objectives of social science are worthy in themselves and need not be subverted by a seductive technological or statistical reductionism.

● *Beware fanciful desires; you may get lucky.*—P. Roth

16.3 ANTHROPOLOGY, STATISTICS, AND COMMON SENSE

● *Next to knowing when to seize an opportunity, the most important thing in life is to know when to forego an advantage.*—B. Disraeli

When asked if he could read music, folk musician Pete Seeger once replied, "Not enough to hurt my playing." This impious attitude can profitably be applied to statistical thinking on the social sciences: Anthropologists should practice just enough statistics not to hurt their anthropology.

This caveat is not a pitch for ignorance. If I didn't think statistics were important for the anthropologist, I wouldn't have written this book. I am merely pointing out that the euphoric refrain of statistical rigor can lead the unwary down a path eventually ending in superficiality and fruitless inquiry. As Bakan has warned (1967),

> We must overcome the myth that if our treatment of our subject matter is mathematical it is therefore precise and valid. We need to overcome the handicap associated with limited competence in mathematics, a competence that makes it possible for us to run tests of significance while it intimidates us with a vision of greater mathematical competence if only one could reach up to it.

I have argued elsewhere in this book that a knowledge of statistics is essential for modern anthropologists so that they will be able to judge when such methods must not be used, as well as when such techniques will be invaluable. It is now time to consider one final statistical test: *Berkson's Interocular Traumatic Test* (Edwards, Lindman, and Savage 1963). The method is quite simple and straightforward, but an elusive test to teach students. The test involves no numbers, no formulas, no tables of probabilities. What could be easier? Berkson's Interocular Traumatic Test states simply: *You know what the data mean when the conclusion hits you between the eyes.* No further statistical methods are involved whenever the Berkson test applies. Learn to apply it well.

● *It requires a very unusual mind to make an analysis of the obvious.*—A. Whitehead

Appendix: Statistical Tables

TABLE A.1   Table of Squares, Square Roots, and Reciprocals of Numbers from 1 to 1000

N	N^2	$\sqrt{N}$	$1/N$	N	N^2	$\sqrt{N}$	$1/N$
1	1	1.0000	1.000000	41	1681	6.4031	.024390
2	4	1.4142	.500000	42	1764	6.4807	.023810
3	9	1.7321	.333333	43	1849	6.5574	.023256
4	16	2.0000	.250000	44	1936	6.6332	.022727
5	25	2.2361	.200000	45	2025	6.7082	.022222
6	36	2.4495	.166667	46	2116	6.7823	.021739
7	49	2.6458	.142857	47	2209	6.8557	.021277
8	64	2.8284	.125000	48	2304	6.9282	.020833
9	81	3.0000	.111111	49	2401	7.0000	.020408
10	100	3.1623	.100000	50	2500	7.0711	.020000
11	121	3.3166	.090909	51	2601	7.1414	.019608
12	144	3.4641	.083333	52	2704	7.2111	.019231
13	169	3.6056	.076923	53	2809	7.2801	.018868
14	196	3.7417	.071429	54	2916	7.3485	.018519
15	225	3.8730	.066667	55	3025	7.4162	.018182
16	256	4.0000	.062500	56	3136	7.4833	.017857
17	289	4.1231	.058824	57	3249	7.5498	.017544
18	324	4.2426	.055556	58	3364	7.6158	.017241
19	361	4.3589	.052632	59	3481	7.6811	.016949
20	400	4.4721	.050000	60	3600	7.7460	.016667
21	441	4.5826	.047619	61	3721	7.8102	.016393
22	484	4.6904	.045455	62	3844	7.8740	.016129
23	529	4.7958	.043478	63	3969	7.9373	.015873
24	576	4.8990	.041667	64	4096	8.0000	.015625
25	625	5.0000	.040000	65	4225	8.0623	.015385
26	676	5.0990	.038462	66	4356	8.1240	.015152
27	729	5.1962	.037037	67	4489	8.1854	.014925
28	784	5.2915	.035714	68	4624	8.2462	.014706
29	841	5.3852	.034483	69	4761	8.3066	.014493
30	900	5.4772	.033333	70	4900	8.3666	.014286
31	961	5.5678	.032258	71	5041	8.4261	.014085
32	1024	5.6569	.031250	72	5184	8.4853	.013889
33	1089	5.7446	.030303	73	5329	8.5440	.013699
34	1156	5.8310	.029412	74	5476	8.6023	.013514
35	1225	5.9161	.028571	75	5625	8.6603	.013333
36	1296	6.0000	.027778	76	5776	8.7178	.013158
37	1369	6.0828	.027027	77	5929	8.7750	.012987
38	1444	6.1644	.026316	78	6084	8.8318	.012821
39	1521	6.2450	.025641	79	6241	8.8882	.012658
40	1600	6.3246	.025000	80	6400	8.9443	.012500

Portions of this table have been reproduced from J. W. Dunlap and A. K. Kurtz. *Handbook of Statistical Nomographs, Tables, and Formulas*, World Book Company, New York (1932), by permission of the authors and publishers.

TABLE A.1   Table of Squares, Square Roots, and Reciprocals of Numbers from 1 to 1000 (cont.)

N	N^2	$\sqrt{N}$	$1/N$	N	N^2	$\sqrt{N}$	$1/N$
81	6561	9.0000	.012346	121	14641	11.0000	.00826446
82	6724	9.0554	.012195	122	14884	11.0454	.00819672
83	6889	9.1104	.012048	123	15129	11.0905	.00813008
84	7056	9.1652	.011905	124	15376	11.1355	.00806452
85	7225	9.2195	.011765	125	15625	11.1803	.00800000
86	7396	9.2736	.011628	126	15876	11.2250	.00793651
87	7569	9.3274	.011494	127	16129	11.2694	.00787402
88	7744	9.3808	.011364	128	16384	11.3137	.00781250
89	7921	9.4340	.011236	129	16641	11.3578	.00775194
90	8100	9.4868	.011111	130	16900	11.4018	.00769231
91	8281	9.5394	.010989	131	17161	11.4455	.00763359
92	8464	9.5917	.010870	132	17424	11.4891	.00757576
93	8649	9.6437	.010753	133	17689	11.5326	.00751880
94	8836	9.6954	.010638	134	17956	11.5758	.00746269
95	9025	9.7468	.010526	135	18225	11.6190	.00740741
96	9216	9.7980	.010417	136	18496	11.6619	.00735294
97	9409	9.8489	.010309	137	18769	11.7047	.00729927
98	9604	9.8995	.010204	138	19044	11.7473	.00724638
99	9801	9.9499	.010101	139	19321	11.7898	.00719424
100	10000	10.0000	.010000	140	19600	11.8322	.00714286
101	10201	10.0499	.00990099	141	19881	11.8743	.00709220
102	10404	10.0995	.00980392	142	20164	11.9164	.00704225
103	10609	10.1489	.00970874	143	20449	11.9583	.00699301
104	10816	10.1980	.00961538	144	20736	12.0000	.00694444
105	11025	10.2470	.00952381	145	21025	12.0416	.00689655
106	11236	10.2956	.00943396	146	21316	12.0830	.00684932
107	11449	10.3441	.00934579	147	21609	12.1244	.00680272
108	11664	10.3923	.00925926	148	21904	12.1655	.00675676
109	11881	10.4403	.00917431	149	22201	12.2066	.00671141
110	12100	10.4881	.00909091	150	22500	12.2474	.00666667
111	12321	10.5357	.00900901	151	22801	12.2882	.00662252
112	12544	10.5830	.00892857	152	23104	12.3288	.00657895
113	12769	10.6301	.00884956	153	23409	12.3693	.00653595
114	12996	10.6771	.00877193	154	23716	12.4097	.00649351
115	13225	10.7238	.00869565	155	24025	12.4499	.00645161
116	13456	10.7703	.00862069	156	24336	12.4900	.00641026
117	13689	10.8167	.00854701	157	24649	12.5300	.00636943
118	13924	10.8628	.00847458	158	24964	12.5698	.00632911
119	14161	10.9087	.00840336	159	25281	12.6095	.00628931
120	14400	10.9545	.00833333	160	25600	12.6491	.00625000

Portions of this table have been reproduced from J. W. Dunlap and A. K. Kurtz. *Handbook of Statistical Nomographs, Tables, and Formulas*, World Book Company, New York (1932), by permission of the authors and publishers.

TABLE A.1 Table of Squares, Square Roots, and Reciprocals of Numbers from 1 to 1000 (*cont*.)

N	N^2	$\sqrt{N}$	$1/N$	N	N^2	$\sqrt{N}$	$1/N$
161	25921	12.6886	.00621118	201	40401	14.1774	.00497512
162	26244	12.7279	.00617284	202	40804	14.2127	.00495050
163	26569	12.7671	.00613497	203	41209	14.2478	.00492611
164	26896	12.8062	.00609756	204	41616	14.2829	.00490196
165	27225	12.8452	.00606061	205	42025	14.3178	.00487805
166	27556	12.8841	.00602410	206	42436	14.3527	.00485437
167	27889	12.9228	.00598802	207	42849	14.3875	.00483092
168	28224	12.9615	.00595238	208	43264	14.4222	.00480769
169	28561	13.0000	.00591716	209	43681	14.4568	.00478469
170	28900	13.0384	.00588235	210	44100	14.4914	.00476190
171	29241	13.0767	.00584795	211	44521	14.5258	.00473934
172	29584	13.1149	.00581395	212	44944	14.5602	.00471698
173	29929	13.1529	.00578035	213	45369	14.5945	.00469484
174	30276	13.1909	.00574713	214	45796	14.6287	.00467290
175	30625	13.2288	.00571429	215	46225	14.6629	.00465116
176	30976	13.2665	.00568182	216	46656	14.6969	.00462963
177	31329	13.3041	.00564972	217	47089	14.7309	.00460829
178	31684	13.3417	.00561798	218	47524	14.7648	.00458716
179	32041	13.3791	.00558659	219	47961	14.7986	.00456621
180	32400	13.4164	.00555556	220	48400	14.8324	.00454545
181	32761	13.4536	.00552486	221	48841	14.8661	.00452489
182	33124	13.4907	.00549451	222	49284	14.8997	.00450450
183	33489	13.5277	.00546448	223	49729	14.9332	.00448430
184	33856	13.5647	.00543478	224	50176	14.9666	.00446429
185	34225	13.6015	.00540541	225	50625	15.0000	.00444444
186	34596	13.6382	.00537634	226	51076	15.0333	.00442478
187	34969	13.6748	.00534759	227	51529	15.0665	.00440529
188	35344	13.7113	.00531915	228	51984	15.0997	.00438596
189	35721	13.7477	.00529101	229	52441	15.1327	.00436681
190	36100	13.7840	.00526316	230	52900	15.1658	.00434783
191	36481	13.8203	.00523560	231	53361	15.1987	.00432900
192	36864	13.8564	.00520833	232	53824	15.2315	.00431034
193	37249	13.8924	.00518135	233	54289	15.2643	.00429185
194	37636	13.9284	.00515464	234	54756	15.2971	.00427350
195	38025	13.9642	.00512821	235	55225	15.3297	.00425532
196	38416	14.0000	.00510204	236	55696	15.3623	.00423729
197	38809	14.0357	.00507614	237	56169	15.3948	.00421941
198	39204	14.0712	.00505051	238	56644	15.4272	.00420168
199	39601	14.1067	.00502513	239	57121	15.4596	.00418410
200	40000	14.1421	.00500000	240	57600	15.4919	.00416667

Portions of this table have been reproduced from J. W. Dunlap and A. K. Kurtz. *Handbook of Statistical Nomographs, Tables, and Formulas*, World Book Company, New York (1932), by permission of the authors and publishers.

TABLE A.1 Table of Squares, Square Roots, and Reciprocals of Numbers from 1 to 1000 (*cont*.)

N	N^2	$\sqrt{N}$	$1/N$	N	N^2	$\sqrt{N}$	$1/N$
241	58081	15.5242	.00414938	281	78961	16.7631	.00355872
242	58564	15.5563	.00413223	282	79524	16.7929	.00354610
243	59049	15.5885	.00411523	283	80089	16.8226	.00353357
244	59536	15.6205	.00409836	284	80656	16.8523	.00352113
245	60025	15.6525	.00408163	285	81225	16.8819	.00350877
246	60516	15.6844	.00406504	286	81796	16.9115	.00349650
247	61009	15.7162	.00404858	287	82369	16.9411	.00348432
248	61504	15.7480	.00403226	288	82944	16.9706	.00347222
249	62001	15.7797	.00401606	289	83521	17.0000	.00346021
250	62500	15.8114	.00400000	290	84100	17 0294	.00344828
251	63001	15.8430	.00398406	291	84681	17.0587	.00343643
252	63504	15.8745	.00396825	292	85264	17.0880	.00342466
253	64009	15.9060	.00395257	293	85849	17.1172	.00341297
254	64516	15.9374	.00393701	294	86436	17.1464	.00340136
255	65025	15.9687	.00392157	295	87025	17.1756	.00338983
256	65536	16.0000	.00390625	296	87616	17.2047	.00337838
257	66049	16.0312	.00389105	297	88209	17.2337	.00336700
258	66564	16.0624	.00387597	298	88804	17.2627	.00335570
259	67081	16.0935	.00386100	299	89401	17.2916	.00334448
260	67600	16.1245	.00384615	300	90000	17.3205	.00333333
261	68121	16.1555	.00383142	301	90601	17.3494	.00332226
262	68644	16.1864	.00381679	302	91204	17.3781	.00331126
263	69169	16.2173	.00380228	303	91809	17.4069	.00330033
264	69696	16.2481	.00378788	304	92416	17.4356	.00328947
265	70225	16.2788	.00377358	305	93025	17.4642	.00327869
266	70756	16.3095	.00375940	306	93636	17.4929	.00326797
267	71289	16.3401	.00374532	307	94249	17.5214	.00325733
268	71824	16.3707	.00373134	308	94864	17.5499	.00324675
269	72361	16.4012	.00371747	309	95481	17.5784	.00323625
270	72900	16.4317	.00370370	310	96100	17.6068	.00322581
271	73441	16.4621	.00369004	311	96721	17.6352	.00321543
272	73984	16.4924	.00367647	312	97344	17.6635	.00320513
273	74529	16.5227	.00366300	313	97969	17.6918	.00319489
274	75076	16.5529	.00364964	314	98596	17.7200	.00318471
275	75625	16.5831	.00363636	315	99225	17.7482	.00317460
276	76176	16.6132	.00362319	316	99856	17.7764	.00316456
277	76729	16.6433	.00361011	317	100489	17.8045	.00315457
278	77284	16.6733	.00359712	318	101124	17.8326	.00314465
279	77841	16.7033	.00358423	319	101761	17.8606	.00313480
280	78400	16.7332	.00357143	320	102400	17.8885	.00312500

Portions of this table have been reproduced from J. W. Dunlap and A. K. Kurtz. *Handbook of Statistical Nomographs, Tables, and Formulas*, World Book Company, New York (1932), by permission of the authors and publishers.

TABLE A.1   Table of Squares, Square Roots, and Reciprocals of Numbers from 1 to 1000 (cont.)

N	N^2	$\sqrt{N}$	$1/N$	N	N^2	$\sqrt{N}$	$1/N$
321	103041	17.9165	.00311526	361	130321	19.0000	.00277008
322	103684	17.9444	.00310559	362	131044	19.0263	.00276243
323	104329	17.9722	.00309598	363	131769	19.0526	.00275482
324	104976	18.0000	.00308642	364	132496	19.0788	.00274725
325	105625	18.0278	.00307692	365	133225	19.1050	.00273973
326	106276	18.0555	.00306748	366	133956	19.1311	.00273224
327	106929	18.0831	.00305810	367	134689	19.1572	.00272480
328	107584	18.1108	.00304878	368	135424	19.1833	.00271739
329	108241	18.1384	.00303951	369	136161	19.2094	.00271003
330	108900	18.1659	.00303030	370	136900	19.2354	.00270270
331	109561	18.1934	.00302115	371	137641	19.2614	.00269542
332	110224	18.2209	.00301205	372	138384	19.2873	.00268817
333	110889	18.2483	.00300300	373	139129	19.3132	.00268097
334	111556	18.2757	.00299401	374	139876	19.3391	.00267380
335	112225	18.3030	.00298507	375	140625	19.3649	.00266667
336	112896	18.3303	.00297619	376	141376	19.3907	.00265957
337	113569	18.3576	.00296736	377	142129	19.4165	.00265252
338	114244	18.3848	.00295858	378	142884	19.4422	.00264550
339	114921	18.4120	.00294985	379	143641	19.4679	.00263852
340	115600	18.4391	.00294118	380	144400	19.4936	.00263158
341	116281	18.4662	.00293255	381	145161	19.5192	.00262467
342	116964	18.4932	.00292398	382	145924	19.5448	.00261780
343	117649	18.5203	.00291545	383	146689	19.5704	.00261097
344	118336	18.5472	.00290698	384	147456	19.5959	.00260417
345	119025	18.5742	.00289855	385	148225	19.6214	.00259740
346	119716	18.6011	.00289017	386	148996	19.6469	.00259067
347	120409	18.6279	.00288184	387	149769	19.6723	.00258398
348	121104	18.6548	.00287356	388	150544	19.6977	.00257732
349	121801	18.6815	.00286533	389	151321	19.7231	.00257069
350	122500	18.7083	.00285714	390	152100	19.7484	.00256410
351	123201	18.7350	.00284900	391	152881	19.7737	.00255754
352	123904	18.7617	.00284091	392	153664	19.7990	.00255102
353	124609	18.7883	.00283286	393	154449	19.8242	.00254453
354	125316	18.8149	.00282486	394	155236	19.8494	.00253807
355	126025	18.8414	.00281690	395	156025	19.8746	.00253165
356	126736	18.8680	.00280899	396	156816	19.8997	.00252525
357	127449	18.8944	.00280112	397	157609	19.9249	.00251889
358	128164	18.9209	.00279330	398	158404	19.9499	.00251256
359	128881	18.9473	.00278552	399	159201	19.9750	.00250627
360	129600	18.9737	.00277778	400	160000	20.0000	.00250000

Portions of this table have been reproduced from J. W. Dunlap and A. K. Kurtz. *Handbook of Statistical Nomographs, Tables, and Formulas*, World Book Company, New York (1932), by permission of the authors and publishers.

TABLE A.1 Table of Squares, Square Roots, and Reciprocals of Numbers from 1 to 1000 (*cont.*)

N	N^2	$\sqrt{N}$	$1/N$	N	N^2	$\sqrt{N}$	$1/N$
401	160801	20.0250	.00249377	441	194481	21.0000	.00226757
402	161604	20.0499	.00248756	442	195364	21.0238	.00226244
403	162409	20.0749	.00248139	443	196249	21.0476	.00225734
404	163216	20.0998	.00247525	444	197136	21.0713	.00225225
405	164025	20.1246	.00246914	445	198025	21.0950	.00224719
406	164836	20.1494	.00246305	446	198916	21.1187	.00224215
407	165649	20.1742	.00245700	447	199809	21.1424	.00223714
408	166464	20.1990	.00245098	448	200704	21.1660	.00223214
409	167281	20.2237	.00244499	449	201601	21.1896	.00222717
410	168100	20.2485	.00243902	450	202500	21.2132	.00222222
411	168921	20.2731	.00243309	451	203401	21.2368	.00221729
412	169744	20.2978	.00242718	452	204304	21.2603	.00221239
413	170569	20.3224	.00242131	453	205209	21.2838	.00220751
414	171396	20.3470	.00241546	454	206116	21.3073	.00220264
415	172225	20.3715	.00240964	455	207025	21.3307	.00219780
416	173056	20.3961	.00240385	456	207936	21.3542	.00219298
417	173889	20.4206	.00239808	457	208849	21.3776	.00218818
418	174724	20.4450	.00239234	458	209764	21.4009	.00218341
419	175561	20.4695	.00238663	459	210681	21.4243	.00217865
420	176400	20.4939	.00238095	460	211600	21.4476	.00217391
421	177241	20.5183	.00237530	461	212521	21.4709	.00216920
422	178084	20.5426	.00236967	462	213444	21.4942	.00216450
423	178929	20.5670	.00236407	463	214369	21.5174	.00215983
424	179776	20.5913	.00235849	464	215296	21.5407	.00215517
425	180625	20.6155	.00235294	465	216225	21.5639	.00215054
426	181476	20.6398	.00234742	466	217156	21.5870	.00214592
427	182329	20.6640	.00234192	467	218089	21.6102	.00214133
428	183184	20.6882	.00233645	468	219024	21.6333	.00213675
429	184041	20.7123	.00233100	469	219961	21.6564	.00213220
430	184900	20.7364	.00232558	470	220900	21.6795	.00212766
431	185761	20.7605	.00232019	471	221841	21.7025	.00212314
432	186624	20.7846	.00231481	472	222784	21.7256	.00211864
433	187489	20.8087	.00230947	473	223729	21.7486	.00211416
434	188356	20.8327	.00230415	474	224676	21.7715	.00210970
435	189225	20.8567	.00229885	475	225625	21.7945	.00210526
436	190096	20.8806	.00229358	476	226576	21.8174	.00210084
437	190969	20.9045	.00228833	477	227529	21.8403	.00209644
438	191844	20.9284	.00228311	478	228484	21.8632	.00209205
439	192721	20.9523	.00227790	479	229441	21.8861	.00208768
440	193600	20.9762	.00227273	480	230400	21.9089	.00208333

Portions of this table have been reproduced from J. W. Dunlap and A. K. Kurtz. *Handbook of Statistical Nomographs, Tables, and Formulas*, World Book Company, New York (1932), by permission of the authors and publishers.

TABLE A.1   Table of Squares, Square Roots, and Reciprocals of Numbers from 1 to 1000
(*cont.*)

N	N^2	$\sqrt{N}$	$1/N$	N	N^2	$\sqrt{N}$	$1/N$
481	231361	21.9317	.00207900	521	271441	22.8254	.00191939
482	232324	21.9545	.00207469	522	272484	22.8473	.00191571
483	233289	21.9773	.00207039	523	273529	22.8692	.00191205
484	234256	22.0000	.00206612	524	274576	22.8910	.00190840
485	235225	22.0227	.00206186	525	275625	22.9129	.00190476
486	236196	22.0454	.00205761	526	276676	22.9347	.00190114
487	237169	22.0681	.00205339	527	277729	22.9565	.00189753
488	238144	22.0907	.00204918	528	278784	22.9783	.00189394
489	239121	22.1133	.00204499	529	279841	23.0000	.00189036
490	240100	22.1359	.00204082	530	280900	23.0217	.00188679
491	241081	22.1585	.00203666	531	281961	23.0434	.00188324
492	242064	22.1811	.00203252	532	283024	23.0651	.00187970
493	243049	22.2036	.00202840	533	284089	23.0868	.00187617
494	244036	22.2261	.00202429	534	285156	23.1084	.00187266
495	245025	22.2486	.00202020	535	286225	23.1301	.00186916
496	246016	22.2711	.00201613	536	287296	23.1517	.00186567
497	247009	22.2935	.00201207	537	288369	23.1733	.00186220
498	248004	22.3159	.00200803	538	289444	23.1948	.00185874
499	249001	22.3383	.00200401	539	290521	23.2164	.00185529
500	250000	22.3607	.00200000	540	291600	23.2379	.00185185
501	251001	22.3830	.00199601	541	292681	23.2594	.00184843
502	252004	22.4054	.00199203	542	293764	23.2809	.00184502
503	253009	22.4277	.00198807	543	294849	23.3024	.00184162
504	254016	22.4499	.00198413	544	295936	23.3238	.00183824
505	255025	22.4722	.00198020	545	297025	23.3452	.00183486
506	256036	22.4944	.00197628	546	298116	23.3666	.00183150
507	257049	22.5167	.00197239	547	299209	23.3880	.00182815
508	258064	22.5389	.00196850	548	300304	23.4094	.00182482
509	259081	22.5610	.00196464	549	301401	23.4307	.00182149
510	260100	22.5832	.00196078	550	302500	23.4521	.00181818
511	261121	22.6053	.00195695	551	303601	23.4734	.00181488
512	262144	22.6274	.00195312	552	304704	23.4947	.00181159
513	263169	22.6495	.00194932	553	305809	23.5160	.00180832
514	264196	22.6716	.00194553	554	306916	23.5372	.00180505
515	265225	22.6936	.00194175	555	308025	23.5584	.00180180
516	266256	22.7156	.00193798	556	309136	23.5797	.00179856
517	267289	22.7376	.00193424	557	310249	23.6008	.00179533
518	268324	22.7596	.00193050	558	311364	23.6220	.00179211
519	269361	22.7816	.00192678	559	312481	23.6432	.00178891
520	270400	22.8035	.00192308	560	313600	23.6643	.00178571

Portions of this table have been reproduced from J. W. Dunlap and A. K. Kurtz. *Handbook of Statistical Nomographs, Tables, and Formulas*, World Book Company, New York (1932), by permission of the authors and publishers.

TABLE A.1 Table of Squares, Square Roots, and Reciprocals of Numbers from 1 to 1000 (*cont.*)

N	N^2	$\sqrt{N}$	$1/N$	N	N^2	$\sqrt{N}$	$1/N$
561	314721	23.6854	.00178253	601	361201	24.5153	.00166389
562	315844	23.7065	.00177936	602	362404	24.5357	.00166113
563	316969	23.7276	.00177620	603	363609	24.5561	.00165837
564	318096	23.7487	.00177305	604	364816	24.5764	.00165563
565	319225	23.7697	.00176991	605	366025	24.5967	.00165289
566	320356	23.7908	.00176678	606	367236	24.6171	.00165017
567	321489	23.8118	.00176367	607	368449	24.6374	.00164745
568	322624	23.8328	.00176056	608	369664	24.6577	.00164474
569	323761	23.8537	.00175747	609	370881	24.6779	.00164204
570	324900	23.8747	.00175439	610	372100	24.6982	.00163934
571	326041	23.8956	.00175131	611	373321	24.7184	.00163666
572	327184	23.9165	.00174825	612	374544	24.7386	.00163399
573	328329	23.9374	.00174520	613	375769	24.7588	.00163132
574	329476	23.9583	.00174216	614	376996	24.7790	.00162866
575	330625	23.9792	.00173913	615	378225	24.7992	.00162602
576	331776	24.0000	.00173611	616	379456	24.8193	.00162338
577	332929	24.0208	.00173310	617	380689	24.8395	.00162075
578	334084	24.0416	.00173010	618	381924	24.8596	.00161812
579	335241	24.0624	.00172712	619	383161	24.8797	.00161551
580	336400	24.0832	.00172414	620	384400	24.8998	.00161290
581	337561	24.1039	.00172117	621	385641	24.9199	.00161031
582	338724	24.1247	.00171821	622	386884	24.9399	.00160772
583	339889	24.1454	.00171527	623	388129	24.9600	.00160514
584	341056	24.1661	.00171233	624	389376	24.9800	.00160256
585	342225	24.1868	.00170940	625	390625	25.0000	.00160000
586	343396	24.2074	.00170648	626	391876	25.0200	.00159744
587	344569	24.2281	.00170358	627	393129	25.0400	.00159490
588	345744	24.2487	.00170068	628	394384	25.0599	.00159236
589	346921	24.2693	.00169779	629	395641	25.0799	.00158983
590	348100	24.2899	.00169492	630	396900	25.0998	.00158730
591	349281	24.3105	.00169205	631	398161	25.1197	.00158479
592	350464	24.3311	.00168919	632	399424	25.1396	.00158228
593	351649	24.3516	.00168634	633	400689	25.1595	.00157978
594	352836	24.3721	.00168350	634	401956	25.1794	.00157729
595	354025	24.3926	.00168067	635	403225	25.1992	.00157480
596	355216	24.4131	.00167785	636	404496	25.2190	.00157233
597	356409	24.4336	.00167504	637	405769	25.2389	.00156986
598	357604	24.4540	.00167224	638	407044	25.2587	.00156740
599	358801	24.4745	.00166945	639	408321	25.2784	.00156495
600	360000	24.4949	.00166667	640	409600	25.2982	.00156250

Portions of this table have been reproduced from J. W. Dunlap and A. K. Kurtz. *Handbook of Statistical Nomographs, Tables, and Formulas*, World Book Company, New York (1932), by permission of the authors and publishers.

TABLE A.1 Table of Squares, Square Roots, and Reciprocals of Numbers from 1 to 1000 (cont.)

N	N^2	$\sqrt{N}$	$1/N$	N	N^2	$\sqrt{N}$	$1/N$
641	410881	25.3180	.00156006	681	463761	26.0960	.00146843
642	412164	25.3377	.00155763	682	465124	26.1151	.00146628
643	413449	25.3574	.00155521	683	466489	26.1343	.00146413
644	414736	25.3772	.00155280	684	467856	26.1534	.00146199
645	416025	25.3969	.00155039	685	469225	26.1725	.00145985
646	417316	25.4165	.00154799	686	470596	26.1916	.00145773
647	418609	25.4362	.00154560	687	471969	26.2107	.00145560
648	419904	25.4558	.00154321	688	473344	26.2298	.00145349
649	421201	25.4755	.00154083	689	474721	26.2488	.00145138
650	422500	25.4951	.00153846	690	476100	26.2679	.00144928
651	423801	25.5147	.00153610	691	477481	26.2869	.00144718
652	425104	25.5343	.00153374	692	478864	26.3059	.00144509
653	426409	25.5539	.00153139	693	480249	26.3249	.00144300
654	427716	25.5734	.00152905	694	481636	26.3439	.00144092
655	429025	25.5930	.00152672	695	483025	26.3629	.00143885
656	430336	25.6125	.00152439	696	484416	26.3818	.00143678
657	431649	25.6320	.00152207	697	485809	26.4008	.00143472
658	432964	25.6515	.00151976	698	487204	26.4197	.00143266
659	434281	25.6710	.00151745	699	488601	26.4386	.00143062
660	435600	25.6905	.00151515	700	490000	26.4575	.00142857
661	436921	25.7099	.00151286	701	491401	26.4764	.00142653
662	438244	25.7294	.00151057	702	492804	26.4953	.00142450
663	439569	25.7488	.00150830	703	494209	26.5141	.00142248
664	440896	25.7682	.00150602	704	495616	26.5330	.00142045
665	442225	25.7876	.00150376	705	497025	26.5518	.00141844
666	443556	25.8070	.00150150	706	498436	26.5707	.00141643
667	444889	25.8263	.00149925	707	499849	26.5895	.00141443
668	446224	25.8457	.00149701	708	501264	26.6083	.00141243
669	447561	25.8650	.00149477	709	502681	26.6271	.00141044
670	448900	25.8844	.00149254	710	504100	26.6458	.00140845
671	450241	25.9037	.00149031	711	505521	26.6646	.00140647
672	451584	25.9230	.00148810	712	506944	26.6833	.00140449
673	452929	25.9422	.00148588	713	508369	26.7021	.00140252
674	454276	25.9615	.00148368	714	509796	26.7208	.00140056
675	455625	25.9808	.00148148	715	511225	26.7395	.00139860
676	456976	26.0000	.00147929	716	512656	26.7582	.00139665
677	458329	26.0192	.00147710	717	514089	26.7769	.00139470
678	459684	26.0384	.00147493	718	515524	26.7955	.00139276
679	461041	26.0576	.00147275	719	516961	26.8142	.00139082
680	462400	26.0768	.00147059	720	518400	26.8328	.00138889

Portions of this table have been reproduced from J. W. Dunlap and A. K. Kurtz. *Handbook of Statistical Nomographs, Tables, and Formulas*, World Book Company, New York (1932), by permission of the authors and publishers.

TABLE A.1   Table of Squares, Square Roots, and Reciprocals of Numbers from 1 to 1000 (*cont.*)

N	N^2	$\sqrt{N}$	$1/N$	N	N^2	$\sqrt{N}$	$1/N$
721	519841	26.8514	.00138696	761	579121	27.5862	.00131406
722	521284	26.8701	.00138504	762	580644	27.6043	.00131234
723	522729	26.8887	.00138313	763	582169	27.6225	.00131062
724	524176	26.9072	.00138122	764	583696	27.6405	.00130890
725	525625	26.9258	.00137931	765	585225	27.6586	.00130719
726	527076	26.9444	.00137741	766	586756	27.6767	.00130548
727	528529	26.9629	.00137552	767	588289	27.6948	.00130378
728	529984	26.9815	.00137363	768	589824	27.7128	.00130208
729	531441	27.0000	.00137174	769	591361	27.7308	.00130039
730	532900	27.0185	.00136986	770	592900	27.7489	.00129870
731	534361	27.0370	.00136799	771	594441	27.7669	.00129702
732	535824	27.0555	.00136612	772	595984	27.7849	.00129534
733	537289	27.0740	.00136426	773	597529	27.8029	.00129366
734	538756	27.0924	.00136240	774	599076	27.8209	.00129199
735	540225	27.1109	.00136054	775	600625	27.8388	.00129032
736	541696	27.1293	.00135870	776	602176	27.8568	.00128866
737	543169	27.1477	.00135685	777	603729	27.8747	.00128700
738	544644	27.1662	.00135501	778	605284	27.8927	.00128535
739	546121	27.1846	.00135318	779	606841	27.9106	.00128370
740	547600	27.2029	.00135135	780	608400	27.9285	.00128205
741	549081	27.2213	.00134953	781	609961	27.9464	.00128041
742	550564	27.2397	.00134771	782	611524	27.9643	.00127877
743	552049	27.2580	.00134590	783	613089	27.9821	.00127714
744	553536	27.2764	.00134409	784	614656	28.0000	.00127551
745	555025	27.2947	.00134228	785	616225	28.0179	.00127389
746	556516	27.3130	.00134048	786	617796	28.0357	.00127226
747	558009	27.3313	.00133869	787	619369	28.0535	.00127065
748	559504	27.3496	.00133690	788	620944	28.0713	.00126904
749	561001	27.3679	.00133511	789	622521	28.0891	.00126743
750	562500	27.3861	.00133333	790	624100	28.1069	.00126582
751	564001	27.4044	.00133156	791	625681	28.1247	.00126422
752	565504	27.4226	.00132979	792	627264	28.1425	.00126263
753	567009	27.4408	.00132802	793	628849	28.1603	.00126103
754	568516	27.4591	.00132626	794	630436	28.1780	.00125945
755	570025	27.4773	.00132450	795	632025	28.1957	.00125786
756	571536	27.4955	.00132275	796	633616	28.2135	.00125628
757	573049	27.5136	.00132100	797	635209	28.2312	.00125471
758	574564	27.5318	.00131926	798	636804	28.2489	.00125313
759	576081	27.5500	.00131752	799	638401	28.2666	.00125156
760	577600	27.5681	.00131579	800	640000	28.2843	.00125000

Portions of this table have been reproduced from J. W. Dunlap and A. K. Kurtz. *Handbook of Statistical Nomographs, Tables, and Formulas*, World Book Company, New York (1932), by permission of the authors and publishers.

TABLE A.1 Table of Squares, Square Roots, and Reciprocals of Numbers from 1 to 1000 (*cont.*)

N	N^2	$\sqrt{N}$	$1/N$	N	N^2	$\sqrt{N}$	$1/N$
801	641601	28.3019	.00124844	841	707281	29.0000	.00118906
802	643204	28.3196	.00124688	842	708964	29.0172	.00118765
803	644809	28.3373	.00124533	843	710649	29.0345	.00118624
804	646416	28.3549	.00124378	844	712336	29.0517	.00118483
805	648025	28.3725	.00124224	845	714025	29.0689	.00118343
806	649636	28.3901	.00124069	846	715716	29.0861	.00118203
807	651249	28.4077	.00123916	847	717409	29.1033	.00118064
808	652864	28.4253	.00123762	848	719104	29.1204	.00117925
809	654481	28.4429	.00123609	849	720801	29.1376	.00117786
810	656100	28.4605	.00123457	850	722500	29.1548	.00117647
811	657721	28.4781	.00123305	851	724201	29.1719	.00117509
812	659344	28.4956	.00123153	852	725904	29.1890	.00117371
813	660969	28.5132	.00123001	853	727609	29.2062	.00117233
814	662596	28.5307	.00122850	854	729316	29.2233	.00117096
815	664225	28.5482	.00122699	855	731025	29.2404	.00116959
816	665856	28.5657	.00122549	856	732736	29.2575	.00116822
817	667489	28.5832	.00122399	857	734449	29.2746	.00116686
818	669124	28.6007	.00122249	858	736164	29.2916	.00116550
819	670761	28.6182	.00122100	859	737881	29.3087	.00116414
820	672400	28.6356	.00121951	860	739600	29.3258	.00116279
821	674041	28.6531	.00121803	861	741321	29.3428	.00116144
822	675684	28.6705	.00121655	862	743044	29.3598	.00116009
823	677329	28.6880	.00121507	863	744769	29.3769	.00115875
824	678976	28.7054	.00121359	864	746496	29.3939	.00115741
825	680625	28.7228	.00121212	865	748225	29.4109	.00115607
826	682276	28.7402	.00121065	866	749956	29.4279	.00115473
827	683929	28.7576	.00120919	867	751689	29.4449	.00115340
828	685584	28.7750	.00120773	868	753424	29.4618	.00115207
829	687241	28.7924	.00120627	869	755161	29.4788	.00115075
830	688900	28.8097	.00120482	870	756900	29.4958	.00114943
831	690561	28.8271	.00120337	871	758641	29.5127	.00114811
832	692224	28.8444	.00120192	872	760384	29.5296	.00114679
833	693889	28.8617	.00120048	873	762129	29.5466	.00114548
834	695556	28.8791	.00119904	874	763876	29.5635	.00114416
835	697225	28.8964	.00119760	875	765625	29.5804	.00114286
836	698896	28.9137	.00119617	876	767376	29.5973	.00114155
837	700569	28.9310	.00119474	877	769129	29.6142	.00114025
838	702244	28.9482	.00119332	878	770384	29.6311	.00113895
839	703921	28.9655	.00119190	879	772641	29.6479	.00113766
840	705600	28.9828	.00119048	880	774400	29.6648	.00113636

Portions of this table have been reproduced from J. W. Dunlap and A. K. Kurtz. *Handbook of Statistical Nomographs, Tables, and Formulas*, World Book Company, New York (1932), by permission of the authors and publishers.

TABLE A.1 Table of Squares, Square Roots, and Reciprocals of Numbers from 1 to 1000 (*cont.*)

N	N^2	$\sqrt{N}$	$1/N$	N	N^2	$\sqrt{N}$	$1/N$
881	776161	29.6816	.00113507	921	848241	30.3480	.00108578
882	777924	29.6985	.00113379	922	850084	30.3645	.00108460
883	779689	29.7153	.00113250	923	851929	30.3809	.00108342
884	781456	29.7321	.00113122	924	853776	30.3974	.00108225
885	783225	29.7489	.00112994	925	855625	30.4138	.00108108
886	784996	29.7658	.00112867	926	857476	30.4302	.00107991
887	786769	29.7825	.00112740	927	859329	30.4467	.00107875
888	788544	29.7993	.00112613	928	861184	30.4631	.00107759
889	790321	29.8161	.00112486	929	863041	30.4795	.00107643
890	792100	29.8329	.00112360	930	864900	30.4959	.00107527
891	793881	29.8496	.00112233	931	866761	30.5123	.00107411
892	795664	29.8664	.00112108	932	868624	30.5287	.00107296
893	797449	29.8831	.00111982	933	870489	30.5450	.00107181
894	799236	29.8998	.00111857	934	872356	30.5614	.00107066
895	801025	29.9166	.00111732	935	874225	30.5778	.00106952
896	802816	29.9333	.00111607	936	876096	30.5941	.00106838
897	804609	29.9500	.00111483	937	877969	30.6105	.00106724
898	806404	29.9666	.00111359	938	879844	30.6268	.00106610
899	808201	29.9833	.00111235	939	881721	30.6431	.00106496
900	810000	30.0000	.00111111	940	883600	30.6594	.00106383
901	811801	30.0167	.00110988	941	885481	30.6757	.00106270
902	813604	30.0333	.00110865	942	887364	30.6920	.00106157
903	815409	30.0500	.00110742	943	889249	30.7083	.00106045
904	817216	30.0666	.00110619	944	891136	30.7246	.00105932
905	819025	30.0832	.00110497	945	893025	30.7409	.00105820
906	820836	30.0998	.00110375	946	894916	30.7571	.00105708
907	822649	30.1164	.00110254	947	896809	30.7734	.00105597
908	824464	30.1330	.00110132	948	898704	30.7896	.00105485
909	826281	30.1496	.00110011	949	900601	30.8058	.00105374
910	828100	30.1662	.00109890	950	902500	30.8221	.00105263
911	829921	30.1828	.00109769	951	904401	30.8383	.00105152
912	831744	30.1993	.00109649	952	906304	30.8545	.00105042
913	833569	30.2159	.00109529	953	908209	30.8707	.00104932
914	835396	30.2324	.00109409	954	910116	30.8869	.00104822
915	837225	30.2490	.00109290	955	912025	30.9031	.00104712
916	839056	30.2655	.00109170	956	913936	30.9192	.00104603
917	840889	30.2820	.00109051	957	915849	30.9354	.00104493
918	842724	30.2985	.00108932	958	917764	30.9516	.00104384
919	844561	30.3150	.00108814	959	919681	30.9677	.00104275
920	846400	30.3315	.00108696	960	921600	30.9839	.00104167

Portions of this table have been reproduced from J. W. Dunlap and A. K. Kurtz. *Handbook of Statistical Nomographs, Tables, and Formulas*, World Book Company, New York (1932), by permission of the authors and publishers.

TABLE A.1   Table of Squares, Square Roots, and Reciprocals of Numbers from 1 to 1000
(*concluded*)

N	N^2	$\sqrt{N}$	$1/N$	N	N^2	$\sqrt{N}$	$1/N$
961	923521	31.0000	.00104058	981	962361	31.3209	.00101937
962	925444	31.0161	.00103950	982	964324	31.3369	.00101833
963	927369	31.0322	.00103842	983	966289	31.3528	.00101729
964	929296	31.0483	.00103734	984	968256	31.3688	.00101626
965	931225	31.0644	.00103627	985	970225	31.3847	.00101523
966	933156	31.0805	.00103520	986	972196	31.4006	.00101420
967	935089	31.0966	.00103413	987	974169	31.4166	.00101317
968	937024	31.1127	.00103306	988	976144	31.4325	.00101215
969	938961	31.1288	.00103199	989	978121	31.4484	.00101112
970	940900	31.1448	.00103093	990	980100	31.4643	.00101010
971	942841	31.1609	.00102987	991	982081	31.4802	.00100908
972	944784	31.1769	.00102881	992	984064	31.4960	.00100806
973	946729	31.1929	.00102775	993	986049	31.5119	.00100705
974	948676	31.2090	.00102669	994	988036	31.5278	.00100604
975	950625	31.2250	.00102564	995	990025	31.5436	.00100503
976	952576	31.2410	.00102459	996	992016	31.5595	.00100402
977	954529	31.2570	.00102354	997	994009	31.5753	.00100301
978	956484	31.2730	.00102249	998	996004	31.5911	.00100200
979	958441	31.2890	.00102145	999	998001	31.6070	.00100100
980	960400	31.3050	.00102041	1000	1000000	31.6228	.00100000

Portions of this table have been reproduced from J. W. Dunlap and A. K. Kurtz. *Handbook of Statistical Nomographs, Tables, and Formulas*, World Book Company, New York (1932), by permission of the authors and publishers.

TABLE A.2 Table of Random Numbers

COLUMN NUMBER

	00000	00000	11111	11111	22222	22222	33333	33333
Row	01234	56789	01234	56789	01234	56789	01234	56789
				1st Thousand				
00	23157	54859	01837	25993	76249	70886	95230	36744
01	05545	55043	10537	43508	90611	83744	10962	21343
02	14871	60350	32404	36223	50051	00322	11543	80834
03	38976	74951	94051	75853	78805	90194	32428	71695
04	97312	61718	99755	30870	94251	25841	54882	10513
05	11742	69381	44339	30872	32797	33118	22647	06850
06	43361	28859	11016	45623	93009	00499	43640	74036
07	93806	20478	38268	04491	55751	18932	58475	52571
08	49540	13181	08429	84187	69538	29661	77738	09527
09	36768	72633	37948	21569	41959	68670	45274	83880
10	07092	52392	24627	12067	06558	45344	67338	45320
11	43310	01081	44863	80307	52555	16148	89742	94647
12	61570	06360	06173	63775	63148	95123	35017	46993
13	31352	83799	10779	18941	31579	76448	62584	86919
14	57048	86526	27795	93692	90529	56546	35065	32254
15	09243	44200	68721	07137	30729	75756	09298	27650
16	97957	35018	40894	88329	52230	82521	22532	61587
17	93732	59570	43781	98885	56671	66826	95996	44569
18	72621	11225	00922	68264	35666	59434	71687	58167
19	61020	74418	45371	20794	95917	37866	99536	19378
20	97839	85474	33055	91718	45473	54144	22034	23000
21	89160	97192	22232	90637	35055	45489	88438	16361
22	25966	88220	62871	79265	02823	52862	84919	54883
23	81443	31719	05049	54806	74690	07567	65017	16543
24	11322	54931	42362	34386	08624	97687	46245	23245

TABLE A.2   Table of Random Numbers (cont.)

			COLUMN NUMBER				
Row	00000 01234	00000 56789	11111 01234	11111 56789	22222 01234	22222 56789	33333 01234	33333 56789
				2nd Thousand				
00	64755	83885	84122	25920	17696	15655	95045	95947
01	10302	52289	77436	34430	38112	49067	07348	23328
02	71017	98495	51308	50374	66591	02887	53765	69149
03	60012	55605	88410	34879	79655	90169	78800	03666
04	37330	94656	49161	42802	48274	54755	44553	65090
05	47869	87001	31591	12273	60626	12822	34691	61212
06	38040	42737	64167	89578	39323	49324	88434	38706
07	73508	30908	83054	80078	86669	30295	56460	45336
08	32623	46474	84061	04324	20628	37319	32356	43969
09	97591	99549	36630	35106	62069	92975	95320	57734
10	74012	31955	59790	96982	66224	24015	96749	07589
11	56754	26457	13351	05014	90966	33674	69096	33488
12	49800	49908	54831	21998	08528	26372	92923	65026
13	43584	89647	24878	56670	00221	50193	99591	62377
14	16653	79664	60325	71301	35742	83636	73058	87229
15	48502	69055	65322	58748	31446	80237	31252	96367
16	96765	54692	36316	86230	48296	38352	23816	64094
17	38923	61550	80357	81784	23444	12463	33992	28128
18	77958	81694	25225	05587	51073	01070	60218	61961
19	17928	28065	25586	08771	02641	85064	65796	48170
20	94036	85978	02318	04499	41054	10531	87431	21596
21	47460	60479	56230	48417	14372	85167	27558	00368
22	47856	56088	51992	82439	40644	17170	13463	18288
23	57616	34653	92298	62018	10375	76515	62986	90756
24	08300	92704	66752	66610	57188	79107	54222	22013

Reproduced from M. G. Kendall and B. B. Smith. Randomness and random sampling numbers. *Journal of the Royal Statistical Society*, 101 (1938), 147–166, by permission of the Royal Statistical Society.

TABLE A.2 Table of Random Numbers (cont.)

COLUMN NUMBER

3rd Thousand

Row	00000 01234	00000 56789	11111 01234	11111 56789	22222 01234	22222 56789	33333 01234	33333 56789
00	89221	02362	65787	74733	51272	30213	92441	39651
01	04005	99818	63918	29032	94012	42363	01261	10650
02	98546	38066	50856	75045	40645	22841	53254	44125
03	41719	84401	59226	01314	54581	40398	49988	65579
04	28733	72489	00785	25843	24613	49797	85567	84471
05	65213	83927	77762	03086	80742	24395	68476	83792
06	65553	12678	90906	90466	43670	26217	69900	31205
07	05668	69080	73029	85746	58332	78231	45986	92998
08	39302	99718	49757	79519	27387	76373	47262	91612
09	64592	32254	45879	29431	38320	05981	18067	87137
10	07513	48792	47314	83660	68907	05336	82579	91582
11	86593	68501	56638	99800	82839	35148	56541	07232
12	83735	22599	97977	81248	36838	99560	32410	67614
13	08595	21826	54655	08204	87990	17033	56258	05384
14	41273	27149	44293	69458	16828	63962	15864	35431
15	00473	75908	56238	12242	72631	76314	47252	06347
16	86131	53789	81383	07868	89132	96182	07009	86432
17	33849	78359	08402	03586	03176	88663	08018	22546
18	61870	41657	07468	08612	98083	97349	20775	45091
19	43898	65923	25078	86129	78491	97653	91500	80786
20	29939	39123	04548	45985	60952	06641	28726	46473
21	38505	85555	14388	55077	18657	94887	67831	70819
22	31824	38431	67125	25511	72044	11562	53279	82268
23	91430	03767	13561	15597	06750	92552	02391	38753
24	38635	68976	25498	97526	96458	03805	04116	63514

Reproduced from M. G. Kendall and B. B. Smith. Randomness and random sampling numbers. *Journal of the Royal Statistical Society*, 101 (1938), 147–166, by permission of the Royal Statistical Society.

TABLE A.2 Table of Random Numbers (cont.)

COLUMN NUMBER

4th Thousand

Row	00000 01234	00000 56789	11111 01234	11111 56789	22222 01234	22222 56789	33333 01234	33333 56789
00	02490	54122	27944	39364	94239	72074	11679	54082
01	11967	36469	60627	83701	09253	30208	01385	37482
02	48256	83465	49699	24079	05403	35154	39613	03136
03	27246	73080	21481	23536	04881	89977	49484	93071
04	32532	77265	72430	70722	86529	18457	92657	10011
05	66757	98955	92375	93431	43204	55825	45443	69265
06	11266	34545	76505	97746	34668	26999	26742	97516
07	17872	39142	45561	80146	93137	48924	64257	59284
08	62561	30365	03408	14754	51798	08133	61010	97730
09	62796	30779	35497	70501	30105	08133	00997	91970
10	75510	21771	04339	33660	42757	62223	87565	48468
11	87439	01691	63517	26590	44437	07217	98706	39032
12	97742	02621	10748	78803	38337	65226	92149	59051
13	98811	06001	21571	02875	21828	83912	85188	61624
14	51264	01852	64607	92553	29004	26695	78583	62998
15	40239	93376	10419	68610	49120	02941	80035	99317
16	26936	59186	51667	27645	46329	44681	94190	66647
17	88502	11716	98299	40974	42394	62200	69094	81646
18	63499	38093	25593	61995	79867	80569	01023	38374
19	36379	81206	03317	78710	73828	31083	60509	44091
20	93801	22322	47479	57017	59334	30647	43061	26660
21	29856	87120	56311	50053	25365	81265	22414	02431
22	97720	87931	88265	13050	71017	15177	06957	92919
23	85237	09105	74601	46377	59938	15647	34177	92753
24	75746	75268	31727	95773	72364	87324	36879	06802

Reproduced from M. G. Kendall and B. B. Smith. Randomness and random sampling numbers. *Journal of the Royal Statistical Society*, 101 (1938), 147–166, by permission of the Royal Statistical Society.

TABLE A.2 Table of Random Numbers *(concluded)*

Row	00000 01234	00000 56789	11111 01234	11111 56789	22222 01234	22222 56789	33333 01234	33333 56789
				COLUMN NUMBER				
				5th Thousand				
00	29935	06971	63175	52579	10478	89379	61428	21363
01	15114	07126	51890	77787	75510	13103	42942	48111
02	03870	43225	10589	87629	22039	94124	38127	65022
03	79390	39188	40756	45269	65959	20640	14284	22960
04	30035	06915	79196	54428	64819	52314	48721	81594
05	29039	99861	28759	79802	68531	39198	38137	24373
06	78196	08108	24107	49777	09599	43569	84820	94956
07	15847	85493	91442	91351	80130	73752	21539	10986
08	36614	62248	49194	97209	92587	92053	41021	80064
09	40549	54884	91465	43862	35541	44466	88894	74180
10	40878	08997	14286	09982	90308	78007	51587	16658
11	10229	49282	41173	31468	59455	18756	08908	06660
12	15918	76787	30624	25928	44124	25088	31137	71614
13	13403	18796	49909	94404	64979	41462	18155	98335
14	66523	94596	74908	90271	10009	98648	17640	68909
15	91665	36469	68343	17870	25975	04662	21272	50620
16	67415	87515	08207	73729	73201	57593	96917	69699
17	76527	96996	23724	33448	63392	32394	60887	90617
18	19815	47789	74348	17147	10954	34355	81194	54407
19	25592	53587	76384	72575	84347	68918	05739	57222
20	55902	45539	63646	31609	95999	82887	40666	66692
21	02470	58376	79794	22482	42423	96162	47491	17264
22	18630	53263	13319	97619	35859	12350	14632	87659
23	89673	38230	16063	92007	59503	38402	76450	33333
24	62986	67364	06595	17427	84623	14565	82860	57300

Reproduced from M. G. Kendall and B. B. Smith. Randomness and random sampling numbers. *Journal of the Royal Statistical Society*, 101 (1938), 147–166, by permission of the Royal Statistical Society.

TABLE A.3   Areas and Ordinates of the Standard Normal Curve

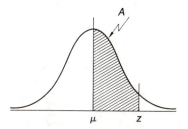
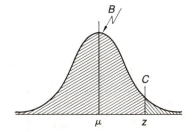

z	A Area from μ to z	B Area in Larger Portion	C Area in Smaller Portion	y Ordinate at z
0.00	.0000	.5000	.5000	.3989
0.01	.0040	.5040	.4960	.3989
0.02	.0080	.5080	.4920	.3989
0.03	.0120	.5120	.4880	.3988
0.04	.0160	.5160	.4840	.3986
0.05	.0199	.5199	.4801	.3984
0.06	.0239	.5239	.4761	.3982
0.07	.0279	.5279	.4721	.3980
0.08	.0319	.5319	.4681	.3977
0.09	.0359	.5359	.4641	.3973
0.10	.0398	.5398	.4602	.3970
0.11	.0438	.5438	.4562	.3965
0.12	.0478	.5478	.4522	.3961
0.13	.0517	.5517	.4483	.3956
0.14	.0557	.5557	.4443	.3951
0.15	.0596	.5596	.4404	.3945
0.16	.0636	.5636	.4364	.3939
0.17	.0675	.5675	.4325	.3932
0.18	.0714	.5714	.4286	.3925
0.19	.0753	.5753	.4247	.3918
0.20	.0793	.5793	.4207	.3910
0.21	.0832	.5832	.4168	.3902
0.22	.0871	.5871	.4129	.3894
0.23	.0910	.5910	.4090	.3885
0.24	.0948	.5948	.4052	.3876
0.25	.0987	.5987	.4013	.3867
0.26	.1026	.6026	.3974	.3857
0.27	.1064	.6064	.3936	.3847
0.28	.1103	.6103	.3897	.3836
0.29	.1141	.6141	.3859	.3825
0.30	.1179	.6179	.3821	.3814
0.31	.1217	.6217	.3783	.3802
0.32	.1255	.6255	.3745	.3790
0.33	.1293	.6293	.3707	.3778
0.34	.1331	.6331	.3669	.3765

TABLE A.3   Areas and Ordinates of the Standard Normal Curve (*cont*.)

z	A AREA FROM μ TO z	B AREA IN LARGER PORTION	C AREA IN SMALLER PORTION	y ORDINATE AT z
0.35	.1368	.6368	.3632	.3752
0.36	.1406	.6406	.3594	.3739
0.37	.1443	.6443	.3557	.3725
0.38	.1480	.6480	.3520	.3712
0.39	.1517	.6517	.3483	.3697
0.40	.1554	.6554	.3446	.3683
0.41	.1591	.6591	.3409	.3668
0.42	.1628	.6628	.3372	.3653
0.43	.1664	.6664	.3336	.3637
0.44	.1700	.6700	.3300	.3621
				.3605
0.45	.1736	.6736	.3264	
0.46	.1772	.6772	.3228	.3589
0.47	.1808	.6808	.3192	.3572
0.48	.1844	.6844	.3156	.3555
0.49	.1879	.6879	.3121	.3538
0.50	.1915	.6915	.3085	.3521
0.51	.1950	.6950	.3050	.3503
0.52	.1985	.6985	.3015	.3485
0.53	.2019	.7019	.2981	.3467
0.54	.2054	.7054	.2946	.3448
0.55	.2088	.7088	.2912	.3429
0.56	.2123	.7123	.2877	.3410
0.57	.2157	.7157	.2843	.3391
0.58	.2190	.7190	.2810	.3372
0.59	.2224	.7224	.2776	.3352
0.60	.2257	.7257	.2743	.3332
0.61	.2291	.7291	.2709	.3312
0.62	.2324	.7324	.2676	.3292
0.63	.2357	.7357	.2643	.3271
0.64	.2389	.7389	.2611	.3251
0.65	.2422	.7422	.2578	.3230
0.66	.2454	.7454	.2546	.3209
0.67	.2486	.7486	.2514	.3187
0.68	.2517	.7517	.2483	.3166
0.69	.2549	.7549	.2451	.3144

TABLE A.3 Areas and Ordinates of the Standard Normal Curve (*cont.*)

z	A AREA FROM μ TO z	B AREA IN LARGER PORTION	C AREA IN SMALLER PORTION	y ORDINATE AT z
0.70	.2580	.7580	.2420	.3123
0.71	.2611	.7611	.2389	.3101
0.72	.2642	.7642	.2358	.3079
0.73	.2673	.7673	.2327	.3056
0.74	.2704	.7704	.2296	.3034
0.75	.2734	.7734	.2266	.3011
0.76	.2764	.7764	.2236	.2989
0.77	.2794	.7794	.2206	.2966
0.78	.2823	.7823	.2177	.2943
0.79	.2852	.7852	.2148	.2920
0.80	.2881	.7881	.2119	.2897
0.81	.2910	.7910	.2090	.2874
0.82	.2939	.7939	.2061	.2850
0.83	.2967	.7967	.2033	.2827
0.84	.2995	.7995	.2005	.2803
0.85	.3023	.8023	.1977	.2780
0.86	.3051	.8051	.1949	.2756
0.87	.3078	.8078	.1922	.2732
0.88	.3106	.8106	.1894	.2709
0.89	.3133	.8133	.1867	.2685
0.90	.3159	.8159	.1841	.2661
0.91	.3186	.8186	.1814	.2637
0.92	.3212	.8212	.1788	.2613
0.93	.3238	.8238	.1762	.2589
0.94	.3264	.8264	.1736	.2565
0.95	.3289	.8289	.1711	.2541
0.96	.3315	.8315	.1685	.2516
0.97	.3340	.8340	.1660	.2492
0.98	.3365	.8365	.1635	.2468
0.99	.3389	.8389	.1611	.2444
1.00	.3413	.8413	.1587	.2420
1.01	.3438	.8438	.1562	.2396
1.02	.3461	.8461	.1539	.2371
1.03	.3485	.8485	.1515	.2347
1.04	.3508	.8508	.1492	.2323

TABLE A.3 Areas and Ordinates of the Standard Normal Curve (cont.)

z	A AREA FROM μ TO z	B AREA IN LARGER PORTION	C AREA IN SMALLER PORTION	y ORDINATE AT z
1.05	.3531	.8531	.1469	.2299
1.06	.3554	.8554	.1446	.2275
1.07	.3577	.8577	.1423	.2251
1.08	.3599	.8599	.1401	.2227
1.09	.3621	.8621	.1379	.2203
1.10	.3643	.8643	.1357	.2179
1.11	.3665	.8665	.1335	.2155
1.12	.3686	.8686	.1314	.2131
1.13	.3708	.8708	.1292	.2107
1.14	.3729	.8729	.1271	.2083
1.15	.3749	.8749	.1251	.2059
1.16	.3770	.8770	.1230	.2036
1.17	.3790	.8790	.1210	.2012
1.18	.3810	.8810	.1190	.1989
1.19	.3830	.8830	.1170	.1965
1.20	.3849	.8849	.1151	.1942
1.21	.3869	.8869	.1131	.1919
1.22	.3888	.8888	.1112	.1895
1.23	.3907	.8907	.1093	.1872
1.24	.3925	.8925	.1075	.1849
1.25	.3944	.8944	.1056	.1826
1.26	.3962	.8962	.1038	.1804
1.27	.3980	.8980	.1020	.1781
1.28	.3997	.8997	.1003	.1758
1.29	.4015	.9015	.0985	.1736
1.30	.4032	.9032	.0968	.1714
1.31	.4049	.9049	.0951	.1691
1.32	.4066	.9066	.0934	.1669
1.33	.4082	.9082	.0918	.1647
1.34	.4099	.9099	.0901	.1626
1.35	.4115	.9115	.0885	.1604
1.36	.4131	.9131	.0869	.1582
1.37	.4147	.9147	.0853	.1561
1.38	.4162	.9162	.0838	.1539
1.39	.4177	.9177	.0823	.1518

TABLE A.3 Areas and Ordinates of the Standard Normal Curve (cont.)

z	A AREA FROM μ TO z	B AREA IN LARGER PORTION	C AREA IN SMALLER PORTION	y ORDINATE AT z
1.40	.4192	.9192	.0808	.1497
1.41	.4207	.9207	.0793	.1476
1.42	.4222	.9222	.0778	.1456
1.43	.4236	.9236	.0764	.1435
1.44	.4251	.9251	.0749	.1415
1.45	.4265	.9265	.0735	.1394
1.46	.4279	.9279	.0721	.1374
1.47	.4292	.9292	.0708	.1354
1.48	.4306	.9306	.0694	.1334
1.49	.4319	.9319	.0681	.1315
1.50	.4332	.9332	.0668	.1295
1.51	.4345	.9345	.0655	.1276
1.52	.4357	.9357	.0643	.1257
1.53	.4370	.9370	.0630	.1238
1.54	.4382	.9382	.0618	.1219
1.55	.4394	.9394	.0606	.1200
1.56	.4406	.9406	.0594	.1182
1.57	.4418	.9418	.0582	.1163
1.58	.4429	.9429	.0571	.1145
1.59	.4441	.9441	.0559	.1127
1.60	.4452	.9452	.0548	.1109
1.61	.4463	.9463	.0537	.1092
1.62	.4474	.9474	.0526	.1074
1.63	.4484	.9484	.0516	.1057
1.64	.4495	.9495	.0505	.1040
1.65	.4505	.9505	.0495	.1023
1.66	.4515	.9515	.0485	.1006
1.67	.4525	.9525	.0475	.0989
1.68	.4535	.9535	.0465	.0973
1.69	.4545	.9545	.0455	.0957
1.70	.4554	.9554	.0446	.0940
1.71	.4564	.9564	.0436	.0925
1.72	.4573	.9573	.0427	.0909
1.73	.4582	.9582	.0418	.0893
1.74	.4591	.9591	.0409	.0878

TABLE A.3 Areas and Ordinates of the Standard Normal Curve (cont.)

z	A AREA FROM μ TO z	B AREA IN LARGER PORTION	C AREA IN SMALLER PORTION	y ORDINATE AT z
1.75	.4599	.9599	.0401	.0863
1.76	.4608	.9608	.0392	.0848
1.77	.4616	.9616	.0384	.0833
1.78	.4625	.9625	.0375	.0818
1.79	.4633	.9633	.0367	.0804
1.80	.4641	.9641	.0359	.0790
1.81	.4649	.9649	.0351	.0775
1.82	.4656	.9656	.0344	.0761
1.83	.4664	.9664	.0336	.0748
1.84	.4671	.9671	.0329	.0734
1.85	.4678	.9678	.0322	.0721
1.86	.4686	.9686	.0314	.0707
1.87	.4693	.9693	.0307	.0694
1.88	.4699	.9699	.0301	.0681
1.89	.4706	.9706	.0294	.0669
1.90	.4713	.9713	.0287	.0656
1.91	.4719	.9719	.0281	.0644
1.92	.4726	.9726	.0274	.0632
1.93	.4732	.9732	.0268	.0620
1.94	.4738	.9738	.0262	.0608
1.95	.4744	.9744	.0256	.0596
1.96	.4750	.9750	.0250	.0584
1.97	.4756	.9756	.0244	.0573
1.98	.4761	.9761	.0239	.0562
1.99	.4767	.9767	.0233	.0551
2.00	.4772	.9772	.0228	.0540
2.01	.4778	.9778	.0222	.0529
2.02	.4783	.9783	.0217	.0519
2.03	.4788	.9788	.0212	.0508
2.04	.4793	.9793	.0207	.0498
2.05	.4798	.9798	.0202	.0488
2.06	.4803	.9803	.0197	.0478
2.07	.4808	.9808	.0192	.0468
2.08	.4812	.9812	.0188	.0459
2.09	.4817	.9817	.0183	.0449

TABLE A.3 Areas and Ordinates of the Standard Normal Curve (*cont*.)

z	A Area from μ to z	B Area in Larger Portion	C Area in Smaller Portion	y Ordinate at z
2.10	.4821	.9821	.0179	.0440
2.11	.4826	.9826	.0174	.0431
2.12	.4830	.9830	.0170	.0422
2.13	.4834	.9834	.0166	.0413
2.14	.4838	.9838	.0162	.0404
2.15	.4842	.9842	.0158	.0396
2.16	.4846	.9846	.0154	.0387
2.17	.4850	.9850	.0150	.0379
2.18	.4854	.9854	.0146	.0371
2.19	.4857	.9857	.0143	.0363
2.20	.4861	.9861	.0139	.0355
2.21	.4864	.9864	.0136	.0347
2.22	.4868	.9868	.0132	.0339
2.23	.4871	.9871	.0129	.0332
2.24	.4875	.9875	.0125	.0325
2.25	.4878	.9878	.0122	.0317
2.26	.4881	.9881	.0119	.0310
2.27	.4884	.9884	.0116	.0303
2.28	.4887	.9887	.0113	.0297
2.29	.4890	.9890	.0110	.0290
2.30	.4893	.9893	.0107	.0283
2.31	.4896	.9896	.0104	.0277
2.32	.4898	.9898	.0102	.0270
2.33	.4901	.9901	.0099	.0264
2.34	.4904	.9904	.0096	.0258
2.35	.4906	.9906	.0094	.0252
2.36	.4909	.9909	.0091	.0246
2.37	.4911	.9911	.0089	.0241
2.38	.4913	.9913	.0087	.0235
2.39	.4916	.9916	.0084	.0229
2.40	.4918	.9918	.0082	.0224
2.41	.4920	.9920	.0080	.0219
2.42	.4922	.9922	.0078	.0213
2.43	.4925	.9925	.0075	.0208
2.44	.4927	.9927	.0073	.0203

TABLE A.3 Areas and Ordinates of the Standard Normal Curve (*cont.*)

z	A AREA FROM μ TO z	B AREA IN LARGER PORTION	C AREA IN SMALLER PORTION	y ORDINATE AT z
2.45	.4929	.9929	.0071	.0198
2.46	.4931	.9931	.0069	.0194
2.47	.4932	.9932	.0068	.0189
2.48	.4934	.9934	.0066	.0184
2.49	.4936	.9936	.0064	.0180
2.50	.4938	.9938	.0062	.0175
2.51	.4940	.9940	.0060	.0171
2.52	.4941	.9941	.0059	.0167
2.53	.4943	.9943	.0057	.0163
2.54	.4945	.9945	.0055	.0158
2.55	.4946	.9946	.0054	.0154
2.56	.4948	.9948	.0052	.0151
2.57	.4949	.9949	.0051	.0147
2.58	.4951	.9951	.0049	.0143
2.59	.4952	.9952	.0048	.0139
2.60	.4953	.9953	.0047	.0136
2.61	.4955	.9955	.0045	.0132
2.62	.4956	.9956	.0044	.0129
2.63	.4957	.9957	.0043	.0126
2.64	.4959	.9959	.0041	.0122
2.65	.4960	.9960	.0040	.0119
2.66	.4961	.9961	.0039	.0116
2.67	.4962	.9962	.0038	.0113
2.68	.4963	.9963	.0037	.0110
2.69	.4964	.9964	.0036	.0107
2.70	.4965	.9965	.0035	.0104
2.71	.4966	.9966	.0034	.0101
2.72	.4967	.9967	.0033	.0099
2.73	.4968	.9968	.0032	.0096
2.74	.4969	.9969	.0031	.0093
2.75	.4970	.9970	.0030	.0091
2.76	.4971	.9971	.0029	.0088
2.77	.4972	.9972	.0028	.0086
2.78	.4973	.9973	.0027	.0084
2.79	.4974	.9974	.0026	.0081

TABLE A.3   Areas and Ordinates of the Standard Normal Curve (*cont.*)

z	A AREA FROM μ TO z	B AREA IN LARGER PORTION	C AREA IN SMALLER PORTION	y ORDINATE AT z
2.80	.4974	.9974	.0026	.0079
2.81	.4975	.9975	.0025	.0077
2.82	.4976	.9976	.0024	.0075
2.83	.4977	.9977	.0023	.0073
2.84	.4977	.9977	.0023	.0071
2.85	.4978	.9978	.0022	.0069
2.86	.4979	.9979	.0021	.0067
2.87	.4979	.9979	.0021	.0065
2.88	.4980	.9980	.0020	.0063
2.89	.4981	.9981	.0019	.0061
2.90	.4981	.9981	.0019	.0060
2.91	.4982	.9982	.0018	.0058
2.92	.4982	.9982	.0018	.0056
2.93	.4983	.9983	.0017	.0055
2.94	.4984	.9984	.0016	.0053
2.95	.4984	.9984	.0016	.0051
2.96	.4985	.9985	.0015	.0050
2.97	.4985	.9985	.0015	.0048
2.98	.4986	.9986	.0014	.0047
2.99	.4986	.9986	.0014	.0046
3.00	.4987	.9987	.0013	.0044
3.01	.4987	.9987	.0013	.0043
3.02	.4987	.9987	.0013	.0042
3.03	.4988	.9988	.0012	.0040
3.04	.4988	.9988	.0012	.0039
3.05	.4989	.9989	.0011	.0038
3.06	.4989	.9989	.0011	.0037
3.07	.4989	.9989	.0011	.0036
3.08	.4990	.9990	.0010	.0035
3.09	.4990	.9990	.0010	.0034
3.10	.4990	.9990	.0010	.0033
3.11	.4991	.9991	.0009	.0032
3.12	.4991	.9991	.0009	.0031
3.13	.4991	.9991	.0009	.0030
3.14	.4992	.9992	.0008	.0029

TABLE A.3 Areas and Ordinates of the Standard Normal Curve (*cont.*)

z	A AREA FROM μ TO z	B AREA IN LARGER PORTION	C AREA IN SMALLER PORTION	y ORDINATE AT z
3.15	.4992	.9992	.0008	.0028
3.16	.4992	.9992	.0008	.0027
3.17	.4992	.9992	.0008	.0026
3.18	.4993	.9993	.0007	.0025
3.19	.4993	.9993	.0007	.0025
3.20	.4993	.9993	.0007	.0024
3.21	.4993	.9993	.0007	.0023
3.22	.4994	.9994	.0006	.0022
3.23	.4994	.9994	.0006	.0022
3.24	.4994	.9994	.0006	.0021
3.30	.4995	.9995	.0005	.0017
3.40	.4997	.9997	.0003	.0012
3.50	.4998	.9998	.0002	.0009
3.60	.4998	.9998	.0002	.0006
3.70	.4999	.9999	.0001	.0004

TABLE A.4   Critical Values of Student's t-Distribution

df\α	0.9	0.5	0.4	0.2	0.1	0.05	0.02	0.01	0.001	α/df
1	.158	1.000	1.376	3.078	6.314	12.706	31.821	63.657	636.619	1
2	.142	.816	1.061	1.886	2.920	4.303	6.965	9.925	31.598	2
3	.137	.765	.978	1.638	2.353	3.182	4.541	5.841	12.924	3
4	.134	.741	.941	1.533	2.132	2.776	3.747	4.604	8.610	4
5	.132	.727	.920	1.476	2.015	2.571	3.365	4.032	6.869	5
6	.131	.718	.906	1.440	1.943	2.447	3.143	3.707	5.959	6
7	.130	.711	.896	1.415	1.895	2.365	2.998	3.499	5.408	7
8	.130	.706	.889	1.397	1.860	2.306	2.896	3.355	5.041	8
9	.129	.703	.883	1.383	1.833	2.262	2.821	3.250	4.781	9
10	.129	.700	.879	1.372	1.812	2.228	2.764	3.169	4.587	10
11	.129	.697	.876	1.363	1.796	2.201	2.718	3.106	4.437	11
12	.128	.695	.873	1.356	1.782	2.179	2.681	3.055	4.318	12
13	.128	.694	.870	1.350	1.771	2.160	2.650	3.012	4.221	13
14	.128	.692	.868	1.345	1.761	2.145	2.624	2.977	4.140	14
15	.128	.691	.866	1.341	1.753	2.131	2.602	2.947	4.073	15
16	.128	.690	.865	1.337	1.746	2.120	2.583	2.921	4.015	16
17	.128	.689	.863	1.333	1.740	2.110	2.567	2.898	3.965	17
18	.127	.688	.862	1.330	1.734	2.101	2.552	2.878	3.922	18
19	.127	.688	.861	1.328	1.729	2.093	2.539	2.861	3.883	19
20	.127	.687	.860	1.325	1.725	2.086	2.528	2.845	3.850	20
21	.127	.686	.859	1.323	1.721	2.080	2.518	2.831	3.819	21
22	.127	.686	.858	1.321	1.717	2.074	2.508	2.819	3.792	22
23	.127	.685	.858	1.319	1.714	2.069	2.500	2.807	3.767	23
24	.127	.685	.857	1.318	1.711	2.064	2.492	2.797	3.745	24
25	.127	.684	.856	1.316	1.708	2.060	2.485	2.787	3.725	25
26	.127	.684	.856	1.315	1.706	2.056	2.479	2.779	3.707	26
27	.127	.684	.855	1.314	1.703	2.052	2.473	2.771	3.690	27
28	.127	.683	.855	1.313	1.701	2.048	2.467	2.763	3.674	28
29	.127	.683	.854	1.311	1.699	2.045	2.462	2.756	3.659	29
30	.127	.683	.854	1.310	1.697	2.042	2.457	2.750	3.646	30
40	.126	.681	.851	1.303	1.684	2.021	2.423	2.704	3.551	40
60	.126	.679	.848	1.296	1.671	2.000	2.390	2.660	3.460	60
120	.126	.677	.845	1.289	1.658	1.980	2.358	2.617	3.373	120
∞	.126	.674	.842	1.282	1.645	1.960	2.326	2.576	3.291	∞

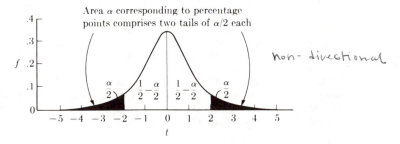

Area α corresponding to percentage points comprises two tails of $\alpha/2$ each

non-directional

From Rohlf and Sokal, 1969, Table Q. Values in this table have been taken from a more extensive one in R. A. Fisher and F. Yates, *Statistical Tables for Biological, Agricultural, and Medical Research*, 5th ed. Edinburgh: Oliver & Boyd, 1958, Table III.

TABLE A.5 Upper Percentage Points of the χ^2 Distribution

ν / Q	0.995	0.990	0.975	0.950	0.900	0.750	0.500
1	$392704 \cdot 10^{-10}$	$157088 \cdot 10^{-9}$	$982069 \cdot 10^{-9}$	$393214 \cdot 10^{-8}$	0.0157908	0.1015308	0.454937
2	0.0100251	0.0201007	0.0506356	0.102587	0.210720	0.575364	1.38629
3	0.0717212	0.114832	0.215795	0.351846	0.584375	1.212534	2.36597
4	0.206990	0.297110	0.484419	0.710721	1.063623	1.92255	3.35670
5	0.411740	0.554300	0.831211	1.145476	1.61031	2.67460	4.35146
6	0.675727	0.872085	1.237347	1.63539	2.20413	3.45460	5.34812
7	0.989265	1.239043	1.68987	2.16735	2.83311	4.25485	6.34581
8	1.344419	1.646482	2.17973	2.73264	3.48954	5.07064	7.34412
9	1.734926	2.087912	2.70039	3.32511	4.16816	5.89883	8.34283
10	2.15585	2.55821	3.24697	3.94030	4.86518	6.73720	9.34182
11	2.60321	3.05347	3.81575	4.57481	5.57779	7.58412	10.3410
12	3.07382	3.57056	4.40379	5.22603	6.30380	8.43842	11.3403
13	3.56503	4.10691	5.00874	5.89186	7.04150	9.29906	12.3398
14	4.07468	4.66043	5.62872	6.57063	7.78953	10.1653	13.3393
15	4.60094	5.22935	6.26214	7.26094	8.54675	11.0365	14.3389
16	5.14224	5.81221	6.90766	7.96164	9.31223	11.9122	15.3385
17	5.69724	6.40776	7.56418	8.67176	10.0852	12.7919	16.3381
18	6.26481	7.01491	8.23075	9.39046	10.8649	13.6753	17.3379
19	6.84398	7.63273	8.90655	10.1170	11.6509	14.5620	18.3376
20	7.43386	8.26040	9.59083	10.8508	12.4426	15.4518	19.3374
21	8.03366	8.89720	10.28293	11.5913	13.2396	16.3444	20.3372
22	8.64272	9.54249	10.9823	12.3380	14.0415	17.2396	21.3370
23	9.26042	10.19567	11.6885	13.0905	14.8479	18.1373	22.3369
24	9.88623	10.8564	12.4011	13.8484	15.6587	19.0372	23.3367
25	10.5197	11.5240	13.1197	14.6114	16.4734	19.9393	24.3366
26	11.1603	12.1981	13.8439	15.3791	17.2919	20.8434	25.3364
27	11.8076	12.8786	14.5733	16.1513	18.1138	21.7494	26.3363
28	12.4613	13.5648	15.3079	16.9279	18.9392	22.6572	27.3363
29	13.1211	14.2565	16.0471	17.7083	19.7677	23.5666	28.3362
30	13.7867	14.9535	16.7908	18.4926	20.5992	24.4776	29.3360
40	20.7065	22.1643	24.4331	26.5093	29.0505	33.6603	39.3354
50	27.9907	29.7067	32.3574	34.7642	37.6886	42.9421	49.3349
60	35.5346	37.4848	40.4817	43.1879	46.4589	52.2938	59.3347
70	43.2752	45.4418	48.7576	51.7393	55.3290	61.6983	69.3344
80	51.1720	53.5400	57.1532	60.3915	64.2778	71.1445	79.3343
90	59.1963	61.7541	65.6466	69.1260	73.2912	80.6247	89.3342
100	67.3276	70.0648	74.2219	77.9295	82.3581	90.1332	99.3341
z_Q	-2.5758	-2.3263	-1.9600	-1.6449	-1.2816	-0.6745	0.0000

TABLE A.5 Upper Percentage Points of the χ^2 Distribution (cont.)

ν \ Q	0.250	0.100	0.050	0.025	0.010	0.005	0.001
1	1.32330	2.70554	3.84146	5.02389	6.63490	7.87944	10.828
2	2.77259	4.60517	5.99147	7.37776	9.21034	10.5966	13.816
3	4.10835	6.25139	7.81473	9.34840	11.3449	12.8381	16.266
4	5.38527	7.77944	9.48773	11.1433	13.2767	14.8602	18.467
5	6.62568	9.23635	11.0705	12.8325	15.0863	16.7496	20.515
6	7.84080	10.6446	12.5916	14.4494	16.8119	18.5476	22.458
7	9.03715	12.0170	14.0671	16.0128	18.4753	20.2777	24.322
8	10.2188	13.3616	15.5073	17.5346	20.0902	21.9550	26.125
9	11.3887	14.6837	16.9190	19.0228	21.6660	23.5893	27.877
10	12.5489	15.9871	18.3070	20.4831	23.2093	25.1882	29.588
11	13.7007	17.2750	19.6751	21.9200	24.7250	26.7569	31.264
12	14.8454	18.5494	21.0261	23.3367	26.2170	28.2995	32.909
13	15.9839	19.8119	22.3621	24.7356	27.6883	29.8194	34.528
14	17.1170	21.0642	23.6848	26.1190	29.1413	31.3193	36.123
15	18.2451	22.3072	24.9958	27.4884	30.5779	32.8013	37.697
16	19.3688	23.5418	26.2962	28.8454	31.9999	34.2672	39.252
17	20.4887	24.7690	27.5871	30.1910	33.4087	35.7185	40.790
18	21.6049	25.9894	28.8693	31.5264	34.8053	37.1564	42.312
19	22.7178	27.2036	30.1435	32.8523	36.1908	38.5822	43.820
20	23.8277	28.4120	31.4104	34.1696	37.5662	39.9968	45.315
21	24.9348	29.6151	32.6705	35.4789	38.9321	41.4010	46.797
22	26.0393	30.8133	33.9244	36.7807	40.2894	42.7956	48.268
23	27.1413	32.0069	35.1725	38.0757	41.6384	44.1813	49.728
24	28.2412	33.1963	36.4151	39.3641	42.9798	45.5585	51.179
25	29.3389	34.3816	37.6525	40.6465	44.3141	46.9278	52.620
26	30.4345	35.5631	38.8852	41.9232	45.6417	48.2899	54.052
27	31.5284	36.7412	40.1133	43.1944	46.9630	49.6449	55.476
28	32.6205	37.9159	41.3372	44.4607	48.2782	50.9933	56.892
29	33.7109	39.0875	42.5569	45.7222	49.5879	52.3356	58.302
30	34.7998	40.2560	43.7729	46.9792	50.8922	53.6720	59.703
40	45.6160	51.8050	55.7585	59.3417	63.6907	66.7659	73.402
50	56.3336	63.1671	67.5048	71.4202	76.1539	79.4900	86.661
60	66.9814	74.3970	79.0819	83.2976	88.3794	91.9517	99.607
70	77.5766	85.5271	90.5312	95.0231	100.425	104.215	112.317
80	88.1303	96.5782	101.879	106.629	112.329	116.321	124.839
90	98.6499	107.565	113.145	118.136	124.116	128.299	137.208
100	109.141	118.498	124.342	129.561	135.807	140.169	149.449
z_Q	+0.6745	+1.2816	+1.6449	+1.9600	+2.3263	+2.5758	+3.0902

From Table 8 of the *Biometrika Tables for Statisticians*, Vol. 1 (ed. 3), edited by E. S. Pearson and H. O. Hartley. Reproduced here with the kind permission of E. S. Pearson and the trustees of *Biometrika*.

TABLE A.6 Wilcoxon Distribution (with no pairing)

Values of U, where $U = W_1 - \tfrac{1}{2}n_1(n_1 + 1)$

n_1	n_2	C_{n,n_1}	0	1	2	3	4	5	6	7	8	9	10	11	12	13	14	15	16	17	18	19	20
3	3	20	1	2	4	7	10	13	16	18	19	20	—	—	—	—	—	—	—	—	—	—	—
3	4	35	1	2	4	7	11	15	20	24	28	31	33	34	35	—	—	—	—	—	—	—	—
4	4	70	1	2	4	7	12	17	24	31	39	46	53	58	63	66	68	69	70	—	—	—	—
3	5	56	1	2	4	7	11	16	22	28	34	40	45	49	52	54	55	56	—	—	—	—	—
4	5	126	1	2	4	7	12	18	26	35	46	57	69	80	91	100	108	114	119	122	124	125	126
5	5	252	1	2	4	7	12	19	28	39	53	69	87	106	126	146	165	183	199	213	224	233	240
3	6	84	1	2	4	7	11	16	23	30	38	46	54	61	68	73	77	80	82	83	84	—	—
4	6	210	1	2	4	7	12	18	27	37	50	64	80	96	114	130	146	160	173	183	192	198	203
5	6	462	1	2	4	7	12	19	29	41	57	76	99	124	153	183	215	247	279	309	338	363	386
6	6	924	1	2	4	7	12	19	30	43	61	83	111	143	182	224	272	323	378	433	491	546	601
3	7	120	1	2	4	7	11	16	23	31	40	50	60	70	80	89	97	104	109	113	116	118	119
4	7	330	1	2	4	7	12	18	27	38	52	68	87	107	130	153	177	200	223	243	262	278	292
5	7	792	1	2	4	7	12	19	29	42	59	80	106	136	171	210	253	299	347	396	445	493	539
6	7	1716	1	2	4	7	12	19	30	44	63	87	118	155	201	253	314	382	458	539	627	717	811
7	7	3432	1	2	4	7	12	19	30	45	65	91	125	167	220	283	358	445	545	657	782	918	1064
3	8	165	1	2	4	7	11	16	23	31	41	52	64	76	89	101	113	124	134	142	149	154	158
4	8	495	1	2	4	7	12	18	27	38	53	70	91	114	141	169	200	231	264	295	326	354	381
5	8	1287	1	2	4	7	12	19	29	42	60	82	110	143	183	228	280	337	400	466	536	607	680
6	8	3003	1	2	4	7	12	19	30	44	64	89	122	162	213	272	343	424	518	621	737	860	994
7	8	6435	1	2	4	7	12	19	30	45	66	93	129	174	232	302	388	489	609	746	904	1080	1277
8	8	12870	1	2	4	7	12	19	30	45	67	95	133	181	244	321	418	534	675	839	1033	1254	1509

The numbers given in this table are the number of cases for which the sum of the ranks of the sample of size n_1 is less than or equal to W_1. From Table H of Hodges and Lehmann: *Basic Concepts of Probability and Statistics*, published by Holden-Day, San Francisco, by permission of the authors and publisher.

TABLE A.7   Critical Values of the Wilcoxon Rank Sum

This table furnishes critical values for the one-tailed test of significance of the rank sum T.

n	nominal α	0.05		0.025		0.01		0.005
		T	α	T	α	T	α	T	α
5		0	.0312						
		1	.0625						
6		2	.0469	0	.0156				
		3	.0781	1	.0312				
7		3	.0391	2	.0234	0	.0078		
		4	.0547	3	.0391	1	.0156		
8		5	.0391	3	.0195	1	.0078	0	.0039
		6	.0547	4	.0273	2	.0117	1	.0078
9		8	.0488	5	.0195	3	.0098	1	.0039
		9	.0645	6	.0273	4	.0137	2	.0059
10		10	.0420	8	.0244	5	.0098	3	.0049
		11	.0527	9	.0322	6	.0137	4	.0068
11		13	.0415	10	.0210	7	.0093	5	.0049
		14	.0508	11	.0269	8	.0122	6	.0068
12		17	.0461	13	.0212	9	.0081	7	.0046
		18	.0549	14	.0261	10	.0105	8	.0061
13		21	.0471	17	.0239	12	.0085	9	.0040
		22	.0549	18	.0287	13	.0107	10	.0052
14		25	.0453	21	.0247	15	.0083	12	.0043
		26	.0520	22	.0290	16	.0101	13	.0054
15		30	.0473	25	.0240	19	.0090	15	.0042
		31	.0535	26	.0277	20	.0108	16	.0051
16		35	.0467	29	.0222	23	.0091	19	.0046
		36	.0523	30	.0253	24	.0107	20	.0055
17		41	.0492	34	.0224	27	.0087	23	.0047
		42	.0544	35	.0253	28	.0101	24	.0055
18		47	.0494	40	.0241	32	.0091	27	.0045
		48	.0542	41	.0269	33	.0104	28	.0052
19		53	.0478	46	.0247	37	.0090	32	.0047
		54	.0521	47	.0273	38	.0102	33	.0054
20		60	.0487	52	.0242	43	.0096	37	.0047
		61	.0527	53	.0266	44	.0107	38	.0053

From Rohlf and Sokal, 1969, Table DD. The table was prepared on a computer using a recursion equation given by D. B. Owen, *Handbook of Statistical Tables*. Reading, Mass.: Addison-Wesley, 1962, p. 325.

TABLE A.7 Critical Values of the Wilcoxon Rank Sum (*cont*.)

This table furnishes critical values for the one-tailed test of significance of the rank sum T.

n	nominal α 0.05		0.025		0.01		0.005	
	T	α	T	α	T	α	T	α
21	67	.0479	58	.0230	49	.0097	42	.0045
	68	.0516	59	.0251	50	.0108	43	.0051
22	75	.0492	65	.0231	55	.0095	48	.0046
	76	.0527	66	.0250	56	.0104	49	.0052
23	83	.0490	73	.0242	62	.0098	54	.0046
	84	.0523	74	.0261	63	.0107	55	.0051
24	91	.0475	81	.0245	69	.0097	61	.0048
	92	.0505	82	.0263	70	.0106	62	.0053
25	100	.0479	89	.0241	76	.0094	68	.0048
	101	.0507	90	.0258	77	.0101	69	.0053
26	110	.0497	98	.0247	84	.0095	75	.0047
	111	.0524	99	.0263	85	.0102	76	.0051
27	119	.0477	107	.0246	92	.0093	83	.0048
	120	.0502	108	.0260	93	.0100	84	.0052
28	130	.0496	116	.0239	101	.0096	91	.0048
	131	.0521	117	.0252	102	.0102	92	.0051
29	140	.0482	126	.0240	110	.0095	100	.0049
	141	.0504	127	.0253	111	.0101	101	.0053
30	151	.0481	137	.0249	120	.0098	109	.0050
	152	.0502	138	.0261	121	.0104	110	.0053
31	163	.0491	147	.0239	130	.0099	118	.0049
	164	.0512	148	.0251	131	.0105	119	.0052
32	175	.0492	159	.0249	140	.0097	128	.0050
	176	.0512	160	.0260	141	.0103	129	.0053
33	187	.0485	170	.0242	151	.0099	138	.0049
	188	.0503	171	.0253	152	.0104	139	.0052
34	200	.0488	182	.0242	162	.0098	148	.0048
	201	.0506	183	.0252	163	.0103	149	.0051
35	213	.0484	195	.0247	173	.0096	159	.0048
	214	.0501	196	.0257	174	.0100	160	.0051

From Rohlf and Sokal, 1969, Table DD. The table was prepared on a computer using a recursion equation given by D. B. Owen, *Handbook of Statistical Tables*. Reading, Mass.: Addison-Wesley, 1962, p. 325.

TABLE A.7 Critical Values of the Wilcoxon Rank Sum (*cont.*)

This table furnishes critical values for the one-tailed test of significance of the rank sum T.

n \ nominal α	0.05 T	α	0.025 T	α	0.01 T	α	0.005 T	α
36	227	.0489	208	.0248	185	.0096	171	.0050
	228	.0505	209	.0258	186	.0100	172	.0052
37	241	.0487	221	.0245	198	.0099	182	.0048
	242	.0503	222	.0254	199	.0103	183	.0050
38	256	.0493	235	.0247	211	.0099	194	.0048
	257	.0509	236	.0256	212	.0104	195	.0050
39	271	.0493	249	.0246	224	.0099	207	.0049
	272	.0507	250	.0254	225	.0103	208	.0051
40	286	.0486	264	.0249	238	.0100	220	.0049
	287	.0500	265	.0257	239	.0104	221	.0051
41	302	.0488	279	.0248	252	.0100	233	.0048
	303	.0501	280	.0256	253	.0103	234	.0050
42	319	.0496	294	.0245	266	.0098	247	.0049
	320	.0509	295	.0252	267	.0102	248	.0051
43	336	.0498	310	.0245	281	.0098	261	.0048
	337	.0511	311	.0252	282	.0102	262	.0050
44	353	.0495	327	.0250	296	.0097	276	.0049
	354	.0507	328	.0257	297	.0101	277	.0051
45	371	.0498	343	.0244	312	.0098	291	.0049
	372	.0510	344	.0251	313	.0101	292	.0051
46	389	.0497	361	.0249	328	.0098	307	.0050
	390	.0508	362	.0256	329	.0101	308	.0052
47	407	.0490	378	.0245	345	.0099	322	.0048
	408	.0501	379	.0251	346	.0102	323	.0050
48	426	.0490	396	.0244	362	.0099	339	.0050
	427	.0500	397	.0251	363	.0102	340	.0051
49	446	.0495	415	.0247	379	.0098	355	.0049
	447	.0505	416	.0253	380	.0100	356	.0050
50	466	.0495	434	.0247	397	.0098	373	.0050
	467	.0506	435	.0253	398	.0101	374	.0051

From Rohlf and Sokal, 1969, Table DD. The table was prepared on a computer using a recursion equation given by D. B. Owen, *Handbook of Statistical Tables*. Reading, Mass.: Addison-Wesley, 1962, p. 325.

TABLE A.8(a) **Table of Critical Values of *D* in the Kolmogorov–Smirnov Two-Sample Test (small samples)**

N	One-tailed test*		Two-tailed test†	
	$\alpha = .05$	$\alpha = .01$	$\alpha = .05$	$\alpha = .01$
3	3	—	—	—
4	4	—	4	—
5	4	5	5	5
6	5	6	5	6
7	5	6	6	6
8	5	6	6	7
9	6	7	6	7
10	6	7	7	8
11	6	8	7	8
12	6	8	7	8
13	7	8	7	9
14	7	8	8	9
15	7	9	8	9
16	7	9	8	10
17	8	9	8	10
18	8	10	9	10
19	8	10	9	10
20	8	10	9	11
21	8	10	9	11
22	9	11	9	11
23	9	11	10	11
24	9	11	10	12
25	9	11	10	12
26	9	11	10	12
27	9	12	10	12
28	10	12	11	13
29	10	12	11	13
30	10	12	11	13
35	11	13	12	
40	11	14	13	

From Siegel, 1956, table L. *Abridged from Goodman, L. A. 1954. Kolmogorov–Smirnov tests for psychological research. *Psychol. Bull*., 51, 167. Copyright 1954 by the American Psychological Association, Reprinted by permission. †Derived from Table 1 of Massey, F. J., Jr. 1951. The distribution of the maximum deviation between two sample cumulative step functions. *Ann. Math. Statist*., 22, 126–127, with the kind permission of the author and the publisher.

TABLE A.8(b)   Table of Critical Values of D in the Kolmogorov–Smirnov Two-Sample Test (large samples; two-tailed test)

Level of significance	Value of D so large as to call for rejection of H_0 at the indicated level of significance.
.10	$1.22 \sqrt{\dfrac{n_1 + n_2}{n_1 n_2}}$
.05	$1.36 \sqrt{\dfrac{n_1 + n_2}{n_1 n_2}}$
.025	$1.48 \sqrt{\dfrac{n_1 + n_2}{n_1 n_2}}$
.01	$1.63 \sqrt{\dfrac{n_1 + n_2}{n_1 n_2}}$
.005	$1.73 \sqrt{\dfrac{n_1 + n_2}{n_1 n_2}}$
.001	$1.95 \sqrt{\dfrac{n_1 + n_2}{n_1 n_2}}$

From Siegel, 1956, table M. Tables for estimating the goodness of fit of empirical distributions. *Ann. Math. Statist.*, 19, 280-281, with the kind permission of the publisher.

TABLE A.9   Table of Critical Values of *D* in the Kolmogorov–Smirnov One-Sample Test

Sample size (N)	Level of significance for D				
	.20	.15	.10	.05	.01
1	.900	.925	.950	.975	.995
2	.684	.726	.776	.842	.929
3	.565	.597	.642	.708	.828
4	.494	.525	.564	.624	.733
5	.446	.474	.510	.565	.669
6	.410	.436	.470	.521	.618
7	.381	.405	.438	.486	.577
8	.358	.381	.411	.457	.543
9	.339	.360	.388	.432	.514
10	.322	.342	.368	.410	.490
11	.307	.326	.352	.391	.468
12	.295	.313	.338	.375	.450
13	.284	.302	.325	.361	.433
14	.274	.292	.314	.349	.418
15	.266	.283	.304	.338	.404
16	.258	.274	.295	.328	.392
17	.250	.266	.286	.318	.381
18	.244	.259	.278	.309	.371
19	.237	.252	.272	.301	.363
20	.231	.246	.264	.294	.356
25	.21	.22	.24	.27	.32
30	.19	.20	.22	.24	.29
35	.18	.19	.21	.23	.27
Over 35	$\dfrac{1.07}{\sqrt{N}}$	$\dfrac{1.14}{\sqrt{N}}$	$\dfrac{1.22}{\sqrt{N}}$	$\dfrac{1.36}{\sqrt{N}}$	$\dfrac{1.63}{\sqrt{N}}$

From Siegel, 1956, table E. Adapted from Massey, F. J., Jr. 1951. The Kolmogorov–Smirnov test for goodness of fit. *J. Amer. Statist. Ass*., 46, 70, with the kind permission of the author and publisher.

TABLE A.10 Critical Values of *r* in the Runs Test, *p* = .05

For the two sample runs test, any value of *r* which is equal to or less than that shown in the body of the table is significant at the .05 level with direction not predicted, or at the .025 level with direction predicted.

N_1 \\ N_2	2	3	4	5	6	7	8	9	10	11	12	13	14	15	16	17	18	19	20
4		2																	
5		2	2	3															
6		2	3	3	3														
7		2	3	3	4	4													
8	2	2	3	3	4	4	5												
9	2	2	3	4	4	5	5	6											
10	2	3	3	4	5	5	6	6	6										
11	2	3	3	4	5	5	6	6	7	7									
12	2	3	4	4	5	6	6	7	7	8	8								
13	2	3	4	4	5	6	6	7	8	8	9	9							
14	2	3	4	5	5	6	7	7	8	8	9	9	10						
15	2	3	4	5	6	6	7	8	8	9	9	10	10	11					
16	2	3	4	5	6	6	7	8	8	9	10	10	11	11	11				
17	2	3	4	5	6	7	7	8	9	9	10	10	11	11	12	12			
18	2	3	4	5	6	7	8	8	9	10	10	11	11	12	12	13	13		
19	2	3	4	5	6	7	8	8	9	10	10	11	12	12	13	13	14	14	
20	2	3	4	5	6	7	8	9	9	10	11	11	12	12	13	13	14	14	15

From F. S. Swed and C. Eisenhart, "Tables for Testing Randomness of Grouping in a Sequence of Alternatives," *Annals of Mathematical Statistics*, vol. 14, pp. 83–86, 1943, with the kind permission of the authors and publisher.

TABLE A.11   Significance Probabilities for the Correlation Coefficient (r)

The body of the table contains values of the correlation coefficient.

df = n−2	.1	.05	.02	.01	.001	df = n−2	.1	.05	.02	.01	.001
1	.98769	.99692	.999507	.999877	.9999988	16	.4000	.4683	.5425	.5897	.7084
2	.90000	.95000	.98000	.990000	.99900	17	.3887	.4555	.5285	.5751	.6932
3	.8054	.8783	.93433	.95873	.99116	18	.3783	.4438	.5155	.5614	.6787
4	.7293	.8114	.8822	.91720	.97406	19	.3687	.4329	.5034	.5487	.6652
5	.6694	.7545	.8329	.8745	.95074	20	.3598	.4227	.4921	.5368	.6524
6	.6215	.7067	.7887	.8343	.92493	25	.3233	.3809	.4451	.4869	.5974
7	.5822	.6664	.7498	.7977	.8982	30	.2960	.3494	.4093	.4487	.5541
8	.5494	.6319	.7155	.7646	.8721	35	.2746	.3246	.3810	.4182	.5189
9	.5214	.6021	.6851	.7348	.8471	40	.2573	.3044	.3578	.3932	.4896
10	.4973	.5760	.6581	.7079	.8233	45	.2428	.2875	.3384	.3721	.4648
11	.4762	.5529	.6339	.6835	.8010	50	.2306	.2732	.3218	.3541	.4433
12	.4575	.5324	.6120	.6614	.7800	60	.2108	.2500	.2948	.3248	.4078
13	.4409	.5139	.5923	.6411	.7603	70	.1954	.2319	.2737	.3017	.3799
14	.4259	.4973	.5742	.6226	.7420	80	.1829	.2172	.2565	.2830	.3568
15	.4124	.4821	.5577	.6055	.7246	90	.1726	.2050	.2422	.2673	.3375
						100	.1638	.1946	.2301	.2540	.3211

Table A-11 is taken (with minor adaptation) from Table VI of Fisher and Yates, *Statistical Tables for Biological, Agricultural, and Medical Research*, published by Oliver & Boyd, Ltd., Edinburgh, by permission of the authors and publishers.

TABLE A.12   Transformation of r to Z $\left(\text{i.e., } Z = \frac{1}{2}\log\frac{1+r}{1-r}\right)$

r	Z	r	Z	r	Z
.00	.000				
.01	.010	.36	.377	.71	.887
.02	.020	.37	.388	.72	.908
.03	.030	.38	.400	.73	.929
.04	.040	.39	.412	.74	.950
.05	.050	.40	.424	.75	973
.06	.060	.41	.436	.76	.996
.07	.070	.42	.448	.77	1.020
.08	.080	.43	.460	.78	1.045
.09	.090	.44	.472	.79	1.071
.10	.100	.45	.485	.80	1.099
.11	.110	.46	.497	.81	1.127
.12	.121	.47	.510	.82	1.157
.13	.131	.48	.523	.83	1.188
.14	.141	.49	.536	.84	1.221
.15	.151	.50	.549	.85	1.256
.16	.161	.51	.563	.86	1.293
.17	.172	.52	.576	.87	1.333
.18	.182	.53	.590	.88	1.376
.19	.192	.54	.604	.89	1.422
.20	.203	.55	.618	.90	1.472
.21	.213	.56	.633	.91	1.528
.22	.224	.57	.648	.92	1.589
.23	.234	.58	.662	.93	1.658
.24	.245	.59	.678	.94	1.738
.25	.255	.60	.693	.95	1.832
.26	.266	.61	.709	.96	1.946
.27	.277	.62	.725	.97	2.092
.28	.288	.63	.741	.98	2.298
.29	.299	.64	.758	.99	2.647
.30	.310	.65	.775		
.31	.321	.66	.793		
.32	.332	.67	.811		
.33	.343	.68	.829		
.34	.354	.69	.848		
.35	.365	.70	.867		

From Alder and Roessler, 1972, table VI. Abridged from Table VII of Fisher and Yates: *Statistical Tables for Biological, Agricultural, and Medical Research*, published by Oliver and Boyd Limited, Edinburgh, by permission of the authors and publishers.

TABLE A.13 Table of Critical Values or r_s, The Spearman Rank Correlation Coefficient

N	Significance level (one-tailed test)	
	.05	.01
4	1.000	
5	.900	1.000
6	.829	.943
7	.714	.893
8	.643	.833
9	.600	.783
10	.564	.746
12	.506	.712
14	.456	.645
16	.425	.601
18	.399	.564
20	.377	.534
22	359	.508
24	.343	.485
26	.329	.465
28	.317	.448
30	.306	.432

From Siegel, 1956, table P. Adapted from Olds, E. G. 1938. Distributions of sums of squares of rank differences for small numbers of individuals. *Ann. Math. Statist.*, 9, 133–148, and from Olds, E. G., 1949. The 5% significance levels for sums of squares of rank differences and a correction. *Ann. Math. Statist.*, 20, 117–118, with the kind permission of the author and publisher.

Answers to Odd-Numbered Exercises

Chapter 3

3.1 (a) $3.5 - 3.9, 4.0 - 4.4$

    (b) $0.015 - 0.019, 0.020 - 0.024$

    (c) $2.8 - 3.2, 3.8 - 4.2$

    (d) $3.55 - 3.95, 4.05 - 4.45$

3.3 (a) $3.7, 4.2$

    (b) $1.95, 2.95$

    (c) $1697, 1702$

    (d) $0.047 - 0.052$

    (e) $15,924.5, 15,974.5$

Chapter 4

4.1 (a) $\sum_{i=3}^{5} W_i$ (c) $\sum_{i=1}^{4} (X_i - 3)$

    (b) $\sum_{i=1}^{4} X_i Y_i$ (d) $\sum_{i=6}^{8} (Y_i - i)$

4.3 (a) 12 (c) -112

    (b) 65

4.5 (a) $\sum_{i=1}^{10} (X_i - 20)$ (c) $\sqrt{\sum X_i (X_i + 4)}$

    (b) $\dfrac{\sqrt{[\sum Y \sum X]^2 + 43}}{n}$

4.7 (a) 3.43 children   (c) 14.45%

    (b) 0.25 children   (d) 3.5 children

4.9 $\sigma^2 = 59.27$

    $\sigma = 7.70$

4.11 (a) $\bar{X} = 0.439$ feet   (b) 0.36 feet

        $S = 0.205$ feet^2 (c) $0.26 - 0.35$ feet

        $CV = 46.70\%$

4.13 (a) $\bar{X} = 117.91$ people   4.17 (a) small standard deviation
$S = 182.59$ people   (b) the mean
(b) 48 people

4.15 (a) 11.14 miles
(b) 130 wives, 25 daughters

Chapter 5

5.1 (a) 40,320   (d) 2
     (b) 1/720   (e) 5
     (c) 45   (f) 56

5.3 (a) $(1/11)^3$
     (b) $(1/11)^3$
     (c) $3!(1/11)^3$
     (d) $(4/11)^3$ (if zero is not considered an even number)
     (e) $1 - (6/11)^3$ or $1 - (7/11)^3$, depending on how zero is figured
     (f) $3(1/11)^2(10/11)$

5.5 $C_{52,5} = \dfrac{52!}{5!47!}$

5.7 $\dfrac{4}{C_{52,5}}$

5.9 $\dfrac{4(C_{13,5})}{C_{52,5}}$

5.11 (a) 15!
      (b) (5!)(10!)

5.13 (a) $p(B_{Science}/A) = .469$
      (b) $p(B_{Nature}/A) = .218$

5.15 $p(B/A) = .27$

5.17 (a) Second archaeologist $p(B_2) = .83$
      (b) $p(B_2/A) = .458$
      (c) $p(\bar{B}_2/A) = .542$

5.19 (a) $p(B_{archaeologist}/A) = 116$
      (b) Who knows?

Chapter 6

6.3   1   12   66   220   495   792   924   792   495   220   66   12   1

6.5 (a) 4   (c) 1.99
     (b) 1.41

6.7 (a) 1/32   (c) 729/10,000
     (b) 1/10

6.9 (a) 90/1024   (c) 5 villages
     (b) 15/1024   (d) 1.25 nontasters

6.11 (a) 17,010/1,048,576   (c) $p = \dfrac{551,123}{1,048,576}$

      (b) No. $(3/4)^{10} = \dfrac{59,048}{1,048,576}$ (d) $(1/4)^{10}$

Chapter 7

7.1 (a) 0.1690   (c) 0.4750   7.9 (a) 0.0143
     (b) 0.0796   (d) 0.9104   (b) 0.8902

7.3 (a) eight   (b) nine   7.11 544

7.5 (a) 286   (b) 0.231   7.13 (a) 0.1749   (c) five

7.7 (a) 48   (b) 187   (b) 0.2318   (d) 48

Chapter 8

8.1 (a) *Homo neanderthalensis* (d) 0.9991
     (b) 0.0035   (e) 129
     (c) 0.0233   (f) 0.1492
8.3 (a) 0.2776   (b) 0.1190
8.5 (a) 0.0183   (b) women
8.7 256

Chapter 10

10.1 Yes. $t = 3.49$
10.3 (a) 9620–10,920 radiocarbon years B.P.
     (b) $10,034 - 12,268$ radiocarbon years B.P.
     (c) $p = 0.2061$
     (d) $p = 0.5314$
     (e) $p = 0.2709$
     (f) $p_{Michigan} = 0.2483$; $p_{Chicago} = 0.2236$
10.5 (a) No. $t = 0.65$
     (b) Yes. $t = 0.80$
     (c) No. $t = 3.24$
10.7 (a) No. $t = 0.278$
     (b) Yes. $t = 3.14$
     (c) Slightly. $CV_{Early} = 33.12\%$
                   $CV_{Late} = 31.05\%$

Chapter 11

11.1 (a) Yes. $\chi^2 = 9.10$
     (b) Yes. $\chi^2 = 12.88$
11.3 (a) Yes. $\chi^2 = 3.305$
11.5 Yes. $\chi^2 = 67.93$
11.7 Yes. $\chi^2 = 15.667$
11.9 No. $p = 0.454$ by Fisher's Exact Method

Chapter 12

12.1 Difference not significant. $p = 0.655$
12.5 No significant effect. $\chi^2 = 4.229$ by a directional Kolmogorov–Smirnov two-sample test.
12.7 Yes. $p = 0.0475$
12.9 The value of $T = 5$ indicates a significant difference between the eleven pairs of monozygotic twins.
12.11 (a) Rectangular houses are not significantly smaller. $p = 0.2611$ by the normal approximation to the Wilcoxon two-sample test.
      (b) Rectangular houses tend to be more ancient than circular houses. $p = 19/3004 = 0.006$ by the Wilcoxon two-sample test.
      (c) Difference significant at $\alpha = 0.05$. $p < 0.071$ for a directional Wilcoxon two-sample test.

12.13 (a) The normal approximation to the Wilcoxon two-sample test produces an almost identical value as that obtained earlier with the t-test. $p = 0.284$.
(b) Result remains significant using the normal approximation to the Wilcoxon two-sample test. $p = 0.0064$.

Chapter 13

13.1 (a) $\hat{Y} = 2.47 + 1.82X$
(b) $Y = 6.1$
(c) $\sigma_{Y.x} = 0.976$
13.3 (a) $\hat{Y} = 10.1 + 2.21X$
(b) $\hat{Y} = 13.6 + 2.41X$
13.5 (a) $\hat{Y} = 642 + 23X$ by Model II regression
(b) 1102 cm^2

Chapter 14

14.1 (a) $r = +0.985$
(b) Yes. $t = 9.887$ with df $= 3$
(c) roughly $0.80 - 1.00$
(d) about 97%
14.3 Yes. $t = 3.597$ with df $= 23$
14.5 Yes. $t = 4.82$ with df $= 93$
14.7 $\tau = +0.507$, a value significant beyond $p < 0.0002$
14.9 (a) Yes. $p = 0.0045$ by Fisher's Exact Method.
(b) The strength of association between agriculture and political organization is $\phi = 0.602$. That between agriculture and economic specialization (exercise 14.8) was slightly stronger.

References

Adam, A., D. Doron, and R. Modan, 1967, Frequencies of Protan and Deutan Alleles in Some Israeli Communities and a Note on the Selection-relaxation Hypothesis. *American Journal of Physical Anthropology*, 26:297–306.

Adkins, Dorothy C., 1964, *Statistics: An Introduction for Students in the Behavioral Sciences*. Columbus: Merrill.

Aikens, C. Melvin, 1970, *Hogup Cave*. University of Utah Anthropological Papers, No. 93.

Alder, Henry L., and Edward B. Roessler, 1972, *Introduction to Probability and Statistics*, 5th ed. San Francisco: Freeman.

Bacon, M. K., H. Barry, III, I. L. Child, and C. R. Snyder, 1965, A Cross-Cultural Study of Drinking: V. Detailed Definitions and Data. *Quarterly Journal of Studies on Alcohol*, Supp. No. 3:78–111.

Bakan, David, 1967, *On Method*. San Francisco: Jossey-Bass.

Barry, H., I. L. Child, and M. K. Bacon, 1959, Relation of Child Training to Subsistence Economy. *American Anthropologist*, 61:51–53.

Barry, H., and L. M. Paxson, 1971, Infancy and Early Childhood: Cross-Cultural Codes 2. *Ethnology*, 10:466–508.

Beardsley, Richard K. (ed.), 1956, Functional and Evolutionary Implications of Community Patterning. *American Antiquity*, 22:129–157.

Benfer, Robert A., 1968, The Desirability of Small Samples for Anthropological Inference. *American Anthropologist*, 70:949–951.

Benjamin, A. C., 1955, *Operationism*. Springfield, Ill.: Charles C Thomas.

Bickel, P. J., E. A. Hammel, and J. W. O'Connell, 1975, Sex Bias in Graduate Admissions: Data from Berkeley, *Science*, 187:398–404.

Binford, Lewis R., 1963, The Pomranky Site: A Late Archaic Burial Station, *Anthropological Papers of the University of Michigan*, No. 19:149–192.

Birdsell, J. B., 1972, *Human Evolution: An Introduction to the New Physical*

Anthropology. Chicago: Rand McNally.

Blakely, Robert L. 1971, Comparison of the Mortality Profiles of Archaic, Middle Woodland, and Middle Mississippian Skeletal Populations, *American Journal of Physical Anthropology,* 34:43–54.

Blalock, Hubert M., 1964, *Causal Inferences in Nonexperimental Research.* Chapel Hill: University of North Carolina Press.

1972, *Social Statistics,* 2d ed. New York: McGraw-Hill.

Bliss, C. I., 1967, *Statistics in Biology,* Vol. I. New York: McGraw-Hill.

Boas, Franz, 1912, *Changes in Bodily Form of Descendants of Immigrants.* New York: Columbia University Press.

1927, Anthropology and Statistics, in W. F. Ogburn and A. Goldenweiser, eds., *The Social Sciences and Their Interrelations.* Boston: Houghton Mifflin, 114–120.

1940, *Race, Language and Culture.* New York: Macmillan.

Bohrer, Vorsila L., 1970, Ethnobotanical Aspects of Snaketown, a Hohokam Village in Southern Arizona, *American Antiquity,* 35:413–430.

Bordes, Francois, 1968, *The Old Stone Age.* London: Weidenfelt and Nicolson.

1972, *A Tale of Two Caves.* New York: Harper & Row.

Boudon, Raymond, 1965, A Method of Linear Causal Analysis, *American Sociological Review,* 30:365–374.

Boyd, William, 1950, *Genetics and the Races of Man.* Boston: Little, Brown.

Brace, C. Loring, 1967, *The Stages of Human Evolution.* Englewood Cliffs, N.J.: Prentice-Hall.

Brim, John A., and David H. Spain, 1974, *Research Design in Anthropology: Paradigms and Pragmatics in the Testing of Hypotheses.* New York: Holt, Rinehart and Winston, Inc.

Brose, David S., 1970, The Summer Island Site, *Case Western Reserve University Studies in Anthropology,* No. 1.

Brose, David S., and Milford H. Wolpoff, 1971, Early Upper Paleolithic Man and Late Middle Paleolothic Tools, *American Anthropologist,* 73:1156–1194.

Brothwell, D. R., 1963, *Digging up Bones.* London: The British Museum (Natural History).

Buchler, I. R. and H. A. Selby, 1968, *Kinship and Social Organization.* New York: Macmillan.

Buettner-Janusch, John, 1973, *Physical Anthropology: A Perspective.* New York: Wiley.

Burr, E. J., 1960, The Distribution of Kendall's Score S for a Pair of Tied Rankings, *Biometrika,* 47:151–17₁.

Burton, Michael, 1970, Computer Applications in Cultural Anthropology, *Computers and the Humanities,* 5:37–46.

Campbell, Stephen K., 1974, *Flaws and Fallacies in Statistical Thinking.* Englewood Cliffs, N.J.: Prentice-Hall.

Carneiro, Robert L., 1973, The Four Faces of Evolution, in J. J. Honigman, ed., *Handbook of Social and Cultural Anthropology.* Chicago: Rand McNally, 89–110.

Chagnon, Napoleon A., 1967, Yanomamö Social Organization and Warfare, in M. Fried, M. Harris, and R. Murphy, eds., *The Anthropology of Armed Conflict and Aggression.* Garden City, N.Y.: Natural History Press, 109–157.

Ciolek-Torrello, Richard, and J. Jefferson Reid, 1974, Change in Household Size at Grasshopper, *The Kiva,* 40:39–48.

Clarke, David L., 1968, *Analytical Archaeology*. London: Methuen.
1972, (ed.) *Models in Archaeology*. London: Methuen.
Cochran, William G., 1947, Some Consequences When the Assumptions for the Analysis of Variance Are Not Satisfied, *Biometrics*, 3:22–38.
1954, Some Methods for Strengthening the Common Tests, *Biometrics*, 10:417–451.
Coe, Michael D., 1966, *The Maya*. Mexico, D.F.: Ediciones Lara.
Cohen, Ronald, and Raoul Naroll, 1970, Method in Cultural Anthropology, in R. Naroll and R. Cohen, eds., *A Handbook of Method in Cultural Anthropology*. Garden City, N.Y.: Natural History Press, 3–24.
Conover, W. J., 1971, *Practical Nonparametric Statistics*. New York: Wiley.
Coon, Carleton S., 1948, *A Reader in General Anthropology*. New York: Holt, Rinehart and Winston, Inc.
1971a, *The Origin of Races*. New York: Knopf.
1971b, A Fossilized Human Mandibular Fragment from Kangatotha, Kenya, East Africa, *American Journal of Physical Anthropology*, 34:157–163.
Cordova, M. S., R. Lisker, and A. Loria, 1967, Studies on Several Genetic Hematological Traits of the Mexican Population, *American Journal of Physical Anthropology*, 26:55–66.
Coult, Alan, 1965, A Note on Fisher's Exact Test, *American Anthropologist*, 67:1537–1541.
Cramér, Harold, 1946, *Mathematical Methods of Statistics*. Princeton, N.J.: Princeton University Press.
Dahlberg, Gunnar, 1926, *Twin Births and Twins from a Hereditary Point of View*. Stockholm: Bokforlags.
Damas, David, 1969, Band Societies, *National Museums of Canada Contributions to Anthropology*, Bull. 228.
Divale, William Tulio, 1972, Systemic Population Control in the Middle and Upper Paleolithic: Inferences based on Contemporary Hunter-Gatherers, *World Archaeology*, 4:222–243.
1974, Migration, External Warfare, and Matrilocal Residence, *Behavior Science Research*, 9:75–133.
Dixon, Wilfred J., and Frank J. Massey, Jr., 1969, *Introduction to Statistical Analysis*, 3d ed. New York: McGraw-Hill.
Dolhinow, Phyllis Jay, 1972, The North Indian Langur, in Phyllis Dolhinow, ed., *Primate Patterns*. New York: Holt, Rinehart and Winston, Inc., 181–238.
Dozier, Edward P., 1970, *The Pueblo Indians of North America*. New York: Holt, Rinehart and Winston, Inc.
Driver, Harold, 1953, Statistics in Anthropology, *American Anthropologist*, 55: 42–59.
Dunning, R. W., 1959, *Social and Economic Change among the Northern Ojibwa*. Toronto: University of Toronto Press.
Edwards, W., H. Lindman, and L. J. Savage, 1963, Bayesian Statistical Inference for Psychological Research, *Psychological Review*, 70:193–242.
Ehrlich, Paul R., and Anne H. Ehrlich, 1972, *Population, Resources, Environment*, 2d ed. San Francisco: Freeman.
Ember, Carol R., and Melvin Ember, 1972, The Conditions Favoring Multilocal Residence, *Southwestern Journal of Anthropology*, 28:382–400.

518

Ember, Melvin, 1963, The Relationship between Economic and Political Development in Nonindustrial Societies, *Ethnology*, 2:228–248.

Ember, Melvin, and Carol R. Ember, 1971, The Conditions Favoring Matrilocal versus Patrilocal Residence, *American Anthropologist*, 73:571–594.

Eveleth, Phyllis B., 1972, An Anthropometric Study of Northeastern Brazilians, *American Journal of Physical Anthropology*, 37:223–232.

Firth, Raymond, 1957, *We, the Tikopia: Kinship in Primitive Polynesia.* Boston: Beacon.

Fisher, Ronald A., 1935, *The Design of Experiments.* London: Oliver and Boyd.

1936, Has Mendel's Work been Rediscovered? *Annals of Science*, 1:115–137.

Fisher, Ronald A., E. B. Ford, and Julian Huxley, 1939, Taste-testing the Anthropoid Apes, *Nature*, 144:750.

Fitting, James E., 1965, A Quantitative Examination of Virginia Fluted Points, *American Antiquity*, 30:484–491.

Freed, Stanley A., 1963, An Objective Method for Determining the Collective Caste Hierarchy of an Indian Village, *American Anthropologist*, 65:879–891.

Freed, Stanley A., and Ruth S. Freed, 1969, Urbanization and Family Types in a North Indian Village, *Southwestern Journal of Anthropology*, 25:342–359.

1973, Status and the Spatial Range of Marriages in a North Indian Area, *Anthropological Quarterly*, 46:92–99.

Galton, Francis, 1885, REGRESSION *towards* MEDIOCRITY *in* HEREDITARY STATURE, *Journal of the Anthropological Institute of Great Britain and Ireland*, XV: 246-263.

Glanville, E. V. and R. A. Geerdink, 1972, Blood Pressure of Amerindians from Surinam, *American Journal of Physical Anthropology*, 37:251–254.

Gnedenko, B. V., and A. YA. Khinchin, 1961, *An Elementary Introduction to the Theory of Probability.* San Francisco: Freeman.

Goodman, L. A., and W. H. Kruskal, 1954, Measures of Association for Cross Classifications, *Journal of the American Statistical Association*, 49:732–764.

1959, Measures of Association for Cross Classifications. II: Further Discussion and References, *Journal of the American Statistical Association*, 54:123–163.

1963, Measures of Association for Cross Classifications. III: Approximate Sampling Theory, *Journal of the American Statistical Association*, 58:310–364.

Goody, Jack, 1970, Cousin Terms, *Southwestern Journal of Anthropology*, 26:125–142.

Greenbaum, Lenora, 1970, Evaluation of a Stratified versus an Unstratified Universe of Cultures in Comparative Research, *Behavior Science Notes*, 5:251–281.

Grizzle, J. E., 1967, Continuity Correction in the χ^2-test for 2×2 Tables, *American Statistician*, 1967:28–32.

Hagood, Margaret Jarman, 1941, *Statistics for Sociologists.* New York: Holt, Rinehart and Winston, Inc.

Harris, J. Arthur, 1930, The Measurement of Man in the Mass, in J. A. Harris, C. M. Jackson, D. G. Patterson, and R. E. Scammon, *The Measurement of Man.* Minneapolis: University of Minnesota Press, 3–76.

Harris, Marvin, 1964, *The Nature of Cultural Things.* New York: Random House, Inc.

1968, *The Rise of Anthropological Theory.* New York: Crowell.

1971, *Culture, Man and Nature.* New York: Crowell.

1972, Warfare Old and New, *Natural History*, LXXXI:18–20.

Harris, H., and H. Kalmus, 1950, The Measure of Taste Sensitivity to Phenyltyourea (P.T.C.), *Annals of Eugenics*, 15:24–31.

Haury, Emil W., E. B. Sayles, and William W. Wasley, 1959, The Lehner Mammoth Site, Southeastern Arizona, *American Antiquity*, 25:2–30.

Hays, William L., 1973, *Statistics for the Social Sciences*, 2d ed. New York: Holt, Rinehart and Winston, Inc.

Heighton, Robert F., and Kathleen A. Deagan, 1971, A New Formula for Dating Kaolin Clay Pipestems, *The Conference on Historic Site Archaeology Papers*, 6:220–229.

Hempel, Carl G., 1966, *Philosophy of Natural Science*. Englewood Cliffs, N.J.: Prentice-Hall.

Hill, James N., 1970, Broken K Pueblo: Prehistoric Social Organization in the American Southwest, *Anthropological Papers of the University of Arizona*, No. 18.

Hodson, F. R., D. G. Kendall, and P. Tăutu (eds.) 1971, *Mathematics in the Archaeological and Historical Sciences*. Chicago: Aldine.

Hoffman, H., 1970, Mathematical Anthropology, in B. J. Siegel, eds., *Biennial Review of Anthropology*. Stanford: Stanford University Press, 41–79.

Hogben, Lancelot, 1968, *Statistical Theory*. New York: Norton.

Hooton, Earnest A., 1930, The Indians of Pecos Pueblo. A Study of the Skeletal Remains, *Papers of the Southwestern Expedition*, No. 4. Andover, Mass.: Phillips Academy.

Hulse, Frederick S., 1963, *The Human Species: An Introduction to Physical Anthropology*. New York: Random House, Inc.

Hymes, Dell, (ed.), 1965, *The Use of Computers in Anthropology*. The Hague: Mouton.

Jennings, J. D., 1957, Danger Cave, *University of Utah Anthropological Papers*, No. 27.

Kay, Paul, 1971, Introduction: Mathematics in Anthropology, in Paul Kay, ed., *Explorations in Mathematical Anthropology*. Cambridge, Mass.: M.I.T. Press, xii–xviii.

Kelso, A. J., 1970, *Physical Anthropology: An Introduction*. Philadelphia: Lippincott.

Kemeny, John G., 1959, *A Philosopher Looks at Science*. New York: Van Nostrand-Reinhold.

Kemeny, John G., and J. Laurie Snell, 1972, *Mathematical Models in the Social Sciences*. Cambridge, Mass.: M.I.T. Press.

Kerlinger, Fred N., 1973, *Foundations of Behavioral Research*, 2d ed. New York: Holt, Rinehart and Winston, Inc.

Kerrich, J. E., and D. L. Clarke, 1967, Notes on the Possible Misuse and Errors of Cumulative Percentage Frequency Graphs for the Comparison of Prehistoric Artefact Assemblages. London: *Proceedings of the Prehistoric Society*, 33:57–69.

Kish, Leslie, 1959, Some Statistical Problems in Research Design, *American Sociological Review*, 24:328–338.

1965, *Survey Sampling*. New York: Wiley.

Köbben, Andre J. F., 1970, Comparativists and Non-Comparativists in Anthropology, in Raoul Naroll and Ronald Cohen, eds., *A Handbook of Method in Cultural Anthropology*. Garden City, N.Y.: Natural History Press, 581–596.

Koertvelyessy, T., 1972, Relationships between the Frontal Sinus and Climatic

Conditions: A Skeletal Approach to Cold Adaptation, *American Journal of Physical Anthropology*, 37:161–172.

Kroeber, A. L., 1925, Handbook of the Indians of California, Bureau of American Ethnology, Bull. 78.

Krogman, Wilton Marion, 1962, *The Human Skeleton in Forensic Medicine*. Springfield, Ill.: Charles C Thomas.

Krumbein, W. C., and Franklin A. Graybill, 1965, *An Introduction to Statistical Models in Geology*. New York: McGraw-Hill.

Labovitz, Sanford, 1968, Criteria for Selecting a Significance Level: A Note on the Sacredness of .05, *The American Sociologist*, 3:200–222.

Langley, Russell, 1971, *Practical Statistics Simply Explained*, rev. ed. New York: Dover.

Leblanc, Steven A., 1971, An Addition to Naroll's Suggested Floor Area and Settlement Population Relationship, *American Antiquity*. 36:210–211.

1973, Two Points of Logic Concerning Data, Hypotheses, General Laws and Systems, in Charles L. Redman, ed., *Research and Theory in Current Archeology*. New York: Wiley, 199–214.

Lee, Richard B., 1969, !Kung Bushman Subsistence: An Input-Output Analysis, in A. P. Vayda, ed., *Environment and Cultural Behavior*. Garden City, N.Y.: Natural History Press, 47–79.

Loflin, Colin, 1972, Galton's Problem as Spatial Autocorrelation: Comments on Ember's Empirical Test, *Ethnology*, 11:425–435.

Long, Austin, and Bruce Rippeteau, 1974, Testing Contemporaneity and Averaging Radiocarbon Dates, *American Antiquity*, 39:205–215.

Lowie, Robert H., 1935, *The Crow Indians*. New York: Holt, Rinehart and Winston, Inc.

1946, Evolution in Cultural Anthropology, *American Anthropologist*, 48:223–233.

McFadden, J. A., 1971, *Physical Concepts of Probability*. New York: Van Nostrand-Reinhold.

McKenzie, Douglas H., 1970, Statistical Analysis of Ohio Fluted Points, *The Ohio Journal of Science*, 70:352.

McKim, Donald, Thomas C. Hutchinson, and James Gavan, 1972, Prenatal Growth of Long Bones in Rhesus and Squirrel Monkeys (*Macaca mulatta* and *Saimiri sciureus*), *American Journal of Physical Anthropology*, 36:353–358.

McNett, Charles W., 1967, The Inference of Socio-Cultural Traits in Archaeology: A Statistical Approach, Ph.D. Dissertation, Tulane University, Ann Arbor, Mich.: University Microfilms.

1970, A Settlement Pattern Scale of Cultural Complexity, in Raoul Naroll and Ronald Cohen, eds., *A Handbook of Method in Cultural Anthropology*. Garden City, N.Y.: Natural History Press, 872–886.

Maresh, Marion M., 1971, Single versus Serial Assessment of Skeletal Age: Either, Both or Neither? *American Journal of Physical Anthropology*, 35:387–392.

Mead, Margaret, 1972, *Blackberry Winter: My Earlier Years*. New York: Simon and Schuster.

Meehl, Paul E., 1967, Theory Testing in Psychology and Physics: A Methodological Paradox, *Philosophy of Science*, 34:103–115.

Mendenhall, William, 1971, *Introduction to Probability and Statistics*, 3d ed. Belmont, Ca.: Duxbury Press.

Minturn, Leigh, Martin Grosse, and Santoah Haider, 1969, Cultural Patterning of Sexual Beliefs and Behavior, *Ethnology*, 8:301–318.

Mood, Alexander M., and Franklin A. Graybill, 1963, *Introduction to the Theory of Statistics*, 2d ed. New York: McGraw-Hill.

Moore, Frank W., (ed.), 1961, *Readings in Cross-Cultural Methodology*. New Haven: Human Relations Area Files Press.

Morgan, Lewis Henry, 1877, *Ancient Society*. New York: World Publishing.

Morrison, Denton E., and Ramon E. Henkel, 1969, Significance Tests Reconsidered, *The American Sociologist*, 4:131–140.

1970, (eds.), *The Significance Test Controversy*. Chicago: Aldine.

Moss, Melvin L., Patricia S. Chase, and Robert I. Howes, 1967, Comparative Odontometry of the Permanent Post-Canine Dentition of American Whites and Negroes, *American Journal Anthropology*, 27:125–142.

Munroe, Robert L., and Ruth H. Munroe, 1969, A Cross-Cultural Study of Sex Gender and Social Structure, *Ethnology*, 8:206–211.

Murdock, George Peter, 1949, *Social Structure*. New York: Macmillan.

1967, *Ethnographic Atlas*. Pittsburgh: University of Pittsburgh Press.

Naroll, Raoul, 1956, A Preliminary Index of Social Development, *American Anthropologist*, 58: 687–715.

1962a, Floor Area and Settlement Population, *American Antiquity*, 27:187–189.

1962b, *Data Quality Control: A New Research Technique*. New York: The Free Press of Glencoe.

1970a, The Culture-Bearing Unit in Cross-Cultural Surveys, in Raoul Naroll and Ronald Cohen, eds., *A Handbook of Method in Cultural Anthropology*. Garden City, N.Y.: Natural History Press, 721–765.

1970b, Galton's Problem, in Raoul Naroll and Ronald Cohen, eds., *A Handbook of Method in Cultural Anthropology*. Garden City, N.Y.: Natural History Press, 974–989.

1970c, Comment on the Second HRAF Cross-cultural Research Conference, *Behavior Science Notes*, 5:162–163.

1971, Review of *The Significance Test Controversy* [by] Denton E. Morrison and Ramon E. Henkel, eds., *American Anthropologist*, 73:1437–1439.

1974, An Exact Test of Significance for Goodman and Kruskal's Gamma, *Behavior Science Research*, 9:27–40.

Naroll, Raoul, and Ludwig von Bertalanffy, 1965, The Principle of Allometry in Biology and the Social Sciences, *General Systems Yearbook of the Society for the Advancement of General Systems Theory*, 1:76–89.

Naroll, Raoul, and Ronald Cohen, 1970, The Logic of Generalization, in Raoul Naroll and Ronald Cohen, eds., *A Handbook of Method in Cultural Anthropology*. Garden City, N.Y.: Natural History Press, 25–50.

Newman, Horatio H., Frank H. Freeman, and Karl J. Holzinger, 1937, *Twins: A Study of Heredity and Environment*. Chicago: University of Chicago Press.

Nie, Norman H., Dale H. Bent, and C. Hadlai Hull, 1970, *Statistical Package for the Social Sciences*. New York: McGraw-Hill.

Noether, Gottfried E., 1972, Distribution-Free Confidence Intervals, *The American Statistician*, 26:39–41.

O'Nell, Carl W., and Henry A. Selby, 1968, Sex Differences in the Incidence of Susto in Two Zapotec Pueblos: An Analysis of the Relationships between Sex Role Expectations and a Folk Illness, *Ethnology*, 7:95–105.

Otterbein, Keith, 1970, *The Evolution of War: A Cross-cultural Study*. New Haven: Human Relations Area Files Press.

Pelto, Pertti J., 1970, *Anthropological Research: The Structure of Inquiry*. New York: Harper & Row.

Pilbeam, David R., 1969, Tertiary Pongidae of East Africa: Evolutionary Relationships and Taxonomy, *Peabody Museum of Natural History Reports*, No. 31.

Rackerby, Frank, 1973, A Statistical Determination of the Black Sand Occupation at the Macoupin Site, Jersey Co., Illinois, *American Antiquity*, 38:96–101.

Ralph, Elizabeth K., 1971, Carbon-14 Dating, in Henry N. Michael and Elizabeth K. Ralph, eds., *Dating Techniques for the Archaeologist*. Cambridge, Mass.; M.I.T. Press, 1–48.

RAND Corporation, 1955, *A Million Random Digits with 100,000 Normal Deviates*. New York: Free Press.

Rappaport, Roy A., 1968, *Pigs for the Ancestors: Ritual in the Ecology of a New Guinea People*. New Haven: Yale University Press.

Riddell, Francis A., and William H. Olsen, 1969, An Early Man Site in the San Joaquin Valley, California, *American Antiquity*, 34:121–131.

Robbins, Michael C., and Richard B. Pollnac, 1969, Drinking Patterns and Acculturation in Rural Buganda, *American Anthropologist*, 71:276–284.

Roberts, D. F., 1953, Body Weight, Race and Climate, *American Journal of Physical Anthropology*, 11:533–558.

Roberts, John M., and Michael L. Forman, 1971, Riddles: Expressive Models of Interrogation, *Ethnology*, 10:509–533.

Rohlf, F. James, and Robert R. Sokal, 1969, *Statistical Tables*. San Francisco: Freeman.

Rosenthal, R., and J. Gaito, 1963, The Interpretation of Levels of Significance by Psychological Researchers, *Journal of Psychology*, 55:33–38.

Sanders, William T., and Joseph Marino, 1970, *New World Prehistory: Archaeology of the American Indian*. Englewood Cliffs, N.J.: Prentice-Hall.

Satterthwaite, Linton, and Elizabeth K. Ralph, 1960, New Radiocarbon Dates and the Maya Correlation Problem, *American Antiquity*, 26:165–184.

Savage, Leonard J., 1954, *The Foundations of Statistics*. New York: Wiley.

Savishinsky, Joel S., 1971, Mobility as an Aspect of Stress in an Arctic Community, *American Anthropologist*, 73:604–618.

Schulman, Edmund, 1956, *Dendroclimatic Changes in Semiarid America*. Tucson: University of Arizona Press.

Selvin, Hanan C., 1957, A Critique of Tests of Significance in Survey Research, *American Sociological Review*, 22:519–527.

Service, Elman, 1962, *Primitive Social Organization*. New York: Random House.

Shapiro, Harry L., 1929, A Correction for Artificial Deformation of Skulls, *Anthropological Papers of the American Museum of Natural History*, 30: 1–38.

1971, The Strange, Unfinished Saga of Peking Man, *Natural History*, LXXX: 8–18, 74–83.

Siegel, Sidney, 1956, *Nonparametric Statistics for the Behavioral Sciences*. New York: McGraw-Hill.

Simpson, George Gaylord, Anne Roe, and Richard C. Lewontin, 1960, *Quantitative Zoology.* New York: Harcourt Brace Jovanovich.

Skipper, James K., Anthony L. Guenther, and Gilbert Nass, 1967, The Sacredness of .05: A Note Concerning the Uses of Statistical Levels of Significance in Social Science, *The American Sociologist,* 2:16–18.

Snedecor, George W., and William Cochran, 1967, *Statistical Methods,* 6th ed. Ames: The Iowa State University Press.

Sokal, Robert R., and F. James Rohlf, 1969, *Biometry.* San Francisco: Freeman.

Southard, Michael D., 1973, A Study of Two Northwest Housepit Populations, *Northwest Anthropological Research Notes,* 7:61–83.

Spaulding, A. C., 1958, The Significance of Differences in Carbon-14 Dates, *American Antiquity,* 23:309–311.

1960, Statistical Description and Comparison of Artifact Assemblages, in R. F. Heizer and S. F. Cook, eds., *Application of Quantitative Methods in Archaeology.* Chicago: Quadrangle, 60–92.

Steger, Joseph A., (ed.), 1971, *Readings in Statistics for the Behavioral Scientist.* New York: Holt, Rinehart and Winston, Inc.

Stevens, S. S., 1951, *Handbook of Experimental Psychology.* New York: Wiley.

Steward, Julian H., 1937, Ecological Aspects of Southwestern Society, *Anthropos,* XXXII:87–104.

1938, Basin-Plateau Aboriginal Sociopolitical Groups, *Bureau of American Ethnology Bull. 120.*

1955, *Theory of Culture Change.* Urbana: University of Illinois Press.

"Student", 1908, The Probable Error of a Mean, *Biometrika,* 6:1–25.

Tatje, Terrence A., and Raoul Naroll, 1970, Two Measures of Social Complexity: An Empirical Cross-Cultural Comparison, in Raoul Naroll and Ronald Cohen, eds., *A Handbook of Method in Cultural Anthropology.* Garden City, N.Y.: Natural History Press, 766–833.

Textor, Robert B., 1966, *A Cross-Cultural Summary.* New Haven: Human Relations Area Files Press.

Thomas, David Hurst, 1969, Regional Sampling in Archaeology: A Pilot Great Basin Research Design, *University of California Archaeological Survey Annual Report,* 11:87–100.

1970, Archaeology's Operational Imperative: Great Basin Projectile Points as a Test Case, *University of California Archaeological Survey Annual Report,* 12:27–60.

1971a, *Prehistoric Subsistence-Settlement Patterns of the Reese River Valley, Central Nevada.* Ph.D. Dissertation, University of California. Ann Arbor: University Microfilms.

1971b, On the Use of Cumulative Curves and Numerical Taxonomy, *American Antiquity,* 36:206–209.

1973, An Empirical Test for Steward's Model of Great Basin Settlement Patterns, *American Antiquity,* 38:155-176.

1974, *Predicting the Past: An Introduction to Anthropological Archaeology.* New York: Holt, Rinehart and Winston, Inc.

Watson, Patty Jo, Steven A. LeBlanc, and Charles Redman, 1971, *Explanation in Archaeology: An Explicitly Scientific Approach.* New York: Columbia University Press.

Welkowitz, Joan, Robert B. Ewen, and Jacob Cohen, 1971, *Introductory Statistics for the Behavioral Sciences*. New York: Academic Press, Inc.

Wendorf, Fred, Alex Krieger, Claude Albritton, and T. Dale Stewart, 1955, *The Midland Discovery*. Austin: University of Texas Press.

Werner, S. Benson, 1974. Coccidioidomycosis among Archaeology Students: Recommendations for Prevention, *American Antiquity*, 39:367-370.

White, Douglas R., 1973, Mathematical Anthropology, in John J. Honigman, ed., *Handbook of Social and Cultural Anthropology*. Chicago: Rand McNally, 369-446.

White, Leslie A., 1940, The Symbol: The Origin and Basis of Human Behavior, *Philosophy of Science*, 7:451-463.

Whiting, Beatrice, 1950, Paiute Sorcery, *Viking Fund Publications in Anthropology, No. 15*. New York; Wenner-Gren Foundation.

Wilcoxon, Frank, 1947, Probability Tables for Individual Comparisons by Ranking Methods, *Biometrics*, 3:119-122.

Willey, Gordon R., and Philip Phillips, 1958, *Method and Theory in American Archaeology*. Chicago: University of Chicago Press.

Williams, Leonard, David Hurst Thomas, and Robert Bettinger, 1973, Notions to Numbers: Great Basin Settlements as Polythetic Sets, in Charles Redman, ed., *Research and Theory in Current Anthropology*. New York: Wiley, 215-237.

Winick, Charles, 1966, *Dictionary of Anthropology*. Totowa: Littlefield, Adams and Co.

Wolpoff, M. H., 1969, Cranial Capacity and Taxonomy of Olduvai Hominid 7, *Nature*, 223:182-183.

Wormington, H. M., 1957, *Ancient Man in North America*, 4th ed. Denver Museum of Natural History, Popular Series No. 4.

Yule, G. Udny, and M. G. Kendall, 1937, *An Introduction to the Theory of Statistics*, 11th ed. London: Griffin.

Index

532